Fodor's

CANCÚN AND THE RIVIERA MAYA

T0049063

Welcome to Cancún and the Riviera Maya

Mexico's Yucatán Peninsula remains enduringly popular with travelers, and there's little wonder why. Stellar attractions include magnificent beaches and the extensive reefs off Cozumel and the southern Yucatán coast, as well as myriad Maya ruins, the remains of a vast empire that ruled here long before the Spanish. Limestone pools called cenotes, great for a swim or dive, dot the countryside, even in Playa del Carmen. All-inclusive resorts predominate in Cancún, but the peninsula also has luxurious boutique hotels, hacienda retreats, and simple guesthouses.

TOP REASONS TO GO

★ **Coral reefs:** Cozumel's are among the best, drawing both divers and snorkelers.

★ **Beaches:** Cancún's are busy and beautiful; the Riviera Maya's are sugary soft and quieter.

★ **Maya ruins:** The pyramids of Chichén Itzá soar; Tulum overlooks a perfect beach.

★ **Nightlife:** Cancún and Playa del Carmen range from raucous to sophisticated.

★ **Spas:** Almost every big resort has a spa, and many are notable for their pampering.

★ **Nature:** Pockets of pristine beauty remain despite widespread development.

Contents

Fodor's Features

MAPS

Chapter 1

EXPERIENCE CANCÚN AND THE RIVIERA MAYA

20 ULTIMATE EXPERIENCES

Cancún and the Riviera Maya offer terrific experiences that should be on every traveler's list. Here are Fodor's top picks for a memorable trip.

1 Marvel at Tulum's Seaside Ruins

While Tulum doesn't have the highest pyramids or the largest ruins, its cliffside setting above the turquoise Caribbean Sea is absolutely breathtaking—and a great backdrop for photos. *(Ch. 5)*

2 Float Your Way through Xcaret

Part Maya ruin, part aquatic theme park, this enormous development has amusement rides, cultural shows, spa treatments, zip-lining, snorkeling, and more. *(Ch. 5)*

3 Wander the Cobblestone Streets of Valladolid

This small city is a great base for exploring the Yucatán, with colonial churches, Mexico's largest private collection of folk art, and a cenote right in the middle of town. *(Ch. 7)*

4 Eat Traditional Yucatecan Cuisine

Try Caribbean and Maya dishes like *cochinita pibil*, marinated roast pork often served on tortillas. *(Chs. 3–7)*

5 Indulge at a Luxury All-Inclusive Resort

With food, nightlife, activities, and spas all within the hotel, you can indulge in the art of laziness. *(Chs. 3–7)*

6 Scuba and Snorkel the Barrier Reef

Sea turtles, lobsters, moray eels, and barracudas congregate around Cozumel, all visible in the clear waters. *(Ch. 6)*

7 Sip Mezcal and Tequila

Mexico is the land of agave plants, and at tequila and mezcal distilleries, you can learn about the production process and pick up some useful souvenirs. *(Chs. 3–7)*

8 Explore Ancient Maya Ruins

There are over three-dozen Maya ruins in the Yucatán Peninsula, including Chichén Itzá's renowned pyramids. *(Chs. 5, 7)*

9 Flock with Flamingoes

One of North America's largest flamingo colonies holds court at the Ría Celestún Biosphere Reserve west of Mérida from November through March. *(Ch. 7)*

10 Campeche City

Campeche City's beautifully preserved and very walkable historic district is filled with sites, museums, and cafés. *(Ch. 7)*

11 Sunbathe at Sian Ka'an Biosphere Reserve

One hundred kilometers (60 miles) of coastline make up this undeveloped stretch of tropical forest framed by white-sand beaches and turquoise water. *(Ch. 5)*

12 Peruse Underwater Art

At the MUSA underwater museum, more than 400 statues sculpted by six artists have been installed over three sites, and the works have turned into a habitat for marine life. *(Chs. 3, 4)*

13 Party Like a Spring-Breaker

Although college students descend on Cancún for several weeks during March and April, the party season really never pauses here. *(Ch. 3)*

14 Chill Out on Isla Mujeres

Golf carts are the main mode of transportation on this sleepy island full of rocky cliffs, turquoise waters, and white sands. *(Ch. 4)*

15 Shop 'til You Drop in Mérida

In Mérida, shops around the main square sell pottery, hand-embroidered clothing, and leather goods. *(Ch. 7)*

16 Escape to Isla Holbox

This under-the-radar island destination is full of boutique hotels, open-air restaurants, and water that's the perfect shade of seafoam green. *(Ch. 7)*

17 Eat at Tulum's Trendiest Restaurants

Tulum has turned into one of the chicest destinations in Mexico, with an abundance of hip dining spots. *(Ch. 5)*

18 Explore the Colorful City of Izamal

This sleepy town in the Yucatán Peninsula is like a ray of sunshine, with every building (including the impressive convent at the center of town) painted a vibrant yellow. *(Ch. 7)*

19 Stay at a Hacienda Hotel

Agave plantations dotted the Yucatán during the colonial era, and many of these haciendas, or ranches, have been repurposed into snazzy places to stay, like the Chablé resort. *(Ch. 7)*

20 Swim in a Cenote

The Yucatán Peninsula has almost 3,000 underground freshwater lagoons, which the ancient Maya believed were passages to the spirit world. *(Chs. 5, 7)*

WHAT'S WHERE

1 Cancún. The gateway to the Riviera Maya, this thriving coastal city is Mexico's most popular beach (and spring break) destination. In its waterfront Zona Hotelera area, high-rise resorts offer creature comforts; inland in El Centro, accommodations are more reasonably priced and authentically Mexican.

2 Isla Mujeres. A quick jaunt across the water from Cancún, this laid-back island is less crowded and cheaper than almost anywhere on the mainland. You can explore it by golf cart, moped, or bike.

3 The Riviera Maya. Dazzling, sugary-white sands and glittering blue waters beckon snorkelers, sunbathers, and spa goers. The seaside ruins of Tulum, the jungle-clad pyramids of Cobá, and the sidewalk cafés of Playa del Carmen are also enticing. Numerous theme parks, dolphin programs, and hidden cenotes cater to families. Farther south, the Costa Maya offers the ultimate in isolation.

4 Cozumel. Ever since Jacques Cousteau made Cozumel's interconnected series of coral

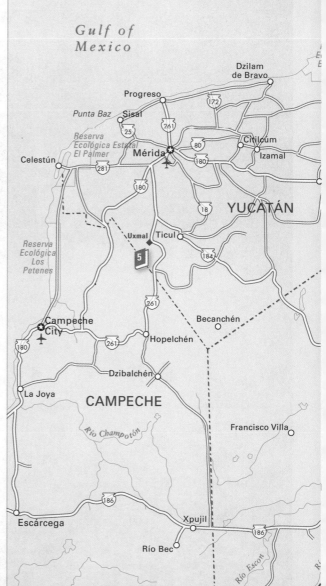

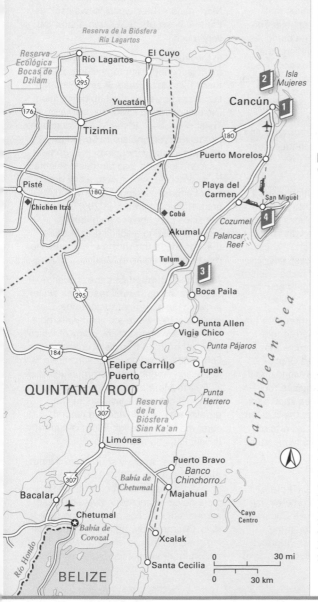

reefs famous in the 1960s, divers and snorkelers have flocked here. Ferries regularly travel from the mainland to the island, which is also popular with cruise-ship passengers. Escape the crowds by visiting Cozumel's windward side to see crumbled monuments to the goddess Ixchel.

5 Yucatán and Campeche States. Rich in art, history, and tradition, Mérida is Yucatán State's capital and the peninsula's cultural and intellectual hub. On the remote north coast, you'll find shell-strewn beaches and charming villages. Yucatán is also renowned for Maya sites that include Chichén Itzá and Uxmal. Campeche's eponymous capital is one of the region's best-kept secrets, with a beautifully preserved and walkable colonial district. Although it's less than an hour's drive southeast and is a significant Maya complex, Edzná sees fewer tour groups than other ruins. Adventurous travelers follow Carretera 186 farther southeast to explore a biosphere reserve where spider monkeys swing from five-story-high ceiba trees and yet another large Maya city, Calakmul, is being excavated.

Yucatán Peninsula Today

GOVERNMENT

Quintana Roo, Yucatán, and Campeche are three of the 32 states (plus Mexico City as the independent capital) that make up Mexico's federal republic. The government consists of three branches: the executive, the legislative, and the judicial. The president of Mexico is elected to a one-time, six-year term by popular vote and holds such extensive power that the position has been coined "the six-year monarchy." Each of Mexico's states is headed by a governor who also serves a single term that cannot exceed six years.

ECONOMY

Tourism has turned tiny fishing villages and farming communities into bustling beach towns. Each year millions of tourists are drawn to the area's waterfront resorts and archaeological sites; these attractions inject a steady cash flow into the economy. This influx of mass tourism created more jobs and a higher standard of living.

Travelers have also shown more interest in local culture. This has spurred the development of historical museums, including the state-of-the-art Gran Museo del Mundo Maya in Mérida, and reawakened interest in exquisite Yucatán crafts, which have long been known for the quality of workmanship. The Yucatán's economy is also helped by exports of henequen products such as twine, rugs, and wall hangings.

TOURISM

The Yucatán Peninsula, B.C. ("before Cancún," that is), really did receive visitors from elsewhere. Jacques Cousteau put Cozumel on divers' radar in the 1960s. Cruise ships called at Progreso on the north coast. The gracious colonial city of Mérida served as the gateway to the peninsula and the launching point to visit Chichén Itzá, Mexico's most famous Maya ruins. (The city still views itself as the true heart of the Yucatán, thank you very much.)

In the late 1960s, the Mexican government launched a strategy to increase tourism in the Yucatán. A site called Kaan Kun was chosen as the hub destination. (No one needs to know that name meant "nest of snakes" in the Mayan language. Not to worry: None are to be found here.) In a totally inorganic development, Cancún's location was famously selected by a computer. As a result, a city grew out of almost nothing to nearly 900,000 population by the early 2020s. Growth has since expanded to neighboring regions, creating a solid infrastructure that has made the Yucatán Peninsula the most visited region in Mexico.

Today, the country faces the challenge of protecting its natural resources while allowing development to continue. Cancún's beaches alone are lined with more than 150 towering hotels, many of which have contributed to coastal erosion. Fortunately, building restrictions are now in place in neighboring communities such as Puerto Morelos. Ecotourism in Tulum and most of Costa Maya has helped protect area wildlife and the natural surroundings, although Tulum is currently developing at a rapid pace.

Mexico never entirely shut down during the height of the COVID-19 pandemic. It did close its land borders; flights were never restricted, however, even if numbers did decline markedly on their own. Countrywide, figures are approaching pre-pandemic levels again with 38 million international tourists arriving in

2022, compared to 45 million in 2019, the last pre-COVID year. Tourism powerhouse Cancún has already surpassed its pre-pandemic totals, welcoming 25 million international visitors, an increase of 2 million over 2019.

One of Mexico's most controversial public-works projects ever will launch operation within the lifespan of this edition. When completed, the Tren Maya ("Maya Train") will travel a 1,525-km loop (950 miles) at 100 miles per hour around the three states covered in this book (Quintana Roo, Yucatán, Campeche) as well as to Tabasco and Chiapas states immediately south. It is expected that tourists will pay train fares up to 20 times higher than local people do. Boosters insist the train will provide much-improved transportation infrastructure within this isolated part of the country; opponents decry the environmental impact on a fragile ecosystem.

RELIGION

Although Mexico has no official religion, 78% of the population consider themselves Roman Catholic. Second only to Brazil, Mexico has more Catholics than anywhere else in the world, even though less than half attend church. Only 8% of the population call themselves Protestant, followed by Eastern Orthodox, Seventh-Day Adventists, Jehovah's Witnesses, and members of the Church of Jesus Christ of Latter-day Saints. (The Yucatán Peninsula counts the highest number of non-Catholic believers in Mexico.) Very few Maya people in the Yucatán Peninsula still practice traditional rituals of offerings and sacrifices of small animals. Central to the Maya religion is the idea of the duality of the soul, one part eternal, and the other supernatural.

CASH CROPS

Although tourism is the Yucatán Peninsula's main source of income, both agriculture and fishing are also great economic contributors. Until 1960 the main crop was henequen, an indigenous plant that produces sisal fiber used to make rope. The Yucatán's henequen once had a global reputation of being "green gold." The advent of similar synthetic fibers destroyed the international market, but henequen is still manufactured in the north-central region. The peninsula's eastern area raises 65% of the state's livestock, while the southern region, near Peto and Tzucacab, is known for corn, citrus, sugarcane, and cattle. Today, the Yucatán Peninsula exports more than 1,500 products, ranging from sponges and oranges to furniture and chocolates.

What to Eat and Drink in Cancún and the Riviera Maya

SOPA DE LIMA
The slight sourness of Yucatán lime soup gives an additional flavor profile to the chicken tortilla soup made elsewhere in Mexico. In this version, shredded chicken, tortilla strips, and local limes are the staple ingredients. The soup is reputed to be an effective hangover cure.

PIBIL
Pibil-style cooking creates what are arguably the Yucatán's signature dishes. Traditionally, *pollo* (chicken) or *cochinita* (a suckling pig) were slow-roasted in banana leaves in a pit; these days, the process more likely takes place in a standard oven, with pork shoulder or loin replacing the whole pig. Key to the recipe are the Yucatecan sour orange and achiote, a smoky, peppery tropical spice that imparts an orange color to the meat.

PAPADZULES
These enchilada-like treats compete with the pibil for a dish that says "quintessential Yucatán." (Papadzules have been around much longer.) Tortillas are dipped in a pumpkin-seed sauce, then hard-boiled eggs are folded inside before baking. They're usually topped with tomato sauce. The end result is a savory, creamy dish, much milder than your standard Mexican enchilada. Almost all establishments—from upscale local restaurants to market vendors—make and serve them, usually three to four to a plate.

POC CHUC
You might dismiss *poc chuc* as nothing more than pork and onions, but the process and additional ingredients make it so much more than that. A sour-orange marinade gives the meat a real tang and a sprinkling of habanero salsa adds just a bit of fire. It's cooked over a grill (the name translates to "roasting on charcoal," after all) and is usually served with sides of pickled onions and cabbage. Black beans and avocados give the plate some color contrast.

CAPIROTADA
Mexican bread pudding, traditionally eaten during Lent, is made from French bread soaked in syrup, sugar, cheese, raisins, and walnuts, and it's downright delicious.

PAN DE CAZÓN
The name of this traditional casserole dish from Campeche state translates to "shark bread." (Don't worry, it won't bite.) It looks like lasagna, but instead of pasta, corn tortillas (usually four at a time) are layered between shredded dogfish- or blacktip-shark meat. Refried black beans and various vegetables form the other layers. It's all covered with tomato sauce, resulting in a distinctive dish little known outside the region.

DULCE DE PAPAYA
The locally grown papaya is the star of this sweet dessert in which the orange fruit is transformed into a compote of sorts. It's soaked in water and lime, then boiled with sugar and cinnamon. The resulting syrupy, caramel-coated treat is usually topped with a dollop of whipped cream.

Papadzules

XTABENTÚN
Comparable to Greek ouzo or the Italian sambuca, this thick and aromatic honey-anise liqueur has been distilled in the Yucatán since ancient Maya times. It's usually ordered straight, on the rocks, or as a shot in sparkling water, coffee, or tequila. Casa D'Aristi in Mérida is the largest distiller. Pronounce the name like "shtab-en-*toon*."

MARQUESITAS
Crepes are fried, rolled like a waffle cone, and filled with shredded cheese and jam or caramel in this sweet treat, once the exclusive province of the children of Yucatán nobility. (A marquis nobleman was a *marqués* in Spanish and his daughters were *marquesitas*.) These days, it's a popular street snack. Dutch Edam, incredibly popular in this region of Mexico, almost always makes up the cheese part of the filling.

QUESO RELLENO
The rind of Edam cheese, so popular here, is stuffed with ground beef, olives, and raisins and steamed in a banana leaf to form a messy but tasty dish, one of the peninsula's most popular. What is the Mexican-Dutch cheese connection? Theories abound. Henequen traders likely brought the Dutch cheese back from trips to Europe. It caught on, and Edam has been a favorite in this region of Mexico ever since.

NARANJADA
The Yucatán sour orange (*naranja agria*), an essential ingredient in pibil-style cooking, is mixed with sparkling water and sugar to make this fresh, sour juice—more like a glass of lemonade than your sweet morning OJ. The thick-rind oranges with large seeds originated in Southeast Asia, and the Spanish intro-duced the fruit to the region in the 16th century.

HUEVOS MOTULEÑOS
Ever ordered huevos rancheros? In the Yucatán variation, eggs are fried, sunny side up, with ham and cheese, and served with a side of black beans, plantains, and tortillas. The dish originated in the town of Motul, east of Mérida, and while the average home serves this dish only on special occasions, it is a morning restaurant staple all over the Yucatán. It promises to fortify you for a morning of sightseeing.

What to Buy in Cancún and the Riviera Maya

HUARACHE SANDALS

The footwear made of hand-braided leather straps and traditionally worn by Mexican farmers was all the rage with hippies on American college campuses in the 1960s. Today, these sandals are popular with people of all cultural backgrounds—counter- or not.

MELIPONA HONEY

The Yucatán's stingless Melipona bees produce a slightly acidic, slightly floral honey that's a bit more syrupy than its stateside counterparts. Traditional Maya healers used Melipona honey, thought to be high in antioxidant and anti-inflammatory properties, to treat all manner of ailments. Many still do. You will more likely find its tangy sweetness a delight when used in your favorite dishes.

TICUL POTTERY

The town of Ticul is the Yucatán's center for pottery and ceramics. The area's red clay imparts a distinctive dark terra-cotta color to the pieces. At 90 km (56 miles) south, the town makes for a quintessential day trip from Mérida, but you'll find the pottery for sale all over the peninsula.

MAYA CHOCOLATE

Chocolate lovers, rejoice! Several businesses in this region double as chocolate shops that let you see the processing of this onetime "food of the gods." History credits the Maya with first harvesting cacao beans and turning them into what we know as chocolate, though it was more likely the neighboring Olmecs. The Maya, however, turned it into a product for mass consumption, even if they preferred it mixed with chili peppers.

HANDBLOWN GLASSWARE

You'll see all manner of handblown and whimsically hand-painted glassware for sale, but this is Mexico, so margarita glasses are especially popular. Credit the Massachusetts-based Libbey company with first importing and popularizing Mexican glassware. Since the glasses are made by hand, expect slight variations in design and color among a set. That's testament to their authenticity.

MOLINILLO WHISKS

Literally, it's a "little mill" in the sense of a mixer or stirrer. Rolled between your hands with a churning motion, it lets you whip up a foam in your hot chocolate with a flair, and, on a cold winter night, it creates a nice remembrance of your trip to the Yucatán. The intricate woodwork designs make a *molinillo* a pleasure to look at when it's simply hanging in your kitchen, too.

CHAC MOOL FIGURES

Chichén Itzá's famous reclined sculpture, now thought to be the Maya rain god Chaac, is reproduced in miniature in wood and stone and sold in markets all over the Yucatán. The god distinctively looks out at a 90-degree angle from the rest of his body. Chac Mool ("thunderous paw"), once mistakenly thought to be a Maya ruler's name, became a generic term for this type of statue, of which there are many in the region.

Huipil blouses and dresses

GUAYABERA SHIRTS

A guayabera shirt is a staple at tropical weddings here, but they'll look sharp for a dressy but informal summer occasion back home. Long or short sleeves? Either works. Most are white, with unadorned vertical pleats. Others contain embroidery, and pastels always stand out from the crowd. Oh, psssst, gents: the hem is straight. You wear a guayabera untucked and never with a jacket or tie.

HUIPIL BLOUSES AND DRESSES

Embroidered tunic-style blouses and dresses are a Maya specialty. A colorful blouse paired with jeans or other slacks might just be that perfect fashion statement to make at a back-home event. We recommend buying, packing, and not wearing this souvenir until you've returned home.

Some communities attach deep importance to huipil designs and look askance at visitors trying to "go native."

XTABENTÚN LIQUEUR

Drink the Yucatán's signature honey-anise-rum liqueur chilled, on the rocks, or as a shot in a cup of coffee. It also pairs well with several spirits: bartenders here mix a shot with tequila and add a twist of lime to create a "Maya margarita." Experiment and let it bring out the mixologist in you. Mérida-based D'Aristi is the best-known brand.

HAMMOCKS

Hamacas are this region's *número uno* souvenir. Use bedding nomenclature. A *sencillo* (single) is perfect for one person. A *doble* sleeps two, albeit crowdedly. A couple might want to upgrade to the larger *matrimonial*. Entire families here sleep in a *familiar*, but that might be too much togetherness. Choose between nylon (faster drying and more colorfast) or cotton (more comfortable).

Best Beaches in Cancún and the Riviera Maya

PLAYA NORTE
At the northern tip of Isla Mujeres, just a 20-minute boat ride from Cancún, Playa Norte has loungers, palms, and practically transparent waters, plus beach bars galore. Make the most of a full day there, or visit in the evening for one of the few over-the-ocean sunsets in the region.

PLAYA GAVIOTA AZUL
In Punta Cancún, at Km 9.5 of the Caribbean side of Cancún's Zona Hotelera beach strip, this public-access beach (also known as Playa Forum) is one of the area's most popular, especially with weekend partiers.

PLAYA TULUM
Tulum's main beach extends for 7 miles. Just north of town lies the so-called Tulum Ruins Beach with its Maya ruins near the water's edge. Visiting this sector is possible only by paying the admission fee to the ruins complex.

PLAYA TORTUGAS
This petite white-sand beach is especially family friendly thanks to a near absence of waves; excellent swimming, snorkeling, and paragliding conditions; and plenty of nearby amenities.

PLAYA LANGOSTA
Like most of the north zone beaches, Playa Langosta is easily accessible on public transport and an ideal spot to enjoy with kids. It's also situated close to the ferry dock—similarly to Playa Tortugas—which makes it an excellent jumping-off point for excursions and tours. The ocean here is swimmable.

PLAYA DELFINES
Moving down the Caribbean coastline—to km 19.5 of the Zona Hotelera, to be precise—you'll find perhaps the most quintessential of all Cancún beaches. Although admittedly not great for swimming—steer clear if you have little kids in tow—Playa Delfines is the perfect place to lounge on the sand.

PLAYA CHAC MOOL
This understated, casual beach has the same white sands, green-blue waters, and spectacular Zona Hotelera views as the neighboring and more vivacious Playa Gaviota Azul.

Tulum

PLAYA PUNTA NIZUC

Shallow waters and coral reefs make this beach—at the extreme south of the Zona Hotelera's Caribbean stretch—an ideal place for swimming, kayaking, and snorkeling. Be on the lookout for *The Gardener of Hope*, an underwater sculpture that's part of the MUSA collection.

PUERTO MORELOS

On the mainland and down the Cancún coastline a bit, Puerto Morelos offers swimmable surf, beach clubs with waiter service and shaded seating, affordable bars and restaurants (don't miss the ceviche), and boats that will shuttle you out to snorkel or scuba dive in the nearby coral reefs.

ISLA BLANCA

Here you can escape the crowds of Cancún's Zona Hotelera beaches without heading to a nearby town or island. Around 30 minutes north of the Cancún epicenter, this often-overlooked peninsula is dominated by jungle, sand, and the Chacmuchuk Lagoon. You'll need to rent a car or hire a taxi to get here, but it's worth it.

Best Snorkeling and Diving in Cancún and the Riviera Maya

CENOTES

Yucatán is noted for its cenotes, or limestone sinkholes, thought by the Maya to be the gateway to the underworld. The stalactites and stalagmites of the Gran Cenote, near Tulum, make it the most famous.

SANTA ROSA WALL

At Cozumel's best-known site for experienced divers, the wall drops steeply and the normally mild current can change at a moment's notice. The reward for braving the strong conditions is the sight of sea turtles and grouper swimming along with you among caves and tunnels.

MANCHONES

Off the southwest coast of Isla Mujeres, this dive site is known for its coral reef and a sunken 1-ton bronze cross (Cruz de la Bahia) that has spurred new coral growth. Shallow conditions make this one of the area's best locations for beginning divers and snorkelers.

PALANCAR REEF

Calm waters, terrific visibility, and proximity to Cozumel make this the Yucatán's ultimate wall dive for beginners. Eagle rays and nurse sharks are among the astounding variety of marine life that hides in the colorful coral reef's cracks, crevices, and tunnels. Reefs—plural—is a better way to describe Palancar, since there are technically four sectors, named "Gardens," "Caves," "Bricks," and "Horseshoe."

COLUMBIA REEF

Grouper, sea turtles, eagle rays, and barracuda populate this sector of reef and its canyons, ravines, and tall coral "pillars." The site, off the southwest coast of Cozumel, has two sections designated Colombia Shallow and Colombia Deep. Both are best suited for experienced divers, and they offer some of the best conditions for underwater photography.

TORMENTOS REEF

The brightly colored section of coral reef here makes a stunning backdrop for underwater photography. Conditions are occasionally good for beginners, but most dive outfitters regard Tormentos as an intermediate dive, owing to sudden changes in current. Barracuda, nurse sharks, and angelfish make up the underwater life you'll see here.

Museo Subacuático de Arte

PARAÍSO REEF
Another great beginner dive, especially for first-time night divers, Paradise Reef has two coral ridges off the west coast of Cozumel. Its crystal clear waters teem with angelfish, sea eels, and yellow rays. The shallower north ridge provides optimal conditions for beginners.

ISLA CONTOY
Experienced divers won't want to miss the Cave of the Sleeping Sharks at this island 32 km (20 miles) north of Isla Mujeres. Here, at 150 feet, you can see the otherwise dangerous creatures "dozing" in a state of relaxed nonaggression. From June to mid-September, divers and snorkelers can swim with docile whale sharks, which can grow up to 50 feet in length. Manta rays, lobster, and barracuda round out Contoy's offerings.

MUSEO SUBACUÁTICO DE ARTE
Unusual underwater sculptures populate this art gallery's three installations, two near Cancún and one off the coast of Isla Mujeres. The sculptures, the most whimsical of which is a life-size VW Beetle, form an artificial reef that attracts marine life. Not into diving or snorkeling? The works are in shallow enough water that you can also see them clearly from glass-bottom boats.

PARED VERDE
One of the region's healthiest sections of reef lies off Playa del Carmen and is home to lobsters, king crabs, and sting rays. The medium to strong current here makes the "Green Wall" a site for advanced divers only.

Top Maya Ruins

SAYIL

South of Uxmal—sometimes referred to as a "suburb" of the larger site—the centerpiece of the "place of the red ants" is its Gran Palacio (Great Palace) a three-story, Late-Classic Period structure perched on top of a hill. Animals and masked figures representing the Maya rain god, Chaac, adorn the palace walls.

CHICHÉN ITZÁ

The most famous of the region's sites features the enormous, oft-photographed El Castillo (Kukulcán) pyramid. One of the largest and most beautiful Maya cities makes for a quintessential day trip from Cancún or Mérida.

COBÁ

The impressive temples and palaces of inland Cobá perpetually live in the shadow of nearby and better-known Tulum. Its many fans are just as happy to keep things that way, although the sprawling forested lakeside site's visitor numbers are growing. Only a small portion of Cobá's estimated 6,000 structures are open to visitors. Three cenotes are nearby.

KOHUNLICH

Giant stucco masks that are about 6 feet tall adorn this site's main structure, the Edificio de los Mascarones (Building of Masks). You can visit 14 of the site's structures, which showcase a mix of architectural styles. It's thought, however, that many more buildings are beneath the numerous burial mounds here.

RESERVA DE LA BIÓSFERA CALAKMUL

Thousands of structures lie buried under the profuse greenery of Mexico's largest ecological corridor at the Calakmul Biosphere Reserve. The reserve's centerpiece is the magnificent Templo II pyramid, the Yucatán's tallest Maya structure.

UXMAL

Along the Ruta Puuc you'll find the most elegant of the peninsula's ruins. Uxmal's perfectly proportioned buildings of the Cuadrángulo de las Monjas (Nun's Quadrangle) make a beautiful "canvas" for facades carved with snakes and the fierce visages of Maya gods.

EK BALAM

At the less visited Ek Balam, just north of Valladolid, huge monster masks guard the mausoleum of Maya ruler Ukit Kan Le'k Tok. Winged figures in full royal regalia gaze down from the amazing friezes. Though the figures look like angels, they probably represent Maya nobility.

TULUM

Tulum is the Yucatán's most visited archaeological site. Although the ruins here aren't as architecturally arresting, a spectacular location on a cliff overlooking the blue-green Caribbean makes Tulum unique.

MUYIL AT SIAN KA'AN

Translating to "where the sky is born," Sian Ka'an's spectacular and undeveloped coastline is home to a 1.3 million-acre reserve with coastal lagoons, mangrove swamps, wildlife, and 22 Maya ruin complexes. Photogenic Muyil sits at the reserve's northern end and is the largest of these. Like nearby Tulum, it's perched on the Caribbean coast. Muyil's 57-foot Castillo is its largest structure.

CHACCHOBEN

This once-thriving ancient city—its name translates to "land of the red corn"—dates from AD 200, but it remained forgotten until 2005. The site's main structure is Templo I, which was dedicated to the Maya sun god Itzamná and once housed a royal tomb, found to be looted when excavated. Pending further exploration, much of the site is closed.

Day Trips Around Cancún and the Riviera Maya

Cancún might have powdery white sands, legendary nightlife, and some of the most luxurious resorts in Mexico, but you're missing out if you don't ditch the pool and the piña coladas for a day trip or two while you're in the region. Whether you're looking to relax on a Caribbean island—there are plenty to choose from—travel back in time at one of the area's many Maya ruins, or make a splash in a freshwater cenote, here are 10 day trips from Cancún you should consider.

MAYA RUINS

Chichén Itzá is by far the most well-known and popular of the Maya ruins within day-trip distance from Cancún. But is this famed New Wonder of the World the best destination for archaeology buffs? Perhaps—as long as you arrive before the busloads of tourists descend for the day. If you want a quieter experience, don't overlook Cobá.

TULUM

Long since overtaken by North American weekenders and Instagram influencers, Tulum is no longer the somewhat secret paradise it once was. Although it's now thronged with exclusive restaurants, jungle cocktail bars, and boutique hotels, Tulum's white sand and palapas remain, and it's an ideal day trip if you're looking for somewhere with a distinctly different vibe to Cancún. Stop by the beaches and clifftop ruins and take a detour to the cool waters of nearby cenotes if you start to feel the heat.

CENOTES

Speaking of cenotes, if you're sick of the salty ocean (remember: while Cancún's beaches look beautiful, they often harbor a nasty undertow) visit a cenote. These freshwater sinkholes, which were sacred to the Maya, speckle the peninsula, so you won't have trouble finding a good one, and entrance fees are usually well under $10 per person. One of the region's most popular is the Gran Cenote, just outside Tulum, although Zacil-Ha, with its aquamarine waters and the made-for-Instagram appeal is a closer-to-Cancún alternative.

VALLADOLID

When the party atmosphere of Cancún all gets just too much, take a break in the colonial city of Valladolid. There, you'll find 16th-century convents, super snackable street foods (be sure to seek out the chocolate and cheese-filled marquesita) and two cenotes (they really are everywhere) in which to cool off—Cenote Zaci and the recently discovered Cenote Chukum-Ha.

SIAN KA'AN BIOSPHERE RESERVE

There are close to 50 Protected Biosphere Reserves in Mexico, and Sian Ka'an in Quintana Roo is widely considered to be one of the best. (As if that wasn't enough, it was also one of the first UNESCO-recognized attractions in the country.) Knotted with mangroves and dotted with lagoons, Sian Ka'an is home to dense jungles, diverse creatures, and even archaeological ruins. At 3½ hours from Cancún, it's not the most convenient day trip, but it's worth the effort.

RÍO LAGARTOS BIOSPHERE RESERVE

Made famous a few years ago thanks to the cotton-candy-pink waters of Los Colorados, the Río Lagartos Biosphere Reserve is another striking natural attraction just over three hours from Cancún. Although you can no longer swim in them, the pink waters are what often draw people but the incredible diversity of the Biosphere Reserve itself is where the real appeal lies. Look out for the flamboyant flamingos in particular.

THE CARIBBEAN ISLANDS

Flee the mainland and make for a Caribbean island off the coast of Cancún. Isla Holbox, known for its laid-back, desert island vibes is a great place to swim with whale sharks from May to September. Though Cozumel is a popular cruise-ship stop, it's still one of the country's top diving destinations. Over on Isla Mujeres—which is just a 20-minute ferry ride from Cancún—you'll find glorious beaches and plenty of opportunities to snorkel with sea turtles. Finally, tiny Isla Contoy (which only accepts 200 visitors a day) is a haven for bird-watchers.

PLAYA DEL CARMEN

When discussing vacations in Quintana Roo, you'll often hear people debating whether to go to Cancún or Playa del Carmen, but why not do both? Just one hour apart, these two cities are a little like eyebrows—sisters, not twins. While Cancún has better nightlife and beaches, Playa is great for shopping and has a more Mexican feel to it. Stroll Quinta Avenida, hang out on Playacar, and catch a Voladores de Papantla performance in Parque Fundadores.

FISHING VILLAGES

If you remain unmoved by the bright lights of Playa del Carmen, ambivalent in the face of Tulum, and reluctant to move inland for your Cancún day trip, consider a visit to one of the region's small(er) coastal towns: Akumal and Puerto Morelos. The former is probably best known for sea turtles, but you can also enjoy a quiet waterfront lunch, windsurfing lessons, and even fishing excursions. Meanwhile, Puerto Morelos is a tranquil gateway to the Mesoamerican Barrier Reef with several nearby cenotes, including the lush Verde Lucero.

ECO THEME PARKS

If you're traveling with children (or just remain young at heart), the trio of water parks that surround Cancún—Xel-Há, Xcaret, and Xplor—are unmissable. Visit one or all three during your vacation but remember that they're all between 1 and 1½ hours from Cancún and share similar attractions—think freshwater rivers, cenotes, jungle walkways, and massive evening spectaculars. True adrenaline chasers may prefer Xplor, families will probably be best suited to Xcaret, and Xel-Há is all about the water activities.

Most Romantic Experiences in Cancún and the Riviera Maya

JOURNEY ALONG THE RÍO SECRETO

Everyone knows secret underground rivers are the very essence of romance. Okay, maybe not. But they are pretty spectacular and make for a cool place to explore alongside your partner while in Cancún. Ideal for adventurous couples, Río Secreto—where you can admire sparkling minerals and dramatic stalactites before biking, hiking, and swimming along the length of this hidden natural phenomenon—offers a more intimate experience than big amusement parks like Xcaret and Xel-Há.

HANG OUT AT A BEACH CLUB

Get out of the resort for the day and hang out at one of Cancún's many beach clubs. Mandala Beach Club—attached to the popular Mandala nightclub—is a favorite of fun-loving friends and couples alike. Grab a poolside lounger, and enjoy the live DJ sets and beachfront pools. Alternatively, for a more low-key, romantic beach club experience, head to Coco's Beach Club. There, snag a private beach bed (or upgrade to the VIP-only lounge), and make the most of the inventive cocktails and refreshing seafood dishes as you admire the ocean views.

GIVE BOB SNORKELING A GO

See the best of the underwater world off the coast of Cancún during a BOB experience. The love child of a scuba suit and a submarine, BOBs (Breathing Observation Bubbles) allow you to submerge and scoot around below water more readily than scuba diving while getting more up-close-and-personal with the marine life than you could while snorkeling.

TAKE A ROMANTIC DINNER CRUISE

You can't go wrong with a sunset dinner cruise when on a romantic vacation for two, and Cancún has a wealth of evening sailing options for loved-up holidaymakers. Take a Columbus Cruise on the Nichupte Lagoon, listen to live music, and make metaphorical heart eyes at your beloved as you enjoy your lobster dinner and drinks.

ESCAPE THE CROWDS ON A CARIBBEAN ISLAND

While popular Isla Mujeres has more of a family-friendly vibe, Isla Holbox—toward the tip of the Yucatán Peninsula—is the ideal place for an intimate day trip for two. Car-free and still hovering under the radar of the average traveler, Holbox is a ready-made romantic idyll where you can sip coconut water and even swim with whale sharks. Meanwhile, animal-loving couples shouldn't pass up the opportunity to visit Isla Contoy, a protected national park that only permits access to 200 travelers per day. At first glance, Cozumel, Mexico's largest Caribbean island, seems all about cruise ships and scuba diving. Walk just one block inland from the waterfront to the central park especially on a weekend. You'll want to grab an ice cream cone, hold hands, and join in the evening *paseo*.

INDULGE IN A COUPLES SPA TREATMENT

If you can't relax while on vacation with your significant other, then when can you? In Cancún, home to some of the best spas in Mexico, take the time to pamper yourself with facials, hydrotherapy circuits, and full-body massages alongside your partner. While there are plenty of places to choose from—your resort may even have an on-site spa—the private couples' suites at Nizuc Spa are incredibly intimate, as are the spa's other state-of-the-art facilities. Similarly, Blanc Spa is a treat for fans of a good massage—opt for the relaxing Aroma Essence Massage.

DINE IN STYLE OVERLOOKING THE WATERFRONT

Cancún may not have the culinary reputation of Mexico City or Puerto Vallarta, but the capital of Quintana Roo has no shortage of romantic fine-dining establishments and waterfront restaurants. Dine overlooking the Nichupte Lagoon at Lorenzillo's, a popular Cancún restaurant that specializes in lobster, or, if you're more of an equal opportunity seafood enthusiast, visit Fred's instead. Prefer turf to surf? Chow down some Kobe sliders at Harry's Grill in Cancún or Playa del Carmen.

TAKE A DIP IN A CENOTE

You can't come to Cancún without visiting a cenote (or two, or three). These freshwater natural sinkholes revered by the Maya are found across the peninsula, although you'll need to travel outside Cancún proper to find some of the best and most easily accessible. Skip the more popular and family-friendly cenotes—such as Cenote Azul and the Gran Cenote–unless you enjoy being splashed by playful toddlers. Instead, combine a trip to Chichén Itzá with a stop at the nearby Cenote Yokdzonot or stay (slightly) closer to Cancún at Cenote Yalahau.

CATCH A SUNSET OVER THE LAGOON

A pesky problem with vacationing on the eastern coastline of Mexico is that the sun sets in the west. Simply put, you can only enjoy a Cancún sunset overlooking the Nichupte Lagoon rather than the Caribbean Sea. Don't let that deter you, though—make a well-timed booking at one of the many waterfront restaurants and enjoy dinner as the sun goes down. And what if you and your partner are early risers? Well, then, make your way down to the beach before the rest of Cancún shakes off its hangover and snatch a rare moment of tranquility as the sun comes up over the sea.

BLAZE A TRAIL TO TULUM

No question: Tulum has been discovered, and this onetime outpost on the Gringo Trail has evolved from the Hippie '60s into the place to see and be seen on the Riviera Maya. Partake of the town's snazzy, romantic boutique hotels and hip, trendy restaurants, all watched over by its stunning seaside Maya ruins. If you're based elsewhere and do Tulum as a day trip now, you might jot down some mental notes about centering your trip here next time.

Weddings and Honeymoons

Imagine exchanging vows on a white sandy beach against a backdrop of swaying palms and turquoise Caribbean waters. Your dream wedding can become a reality as long as you know the necessary steps to take when saying "I do" in Mexico.

We strongly suggest you enlist a local wedding planner and make initial contact several months in advance. Many big resorts have one on staff. The red tape is not onerous, but one missing step, one forgotten piece of paper and, boom, no wedding.

All marriage in Mexico is civil and must be performed by a judge from the state Oficina de Registro Civil (Civil Registry Office). You may hold a religious wedding or a ceremony of your own design, but without the judge, it won't be legal. You can take care of the legalities at the registry office, or the judge can come to your ceremony. The judge's formalities will be fixed and will be in Spanish, although an interpreter can be supplied. As of 2022, all Mexican states recognize and perform same-sex marriages.

Couples need to bring passports, original birth certificates, tourist cards, and results of blood tests taken in Mexico 14 days before the wedding. Most clinics charge MX$3,000 per couple for the required RPR, HIV, and blood-type tests. A judge's fee of MX$8,000 must be paid in advance, and, if all documents are not presented, the judge will not perform the ceremony.

You also must have four witnesses at the ceremony, all of whom must be over 18 and have passports. If either of the couple was previously married, the divorce decree or death certificate of the former spouse must be translated into Spanish and notarized. In such cases, you must wait a full year to remarry. There is no way around this arcane requirement, designed to ensure no pregnancy lingers from a prior marriage. It doesn't matter if you are 25 or 75.

BEAUTIFUL BACKDROPS

The Yucatán Peninsula is one of the most sought-after spots for destination weddings. It's no wonder: the region not only makes for an incredible backdrop—whether you choose a white sandy beach in Cozumel or a colorful hacienda in Mérida—but it's also a great place to combine a wedding and honeymoon.

Surprisingly, exchanging vows in Mexico can be much cheaper than a traditional wedding back home. Some smaller hotels can organize beautiful ceremonies, including food and music, for under $5,000. If you book your entire wedding party at the hotel, special rates and upgrades are generally available, and you can have the entire place to yourselves. Between May and November, rates are at their lowest, but you might end up with a soggy ceremony, especially during prime hurricane period—July through September.

HONEYMOONS

The peninsula's countless treasures, ranging from Maya ruins to fishing villages, make it a haven for honeymooners. Beach-bound newlyweds have plenty of resort options along the Riviera Maya, many of which have luxury spas with treatments for two. Ideal for both weddings and honeymoons, Tulum offers ancient ruins, beautiful beaches, and dozens of eco-lodges willing to host simple weddings with vegetarian buffets and yoga classes between events.

Kids and Families

The Yucatán Peninsula has plenty of activities for the entire family. The warm Caribbean waters are ideal for water sports such as swimming, snorkeling, and kayaking, and some areas even have roped-off sections designated for children. If you're vacationing in Cancún, beaches facing Bahía de Mujeres tend to have calmer waters and softer sand than those facing the Caribbean. Farther out, there may be undertows or riptides, so take note of warning signs and colored flags posted daily.

KID-FRIENDLY ACTIVITIES

For teens, there are adrenaline-pumping water activities like Jet Skiing, banana boat rides, parasailing, and diving. Smaller children may prefer interactive programs like those available at Dolphin Discovery, with locations in Isla Mujeres, Cozumel, Playa del Carmen, Costa Maya, Akumal, and Puerto Aventuras; the tour includes encounters with manatees and sea lions, plus a chance to swim with the dolphins.

For parents wanting to introduce their children to history, combine a tour of the Tulum ruins with a day at the beach, or opt for the Cobá ruins, where your entire family can explore jungle trails by mountain bike. Cancún's all-inclusive resorts have plenty to keep the kids busy, including swimming pools, children's programs, and on-site water sports. Nearby La Isla Shopping Village has an interactive aquarium. Also located in Zona Hotelera is Plaza Kukulcán, an upscale mall with a food court and play area on the second floor. In the Riviera Maya, Joyà by Cirque du Soleil is a whimsical show filled with entertainment and acrobatics for the entire family.

Isla Mujeres is home to Garrafón Natural Reef Park, where you can go snorkeling, swimming, hiking, or biking.

CHOOSING A DESTINATION

Just 16 km (10 miles) south of Tulum, the Reserva de la Biósfera Sian Ka'an has hundreds of species of wildlife in their freshwater lagoons, mangrove swamps, and tropical forests. The beaches here are excellent for swimming, snorkeling, and camping.

The colorful city of Mérida has folkloric shows, free concerts, and open-air markets where local crafts are sold. South of Mérida are the impressive Grutas de Loltún, one of the largest cave systems on the Yucatán Peninsula.

The quaint fishing villages of Puerto Morelos and Puerto Aventuras are excellent for families and close to the 250-acre ecological theme park, Xcaret. Here families can experience a butterfly pavilion, aviary, and dozens of water activities. Catering to adventure seekers, the neighboring Xplor lets you swim in a stalactite river, ride in an amphibious vehicle, or soar across the park on 14 zip lines.

To escape the heat, families can visit Xel-Há (the natural aquarium park) or take a dip in one of the hundreds of cenotes that dot the peninsula. These freshwater pools are ideal for snorkeling and swimming.

The People of the Yucatán Peninsula

The Maya people, whose ancient ruins have made the Yucatán a world-renowned travel destination, also make up the bulk of the peninsula's population and are the single largest indigenous group on the entire North American continent. Although predominantly located in Yucatán state, members of this group have also settled in other Mexican states such as Campeche, Quintana Roo, Tabasco, and Chiapas. Outside Mexico, the Maya can be found in Guatemala, Belize, Honduras, and El Salvador. Their total population is estimated at about 6 million, with 1.2 million living on the Yucatán Peninsula.

Linguists have associated 32 distinct indigenous languages among the Maya. Most of the Maya in this area speak Yucatec Maya and might be able to use Spanish only as a second language. While neighboring Guatemala makes a big deal of identifying its Maya population by different ethnic subdivisions, Mexico's corresponding population typically self-identifies as simply "Maya." Guatemala's program of genocide against its highland indigenous population in the 1980s caused the flight of much of its Maya population to Mexico and resulted in an increased number of non-Yucatec speakers.

The Maya are rightfully proud of their history, which dates back to a period immediately following the rise of the Olmec culture. After the fall of the Olmecs, the Maya rose to power and settled in the Yucatán Peninsula, where they developed several city-states including that of Chichén Itzá. Maya architecture, much of it ceremonial in nature, has been archaeologically classified as dating back some 3,000 years. Well-preserved hieroglyphs found in the Yucatán trace the presence of the Maya to 200 BC or before. More than 100 ancient Maya ruins still exist today, many of them drawing travelers from around the world to the Yucatán each year.

The Spanish fought to colonize the Yucatán well into the 1500s, achieving victory by the middle of that century. But long before the Spanish arrived, the once-powerful Maya civilization was already in decline, and no one really knows why—possibly disease, war, or famine. But while historians speak of the "waning" of Maya society, that pertains only to the military power it once wielded over Mesoamerica. The Maya have evolved and adapted to modern civilization.

The Maya continue to blend the elements of their ancient worship practices and rituals (minus the live sacrifice) with more contemporary religious practices. In addition, many people here still wear traditional clothing, and construct the oblong, thatched-roof houses of their forebears. The Maya passion to preserve its long history can be seen in the highly valued handicrafts that they create with the same skill and artistry as their ancestors. We recommend any excursion that allows you to experience this fascinating history and culture. Even if you're ensconced at a flashy beach resort, Maya villages and ruins are never far away.

Chapter 2

TRAVEL SMART

Updated by
Jeffrey Van Fleet

★ **MAJOR CITIES:**
Cancún, Playa del Carmen, Mérida

♛ **POPULATION:**
Quintana Roo state 1.86 million; Yucatán state 2.32 million

💬 **LANGUAGE:**
Spanish; English spoken in tourism industry

$ **CURRENCY:**
Peso

☎ **COUNTRY CODE:**
52

⚠ **EMERGENCIES:**
911

🚗 **DRIVING:**
On the right

⚡ **ELECTRICITY:**
120–220 v/60 cycles; plugs have two or three rectangular prongs

🕐 **TIME:**
Quintana Roo state: winter, same as New York; summer one hour behind New York. Yucatán: winter, same as Chicago; summer, one hour behind Chicago

🌐 **WEB RESOURCES:**
www.visitmexico.com

✈ **AIRPORT:**
Cancún (CUN), Cozumel (CZM), Mérida (MID)

Know Before You Go

Is it safe? Can you drink the water? Do you need special documents to enter the country? You may have a few questions before your trip to Mexico. We've got answers and a few insider tips to help you make the most of your visit, so you can rest easy in paradise.

THE "IS MEXICO SAFE?" QUESTION DOESN'T HAVE AN EASY ANSWER.

We've all heard the accounts of Mexico's drug-cartel violence. They've put once-popular travel spots in the northern part of the country off limits, and they have even affected travel to storied destinations such as Acapulco. The occasional drug-related killing grabs headlines here, but the Yucatán has largely been spared such problems and remains one of the safest regions of the country. Let common sense be your guide: leave the flashy jewelry at home, use ATMs during the day, store valuables in hotel safes, keep an eye on your belongings, watch your drink in public, and avoid Cancún's center city late at night. You should have a safe and enjoyable time here.

ENTRY AND EXIT GET EASIER ALL THE TIME.

You must have a valid passport to enter Mexico for up to 180 days and to reenter the United States. Cancún (CUN) and Cozumel (CZM) airports are two of five nationwide now permitted to do away with the tourist card (FMM or Forma Migratoria Multiple) for most visitors. If you fly into and out of the same airport, you don't have to fill out a form. If you don't meet those conditions, you'll still be required to fill out the FMM and will also need to present it when you leave Mexico. The news gets better: Cancún airport is one of two in Mexico now to offer "e-gate" entry to U.S. and Canadian tourists. As long as you visit as a tourist, have no one under 18 in your party, and have a biometric passport, you scan that passport, a machine takes your fingerprint and photo, and the gate swings open and welcomes you to Mexico. Alas, CUN baggage claim can still be the same old bottleneck it has been for years.

IT'S A CINCH TO GET AROUND.

Compared to other parts of Mexico, the roads in the Yucatán Peninsula are safe, flat, and well maintained. The main highway between Cancún and Belize, known as Carretera 307, is clearly marked and well paved. Toll road 180D runs between Cancún and Mérida—you can do it in four hours—and is by far your safest, fastest east–west option. In addition, Mexico's bus system (particularly the deluxe buses) is excellent, and now you can even take the train! The new-in-2024 Tren Maya (Maya Train) makes a grand loop in the states of Quintana Roo, Yucatán, and Campeche.

YOU MUST TAKE THE CAR INSURANCE.

Regardless of what coverage you have from your credit card or travel insurance, you must (by law) have additional Mexican auto insurance to rent a car. Average daily insurance rates start around $45, which is often more than the daily rental fee if you happened to find a good deal online. When renting a car, make sure that your insurance coverage includes an attorney and claims adjusters who will come to the scene of an accident.

CONSIDER AN ALL-INCLUSIVE PACKAGE.

Cancún and the Riviera Maya pioneered the all-inclusive concept in Mexico. Fly in planeloads of visitors for a week or two, house them at a flashy beach resort, throw in all (or most) of their food and drink, and provide them with all the activities they could desire. (Rest assured that if you seek a relaxing vacation, you can eschew your lodging's activities.) The resorts here do it well, and they roll everything into a fair price. Even the toniest Cancún beach property can be more reasonably priced than comparable facilities on a Caribbean island. We do recommend getting off the resort a time or two during your stay and sampling the region's many offerings.

BUT OTHER PLACES, DO IT À LA CARTE.

The farther you get from the beach, the scarcer the all-inclusive options become, and that's okay, too. Mérida, Valladolid, Campeche City, and the towns of the peninsula are the province of small but stylish colonial-era inns that once served as palaces, convents, or haciendas. Something lurks behind those walls and the gates; it takes peering inside to see the sumptuous rooms and lovely gardens. Rates include breakfast but rarely other meals.

YOU SHOULD CARRY SOME CASH.

Outside of remote areas like Xcalak and Mahahual, most tourist-oriented businesses accept Visa and Master-Card, but some places charge 5% to 10% more for credit-card payments to help offset high processing fees. It's always best to have at least some cash on hand. Remember: if you plan to bargain in a traditional market, cash in pesos gives you better leverage. A merchant likely won't give you a price break if you wish to pay by card or in U.S. dollars. Most ATMs in Mexico accept U.S. credit and debit cards. Before your trip, make sure your PIN has only four numbers, since ATMs in Mexico do not recognize more digits. Foreign transaction fees can be high, as much as MX$150 per withdrawal.

EXPAND YOUR DEFINI-TION OF MEXICAN FOOD.

Tacos, enchiladas, fajitas, nachos, burritos... they're all here, but Yucatecan cooks will give you a whole new notion of what south-of-the-border cuisine looks like and tastes like. Your morning *huevos rancheros* give way here to *huevos motuleños*, eggs with ham and cheese, black beans, and plantains. *Pibil*-style cooking, a Maya specialty, bakes chicken (*pollo*) or pork (*cochinita*) in an oven or casserole with fruits and spices. Top off your evening with a standard Mexican tequila, but fortify it with a dash of *xtabentún*, a honey-anise liqueur distilled here since ancient Maya times.

LIGHTING UP JUST GOT A LOT TOUGHER.

Mexico implemented one of the world's strictest no-smoking laws nation-wide in 2023. Lighting up is prohibited in all public spaces, indoors and outdoors. That includes beaches and parks, in addition to hotels and resorts—that means your room, too—bars, restaurants, clubs, and stores. Fines are steep (up to MX$5,000).

YOU CAN NO LONGER CLIMB THE PYRAMIDS.

At this writing, climbing pyramids is prohibited at all Maya sites, a wise decision, we think, that preserves both your safety and the ruins' structural integrity.

Helpful Phrases in Spanish

BASICS

Hello	Hola	**oh**-lah
Yes/no	Sí/no	see/no
Please	Por favor	pore fah-**vore**
May I?	¿Puedo?	**Pweh**-doh
Thank you	Gracias	**Grah**-see-as
You're welcome	De nada	day **nah**-dah
I'm sorry	Lo siento	lo see-**en**-toh
Good morning!	¡Buenos días!	**bway**-nohs dee-ahs
Good evening!	¡Buenas tardes! (after 2pm)	**bway**-nahs-**tar**-dess
	¡Buenas noches! (after 8pm)	**bway**-nahs no-chess
Good-bye!	¡Adiós!/¡Hasta luego!	ah-dee-**ohss/ah** -stah **lwe**-go
Mr./Mrs.	Señor/Señora	sen-**yor**/sen-**yohr**-ah
Miss	Señorita	sen-yo-**ree**-tah
Pleased to meet you	Mucho gusto	**moo**-cho **goose**-toh
How are you?	¿Cómo estás?	**koh**-moh ehs-**tahs**

NUMBERS

one	un, uno	oon, **oo**-no
two	dos	dos
three	tres	tress
four	cuatro	**kwah**-tro
five	cinco	**sink**-oh
six	seis	saice
seven	siete	see-**et**-eh
eight	ocho	**o**-cho
nine	nueve	new-**eh**-vey
ten	diez	dee-**es**
eleven	once	**ohn**-seh
twelve	doce	**doh**-seh
thirteen	trece	**treh**-seh
fourteen	catorce	ka-**tohr**-seh
fifteen	quince	**keen**-seh
sixteen	dieciséis	dee-es-ee-**saice**
seventeen	diecisiete	dee-**es**-ee-see-**et**-eh
eighteen	dieciocho	dee-**es**-ee-**o**-cho
nineteen	diecinueve	dee-**es**-ee-new-**ev**-eh
twenty	veinte	**vain**-teh
twenty-one	veintiuno	**vain**-te-oo-noh
thirty	treinta	**train**-tah
forty	cuarenta	kwah-**ren**-tah
fifty	cincuenta	seen-**kwen**-tah
sixty	sesenta	sess-**en**-tah
seventy	setenta	set-**en**-tah
eighty	ochenta	oh-**chen**-tah
ninety	noventa	no-**ven**-tah
one hundred	cien	see-**en**
one thousand	mil	meel
one million	un millón	oon meel-**yohn**

COLORS

black	negro	**neh**-groh
blue	azul	ah-**sool**
brown	café	kah-**fehg**
green	verde	**ver**-deh
orange	naranja	na-**rahn**-hah
red	rojo	**roh**-hoh
white	blanco	**blahn**-koh
yellow	amarillo	ah-mah-**ree**-yoh

DAYS OF THE WEEK

Sunday	domingo	doe-**meen**-goh
Monday	lunes	**loo**-ness
Tuesday	martes	**mahr**-tess
Wednesday	miércoles	me-**air**-koh-less
Thursday	jueves	hoo-**ev**-ess
Friday	viernes	vee-**air**-ness
Saturday	sábado	**sah**-bah-doh

MONTHS

January	enero	eh-**neh**-roh
February	febrero	feh-**breh**-roh
March	marzo	**mahr**-soh
April	abril	ah-**breel**
May	mayo	**my**-oh
June	junio	**hoo**-nee-oh
July	julio	**hoo**-lee-yoh
August	agosto	ah-**ghost**-toh
September	septiembre	sep-tee-**em**-breh
October	octubre	oak-**too**-breh
November	noviembre	no-vee-**em**-breh
December	diciembre	dee-see-**em**-breh

USEFUL WORDS AND PHRASES

Do you speak English?	¿Habla Inglés?	**ah**-blah in-**glehs**
I don't speak Spanish.	No hablo español	no **ah**-bloh es-pahn-**yol**
I don't understand.	No entiendo	no en-tee-**en**-doh
I understand.	Entiendo	en-tee-**en**-doh
I don't know.	No sé	no **seh**
I'm American.	Soy americano (americana)	soy ah-meh-ree-**kah**-no (ah-meh-ree-**kah**-nah)
What's your name?	¿Cómo se llama ?	koh-mo seh **yah**-mah
My name is . . .	Me llamo . . .	may **yah**-moh
What time is it?	¿Qué hora es?	keh **o**-rah es
How?	¿Cómo?	**koh**-mo
When?	¿Cuándo?	**kwahn**-doh
Yesterday	Ayer	ah-**yehr**
Today	hoy	oy
Tomorrow	mañana	mahn-**yah**-nah
Tonight	Esta noche	es-tah **no**-cheh
What?	¿Qué?	keh

What is it?	¿Qué es esto?	keh es **es**-toh
Why?	¿Por qué?	pore **keh**
Who?	¿Quién?	kee-**yen**
Where is . . .	¿Dónde está . . .	**dohn**-deh es-**tah**
. . . the bus station?	la central de autobuses?	lah sehn-**trahl** deh ow-toh-**boo**-sehs
. . . the subway station?	estación de metro	la es-ta-see-**on** del **meh**-tro
. . . the bus stop?	la parada del autobus?	la pah-**rah**-dah del ow-toh-**boos**
. . . the terminal? (airport)	el aeropuerto	el air-oh-**pwar**-toh
. . . the post office?	la oficina de correos?	la oh-fee-**see**- nah deh koh-**rreh**-os
. . . the bank?	el banco?	el **bahn**-koh
. . . the hotel?	el hotel?	el oh-**tel**
. . . the museum?	el museo?	el moo-**seh**-oh
. . . the hospital?	el hospital?	el ohss-pee-**tal**
. . . the elevator?	el elevador?	ehl eh-leh-bah-**dohr**
Where are the restrooms?	el baño?	el **bahn**-yoh
Here/there	Aquí/allí	ah-**key**/ah-**yee**
Open/closed	Abierto/cerrado	ah-bee-**er**-toh/ ser-**ah**-doh
Left/right	Izquierda/derecha	iss-key-**eh**-dah/ dare-**eh**-chah
Is it near?	¿Está cerca?	es-**tah** sehr-kah
Is it far?	¿Está lejos?	es-**tah** leh-hoss
I'd like . . .	Quisiera . . .	kee-see-**ehr**-ah
. . . a room	un cuarto/una habitación	oon **kwahr**- toh/**oo**-nah ah-bee-tah-see-**on**
. . . the key	la llave	lah **yah**-veh
. . . a newspaper	un periódico	oon pehr-ee-**oh**- dee-koh
. . . a stamp	un sello de correo	oon **seh**-yo deh korr-**oh**-oh
I'd like to buy . . .	Quisiera comprar . . .	kee-see-**ehr**-ah kohm-**prahr**
. . . soap	jabón	hah-**bohn**
. . . suntan lotion	bronceador	brohn-seh-ah-**dohr**
. . . envelopes	sobres	**so**-brehs
. . . writing paper	papel	pah-**pel**
. . . a postcard	una postal	**oo**-nah pohs-**tahl**
. . . a ticket	un billete (travel)	oon bee-**yee**-teh
	una entrada (concert etc.)	oona en-**trah**-dah
How much is it?	¿Cuánto cuesta?	**kwahn**-toh **kwes**-tah
It's expensive/ cheap	Es caro/barato	es **kah**-roh/ bah-**rah**-toh
A little/a lot	Un poquito/mucho	oon poh-**kee**-toh/ **moo**-choh
More/less	Más/menos	mahss/**men**-ohss
Enough/too (much)	Suficiente/	soo-fee-see-**en**-teh/
I am ill/sick	Estoy enfermo(a)	es-**toy** en-**fehr**-moh(mah)

Call a doctor	Llame a un medico	ya-meh ah oon **med**-ee-koh
Help!	Ayuda	ah-**yoo**-dah
Stop!	Pare	**pah**-reh
DINING OUT		
I'd like to reserve a table . . .	Quisiera reservar una mesa . . .	kee-**syeh**-rah rreh- sehr-**bahr** oo-nah **meh**-sah . . .
. . . for two people.	para dos personas.	**pah**-rah dohs pehr-**soh**-nahs
. . . for this evening.	para esta noche.	**pah**-rah ehs-tah **noh**-cheh
. . . for 8 PM	para las ocho de la noche.	**pah**-rah lahs **oh**-choh deh lah **noh**-cheh
A bottle of . . .	Una botella de . . .	oo-nah bo-**teh**-yah deh
A cup of . . .	Una taza de . . .	oo-nah **tah**-sah deh
A glass of . . .	Un vaso (water, soda, etc.) de...	oon **vah**-so deh
	Una copa (wine, spirits, etc.) de...	oona **coh**-pah deh
Bill/check	La cuenta	lah **kwen**-tah
Bread	Pan	pahn
Breakfast	El desayuno	el deh-sah-**yoon**-oh
Butter	mantequilla	man-teh-**kee**-yah
Coffee	Café	kah-**feh**
Dinner	La cena	lah **seh**-nah
Fork	tenedor	ten-eh-**dor**
I don't eat meat	No como carne	noh koh-moh **kahr**-neh
I cannot eat . . .	No puedo comer . . .	noh **pweh**-doh koh-**mehr**
I'd like to order . . .	Quiero pedir . . .	**kee**-yehr-oh peh-**deer**
I'd like . . .	Me gustaría . . .	Meh goo-stah-**ee**-ah
I'm hungry/thirsty	Tengo hambre/sed	**Tehn**-goh **hahm**-breh/seth
Is service/the tip included?	¿Está incluida la propina?	es-**tah** in-cloo-**ee**- dah lah pro-**pee**-nah
Knife	cuchillo	koo-**chee**-yo
Lunch	La comida	lah koh-**mee**-dah
Menu	La carta, el menú	lah **cart**-ah, el meh-**noo**
Napkin	servilleta	sehr-vee-**yet**-ah
Pepper	pimienta	pee-mee-**en**-tah
Plate	plato	
Please give me . . .	Me da por favor . . .	meh dah pohr fah-**bohr**
Salt	sal	sahl
Spoon	cuchara	koo-**chah**-rah
Sugar	ázucar	ah-**su**-kar
Tea	té	teh
Water	agua	**ah**-gwah
Wine	vino	**vee**-noh

Getting Here and Around

Air

Cancún is 4½ hours from New York and Chicago, 5 hours from Los Angeles, 3 hours from Dallas, and 2 hours from Miami. Flights to Cozumel and Mérida are comparable in length, but many fewer in number. There are direct flights to Cancún from hub airports such as Atlanta, Boston, Charlotte, Chicago, Dallas, Denver, Detroit, Fort Lauderdale, Houston, Los Angeles, Miami, New York, Newark, Orlando, Philadelphia, Phoenix, San Francisco, Seattle, Toronto, and Washington, D.C. You can reach it from other locales on connecting flights; some arrive via Mexico City, where you must pass through immigration and customs before transferring to a domestic flight to Cancún.

Charter flights, especially those leaving from Cancún, are notorious for last-minute changes. Be sure to ask for an updated telephone number from your charter company before you leave, so you can verify departures times. Most recommend that you call within 48 hours of departure. Commercial airlines usually have more dependable departure times; any changes are usually due to weather conditions.

Flying within the Yucatán is neither cost-effective nor time-efficient. Given the additional time needed for check-in, you might as well drive or take a bus to your destination, unless you're continuing on by plane.

AIRPORTS

The Aeropuerto Internacional de Cancún (CUN) is Mexico's second busiest airport and the Yucatán Peninsula's major gateway, offering the best selection of flights and fares. It sprawls over four unconnected terminals (most domestic Mexican airlines use Terminal 2), and, in peak season, passenger waiting lines can be long, especially on weekends. Plan accordingly.

Note, too, that your first encounter with Cancún's ubiquitous time-share sales reps will be here, as they are permitted to position themselves in the airport arrivals area. Learn to say no, and walk right on by. They are not your hotel transport or your baggage handler or your tour guide. Don't let them muscle their way into any of those roles.

Several North American hubs also offer nonstop flights to the Aeropuerto Internacional de Cozumel (CZM). The inland Aeropuerto Internacional Manuel Crescencio Rejón (MID), in Mérida, is smaller but closer to most major Mayan ruins. Tulum (TUY), Chetumal (CTM), and Campeche (CPE) have very small airports served by domestic carriers only.

It's 20 to 30 minutes from the Zona Hotelera to the Cancún airport or from downtown Mérida or Campeche to theirs. Allow 1½ hours from Playa del Carmen to the Cancún airport. The Cozumel airport is less than 10 minutes from downtown Cozumel.

AIRLINES

International, national, and regional carriers serve the Yucatán Peninsula. The most convenient flight from the United States is nonstop on either a U.S. or Mexican airline.

Since all the major airlines listed here fly to Cancún—and often have the cheapest and most frequent flights there—it's worthwhile to consider it as a jumping-off point even if you don't plan on visiting the city. At this writing, more than 450 flights land daily in Cancún. Airlines that serve it include Aeroméxico, Air Canada and Air Canada Rouge, Alaska, American, Delta, Frontier, JetBlue, Southwest, Spirit, United, Viva Aerobús, Volaris, and WestJet. Air Canada Rouge, American,

Delta, Frontier, Southwest, United, Volaris, Viva Aerobus, and WestJet also fly to Cozumel. Aeroméxico, American, United, Viva Aerobús, and Volaris fly to Mérida.

AIRPORT TRANSFERS

As you exit the Cancún airport, transportation operators can be overwhelming as they eagerly wave signs and yell names to arriving passengers. There are taxi and shuttle desks in the baggage-claim area, just before you exit the terminal. Go to the ones with posted prices, but keep in mind that rates are much higher for last-minute bookings as opposed to pre-arranged ground transportation reserved online.

It's not uncommon to be told that you just missed the last bus, taxi, or van to your destination. This is actually a ploy to get you to use the transportation company that is "assisting" you. Ask around if you're not entirely sure. Always arrive with small bills for taxi or bus fare; otherwise, you're liable to get ripped off. Check the identification of transportation operators, and don't allow anyone to "help" you with your luggage. Many people perform this task on commission for specific transportation companies. Worse yet, they might end up disappearing into the crowd with your baggage.

BUS AND SHUTTLE

All four terminals have an ADO kiosk (the name of the company) outside selling bus tickets into the city. A bus leaves every hour from the airport to the ADO terminal in downtown Cancún.

Some major hotels send shuttles to pick up arriving guests; it's worth checking before you arrive at the airport. Private taxis from the airport charge reasonable rates within Cancún. Airport shuttle vans, which charge set rates based on your destination, are another option; however, they sometimes take forever before

filling up and getting under way. For round-trip transportation from the airport to the Riviera Maya, it's worth looking for a shuttle service, as a private taxi can be prohibitively expensive. Some can be arranged beforehand by phone or online.

Cancún Valet rents per van, rather than per person, for up to 10 passengers, making it a good value for couples and groups. Prices from the airport to the Zona Hotelera, Playa del Carmen, and Tulum, as well as intermittent points are reasonable: MX$800 to Cancún (MX$1,400 round-trip) or MX$1,500 to Playa del Carmen (MX$2,700 round-trip), for example.

Van Travel charges MX$700 per couple or individual, one way, to the Zona Hotelera (MX$1,100 round-trip) or MX$1,200 to Playa del Carmen (MX$2,200 round-trip). Despite their names, anyone may use the services of USA Transfers and Canada Transfers. Both companies get high marks for dependable service. Expect to pay MX$1,000 one way to Cancún's hotel zone and MX$1,900 to Playa del Carmen.

TAXI

For safety, you should only take the authorized taxi service from most airports. A metered taxi has a *taxímetro,* and if a cab has one, ask the driver what the rates are. If not, agree on a fare before setting out. Tipping isn't customary unless the driver helps you with your bags.

⚓ Boat

The Yucatán is served by a number of ferries and boats. Most popular are the efficient speedboats that run between Playa del Carmen and Cozumel or from Puerto Juárez, Punta Sam, and Isla Mujeres. Vessels also run from Chiquila to Isla Holbox. Most carriers follow set

Getting Here and Around

schedules, with the exception of those going to the smaller, less visited islands. But departure times can vary with the weather and with the number of passengers. You can check ⊕ *visitcancun.com, travelyucatan.com,* and *granpuerto.com. mx* for information on water taxis and ferries, though always confirm the details before heading down to the docks.

Bus

If you are nervous about driving, the extensive Mexican bus network is a great and affordable means of getting around, though you'll have to either walk or organize additional transportation from the bus station or stop. Regardless, bus service is frequent, and you can buy tickets on the spot (except during holidays and on long weekends, when advance purchase is crucial). Bring something to eat on long trips in case you don't like the restaurant or market where the bus stops. Also, bring toilet tissue, and wear a sweater, as the air-conditioning is often set on high. Most buses play videos or television until midnight, so bring earplugs if you're bothered by noise. Smoking is prohibited on Mexican buses.

Bus companies here offer several classes of service: first-class (*primera clase*), deluxe or executive class (*de lujo* or *ejecutivo*), and second class (*segunda*). First- and executive-class buses are generally punctual and have air-conditioned coaches with bathrooms, movies, reclining seats with seat belts, and refreshments. They take the fastest route (usually on safer, well-paved toll roads) and make few stops between points. Less desirable, second-class vehicles connect smaller, secondary routes; they also run along some long-distance routes, often taking slower, local roads. They're tolerable but are usually cramped

and make many stops. If you're staying in the Riviera Maya, *colectivos* (minibuses) run along Carretera 307 from Cancún to Tulum.

The class of travel will be listed on your printed ticket—if you see "económico" printed next to "servicio," you've been booked on a second-class bus. At many bus stations, one counter will represent several lines and classes of service, and mistakes do happen. ADO is the Yucatán's principal first-class bus company, and Mayab (operated by ADO) is the second-class line. Most bus tickets, including first-class (or executive) and second-class, can be reserved ahead of time in person at ticket offices. ADO also allows you to reserve tickets online 48 hours in advance.

Schedules are posted at bus stations; the bus leaves more or less around the listed time. Occasionally, if all the seats have been sold, the bus will leave early. Typical times and fares on first-class buses are: Cancún to Playa del Carmen, 1½ hours, MX$240; Cancún to Mérida, 4 hours, MX$615; Mérida to Campeche, 2½ hours, MX$330; and Cancún to Mexico City, 28 hours, MX$1,990.

🚗 Car

The most practical way to explore the Yucatán Peninsula is to fly to your region and rent a car for the duration of your stay. The best flight deals, however, usually arrive and depart from the Cancún airport, where, alas, rental cars can be expensive. Consider whether your itinerary even requires a rental car.

If you're not traveling far afield, don't bother to rent, as you can arrange taxi service to nearby sights through your hotel. For longer trips—to Playa del Carmen, for instance—taxis can be pricey, so renting a car for a day or two of exploring may be more economical. Alternatively, you can hop on one of the colectivos (minibuses) that run along Carretera 307 from Cancún to Tulum or travel via the luxury ADO buses that serve the peninsula.

You won't need a car on Isla Mujeres or Isla Holbox, which are too small to make driving practical. (Electric golf carts are a popular way to get around Isla Mujeres, and you can rent one.) Playa del Carmen's downtown area is quite compact, and the main street is blocked off to vehicles. Cars can feel like a burden in Mérida and Campeche City because of the narrow cobbled streets and the lack of parking spaces. You'll need a car in Cozumel only if you wish to explore the less-developed eastern side of the island.

BORDER CROSSINGS BY CAR

You probably won't be driving to the Yucatán Peninsula from the United States, but, on the rare chance that you do, there are two absolutely essential points to remember. First and foremost is to carry Mexican auto insurance (we can't stress this enough). If you injure anyone in an accident, you could be jailed—whether it was your fault or not—unless you have this insurance. Second, the high rate of U.S. vehicles being sold illegally in Mexico has caused the Mexican government to enact stringent regulations for bringing a car into the country.

So, if you enter Mexico with a car, you must leave with it. You must also be in your foreign vehicle at all times when it's driven. You cannot lend it to another person. Do not, under any circumstances, let a national drive your car. It's illegal for Mexicans to drive foreign-owned cars; if a national is caught driving your car, the car will be impounded by customs, and you will receive a stiff fine. Newer

models of vans, SUVs, and pickup trucks can be impossible to get back once impounded.

To cross the border you'll need the following documents: title or registration for your vehicle, a valid passport, proof of insurance, a credit card (MasterCard or Visa only), and a valid driver's license with a photo. You'll also need a temporary car-importation permit and an FMM (tourist permit). The title-holder, driver, and credit-card owner must be one and the same—that is, if your spouse's name is on the title of the car and yours isn't, you cannot be the one to bring the car into the country. For financed, leased, rental, or company cars, you must bring a notarized letter of permission from the bank, lien holder, rental agency, or company.

When you submit your paperwork at the border and pay the approximate US$60 charge on your credit card, you'll receive a car permit and a sticker to put on your vehicle. The permit is valid for the same amount of time as your tourist visa, which is up to 180 days. You may go back and forth across the border during this six-month period, as long as you check with immigration and bring all your permit paperwork with you. If you're planning to stay and keep your car in Mexico for longer than six months, however, you'll have to get a new permit before the original one expires.

In addition to the permit fee, your credit card will be charged a deposit based on the age of your car. This fee is to guarantee return of the vehicle to U.S. territory. If your car is older than 2000, you'll pay $200; cars between 2001 and 2006 will be charged $300; and anything newer than 2007 will cost $400. This amount is refunded in full 24 hours after you cancel your permit, unless you have passed the expiration date or left your car in Mexico.

Getting Here and Around

Upon your departure from Mexico, the permit for temporary importation must be canceled at customs or you will not receive your refunded deposit.

■ TIP→ **One way to minimize hassle when you cross the border with a car is to have your paperwork done in advance at a branch of Sanborn's Mexico Auto Insurance.** You'll find an office in almost every town on the U.S.–Mexico border. Average daily insurance rates start around $45. The fact that you drove in with a car is stamped on your tourist card, which you must give to immigration authorities at departure. If an emergency arises and you must fly home, there are complicated customs procedures to face.

CAR INSURANCE

Car-rental agencies in Mexico require you to purchase a CDW or Collision Damage Waiver (starting at $30 per day), and Mexico Liability Auto Insurance (starting at $15 per day). △ **Regardless of any coverage afforded by your credit-card company, you must purchase liability insurance.** If you are caught without coverage, fines start at $200. Keep in mind that although you might have reserved a rental car for only $20 per day, full coverage insurance will cost you about $50 per day. Additional theft protection and personal injury policies are optional. Since most U.S. insurance policies aren't recognized in Mexico (including those purchased online at time of booking), it is best to buy insurance directly at the counter with the rental car provider.

Be sure that you've been provided with proof of such insurance; if you drive without it, you're not only liable for damages, but you're also breaking the law. If you're in a car accident and you don't have insurance, you may be placed in jail until you're proven innocent. If anyone is injured you'll remain in jail until you make retribution to all injured parties and their families—which will likely cost you thousands of dollars. Mexican laws seem to favor nationals.

Even if you're absolutely certain you're fully covered by your credit-card company, we recommend you purchase full coverage insurance in Mexico. Getting into a car accident in Mexico would be harrowing enough without having to navigate the bureaucracy of your credit-card company to clear things up with Mexican authorities. Make sure that your insurance covers the cost for an attorney and claims adjusters who will come to the scene of an accident. Buying insurance makes renting a car in Mexico one of the most expensive parts of the trip, but in this case it's better to be safe than frugal.

CAR RENTAL

In Mexico the minimum driving age is 18, but most rental-car agencies have a minimum age requirement between 21 and 25; some have a surcharge for drivers under 25. Your own driver's license is acceptable; there's no reason to get an international driver's license.

As a rule, local agencies have better rates than major companies, but if you're looking for a reliable car, stick with a brand you recognize. You can get the same kind of midsize and luxury cars in Mexico that you can rent in the United States. Economy usually refers to a small car barely fitting four passengers, which may or may not come with air-conditioning.

Pancake-flat Yucatán makes for fairly easy driving, although side roads may have inadequate (or no) signposting; four-wheel-drive vehicles aren't necessary unless you plan on traveling to sites far off the beaten path in rainy season. If you'll require a child's car seat, request one when booking.

GASOLINE

Pemex, Mexico's government-owned petroleum monopoly, franchises all gas stations, so prices throughout the Yucatán—and the country—are the same. Overall, gas prices run around 25% higher than in the United States. Gas is always sold in liters. High-octane unleaded (called *premium*), the red pump, and regular unleaded (*magna*), the green pump, are available nationwide. Fuel quality is generally lower than that in the United States and Europe, but it has improved enough so that your car will run acceptably.

There are no self-service stations in Mexico. Ask the attendant to fill your tank ("*lleno* [*yay*-noh], *por favor*") or ask for a specific amount in pesos to avoid being overcharged. Check that the attendant has set the meter back to zero and that the price is shown. Watch the attendant check the oil as well—to make sure you actually need it—and watch while they pour it into your car. Never pay before the gas is pumped, even if the attendant asks you to. Always tip your attendant a few pesos.

A few stations in Cancún accept U.S. dollars, but most do not. Some stations accept credit cards, and a few have ATMs, but don't count on it. Plan to pay in pesos, which is best anyway since attendants have been known to run credit cards through twice, claiming it didn't work the first time, thus leaving you with two charges on your statement. If you do pay by credit card, don't be surprised if the attendant makes a photocopy of your passport since this is a normal practice, and always ask for a *recibo* (receipt), just in case you need to present it to your credit card company for evidence.

■ TIP➔ **Keep your gas tank full, because stations aren't plentiful in this region.** If you run out of gas in a small village and there's no gas station for miles, ask if there's a store that sells gas from containers. Do everything you can to avoid having to use this option; you run a risk of such gas being less clean.

MEXICAN DRIVERS

Mexicans are generally skilled drivers, but they do drive quite fast, even on twisting or extraordinarily dark roads, and often think nothing of tailgating, speeding, and weaving in and out of traffic. Drive defensively and keep your cool.

All that said, Mexicans motorists are, in some ways, more courteous than U.S. ones. It's customary, for example, for drivers to put on their hazard lights to warn the cars behind them of poor road conditions, slow-downs, or upcoming speed bumps; oncoming cars may flash their lights at you for the same reasons.

PARKING

A circle with a diagonal line superimposed on the letter *E* (for *estacionamiento*) means "no parking." A red curb means parking is restricted at all times, and a white curb is designated for loading and unloading only. A blue curb is for handicap parking, a green curb allows parking during specific hours, and a yellow curb means that the parking space is private. If you're ticketed, your license plate will be taken to a nearby police station and will only be returned upon payment of the infraction.

■ TIP➔ **Never park overnight on the street, and never leave anything of value in an unattended car.** When in doubt, choose a parking lot; it will probably be safer anyway. Lots are plentiful, though not always clearly marked, and fees are reasonable—as little as MX$60 for a half day. Sometimes you park your own car; more often, though, you hand the keys over to an attendant. Tip him and ask that he look after your vehicle.

Getting Here and Around

ROAD CONDITIONS

Compared to other parts of Mexico, main roads in the Yucatán Peninsula are nicely paved. Carretera 307 serves as the coastal route between Cancún and the Belize border, but this stretch of highway is known for its speed traps and large *topes* (speed bumps). Toll road 180D, the four-lane highway from Cancún to Mérida, is smooth going, sometimes with long stretches between off-ramps. The colonial city of Valladolid and the Maya ruins of Chichén Itzá have their own exits.

From Cancún, you can reach Mérida in about four hours. You will pay MX$609 in tolls, a bit pricey, but look at it as an investment in terms of time and ease of driving. (Tolls must be paid in cash in pesos.) A free section of Highway 180 continues southwest to Campeche and the rest of Mexico.

The winding, more scenic Carretera 261 also leads from Mérida to some of the more off-the-beaten-track archaeological sites on the way south to Campeche and Escárcega, where it joins Carretera 186 going east to Chetumal. These highways are two-lane roads. Carretera 295 (from the north coast to Valladolid and Felipe Carrillo Puerto) is also a good two-lane road.

Some secondary roads are unpaved, unmarked, and full of potholes. If you must take one of these, travel only by day and allow plenty of time. Slow down when approaching towns, where you'll encounter pedestrians and animals as well as *topes* (speed bumps). Note, too, that locals selling produce or candy will almost certainly approach your car.

ROADSIDE EMERGENCIES

The Mexican Tourism Ministry operates a fleet of some 1,800 pickup trucks, known as Angeles Verdes, or the Green Angels, an organization in existence since 1960 that assists motorists on major highways. Dial ☎ *078* from any cell phone or Telmex phone booth and your call will be routed to the Green Angels' dispatch office. The bilingual drivers provide mechanical help, first aid, radio-telephone communication, basic supplies and small parts, towing, and tourist information. Services are free, and spare parts, fuel, and lubricants are provided at cost. Tips are always appreciated and are sometimes openly solicited.

The Green Angels patrol fixed sections of the major highways twice daily 8 am to dusk, later on holiday weekends. If your car breaks down, pull as far as possible off the road, lift the hood, hail a passing vehicle, and ask the driver to notify the patrol. Don't accept rides from strangers. If you witness an accident, don't stop to help since witnesses are often detained for questioning for long periods of time. Instead find the nearest official.

RULES OF THE ROAD

When you sign up for Mexican car insurance, you should receive a booklet on Mexican rules of the road, and it really is a good idea to read it. Here we've provided just a few highlights.

Right turns on red are not allowed, and phoning or texting while driving is not permitted. Seat belts are required by law throughout Mexico.

If an oncoming vehicle flicks its lights at you in the daytime, slow down: it could mean trouble ahead. When approaching a narrow bridge, the first vehicle to flash its lights has right of way. One-way streets are common. One-way traffic is indicated by an arrow; two-way, by a double-pointed arrow. Other road signs follow the widespread system of international symbols.

Mileage and speed limits are given in kilometers: 100 kph and 80 kph (60 mph and 50 mph, respectively) are the most common maximums. A few of the toll roads allow 110 kph (65 mph). In cities and small towns, observe the posted speed limits, which can be as low as 20 kph (12 mph). Foreigners must pay on-the-spot speeding penalties, which can be steep. Some minor traffic violations, however, can be dismissed until you return your rental car by simply showing your "Tourist Traffic Card" available from several car-rental agencies.

Drunk-driving laws are harsh in Mexico, and if you're caught, you'll go to jail immediately. Quintana Roo, Yucatán, and Campeche states impose a blood-alcohol limit of 0.08, but transit police often apply that number more strictly. The best way to avoid any problems is simply not to drink and drive.

If you encounter a police checkpoint, stay calm. These are simply routine checks for weapons and drugs; customarily they'll review the car's registration and look in the back seat, the trunk, and at the undercarriage with a mirror.

SAFETY ON THE ROAD
Before setting out on any car trip, check your vehicle's fuel, oil, fluids, tires, windshield wipers, and lights. Consult a map and have your route in mind as you drive.

When stopping for traffic or at a red light, always leave sufficient room between your car and the one ahead so you can maneuver to safety if necessary. On the highway, a left-turn signal in Mexico means the driver is signaling those behind that it's safe to pass. Blinking hazard lights means that traffic is stopped up ahead and to slow down.

⚠ **Avoid driving at night, especially in remote and rural areas.** Although there are few *bandidos* on the roads here, there will probably be a dearth of streetlights making it hard to see the inevitable potholes, free-roaming animals, and cars with no working lights. Road-hogging trucks are also a concern. If you must travel at night, use toll roads when possible; although costly, they're much safer.

Some of the biggest road-trip hassles might be from police who pull you over for supposedly breaking the law or for being a good prospect for a scam. Remember to be polite—displays of anger will only make matters worse—and be aware that a police officer might be pulling you over for something you didn't do. Although efforts are being made to fight corruption, it's still a fact of life in Mexico. The MX$100 (and up) it costs to get your license back is definitely supplementary income for the officer who pulled you over with no intention of taking you down to police headquarters.

🚢 Cruise Ship
As this region is included on many western Caribbean itineraries, a lot of travelers arrive by ship at the ports of Cancún, Cozumel, Calica, Costa Maya, and Progreso. A few cruise lines include multiple stops in Cancún, Playa del Carmen, and Cozumel.

Cozumel technically has three ports—Punta Langosta, Puerto Maya, and the International Terminal—each catering to its own cruise lines. Large ships dock in Calica, south of Playa del Carmen, although a few call at Carmen's small downtown port itself. Mahahual (aka Puerto Costa Maya) is a self-contained port facility. Progreso (near Mérida) is known for its 8-km (5-mile) pier, reputedly the world's longest.

Getting Here and Around

🚗 Ride-Sharing

Uber operates in a few localities here. That said, service can be unreliable owing to pushback and legal challenges from the taxi unions, which want to keep Uber out of the open market and complain that it doesn't procure proper government permits.

Tales abound of Uber drivers being unable to enter Cancún airport or the Zona Hotelera and having to drop off travelers several blocks away, or of authorities stopping and seizing vehicles with passengers inside. Until all is resolved, it's best to avoid using the service.

🚕 Taxi

Taxis are ubiquitous in both cities and larger towns. The standard taxi is a mid-size, four-door sedan. Drivers generally speak English, either enough to negotiate the fare or, in some cases, enough for a lively discussion of national politics.

Most taxis, particularly those in resort areas, are unmetered, so confirm the fare before setting out. Major hotels post rate sheets, or you can ask someone at the front desk what the fare should be. Note that if a cabbie asks for more than the posted rates, which are inflated to begin with, you're being grossly overcharged. Regardless, don't be shy about trying to negotiate a better price. That said, a surcharge of 20% to 40% may be added at night, usually after 11 pm.

If a driver doesn't know the address you give him, he'll radio either a dispatcher or other cabbie to get the info, or drive to the neighborhood and ask around. When you've negotiated the fare before starting, you needn't pay extra if the cabbie has to drive around a bit.

In addition to private taxis, many cities have bargain-price collective taxi services using minibuses and sedans. The service is called *colectivo* or *pesero*. Such vehicles run along fixed routes, and you hail them on the street and tell the driver where you're headed. He charges you based on how far you're going on that route. Paying the exact fare can make your ride smoother as drivers often run out of change.

🚆 Train

The new-in-2024 Tren Maya (Maya Train) was designed to provide a previously unknown mode of transport around this region. The 1,525-km (950-mile) network makes a grand loop—at speeds of up to 160 kph (100 mph)—through the states of Quintana Roo, Yucatán, and Campeche.

From Cancún, the route heads south to Playa del Carmen, Tulum, and Chetumal at the Belizean border. West from Cancún, service connects Valladolid, Chichén Itzá, Izamal, Mérida, and Campeche. Both portions of the loop meet in southern Campeche State and continue south through Tabasco and Chiapas states, where the network terminates near the famous Maya ruins of Palenque.

Fares for locals are lower than those for tourists. That said, tourist service includes things like checked baggage and dining cars.

Essentials

🍴 Dining

If you're here on an all-inclusive package, your meals will likely be covered (though you should check carefully for exclusions). The downside is that you may feel locked into your dining options. We recommend enjoying a meal or two outside your resort to experience Cancún and the Riviera Maya's amazing dining scenes.

Mexican law prohibits smoking in all restaurants, both in indoor- and outdoor-seating areas.

MEALS AND MEALTIMES

Desayuno can be either a breakfast sweet roll and coffee or milk or a full breakfast of an egg dish such as *huevos a la mexicana* (scrambled eggs with chopped tomato, onion, and chiles), *huevos rancheros* (fried eggs on a tortilla covered with salsa), or *huevos con jamón* (scrambled eggs with ham), plus juice and toast or tortillas. Some cafés don't open until 8 or 8:30, in which case hotel restaurants are the best bets for early risers. *Panaderías* (bakeries) open early and provide the cheapest breakfast you'll find—a bag of assorted rolls and pastries will likely cost less than MP100.

Traditionally, lunch is called *comida* or *almuerzo* and is the biggest meal of the day. Most restaurants start serving lunch no earlier than 1 pm and traditional businesses close between 2 pm and 4 pm for this meal. It usually includes soup, a main dish, and dessert. Regional specialties include *pan de cazón* (baby shark shredded and layered with tortillas, black beans, and tomato sauce) in Campeche; *pollo pibil* (chicken baked in banana leaves) in Mérida; and *tikin xic* (fish in a sour-orange sauce) on the coast. Restaurants in tourist areas also serve American-style food such as hamburgers, pizza, and pasta. The evening meal is called *cena*, which is sometimes replaced by *merienda*, a lighter meal between lunch and dinner.

Most restaurants are open daily for lunch and dinner during high season (late November through April), but hours may be reduced during the rest of the year. It's always a good idea to phone ahead.

⇨ *Unless otherwise noted, the restaurants listed in this guide are open daily for lunch and dinner.*

PAYING

Most small restaurants do not take credit cards. Larger restaurants and those catering to tourists typically accept MasterCard and Visa. Prices are generally in pesos, which might be indicated on menus with just a dollar sign ($). When in doubt, ask if the prices are in Mexican pesos or U.S. dollars.

⇨ *Throughout this guide, restaurant prices are cited in pesos, indicated with the "MP" designation.*

RESERVATIONS AND DRESS

During high season, it's a good idea to make a reservation if you can. In Cancún, for example, they're expected at the nicer restaurants. Some restaurants accept online reservations, although it's always wise to confirm by phone. Large parties should always call ahead to check the reservations policy.

⇨ *Throughout this guide, we mention reservations only when they're essential (there's no other way you'll ever get a table) or when they're not accepted. We mention dress only when men are required to wear a jacket.*

Essentials

⚠ Emergencies

It's helpful, albeit daunting, to know ahead of time that you're not protected by the laws of your native land once you're on Mexican soil. Nevertheless, if you get into a scrape with the law, you can call the Citizens' Emergency Center in the United States.

In Mexico, you can also call INFOTUR, the 24-hour English-speaking hotline of the Mexico Ministry of Tourism (Sectur). The hotline can provide immediate assistance as well as general, nonemergency guidance. Mexico uses a *911* emergency number nationwide for police, fire, and ambulance. Operators speak Spanish and English.

➕ Health

According to the U.S. government's Centers for Disease Control and Prevention (CDC) there's a limited risk of malaria in certain rural areas of the Yucatán Peninsula, in the states of Campeche and Quintana Roo. Dengue fever is also a limited risk along the Caribbean Coast. Travelers in mostly urban areas need not worry, nor do travelers who rarely leave resort environs.

To safeguard yourself against mosquito-borne diseases like malaria and dengue, use mosquito nets (provided at most beach and jungle properties), wear clothing that covers the body, apply repellent containing DEET, and use spray for flying insects in living and sleeping areas. The CDC recommends mosquito avoidance for this region of Mexico rather than a regimen of antimalarial pills. There's no vaccine to combat dengue.

COVID-19

Mexico in general and Cancún in particular have staged remarkable tourism recoveries after the disastrous COVID-infused years of 2020 and 2021. Visitor numbers are at or exceed pre-pandemic levels. Still, no one should pronounce the pandemic "over." Although the illness is mild in most people, some older adults (especially those over 65), people with weakened immune systems, and people with certain medical conditions (e.g., diabetes, asthma, kidney or liver disease, heart conditions) are still at risk for experiencing severe and even life-threatening complications.

Starting two weeks before a trip, be on the lookout for some of the following symptoms: cough, fever, chills, trouble breathing, muscle pain, sore throat, new loss of smell or taste. If you experience any of these, you should not travel. Consider protecting yourself by purchasing a travel insurance policy that will reimburse you for any cancellation costs related to COVID-19. Not all travel insurance policies protect against pandemic-related cancellations, so always read the fine print.

While traveling, do your best to avoid contact with people showing symptoms. Wash your hands often with soap and water. Limit your time in public places, and, when you are out and about, wear a face mask that covers your nose and mouth. Indeed, a mask may still be required in some places, such as on an airplane or in a confined space like a theater. You may wish to carry extra supplies, such as disinfecting wipes, hand sanitizer, and a first-aid kit with a thermometer.

FOOD AND DRINK

In Mexico the biggest health risk is traveler's diarrhea caused by consuming contaminated fruit, vegetables, water (ice included), and unpasteurized milk or milk products.

Drink only bottled water or water that has been boiled for at least 10 minutes, even when you're brushing your teeth. At restaurants, particularly those off the beaten path, ask for *agua mineral* (mineral water) or *agua purificada* (purified water). When ordering cold drinks, skip the ice: *sin hielo*. Hotels with water-purification systems will post signs to that effect in the rooms; even then, be wary.

Although salads in tourist-oriented areas have usually been hygienically prepared, when in doubt don't eat any raw vegetables or fruits that haven't been, or can't be, peeled (e.g., lettuce and tomatoes). In coastal towns like Celestún, the shrimp may be fresh, but it has been known to cause traveler's diarrhea in people with sensitive stomachs.

IMMUNIZATIONS

At this writing, no immunizations are required for travel between the United States and Mexico. The CDC recommends being up to date on all routine immunizations (tetanus, mumps, measles, varicella, seasonal flu, shingles, and COVID).

PESTS

It's best to be cautious and go indoors at dusk (called the "mosquito hour" by locals). An excellent brand of *repelente de insectos* (insect repellent) called Autan is readily available; don't use it on children under age two. If you want to bring a mosquito repellent from home, make sure it has at least 20% DEET or it won't be effective. If you're hiking in the jungle or near standing water, wear repellent and/or long pants and sleeves;

if you're camping in the jungle, use a mosquito net and invest in a package of mosquito coils (sold in most stores).

Isla Holbox is often riddled with tiny mosquitoes and "no-seeums" after the rains. Island locals use baby oil as a natural repellent. If you plan on visiting one of the many *cenotes* (subterranean water bodies) throughout the Yucatán, be sure to bring waterproof insect repellent.

Another local flying pest is the *tabaño*, a type of deer fly that resembles a common household fly with yellow stripes. Some people swell up after being bitten, but taking an antihistamine can help. Watch out for the small red ants, as their bites can be quite irritating. Clean all bites and cuts carefully (especially those produced by coral), as the rate of infection is much higher here.

Scorpions also live in the region; their sting is similar to a bee sting. They're rarely fatal, but can cause strong reactions in small children and the elderly. The Yucatán has many poisonous snakes. The coral snake, easily identified by its black-and-red markings, should be avoided at all costs since its bite is fatal. If you're planning any jungle hikes, be sure to wear hard-sole shoes and stay on the path. For more remote areas, hire a guide and make sure there's an antivenom kit accompanying you on the trip.

REMEDIES

Mild cases of diarrhea may respond to Imodium (known generically as loperamide) or Pepto-Bismol (not as strong), both of which you can buy over the counter. Keep in mind, though, that these drugs can complicate more serious illnesses. Drink plenty of bottled water or tea. Chamomile tea (*té de manzanilla*) is a good remedy, and it's readily available in restaurants throughout Mexico.

2

Travel Smart ESSENTIALS

Essentials

In severe cases, hydrate with Gatorade or a salt-sugar solution (½ teaspoon salt and 4 tablespoons sugar per quart of water). You can also balance out your pH levels by drinking a glass of water with a tablespoon of baking soda, which acts as a natural antacid. If your fever and diarrhea last more than three days, see a doctor—you may have picked up a parasite that requires prescription medication.

SUNBURN

The sun is strong here; it takes fewer than 20 minutes to get a serious burn. Wear a hat and use sunscreen, preferably something with zinc oxide.

To prevent sunburn—as well as dehydration or heat exhaustion (the first signs of which are dizziness, extreme irritability, and fatigue)—try to avoid the sun between 11 am and 3 pm. Also drink more fluids than you do at home—Mexico is probably hotter than what you're used to, and you'll perspire more.

TRIP INSURANCE

Neither Medicare nor some private insurers cover medical expenses anywhere outside the United States. If you aren't interested in purchasing comprehensive trip coverage, consider buying medical-only travel insurance. Such policies typically reimburse you for medical care (excluding that related to preexisting conditions) and hospitalization abroad. You still have to pay the bills and await reimbursement from the insurer, though.

Another option is to sign up with a medical-evacuation assistance company. A membership in one of these gets you doctor referrals, emergency evacuation or repatriation, 24-hour hotlines for medical consultation, and other assistance. International SOS and AirMed provide evacuation services and medical referrals. Medjet offers medical evacuation.

🛏 Lodging

The price and quality of accommodations in the Yucatán Peninsula vary from luxury resorts and coastal villas to seedy hostels and eco-friendly cabanas. Near Mérida and Campeche, many historic haciendas have been converted into luxury accommodations. You may find bargains while you're on the road, but if your comfort threshold is high, look for an English-speaking staff, guaranteed dollar rates, and toll-free reservation numbers. In addition, note that all-inclusive hotels are a good option for families since the price of the room usually includes children's activities and meals.

Mexico doesn't have an official star-rating system, but the usual number of stars (five being the ultimate) denotes the most luxury and amenities, while a two-star hotel might have a ceiling fan and TV with local channels only. "Gran turismo" is a special category of hotel that may or may not have all the accoutrements of a five-star hotel (such as minibars) but is nonetheless at the top of the heap, both in price and level of service and sophistication.

Mexican law prohibits smoking in all hotels and resorts, both in rooms and in public areas, indoors and outdoors.

APARTMENT AND HOUSE RENTALS

Local agencies that specialize in renting out apartments, condos, villas, and private homes can be found in many tourist locales. International agencies are another option, and rental websites such as ⊕ www.airbnb.com or ⊕ www.vrbo.com are increasingly popular.

HOTELS

Hotel rates are subject to the 16% value-added tax, in addition to a 2% (Yucatán and Campeche states) to 3%

(Quintana Roo state) hotel tax. Service charges and meals generally aren't included in the quoted rates. Make sure to ask if tax is included and take this into account when comparing properties.

⇨ *Unless otherwise noted, prices throughout this guide are cited in U.S. dollars ($), which is how they're usually quoted on hotel and other booking websites.*

High- and low-season rates can vary significantly. In the off-season, Cancún hotels can cost one-third to one-half what they cost during peak periods. Keep in mind, however, that this is also the time that many hotels undergo necessary repairs or renovations.

Hotels in this guide have private bathrooms with showers, unless stated otherwise; bathtubs aren't common in inexpensive hotels and properties in smaller towns.

Reservations are easy to make online. If you choose this route, be sure to book at least two days in advance of your stay, and always print out your confirmation. Although major resorts are generally efficient at keeping up with online bookings, there's often a lag, and the reservation desks that handle such things may be closed on weekends. If you prefer to make phone reservations, hotels in the larger urban areas will have someone on staff who speaks English. In smaller destinations, you'll have to make your reservations in Spanish. In more remote areas (like Xcalak), you'll have to make reservations by email since most properties don't have telephones.

It's essential to reserve in advance if you're traveling to the resort areas in high season (late November through Easter), and it's recommended, though not always necessary, to do so elsewhere during high season. Resorts popular with college students tend to fill up in the summer months and during spring break (generally March through April). Overbooking is a common practice in some parts, especially in Cancún. To protect yourself, get a written confirmation via email.

$ Money

The Mexican currency is the peso, which comes in denominations of 20-, 50-, 100-, 200-, 500-, 1,000-, and 2,000-peso bills. The latter two are not commonly seen, and many establishments refuse to accept them due to a lack of change. Indeed, it's best to have smaller peso denominations (i.e., MX$50 or less) on hand to pay tips, bus fare, taxis, highway tolls, and the like. Coins officially come in denominations of 1, 2, 5, and 10 pesos, although you will likely not see anything less than a 5. Many of the coins are very similar, so check carefully. ■TIP➔ **Do not accept damaged pesos, which are of no value to merchants or banks.**

Like many countries, Mexico uses the dollar sign ($) to indicate pesos, though you'll also see MXN, Mex$, MX$, and MP. ■TIP➔ **As some places might actually be citing prices in U.S. dollars, when in doubt, ask which currency is being displayed.**

U.S. dollar bills (but never coins) are widely accepted in many tourist destinations of the Yucatán, particularly in Cancún and Cozumel; however, you will likely get your change back in pesos. Many restaurants, tourist shops, and market vendors, as well as virtually all hotel service personnel, also accept dollars. Wherever you are, though, watch out for bad exchange rates—you'll generally do better paying in pesos.

Essentials

⇨ *Throughout this guide, we use MX$ or MP to indicate pesos and just the dollar sign ($) to indicate U.S. dollars.*

ATMS

ATMs (*cajeros automáticos*) are the easiest way to get pesos. In key tourist destinations, airports (though not bus stations) and many gas stations and larger resorts have them. In rural locales, however, ATMs can be hard to find, and, when you do, they might be broken or out of cash. What's more, truly remote areas, like Xcalak near Belize, don't have ATMs or banks, and businesses there don't accept credit cards, so plan accordingly.

Cirrus and Plus are the most frequently found networks. Your own bank will probably charge a transaction fee for withdrawing money in Mexico (up to $8 a pop); the foreign bank you use may also charge a fee. Before you leave home, ask your bank if they have an agreement with a Mexican counterpart to waive or charge reduced fees for cash withdrawals. For example, Bank of America has such an agreement with Scotiabank. Regardless of the fee, you'll usually get a better rate of exchange at an ATM than you will at a currency-exchange office or even at a a bank.

■TIP➜ **PINs with more than four digits are not recognized at ATMs in Mexico. If your PIN has five or more numbers, get it changed before you leave.**

CREDIT CARDS

Major credit cards are accepted in most tourist areas, though businesses may add a surcharge to compensate for their own high processing fee. Note, too, that some credit-card companies *and* the banks that issue them add substantial percentages to all foreign transactions. Check on these fees before leaving home, so there won't be any surprises when you get the bill.

Smaller, less-expensive restaurants and shops tend to take only cash. In general, credit cards aren't accepted in small towns and villages.

⇨ *Throughout this guide, it's safe to assume that businesses accept major credit cards unless you see the "no credit cards" notation.*

The most widely accepted cards are MasterCard and Visa; American Express is not widely accepted in Mexico outside of large international chain hotels and resorts. When shopping in traditional markets, where bargaining might be acceptable, you can usually get better prices if you pay with cash.

To avoid fraud on credit-card charges, make sure that "pesos" or the notation *M.N.* (*moneda nacional,* or national currency) is clearly marked on all receipts, unless the charge was made in U.S. dollars. Also, inform your credit-card company before you travel to Mexico, especially if you don't travel internationally very often. Otherwise, the credit-card company might put a hold on your card owing to unusual activity—not a good thing halfway through your trip. Finally, record all your credit-card numbers—as well as the phone numbers to call if your cards are lost or stolen—in a safe place, so you're prepared should something go wrong.

CURRENCY EXCHANGE

Exchange rates have hovered at US$1 = MX$16–MX$18 in recent years, but check with your bank or online for current rates. Bank rates of exchange are regulated by Mexico's federal government but vary slightly from one establishment to the next. *Casas de cambio* (private exchange offices) have slightly more variable rates. Most banks change money only on weekdays until noon (though they stay open until 5), whereas *casas de cambio* generally stay open until 6 or 9 and often operate on weekends.

A passport is required wherever you are exchanging U.S. dollars or traveler's checks, which have have become increasingly difficult to cash in Mexico. We advise against using them; though they can be exchanged at some banks, this might require a processing fee as well as a hefty chunk of your time.

Foreign travelers may not exchange more than US$1,500 (cash) per person, per month into Mexican pesos. (Mexican travelers are also limited to US$1,500 cash per person, per month, with the added restriction of no more than US$300 cash per day.) Other methods of payment including credit cards, traveler's checks, and non-American foreign currencies are not affected by this law.

Many shop and restaurant owners are unable to make change for large bills. ■TIP→ It's best to request *billetes chicos* (small bills) when you exchange money.

⊡ Packing

Cancún is the dressiest spot on the peninsula; however, even fancy restaurants there don't usually require men to wear jackets, opting instead for a "resort elegant" dress code. For trips to rural areas or Mérida, where dress is typically more conservative and shorts are considered inappropriate, make sure you have at least one pair of slacks.

Also on your packing list should be lightweight clothes, bathing suits, beach cover-ups, sun hats, sunscreen, sunglasses, and a light jacket or sweater to wear in chilly, air-conditioned restaurants or to tide you over during a shower or

an unusual cool spell. If you're traveling during the rainy season, lightweight rain gear and an umbrella are a good idea. Comfortable walking shoes with rubber soles are a must, both for exploring ruins and for walking around cities.

Other handy items—especially if you're staying in budget hotels, frequenting inexpensive restaurants, or going off the beaten path—include toilet paper, tissues, hand sanitizer, a plastic water bottle, and a flashlight (for occasional power outages). Snorkelers should consider bringing their own equipment unless traveling light is a priority; reef shoes with rubber soles for rocky underwater surfaces are also advised.

To avoid problems at customs, bring your prescription drugs in the original pill bottle or with a current prescription. Don't count on purchasing necessary OTC or prescription meds (such as sleeping pills); the same brands are not always available in Mexico.

Regardless, pack lightly to save space in your suitcase for purchases. The Yucatán is filled with bargains on clothing, leather goods, jewelry, and other crafts. If you purchase pottery or ceramics, make sure they're carefully wrapped in your check-in luggage since a few airlines prohibit these items from being in your carry-on.

⊕ Passports and Visas

Visitors to Mexico from the United States and Canada require a valid passport to enter for up to 180 days. Cancún and Cozumel airports no longer issue tourist cards (FMM or Forma Migratoria Multiple) as long as you fly into and out of the same airport. If you don't qualify that way, you do need to fill out the FMM—they're available at airport arrival just before immigration, and you'll need your own

Essentials

pen—and present it with your passport to the official. A portion will be returned to you which you will be required to present upon departure from Mexico. Don't lose it. If you are doing anything "out of the ordinary" while in Mexico you'll need a tourist card. Are you getting married or witnessing a wedding here? Do you plan to file for a partial refund on Mexican sales taxes on your souvenir purchases? Pick up a card and fill it out if one was not given to you on the plane.

U.S. and Canadian tourists arriving internationally at Terminals 3 and 4 of Cancún airport scan in their passports themselves at the Automated Border Control, the so-called "e-gates." You must have a biometric (machine-readable) passport. (Look for the rectangular camera-like symbol on the cover.) You must not be traveling with anyone under 18. A machine snaps your photo and takes your fingerprint. Unless you are pulled aside for a spot check, you'll have entered Mexico without talking to an official. ⚠ **Do not under any circumstances try to use an e-gate if you are not a visiting tourist and do not meet the above qualifications. Correcting the mistake will be a nightmare.**

Customs is not as slick. Baggage claim at Cancún is legendarily slow. You will be required to fill out a short declaration form—have a pen handy—and give it to the customs official.

✚ Safety

Unfortunately, Mexico as a whole has seen a dramatic increase in violence over the past few years, but most of this has been concentrated along border zones and in less-touristed areas. Sporadic murders have taken place around Cancún and the Riviera Maya—all of which were drug related. Nevertheless, the Yucatán Peninsula remains one of the safest regions of the country.

Cancún's Zona Hotelera (Hotel Zone) is a highly trafficked tourist area, making it extremely safe for those who want to relax at the beach or explore the string of shops and restaurants that line Boulevard Kukulcán. Security has increased on this main strip, which means you'll most likely see armed tourist police driving up and down the boulevard. There is also a security checkpoint that marks the entrance to the Zona Hotelera on Boulevard Kukulcán in front of Playa Delfines. Tourists are rarely stopped here.

Less visited by tourists, El Centro (downtown Cancún) should be avoided late at night. Video cameras survey activity in strategic points throughout the city.

BEACHES

Be aware that the calmest-looking waters can still have currents and riptides. Waves are most powerful during December, and hurricane season lasts from June through November.

Most resorts notify beachgoers of coastal conditions by displaying colored flags. ■**TIP→ Don't swim when the black danger flag flies; a red or yellow flag indicates that you should proceed with caution, and a green flag means the waters are safe.** You will seldom see the green flag—even when the water is tranquil—so swim cautiously. Ignoring these warning flags has resulted in at least one tourist drowning each season.

If visiting isolated beaches, bring sunscreen and drinking water to avoid sunburn and dehydration. Finally, note that Mexico has laws against topless sunbathing on public beaches.

CRIME

Petty crime can be an issue, so use common sense. Take advantage of hotel safes when available, and carry your own baggage whenever possible unless you're checking into a hotel. Leave expensive jewelry at home, since it often entices thieves and will mark you as a *turista* who can afford to be robbed.

Keep an eye on your belongings at all times, and, when in public, do not reach for your cash, credit cards, ID, and other valuables, all of which should be distributed between a deep front pocket, an inside jacket or vest pocket, and a hidden money pouch. If you carry a purse, choose one with a zipper and a thick strap that you can drape across your body; adjust the length so that the purse sits in front of you at or above hip level.

Use ATMs during the day and in big commercial areas. Avoid the glass-enclosed street variety where you may be more vulnerable to thieves who force you to withdraw money for them.

Note that empty coastlines can be susceptible to car break-ins and theft. In addition, there have been reports of travelers being victimized after imbibing drinks that have been drugged in Cancún nightclubs and even in a few of the resorts here. Never drink alone with strangers, watch your drink being poured, and keep your eye on it at all times. Finally, don't drive on desolate streets or travel at night, and never pick up hitchhikers or hitchhike yourself.

Bear in mind that reporting a crime to the police is often a frustrating experience unless you speak excellent Spanish and have a great deal of patience. If you're victimized, contact your local consular agent or the consular section of your country's embassy in Mexico City.

HARASSMENT

Part of the machismo culture is being flirtatious and showing off, and women might be subjected to catcalls, although this is less true in the Yucatán than in other parts of Mexico. It's best not to enter into a discussion with harassers, even if you speak Spanish. When the person is persistent, say "no" to whatever is said, and leave immediately—walking away briskly—for a safe place, such as a nearby store. Dressing conservatively might also help deter would-be harassers.

A woman traveling alone will, in particular, be the subject of much curiosity, since it is uncommon in Mexico. Don't walk on deserted beaches by yourself, and make sure your hotel room is securely locked when you retire.

🔟 Shipping

Mail can be sent from your hotel or the *oficina de correos* (post office). Be forewarned, however, that mail service to, within, and from Mexico is notoriously slow and can take anywhere from 10 days to, well, never. Don't send anything of value to or from Mexico via mail, including cash, checks, or credit-card numbers.

Hotel concierges can recommend international carriers, such as DHL, Estafeta, or FedEx, which give your package a tracking number and ensure its arrival back home.

💲 Taxes

An air-departure tax of around US$65 is almost always included as part of your ticket price. Check with your airline if you're unsure; a few charter airlines do not collect the tax. In the rare case it's

Essentials

not included, you must pay the tax in cash at the airport.

Mexico has a value-added tax (V.A.T.) or IVA (*impuesto al valor agregado*), of 16%. Many establishments already include the IVA in their quoted price. When comparing rates, it's important to know whether yours does. Occasionally (and illegally) it may be waived for cash purchases; this is nothing for you to worry about. Hotel taxes also apply. The amount is the V.A.T. plus 3% in Quintana Roo, plus 2% in the states of Yucatán and Campeche.

Quintana Roo state (Cancún, Cozumel, Isla Mujeres, Tulum, Riviera Maya) implemented a new tourist tax in 2021. The so-called Visitax is a separate unbundled fee of MX$224 (approximately $14) that must be paid for each visitor 15 years old and over. Payment can be made online (⊕ *www.visitax.gob.mx*) before arrival or during your stay. A few resorts will collect the tax on your behalf. The deadline for payment is when you pass through airport security upon departure.

A QR code on your smartphone is your receipt to present to airport authorities. There is often no one staffing the Visitax kiosks at Cancún and Cozumel airports to accept payment. Frequently, no one checks to see if you've paid at all. Many visitors report skipping out on the tax, even with every intention of paying. To be on the safe side, we recommend making the online payment.

If you depart Mexico by air or cruise ship, you are eligible for partial reimbursement of the value-added tax you paid on items bought in participating Mexican stores. When making purchases, you must show your passport and get a receipt and refund form. The refund pertains only to items you take out of Mexico; taxes on hotel and restaurant bills do not apply. In addition, your purchases must have been paid by cash or a Visa or MasterCard issued outside Mexico, and they must total at least MX$1,200 per individual receipt.

A private company called MoneyBack administers the tax-refund scheme. On departure, look for its orange-white-black logo in stores at the Cancún, Cozumel, or Mérida airports or a cruise port, where you can arrange to receive about half the tax (8.9%) credited to your credit card, a step that takes 45 business days. You can also initiate the process after you return home by downloading MoneyBack's app to your smartphone. Many visitors have reported problems with the system, and for small purchases, it is probably not worth your time.

💲 Tipping

When tipping in Mexico, remember that the minimum wage is only about $5 a day and that many in the tourism industry don't earn much more. Many tourism workers think in dollars and know, for example, that in the United States porters are tipped $1 to $2 a bag. They therefore expect the peso equivalent from visitors.

Though dollars are widely accepted in Cancún and Cozumel, it's best to tip using local currency whenever possible, so that service personnel aren't stuck going to the bank to exchange dollars for pesos. Never leave U.S. coins; they are worthless here.

What follows are some guidelines. Naturally, larger gratuities are always welcome. Tip porters and bellhops MX$20 per bag at airports and moderate and inexpensive hotels and MX$40 per person per bag at expensive hotels. Leave maids MX$20 per night (all hotels).

For spa attendants, plan on tipping 15% to 20% of the total bill.

In all restaurants, be sure a service charge hasn't already been added, a practice that's particularly common in resorts. Otherwise, tip waiters and bartenders 15% to 20% of the bill.

Tipping cabbies isn't usual, and they sometimes overcharge tourists. If, however, the taxi driver helps you with your bags, give them MX$20. Tip tour guides MX$100 per half day, MX$200 for a full day; drivers about half as much. Gas-station attendants expect MX$10 unless they check the oil, tires, and so on, in which case tip more. Parking attendants should get MX$10 to MX$20, even if it's for valet parking at a theater or restaurant that charges for the service.

🧭 Tours

Old standby Gray Line Cancún covers the entire peninsula with a broad range of packages for both day trips and overnight junkets. It can deliver most experiences on the typical tourist wish list. Mérida-based Ecoturismo Yucatán leads guided tours that hit the region's archaeological and cultural highlights; other options focus on nature, cuisine, and active pursuits. Alltournative is recommended for sustainable adventure tours on the coast; it specializes in archaeological and eco-oriented excursions. EcoColors runs single- and multiday trips to the wildlife reserves at Isla Holbox and Sian Ka'an, and to remote Mayan ruin sites; bird-watching and biking excursions are also available.

🇺🇸 U.S. Embassy/Consulate

The work of the United States Embassy in Mexico City is supplemented by 10 consulates around the country, one of which is in Mérida and serves this region. Mérida, in turn, operates two branch consular agencies (Cancún and Playa del Carmen) which keep shorter hours and can tend to routine matters.

📅 When to Go

Low season: You can save 20% to 50% during low season (the day after Easter to late November).

Shoulder season: Post-Easter through the end of May still offers plenty of morning sunshine.

High season: High season lasts from late November through Easter, with Christmas and Holy Week holiday prices being up to 50% above regular rates. Beach resorts—particularly in Cancún—tend to fill up with college students during summer months and spring break (primarily March and April). European travelers flock here during the summer months, too.

WEATHER

November through March, winter temperatures hover around 27°C (80°F). Occasional winter fronts called *nortes* can bring blustery skies and sharp winds that make air temperatures drop and swimming unappealing. The spring (especially April and May) sees a period of intense heat that tapers off in June. The most active part of hurricane season—July through the end of September—is also hot and humid.

Great Itineraries

Cancún and Day Trips

You'll likely start your visit in Cancún. If sunbathing, water sports, and parties that last until the wee hours are what you're after, you won't need to set foot outside the Zona Hotelera (or even your resort). If you're staying for a week or so, though, do check out some of the attractions that are an easy day trip from Cancún.

DAYS 1 AND 2: CANCÚN

If you stay at an all-inclusive resort, your Cancún lodging becomes, in many ways, your primary tourist attraction, with its restaurants, bars, pools, spas, and myriad activities to keep you occupied for a week. Spend your first day or two doing what comes naturally: lounging at the hotel pool, playing in the waves, and going out for dinner and drinks, or more. (The city's nightlife is legendary, you may have heard.)

If you start to feel restless your second day, you can head to Cancún's very own **El Rey** ruins and follow it up with a tequila tasting at **La Destilería**. Taxi into **El Centro** (downtown Cancún) to browse the shops and open-air markets along **Avenida Tulum** and grab some local Mexican food.

DAY 3: ISLA MUJERES

One of Cancún's most popular day trips takes you to tiny **Isla Mujeres**, a 30-minute ferry ride from the Embarcadero Dock at Playa Linda. The island makes the perfect break from high-powered Cancún. You get around by golf cart here, either as an informal taxi system or by you renting one for a few hours.

Head for **Playa Norte** on the north end of the island for a laid-back meal of freshly grilled seafood in an open-air dining spot with a *palapa* (thatch roof), the quintessential Isla Mujeres experience. A whimsical take on an art museum, the **Isla Mujeres Underwater Museum** (also known as the Museo Subacuático de Arte or **MUSA**) has installed some of its sculptures at Manchones Reef, off the island's southwest shore. You can view them on diving, snorkeling, or glass-bottom-boat excursions. (This is one of three MUSA installations; the other two are in the waters near Cancún.)

DAY 4: VALLADOLID AND CHICHÉN ITZÁ

Get up early, board your tour van, and head inland two hours to the peninsula's most famous sight: the splendid Maya ruins of **Chichén Itzá**. You've seen countless photos of its **El Castillo** (Kukulkan) pyramid, but they don't compare to seeing it in person.

Most day tours to the area include a breakfast or lunch stop in the charming colonial city of **Valladolid**, about 30 minutes from the ruins, and a chance to explore a bit. The city's **Casa de los Venados** holds the country's largest private collection of folk art. Day trips sometimes include a dip in the right-in-town **Cenote Zaci**. Pack your swimwear if yours does.

DAY 5: XCARET

In the morning, pack your bathing suit and join an excursion to the **Xcaret** nature park. You'll see the signs for the mammoth complex from the moment you arrive at Cancún airport, and you'll continue to encounter its brochures and publicity everywhere. By the time you actually arrive, you'll feel like you already know the place. Touristed it is, but it's also great fun, and it has become one of the Yucatán's top visitor attractions.

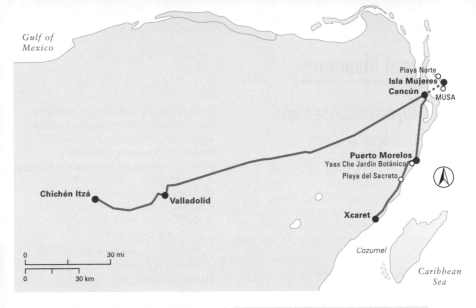

You can easily spend an entire day here snorkeling through underwater caves, visiting the butterfly pavilion, sea-turtle nursery, and reef aquarium, and bonding with dolphins. (Reserve a spot early for that last one.)

DAY 6: PUERTO MORELOS

One of the last vestiges of the pre-1970 (pre-Cancún, in other words) coast is the still-quaint fishing village of **Puerto Morelos,** 36 km (22 miles) south and the first real community you encounter on Carretera 307. The **Mesoamerican Barrier Reef** is a mere 1,800 feet offshore, making this and outstanding place for snorkeling.

Puerto Morelos's beach is ho-hum, but south of town lies **Playa del Secreto**, whose many fans rate it as the most beautiful beach on the Yucatán Peninsula. Also south of town is the **Yaax Che Jardín Botánico**, Mexico's largest botanical gardens, which offer an impressive everything-you-want-to-know lesson about plant life in the Yucatán.

Tips

■ If you stay at an all-inclusive, you likely are not renting a car. Most resorts can arrange day excursions to area attractions for their guests.

■ Remember that any crossing between Quintana Roo and Yucatán states (to Chichén Itzá and Valladolid) entails a change in time zone. Set your watch back one hour traveling west, but then move it forward one hour when you return to Cancún at the end of the day.

Great Itineraries

Playa del Carmen and the Riviera Maya

Tourism booms along the Yucatán Peninsula's Caribbean coast, yet zoning efforts have kept the Riviera Maya a bit lower key. Things here haven't turned into Cancún—so far, at least. Cancún airport, just 1½ hours north of Playa del Carmen, serves as your gateway.

DAYS 1 AND 2: PLAYA DEL CARMEN

Hop in your rental car and drive southwest along Carretera 307 toward **Playa del Carmen**, Mexico's fastest growing city. Take a day or two to get oriented. The place has no sights per se, but its many fans revel in the Playa vibe—15 minutes here and you'll shorthand the name like everybody else does.

Head for **Avenida 5**, where you can choose from dozens of waterfront lunch spots in the eminently walkable downtown. Then spend the afternoon wandering among the shops and cafés. Playa has perfected the art and science of the beach club, a place you can go to enjoy the beach in relative privacy for either an outright admission price or the price of a meal and drinks. (Technically, all beaches in Mexico are public, so things can't be totally walled off.)

DAY 3: XCARET AND XPLOR

You can spend a whole day at the area's two powerhouse theme parks just a few miles south of Playa del Carmen, and various mix-and-match packages let you take in both. The nature-themed **Xcaret** sits on the site of a Maya city and port, and Xcaret's ruins anchor all manner of water-, dolphin-, bat-, garden-, and culture-themed activities.

Gauge your own abilities and tolerance for a half-day at the adventure-themed **Xplor**, Xcaret's sister property a mile away, with its swimming, rafting, and zip-lining offerings. A separate **Xplor Fuego** admission offers night-themed adventure activities. The parks do offer their own lodgings, or you can continue to base yourself back in Playa del Carmen.

DAY 4: COZUMEL

The Mexican Caribbean's largest island makes the quintessential day trip from Playa del Carmen, but it's worth an overnight if your schedule permits. Car and passenger-only ferries ply the 29-km (18-mile) crossing to the island, where more than 100 scuba and snorkeling outfitters all offer trips out to the spectacular **Mesoamerican Barrier Reef**.

Cozumel is Mexico's largest cruise destination, so you will rub shoulders with other day-trippers just off their ships. But a block inland from the tourist hubbub of the island's seaside boulevard is **San Miguel**, a charming Mexican town brimming with local flavor, especially on weekends when couples and families turn out for an evening stroll around the **Plaza Benito Juárez**. The crashing surf gives Cozumel's wild and woolly **Windward Coast** an end-of-the-world feel.

DAYS 5 AND 6: TULUM AND COBÁ

It's worth spending a day at each of these beautiful Maya ruins south of Playa del Carmen; they are entirely different from one another. Purely objectively, **Tulum** 's ruins are impressive primarily because of their seaside setting, the only such installation in this part of the country. The surrounding town itself has evolved from "hippie" to "hip." The '60s counterculture vibe of old is still here, but trendy restaurants, boutique hotels, and art galleries have taken over and made

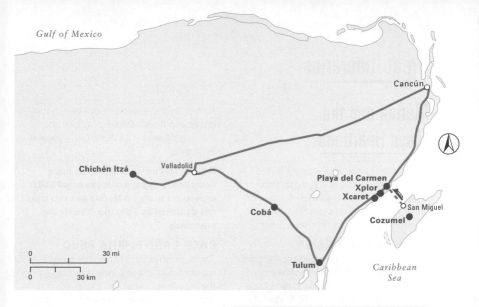

Gulf of Mexico

Cancún

Chichén Itzá   Valladolid

Playa del Carmen
Xplor
Xcaret
San Miguel
Cobá
Cozumel

0   30 mi

0   30 km

Tulum   Caribbean
Sea

today's Tulum the place to see and be seen. **Cobá**, which is about a half-hour's drive west of Tulum, is a less-visited, but spectacular, ancient city surrounded by jungle.

DAY 7: CHICHÉN ITZÁ

Coming to the Yucatán and not visiting its star attraction might be akin to going to Paris and skipping the Eiffel Towel. The ruins of **Chichén Itzá** can be approached from multiple directions.

Rather than going all the way back to Cancún and heading west, the tolled Carretera 305D heads northwest from Playa del Carmen and connects with the east-west 180D highway, which takes you directly to the complex. Approaching from Tulum, the two-lane Carretera 109 heads northwest to the colonial city of **Valladolid**, about 30 minutes from Chichén Itzá.

■ TIP→ In true "leave the driving to them" fashion, tour operators in Tulum and Playa del Carmen and many other touristed communities along the coast offer day trips to the ruins.

Tips

■ Highway 307 runs northeast to southwest, from Cancún to the Belizean border, conveniently laying out the Riviera Maya's attractions in a straight line along the coast. A jaunt inland to Chichén Itzá takes you off that track.

■ Two companies operate the ferries between the mainland and Cozumel. Fares and amenities are similar. Grab the one that suits your schedule.

■ This entire itinerary can be accomplished without a car. ADO's comfy tourist-class buses are the workhorse of public transportation in this part of the country.

Great Itineraries

Mérida and the Maya Heartland

Perhaps you have little interest in the beach at all. Inland, the Yucatán Peninsula is one of Mexico's great repositories of history and culture, and it feels worlds away from the more touristed coast.

DAYS 1 AND 2: MÉRIDA

Launch any history-oriented Yucatán itinerary in the gracious old colonial city of Mérida. Wander the **Zócalo** (main plaza) and surrounding streets. (Both the city and Yucatán State operate phenomenal tourist offices on the plaza if you need help.) Spend the next day shopping, visiting museums, and enjoying Mérida's vibrant city scene.

As fabulous as Mérida is, it is still a busy city of 900,000 people, and the more authentic Yucatán beckons. Before heading out to the indigenous hinterlands, your best Maya 101 intro will be the **Gran Museo del Mundo Maya** (Great museum of the Maya World). Its takeaway message is that "Maya" refers to a living, breathing, contemporary, evolving culture in addition to the pyramids and ruins of the distant past—an important point to bear in mind as you begin your explorations.

DAY 3: IZAMAL

Get an early start, and head east to Izamal, a charming town famous for its bright yellow buildings. Take a *calesa* (horse-drawn carriage) tour of artisans' shops, and visit the stately 16th-century **Iglesia de San Antonio de Padua**. The church is on the main plaza—it's also yellow, of course—and it dominates the town. It previously had served as a convent and is famous for its enormous colonnaded

atrium. In the afternoon, check out the crumbling **Kinich Kakmó** pyramid, once the largest such structure in the Yucatán Peninsula.

■ **TIP→ This much smaller town has a limited lodging selection; you might find it convenient to stay in Mérida an extra night and do Izamal as a day trip. It's only one hour away.**

DAYS 4 AND 5: RUTA PUUC

The Yucatán is largely flat, but *puuc* means "hill" in the Mayan language, and that's, indeed, what you'll find along this scenic route in the south-central region of the peninsula. **Uxmal**, with its ornate ruins, makes a good base for a pair of days. Many of the Maya structures here are still being excavated. Uxmal's **Adivino Pyramid** ("magician pyramid") is known for its softer rounded corners, a rarity in Maya architectural style. Take in **Ticul**, famous for its dark pottery, and friendly market town **Oxcutzcab**, which anchors this fertile agricultural region and brims with fruits and vegetables. You'll find the peninsula's most extensive cave system at the **Grutas de Loltún**. Wear sturdy shoes that don't slip and invest in the services of a guide.

DAY 6: CHICHÉN ITZÁ

Get up early, check out of your hotel, and head back east along Carretera 180D toward the world-renowned Chichén Itzá ruins. (Chichén Itzá and Valladolid, below, have their own exits on the toll highway.) Check into one of the area hotels, then spend the day exploring the site before it closes at 5 pm. Visit **El Castillo**—no, you can't climb the structure—and check out the former marketplace, steam bath, observatory, and temples honoring formidable Maya gods.

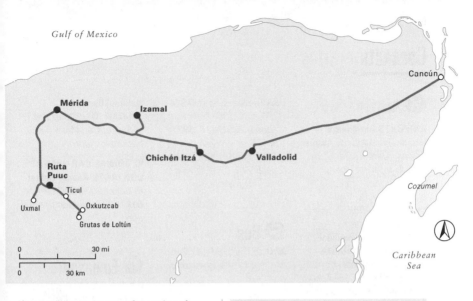

If you still have energy after a day of navigating the ruins, take in **Kukulkan Nights**, the site's 30-minute evening sound-and-light show. Schedules vary widely depending on the season and, quite frankly, if the equipment is working. Otherwise, turn in after dinner at your hotel.

DAY 7: VALLADOLID

Yucatán state's second-largest city sits just 30 minutes east of Chichén Itzá. Arrive in time for the daily 10 am tour of the sumptuous **Casa de los Venados**, a converted mansion housing Mexico's largest private collection of folk art. Stop for lunch at the casual eatery at **Cenote Zaci,** where you can also swim in the lovely jade-green cenote, right in town and perhaps the best known of the many such underground sinkholes that dot the peninsula.

Five blocks off the main square, the **Iglesia de San Bernardino** is the most ornate of Valladolid's churches. Back on the square, the limestone **Iglesia de San Servacio** might be plain inside but is bathed in light nightly, an impressive sight to end a Valladolid day.

Tips

■ Mérida has its own small airport, but Cancún airport's 450 daily flights give an infinitely better selection often at more competitive fares. Savings could be substantial. Do compare.

■ Most Mérida tour operators zip through the Ruta Puuc sights in a tiring day; two days with your own transport lets you soak up things more leisurely.

■ Valladolid and Chichén Itzá sit a mere 30 minutes apart. You can stay at one place or the other and take in both.

Contacts

✈ Air

AIRPORTS Aeropuerto Internacional Alberto Acuña Ongay. *(Campeche Aeropuerto Internacional).* ✉ *Av. Lopez Portillo s/n, Campeche City* ☎ *981/823–4059* ⊕ *www. aeropuertosasa.mx.* **Aeropuerto Internacional de Cancún.** ✉ *Carretera Cancún-Chetumal, Km 22, Cancún* ☎ *998/848–7200* ⊕ *www.asur.com.mx.* **Aeropuerto Internacional de Chetumal.** ✉ *Prolong Av. Efrain Aguila, Chetumal* ☎ *983/834–5013* ⊕ *www. aeropuertosasa.mx.* **Aeropuerto Internacional de Cozumel.** *(CZM).* ✉ *Av. 65 and Blvd. Aeropuerto, Cozumel* ☎ *987/872–2081* ⊕ *airport-cozumel.com.* **Aeropuerto Internacional Manuel Crescencio Rejón.** *(Mérida Aeropuerto Internacional).* ✉ *Av. Itzáes, Km 14.5, Mérida* ☎ *999/940–6090* ⊕ *www. asur.com.mx.*

TRANSFERS Canada Transfers. ☎ *998/478–2994, 866/751–7012 in the U.S. and Canada* ⊕ *www. canadatransfers.com.* **Cancún Valet.** ☎ *888/479–9095 in the U.S., 998/848–3634* ⊕ *www. cancunvalet.com.*

USA Transfers. ☎ *998/914–0290, 587/600–7587 in Canada, 209/382–7587 in the U.S.* ⊕ *www.usa-transfers.com.* **Van Travel.** ☎ *998/210–3317* ⊕ *www. cancuntransfers.com.*

🚌 Bus

ADO. ☎ *55/5784–4652 in Mexico City* ⊕ *www.ado. com.mx.*

🚗 Car

EMERGENCY SERVICE CONTACTS Angeles Verdes. *(Green Angels).* ☎ *078* ⊕ *www.gob.mx/sectur/ angelesverdes.*

INSURANCE Sanborn's Mexico Auto Insurance. ☎ *800/222–0158 in the U.S. and Canada* ⊕ *www. sanborns.com.*

MAJOR CAR RENTAL CONTACTS Alamo. ☎ *855/533–1196* ⊕ *www.alamo.com.* **Avis.** ☎ *888/583–6369 in the U.S. and Canada, 01800/288–8888 toll-free in Mexico* ⊕ *www.avis. com.* **Budget.** ☎ *877/467–7518 in the U.S. and Canada* ⊕ *www.budget.com.* **Hertz.** ☎ *800/654–3001 in the U.S. and Canada* ⊕ *www.hertz.com.*

National Car Rental. ☎ *800/227–7368 in the U.S. and Canada* ⊕ *www. nationalcar.com.*

REGIONAL CAR RENTAL CONTACTS Adocar Rental. ✉ *Cancún* ☎ *998/253–6113* ⊕ *www.adocarrental. com.*

🏛 Embassy

U.S. Consular Agency Cancún. ✉ *Blvd. Kukulcán, Km 13, Zona Hotelera* ☎ *999/942–5700.* **U.S. Consular Agency Playa del Carmen.** ✉ *Plaza Progreso, Carretera Puerto Juárez-Chetumal 293, Playa del Carmen* ☎ *999/942–5700.* **U.S. Consulate.** ✉ *Calle 60 No. 338, Col. Alcala Martin, Centro* ☎ *999/942–5700* ⊕ *mx. usembassy.gov/embassy-consulates/merida.* **U.S. Embassy.** ✉ *Paseo de la Reforma 305, Col. Cuauhtémoc* ☎ *55/5080–2000, 55/8526–2561 for emergency assistance in Mexico, 844/528-6611 for emergency assistance from the U.S.* ⊕ *mx.usembassy.gov.*

➕ Health

MEDICAL ASSISTANCE COMPANIES AirMed.
☎ 205/443–4840, 800/356–2161 in the U.S. and Canada ⊕ www.airmed.com. **International SOS.** ☎ 215/942–8342 ⊕ www.internationalsos.com. **Medjet.** ☎ 800/527–7478 in the U.S. and Canada ⊕ medjetassist.com.

MEDICAL-ONLY INSURERS International Medical Group. *(IMG).* ☎ 317/655–9796 in the U.S. and Canada ⊕ www.imglobal.com. **Wallach & Company.** ☎ 800/237–6615 in the U.S. and Canada, 540/687–3166 ⊕ wallach.com.

🛏 Lodging

APARTMENT AND HOUSE RENTALS Akumal Villas. ☎ 866/535–1324 in the U.S. and Canada, 984/875–9088 in Mexico ⊕ www.akumal-villas.com. **Caribbean Realty.** ☎ 910/543–0019, 984/873–5218 in Mexico ⊕ www.puertoaventurasrentals.com. **Cozumel Villas.** ☎ 507/281–0961 in the U.S. and Canada ⊕ www.cozumelvillas.com.

Lost Oasis. ☎ 998/888–0211 in Mexico, 226/298–0504 in the U.S. and Canada ⊕ lostoasis.net. **Villas of Distinction.** ☎ 800/289–0900 in the U.S. and Canada ⊕ www.villasofdistinction.com.

🧭 Tours

RECOMMENDED COMPANIES Alltournative. ✉ Carretera Cancún-Tulum Juarez, Km 287, Playa del Carmen ☎ 01800/466–2848 toll-free in Mexico, 877/437–4990 in the U.S. and Canada ⊕ alltournative.com. **EcoColors.** ✉ Calle Camaron 32, Smz 27, El Centro ☎ 998/884–3667 in Mexico ⊕ ecotravelmexico.com. **Ecoturismo Yucatán.** ✉ Calle 3 No. 235, between 32A and 34, Col. Pensiones, Mérida ☎ 999/920–2772 ⊕ www.ecoyuc.com.mx. **Gray Line Cancún.** ☎ 9980/887–2495 in Mexico, 877/240–5864 in the U.S. and Canada ⊕ graylinecancun.com.

On the Calendar

JANUARY
El Día de los Tres Reyes (Three Kings Day).
Tradition says the Three Kings brought gifts to the infant Jesus on January 6. So, too, do families present gifts to their children to mark what is almost a "second Christmas." Look for Magi processions and the *rosca*, a traditional sweet fruit bread.

FEBRUARY
Carnaval festivities occur the week before Lent with parades, fireworks, and much revelry. They're especially spirited in Mérida, Cozumel, Isla Mujeres, and Campeche.

MARCH
Equinoccio de Primavera (Spring Equinox).
The Maya were meticulous astronomers, and they constructed Chichén Itzá's Kukulkán (El Castillo) pyramid to display a twice-a-year (March and September) optical illusion. As spring begins, a mirage of a serpent shadow "descends" the pyramid. The serpent is said to fertilize the land when it reaches the ground.

Spring Break. No place does spring break quite like Cancún does. Depending on your proclivities, you might think "Let's party!" or "Thanks for the warning!" Staggered mid-semester breaks at North American colleges mean that the debauchery rolls through March and early April. (Mexico's drinking age is 18.)

APRIL
Semana Santa. Reenactments of the Passion, family parties and meals, and religious services are held during the week leading up to Easter Sunday (March or April). For many Mexicans this means a holiday at the beach, resulting in fully booked oceanside hotels.

AUGUST
Founder's Day. In mid-August, Isla Mujeres celebrates its founding with six days of races, folk dances, music, and food.

SEPTEMBER
Día de Independencia (Independence Day) is celebrated throughout Mexico with fireworks and parties beginning at 11 pm on the 15th and continuing through the 16th.

Fiesta del Cristo de las Ampollas (Feast of the Christ of the Blisters) is an important religious event that falls in late September or early October. People dress in traditional clothing; partake in daily mass and processions; and enjoy dances, fireworks, and other events.

OCTOBER
Fiesta del Cristo de Sitilpech. Ten days of festivities and a solemn parade mark this religious event, during which the Christ image of Sitilpech village is carried to Izamal. The biggest dances (with fireworks) happen around October 28.

NOVEMBER
Día de los Muertos (Day of the Dead), called Hanal Pixan in Mayan, is a joyous holiday when graves are refurbished and symbolic meals are prepared to welcome the spirits of family members back to Earth for the day. Deceased children are honored on All Saints Day (Nov. 1); adults are feted on All Souls Day (Nov. 2).

DECEMBER
Navidad. Among the many Christmas events are *posadas*, during which families gather to eat, sing, and enjoy lively parades, culminating December 24, on **Nochebuena (Christmas Eve).**

Chapter 3

CANCÚN

Updated by
Luis F. Dominguez

● Sights	🍴 Restaurants	🛏 Hotels	💼 Shopping	🍸 Nightlife
★★★★☆	★★★★★	★★★★★	★★★★☆	★★★★★

WELCOME TO CANCÚN

TOP REASONS TO GO

★ **Dancing the night away:** Salsa, cumbia, reggae, mariachi, hip-hop, and electronic music dizzy the air of the Zona Hotelera's many nightclubs.

★ **Exploring the nearby Maya ruins:** Trips to remarkable sites like Tulum, Cobá, and Chichén Itzá can easily be accomplished in a day.

★ **Getting wild on the water:** Rent a WaveRunner, jungle boat, stand-up paddleboard, or kayak, then skim across the sea or Laguna Nichupté.

★ **Browsing for Mexican crafts:** The colorful stalls of Mercado Veintiocho and Coral Negro will certainly hold something that catches your eye.

★ **Indulging in local flavor:** Dishes like lime soup and *poc chuc* (pork in a sour orange sauce) and drinks like tamarind margaritas pay respect to traditional cuisine.

Over the past five decades, Cancún has turned into the Miami of the south, with international investors pouring money into property development. The main attractions for most visitors lie along the Zona Hotelera, a barrier island shaped roughly like the number 7. To the east is the Caribbean, and to the west you'll find a system of lagoons, the largest of which is Laguna Nichupté. Downtown Cancún—aka El Centro—is 4 km (2½ miles) west of the Zona Hotelera on the mainland.

1 El Centro. Cancún's mainland commercial center provides an authentic glimpse into modern-day Mexico and a colorful alternative to the Zona Hotelera. Many of the restaurants scattered throughout this downtown area offer surprising bursts of culture and Mexican flavor. With more than 800,000 permanent residents, Cancún is full of shops, cafés, and open-air markets that cater mainly to locals. Although most tourists bask on the beaches, those who venture into the heart of El Centro will be glad they did—prices are much more reasonable than elsewhere, and the food is outstanding.

2 Punta Sam. A separate strip called Punta Sam, north of Puerto Juárez, is sometimes billed as the Zona Hotelera Norte (Northern Hotel Zone) or Playa Mujeres. This area is quieter than the main Zona, but there are some newer resorts, marinas, restaurants, and a golf course. This is also a good launch point for those heading to the nearby Isla Mujeres.

3 Zona Hotelera. The Hotel Zone is structured along a 25-km (15½-mile) stretch known as Boulevard Kukulcán. On the Caribbean side, dozens of resorts and condominiums line the beachfront like a tight row of Legos. On the inland side, Laguna Nichupté is home to water sports, shopping malls, restaurants, and golf courses. At the northern tip of this main thoroughfare, near Punta Cancún, is a pack of nightclubs, discos, and bars—a nighttime favorite for those who like to party. For quieter accommodations, opt for a hotel near Punta Nizuc (at the southern tip of Kukulcán Boulevard) or PokTaPok (a small inlet halfway between Punta Cancún and El Centro).

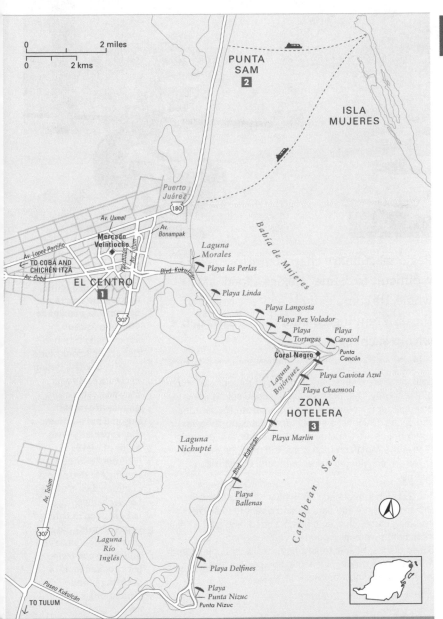

0   2 miles

0   2 kms

PUNTA
SAM
2

ISLA
MUJERES

Puerto
Juárez
(180)

Av. Uxmal

Av.
Bonampak

Mercado
Veintiocho

Av. López Portillo

TO COBÁ AND
CHICHÉN ITZÁ

Av. Cobá

Laguna
Morales

Bahía de Mujeres

Blvd. Kukulcán

Playa las Perlas

EL CENTRO
1

(307)

Playa Linda

Playa Langosta

Playa Pez Volador

Playa
Tortugas

Playa
Caracol

Coral Negro

Punta
Cancún

Playa Gaviota Azul

Laguna
Bojórquez

Playa Chacmool

ZONA
HOTELERA
3

Laguna
Nichupté

Blvd. Kukulcán

Playa Marlin

Av. Tulum

Caribbean Sea

(307)

Playa
Ballenas

Laguna
Río
Inglés

Playa Delfines

Paseo Kukulcán

Playa
Punta Nizuc

TO TULUM

Punta Nizuc

MEXICAN FOOD PRIMER

Regional culinary characteristics make it difficult to define "Mexican food" as a whole. Its complexity is a direct result of the different ingredients that are available within each region.

Still, there are overlapping items used throughout much of the county. The most frequently used spices are chile powder, cumin, oregano, cilantro, epazote, cinnamon, and cocoa. Chipotle, a smoke-dried jalapeño chile, is common, as are tomatoes, garlic, onions, and peppers. Rice is the most common grain, but corn, beans, and chiles are considered the cornerstones of Mexican cuisine.

The Spanish introduced rice, wheat, olive oil, nuts, cinnamon, wine, and parsley, and a variety of animals including cattle, chickens, goats, sheep, and pigs. These ingredients were incorporated with indigenous corn-based dishes, beans, turkey, fish, vanilla, chocolate, and fruits such as guava, pineapple, and papaya, giving us what we now know as Mexican food.

JUST DESSERTS

Locally grown fruits like mango, mamey, cherimoya, pomegranate, *tuna* (cactus apple), and strawberries are delicious alone or served with a dollop of cream and sugar. Stewed peaches and guavas are refreshing on a hot summer day, especially with a side of *nieves* (sherbet or sorbet). Among Mexico's most common desserts are *tres leches* (sponge cake soaked in three types of milk), churros (fried-dough pastry), and *arroz con leche* (rice cooked in milk with sugar and cinnamon).

REGIONAL CUISINES

Mexican food is much more than burritos, tacos, and rice and beans. Traditional recipes reach far beyond these stereotypical dishes, varying by region as a result of the climate, geography, local ingredients, and cultural differences among the inhabitants.

Yucatán Peninsula. The cuisine of the Yucatán Peninsula has both strong European and Maya influences. Specialties of the region include *cochinita pibil* (seasoned pork colored with annatto seed and wrapped in banana leaves), turkey with black stuffing, and *papadzules* (tortillas filled with hard-boiled eggs and topped with a pumpkin-seed sauce). Unique to Yucatán's cooking is the earthen pit oven where meats are slowly cooked with *recado negro* or *chilmole* (a blend of dried chiles that are set aflame and ground with spices to create a paste).

Mexico City and Environs (including Puebla). Largely influenced by the rest of the country, Mexico City still has original dishes such as *carnitas* (braised or roasted pork), *menudos* (tripe stew), and *pozole* (pork and hominy soup). Mexico City is also known for its incredible cheeses, tamales, and yellow-corn tortillas. The favored *mixiote* (mutton wrapped in maguey leaves) is slowly

Cochinita pibil

steam-baked in a pit oven. Puebla produces various species of cacti including maguey and nopal, which can be eaten as a vegetable (de-spined, of course) or used to make juices and sorbets. Puebla is best known for *mole poblano* (thick, chocolate-tinged sauce).

Oaxaca. With a strong pre-Hispanic influence, the state of Oaxaca has the second-highest percentage of indigenous residents in Mexico, exceeded only by the Yucatán. *Gusanos de maguey* (worms) and *chapulines* (grasshoppers), originally indigenous foods, are fried and eaten like roasted peanuts or sprinkled onto tacos. Oaxaca takes pride in its assortment of chiles, including yellow and black *chilhuacles, costeños,* and light-green *chiles de agua.*

Veracruz. Spanning the coast of the Gulf of Mexico, the cuisine here is characterized geographically by fish and seafood. It is also one of the most versatile agricultural regions of Mexico. Nut- and seed-based sauces are very popular, as are spicy chicken and vegetable dishes.

Cancún's famous tacos

Cancún is a great place to experience 21st-century Mexico, because it has everything you'd want in a vacation: shopping, sports, spas, and beaches. Here you'll find five-star resorts, exceptional food, Mexican culture, and natural beauty, all within day-trip distance of the world-famous Maya ruins.

The locals—most of whom have embraced the accoutrements of urban middle-class life—typically live on the mainland in a part of the city called El Centro, but they work in the Zona Hotelera's tourist hub. The zone's main drag is Boulevard Kukulcán, and kilometer markers along it indicate where you are, from Km 1 near El Centro to Km 25 at the southern tip of Punta Nizuc. The area in between consists entirely of hotels, restaurants, shopping complexes, marinas, and time-share condominiums. Most travelers base themselves in this 25-km (15½-mile) stretch of paradise.

The party atmosphere of Zona Hotelera has inevitably earned it the title "Spring Break Capital of the World." Dozens of bars and nightclubs cater to college students just south of Punta Cancún at Km 9. Fortunately, this late-night/early-morning scene is contained within a small area, far from the larger resorts. Cancún, though, isn't just a magnet for youth on the loose. Adults with more sophisticated tastes appreciate its posh restaurants and world-class spas, while families are drawn to the limitless water sports and a plethora of children's activities.

If you believe that local flavor trumps the Zona Hotelera's pristine beaches, El Centro beckons. Although less visited by vacationers, the downtown area holds cultural gems that will remind you that you really are in Mexico. Hole-in-the-wall cantinas promise authentic regional food; evocative markets offer bargain-priced goods; and the hotels, while much more modest in terms of scale and amenities, provide true Mexican ambience for more modest prices, too.

Planning

When to Go

The sun shines an average of 253 days a year in Cancún. During high season (late November to April), the weather is nearly perfect, with temperatures hovering around 29°C (84°F) during the day and 18°C (64°F) at night. Hotel prices hit their peak between December 15 and January 5. If you plan to visit during Christmas, spring break, or Easter, book at least three months in advance.

Vacationers with travel-date flexibility can avoid the crowds and save 20% to 50% on accommodations during the remaining months. Be advised, though, that May through September are hot and humid, with temperatures that can top 36°C (97°F). The rainy season starts in mid-September and lasts until mid-November, bringing afternoon downpours that can last anywhere from 30 minutes to two hours. El Centro's streets often get flooded during these storms, and traffic can grind to a halt.

PLANNING YOUR TIME

Understandably, many visitors stay here a week, or longer, without ever leaving the silky sands and seductive comforts of their resorts. If you're game to do some exploring, though, allow time for day trips to nearby eco-parks and archaeological sites.

Getting Here and Around

You might find El Centro's layout confusing as it's based on a circular pattern rather than a grid. In addition, the whole city is divided into districts called Super Manzanas (abbreviated "Sm"), each with its own central square or park.

Walks through downtown can be unpleasant, with whizzing cars, corroded pathways, and overgrown weeds. Sidewalks sometimes disappear, forcing pedestrians to cross grassy inlets and thin strips of land separating four lanes of traffic. Few people, even residents, seem to know exactly where anything is. When exploring on foot, expect to get lost at least once. Taxis are always a good bet for exploring downtown Cancún.

For a taste of downtown culture, start at the colorful Mercado Veintiocho or Parque de las Palapas. To return to the Zona Hotelera, take a taxi to the Chedraui on Avenida Tulum and then catch the bus that passes every few minutes toward the Zona. (At night, the buses come alive with amateur performers—from accordionists to jugglers—hoping to earn a few pesos.)

South of Punta Cancún, Boulevard Kukulcán becomes a busy road and is difficult for pedestrians to cross. It's also punctuated by steeply inclined driveways for hotels, most of which are set back at least 100 yards from the road. The boulevard's lagoon side consists of scrubby stretches of land alternating with marinas, shopping centers, and restaurants.

AIR

Located 16 km (9 miles) southwest of the heart of Cancún and 10 km (6 miles) from the Zona Hotelera's southernmost point, Cancún Aeropuerto Internacional (CUN) receives direct scheduled flights from many cities, including New York, Washington, D.C., Houston, Dallas, Miami, Chicago, Los Angeles, Orlando, Fort Lauderdale, Charlotte, Atlanta, Toronto, and Montreal. An increasing number of direct charter flights from other locales are also available.

Hourly buses link the airport to downtown Cancún, as do taxis, *colectivos* (minibuses), and hotel shuttles.

BICYCLE

A cycling and walking path that starts downtown, at the beginning of the Zona Hotelera, continues to Punta Nizuc. The beginning of the path parallels a grassy strip of Boulevard Kukulcán that's decorated with reproductions of ancient Mexican art.

BUS

For travel within the Zona Hotelera, buses R1, R2, R15, and R27 stop every five minutes along Boulevard Kukulcán and cost a flat MX$10 no matter where you get on or off. The R2 and R15 continue to El Centro's Walmart and Mercado Veintiocho; the R1 goes as far as Puerto Juárez and the main bus terminal in El Centro.

Buses for farther-flung destinations leave from El Centro's terminal. One of the oldest bus lines in Mexico, ADO has first-class buses that make stops in Puerto Morelos, Playa del Carmen, Tulum, Felipe

Carrillo Puerto, Limones, and Chetumal. The full trip (concluding in Chetumal) takes five hours and 45 minutes and costs MX$370. Fifteen buses make the trip daily, departing between 6 am and midnight. Mayab, a division of ADO, has second-class buses leaving for destinations along the Riviera Maya every hour.

BUS CONTACTS ADO. ☎ *555/784–4652* ⊕ *www.ado.com.mx.* **Terminal de Autobuses.** ✉ *Calle Pino, Super Mzna. 2, El Centro* ☎ *998/132–9562.*

CAR

If you are planning to visit only Cancún, you don't need to (and probably shouldn't) rent a car. But if you want to explore the region, a car can be convenient if expensive. Be sure to read our extensive guidelines regarding road conditions, insurance requirements, and costs (⇨ *see Car in Travel Smart*) so that you can make an informed decision.

TAXI

Taxis are easy to find, and rides cost MX$140–MX$290 within the Zona Hotelera and MX$70–MX$140 within El Centro. Fares between the two run around MX$290. A ride to the ferries at Punta Sam or Puerto Juárez will set you back MX$350 or more. Make sure you check the fare before accepting a ride; a list of rates can be found in the lobby of most hotels, or you can ask the concierge.

The ride-hailing service Uber has legal permission to operate in Cancún, however, the local taxi union wasn't pleased by the decision and has created a lot of trouble for Uber drivers. Accounts abound of Uber drivers unable to enter the airport and the Zona Hotelera, leaving passengers stranded. Until Uber and the taxi union work out their differences, we recommend not using its services.

TRAIN

The Tren Maya (Maya Train), one of the federal government's flagship projects, aims to connect destinations within southeastern Mexico in general and those within the Yucatán Peninsula in particular. In total, the rail network covers 1,525 kilometers (950 miles) over five Mexican states, with the Cancún station, situated next to the airport, being the largest and serving as headquarters. West from Cancún trains will travel to Valladolid, Chichén Itzá, Izamal, and Mérida. To the south, the network will run to Puerto Morelos, Playa del Carmen, Tulum, and all the way to Chetumal near the border with Belize.

Beaches

All beaches can be reached by public transportation; just let the driver know where you're headed. If you're traveling with young children, opt for beaches facing Bahía de Mujeres at the top of the "7," which tend to be less crowded and more sheltered than those on the Caribbean side. Wide beaches and shallow waters make the northern tip ideal for snorkeling or swimming. Forming the right side of the "7" are beaches facing the Caribbean Sea. Here riptides and currents can be somewhat dangerous, especially when the surf is high.

⚠ **Don't swim when the black danger flag flies; a red or yellow flag indicates that you should proceed with caution; and a green flag means the waters are calm. Most likely, you will always see a red or yellow flag posted on the shores.**

The snorkeling is also good at the southern end of Boulevard Kukulcán near the Westin Hotel. In the saltwater lagoon, jungle boats and WaveRunners rule the waters by day and adult crocodiles wade the banks by night. Note, too, that beaches not maintained by hotels will have seaweed on their shores.

Hotels

You might find it bewildering to choose among Cancún's many hotels, not least because brochures and websites make them sound—and look—almost exactly alike. For luxury and amenities, the Zona Hotelera is the place to stay. If you want to be in the heart of the action, northern hotels near Punta Cancún are within walking distance of the nightclubs. Quieter properties are located at the southern end of Boulevard Kukulcán and on the residential streets between El Centro and the Zona Hotelera at Laguna Nichupté. In the modest Centro, local color outweighs facilities. Downtown hotels here are more basic and much less expensive than those in the Zona.

Many hotels have all-inclusive packages, as well as theme-night parties complete with food, beverages, activities, and games. Take note: generally the larger the all-inclusive resort, the blander the food (and the more watered-down the cocktails). For more memorable meals, you may need to dine off-site and essentially pay for food you're not consuming at your resort.

Many of the larger and more popular all-inclusives will not guarantee an ocean-view room when you make your reservation. If this is important to you, check that all rooms have ocean views at your chosen hotel, or book only at places that will guarantee one. Be sure to bring your confirmation information with you to prove you paid for an ocean-view room. Also be careful about lost wristbands and unreturned towels, since many resorts charge up to $150 per day for the former and $25 for the latter. When checking out, make sure the hotel hasn't tacked on excessive phone or minibar charges, as a few tend to do.

■TIP➜ Hotels generally cite rates in U.S. dollars ($), rather than Mexican pesos (MP or MX$), especially online. Also, when booking an all-inclusive stay, ask if the rate includes tips—some resorts automatically add 15% gratuities—and resort fees, which tend to be hidden supplementary charges.

Cancún is the consummate spring-break destination, but many lodgings don't accept partying college students as guests, no matter the season.

⇨ Hotel reviews have been shortened. For full information, visit Fodors.com. Hotel prices are the lowest cost of a standard double room in high season.

What It Costs in U.S. Dollars			
$	$$	$$$	$$$$
HOTELS			
under $200	$200–$350	$351–$500	over $500

Nightlife

We're not here to judge: we know that most people come to Cancún to party. If you want fine dining and dancing under the stars, you'll definitely find it here. But if your tastes run more toward bikini contests, all-night chug-a-thons, or cross-dressing Cher impersonators, rest assured: Cancún has plenty of those, too. For all its raucous reputation, Cancún concentrates its party-hearty nightlife along a relatively small strip of the Zona Hotelera, south of the convention center. It's as easy to avoid as it is to find.

Indoor areas of all venues are no-smoking. Carrying open containers of alcohol outside bars and restaurants is against the law.

■TIP➜ If you want to avoid rowdy spring breakers, stay clear of "open-bar" establishments and chain restaurants like Señor Frog's. They'll likely be packed with party animals on the loose.

Restaurants

Even at all-inclusives, some on-site restaurants may not be included in your rate, and Cancún has a great dining scene, so you'll be rewarded if you leave your hotel grounds for a meal or two. Large breakfast and brunch buffets are among the most popular meals in the Zona Hotelera, with prices ranging from MX$200 to MX$400 per person. El Centro offers an impressive selection of restaurants, all just a taxi ride away from the Zona Hotelera.

Most local restaurants open for lunch around 2 pm and generally stay open until midnight. When choosing one, be aware that those lining Avenidas Tulum and Yaxchilán are often noisy and crowded, and gas fumes make it hard to enjoy meals alfresco. Many of the finer options are on Avenida Bonampak. Eateries in the Parque de las Palapas, just off Avenida Tulum, serve expertly prepared Mexican food. Deeper into the city center, you can find fresh seafood and traditional fare at Mercado Veintiocho (Market 28).

Although many restaurants do not allow bare feet, short shorts, or bathing suits, dress is casual. Even at the fanciest places, suggested attire is "resort elegant," meaning long pants, collared shirts, and closed shoes for gentlemen. For women, a dress or skirt and blouse with chichi sandals or heels will suffice. The indoor portions of all restaurants are no-smoking.

■TIP→ **Upscale resorts in the Zona Hotelera typically purify their tap water; however, ask in advance whether it's safe to drink.**

⇨ *Restaurant reviews have been shortened. For full information, visit Fodors. com. Restaurant prices are the average cost of a main course at dinner, or if dinner is not served, at lunch.*

What It Costs in Mexican Pesos

	$	$$	$$$	$$$$
RESTAURANTS				
	under MP150	MP150– MP300	MP301– MP400	over MP400

Safety

Although it's wise to exercise caution and use common sense while moving about, Cancún is one of Mexico's safest cities. The violence in the country that's greatly reported in the news generally takes place along the U.S.–Mexico border, north of Cancún by some 2,090 km (1,300 miles)—the same distance as New York is from Texas.

Don't be surprised to see Tourist Police patrolling the Zona Hotelera, especially during the holidays and high season when security is increased. The C4 Surveillance and Rescue Center monitors the tourist area through video cameras installed at strategic points throughout the city, and an emergency 911 call center is available.

Shopping

The *centros comerciales* (malls) in Cancún are fully air-conditioned and as well kept as similar establishments in the United States or Canada. Like their northerly counterparts, they also sell just about everything: designer clothing, beachwear (including raunchy T-shirts aimed at the spring break crowd), sportswear, jewelry, music, electronics, household items, shoes, and books. Some even have the same terrible mall food that's standard north of the border.

Prices are fixed in shops. They're also generally—but not always—higher than in the markets, where bargaining is a given. Perfumes in Cancún are considerably less expensive than at home (and even than at the duty-free shops at the airport). Tequila is a bargain here as well, but make sure you buy at the supermarket rather than at a souvenir shop.

Lots of duty-free stores sell designer goods at prices that can be as much as 30% or 40% below retail. You can find handwoven textiles, leather goods, and handcrafted silver jewelry, although prices are higher than in other cities, and the selection is limited.

Monday through Saturday, shop hours are generally from 10 am to 7 pm. Many open on Sunday as well. Centros comerciales tend to be open daily from 10 or 11 am to 8 or 9 pm.

Tours

BOAT TOURS
AquaWorld
BOAT TOURS | FAMILY | In addition to renting two-person speedboats, WaveRunners, and cool water toys like flyboards and hoverboards, this operator offers Nichupté lagoon outings, Isla Mujeres day trips, and tours on the Paradise Sub-See—a glass-bottom boat that submerges halfway into the water. On the short journey to Punta Nizuc, you'll see turtles, fish, coral, and a few statues in the Underwater Museum. ⊠ *Blvd. Kukulcán, Km 15.2, Zona Hotelera* ☎ *554/166–3092, 866/210–1236 in the U.S.* ⊕ *www. aquaworld.com.mx* ⊠ *Flyboard USD$70; SubSee Explorer from USD$50; other tours from USD$95.*

Asterix Tours
BOAT TOURS | FAMILY | This is one of the few companies permitted to depart from the Zona Hotelera on tours to Isla Contoy and the underwater gardens of Isla Mujeres. Excursions, which first go to Isla Mujeres and then Isla Contoy, depart at 9 am and return at 5 pm from Tuesday to Sunday. Day- and nighttime fishing trips run three times a week. ⊠ *Blvd. Kukulcán, Km 5.5, Zona Hotelera*

☎ *998/886–4270* ⊕ *www.contoytours. com* ⊠ *Isla Contoy tours USD$119.*

Kolumbus Tours
BOAT TOURS | FAMILY | Excursions to Isla Contoy and Isla Mujeres on the same day are available daily (less frequently May–October) on a double-decker trawler. ⊠ *Punta Conoco 36, Sm 24, El Centro* ☎ *998/885–5333* ⊕ *www.kolumbustours. com* ⊠ *From MX$1,294.*

Sea Passion by Cancun Sailing
BOAT TOURS | Day trips to Isla Mujeres and Isla Contoy onboard a beautiful catamaran (which includes a buffet lunch, open bar, and snorkel equipment) are available by reservation. ⊠ *Hotel Imperial Las Perlas, Blvd. Kukulcán, Km 2.5, Zona Hotelera* ☎ *998/626–8961* ⊕ *www.cancunsailing.com* ⊠ *From USD$114.*

ECOTOURS
Eco Colors
ECOTOURISM | FAMILY | Bike tours, butterfly- and bird-watching adventures, as well as kayaking, diving, and eco-oriented snorkeling trips can be booked through Eco Colors. It also specializes in cultural programs and volunteer opportunities. ⊠ *Av. Chapultepec 42, El Centro* ☎ *998/884–3667* ⊕ *ecotravelmexico.com* ⊠ *From USD$125.*

Odigoo Travel
ECOTOURISM | FAMILY | Odigoo Travel provides a wide array of travel-related services in Cancún and the Riviera Maya region. Its tours are centered on the idea of sustainable tourism and reconnection with nature. Top offerings include bird-watching expeditions, snorkeling in stunning lagoons, and catamaran sails to Isla Mujeres. ⊠ *Calle Tejón Sm 20, Mz 3, Lote 16, Local 100, El Centro* ☎ *998/197–3240* ⊕ *www.odigootravel.com* ⊠ *From USD$89.*

GENERAL TOURS
Discova
ADVENTURE TOURS | Specializing in outings in Cancún and the whole Riviera Maya, this agency's options run the gamut from

ATV and extreme Tulum tours to snorkeling VIP experiences and luxury sailing. It will also book reservations for Xcaret, Xel-Há, and other area adventure parks. ✉ *Blvd. Luis Donaldo Colosio Sm 307, Mz 305, Lote 2-09, Edificio Cunstorage, El Centro* 🌐 *www.discova.com.*

Gray Line Cancún

SPECIAL-INTEREST TOURS | FAMILY | Cancún's Gray Line office offers everything from luxury airport transportation and dolphin adventures to sunset or dinner cruises and tours of Chichén Itzá. ✉ *Calle Robalo 30, Local 41* ☎ *877/240–5864 toll-free in the U.S., 998/887–2495, 800/719–5465 toll-free in Mexico* 🌐 *graylinecancun.com* 🎫 *From MX$680.*

Visitor Information

CONTACT Cancún Convention & Visitors Bureau. (*CVB*) ✉ *Zona Hotelera, Blvd. Kukulcán, Km 9, Cancun Center* ☎ *998/881–0400* 🌐 *cancuncenter.com.*

El Centro

There really is a downtown Cancún, and its malls and markets offer a glimpse of Mexico's urban lifestyle. Avenida Tulum, El Centro's main drag, is marked by a huge sculpture of shells and starfish in the middle of a traffic circle. This iconic sight, which locals refer to as El Ceviche, is particularly dramatic at night when the lights are turned on.

El Centro is also home to many restaurants and bars. (We recommend taking a taxi to and from at night.) You'll also find Mercado Veintiocho (Market 28), an enormous crafts market just off Avenidas Yaxchilán and Sunyaxchén, and the nearby Mercado Veintitres (Market 23) for a fun look at a local produce market. For bargain shopping, hit the stores and small strip malls along Avenida Tulum.

■ TIP→ The built-up area in the Zona Hotelera near the convention center at the sharply angled bend of Boulevard Kukulcán is not El Centro.

🍴 Restaurants

Bandoneón

$$$$ | ARGENTINE | Every detail here evokes the streets of Buenos Aires, right down to the cobblestone floors, the dramatic tango music, and the walls adorned with antique *bandoneons* (concertinas). Although the star offering is steak, the broad menu also features starters like smoked marlin and charcoal-grilled provolone cheese and mains that include pasta, fish, and chicken dishes. **Known for:** impeccably prepared steaks; enormous wine selection; cool Argentine atmosphere. [$] *Average main: MP580* ✉ *Av. Bonampak at Nichupté, El Centro* ☎ *998/889–9500, 305/200–5606* 🌐 *www.bandoneonrestaurantes.com.*

Café con Gracia

$ | CAFÉ | FAMILY | This adorable downtown café with an outdoor garden is a local favorite for breakfast. It serves an extensive selection of coffees alongside yummy pancakes, crepes, bagels, waffles, and paninis. **Known for:** informal café setting; all-day breakfast menu; hot and cold drinks. [$] *Average main: MP99* ✉ *Av. Tankah 69, Mz 1, Lote 24, El Centro* ☎ *998/884–9850* 🌐 *cafecongracia.com.*

El Cejas

$$ | SEAFOOD | The clientele is lively, and the seafood is fresh at this open-air eatery in the bustling Mercado Veintiocho. The kitchen serves crab (stuffed, steamed, or fried) and whole fried fish that's crispy outside and moist inside. **Known for:** quality crab and fried fish; fun atmosphere in a local market; strolling musicians. [$] *Average main: MP250* ✉ *Mercado Veintiocho, Sm 26, Local 90–100, El Centro* ✥ *Inside Market 28* ☎ *998/884-0401* 🌐 *facebook.com/ElCejasRestaurante.*

El Oasis

$$$ | **SEAFOOD** | **FAMILY** | This aptly named eatery is a welcome respite from El Centro's busy streets. House specials include grilled seafood with rice, fish fillet with coconut cream, and smaller dishes like ceviche or *aguachiles* (spicy lime shrimp). **Known for:** relaxing setting; colorful decorations; dishes grilled to perfection. [$] *Average main: MP315* ✉ *Av. Yaxchilan, Sm 17, Mz 2, Lote 3, across from Costco, El Centro* ☎ *998/136–3094, 998/478-4810 WhatsApp* 🌐 *eloasismariscos.com.*

Herbívoro

$$ | **VEGETARIAN** | **FAMILY** | One of the few vegan restaurants in Cancún is popular with locals thanks to its wide variety of juices, smoothies, and fruit bowls. Its menu also features excellent vegan versions of traditional Mexican breakfasts such as enchiladas, chilaquiles, and burritos. **Known for:** wide range of smoothies; delicious avocado toast; vegan tacos. [$] *Average main: MP170* ✉ *Av. Tulum esq. Calle Liebre, Sm 20, El Centro* ☎ *998/336–1178* 🌐 *facebook.com/soyherbivoro.*

★ La Dolce Vita

$$$ | **ITALIAN** | The grande dame of Cancún restaurants delivers on the promise of its name, with candlelit tables and discreet waiters who will make you feel as if you've been transported to Italy. The fare includes homemade pizzas and pastas such as Bolognese-style lasagna; veal scaloppine and calamari steak in shrimp and lobster sauce are other options. **Known for:** excellent wine list; chocolate desserts; slow service. [$] *Average main: MP390* ✉ *Av. Cobá 87, Sm 3, El Centro* ☎ *998/884–3393* 🌐 *ladolcevitacancun.com* 🕓 *Closed Sun.*

La Habichuela

$$ | **CARIBBEAN** | This much-loved restaurant, "The Bean," has an elegant yet cozy indoor dining room plus an outdoor area full of Mayan sculptures and local flora. Although the menu includes chicken, pasta, and grilled kabobs, this is a good place to satisfy your seafood cravings with Caribbean lobster tail or giant shrimp prepared 10 different ways. **Known for:** ample seafood portions; cozy elegance; lush surroundings. [$] *Average main: MP290* ✉ *Av. Margaritas 25, Sm 22, El Centro* ☎ *998/884–3158* 🌐 *facebook.com/LaHabichuelaRest.*

La Parrilla

$$ | **MEXICAN** | With its flamboyant live mariachi music and energetic waiters, this place is a Cancún classic. The menu isn't fancy, but it offers good, basic Mexican food—including sizzling fajitas, thick burritos, and 30 different taco dishes. **Known for:** solid Mexican menu; showy service; great tequila selection. [$] *Average main: MP290* ✉ *Av. Yaxchilán 51, Sm 22, El Centro* ☎ *998/287–8118* 🌐 *laparrilla.com.mx.*

Locanda Paolo

$$$ | **ITALIAN** | Flowers and artwork lend warmth to this sophisticated Italian restaurant, where the cuisine includes linguine with lobster, angel-hair pasta with seafood, specialty lasagnas, plus assorted meat and fish dishes. The waiters are laid-back and seem to know everyone who walks in the door. (Most patrons are locals who've been dining here for more than 20 years.) On any given night, many of chef Paolo Ceravolo's offerings are colorful and innovative specials that do not appear on the menu. **Known for:** careful attention to Italian dishes; friendly service in formal setting; terrific international wine menu. [$] *Average main: MP360* ✉ *Av. Bonampak 145, Sm 3, corner of Calle Jurel, El Centro* ☎ *998/887–2627, 998/884–8396* 🌐 *locandapaolo.com.*

100% Natural

$$ | **CAFÉ** | **FAMILY** | Start the day at this open-air restaurant with a signature omelet and a *bebida inteligente* ("intelligent drink"), which combines fruit juice with ginseng. Sandwiches, soy burgers, and stuffed pitas are prepared with fresh-baked breads. **Known for:** vegetarian

Restaurants ▼

1 Bandoneón. **D8**
2 Café con
  Gracia....... **A4**
3 El Cejas **A3**
4 El Oasis **A7**
5 Herbívoro... **C6**
6 La Dolce
  Vita **D5**
7 La
  Habichuela . **B3**
8 La
  Parrilla **B3**
9 Locanda
  Paolo........ **D4**
10 100%
  Natural...... **B3**
11 Peter's
  Restaurant.. **D5**
12 Rolandi's
  Pizzeria **C5**
13 Ty-Coz....... **C2**
14 Yamamoto .. **D3**

Hotels ▼

1 Ambiance
  Suites
  Cancún...... **C6**
2 El Rey
  del Caribe... **D3**
3 Hotel Adhara
  Cancún...... **C2**
4 Ibis Cancún
  Centro....... **C8**
5 Oh! Cancún
  The Urban
  Oasis **C5**
6 Smart Cancún
  by Oasis..... **C5**
7 Xbalamqué
  Hotel
  & Spa........ **B3**

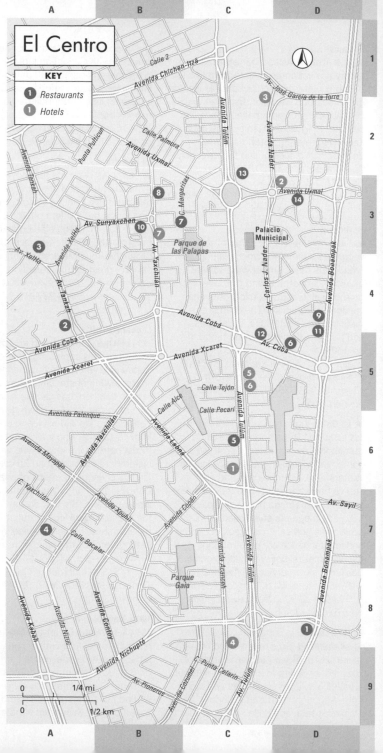

El Centro

KEY

1 Restaurants
1 Hotels

cuisine; fresh fruit juices; relaxing, plant-filled surroundings. $ *Average main: MP300* ✉ *Av. Sunyaxchén, Sm 25, Mz 6, Lote 62, El Centro* ☎ *998/884–0102* ⊕ *www.100natural.com.*

★ Peter's Restaurant
$$$$ | INTERNATIONAL | Although it has only six tables, Peter's has an impressive menu that gives international dishes a Mexican twist—think foie gras with apple and yam bean salad or smoked salmon with potato-chipotle mash. Portions are generous, flavors are outstanding, and prices aren't too bad. **Known for:** key lime pie; cozy, intimate atmosphere; expat hangout. $ *Average main: MP465* ✉ *Av. Bonampak, Sm 3, between Robalo and Sierra, El Centro* ☎ *998/251–9310* ⊕ *facebook.com/peterscancun* ☾ *Closed Sun. and Mon. June–Nov. No lunch.*

Rolandi's Pizzeria
$$ | PIZZA | FAMILY | This Cancún landmark since almost the beginning draws crowds with its scrumptious wood-fired pizzas. The most popular, Pizza Del Padrone, is topped with tomatoes, prosciutto, arugula, and mascarpone cheese. **Known for:** 20 pizza varieties; calzones with fresh ingredients; friendly service. $ *Average main: MP289* ✉ *Av. Cobá 12, Sm 5, El Centro* ☎ *998/884–4047* ⊕ *rolandispizzeria.mx.*

Ty-Coz
$ | SANDWICHES | FAMILY | The inexpensive croissants and freshly brewed coffee make a delicious breakfast combo at this place tucked behind the Soriana grocery store on Avenida Tulum. At lunchtime, stop in for a huge sandwich stuffed with all the deli classics, but be prepared to wait awhile since lines are long. **Known for:** monster sandwiches; dirt-cheap prices; local atmosphere. $ *Average main: MP81* ✉ *Av. Tulum, Sm 2, El Centro* ☎ *998/884–6060, 998/883-5394.*

Yamamoto
$$ | JAPANESE | The oldest Japanese restaurant in Cancún serves the best sushi and sashimi in El Centro with a menu of traditional Japanese dishes like chicken teriyaki and tempura for those who prefer their food cooked. Large groups can order combination platters of sushi, sashimi, kushikatsu, and gyoza. **Known for:** terrific sushi variety; Japanese decor; delivery to El Centro hotels. $ *Average main: MP230* ✉ *Av. Uxmal 31, Sm 3, El Centro* ☎ *998/812–1245* ⊕ *restauranteyamamoto.com.*

🛏 Hotels

Ambiance Suites Cancún
$ | HOTEL | Branding itself as "your home and office" and catering mostly to business travelers, this modern hotel just two blocks from the Plaza Las Américas shopping center has guest rooms with a plasma TV, minibar, coffeemaker, and Wi-Fi. **Pros:** small but charming courtyard pool; convenient El Centro location; good value. **Cons:** outdated decor; unfriendly staff; far from the beach. $ *Rooms from: $75* ✉ *Av. Tulum 227, Sm 20, El Centro* ☎ *998/892–0392* ⊕ *www.ambiancecancun.com* ⇆ *48 rooms* ❍ *Free Breakfast.*

El Rey del Caribe
$ | HOTEL | FAMILY | Thanks to the use of solar energy, a water-recycling system, and composting toilets, this tranquil hotel has little impact on the environment—and its luxuriant garden blocks the heat and noise of downtown. **Pros:** eco-friendly; affordable spa; walking distance to El Centro's shops and restaurants. **Cons:** simple and musty rooms; alcohol is not served at the hotel restaurant; mosquitoes in common areas. $ *Rooms from: $92* ✉ *Av. Uxmal 24, Sm 2A, at Náder, El Centro* ☎ *998/884–2028, 800/508–1864* ⊕ *www.elreydelcaribe.com* ⇆ *31 rooms* ❍ *Free Breakfast* ☞ *Visa and Mastercard only, no American Express.*

Hotel Adhara Cancún
$ | HOTEL | Not only does the circular lobby of this hip, hacienda-style property have a martini bar but it's also decorated with

illuminated onyx stone, marble floors, and teak furnishings accented with gray and cream cushions. **Pros:** well-equipped business center; state-of-the-art gym equipment; available handicapped-accessible units. **Cons:** east-facing rooms tend to have street noise; lights in rooms are movement triggered; far from the beach. [$] *Rooms from: $119* ✉ *Av. Náder 1, El Centro* ☎ *998/881–6500, 998/122–1861 WhatsApp* 🌐 *adharacancun.com* 🛏 *247 rooms* 🍴 *Free Breakfast.*

Ibis Cancún Centro

$ | **HOTEL** | Within walking distance of Las Américas Shopping Center and next to a grocery store, this hotel is perfect for mixing business with pleasure at a very reasonable price. **Pros:** clean, bright rooms; free underground parking; car rental agency and tour operator on-site. **Cons:** no pool; mainly caters to business and budget travelers; hotel will not sell alcohol on Sunday. [$] *Rooms from: $67* ✉ *Avs. Tulum and Nichupté, Sm 11, El Centro* ☎ *998/272–8500* 🌐 *all.accor.com* 🛏 *190 rooms* 🍴 *No Meals.*

Oh! Cancún The Urban Oasis

$ | **HOTEL** | This fresh, hip hotel greets you with a pop art–style lobby and vibrant hallways that lead to guest rooms with marble floors, 42-inch flat-screen TVs, minibars, and small balconies. **Pros:** adults-only; buffet breakfast included; lovely pool area. **Cons:** no spa within the facilities; not on the beach; not suitable for families. [$] *Rooms from: $125* ✉ *Av. Tulum, Sm 4, corner of Brisa, El Centro* ☎ *55/4170-9258, 998/287–4478 WhatsApp* 🌐 *oasishoteles.com* 🛏 *62 rooms* 🍴 *Free Breakfast.*

Smart Cancún by Oasis

$ | **HOTEL** | **FAMILY** | Oasis Smart caters to business travelers with a location 20 minutes from the airport and 10 minutes from the Zona Hotelera. **Pros:** peaceful atmosphere; walking distance from main avenues; free shuttle to Zona Hotelera sister properties. **Cons:** not on the beach; small bathrooms; seemingly safe but old elevators. [$] *Rooms from: MP112* ✉ *Av. Tulum 4, Sm 4, Lote 113, El Centro* ☎ *55/4170–9258, 998/287–4478 WhatsApp* 🌐 *oasishoteles.com* 🛏 *132 rooms* 🍴 *Free Breakfast.*

Xbalamqué Hotel & Spa

$ | **HOTEL** | This refreshing retreat from El Centro's bustling streets reflects Maya culture through murals, statues, and reliefs and forms part of a complex that also includes two restaurants and a snack shop open to the general public. **Pros:** small on-site spa and beauty salon; good El Centro location; kids under 11 stay free. **Cons:** street noise audible from front rooms; intermittent hot water; patchy Wi-Fi. [$] *Rooms from: $55* ✉ *Av. Yaxchilan 31, Sm 22, Mz 18, El Centro* ☎ *998/892–3377, 998/283–3353 reservations* 🌐 *www.xbalamque.com* 🛏 *91 rooms* 🍴 *No Meals.*

🍸 Nightlife

Laser Hot Bar

BARS | The oldest gay bar in Cancún has been operating for more than 15 years. Doors open at 10 pm, but don't expect things to get underway until midnight. ✉ *Plaza Galerias, Av. Tulum 45, El Centro* ☎ *998/860–0426* 🌐 *www.facebook.com/laserhot* 🕒 *Closed Mon. and Tues.*

McCarthy's Irish Pub Cancún

PUBS | This traditional Irish pub in Cancún's downtown is a favorite of locals who come for the great variety of national and international beers and stay for the live music. It's open every day until 3 am. ✉ *Av. Bonampak Esq. Av. Sayil, Plaza Solare Local 222, El Centro* ☎ *998/267–7260* 🌐 *www.mccarthyspub.com.mx.*

Parque de las Palapas

GATHERING PLACES | **FAMILY** | To mingle with locals and hear great music for free, head to the Parque de las Palapas. Every Friday night at 7:30 there's live music that ranges from jazz to salsa; lots of locals show up to dance. On Sunday afternoon the Cancún Municipal Orchestra plays.

Ciruela 27, El Centro ⊕ *www.facebook. com/Parquedelaspalapas.*

🛍 Shopping

There are a few interesting shops along Avenida Tulum between Avenidas Cobá and Uxmal. For the best selection in downtown, however, head to the Plaza Las Américas shopping center.

GROCERY STORES

Chedraui

CHAIN | FAMILY | With several locations in El Centro, this popular superstore (a Mexican version of Walmart) has a large selection of local and American products. ⊠ *Av. Tulum 260, El Centro* ☎ *998/884–1024* ⊕ *www.chedraui.com.mx.*

Soriana

CHAIN | FAMILY | One of the major Mexican grocery-store chains, Soriana has multiple locations. The most convenient is at Avenidas Tulum and Uxmal, across from the bus station; its largest store, farther north on Avenida Kabah, is open 24 hours. ⊠ *Avs. Tulum and Uxmal, Mz 1, El Centro* ☎ *81/8329–9252* ⊕ *www. soriana.com.*

Súper Akí

CHAIN | FAMILY | This is a smaller grocery store with several branches throughout downtown Cancún. ⊠ *Av. José López Portillo s/n, Mz 1, Lote 31, El Centro* ☎ *998/892–4690* ⊕ *www.superaki.mx.*

MARKETS AND MALLS

★ **Mercado 28** (*Mercado Veintiocho*)

MARKET | FAMILY | Mercado 28 is Cancún's largest open-air market. In addition to a few small restaurants, it has about 100 stalls where you can buy many of the same items found in the Zona Hotelera at a fraction of the cost. Expect to be confronted by aggressive vendors trying to coax you into their shop. This is a great place to haggle, and usually you can end up paying half of the initial asking price. ⊠ *Xel-ha Mz 13, El Centro* ☎ *998/892–4303* ⊕ *www.facebook.com/ ofismercado28.*

Mercado Veintitrés (*Mercado 23*)

MARKET | FAMILY | If Mercado 28 (Veintiocho) is El Centro's large local Mexican crafts market, Mercado Veintitrés (open daily) goes more local still. Here's where the typical Cancunese comes to shop for produce, although you'll find a selection of souvenirs here, too. This market provides a healthy dose of local color, but speaking Spanish is a must here. ⊠ *Ciricote 23, at Cedro, El Centro.*

Plaza Las Américas

MALL | FAMILY | With 100-plus shops, several big department stores and restaurants, two movie theaters, a video arcade, and plenty of fast-food outlets El Centro's shopping mecca will—for better or worse—make you feel right at home. The mall is intolerably crowded on weekends. ⊠ *Av. Tulum Sur 7, Sm 4 and Sm 9, El Centro* ☎ *998/887–3863* ⊕ *www. lasamericascentrocomercial.com.mx.*

Punta Sam

👁 Sights

★ **Cancún Underwater Museum** (*Museo Subacuático de Arte/MUSA*)

NAUTICAL SIGHT | FAMILY | The collection at what is known locally as the Museo Subacuático de Arte (MUSA) consists of more than 400 lifelike statues that create marine-life habitats in three locations: off the shores of Punta Sam, Punta Nizuc, and Manchones Reef near Isla Mujeres. The sculptures at the Manchones site are 26 feet deep and best observed on a scuba dive. The two sites closer to Cancún, at half that depth or less, can easily be viewed on snorkeling or glass-bottom-boat excursions. ⊠ *Punta Cancún, Punta Nizuc, and Manchones Reef in Isla Mujeres, Cancún* ☎ *998/206–0182* ⊕ *musamexico.org* 🆓 *Free.*

🛏 Hotels

The area north of Cancún is slowly being developed into an alternative hotel zone, known informally as the Zona Hotelera Norte or Playa Mujeres (a term that has nothing to do with the island of Isla Mujeres). This is an ideal area for a tranquil beach vacation, because the shops, eateries, and nightlife of Cancún are about 30 minutes away by cab. If you decide against an all-inclusive plan, be sure to factor in about MX$540 in cab fees (each way) from Punta Sam to Cancún restaurants.

★ Beloved Playa Mujeres

$$$$ | **RESORT** | One of the region's few boutique-style all-inclusives, this modern sugar-cube-like structure is stylishly decorated in creams and whites, and offers the perfect balance of luxury and comfort. **Pros:** outstanding dining options and a large spa; personalized service; adults-only. **Cons:** narrow beach lined with sea grass; swim-up bar is in the shade; one-way cab fare to Cancún is an additional cost. $ *Rooms from: $571 ✉ Vialidad Paseo Mujeres, Sm 3, Mz 1, Lote 10, Punta Sam ☎ 998/872–8730, 866/211–6223 toll free from the U.S.* ⊕ *www.belovedhotels.com* ⥂ *109 rooms* ✝⊙✝ *All-Inclusive.*

Excellence Playa Mujeres

$$$$ | **ALL-INCLUSIVE** | Onyx pillars rising from two-tone marble floors, overshadowed only by a massive stained-glass ceiling illuminated from above, are your first indication of luxury at this adults-only resort, where every room has a terrace, hot tub, walk-in closet, and drop box for discreet room-service delivery. **Pros:** beautiful property; never feels crowded; doesn't operate as a time-share. **Cons:** $50 charge for spa facilities; 15-minute drive to El Centro, 30-minute drive to Zona Hotelera; no children under 18. $ *Rooms from: $620 ✉ Prolongación Bonampak s/n, Sm 003, Mz 001, Lote Terrenos 001, Punta Sam ☎ 866/211–6223*

in the U.S., 800/953–2142 in Mexico ⊕ *www.excellenceresorts.com* ⥂ *450 rooms* ✝⊙✝ *All-Inclusive.*

★ Garza Blanca Resort & Spa

$$ | **ALL-INCLUSIVE** | **FAMILY** | Top-notch luxury, extraordinary gastronomy, and a state-of-the-art spa are some of the attributes of this sprawling property in Cancún's up-and-coming Punta Sam area. **Pros:** great family package; outstanding dining offer; fantastic hydrotherapy circuit. **Cons:** not all rooms have ocean views; timeshare vibes; far from the Cancún action. $ *Rooms from: $315 ✉ Carretera a Punta Sam, Km 5.2, Mz 9, Lote 3, Punta Sam ☎ 800/927–0503 in the U.S. and Canada, 998/193–2930* ⊕ *www.garzablancaresort. com* ⥂ *452 suites* ✝⊙✝ *All-Inclusive.*

★ TRS Coral Hotel

$$$ | **ALL-INCLUSIVE** | Expect five-star service at this adults-only Palladium Hotel Group property (a member of The Leading Hotels of the World), where your every need is attended to by your butler and other well-trained, courteous staffers. **Pros:** attentive staff; access to tennis center and other facilities at adjacent Grand Palladium Costa Mujeres Resort & Spa; elegant, minimalist decor. **Cons:** property is spread out; 30-minute drive to Zona Hotelera; no kids under 18 allowed. $ *Rooms from: $475 ✉ Vialidad Paseo Mujeres, Mz 1, Punta Sam ☎ 888/660–9070 in the U.S., 800/990–1234* ⊕ *www. palladiumhotelgroup.com/en* ⥂ *469 suites* ✝⊙✝ *All-Inclusive.*

Villa del Palmar Cancún

$$ | **RESORT** | **FAMILY** | This five-star resort, which blends Maya and modern architecture, makes you feel right at home in apartment-like rooms with full kitchens, living rooms, dining areas, and spacious balconies draped with hammocks. **Pros:** on-site activities and minimart; complimentary Cancún shuttle; walking distance to Isla Mujeres ferry. **Cons:** away from the action; plenty of mosquitoes at night; seaweed in water. $ *Rooms from: $250 ✉ Carretera Punta Sam, Km 5.2,*

Punta Sam ☎ 998/193–2600, 800/931–4608 toll-free in the U.S. and Canada ⊕ www.villapalmarcancun.com ⇌ 415 rooms ❘◉❘ All-Inclusive.

⚡ Activities

Cancun Adventures

BOAT TOURS | FAMILY | Cancun Adventures provides a variety of excursions in the Riviera Maya, including catamaran sailings to the Isla Mujeres. The 5½-hour voyage departs from the Marina Cancún and includes lunch, an open bar onboard, snorkeling, and free time to explore Isla Mujeres. You also have time to visit Playa Norte, one of the most beautiful beaches in Cancún. Round-trip transportation to the dock is included from select hotels if you book 24 hours in advance. Knowledgeable, bilingual guides accompany guests on every tour. ⊠ Vialidad Paseo Mujeres MZ1, LT1 SM 3, Punta Sam ⊹ Condominio Playa Mujeres, Marina Cancún ☎ 984/854–3460, 866/854–3460 in the U.S. ⊕ cancun-adventure.com ▧ From $69.

Eco Tours Adventure

BOAT TOURS | FAMILY | Led by marine biologists and certified guides, this tour company is dedicated to delivering a fun and safe experience, without exploiting the natural environment by respecting animal rights and the conservation of nature. The Whale Shark Tour is an easy excursion that the whole family can enjoy. In addition to snorkeling with the whale sharks, there's also time to snorkel at Isla Mujeres. Breakfast, lunch, mask, fins, and safety jackets are included, as is transportation from and to any hotel. ⊠ Carr. a Punta Sam 84, Punta Sam ☎ 984/147–9678 ⊕ ecotoursadventure.com ▧ From $120.

Playa Mujeres Golf Club

GOLF | Designed by Greg Norman, this course was constructed in an environmentally sensitive way that preserved existing ecosystems and indigenous flora. The front nine holes take you between mangroves and wetlands adjacent to Laguna Chacmochuk. The back nine holes open up through natural sand dunes and lead to the Caribbean, with spectacular turquoise water and distant Isla Mujeres views. The lush, well-kept fairways and true-rolling greens are swept by daily trade winds, demanding pinpoint accuracy and challenging even the most experienced golfer. On the day of play, you have access to golf carts with Visage GPS systems, as well as the driving range and putting greens. Guest of Dreams Playa Mujeres enjoy complimentary greens fees. ⊠ Prolongación Bonampak, Carretera a Punta Sam s/n, Punta Sam ☎ 998/800–3892, 998/234–0430 ⊕ golfplayamujeres.com ▧ $250 for 18 holes ⅄ 18 holes, 7218 yards, par 72.

Zona Hotelera

◉ Sights

Cancún Scenic Tower (Torre Escénica de Cancún)

OBSERVATORY | FAMILY | This 262-foot rotating tower has a bird's-eye view of Cancún and the bay. The experience—which includes the ascent, a few rotations at the top, and the descent—takes about 10 minutes and is accompanied by Spanish-English narration. ⊠ Blvd. Kulkulcán, Km 4.5, Zona Hotelera ☎ 998/883–3143, 855/326–0682 in the U.S. ⊕ www.xcaret.com/en ▧ $20.

Interactive Aquarium Cancún (Acuario Interactivo de Cancún)

AQUARIUM | FAMILY | The enthusiastic staff at this small aquarium incorporate concern for the environment into their presentations, and the animals are well looked after. For added fees, you can participate in an aquarium trek, a dolphin presentation, or a swim with the dolphins. ⊠ La Isla Shopping Village, Blvd. Kukulcán, Km 12.5, Zona Hotelera

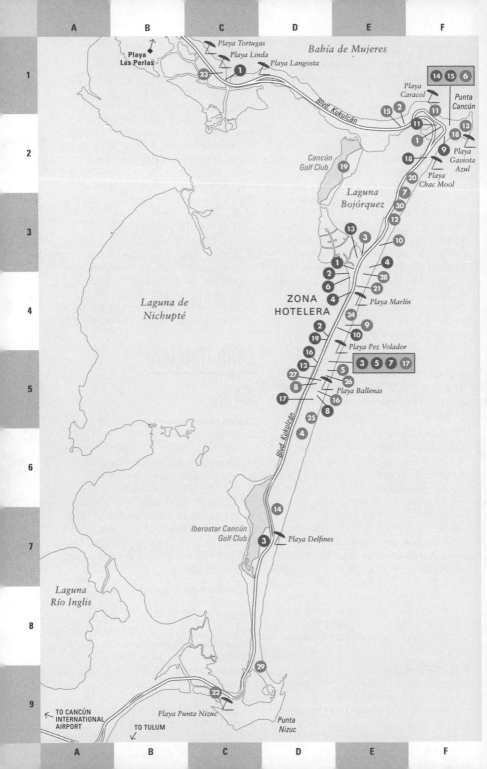

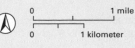

0   1 mile

0   1 kilometer

Caribbean Sea

KEY

1 *Sights*

1 *Restaurants*

1 *Hotels*

Zona Hotelera

998/251–6581 ⊕ www.interactiveaquariumcancun.com/en ≊ $15.

Ruinas El Rey

RUINS | FAMILY | Large signs on the Zona Hotelera's lagoon side, roughly opposite Playa Delfines, point out the so-called Ruins of the King, though the noble who held court here may or may not have been a king. Although much smaller than famous archaeological sites like Tulum and Chichén Itzá, this site is nevertheless worth a visit.

First entered into Western chronicles in a 16th-century travelogue, El Rey's ruins weren't explored by archaeologists until 1910, and excavations didn't begin until 1954. In 1975, archaeologists began restoration work on the 47 structures with the help of the Mexican government. In 2006, workmen unearthed an ancient Maya skeleton on the outskirts of the park.

Dating from the 3rd to 2nd century BC, El Rey is notable for having two main plazas bounded by two streets. (Most other Maya cities contain only one plaza.) Originally named Kin Ich Ahau Bonil, Mayan for "king of the solar countenance," the site was linked to astronomical practices. The pyramid is topped by a platform, and inside its vault are paintings on stucco. Skeletons interred at the apex and at the base indicate the site may have been a royal burial ground. ⊠ Blvd. Kukulcán, Km 17, Zona Hotelera 998/849–2880, 983/837–2411 ⊕ inah.gob.mx ≊ MX$70.

Yamil Lu'um

RUINS | FAMILY | Located on Cancún's highest point (the name means "hilly land"), this archaeological site is on the grounds of the Park Royal Cancún and Westin Lagunamar, which means that nonguests can visit only from the beachside. The concierges at either hotel may let you enter through their property if you ask nicely, but otherwise head to Playa Marlín and admire the ruins from a distance. Although it consists of two

structures—one probably a temple, the other probably a lighthouse—this is the smallest of Cancún's few archaeological sites. Discovered in 1842 by John Lloyd Stephens, the ruins date from the late 13th or early 14th century. Keep an eye out for roaming iguanas. ⊠ Blvd. Kukulcán, Km 12, Zona Hotelera ≊ Free.

🏖 Beaches

Playa Ballenas

BEACH | FAMILY | Also known as Whale Beach, this Blue Flag Beach is a raw stretch of sand and crystal water at Km 14.5 between the Hard Rock Hotel and Secrets The Vine. Jet Skiers often zoom through the water, and the strong wind makes the surf rough. The beach is open to the public; parking and beach access are at Calle Ballenas. Food and drinks are available at any of the resorts along this stretch, including the Hard Rock, Secrets The Vine, and Sandos Cancún—but keep in mind these all-inclusives cater only to hotel guests. **Amenities:** parking (no fee); water sports. **Best for:** sunrise; walking; windsurfing. ⊠ Blvd. Kukulcán, Km 14.5, Zona Hotelera.

Playa Caracol

BEACH | FAMILY | The last "real beach" along the east–west stretch of the Zona Hotelera is near Plaza Caracol and the Xcaret dock. Located at Km 8.5, the whole area has been eaten up by development, in particular the high-rise condominium complex next to the entrance. Playa Caracol (caracol means "snail") is also hindered by the rocks that jut out from the water to mark the beginning of Punta Cancún, where Boulevard Kukulcán turns south. There are several hotels along here and a few sports rental outfits. It's also the launching point for trips to Contoy Island. ■TIP➔ **Closer to the Fiesta Americana Grand Coral Beach hotel, the water is calm because of the jetty that blocks the wind and waves.** **Amenities:** food and drink; water sports.

Best for: swimming; windsurfing. ⊠ *Blvd. Kukulcán, Km 8.5, Zona Hotelera.*

Playa Chac Mool

BEACH | FAMILY | Located at Km 10 on Boulevard Kukulcán, this Blue Flag Beach can be accessed through the beach entrance across the street from Señor Frog's. As at Playa Caracol, development has greatly encroached on the shores here. There are a lot of rocks, but the water is a stunning turquoise; moreover, the beach is close to shopping centers and the party zone, so you'll find plenty of restaurants nearby. The short stretch to the south has gentler waters and fewer rocks. Public changing rooms and limited free parking are also available. The clear, shallow water makes it tempting to walk far out, but be careful—there's a strong current and undertow. Lifeguards are on duty until 5 pm. The closest hotel to Playa Chac Mool is Le Blanc Resort. **Amenities:** food and drink; lifeguards; parking (free); toilets. **Best for:** partiers; sunrise. ⊠ *Blvd. Kukulcán, Km 10, Zona Hotelera.*

★ Playa Delfines (*Dolphins Beach*)

BEACH | Near Ruinas del Rey, where Boulevard Kukulcán curves into a hill, this local favorite is one of the last before Punta Nizuc. Hotels have yet to dominate this small section of coastline that's considered a Blue Flag Beach. ("Yet" is, unfortunately, the operative word here.) Delfines showcases an incredible lookout and the iconic sign with large letters painted in bright colors that spell "Cancún." It's a popular photo op, so you may have to wait in line to get a picture. The sand is darker and more granular here than on other Cancún beaches, and on a clear day you can see at least four shades of blue in the water. Swimming is treacherous unless a green flag is posted, but you'll find plenty of sand and waves. It's one of the few places in Cancún you'll see a surfer, though even during hurricane season, waves seldom hit "epic" status; at best, you might find choppy, inconsistent surf. **Amenities:**

lifeguard; parking (no fee); toilets. **Best for:** sunrise; surfing. ⊠ *Blvd. Kukulcán, Km 18, Zona Hotelera.*

Playa Gaviota Azul (*Blue Seagull Beach*)

BEACH | Heading down from Punta Cancún onto the long, southerly stretch of the island, Playa Gaviota Azul (meaning Blue Seagull Beach, but also commonly called City Beach or Forum Beach) is the first on the Caribbean's open waters. Closer to Km 9, the waves break up to 6 feet during hurricane season, making it one of the few surfing spots in Cancún; lessons are offered by the 360 Surf School (⊕ *www.360surfschoolcancun. com*). If you'd rather just relax, ascend a short flight of steps to Mandala Beach Club at Km 9.5, where you can enjoy the full resort experience without booking into a hotel. There is paid parking at Plaza Forum plus minimal street parking. The closest hotels—Krystal Grand Punta Cancún and Aloft—are across the street from the beach. **Amenities:** food and drink; parking (fee); toilets; water sports. **Best for:** partiers; sunrise: surfing; swimming. ⊠ *Blvd. Kukulcán, Km 9.5, Zona Hotelera.*

Playa Langosta

BEACH | FAMILY | Small, placid Lobster Beach has safe waters and gentle waves that make it a popular swimming spot for families and spring breakers alike. On weekends, you'll be lucky if you can find a space on the sand. There's an entrance to the beach at Boulevard Kukulcán's Km 5. A dock juts out in the middle of the water, but swimming areas are marked off with ropes and buoys. Next to the beach is a small building with a restaurant, an ice-cream shop, and an ATM. **Amenities:** food and drink; toilets. **Best for:** swimming. ⊠ *Blvd. Kukulcán, Km 5, Zona Hotelera.*

Playa Las Perlas

BEACH | FAMILY | Pearl Beach is the first heading east from El Centro along Boulevard Kukulcán. Located at Km 2.5, between the Cancún mainland and the bridge, this Blue Flag Beach is a relatively

small beach on the protected waters of the Bahía de Mujeres, and is popular with locals. There are several restaurants lining the sand, but most of the water-sports activities are only available to those staying at the nearby lodgings like the Imperial las Perlas. There's a small store beside that resort where you can buy sandwiches and drinks if you want to have a beach picnic. ■TIP→ **Parking is limited. Amenities:** food and drink; lifeguards; parking (no fee); water sports. **Best for:** swimming. ⊠ *Blvd. Kukulcán, Km 2.5, Zona Hotelera.*

Playa Linda

BEACH | At Km 4 on Boulevard Kukulcán, Pretty Beach is where the ocean meets the freshwater of Laguna Nichupté to create the Nichupté Channel. Restaurants and changing rooms are available near the launching dock. Playa Linda is situated between the Barceló Costa Cancún and Sotavento Hotel. There's lots of boat activity along the channel, and the ferry to Isla Mujeres leaves from the adjoining Embarcadero marina, so the area isn't safe for swimming. It is, however, a great place to people-watch, with a 300-foot rotating scenic tower nearby that offers a 360-degree view. **Amenities:** food and drink; parking (no fee); toilets. **Best for:** walking. ⊠ *Blvd. Kukulcán, Km 4, Zona Hotelera.*

Playa Marlín

BEACH | FAMILY | Accessible via a road next to Kukulcán Plaza, Marlin Beach is a seductive stretch of sand in the heart of the Zona Hotelera at Km 13. Despite its turquoise waters and silky sands, the waves are strong and the currents are dangerous. If this Blue Flag Beach is crowded, you can walk in either direction to find quieter spots. There's also a small tent where you can rent boogie boards, snorkel gear, and motorized sports equipment. Although there are currently no public facilities, you can always walk over to Kukulcán Plaza if you need a restroom and to the nearby Oxxo, Mexico's

convenience-store chain, for a snack or beverage. **Amenities:** water sports. **Best for:** snorkeling; sunrise; surfing; walking. ⊠ *Blvd. Kukulcán, Km 13, Zona Hotelera.*

Playa Pez Volador

BEACH | FAMILY | The calm surf and relaxing shallows of Playa Pez Volador—the name translates as Flying Fish Beach—make it an aquatic playground for families with young children. Marked by a huge Mexican flag at Km 5.5, the wide beach is popular with locals, as many tourists tend to head to the more active Playa Langosta. Seagrass occasionally washes ashore here, but by early morning it is cleared away by the staff of the neighboring Casa Maya Hotel. **Amenities:** none. **Best for:** swimming. ⊠ *Blvd. Kukulcán, Km 5.5, Zona Hotelera.*

Playa Punta Nizuc

BEACH | You'll find Cancún's most isolated and deserted beach on the southern tip of the peninsula. Far from the crowds and party scene, Playa Punta Nizuc has few amenities other than those available to guests at the nearby Wet 'n Wild Waterpark (Km 25), Nizuc Resort (Km 21), or Club Med (Km 21.5). The lack of beach traffic helps keep the white sands clean and the waters sparkling, except when seagrass washes up. Bordered by jungle to the south, Playa Punta Nizuc can be accessed directly from Boulevard Kukulcán, so there's plenty of street parking—but make sure you bring water, snacks, sunscreen, and an umbrella for shade. ■TIP→ **This is a great place to collect shells or swim, since waves crash only on stormy days. Amenities:** parking (no fee). **Best for:** solitude; snorkeling; swimming; walking. ⊠ *Blvd. Kukulcán, Km 24, Cancún.*

Playa Tortugas

BEACH | FAMILY | Don't be fooled by the name—this spot is seldom frequented by *tortugas*. It's the opportunity to swim, snorkel, kayak, paraglide, and ride WaveRunners that really brings folks to Turtle Beach. The water is deep, but the beach itself (the nicest section of which is on the far right, just past the rocks) can get very crowded. Passengers usually grab a drink or snack here before catching the ferry to Isla Mujeres, and locals from El Centro will spend their entire weekend on the sand. If you are looking for isolation, head elsewhere. ■ **TIP→ There's an over-the-water bungee-jumping tower where your head will actually touch the water.** **Amenities:** food and drink; water sports. **Best for:** partiers; snorkeling; swimming. ✉ *Blvd. Kukulcán, Km 6.5, Zona Hotelera.*

🍴 Restaurants

Cambalache

$$$$ | **ARGENTINE** | This Argentinean steak house is rustic yet elegant, with dark wooden tables and arched brick ceilings. Not surprisingly, steak is the most popular main. although the local fish and lamb skewers grilled over a brick fire are other good choices. **Known for:** tango music; cool Argentine atmosphere; lively—sometimes loud—surroundings. [$] *Average main: MP450* ✉ *La Isla Cancún Shopping Village, Blvd. Kukulcán, Km 12.5, Zona Hotelera* ☎ *998/883–0902, 998/883–0897* 🌐 *www.cambalacherestaurantes.com* ☞ *Valet parking.*

Casa Rolandi

$$$$ | **EUROPEAN** | The secret to this restaurant's success is its creative handling of Italian and Swiss cuisine, which explains why both carpaccio *de pulpo* (thin slices of fresh octopus) and lettuce taco with sautéed duck breast appear on the menu. Appetizers are tempting, too—there's puff bread from a wood-burning oven plus a salad and antipasto bar. **Known for:** attentive service; pleasant dining room; jumbo shrimp baked in banana leaves. [$] *Average main: MP500* ✉ *Plaza Caracol, Blvd. Kukulcán 7500, Zona Hotelera* ☎ *998/883–2557* 🌐 *casarolandi.mx.*

Casitas

$$$$ | **SEAFOOD** | Sink your toes into the sand at Cancún's only on-the-beach restaurant where impeccable service matches an incredible setting. The romantic setting caters to couples—silk curtains drape palapas, each centered with an illuminated table adorned with seashells—and many of the seafood dishes are created for two. **Known for:** platter of shrimp, oysters, tuna tartare, king crab, and lobster tail; flawless service; rare beach setting. [$] *Average main: MP1,950* ✉ *Kempinski Hotel Cancún, Retorno del Rey 36, off Blvd. Kukulcán, Km 13.5, Zona Hotelera* ☎ *998/881–0808* 🌐 *www.kempinski.com/en/hotel-cancun/restaurants-bars* 🕒 *No lunch.*

Cenacolo

$$$ | **ITALIAN** | Brick-oven pizza and excellent pasta dishes, handmade in full view, have made this fine Italian restaurant a Cancún favorite. Best bets include the melt-in-your-mouth-tender beef or octopus carpaccio appetizers and such stellar pasta dishes as the "green hats"—little pieces of handmade pasta filled with ricotta cheese, butter, and fresh sage. **Known for:** elegant Italian cuisine; wine cave; romantic setting. [$] *Average main: MP379* ✉ *Blvd. Kukulcán, Km 12.6, Zona Hotelera* ☎ *998/885–3603, 998/214–2356 reservations* 🌐 *cenacolo.com.mx.*

★ The Club Grill

$$$$ | **INTERNATIONAL** | Begin the evening at The Club Grill with a special cocktail at the champagne bar before ordering from a continental menu that includes starters like beef tartar and mains like roasted duck with tequila and agave honey sauce; a multicourse tasting menu, paired with boutique Mexican wines, is available, too. For dessert, try one of the signature soufflés—chocolate, coconut cream, or Grand Marnier. **Known for:** silver serving platters; chocolate soufflé; romantic, elegant surroundings. [$] *Average main: MP680* ✉ *Kempinski Hotel Cancún, Retorno del Rey 36, off Blvd. Kukulcán,*

Km 13.5, Zona Hotelera ☎ *998/881–0808* 🌐 *www.kempinski.com/en/hotel-cancun/restaurants-bars* 🕓 *No lunch.*

Elefanthai

$$$$ | **THAI** | The individual huts with thatched roofs at this garden oasis provide an intimate setting to sample spicy Thai dishes like roasted duck in coconut red curry or the house favorite, a deep-fried fish fillet prepared with ginger, garlic, and a tamarind-chile sauce. The menu also features traditional Indian dishes such as chicken tikka masala, Kasundi shrimp with coconut sauce, and tandoori-style New Zealand lamb. **Known for:** intimate garden setting; sunset views over lagoon; palapa casitas perched over the water. [$] *Average main: MP490* ✉ *La Isla Cancún Shopping Village, Blvd. Kukulcán, Km 12.5, Zona Hotelera* ☎ *998/144–0364* 🌐 *www.asiagourmetcancun.com* 🕓 *No lunch.*

Fantino

$$$$ | **MEDITERRANEAN** | Expect fine dining and culinary excellence, with rich-in-flavor ingredients, at this Mediterranean restaurant; consider the tasting menu for the full Fantino experience. With synchronized precision, servers unveil each plate with beautiful, if not artistic, execution. **Known for:** ballroom setting; polished service; careful attention to ingredient selection. [$] *Average main: MP750* ✉ *Kempinski Hotel Cancún, Retorno del Rey 36, Zona Hotelera* ☎ *998/881–0808* 🌐 *www.kempinski.com/en/hotel-cancun/restaurants-bars* 🕓 *No lunch.*

Gustino Italian Grill

$$$$ | **ITALIAN** | As soon as you walk down the dramatic staircase at this elegant restaurant, you know you're in for a memorable experience. The *gamberi saltati* (sautéed shrimp with spinach, artichoke, and Asiago cheese) appetizer is a standout here, as are entrées such as the fettuccine carbonara in truffle sauce or the risotto. **Known for:** wine cellar; great Italian and seafood selections; impeccable service. [$] *Average main: MP520* ✉ *JW Marriott Resort, Blvd. Kukulcán, Km 14.5, Zona Hotelera* ☎ *998/848–9600* 🌐 *www.marriott.com* 🕓 *No lunch.*

Hacienda el Mortero

$$$$ | **MEXICAN** | The main draw at one of Cancún's first restaurants is the setting—namely, in a replica of a 17th-century hacienda, complete with a courtyard fountain, flowering garden, and strolling mariachi band. The traditional menu includes tortilla soup, tasty chicken fajitas, and rib-eye steaks. **Known for:** traditional setting; astounding variety of tequila; block of fish "tikin-xic-style" with achiote and sour orange. [$] *Average main: MP750* ✉ *Blvd. Kukulcán, Km 9.5, Zona Hotelera* ☎ *998/848–9800, 998/201–5263 WhatsApp* 🌐 *restaurantehaciendaelmortero.com* 🕓 *Closed Mon. No lunch Tues.–Sat.*

Hacienda Sisal

$$$$ | **MEXICAN** | **FAMILY** | Built to resemble a sprawling hacienda, this restaurant is warm and intimate, with comfortable high-backed chairs and Mexican paintings. Menu highlights include the goat-cheese-and-mango salad, Tampico chicken breast, New York steak with stuffed pepper, and annatto-seasoned grilled pork chops; a kids' menu is also available. **Known for:** faux hacienda vibe; Sunday breakfast buffet; weeknight music and dance performances. [$] *Average main: MP445* ✉ *Blvd. Kukulcán, Km 13.5, next to Royal Sands Resort, Zona Hotelera* ☎ *998/848–8220* 🌐 *haciendasisal.com* 🕓 *No lunch.*

★ **Hanaichi**

$$ | **JAPANESE** | It might look like a hole-in-the-wall, but this small Japanese restaurant has some of Cancún's best sushi. Expect sashimi, nigiri, and every type of roll imaginable; house specialties include the Copán roll (deep-fried shrimp wrapped in cucumber) and the Cancún roll (stuffed with eel and scallops). **Known for:** inexpensive menu; great sushi selection; casual surroundings. [$] *Average main: MP260* ✉ *Blvd. Kukulcán, Km*

9, across from Plaza Caracol, Cancún ☎ 998/204–6452 reservations, 998/883–2804 ⊕ facebook.com/hanaichicancun.

Harry's

$$$$ | STEAKHOUSE | High-profile locals and visitors alike are drawn to this contemporary steak house's Vegas–meets–Beverly Hills style. The spectacular menu features glazed duck, Maine lobster, and Kobe beef served with aged Vermont cheddar cheese. **Known for:** atmospheric, dimly lit setting; house-aged steaks grilled to perfection; cotton candy that comes with the check. $ *Average main: MP677* ✉ *Blvd. Kukulcán, Km 14.2, across from Kempinski Hotel, Zona Hotelera* ☎ *998/840–6550* ⊕ *harrys.com.mx.*

KAI

$$$ | JAPANESE | Don't be put off by the shopping mall location or shared entrance with the Macao casino, because this modern Japanese restaurant serves truly fresh sashimi and sushi with unique toppings such as miso foie grass, black truffles, or lemon caviar. The excellently trained servers guide you through the extensive menu and offer cocktail suggestions to complement the myriad of main courses and roll choices—from uramaki to futomaki. **Known for:** umami roll; Waygu burgers; Shinkai speakeasy (make reservations) open on Friday and Saturday nights. $ *Average main: MP350* ✉ *Plaza, La Isla, II, Zona Hotelera* ☎ *998/159–7999* ⊕ *kai. restaurant.*

La Joya

$$$$ | MEXICAN | Soaring stained-glass windows, a fountain, artwork, and beautiful furniture from the central part of the country lend drama to this restaurant. The food is both traditional and creative, with dishes like grilled Tampiqueña-style beef or sea bass wrapped in maguey leaves. **Known for:** Oaxacan cuisine; performances by a 10-piece Mariachi band; traditional Mexican decor. $ *Average main: MP406* ✉ *Grand Fiesta Americana Coral Beach Cancún, Blvd. Kukulcán,*

Km 9.5, Zona Hotelera ☎ 443/137–8728 ⊕ www.coralbeachcancunresort.com/ dining ۞ No lunch.

★ Le Basilic

$$$$ | MEDITERRANEAN | Arched bay windows, checkered marble floors, live jazz, and exquisite garden views create a stunning backdrop to your dining experience here. The menu changes every four months but always consists of fine French-Mediterranean cuisine served beneath silver domes by tuxedoed waiters. **Known for:** attentive service; centerpiece gazebo with orchids; art gallery. $ *Average main: MP550* ✉ *Grand Fiesta Americana Coral Beach, Blvd. Kukulcán, Km 9.5, Zona Hotelera* ☎ *443/137–8728* ⊕ *www.coralbeachcancunresort.com/ dining* ۞ *Closed Sun. No lunch.*

★ Puerto Madero

$$$$ | STEAKHOUSE | Modeled after the dock warehouses that have been converted into modern eateries in Argentina's Puerto Madero, this steak-and-seafood restaurant gets rave reviews from locals. The grilled octopus seasoned with paprika is exceptional, as are the thin tuna rolls filled with Alaskan crab meat and Maine lobster. **Known for:** fun-loving staff; crackly soufflé potatoes; chic appetizers. $ *Average main: MP540* ✉ *Blvd. Kukulcán, Km 14.1, Zona Hotelera* ☎ *998/885–2829* ⊕ *www.puertomaderestaurantes.com.*

Sasi Thai

$$$$ | THAI | Six thatch-roofed cabanas—each housing four tables—are staggered on a hill and dimly lit with candles and lanterns. The menu features traditional Thai cuisine such as spring rolls, pork dumplings, red duck curry, and pad Thai with chicken or shrimp. **Known for:** open-air setting; mango crème brûlée with ginger sorbet; bamboo decor. $ *Average main: MP474* ✉ *JW Magna Marriott, Blvd. Kukulcán, Km 14.5, Zona Hotelera* ☎ *998/881–2092* ⊕ *www.marriott.com* ۞ *No lunch.*

The Surfin' Burrito

$$ | **MEXICAN** | **FAMILY** | A truly local joint that seems out of place in the Zona Hotelera draws crowds in the morning for its smoothie bowls and later on for its tacos and burritos. Forget your own private booth at this 24-hour place—you'll eat at long tables and really get to know your fellow diners. **Known for:** California-style burritos; informal late-night eats; friendly service. [$] *Average main: MP195* ✉ *Blvd. Kukulcán, Km 9.5, Zona Hotelera* ☎ *998/883–0083, 998/490–2217 WhatsApp* 🌐 *www.facebook.com/thesurfinburrito.*

★ **Taboo**

$$$$ | **MEDITERRANEAN** | This sophisticated Mediterranean restaurant enjoys an enviable location at the heart of the Zona Hotelera and with breathtaking views of the Nichupté Lagoon. Start with the Alaskan king crabs marinated in lime or the Omega mussels with white wine and Sicilian lemon; continue with wood-fired Mediterranean shrimp or a New Zealand rack of lamb. **Known for:** Wagyu meats; champagne parades; giant shellfish sold by weight. [$] *Average main: MP560* ✉ *Blvd. Kukulcán, Km 13.5, Zona Hotelera* ☎ *998/234–2528* 🌐 *taboorestaurant.com.mx.*

Hotels

Aloft Cancún

$ | **HOTEL** | **FAMILY** | This hip Marriott property near the convention center has a fresh, modern concept that generates quite a social scene. **Pros:** free parking and Wi-Fi; pet- and child-friendly; within walking distance to main clubs. **Cons:** small rooms; not on beach; meals not included. [$] *Rooms from: $178* ✉ *Blvd. Kukulcán, Km 9, across from Fiesta Americana Grand Coral Beach, Zona Hotelera* ☎ *998/848–9900* 🌐 *www.marriott.com* 🛏 *177 rooms* 🍴 *No Meals.*

Beachscape Kin-Ha Villas & Suites

$$ | **HOTEL** | **FAMILY** | Sandwiched amid several looming resorts, this low-rise condo-hotel complex is a wonderful place for families thanks to its nicely planted grounds, tranquil beach, and relaxed atmosphere. **Pros:** all rooms have balconies; peaceful; on one of Cancún's best beaches. **Cons:** some rooms don't have ocean views; three-story hotel has no elevator; no children's programs. [$] *Rooms from: $219* ✉ *Blvd. Kukulcán, Km 8.5, Zona Hotelera* ☎ *998/891–5400* 🌐 *beachscape.com.mx* 🛏 *132 rooms* 🍴 *No Meals.*

Canopy by Hilton Cancún La Isla

$$ | **HOTEL** | Shopaholics will love staying at this luxury lifestyle hotel overlooking Laguna Nichupté and with direct access to the trendy shops of La Isla Entertainment Village. **Pros:** rooftop pool; free transportation to Mandala Beach Club; complimentary bikes. **Cons:** not on the beach; no meals included; close to a big mall, lacks privacy. [$] *Rooms from: $229* ✉ *Blvd. Kukulcán s/n, Km 12.5, Zona Hotelera* ✣ *Adjacent to La Isla Shopping Village* ☎ *998/689–1193* 🌐 *www.hilton.com* 🛏 *174 rooms* 🍴 *No Meals.*

Fiesta Americana Condesa Cancún

$$$ | **ALL-INCLUSIVE** | **FAMILY** | Part of a reliable Mexican chain and more laid-back than its sister property, the Grand Fiesta Americana Coral Beach, this hotel is easily recognized by the 118-foot-tall palapa that covers its lobby. **Pros:** friendly staff; scheduled activities on the hour; smaller pools designated for children. **Cons:** halls get slippery when it rains; sound carries between floors; popular with convention goers and tour groups. [$] *Rooms from: $360* ✉ *Blvd. Kukulcán, Km 16.5, Zona Hotelera* ☎ *443/310–8137* 🌐 *www.fiestamericana.com/destinos/cancun* 🛏 *502 rooms* 🍴 *All-Inclusive.*

Golden Parnassus All Inclusive Resort & Spa

$$ | **ALL-INCLUSIVE** | Accommodations at this adults-only resort have rich wood furnishings and a cream-and-plum palette and feature small sitting areas that open onto balconies overlooking the lagoon or ocean. **Pros:** free shuttle to sister property Great Parnassus Resort & Spa; great tiki bar; evening entertainment. **Cons:** no kids under 18; thin towels and poor lighting; dated common areas. [$] *Rooms from: $273* ✉ *Blvd. Kukulcán, Km 14.5, Retorno San Miguelito, Lote 37, Zona Hotelera* ☎ *786/673–6442* 🌐 *www.goldenparnassusresortspa.com* 🛏 *214 rooms* 🍴 *All-Inclusive.*

Grand Fiesta Americana Coral Beach Cancún All-Inclusive Spa Resort

$$$$ | **ALL-INCLUSIVE** | **FAMILY** | Those who love the trappings of traditional luxury—stained-glass skylights, mahogany furniture, stunning floral arrangements—will feel at home at this all-suites hotel, which also has the award-winning Le Basilic restaurant and the enormous Gem Spa. The hotel's W shape means all rooms have ocean views in addition to marble floors, sunken living rooms, and infinity balconies; upgrading to the Grand Club Level gets you private check-in, an open bar, beach service, breakfast, and appetizers throughout the day. **Pros:** complimentary kids' club; business center with private offices; stellar spa and restaurant. **Cons:** pool is only heated October to March; extra charge for use of the spa facilities; too big for some. [$] *Rooms from: $550* ✉ *Blvd. Kukulcán, Km 9.5, Zona Hotelera* ☎ *443/310–8137* 🌐 *www.grandfiestamericana.com* 🛏 *602 suites* 🍴 *All-Inclusive.*

Grand Park Royal Cancún

$$ | **ALL-INCLUSIVE** | **FAMILY** | You'll find a wide variety of accommodations at the Grand Park Royal, including villas with a private beach area and personal concierge. **Pros:** most rooms face ocean; excellent pool areas; kids' club. **Cons:** gym costs extra; intrusive time-share salespeople; reservations required at restaurants. [$] *Rooms from: $289* ✉ *Blvd. Kukulcán, Km 10.5, Zona Hotelera* ☎ *800/872–7275, 800/890–3798 in the U.S.* 🌐 *www.park-royalhotels.com* 🛏 *346 rooms* 🍴 *All-Inclusive.*

Hard Rock Hotel Cancún

$$$ | **RESORT** | **FAMILY** | In keeping with Hard Rock tradition and fitting right into Cancún's energetic atmosphere, this property showcases musical memorabilia, offers a variety of entertainment experiences, and hosts an ongoing slate of celebrity-driven soirees. **Pros:** two tennis courts; excellent Japanese restaurant; activities for children and teens. **Cons:** some rooms lack ocean views; no water sports; hard mattresses. [$] *Rooms from: $418* ✉ *Blvd. Kukulcán, Km 14.5, Zona Hotelera* ☎ *998/881–3600, 817/567–7516 in the U.S.* 🌐 *www.hardrockhotels.com/cancun* 🛏 *625 rooms* 🍴 *All-Inclusive.*

Hotel Casa Turquesa

$ | **HOTEL** | On a hill overlooking the ocean, this all-suites boutique hotel doubles as an impressive gallery showcasing works by famous artists. **Pros:** lighted tennis court; 24-hour room service; intimate, personalized feel. **Cons:** ground-floor rooms lack full ocean views; not child-friendly; outdated decor. [$] *Rooms from: $150* ✉ *Blvd. Kukulcán, Km 13.5, Zona Hotelera* ☎ *998/193–2260* 🌐 *www.casaturquesa.com* 🛏 *29 rooms* 🍴 *No Meals.*

Hotel NYX Cancún

$ | **RESORT** | Here's a hotel that's funky and fun, catering to young adults with its chic lounge bar, ambient music, and hot-pink billiard tables and rugs that match the property's bright exterior. **Pros:** gracious staff; reasonable rates; close to shops. **Cons:** no elevator; some rooms don't have ocean views; facilities have seen better days. [$] *Rooms from: $181* ✉ *Blvd. Kukulcán, Km 11.5, Zona Hotelera* ☎ *998/848–9300* 🌐 *www.nyxhotels.com* 🛏 *196 rooms* 🍴 *Free Breakfast.*

Cancún's beautiful JW Marriott resort is the only local property designed to withstand a Category 5 hurricane.

Hotel Riu Palace Las Américas

$$$ | ALL-INCLUSIVE | The most upscale of Cancún's Riu properties, this colossal eight-story resort at the north end of the Zona Hotelera is visually stunning. **Pros:** spacious suites; access to sister properties in Cancún and Playa del Carmen; 24-hour room service. **Cons:** small pools and tiny beach; not much late-afternoon sun by the pool or beach; no kids under 18. $ *Rooms from: $410* ✉ *Blvd. Kukulcán, Km 8.5, Zona Hotelera* ☎ *998/891–4300, 808/780–809* ⊕ *riu.com* ⤳ *350 suites* ❍ *All-Inclusive.*

★ Hyatt Zilara Cancún

$$$ | ALL-INCLUSIVE | Luxury is the focus at this high-end, adults-only resort, where all the accommodations have mahogany furniture, whirlpool tubs, ocean views, balconies with hammocks, and "magic boxes" that allow for room-service delivery without having to open the door. **Pros:** extraordinary dining options; two-person whirlpool tubs in suites; great ocean views. **Cons:** no children under 18; time-share sales pitch; sleepless nights for

those in rooms near the pool and lobby. $ *Rooms from: $472* ✉ *Blvd. Kukulcán, Km 11.5, Zona Hotelera* ☎ *998/881–5600, 800/323–7249 in the U.S.* ⊕ *www.hyatt. com* ⤳ *310 suites* ❍ *All-Inclusive.*

★ Hyatt Ziva Cancún

$$$$ | ALL-INCLUSIVE | This luxury resort, perched at the very point where Caribbean and Gulf of Mexico meet, caters to families and adults, and manages to do so by keeping them separate. **Pros:** impeccable service; teen and kids club included; exclusivity of adults-only tower. **Cons:** restaurant fare is uninspiring; swim-up suites don't allow kids under 13; a bit pricey. $ *Rooms from: $724* ✉ *Blvd. Kukulcán, Mz 51, Lote 7, Punta Cancún, Cancún* ☎ *998/848–7000, 833/884–9288 in the U.S.* ⊕ *www.hyatt.com* ⤳ *547 rooms* ❍ *All-Inclusive.*

Iberostar Selection Cancún

$$ | ALL-INCLUSIVE | FAMILY | This all-inclusive resort's lush 150-acre grounds are complete with palapa huts, hammocks, and a series of lavish, interconnected swimming pools that wind through palm-dotted lawns to Playa Delfines. **Pros:** all standard rooms have ocean views; angled pool area gets all-day sunshine; tennis courts. **Cons:** loud poolside music; only one heated pool; some villas lack ocean views. $ *Rooms from: $272* ✉ *Blvd. Kukulcán, Km 17, Zona Hotelera* ☎ *998/881–8000, 800/781–411* ⊕ *www.iberostar.com* ➥ *531 rooms* ❑ *All-Inclusive.*

InterContinental Presidente Cancún Resort

$$ | **RESORT** | The atmosphere at this contemporary, service-oriented hotel on one of Cancún's best beaches is more conservative than at other Zona Hotelera properties, so you're likely to have a relaxed stay. **Pros:** short walk to shops and restaurants; IKAL Spa offers massages that blend ancient Maya and Eastern techniques; virtually currentless beach is great for families. **Cons:** focus on business travelers and conventions; unimpressive dining options; palm trees block ocean view in some lower-level rooms. $ *Rooms from: $235* ✉ *Blvd. Kukulcán, Km 7.5, Zona Hotelera* ☎ *998/848–8700, 800/450–076* ⊕ *www.ihg.com* ➥ *300 rooms* ❑ *No Meals.*

JW Marriott Cancún Resort & Spa

$$$ | **RESORT** | A three-level, 35,000-square-foot spa, which has an indoor pool, and a 20-foot dive pool, where you can practice snorkeling and scuba diving in an artificial reef, are among the draws at this towering beach resort. **Pros:** top-notch service; huge spa; rainfall showers. **Cons:** fee for Wi-Fi; lacks the festive mood of other hotels on the strip; extra charge for the Kids' Club. $ *Rooms from: $417* ✉ *Blvd. Kukulcán, Km 14.5, Lote 40A, Zona Hotelera* ☎ *998/848–9600, 888/813–2776* ⊕ *www.marriott.com* ➥ *447 rooms* ❑ *No Meals.*

★ Kempinski Hotel Cancún

$$$ | **RESORT** | Renovations at this Kempinski property, formerly the Ritz-Carlton, maintained a classic style and added a layer of modern comfort and luxury, as evidenced by guest rooms done up in neutral colors and featuring Salvatore Ferragamo bath amenities. **Pros:** two award-winning restaurants; tennis and pickleball courts; all rooms have sea views. **Cons:** formal atmosphere; quite expensive; extra charge for beach villas (luxury palapas). $ *Rooms from: $468* ✉ *Retorno del Rey 36, off Blvd. Kukulcán at Km 13.5, Zona Hotelera* ☎ *998/881–0808, 855/277–7439 in the U.S.* ⊕ *www.kempinski.com* ➥ *365 rooms* ❑ *No Meals.*

Krystal Cancún Hotel

$$ | **RESORT** | **FAMILY** | On the tip of Punta Cancún, this contemporary, 14-story hotel offers some of the Zona Hotelera's best views—west-facing rooms enjoy sunsets over the lagoon and bay, while east-facing rooms take in sunrises over Isla Mujeres and the Caribbean. **Pros:** excellent views; on-site beauty salon and car rental; great restaurants. **Cons:** bathrooms have showers only; uninspiring decoration; extra charge for Kids' Club. $ *Rooms from: $280* ✉ *Blvd. Kukulcán, Km 8.5, Zona Hotelera* ☎ *998/891–5555* ⊕ *www.krystal-hotels.com* ➥ *398 rooms* ❑ *All-Inclusive.*

Laguna Suites

$$ | **HOTEL** | **FAMILY** | At this tranquil resort, 12 white-stucco buildings house spacious suites equipped with kitchens, dining areas, and living rooms that have 42-inch flat-screen TVs and pullout couches. **Pros:** great for families and other groups; all-inclusive plan available; free hourly shuttle to the beach. **Cons:** menu is repetitive if you select all-inclusive package; no children's activities; far from the beach. $ *Rooms from: $280* ✉ *Paseo Pok Ta Pok 3, Zona Hotelera* ☎ *998/848–7174, 800/986–9359 in the U.S.* ⊕ *www.sunsetworldresorts.com* ➥ *47 suites* ❑ *All-Inclusive.*

★ Le Blanc Spa Resort Cancún

$$$$ | **ALL-INCLUSIVE** | What is perhaps Cancún's most luxurious adults-only all-inclusive has a chic, modern decor and caters mainly to couples who like

The NIZUC Resort & Spa has a beautiful infinity pool looking out onto Punta Nizuc.

to dress their best for evening meals at one of the various on-site eateries, including an impressive French restaurant with a seven-course tasting menu. **Pros:** excellent spa; complimentary use of hydrotherapy; personal butler. **Cons:** no kids allowed; super-pricey; some rooms have small French balconies only. [$] *Rooms from: $813* ✉ *Blvd. Kukulcán, Km 10, Punta Cancún, Zona Hotelera* ☎ *998/881–4740, 888/702–0913* 🌐 *cancun.leblancsparesorts.com* 🛏 *260 rooms* 🍴 *All-Inclusive.*

★ Live Aqua Beach Resort Cancún

$$$ | **RESORT** | Ambient music, aromatherapy, water features, soothing hues, and airy guest quarters are among the things that lend a Zen vibe to this resort, which attracts luxury-minded, thirtysomething sun-worshippers. **Pros:** huge suites; gratuities included; 24-hour in-room dinning. **Cons:** no nightly entertainment; fee for beach or poolside cabanas; some hallway noise carries into rooms. [$] *Rooms from: $429* ✉ *Blvd. Kukulcán, Km 12.5, Zona Hotelera* ☎ *998/881–7600, 443/310–8137* 🌐 *www.liveaqua.com* 🛏 *407 rooms* 🍴 *No Meals.*

★ NIZUC Resort & Spa

$$$$ | **RESORT** | Tucked away on a beach sheltered by mangroves and facing the Mesoamerican Barrier Reef, this stylish 29-acre resort has the most secluded location in Cancún. **Pros:** top-tier restaurants; excellent service; only private beach in Cancún. **Cons:** occasional airplane noise; 18% service charge added to bill; sprawling property means long walks or golf-cart trips. [$] *Rooms from: $710* ✉ *Blvd. Kukulcán, Km 21.26, Zona Hotelera* ☎ *998/891–5700, 855/696-4982 in the U.S.* 🌐 *www.nizuc.com* 🛏 *274 rooms* 🍴 *No Meals.*

Occidental Costa Cancún

$$ | **RESORT** | **FAMILY** | Situated just steps from the ferries to Isla Mujeres, this family-friendly property has lots of pool-side activities, as well as a roomy kids' clubhouse with a small outdoor play area. **Pros:** great for kids; close to El Embarcadero; good water-sports center. **Cons:** no a/c in lobby; small beach area

with boats often passing by; lobby can be chaotic during check-in/check-out times. [$] *Rooms from: $238* ✉ *Blvd. Kukulcán, Km 4.5, Zona Hotelera* ☎ *998/193–0850, 800/227–2356 in the U.S.* 🌐 *www.barcelo.com* 🛏 *358 rooms* 🍴 *All-Inclusive.*

Occidental Tucancún

$$ | **RESORT** | **FAMILY** | Shoppers appreciate this lively resort's proximity to a couple of malls, but there's plenty here to keep non-shoppers occupied, too—including volleyball games and water-polo matches in the activities pool. **Pros:** near two of Cancún's biggest malls; wide range of activities for children and adults; four handicapped-accessible rooms. **Cons:** only half the rooms have water views; hotel feels dated; chaotic lobby during check-in/check-out times. [$] *Rooms from: $210* ✉ *Blvd. Kukulcán, Km 14, Zona Hotelera* ☎ *998/891–5900, 800/227–2356 in the U.S.* 🌐 *www.barcelo.com/en-us/occidental-tucancun* 🛏 *332 rooms* 🍴 *All-Inclusive.*

Paradisus Cancún

$$$ | **RESORT** | **FAMILY** | Resembling a Maya temple, this enormous, modern beachfront property features atriums topped by pyramid-shaped skylights and spacious rooms that are decorated with hints of orange and have marble floors, balconies, and lagoon or ocean views. **Pros:** three play zones for babies, kids, and teens; privacy of The Reserve VIP area; free golf course exclusively for guests. **Cons:** some buildings are a bit outdated; no children allowed at several restaurants; top-shelf alcohol and Tempo restaurant not part of the all-inclusive plan. [$] *Rooms from: $420* ✉ *Blvd. Kukulcán, Km 16.5, Zona Hotelera* ☎ *998/881–1100* 🌐 *www.melia.com* 🛏 *668 suites* 🍴 *All-Inclusive.*

Sandos Cancún

$$$ | **RESORT** | High on a hill off the main boulevard, this refined yet relaxed hotel offers personalized service and rooms that blend art deco and Maya styles, are done in soothing shades of cream and mauve, and have either ocean or lagoon views. **Pros:** near one of Cancún's best malls; good fitness facilities; all rooms have water views. **Cons:** lack of activities at night; shady pool by early afternoon; not all rooms have balconies. [$] *Rooms from: $407* ✉ *Retorno del Rey, Mz 53, Lote 37, off Blvd. Kukulcán at Km 14, Zona Hotelera* ☎ *998/881–2200, 863/223–4530 in the U.S.* 🌐 *www.sandos.com* 🛏 *214 rooms* 🍴 *All-Inclusive.*

Secrets The Vine Cancún

$$$ | **RESORT** | This adults-only resort offers "unlimited luxury," so even butler service, international calls, 24-hour room service, taxes, and gratuities are included in the rate. **Pros:** free fitness classes; great restaurants; access to Riviera Maya sister properties. **Cons:** thin walls; only suites have full ocean views; no children under 18. [$] *Rooms from: $420* ✉ *Retorno del Rey, Mz 13, Lote 38 and 38B, off Blvd. Kukulcán, Km 14.5, Zona Hotelera* ☎ *998/848–9400, 866/467–3273 in the U.S.* 🌐 *www.hyatt.com/en-US/hotel/mexico/vine-cancun/sevcu* 🛏 *495 rooms* 🍴 *All-Inclusive.*

The Westin Lagunamar Ocean Resort Villas & Spa, Cancún

$$ | **RESORT** | **FAMILY** | Every unit here—four-person studio or eight-person villa—is oceanfront and equipped with a washer and dryer, full kitchen, whirlpool tub, and delightful design touches like recessed lighting and built-in shelves displaying Mexican pottery. **Pros:** beautiful infinity pool; all the comforts of home; great for families. **Cons:** time-share pitch; spotty Wi-Fi; no all-inclusive plan. [$] *Rooms from: $230* ✉ *Blvd Kukulcán, Km 12.5, Zona Hotelera* ☎ *998/891–4200* 🌐 *www.marriott.com* 🛏 *580 units* 🍴 *No Meals.*

The Westin Resort & Spa Cancún

$$ | **RESORT** | **FAMILY** | Pampering touches—like the white-tea mist that periodically sprays in the lobby and the beds so heavenly that some guests buy them for their own homes—are what make this hotel extraordinary. **Pros:** two beaches;

natural reef great for snorkeling; all-inclusive plan available. **Cons:** some rooms don't have a balcony; driving distance to off-site shops and restaurants; only odd-numbered rooms have ocean views. *[$] Rooms from: $213 ✉ Blvd. Kukulcán, Km 20, Zona Hotelera ☎ 998/848–7400, 800/545–7964 in the U.S. 🌐 www.marriott.com 🛏 379 rooms 🍴 No Meals.*

Wyndham Alltra Cancún

$$ | RESORT | FAMILY | The most basic lodging option at this resort is a spacious junior suite with a sofa bed, sitting area, flat-screen TV, stocked minibar, and balcony; family suites have bunk beds and direct access to the Kids' Club via sliding glass doors. **Pros:** wide array of activities; gym has yoga and spin classes; access to an adults-only sister property in Playa del Carmen. **Cons:** annoying time-share presentations; mediocre restaurants; pools tend to get crowded and rowdy. *[$] Rooms from: $329 ✉ Blvd. Kukulcán, Km 11.5, Zona Hotelera ☎ 998/881–6750, 833/349–2088 in the U.S. 🌐 alltrabyplaya.com 🛏 458 suites 🍴 All-Inclusive.*

🍸 Nightlife

BARS

Many bars daylight as restaurants, but after sunset the party kicks up with pulsating music and waiters who don't so much encourage crowd participation as demand it. Just remember: it's all in good fun.

Señor Frog's

BARS | Known for its over-the-top drinks, Señor Frog's serves up foot-long funnel glasses filled with margaritas, daiquiris, or beer, which you can take home as souvenirs once you've chugged them dry. Spring breakers adore this place and often stagger back night after night. For $29 you get your entrance cover, food menu, and a yard of beer. *✉ Blvd. Kukulcán, Km 9.5, Zona Hotelera ✥ Across from Coco Bongo ☎ 998/883–1862 🌐 senorfrogs.com.*

DANCE CLUBS

Cancún wouldn't be Cancún without clubs—both glittering and raucous. Though most open at around 10 pm, things generally don't start happening until about midnight, with the goings-on continuing until 6 am. As the hours roll on, frenzied dancing seems to quake the building and the floor beneath.

Most clubs offer open-bar tickets (MX$600–MX$1,100) that cover admission and unlimited drinks until 3 am. (The fine print usually specifies unlimited domestic—meaning Mexican—alcohol. In any case, check carefully what your ticket buys you.) If you stay past 3, you're on your own for beverages. You can also pay a lower cover charge of MX$200–MX$500 and buy drinks separately. Typical prices range from MX$100 for a shot to MX$200 for a cocktail.

★ The City

DANCE CLUBS | Open only on Friday nights, The City is a giant party complex with several large bars selling overpriced drinks and a cavernous dance floor with stadium seating. Dancing and live shows are the main draw during the legendary foam parties. This is by far the loudest club in the Zona Hotelera, so don't be surprised if you go home with your ears ringing. Doors open at 10 pm; expect to pay a MX$500 cover or MX$1,300 for open-bar entry. *✉ Blvd. Kukulcán, Km 9.5, Zona Hotelera ☎ 998/883–3333 🌐 mandalatickets.com/en/cancun/disco/the-city 🕑 Closed Sat.–Thurs.*

★ Coco Bongo

DANCE CLUBS | The wild Coco Bongo has no chairs, but there are plenty of tables that everyone dances on and capacity for 1,800 people. There's also a popular show billed as "Las Vegas meets Hollywood," featuring celebrity impersonators and an amazing gravity-defying acrobatic performance with an accompanying 12-piece orchestra. After the shows, the techno gets turned up to full volume, and everyone gets up to get down.

Doors open at 10:30 pm. Tickets are MX$1,400–MX$2,600 for open bar and shows. ✉ *Forum Cancún, Blvd. Kukulcán, Km 9.5, Zona Hotelera* ☎ *998/883–2373* ⊕ *www.cocobongo.com.*

Congo Bar

DANCE CLUBS | Brought to you by the makers of the famed Coco Bongo, Congo Bar is hard to miss. This spot stops traffic due to the go-go dancers who perform on open platforms lining the street. Expect Jell-O shots, confetti showers, and loud music. A regular dance floor ticket costs $47. ✉ *Blvd. Kukulcán, Km 9, Zona Hotelera* ✛ *Diagonally across from Coco Bongo* ☎ *800/841–4636 toll-free in Mexico, 998/883–2373* ⊕ *www.facebook. com/CongoBarOficial.*

D'Cave

DANCE CLUBS | Previously known as Dady'O, Cancún's original dance club has rebranded itself as D'Cave and is still very "in" with the younger set. A giant screen projects music videos above the always-packed dance floor, while laser lights whirl across the crowd. During spring break, Hawaiian Bikini contests make the place even livelier. It's only open on Saturday from 9:30 pm to 3 am, and a general access ticket costs $30. ✉ *Blvd. Kukulcán, Km 9.5; Zona Hotelera* ✛ *Across from Coco Bongo* ☎ *998/883–3333* ⊕ *www.facebook.com/DCave.mx* ☾ *Closed Sun.–Fri.*

Mandala Cancún/Mandala Beach Club

DANCE CLUBS | This Balinese-style party place is a buzzing beach retreat by day and a more upscale nightclub after dark. Both have bikini contests, DJs, pool parties, and bottle service. Don't forget your swimsuit and beach-appropriate shoes. Expect to pay a $20 cover. ✉ *Blvd. Kukulcán, Km 9, Zona Hotelera* ☎ *998/883–3333* ⊕ *www.mandalabeach.com.*

Avoid Tortoiseshell ⬤

Refrain from buying anything made from tortoiseshell. The *carey*, or hawksbill turtle from which most of it comes, is an endangered species, and it's illegal to bring tortoiseshell products into the United States and several other countries. Also be aware that there are some restrictions regarding black coral. For one, you must purchase it from a recognized dealer.

⬤ Shopping

Coral Negro

MARKET | **FAMILY** | Next to the convention center, this open-air market has about 50 stalls selling crafts and souvenirs. Everything here is overpriced, and vendors are pushy, but you can try bargaining. Stalls deeper in the market tend to have better deals than those around the periphery. ✉ *Blvd. Kukulcán, Km 9, Zona Hotelera* ☎ *998/984–8531* ⊕ *www. facebook.com/coralnegrocun.*

Forum by the Sea

MALL | **FAMILY** | This three-level entertainment and shopping plaza features brand-name restaurants, upscale clothing boutiques, a food court, and chain stores, all in a circus-like atmosphere. For spring breakers the main draws are the nightclubs, Coco Bongo and Señor Frog's. The bungee trampolines set up here during high season are especially popular with children. You will also find several ATMs. ✉ *Blvd. Kukulcán, Km 9.5, Zona Hotelera* ☎ *998/883–4425.*

★ La Isla Paradise Experience

MALL | **FAMILY** | Situated on Laguna Nichupté, the sleek, white, ultratrendy La Isla has myriad international designer and other big-name retailers as well as both sit-down and fast-food restaurants. If you're interested in doing more than just shopping and dining, attractions include a cinema, a Ferris wheel, a tequila museum, and an interactive aquarium where you can swim with the dolphins and feed the sharks. ⊠ *Blvd. Kukulcán, Km 12.5, Zona Hotelera* ☎ *998/883–5025* ⊕ *www. laislacancun.mx.*

Plaza Caracol

MALL | **FAMILY** | North of the convention center, the two-story Plaza Caracol has chain stores, souvenir shops, jewelry boutiques, and pharmacies. If you work up an appetite, it also has a food court. ■**TIP**→ **Free Wi-Fi is available at the Häagen-Dazs ice cream shop.** ⊠ *Blvd. Kukulcán, Km 8.5, Zona Hotelera* ☎ *998/883– 4760* ⊕ *www.plazacaracol.mx/en.*

Plaza Kukulcán

MALL | **FAMILY** | In addition to housing about 30 shops and restaurants, this mall also hosts art exhibits and other cultural events. ■**TIP**→ **While parents shop, kids can enjoy the games arcade and play area.** ⊠ *Blvd. Kukulcán, Km 13, Zona Hotelera* ☎ *998/193–0160* ⊕ *kukulcanplaza.mx.*

Plaza la Fiesta (*Mexican Outlet*)

MARKET | **FAMILY** | Near the convention center, the large Plaza la Fiesta probably has the Zona Hotelera's widest selection of Mexican goods, including jewelry, clothing, handicrafts, alcohol, and other assorted souvenirs. ■**TIP**→ **Look carefully at what you buy, though: not everything here is made in Mexico. There are some good bargains, but this is not a place to haggle.** ⊠ *Blvd. Kukulcán, Km 9, Zona Hotelera.*

 Activities

BOATING AND SAILING

El Embarcadero Por Xcaret

BOAT TOURS | **FAMILY** | The marina complex at Playa Linda, El Embarcadero is the departure point for the tourist-oriented ferries to Isla Mujeres and several other tour boats. ⊠ *Playa Linda, Blvd. Kukulcán, Km 4, Zona Hotelera* ☎ *998/883–3143, 855/326–0682 in the U.S.* ⊕ *xailing.com.*

Jungle Tour Barracuda

BOAT TOURS | **FAMILY** | Jungle boats for two to three passengers can be rented through Jungle Tour Barracuda. Book mangrove or jungle tour. Private tours to Isla Mujeres, with a captain, and up to 10 passengers can also be arranged. ⊠ *Blvd. Kukulcán, Km 14.1, Marina Puerto Madero, Zona Hotelera* ☎ *998/885–2444* ⊕ *jungletourbarracuda.com* ⊠ *From $45.*

DINNER CRUISES

Sunset boat cruises that include dinner, drinks, music, and sometimes dancing are popular in Cancún—especially among couples looking for a romantic evening and visitors who'd rather avoid the carnival atmosphere of the clubs and discos.

Capitán Hook

ENTERTAINMENT CRUISE | **FAMILY** | This outfit's three-hour sunset cruises aboard a replica 18th-century Spanish galleon include dinner (lobster or steak), drinks, and a show. Trips are offered daily and run from 7 to 10:30 pm, but you must arrive 45 minutes before departure time. ⊠ *Blvd. Kukulcán, Km 5, Zona Hotelera* ☎ *998/849–4931, 998/849-4933* ⊕ *capitanhook.com* ⊠ *From MX$1,520.*

Columbus Cancún

ENTERTAINMENT CRUISE | This company offers cruises on a 62-foot galleon. Advertised as a "romance tour," it has some elements of a booze cruise (including watered-down cocktails). But it's still worth it for the fresh lobster dinner and sunset views over Laguna Nichupté; afterward, the boat trip continues so you can stargaze. Departures take place at 5 and 8 pm. The outings are geared to couples, but families are welcome though no children under 14 are permitted.

Water Sports in Cancún

With the Caribbean on one side and the still waters of Laguna Nichupté on the other, it's no wonder that Cancún is one of the world's water sports capitals. The top activities are snorkeling and diving along the coral reef just off the coast.

Kiteboarding and windsurfing are also popular, although the waves are not as constant as on Mexico's Pacific coast. For the beach-break surfer, the sandbars are best at Playa Gaviota Azul and Playa Delfines, but waves are generally choppy and created by wind swells. Thirty-two kilometers (20 miles) south of Cancún are several point breaks off the coast of Puerto Morelos and Punta Brava.

If you want to view the mysterious underwater world but don't want to get your feet wet, a glass-bottom boat or "submarine" is the ticket. You can also go fishing, parasailing, or try your balancing skills on a stand-up paddleboard. Paddleboats, kayaks, catamarans, and banana boats are readily available, too.

Because the beaches along the Zona Hotelera can have a strong undertow, always respect the flags posted in the area. A black flag means no swimming at all. A red flag means you can swim but only with extreme caution. Yellow means approach with caution, while green means water conditions are safe. You'll most likely always see a red or yellow flag, even when the water is calm.

Unfortunately, there's very little wildlife in the Laguna Nichupté, so most advertised jungle tours are glorified Jet Ski romps where you drive around fast, make a lot of noise, and don't see many animals. American crocodiles still reside in these waters though, so don't stand or swim in them.

Although the coral reef in this area is not as spectacular as that farther south, there's still marine life. It's quite common to spot angelfish, parrot fish, blue tang, sea turtles, and the occasional moray eel. To be a good world citizen, follow the six golden rules for snorkeling or scuba diving:

1. Don't throw garbage into the sea, as the marine life will assume it's food, an often lethal mistake.

2. Never stand on the coral.

3. Secure all cameras and gear onto your body so you don't drop anything onto the fragile reef.

4. Never take anything from the sea.

5. Don't feed any of the marine animals.

6. Avoid applying sunblock, tanning lotion, or mosquito repellent just before you visit the reef.

✉ *Marina Aquatours, Blvd. Kukulcán, Km 6.5, Zona Hotelera* ✛ *In front of Playa Tortugas–Turtles beach, also known as the Fat Tuesday beach* ☎ *866/393–5158 in the U.S., 800/727–5391 toll-free in Mexico* ⊕ *www.columbuscancun.com. mx* 🎫 *From $89.*

Jolly Roger Pirate Show
ENTERTAINMENT CRUISE | FAMILY | Enjoy a three-hour sailing trip on the Caribbean Sea aboard a 112-feet galleon full of scary pirates who are actually quite fun once you get to see them performing. In addition to acrobatic fights and live music, the experience features a gourmet

dinner and an open bar. Departures are at 4 and 8:30 pm on both Wednesday and Saturday. ⊠ *Blvd. Kukulkán, Km 4.5, Embarcadero Playa Linda, Zona Hotelera* ☎ *998/849-4247* ⊕ *pirateshowcancun. com* ✉ *From $108.*

★ Xoximilco

ENTERTAINMENT CRUISE | The creators of Xcaret are behind this three-hour dinner-cruise experience, which offers a fiesta like no other. The entire setup is modeled on the famous Xochimilco floating gardens near Mexico City, so sails are aboard colorful *trajineras* (gondola-like boats). While floating along the freshwater canals, you're treated to live music, an open bar (tequila and beer), and various dishes from around the country. Departures are at 7 pm. ■**TIP→ Bring mosquito repellent.** ⊠ *Carretera 307, Km 338, Carretera Cancún-Aeropuerto* ⊹ *5 mins from Cancún Airport* ☎ *998/883–3143 in Mexico, 855/326–0682 in the U.S.* ⊕ *www.xoximilco.com* ✉ *From $99.*

FISHING

Some 500 species—including sailfish, wahoo, bluefin, marlin, barracuda, and red snapper—live in the waters off Cancún. You can charter deep-sea fishing boats for four to eight hours; rates generally include a captain and first mate, gear, bait, and beverages.

Charter Fishing Cancún

FISHING | This outfit offers sportfishing trips between the mainland and Isla Mujeres, where possible catches include mahimahi, sailfish, barracuda, king mackerel, wahoo, tuna, grouper, snapper, and shark. Boats, ranging in size from 31 to 54 feet, can be chartered for four, six, eight, or ten hours. Shared boats with a maximum of six anglers are also available. ⊠ *Marina Aquatours, Blvd. Kukulcán, Km 6.5, Zona Hotelera* ☎ *998/200–3240* ⊕ *www.charterfishingcancun.com* ✉ *Shared fishing from $175; boats from $600.*

Scuba Cancún

FISHING | In addition to diving trips and instruction, Scuba Cancún offers deep-sea fishing expeditions that last from four to eight hours. Whale-shark snorkeling tours and trips to Isla Contoy are also available. ⊠ *Playa Langosta, Blvd. Kukulcán, Km 5, Zona Hotelera* ☎ *998/849–7508* ⊕ *scubacancun.com.mx* ✉ *Fishing trips from $660.*

GOLF

All courses here enforce a moderate dress code: collared shirts, skirts or shorts that extend to at least mid-thigh, and no jeans or swimwear.

El Tinto

GOLF | The Cancún Country Club's well-maintained, 18-hole course is just 10 minutes south of the airport. Designed by world-renowned professional Nick Price, it has 84 bunkers, five lakes, and wide fairways. The yardage length, coupled with multiple sets of tee markers, challenges golfers of all abilities. Greens fees include a golf cart (mandatory), water bottle, and game accessories. On-site facilities include a practice area and a golf academy. ⊠ *Carretera Federal 307, Sm 46, Mz 1, Lote 1-08, Km 388, Carretera Cancún-Aeropuerto* ☎ *998/886–2815* ⊕ *cancuncountryclub.com* ✉ *$180* ⛳ *18 holes, 7435 yards, Par 72.*

★ Iberostar Selection Cancún Golf Club

GOLF | Designed by legendary golfer Isao Aoki, Cancún's only 18-hole championship course has four sets of tees that stretch from 5,000 yards to 6,800 yards over 150 lush acres along the Nichupté Lagoon. You're likely to see birds, iguanas, crocodiles, and other wildlife as you play, and the 16th hole overlooks the Maya Ruinas El Rey. Other than a few holes lined by jungle and water, the course is wide open, and the fairways are fast. There's also a practice facility with a driving range and a putting green. The greens fee includes a golf cart, unlimited food and beverage service, and transfers between the course and Zona Hotelera

Cancún may not be the best destination for serious golfers, but it has several beautiful and challenging courses.

properties for a minimum of two people. Those staying at the Iberostar hotel receive 60% discounts. ⊠ *Iberostar, Blvd. Kukulcán, Km 17, Zona Hotelera* ☎ *998/881–8016* ⊕ *www.iberostar.com* 🖾 *$199* ⅄ *18 holes, 6735 yards. Par 72.*

Moon Palace Golf Club

GOLF | Designed by Jack Nicklaus, this is the only exclusive 27-hole par 72 course in the Mexican Caribbean. It's spread over three nine-hole courses—the Jungle, the Lakes, and the Dunes—each with four sets of tees with mangroves, wetlands, and strategically placed bunkers. Eighteen-hole play consists of three combinations: Dunes and Jungle, Jungle and Lakes, or Lakes and Dunes. The 18-hole greens fee includes a cart and food and drink service. If you're staying at any of the Palace Resorts, inquire about all-inclusive golf packages. Lessons are available. ⊠ *Moon Palace Cancun, Carretera Cancún-Chetumal, Km 340, Cancún* ✛ *About 15 mins from airport* ☎ *998/881–0285* ⊕ *www.moonpalace-cancun.com/golf* 🖾 *$303 for 18 holes*

(choice of 2 courses) ⅄ *27 holes, 7165 yards, par 72.*

Puerto Cancún Club

GOLF | Midway between the Zona Hotelera and El Centro, this 18-hole course designed by British Open Champion Tom Weiskopf stretches over 185 acres that feature ocean views and two holes that play on a marina. Winding fairways test your skills on distance and short game swings, and strategically placed bunkers demand considerable accuracy. Stay focused on the final hole, which is on an island in a canal. The course offers access to the Puerto Cancún youth golf program. ⊠ *Av. Bonampak, Mz 27, Lote 1-02, Calle Puerto Acapulco, Zona Hotelera* ☎ *998/892–1958* ⊕ *www.puertocancun. com* 🖾 *$155 for 18 holes* ⅄ *18 holes, 7241 yards, par 72* ☺ *Closed Mon.*

Riviera Cancún Golf Club

GOLF | Designed by Jack Nicklaus, this signature 18-hole golf course has strategic bunkering, immaculate greens, wooden bridges, and incredible ocean views on holes 14 and 15. Surrounded by mangroves, dunes, and lakes, it's a challenging course. Bring more balls than you think you need, as you'll encounter water at nearly every hole. The contemporary Mexican-style clubhouse has a restaurant and fantastic views of the 18th hole. Other on-site amenities include a driving range and putting and chipping greens. ✉ *Blvd. Kulkucán, Km 25.3, Zona Hotelera* ✛ *At southern end of Kukulcán near Punta Nizuc* ☎ *998/294–2742* ⊕ *rivieracancungolfclub.com* ✐ *$236 for 18 holes* ⚘ *18 holes, 7060 yards, par 72.*

SCUBA DIVING AND SNORKELING

Scuba diving is popular in Cancún, though it's not as spectacular as in Cozumel. Look for a company that will give you lots of personal attention. (Smaller outfits are often better at this than larger ones.) Regardless, ask to meet the dive master, and check the equipment and certifications thoroughly.

The snorkeling is best at Punta Nizuc, Punta Cancún, and Playa Tortugas, although you should be careful of the strong currents at Tortugas. You can rent gear from many of the diving places as well as at many hotels.

■TIP➜ The one-hour courses that many resorts offer for free do not prepare you to dive in the open ocean—only in shallow water where you can easily surface without danger. They are meant only to whet your appetite. If you've caught the scuba bug and want to take deep-water or boat dives, prepare yourself properly by investing in a full certification course.

Aquafun Marina & Plaza
SNORKELING | FAMILY | This company is a marina/shopping center/tour operator with an outstanding location right at the heart of the Zona Hotelera. Here, you can not only take scuba diving lessons, but also splash in a swimming pool or even pamper yourself in a small but well-appointed spa. A highlight, though, is the two-hour mangrove tour aboard easy-to-drive, two-person boats that includes

snorkeling at the Punta Nizuc reef. Reservations are required for the tours, which take place on Monday, Wednesday, and Friday at 10 am, 1 pm, and 3 pm. ✉ *Blvd. Kukulcán, Km 16.5, Zona Hotelera* ☎ *998/885–1682* ⊕ *aquafun. com.mx* ✐ *MX$1,400.*

AquaWorld
SCUBA DIVING | FAMILY | In addition to snorkeling and scuba trips to the Cancún Underwater Museum off Punta Sam, AquaWorld organizes dive explorations of boat wrecks. ✉ *Blvd. Kukulcán, Km 15.2, Zona Hotelera* ☎ *554/166–3092, 866/210–1236 in the U.S.* ⊕ *aquaworld. com.mx* ✐ *Snorkeling trips from $70; dive trips from $89.*

Scuba Cancún
SCUBA DIVING | Long-established Scuba Cancún specializes in diving trips and PADI instruction. ✉ *Playa Langosta, Blvd. Kukulcán, Km 5, Zona Hotelera* ☎ *998/849–7508* ⊕ *scubacancun.com.mx* ✐ *Dives from $89.*

Solo Buceo
SCUBA DIVING | Options with this operator include PADI instruction, one- and two-tank dives, and whale-shark snorkeling excursions. ✉ *Hotel Real Inn, Blvd. Kukulcán, Km 5.5, Zona Hotelera* ☎ *998/260–4995, 305/912–9378 in the U.S.* ⊕ *solobuceo.com* ✐ *Dives from $87; instruction from $120.*

SPAS
★ Blanc Spa
SPAS | This massive facility takes pampering to a whole new level. Arrive early and linger in one of the dimly lighted relaxation rooms, nibble on fresh cookies, and sip agua fresca flavored with hibiscus or cucumber. Before your treatment, utilize the hydrotherapy area with hot/cold plunge pools, sauna, herbal steam room, ice room, sauna therapy, and relaxation lounge. A vast array of treatments—from facials and body wraps to intensive four-handed couples' massages—are offered in oversized suites. ✉ *Le Blanc*

Spa Resort, Blvd. Kukulcán, Km 10, Zona Hotelera ☏ *998/881–4740* ⊕ *cancun. leblancsparesorts.com/spa.*

★ Coral Beach Gem Spa

SPAS | With 40,000 square feet and 26 treatment rooms, this is one of Latin America's largest spas. The experience begins with a 90-minute, 10-step hydro-therapy ritual that detoxifies the skin and incorporates an aromatherapy steam room, multi-jet shower, clay steam room, rain shower, sauna, ice room, whirlpool, cold plunge pool, and pebble walkway with warm water jets. Treatments—rang-ing from a diamond-dust body exfoliation to an amber-and-gold facial—are inspired by the healing energy of gemstones. The 80-minute Seventh Wonder Luxury Massage, during which quartz crystals are placed on seven chakras, is worth the splurge. Guest must be 16 years or older. ⊠ *Grand Fiesta Americana Coral Beach, Blvd. Kukulcán, Km 9.5, Zona Hotelera* ☏ *443/310–8137* ⊕ *www.coralbeachcan-cunresort.com/gem-spa.*

Feel Harmony Spa by Live Aqua

SPAS | It may be one of the smaller Zona Hotelera spas, but Feel Harmony Spa by Live Aqua has experienced therapists who attract repeat clients from neighbor-ing resorts. Treatments begin with a foot bath, hand massage, and your choice of chlorophyll water or green tea. A hydro-therapy ritual is included with treatments like the coffee exfoliation, coconut–choc-olate wrap, and honey scrub. For the ulti-mate in pampering, request a diamond facial that uses more than 30 botanical ingredients and a powerful deep-sea antioxidant that enhances skin firmness. ⊠ *Live Aqua Beach Resort Cancún, Blvd. Kukulcán, Km 12.5, Zona Hotelera* ☏ *443/310–8137* ⊕ *www.liveaqua.com.*

Kayantá Spa

SPAS | Indigenous Yucatán ingredients are used in Maya-inspired treatments at this spa, which also offers nanotechnology facials and hydrotherapy. Consider trying the namesake Kayantá massage featur-ing hot stones, lomilomi technique, and acupressure. ⊠ *Kempinski Hotel Cancún, Retorno del Rey 36, Zona Hotelera* ☏ *998/881–0808 Ext. 5228* ⊕ *www.kem-pinski.com/en/hotel-cancun/kayanta-spa* ⊠ *Massages from USD$169.*

Sens-Yah Spa at JW Marriott Resort

SPAS | This 35,000-square-foot spa has breathtaking ocean views and Maya-in-spired facials and body treatments, including those for men, expectant moth-ers, couples, and teens. Fitness classes are also offered. ⊠ *JW Marriott, Blvd. Kukulcán, Km 14.5, Cancún* ☏ *998/848–9700* ⊕ *www.marriott.com.*

Chapter 4

ISLA MUJERES

Updated by
Luis F. Dominguez

● Sights	ⓘ Restaurants	🛏 Hotels	🛍 Shopping	🍸 Nightlife
★★★★☆	★★★★☆	★★★★☆	★★★☆☆	★★★☆☆

WELCOME TO ISLA MUJERES

TOP REASONS TO GO

★ **Getting away from the crowd:** Although Isla Mujeres is just across the bay from Cancún, the peace and quiet make it seem like another universe.

★ **Exploring the southeastern coast:** Bump along in a golf cart where craggy cliffs meet the blue Caribbean.

★ **Eating freshly grilled seafood:** For some reason it always tastes best under a beachfront *palapa* (thatched roof) at lovely Playa Norte.

★ **Diving with "sleeping sharks":** Plunge into the underwater caverns off Isla, where these gentle giants sleep.

★ **Taking a boat trip to Isla Contoy:** On this even smaller island, more than 150 species of birds make their home.

Isla Mujeres is still quiet by Riviera Maya standards, with a small-town feel that makes it a great escape from Cancún. (Don't mention that to locals, who will tell you that the influx of big hotels has changed it forever.) Just 8 km (5 miles) long and 1 km (½ mile) wide, its landscapes include flat sandy beaches in the north and steep rocky bluffs to the south. The liveliest activities here are swimming, snorkeling, exploring the remnants of the island's past, drinking cold beer, eating fresh seafood, and lazing under palapas.

1 El Pueblo. Directly in front of the ferry piers, El Pueblo is Isla's only town. It extends the full width of the island's northern end, sandwiched between sand and sea to the south, west, and northeast. The *zócalo* (main square) is the hub of *Isleño* life.

2 Playa Norte. With its waist-deep turquoise waters and wide soft sands, Playa Norte is the northernmost beach on Isla Mujeres, and the most beautiful. The bulk of the island's resorts and hotels are here, and the town center and historic cemetery are both just a short walk away.

3 Greater Isla Mujeres. Midway along the western coast of Isla you can glimpse the lovely Laguna Makax. At the lagoon's southeastern end are the shady stretches of Playa Tiburón and Playa Lancheros. At Isla's southernmost tip is Garrafón Natural Reef Park.

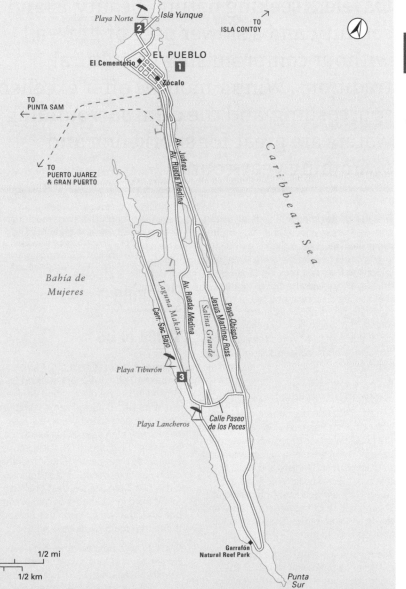

Playa Norte
Isla Yunque
2
TO
ISLA CONTOY

EL PUEBLO
1
El Cementerio ◆

● *Zócalo*

TO
PUNTA SAM

TO
PUERTO JUAREZ
& GRAN PUERTO

C a r i b b e a n   S e a

Av. Juárez
Av. Rueda Medina

*Bahía de
Mujeres*

Payo Obispo
Jesús Martínez Ross
Salina Grande

Av. Rueda Medina

Laguna Makax

Carr. Sac Bajo

Playa Tiburón
3

Playa Lancheros
*Calle Paseo
de los Peces*

0   1/2 mi
0   1/2 km

◆ Garrafón
Natural Reef Park

Punta
Sur

Once a small fishing village, colorful Isla Mujeres (meaning "Island of Women") has become a favorite for travelers seeking natural beauty, island serenity, and a slower pace of life—all without compromising its cultural traditions. Winter months offer excellent sportfishing, and the calm surrounding waters are great for snorkeling and swimming year-round.

During high season, boatloads of visitors pop over from Cancún for a taste of the island life. The midday rush is a boon for vendors and hagglers offering every kind of service from hair braiding to beach massages. By late afternoon, though, the masses disappear and return to their big-city nightlife and the comforts of the mainland. Those who stay behind discover that on Isla Mujeres (*ees*-lah moo-*hair*-ays), worldly concerns fade with the setting sun.

Isla—after 10 minutes here, you'll shorthand the name like everyone else does—has about 12,000 permanent residents, many of whom earn a living selling fish at the docks or plates of food outside their homes. There are plenty of opportunities to practice your Spanish, and you'll find that most locals beam when you try. Taxi drivers are genuinely interested in sharing details of the island's history and telling you about their families who were born and raised here.

The minute you step off the boat, you'll get a sense of how small Isla is. The sights and properties are strung along the coasts, and there's not much to the interior except for two briny marshes where the Maya harvested salt centuries ago.

Planning

When to Go

When you factor in an international contingent of vacationers seeking winter sunshine and the day-tripping college students who flock in from neighboring Cancún during spring break, it's easy to see why high season here extends from late November (U.S. Thanksgiving) straight through Easter. Other months qualify as low season, and prices may be cut in half. Some of the best deals can be found from late October to mid-November, after the rainy season has passed but before the crowds have arrived.

Isla enjoys its best weather between November and May, when temperatures usually hover around 27°C (80°F). June, July, and August are the hottest and most humid months, with daytime highs routinely over 35°C (95°F). A few festivals and holidays are worth keeping in mind while you're planning your trip: Carnaval in either February or March (the week before Lent); the Sol a Sol Regatta in late April; Founder's Day on August 17; the Day of the Virgin de la Caridad del Cobre, patron saint of local fishermen, on September 8; the Day of the Dead from October 31 to November 2; and the Feast of the Immaculate Conception on December 8. Be sure to book well in advance if you're planning to visit on any of these days.

PLANNING YOUR TIME

Although most mainland travelers visit Isla only for the day, it's definitely worth spending the night if you're looking for a mix of culture, tranquility, good food, and island atmosphere. In a single afternoon you can visit all the best beaches and major attractions. You may even have enough time to snorkel or swim.

If you're interested in taking a DIY driving tour of Isla Mujeres, start by looping the island's perimeter, stopping midway at the southernmost tip. Here you can walk down to the rocky shores where waves crash at your feet. The views from Punta Sur are magnificent, and the temple of Goddess Ixchel is worth a visit. Head back north and explore colorful neighborhoods on the outskirts of town, with a stop at the excellent Mango Cafe for lunch.

If you prefer the beach, relax at peaceful Playa Lancheros on the island's west side and see the area's dolphins, turtles, or nurse sharks before enjoying a traditional Mayan lunch at Playa Tiburón. Finish your tour with a sunset cocktail at Playa Norte before going downtown for dinner and live music.

Getting Here and Around

To get your bearings, picture the island as a long fish: the head is the southeastern tip, the tail is the northwest prong. Eight kilometers (5 miles) long and 1 km (½ mile) wide, Isla Mujeres is easy to explore in a single day. If you take your time, however, you'll discover that the island is not a destination to be rushed.

Mopeds and golf carts are the most popular modes of transportation on Isla's virtually car-free dirt roads. If you're staying at one of the remote hotels on the southern tip, a taxi will take you from one end of the island to the other for roughly MX$140.

BOAT AND FERRY

Isla ferries are typically two-story passenger cruisers that run between the mainland and the island's main dock. The ride gets a bit choppier with evening crossings.

Between 9:30 and early evening, Ultramar ferries to Isla's main dock depart from three locations in Cancún's Zona Hotelera: El Embarcadero marina complex at Playa Linda (approximately hourly), Playa Tortugas (approximately hourly), and Playa Caracol (approximately every two hours). The voyage costs MX$270 one way and takes about 30 minutes. Services from the hotel zone are more geared to day-trippers to and from Cancún. Local people are more apt to use the half-hourly service that departs from Cancún's Puerto Juárez from 5 am to midnight. (You can, too.) Fares are the same.

If you have a vehicle—and you really don't need one on the island—the Ultramar Vehicle Ferry leaves from Punta Sam, a dock north of Puerto Juárez. The ride takes about 45 minutes, and the fare is MX$420 per family car including the driver, although prices might vary for bigger cars and more passengers. If you're staying at Zoëtry Villa Rolandi or Isla Mujeres

Palace, transportation by private boat is included in your room rate.

CONTACTS Ultramar. ⊠ *Terminal Marítima Ultramar, Av. López Portillo, Sm 84, Mz 5, Lote 6, Puerto Juárez, El Centro* ☏ *984/881–5890* ⊕ *ultramarferry.com.*

GOLF CART

Golf carts are a fun way to get around the island, especially if you're traveling with kids. Due to *topes* (speed bumps), potholes, and the occasional gusty winds, they're also a much safer option than exploring by moped or bike. The downside is you can't lock them. (Never leave anything of value inside.)

There are more than a dozen rental agencies, although not all golf carts are created equal. Bypass the rusty cream-color carts, and opt for those with thick tires made by familiar brands like Jeep Wrangler. Most companies allow prebooking online and will deliver your golf cart directly to your hotel. This, however, limits your ability to haggle over the price. Rates start at approximately $65 USD for 24 hours, with prorated rates for shorter periods, depending on the season.

CONTACTS Golf Carts Indios. (*Apache's*) ⊠ *Av. Juárez 67, Sm 1, Mz 15, Lote 12, Matamoros y Abasolo, Downtown* ☏ *999/777–0003* ⊕ *indios-golfcarts. com.* **Isla Mujeres Golf Cart Rentals.** ⊠ *Miguel Hidalgo, Sm 1, Downtown* ☏ *998/578–5266, 281/587–7725 in the U.S.* ⊕ *islamujeresgolfcartrentals.com.* **Pepe's Moto Rent.** ⊠ *Miguel Hidalgo, Sm 1, Downtown* ☏ *998/525–7729* ⊕ *rentadora-ppes.negocio.site.*

MOPED AND BICYCLE

If you need your own wheels—and you really don't here on Isla—we strongly recommend you rent a golf cart rather than a scooter, for safety reasons. If you absolutely want two wheels rather than four, Avenida Rueda Medina, directly across from the dock, is lined with shops where you can rent mopeds. Most charge $35 a day including tax and complimentary gas

refills, but the final price will depend on the vehicle's make and condition and your own haggling skills.

Some also offer bike rentals, with daily rates starting at MX$250 for beaters and MX$350 for mountain bikes. If you are interested in cycling, be advised that it's hot here and you'll encounter plenty of speed bumps and the occasional wind gusts. Don't ride at night, since many roads don't have streetlights, and make sure your bike comes with a lock to keep it from wandering off.

■TIP→ **Before leaving the rental agency, check your moped or golf cart for scratches and dings. You may even want to take a photo for additional proof of the original condition. Otherwise, you'll pay dearly for any damage that was not noted prior to your rental agreement.**

Banks and Currency Exchange

Isla Mujeres banks rarely change U.S. dollars into Mexican pesos, but many *casas de cambio* (exchange houses) will; note, too, that there's one at the Ultramar ferry dock in Cancún. Alternatively, you can withdraw pesos at several on-island ATMs, including those at the Super Aki store on the town square, the Citybanamex at the corner of Juarez and Morelos, and the HSBC across from the ferry port. Note, however, that these machines tend to have long lines and can run out of money on busy weekends and holidays.

Although most businesses accept U.S. dollars, you should expect to get change back in pesos at a less-than-favorable exchange rate. A minority of establishments accept credit cards (mostly MasterCard and Visa, and often with a 5% service fee attached), though this number is growing.

Beaches

Despite being surrounded by water, Isla Mujeres really has only three beaches suitable for visitors: Playa Norte on the north end, and Playa Lancheros and Playa Tiburón on the west side. With its crystal clear water, Playa Norte is generally tranquil and better for swimming than eastern beaches facing the Caribbean, which are rocky and susceptible to strong winds and riptides.

Western beaches always have a subtle south-to-north current, which can be dangerous if you're not alert. The southern part of the island has several secluded beaches, but they, too, have exposed reefs and strong currents and are often littered with seagrass and ocean debris.

Isla's sandy beaches have experienced erosion due to high winds and stormy seas in the past few decades and have never fully recovered. Property owners have worked to minimize erosion with Geotubes placed along Playa Norte's shores.

Hotels

Hotels here range from bed-and-breakfasts and boutique properties to all-inclusive resorts. Even the largest of the latter are small compared to mainland resorts, and, with so many restaurants around, it's not worth paying for an all-inclusive package unless you'd rather not venture off-site. In addition, several agencies can help you find a vacation rental. For instance, Everything Isla (⊕ *www. everythingislamujeres.com*), which also handles hotel-room reservations, lists fully equipped apartments and houses.

Properties on the north end near El Pueblo are within walking distance of shops, eateries, and the calm waters of Playa Norte. Budget digs can be found in the center of town—just bear in mind they get street noise from the pedestrian traffic on Avenida Hidalgo. Lodgings elsewhere on the island are more private but aren't as convenient and might lack beaches.

Many of Isla's smaller hotels don't accept credit cards, and some add a 5%–10% surcharge if you use one. Hoteliers here have also been tightening up cancellation policies, so inquire about fees for changing reservations. ■TIP→ **Before paying, ask to see your room to make sure everything is satisfactory—especially at the smaller hotels.**

⇨ *Hotel reviews have been shortened. For full information, visit Fodors.com. Hotel prices are the lowest cost of a standard double room in high season.*

What It Costs in U.S. Dollars			
$	$$	$$$	$$$$
HOTELS			
under $100	$100–$200	$201–$300	over $300

Nightlife

This sleepy island has a surprisingly robust and varied nightlife scene. Most bars close by midnight, but the party continues at a few nightclubs until 2 am. Most venues are within downtown's four-block radius, with a few others along Playa Norte. The proximity makes barhopping on foot perilously convenient.

Isleños also celebrate many holidays and festivals in El Pueblo, usually with live entertainment. Carnaval, held annually in February or March (the week before Lent), turns sleepy Isla Mujeres into party central with music, dancing, and colorful parades in the zócalo. Other popular events include Founder's Day (August 17), which marks the island's official founding by the Mexican government. From October 31 to November 2, locals head to the cemetery to honor their dearly departed during Día de los Muertos (Day of the Dead) celebrations.

Restaurants

Restaurants tend to serve simple food like seafood, pizza, salads, and Mexican dishes. Prices that are lower than in Cancún, fresh ingredients, and hospitable waiters make up for the lack of elaborate menus and master chefs.

Though informal, most indoor restaurants request that you at least wear a shirt and shoes. Some outdoor terrace and palapa restaurants also require shoes and some sort of cover-up over your bathing suit. Expect to have some of the island's stray dogs looking you in the eye if you dine outdoors. It's part of the casual life on Isla.

It's cash-only in most restaurants. If credit cards are accepted, you'll most likely pay an additional 5% service charge. It's customary in Mexico for the waiter to bring the bill only when you ask for it ("la cuenta, por favor"). Always check to make sure you didn't get charged for something you didn't order and to ensure the math is correct. The "tax" on the bill is often a service charge, a sort of guaranteed tip.

⇨ Restaurant reviews have been shortened. For full information, visit Fodors. com. Restaurant prices are the average cost of a main course at dinner, or if dinner is not served, at lunch.

What It Costs in Mexican Pesos			
$	$$	$$$	$$$$
RESTAURANTS			
under MP150	MP150– MP300	MP301– MP400	over MP400

Safety

The presence of a Mexican naval base contributes to a sense of safety here. There's little crime on this small island, making it an excellent choice for solo travelers. But common-sense precautions do apply: stay clear of drugs; don't leave personal items unattended on the beach or in a golf cart; and lock your hotel room when you leave.

Dehydration is a concern, so drink plenty of bottled water and order beverages without ice unless you're at a restaurant that uses purified water. Be careful when driving along the narrow roads, especially since many have gravel surfaces and potholes.

Visitor Information

CONTACTS Tourist Office. ✉ Av. Rueda Medina 130, Downtown ☎ 998/877–0307.

El Pueblo

◉ Sights

Aquatic Funday Park

WATER PARK | FAMILY | As its name suggests, this water park is the way to spend a fun day by the beach. Play beach volleyball, ride a bike through the quaint streets of Isla, explore the calm waters of the Caribbean in a kayak, or let the adrenaline pump through your veins as you slide down one of four slides that end directly into the sea. All the while, you can enjoy a good buffet and an even better open bar. The place is in constant renovation, so note that while some areas are top-notch, others are in need of a face-lift. ✉ Carretera Longitudinal, Km 4, Lote 8A, Sac Bajo, El Pueblo ☎ 998/123–7310 ⊕ www.aquaticfundaypark.com ⊠ From $31.50.

Iglesia de Concepción Inmaculada (*Church of the Immaculate Conception*)
CHURCH | FAMILY | In 1890, local fishermen landed at a deserted colonial settlement known as Ecab, where they found three identical statues of the Virgin Mary, each carved from wood with porcelain face and hands. No one knows where the statues came from, but it's widely believed they were gifts from the Spanish during a visit in 1770. One statue went to the city of Izamal in the Yucatán, and another was sent to Kantunikin in Quintana Roo. The third remained on the island. It was housed in a small wooden chapel while this church was being built; legend has it that the chapel burst into flames when the statue was removed. Some islanders still believe the statue walks on the water around the island from dusk until dawn, looking for her sisters. You can pay your respects daily between 11 am and 4 pm or between 6 pm and 8 pm, or attend mass, mostly in Spanish, with a few services in English throughout the week. ✉ *Av. Nicolas Bravo 15, Sm 1, Downtown* 🌐 *www.diocesiscancunchetumal.org* 🎟 *Free.*

🍴 Restaurants

Amigos
$$ | ECLECTIC | This easy-to-miss eatery offers a little bit of everything from fish and meat to pastas and vegetarian dishes, but it's best known for its superb pizza. Breakfasts, featuring delicious omelets and strong coffee, are also served. **Known for:** local vibe; street-side dining; big portions. [$] *Average main: MP210* ✉ *Av. Hidalgo 19, between Avs. Matamoros and Abasolo, Downtown* ☎ *998/877–0624* 🌐 *amigos.restaurantwebexperts.com.*

Angelo
$$ | ITALIAN | FAMILY | Named for its Italian chef Angelo Sanna, this charming bistro on Hidalgo's busy main strip is done up with soft lighting and a wood-fired oven. Come for the pizza, which has a thin crispy crust and is quite delicious. **Known for:** late night pizza; Italian classics; friendly atmosphere. [$] *Average main: MP300* ✉ *Av. Hidalgo 14, Isla Mujeres* ☎ *998/877–1273* 🕒 *Closed Sept.*

Café Cito
$ | CAFÉ | FAMILY | Cheery, seashell-decorated Cito was one of Isla's first cafés, and it's still among the best breakfast spots on the island. The menu includes pancakes, waffles, fruit-filled crepes, and egg dishes, as well as great cappuccino and espresso. **Known for:** fresh-squeezed orange juice; Mexican breakfasts; homemade coffee. [$] *Average main: MP110* ✉ *Avs. Juárez and Matamoros, El Pueblo* ☎ *998/225–0188* 🕒 *No dinner.*

Café Mogagua
$$ | ECLECTIC | FAMILY | Whether you come for breakfast or lunch, you'll enjoy the relaxed vibe at this open-air café. Its menu ranges from Mexican classics like chilaquiles and *huevos divorciados* (eggs with chile sauce), to pizza, grilled meats, and fish later in the day. **Known for:** organic coffee; friendly service; delicious chilaquiles. [$] *Average main: MP250* ✉ *Av. Juárez at Madero, El Pueblo* ☎ *998/877–0127* 🌐 *www.facebook.com/cafe.mogagua.*

Cocktelería Picus
$$ | SEAFOOD | Kick off your shoes, and settle back with a beer at this charming beachside restaurant near the ferry docks, where you can watch the fishing boats come and go while you wait for some of the island's freshest seafood. The grilled fish and lobster with garlic butter are both excellent, as are the shrimp fajitas—but the real showstopper is the ceviche, which might include conch, shrimp, abalone, fish, or octopus. **Known for:** Yucatecan pescado tikinxic; extraordinary ceviche; waterfront location. [$] *Average main: MP195* ✉ *Av. Rueda Medina 318, El Pueblo* ✣ *1 block northwest of ferry docks* ☎ *998/274–0083* 🕒 *No dinner.*

Isla's History

The name Isla Mujeres means "Island of Women," although no one knows who dubbed it that. Many believe it was the ancient Maya, who were said to use the island as a religious center for worshipping Ixchel (the "Rainbow Goddess"), the tide-controlling Mayan patroness of fertility, childbirth, and healing. Another popular legend has it that the Spanish conquistador Hernández de Córdoba named the island when he landed here in 1517 and found hundreds of female-shaped clay idols dedicated to Ixchel and her daughters. Still others say the name dates from the 1600s, when visiting pirates left women on Isla before sailing out to pillage merchant ships. (Reputedly both Henry Morgan and Jean Lafitte buried treasure here, although no one has ever found any pirate's gold.) Pick the story you like best.

Settlement began in earnest in the mid-19th century. Refugees from the Caste War of the Yucatán fled to the island and built its first official village of Dolores. By 1858, Fermín Mundaca de Marechaja, a slave trader turned pirate, began building an estate that took up 40% of the island. By the end of the century the population had risen to 650, and residents began to establish trade with the mainland, mostly by supplying fish to the owners of chicle and coconut plantations on the coast. In 1949, the Mexican navy built a base on Isla's northwestern coast. Around this time the island also caught the eye of some wealthy Mexican sportsmen, who began using it as a vacation spot.

Tourism flourished on Isla during the latter half of the 20th century, partly due to the island's most famous resident, Ramón Bravo (1927–98). A diver, cinematographer, ecologist, and colleague of Jacques Cousteau, Bravo was the first underwater photographer to explore the area. He contributed to the discovery of the now-famous Cave of the Sleeping Sharks and produced dozens of underwater documentaries for American, European, and Mexican television. Bravo's efforts to maintain the ecology on Isla have helped keep development here to a minimum. Even today, Bravo remains an iconic figure to many *Isleños* (ees-*lay*-nyos); his statue can be found where Avenida Rueda Medina becomes the Carretera Garrafón, and there's a museum named after him on nearby Isla Contoy.

Coco Restaurant & Beach Bar
$$$ | **INTERNATIONAL** | **FAMILY** | Open daily from 7:30 am to 10 pm, this restaurant by the beach is a great spot to enjoy any meal of the day while making the most of the Caribbean lifestyle. The breakfast buffet, served Friday through Sunday, is very popular, but in the evening, the catch of the day is your best bet. **Known for:** beautiful sunset views; live music; great variety of margaritas. [$] *Average main: $320* ✉ *Av. Rueda Medina, El Pueblo* ☎ *998/274–2544* 🌐 *www.facebook.com/cocorestaurantandbeachbar.*

El Patio Casa de la Música
$$$ | **ECLECTIC** | This low-key open-air oasis in the heart of El Pueblo has chit palms and ocean grape trees wrapped in fairy lights and adorned with seashell lanterns. House specialties like chicken mole and grilled octopus are served with a choice of two side dishes. ■ **TIP→ Head to the rooftop lounge for live music and frozen mojitos.** **Known for:** live music; happy hour;

frozen mojitos. $ *Average main: MP350* ⊠ *Av. Hidalgo 17, El Pueblo* ☎ *207/514–3385* ⊕ *elpatioislamujeres.com.*

Fredy's Restaurant & Bar

$$ | **MEXICAN** | This family-run restaurant specializes in simple seafood and Mexican dishes like fajitas and oven-baked shrimp. There isn't much here in the way of decor, but the staff is friendly, the food is fresh, the beer is cold, and the value is good. **Known for:** local vibe; famous margaritas; seafood dishes. $ *Average main: MP275* ⊠ *Av. Hidalgo 13, between Avs. Matamoros and López Mateo, El Pueblo* ☎ *998/167–4000, 998/190–8183* ⊕ *www. facebook.com/restaurantfredys.*

Javi's Cantina

$$$ | **AMERICAN** | There's nothing fancy about one of Isla's most popular restaurants—think plastic tables and chairs with bright tablecloths and furnishings— but Javi's captures that island informality perfectly. Seafood is the specialty here, with cilantro-chile-lime shrimp, grilled octopus, or Alfredo lobster among the don't-miss dishes. **Known for:** courtyard dining; live music; outstanding seafood. $ *Average main: MP340* ⊠ *Av. Juárez, between Av. Madero and C. Abasolo, El Pueblo* ☎ *998/414–2055* ⊕ *javiscantina. com* ☾ *Closed Wed. No lunch.*

La Lomita

$$ | **MEXICAN** | This hole-in-the-wall, with its red plastic tables and chairs, is a perennial local favorite. Expect enormous portions of the beloved *sopa de frijoles* (black bean soup made with onions, tomatoes, lime, and fresh cheese) and *chiles rellenos* (stuffed chiles lightly battered, fried, and served with a side of pickled cabbage and rice). **Known for:** best chicken mole on the island; seafood dishes; no-frills setting. $ *Average main: MP150* ⊠ *Av. Juárez Sur 25B, at Av. Allende, El Pueblo* ☎ *998/939–2331* ⊕ *www. facebook.com/RestaurantLaLomita.*

★ Lola Valentina

$$$ | **CARIBBEAN** | **FAMILY** | Chef Lori Dumm provides a unique take on Caribbean-fusion cuisine here, creating all of her own recipes and making every menu item from scratch. Starters like hibiscus flower empanadas served with avocado-xnipec dipping sauce make way for fried fish of the day served with jasmine rice and passion-fruit sauce or coconut shrimp with grilled pineapple. **Known for:** passion-fruit salmon; decadent breakfasts; Cuban salsa. $ *Average main: MP340* ⊠ *N. Av. Hidalgo 27, El Pueblo* ☎ *998/104–7643* ⊕ *www.facebook.com/lolavalentinaislamujeres* ⊟ *No credit cards.*

★ Olivia

$$$ | **MEDITERRANEAN** | The delightful dishes at this Mediterranean restaurant are combinations of Moroccan, Greek, and Turkish flavors based on owners Lior and Yaron Zelzer's family recipes. Start with the Greek or Moroccan tapas and move on to house favorites like the shawarma pita wrap filled with grilled chicken, hummus, tahini, and fried eggplant or the *moussaka,* a Balkan casserole with layers of ground beef and eggplant baked in a Parmesan béchamel sauce. **Known for:** homemade pastries; romantic setting; cherry ice cream. $ *Average main: MP315* ⊠ *Matamoros 11, between Avs. Juárez and Rueda Medina, El Pueblo* ☎ *998/877–1765* ⊕ *www.olivia-isla-mujeres.com* ⊟ *No credit cards* ☾ *Closed Sun. and 3–4 wks. in Sept. and/or Oct. No lunch.*

Qubano

$$ | **CUBAN** | This delightful restaurant is known for its delicious Cuban food. The grilled tostones sandwiches, which use fried plantains instead of bread, are topped with a finger-licking onion-and-orange sauce, and the juicy hamburgers are stuffed with goat cheese and served with yucca fries. **Known for:** Cuban food; amazing mojitos; vegetarian options. $ *Average main: MP220* ⊠ *Av. Hidalgo, across from Angelo, El Pueblo*

☎ *998/214–2118* 🌐 *www.facebook.com/qubanorestaurant* ⏲ *Closed Sun.*

Coffee and Quick Bites

Gelateria Montebianco
$ | **ICE CREAM** | **FAMILY** | Run by an Italian couple who have lived on the island since 2005, Gelateria Montebianco serves a wide variety of gelatos, as well as tasty desserts like tiramisu. It's the place to take a break and enjoy what many consider the best ice cream on the island. **Known for:** variety of gelatos; delicious tiramisu; zuppa inglese. [$] *Average main: $100* ✉ *Av. Matamoros 316, El Pueblo* ☎ *998/149–3109.*

Hotels

★ Casa El Pío
$ | **HOTEL** | Off the town square, this boutique hotel is bursting with character, charm, and creativity, ideally suited for independent travelers who don't need 24-hour service but who appreciate value, comfort, and modern design. **Pros:** unlimited fresh drinking water; spotless property; excellent rates. **Cons:** no meals; adults only; minimum stay of three nights. [$] *Rooms from: $95* ✉ *Av. Hidalgo 3, between Avs. Nicolas Bravo and Allende, El Pueblo* ☎ *998/152–8669* 🌐 *casaelpio.com* 🛏 *5 rooms* 🍴 *No Meals.*

Hotel Secreto
$$ | **HOTEL** | One of Isla's few luxury boutique hotels is intimate, contemporary, and notable for its long infinity pool and its guest rooms with floor-to-ceiling windows and balconies overlooking Half Moon Bay. The most affordable accommodations are on the ground floor; those on the top floor have better views, but the four-flight climb might be too much for some. **Pros:** pool overlooks ocean; private and secure; great fitness center. **Cons:** no elevator or restaurant; rocky beach; property could use renovation. [$] *Rooms from: $178* ✉ *Half Moon Beach, Sección Rocas, Lote 11, El Pueblo* ☎ *998/877–1039* 🌐 *www.hotelsecreto.com* 🛏 *12 rooms* 🍴 *Free Breakfast.*

Mía Reef Isla Mujeres
$$$$ | **RESORT** | Situated on tiny Isla Yunque, which is connected to the northern tip of Isla Mujeres by a long wooden bridge, this is one of the island's best all-inclusive options, where many of the studios have ocean-view balconies. **Pros:** beautiful location; calm bay great for swimming; small but well-appointed spa. **Cons:** mosquitos can be a problem; some rooms lack views; uninspiring dining options. [$] *Rooms from: $457* ✉ *Calle Zazil-Ha s/n, Isla Yunque, El Pueblo* ☎ *998/999–2050, 877/243–7883 in the U.S.* 🌐 *hotelmiareefislamujeres.com* 🛏 *164 rooms* 🍴 *All-Inclusive.*

Na Balam
$$ | **HOTEL** | Elegant without being pretentious, this tranquil hotel is a true sanctuary with sandy pathways winding through a jungle setting that spills onto the beach. **Pros:** good restaurant; beautiful beach; 24-hour security. **Cons:** not all rooms are on the beach; lots of mosquitoes; Wi-Fi in common areas only. [$] *Rooms from: $150* ✉ *Calle Zazil-Ha 118, El Pueblo* ☎ *998/881–4772, 866/719–2138 in the U.S. and Canada* 🌐 *www.nabalam.com* 🛏 *35 rooms* 🍴 *Free Breakfast.*

Playa La Media Luna Hotel
$$ | **HOTEL** | This breezy palapa-roofed hotel on Half Moon Beach has rooms decorated in neutral colors, with hammocks, king-size beds, and balconies or terraces overlooking the pool and ocean beyond. **Pros:** some deluxe rooms have whirlpool tubs; nearby beach is calm and shallow; balconies with hammocks. **Cons:** pool bar seldom open; a few rooms could stand renovating; no elevator. [$] *Rooms from: $125* ✉ *Half Moon Beach, Sección Rocas, Lote 9/10, El Pueblo* ☎ *998/877–0759* 🌐 *playamedialuna.com* 🛏 *33 rooms* 🍴 *Free Breakfast.*

Rocamar Hotel Panorámico

$ | **HOTEL** | You can smell, hear, and see the ocean from the starkly minimalist, blue-and-white rooms at this hotel, which is on the eastern *malecón* (boardwalk) and is one of the few on the island that overlooks the Caribbean. **Pros:** steps from the water; helpful staff; communal lounge with TV and library. **Cons:** no elevator; not all rooms enjoy ocean views; 10-minute walk to beach. $ *Rooms from: $85* ⊠ *Av. Nicolas Bravo 2, El Pueblo* ☎ *998/877–0101* ⊕ *www.rocamar-hotel.com* ⇄ *32 rooms* ĭOĭ *No Meals.*

Selina Isla Mujeres PocNa

$$ | **HOTEL** | The first hostel in Latin America has been renovated by trendy travel and co-working brand Selina and is now the kind of place we all dreamed existed when we were young—one whose options range from cute and comfortable private rooms with en-suite baths to dorms for 4 to 12 people with shared bathrooms. **Pros:** on the beach; co-working area; daily entertainment activities. **Cons:** some rooms share bathroom; dorms of up to 12 people; no restaurant. $ *Rooms from: $148* ⊠ *Matamoros 15, El Pueblo* ☎ *998/224–1155* ⊕ *www.selina.com/mexico/isla-mujeres* ⇄ *84 rooms* ĭOĭ *Free Breakfast.*

🅨 Nightlife

★ Fayne's Bar and Grill

LIVE MUSIC | Best known for its terrific cocktails and live music, Fayne's is a brightly painted place with a hip, energetic personality. The party kicks off nightly at 8 with everything from American rock to Caribbean rhythms providing the soundtrack. Bring your dancing shoes. ⊠ *Av. Hidalgo 12A, between Avs. Mateos and Matamoros, El Pueblo* ☎ *998/877–0525* ⊕ *www.facebook.com/faynesbar.*

Jax Bar & Grill

BARS | When you're looking for live music, cold beer, good bar food, and a satellite TV that's always tuned to the current game, make tracks for Jax, open daily until 11 pm. ⊠ *Av. Adolfo López Mateos 42, near lighthouse, El Pueblo* ☎ *998/877–1218* ⊕ *www.facebook.com/jaxislamujeres.*

Snapper's

BARS | There must be a bar like Snapper's in every Mexican beach town—namely, a place where every American and Canadian visitor goes to watch their favorite sport games and enjoy a cold beer and a tasty burger. Snapper's is open every day until midnight. ⊠ *Avs. Carlos Lazo and Adolfo López Mateos, El Pueblo* ☎ *998/705–9005* ⊕ *www.snappersislamujeres.com.*

🛍 Shopping

Although Isla produces few local crafts, and its streets are filled with souvenir shops selling cheap T-shirts, garish ceramics, and a variety of objects with seashells glued onto them, amid all the junk you may find good Mexican folk art, hammocks, textiles, and silver jewelry. In terms of jewelry, which ranges from tasteful to tacky, bargains are available, but beware of street vendors—most of their wares, especially the amber, are fake.

Most stores are small family operations that don't take credit cards, but almost everyone gladly accepts U.S. dollars, albeit at a slightly disadvantageous exchange rate. Stores that do take credit cards often tack on a fee to offset the commission they must pay. Hours are generally Monday through Saturday 10–1 and 4–7, although many stores stay open during the midday siesta.

CLOTHING

Gladys Galdamez Beachwear

SWIMWEAR | Gladys Galdamez's eponymous shop carries Isla-designed and manufactured beachwear for both men and women. Select something off the rack, or bring a photograph of your dream bikini and she'll sew a bespoke version

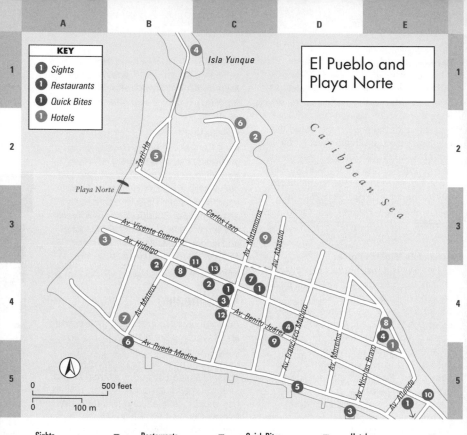

Isla Yunque

C a r i b b e a n   S e a

El Pueblo and Playa Norte

KEY
- **1** Sights
- **1** Restaurants
- **1** Quick Bites
- **1** Hotels

Playa Norte

Zazil-Ha

Carlos Lazo

Av. Vicente Guerrero

Av. Hidalgo

Av. Matamoros

Av. Abasolo

Av. Mateos

Av. Benito Juárez

Av. Francisco Madero

Av. Rueda Medina

Av. Morelos

Av. Nicolas Bravo

Av. Allende

0 ——— 500 feet
0 ——— 100 m

Sights ▼	Restaurants ▼	Quick Bites ▼	Hotels ▼
1 Aquatic Funday Park.... **E5**	1 Amigos.................... **C4**	1 Gelateria Montebianco............. **C4**	1 Casa El Pío................ **E5**
2 El Cementerio **B4**	2 Angelo **C4**		2 Hotel Secreto **C2**
3 El Malecón **D5**	3 Café Cito **C4**		3 Ixchel Beach Hotel **A3**
4 Iglesia de Concepción Inmaculada............... **E4**	4 Café Mogagua **D4**		4 Mía Reef Isla Mujeres.............. **C1**
	5 Coctelería Picus....... **D5**		5 Na Balam................ **B2**
	6 Coco Restaurant & Beach Bar **B5**		6 Playa La Media Luna Hotel................ **C2**
	7 El Patio Casa de la Música.................... **C4**		7 Privilege Aluxes......... **B4**
	8 Fredy's Restaurant & Bar..................... **B4**		8 Rocamar Hotel Panorámico **E4**
	9 Javi's Cantina **D4**		9 Selina Isla Mujeres PocNa.................... **C3**
	10 La Lomita **E5**		
	11 Lola Valentina **C3**		
	12 Olivia **C4**		
	13 Qubano.................... **C4**		

for you. ✉ *Punta Sur, Playa Caracol, entre Tortuga y Manatí, Downtown* ☎ *998/147–1115* ⊕ *www.facebook.com/Gladysbeachwear* ☯ *Closed Tues.*

CRAFTS

Galería de Arte Mexicano

JEWELRY & WATCHES | Bypass the street vendors and come directly to this lovely shop for the best quality silver in town. It also sells Talavera and custom-made jewelry at amazing prices. Don't be afraid to haggle. ✉ *Avs. Morelos and Guerrero, Sm 1, Downtown* ☎ *998/877–1272* ⊕ *www.facebook.com/GaleriaDeArteMexicano.*

Galería Elemento Arte

CRAFTS | For authentic made-in-Isla gifts—including wooden boxes, hand-carved sculptures, and ceramics—head to Galeria Elemento Arte. Jewelry is another top draw: pick your stone, setting, and clasp, then watch the masters make a custom piece before your eyes. ✉ *Av. Hidalgo, at Plaza los Almendros, El Pueblo* ☎ *998/214–0664* ⊕ *www.facebook.com/galeriaLmentoarte.*

Isla Mujeres Artist Fair

MARKET | Held every Thursday from November through April, this community event showcases the work of resident artists, designers, and authors. It's a great place to buy jewelry, clothing, and artwork or even have your palm read—all to the benefit of local nonprofits. Food vendors and musicians also take part in the fair, which runs from 4 pm to 8 pm. ✉ *Casa de la Cultura, Abasolo s/n, El Pueblo* ☯ *Closed Fri.–Wed. and May–Oct.*

Women's Beading Cooperative (*Taller Artesanias de Mujeres*)

JEWELRY & WATCHES | Nearly 60 local women are part of this beading cooperative, which creates handcrafted jewelry and sells it for a very reasonable price. It's worth the drive to the middle of the island to see these talented artisans at work. ✉ *Colonia La Gloria, Paseo de los Peces, Mz 160, Lote 5, La Gloria, Downtown* ☎ *998/161–9659* ⊕ *www.facebook.com/IslaMujeresBeadingCoop.*

GROCERY STORES

Chedraui

SUPERMARKET | FAMILY | Selling everything from food and clothing to appliances and medicine, and keeping long hours, this Mexican grocery chain is about as close as you can get to the Walmart experience. You'll find the island's best selection of groceries here. ✉ *Mid-island, at Salina Chica, Rueda Medina, Downtown* ✛ *South of the hospital, near the baseball field* ☎ *998/888–0175.*

Mercado Municipal (*Mercado Audomaro Magaña*)

MARKET | FAMILY | For fresh produce, the Mercado Municipal is your best bet. It's open daily from 6 am until 2 pm. ■ **TIP**➔ **A second market (Mercado Javier Rojo Gomez) operates during the same hours on Avenida Guerrero between Mateos and Matamoros.** ✉ *Guerrero, Sm 1, El Pueblo* ☯ *Closed Sun. and Mon.*

Super Aki

SUPERMARKET | FAMILY | One of two main grocery stores on the island, Super Aki is well stocked with all the basics and is a good in-town option if you can't make it out to Chedraui. ✉ *Av. Morelos 3, between Avs. Hidalgo and Guerrero, El Pueblo* ☎ *998/877–1092.*

Playa Norte

⊙ Sights

El Cementerio

CEMETERY | Isla's cemetery is on Avenida López Mateos, the road that runs parallel to Playa Norte. Many of the century-old gravestones are covered with carved angels and flowers, with the most elaborate and beautiful marking the graves of children. Hidden among them is the

In Search of the Dead

El Día de los Muertos (the Day of the Dead) is often described as a Mexican version of Halloween, but it's much more than that. The festival, which runs from October 31 to November 2, is a hybrid of pre-Hispanic and Christian beliefs that honors the cyclical nature of life and death. Local celebrations are as varied as they are dynamic, often laced with warm tributes and dark humor.

To honor departed loved ones at this time of year, families and friends create *ofrendas*, altars adorned with photos, flowers, candles, liquor, and other items whose colors, smells, and potent nostalgia are meant to lure spirits back for a family reunion. The favorite foods of the deceased are prepared with extra spice so that the souls can absorb the essence of the offerings. Although the ofrendas and the colorful *calaveritas* (sugar skulls and skeletons) are common everywhere, the holiday is observed in so many ways that a definition of it depends entirely on what part of Mexico you visit. In the Yucatán Peninsula, the cultural center of Mérida is where most people gather to honor the dead.

On Isla Mujeres, reverence is paid at the historic cemetery, where locals like Marta rest on a fanciful tomb in the late-afternoon sun. "She is my sister," Marta says, motioning toward the teal-and-blue tomb. "I painted this today." Instead of mourning, she's smiling, happy to be spending the day with her sibling.

Nearby, Juan puts the final touches—vases made from shells he's collected—on his father's colorful tomb. A glass box holds a red candle and a statue of the Virgin Mary, her outstretched arms pressing against the glass as if trying to escape the flame. "This is all for him," Juan says, motioning to his masterpiece, "because he is a good man."

tomb of the notorious Fermín Mundaca de Marechaja, a 19th-century slave trader—often billed more glamorously as a pirate—who carved his own skull-and-crossbones gravestone with the ominous epitaph: "As you are, I once was; as I am, so shall you be." Ironically, his remains actually lie in Mérida, where he died. The monument is tough to find, so ask a local to point out the marker. ⊠ *Av. López Mateos, Sm 1, Playa Norte* ☎ *998/877–0082* ⊕ *islamujeres.gob.mx* ⊠ *Free.*

El Malecón
PROMENADE | FAMILY | To enjoy the drama of Isla's western shore while soaking up some rays, stroll along this 1½-km-long (1-mile-long) boardwalk. It runs from the Ultramar pier to Playa Norte and has several benches and lookout points. Check out El Monumento del Marlin Azul y la Barracuda (Blue Marlin and Barracuda Monument) along the way. ⊠ *Av. Rueda Medina s/n, Playa Norte* ⊠ *Free.*

🏖 Beaches

★ Playa Norte (*North Beach*)
BEACH | FAMILY | North Beach is easy to find: simply head north on any of the north–south streets in town until you hit it. The turquoise sea is as calm as a lake here, though developers have built along most of the coast. The small cove between Mia Reef Resort and the Caribbean is the nicest section. Relatively shallow, the water flows directly from the open sea, so it's clean and good for

Playa Norte is a superb beach for strolling in the sun.

snorkeling; tour guides often lure the fish with food. A food or drink purchase from the Playa Norte Beach Club gives you access to beach beds and changing facilities at Privilege Aluxes Resort. Alternately, you can enjoy a libation at one of the palapa bars where wooden swings take the place of bar stools; Buho's is especially popular, as MX$100 lounge chairs and MX$200 beach beds come with a free drink ticket. At Sunset Grill, lounge chairs, umbrellas, towels, toilets, and showers are included when you spend MX$300 on food or drink. **Amenities:** food and drink; parking; showers; toilets. **Best for:** snorkeling; sunset; swimming; walking. ✉ *Calle Zazil-Há, Playa Norte* ✥ *Along the northern end of the island, just before Mia Reef Resort* 🎫 *Free.*

Hotels

Ixchel Beach Hotel

$$$ | **HOTEL** | With a location—on a beach with clear, calm water—that can't be beat, this property consists of two condo-style buildings that face one another—the slightly newer, five-story East Wing has 48 units, and the six-story West Wing has 69 units. **Pros:** reasonable rates; on-site restaurant; beachfront. **Cons:** small pool; no meals; some rooms are very humid. [$] *Rooms from: $248* ✉ *Calle Guerrero, Sm 1, Playa Norte* ☎ *998/802–1014 Ext. 2, 800/638–5061 in the U.S. and Canada* 🌐 *www.ixchelbeachhotel.com* 🛏 *117 rooms* 🍴 *No Meals.*

Privilege Aluxes

$$$ | **ALL-INCLUSIVE** | Perched on the sugary shores of Playa Norte, this five-story resort is one of the island's largest and one of the few to offer an all-inclusive plan. **Pros:** excellent location; Wi-Fi on the beach; spa and gym. **Cons:** some rooms have cemetery views; standard rooms lack tubs; adults only. [$] *Rooms from: $229* ✉ *Av. López Mateos, Playa Norte* ☎ *998/848–8470* 🌐 *www.privilegehotels.com* 🛏 *124 rooms* 🍴 *All-Inclusive.*

Who Was Ixchel?

Ixchel (ee-*shell*) is a principal figure in the pantheon of Mayan gods. Sometimes called the "Rainbow Goddess" or the "Red Goddess," she is the patroness of childbirth, fertility, and healing, and is said to control the tides and all water on Earth. Originally married to the Earth god Voltan, Ixchel fell in love with the moon god Itzamna, considered the founder of the Maya because he taught them how to read, write, and grow corn. When Ixchel became his consort, she gave birth to four powerful sons known as the Bacabs, who continue to hold up the sky in each of the four directions.

Often portrayed as a wise crone, Ixchel can be seen wearing a skirt decorated with crossbones and a crown of serpents while carrying a jug of water. The crossbones are a symbol of her role as the giver of new life and keeper of dead souls. The serpents represent her wisdom and power to rejuvenate, and the water jug alludes to her dual role as both a benign and destructive deity. Although she gives mankind the continual gift of water—the most essential element of life—according to Mayan myth Ixchel also sent floods to cleanse the Earth of wicked people who had stopped thanking the gods. She is said to give special protection to those making the sacred pilgrimage to her sites on Cozumel and Isla Mujeres.

Nightlife

Playa Norte Beach Club

LIVE MUSIC | Although it caters mostly to guests of the Privilege Aluxes hotel, you can also visit this architecturally modern bar that plays chill-out music by day and has live music at night, just make sure to book a table (or a palapa) in advance via email. The fish tacos are a perfect cerveza accompaniment. Try to stop by for the gorgeous sunset. ⊠ *Av. López Mateos, Playa Norte* ☎ *998/848–8470* ⊕ *www.privilegehotels.com* ⌕ *Bookings: reservations.aluxes@privilegehotels.com.*

Greater Isla Mujeres

Sights

Garrafón Natural Reef Park

REEF | **FAMILY** | Despite the widely publicized Garrafón reef restoration project, much of the coral at this national marine park is dead—the result of hurricanes, boat anchors, and too many careless tourists. There are still colorful fish, but many of them will come near only if bribed with food. Although there's not much for snorkelers anymore, the park—part nature, part amusement—does have kayaks, restaurants, zip lines, bathrooms, and a gift shop.

Be prepared to spend over $89 for the basic Royal Garrafón package, which includes snorkeling gear, breakfast, lunch, kayaks, transportation from Cancún, a bike tour, and an open bar. Another option is Dolphin Encounter ($129), which lets you use the park amenities and swim with dolphins. ■TIP→ **The neighboring Beach Club Garrafón de Castilla is a much cheaper alternative; the snorkeling is at least equal to that available in the park, and a day pass is just MX$50. You can take a taxi from town.**

El Garrafón Natural Reef Park is also home to the Santuario Maya a la Diosa Ixchel, the sad vestiges of a Mayan temple once dedicated to the goddess Ixchel. This southern point is where the

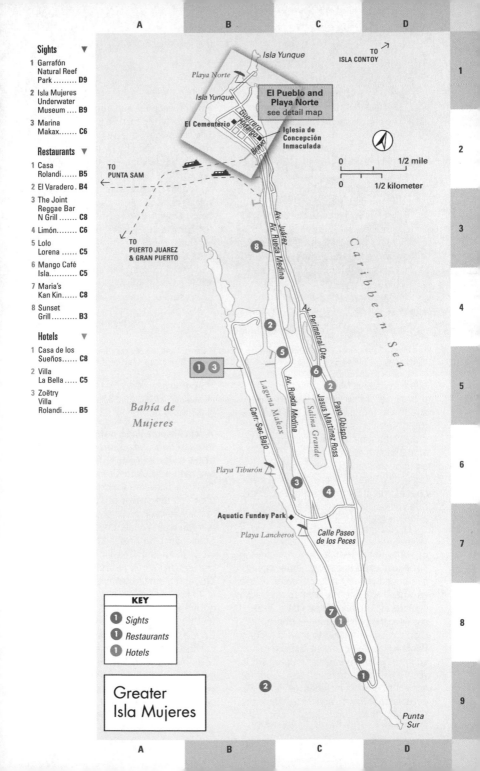

Sights ▼

1 Garrafón Natural Reef Park **D9**
2 Isla Mujeres Underwater Museum **B9**
3 Marina Makax....... **C6**

Restaurants ▼

1 Casa Rolandi...... **B5**
2 El Varadero . **B4**
3 The Joint Reggae Bar N Grill **C8**
4 Limón........ **C6**
5 Lolo Lorena **C5**
6 Mango Café Isla........... **C5**
7 Maria's Kan Kin...... **C8**
8 Sunset Grill **B3**

Hotels ▼

1 Casa de los Sueños...... **C8**
2 Villa La Bella **C5**
3 Zoëtry Villa Rolandi...... **B5**

Isla Yunque

TO ISLA CONTOY

Playa Norte

Isla Yunque

El Pueblo and Playa Norte
see detail map

El Cementerio

Iglesia de Concepción Inmaculada

Guerrero
Hidalgo
Bravo

0   1/2 mile

0   1/2 kilometer

TO PUNTA SAM

TO PUERTO JUAREZ & GRAN PUERTO

Caribbean Sea

Av. Juárez
Av. Rueda Medina

Av. Perimetral Ote.

Payo Obispo

Jesus Martinez Ross

Av. Rueda Medina

Salina Grande

Bahía de Mujeres

Laguna Makax

Carr. Sac Bajo

Playa Tiburón

Aquatic Funday Park ◆

Playa Lancheros

Calle Paseo de los Peces

KEY

1 Sights
1 Restaurants
1 Hotels

Greater Isla Mujeres

Punta Sur

The Museo Subacuático de Arte (MUSA), off the coasts of Cancún and Isla Mujeres, has more than 480 underwater sculptures—including a full-scale VW Beetle made from 8 tons of pH-neutral concrete.

sun first rises in Mexico, meaning that thousands of travelers make a pilgrimage to the temple on New Year's to see the country awaken. A lovely walkway around the area remains, but the natural arch beneath the ruin has been blasted open and repaired with concrete badly disguised as rocks. The views are spectacular, though: you can look to the open ocean, where waves crash against dramatic cliffs on one side and the Bahía de Mujeres (Bay of Women) on the other.

En route to the temple there's a cutesy Caribbean-style shopping center selling overpriced jewelry and souvenirs, as well as a park with brightly painted abstract sculptures. The ruins (open daily 9–5) are near the old lighthouse, where the road turns northeast into the Corredor Panorámico. You can visit just the ruins and the sculpture park for roughly $4; if you've paid the admission to El Garrafón, access to them is included. ⊠ *Punta Sur, southeast of Playa Lancheros, Carretera Garrafón, Km 6, Sm 9, Mz 41, Lote 12,*

Downtown ☎ *800/727–5391 toll-free in Mexico, 866/393–5158 in the U.S.* ⊕ *www.garrafon.com* ✉ *$89.*

★ **Isla Mujeres Underwater Museum** (*Museo Subacuático de Arte/MUSA*) **OTHER MUSEUM | FAMILY |** Combining art and nature, sculptor Jason de Caires Taylor has created "underwater museums" off the shores of Punta Cancún, Punta Nizuc, and Manchones Reef near Isla Mujeres. Locally known as Museo Subacuático de Arte (MUSA), his main work features more than 480 lifelike statues that serve as artificial reefs to attract marine life. Within the 12 galleries is *The Silent Evolution*, a 120-ton work of more than 400 individual statues, as well as *Anthropocene*, a full-scale VW Beetle made from 8 tons of pH-neutral concrete. The displays have conveniently been placed in shallow areas for viewing by divers, snorkelers, and glass-bottom boats. The unusual artificial habitat also helps restore the natural reefs that have suffered damage over the years. Most local dive shops can organize excursions to the site starting at $95. ✉ *Punta Cancún, Punta Nizuc, and Manchones Reef in Isla Mujeres, Isla Mujeres* ☎ *998/206–0182* 🌐 *musamexico.org* 🎟 *From $95.*

Marina Makax

MARINA/PIER | Pirates are said to have anchored their ships in this lagoon while waiting to ambush hapless vessels crossing the Spanish Main. Today it houses a local marina and provides a safe harbor for boats during hurricane season. ✉ *Carretera Garrafón, Mz 121, Lote 5, Col. El Cañotal, Downtown* ↕ *About 2½ km (1½ miles) south of town* ☎ *998/888–0973* 🌐 *marinamakaxcancun.com.*

Beaches

Playa Lancheros (*Boatman's Beach*)

BEACH | FAMILY | On the western side of the island, this stretch between Laguna Makax and Garrafón Natural Reef Park is a popular spot with an open-air restaurant where locals gather to eat freshly grilled *tikin xic* (whole fish marinated with *adobo de achiote* and sour oranges, then wrapped in a banana leaf and cooked over an open flame). Playa Lancheros has grittier sand than Playa Norte but more palm trees. Calm water makes it good for children, but keep them close to shore as the bottom drops off steeply. Souvenir stands here are fairly low-key, and most bars and restaurants will give you access to their beach facilities provided you order a drink. The closest hotel is Isla Mujeres Palace, an all-inclusive resort open to hotel guests only. **■TIP→ There's a small pen with tame *tiburones gatos* (nurse sharks). You can swim with them or just get your picture taken for an MX$20 tip. Amenities:** food and drink; parking (no fee); showers; toilets; water sports. **Best for:** snorkeling; sunset; swimming. ✉ *Carretera Garrafón, Km 4.6, near Hacienda Mundaca, Downtown.*

A Shell House?

When exploring the southeastern tip of Isla Mujeres, be sure to check out the unique house located on Corredor Panorámico. Owned by artist Octavio Ocampo, it resembles an enormous conch shell both inside and out.

Playa Tiburón (*Shark Beach*)

BEACH | FAMILY | Like Playa Lancheros, this beach on the west side of the island faces Bahía de Mujeres, so the water is exceptionally calm. Once a respite from the crowds, it has become more developed, with a large restaurant (through which you actually enter the beach) that serves burgers, hot dogs, and fish. There are several souvenir stands selling handmade seashell jewelry. On certain days you can find women who will braid your hair or give you a henna tattoo. Many people visit to swim or take photos with tame nurse sharks (MX$50), but the tiny pen entrapping the large creatures is rather sad. **■TIP→ Although there are public restrooms, you have to pay for toilet paper. Amenities:** food and drink; parking (no fee); toilets; water sports. **Best for:** snorkeling; sunset; swimming. ✉ *Carretera Sac Bajo, Downtown.*

Restaurants

★ Casa Rolandi

$$$$ | ITALIAN | This quietly sophisticated hotel restaurant has an open-air dining room connected to a deck overlooking the water. A northern Italian menu includes wonderful carpaccio *di tonno alla Giorgio* (thin slices of tuna with extra-virgin olive oil and lime juice), along with excellent pastas. **Known for:** fine dining; seafood risotto; spectacular views. [$] *Average main: MP420* ✉ *Zoëtry Villa Rolandi, Fracc. Laguna Mar, Sm 7, Mz 75,*

Isla's Salt Mines

The ancient salt mines in Isla's interior were worked during the Postclassic period of Mayan history (roughly AD 1000–1500). Salt was an important commodity for the Maya, who used it not only for preserving and flavoring food but also for making armor. Since the Maya had no metal, they soaked cotton cloth in salt until it formed a hard coating.

There's little to see today: simply two shallow marshes called Salina Chica (Small Salt Mine) and Salina Grande (Big Salt Mine) with murky water and quite a few mosquitoes at dusk. But since both of the island's main roads (Avenida Rueda Medina and the Corredor Panorámico) pass by them, you can have a look on your way to other parts of Isla.

Lotes 15 and 16, Downtown ☎ 998/999–2000 🌐 www.hyattinclusivecollection.com ☞ Reservations required.

El Varadero

$$ | **CUBAN** | Located off the beaten path, in a weathered, palapa-topped fisherman's cottage, this local favorite is known for its fresh mojitos, but its reasonably priced, family-style plates of grilled or fried fish are an even bigger draw. The day's catch might include anything from grouper to lobster (order them with creole sauce if it's being served). **Known for:** lobster; Cuban specialties; early dinners. [$] *Average main: MP275 ✉ Calle 16 de Septiembre, Sm 3, Col. Electricistas, Downtown ☎ 998/877–1600 ⏲ Closed Mon.*

The Joint Reggae Bar N Grill

$$ | **CARIBBEAN** | One of the island's coolest and liveliest spots has an eclectic Caribbean, Mexican, seafood menu that includes gems such as jerk chicken skewers and buffalo shrimp, as well as delicious pizzas at the adjacent Pizza Joint. The main attraction, though, is the live music—particularly reggae and other Caribbean styles—which plays almost nonstop. **Known for:** live reggae bands; best pizzas in the island; special events. [$] *Average main: MP240 ✉ Col. Mar Turquesa Sm 9, Mz 42, Carretera Garrafón, El Pueblo ☎ 998/243–4475 🌐 thejointisla.com.*

★ Limón

$$$$ | **MEXICAN** | Inspired by "mom's recipes," chef Sergio makes freshness a top priority—nothing here is ever frozen. The Mexican-fusion menu features dishes like slightly sweet hibiscus-filled tacos, impressive tomato towers with mozzarella cheese, and shrimp with a four-chile sauce. **Known for:** Maya fusion; grilled fish and steaks; pineapple flambé. [$] *Average main: MP450 ✉ Colonia la Gloria, Calle Lizeta 159, near Super Express, Downtown ☎ 998/130–1924 🌐 limonislamujeres.com 💳 No credit cards ⏲ Closed weekends. No lunch.*

★ Lolo Lorena

$$$$ | **MEDITERRANEAN** | Join the dinner party at Lolo's, where the multicourse, prix-fixe menu varies each night but might include lobster carpaccio or gnocchi with truffle sauce, served in an outdoor courtyard. There are a few catches, though—you must bring your own wine (there's no corking fee), dining is at communal tables, and you must make reservations. **Known for:** strict reservation policy; unique dining experience; Lolo, a local celebrity. [$] *Average main: MP700 ✉ Av. Rueda Medina 484, Downtown ☎ 998/704–4392 🌐 www.facebook.com/lololorena62 ⏲ Closed June–Aug. No lunch.*

★ Mango Café Isla

$$ | ECLECTIC | FAMILY | Warm and inviting, with wooden tables and colorful chalkboards announcing the day's aguas frescas, this 10-table hot spot is a must if you're looking for an unbeatable breakfast or lunch. Standouts include traditional chiles rellenos, fish tacos, and delicious French toast. **Known for:** Mexican-inspired classics; massive portions; vegan menu. $ *Average main: MP180* ✉ *Payo Obispo, Lote 1, Suite 725, across from Guadalupe Church, Isla Mujeres* ☎ *998/274–0118* ⊕ *www.facebook.com/ mangocafeisla* ☺ *No dinner.*

Maria's Kan Kin

$$$ | SEAFOOD | The difference between a memorable evening here and an unforgettable one is reserving a table for two at the water's edge—otherwise, you'll be sitting beneath a palapa roof overlooking an infinity pool and the crystal bay, which is, of course, a spectacular runner-up. The minimal menu presents the best local seafood in dishes like red snapper with herb sauce; shrimp skewers with lime; and grouper with tomatoes, olives, and basil. **Known for:** grilled lobster; caramel lava cake; unbelievable setting. $ *Average main: MP340* ✉ *Carretera Garrafón, Km 4.5, Isla Mujeres* ☎ *998/877–0015* ⊕ *www.mariaskankin.com.*

Sunset Grill

$$$$ | SEAFOOD | FAMILY | With an enormous menu (as well as a kids' menu) to satisfy every appetite, this elegant palapa restaurant is the perfect place to savor the sunset. The wide range of dinner dishes includes grilled tuna, coconut shrimp, paella, and grouper in a creamy dill-and-wine sauce. **Known for:** romantic ambience; oceanfront dining; fresh seafood. $ *Average main: MP440* ✉ *Av. Rueda Medina, Sm 2, Mz 88, Lote 9, El Pueblo* ☎ *998/865–4148* ⊕ *sunsetgrill. com.mx* ☺ *Closed Tues. No lunch.*

🛏 Hotels

★ Casa de los Sueños

$$$ | HOTEL | Walking into the open-air sunken lobby of this gorgeous hotel feels like walking into a friend's fabulous vacation hacienda—it's colorful and cozy, yet modern and chic. **Pros:** exceptional breakfast served until noon; three swimming pools; intimate atmosphere. **Cons:** not child-friendly; far from town; no beach. $ *Rooms from: $213* ✉ *Fracc. Turquesa, Lote 9A and B, Isla Mujeres* ☎ *998/877–0708* ⊕ *hotelcasasuenos.com* ⤴ *12 rooms* ❑ *Free Breakfast.*

Villa La Bella

$$$ | B&B/INN | This romantic, laid-back B&B on the east coast has fantastic sea views and funky designs—bungalow rooms are equipped with king-size beds and conch showerheads and bamboo faucets, rooms with palapa roofs have beds swinging from ropes, and the grounds feature remarkable stonework. **Pros:** welcoming owners; relaxing atmosphere; tasty breakfasts. **Cons:** taxi ride from downtown; kids under 18 not allowed; no on-site restaurant. $ *Rooms from: $220* ✉ *Av. Perimetral Oriente, Sm 4, Mz 91, Isla Mujeres* ⊕ *villalabella. com* ✎ *info@villalabella.com* ⤴ *6 rooms* ❑ *Free Breakfast.*

Zoëtry Villa Rolandi

$$$$ | HOTEL | The luxury starts with a private yacht that delivers you to this all-inclusive hotel from Cancún's Embarcadero Marina, and it continues throughout your stay. **Pros:** attentive staff; great views; luxurious amenities. **Cons:** expensive travel experience; must drive to main town; children under 13 not allowed. $ *Rooms from: $797* ✉ *Fracc. Laguna Mar, Sm 7, Mz 75, Lotes 15 and 16, Isla Mujeres* ☎ *998/999–2000, 888/496–3879 reservations in the U.S.* ⊕ *www.hyattinclusivecollection.com* ⤴ *35 suites* ❑ *All-Inclusive.*

Shhh . . . Don't Wake the Sharks

The underwater caverns off Isla Mujeres attract reef sharks, a dangerous species. Once the sharks swim into the caves, though, they enter a state of relaxed nonaggression seen nowhere else. Naturalists have two explanations, both involving the composition of the water inside the caves, which contains more oxygen, more carbon dioxide, and less salt than usual.

According to the first theory, the decreased salinity causes the parasites that plague sharks to loosen their grip, allowing the remora fish (sharks' personal vacuum cleaners) to eat the parasites more easily. Perhaps the sharks relax to make the cleaning easier, or maybe it's the aftereffect of

a good scrubbing. Another theory is that the caves' combination of fresh- and saltwater produces a euphoria similar to the "nitrogen narcosis" scuba divers experience on deep dives.

Whatever the sharks experience while "sleeping" in the caves, they pay a heavy price for it. A swimming shark breathes automatically and without effort as water flows through its gills, but a stationary shark must laboriously pump water to continue breathing. If you dive in the Cave of the Sleeping Sharks, be cautious: many are reef sharks, the species responsible for the largest number of attacks on humans. Dive with a reliable guide and be on your best underwater behavior.

Activities

FISHING

Cooperativa Isla Mujeres

FISHING | FAMILY | This fishermen's cooperative rents boats for a maximum of four hours and six people. Excursions to Isla Contoy (lunch included) and to swim with whale sharks are also available. ⊠ Pier 7, Av. Rueda Medina, Downtown ☎ 998/240–4721 ⊕ islamujerestours. com.mx 🖾 Offshore sportfishing from $750.

Keen M International Blue Water Encounters

FISHING | Captain Anthony Mendillo Jr. runs specialized fishing trips all year round aboard several vessels, which range from 34 to 41 feet. ⊠ Sección Rocas, Punta Norte, Lote 10, Int. B2, Downtown ☎ 998/877–0759 ⊕ www. islamujeressportfishing.com 🖾 From $500 for up to 4 anglers.

Sea Hawk Divers

FISHING | If you're interested in either offshore or deep-sea fishing, try Sea Hawk Divers, which offers trips daily from 9 am to 1 pm. Scuba diving and snorkeling tours are also available. ⊠ Av. Arq. Carlos Lazo, Mz 30, Lote 19, near Playa Norte, Isla Mujeres ☎ 998/877–1233, 998/137–9585 ⊕ www.seahawkislamujeres.com 🖾 Offshore fishing from $350.

SNORKELING AND SCUBA DIVING

There are numerous dive spots on the island but make sure you follow local laws and rules to help preserve them. Coral reefs at Garrafón Natural Reef Park have suffered tremendously from a variety of factors, some unavoidable (hurricanes) and some all-too-avoidable (boats dropping anchors onto soft coral, a practice now outlawed). Some good snorkeling can be found near Playa Norte on the north end.

Isla is a good place for learning to dive, since dive areas are close to shore. Offshore, there is excellent diving and snorkeling at Xlaches (pronounced *ees-lah-chays*) reef, due north on the way to Isla Contoy. One of Contoy's most alluring dives is a cave full of sharks off the northern tip. Discovered in 1969 by a local fisherman, the cave was extensively explored by Ramón Bravo, a local diver, cinematographer, and Mexico's foremost expert on sharks. It's a fascinating 150-foot dive for experienced divers only.

At 30–40 feet deep and 3,300 feet off the southwestern coast, the coral reef known as Manchones is a good dive site. During the summer of 1994, an ecological group hoping to divert divers and snorkelers from Garrafón commissioned a 1-ton, 9¾-foot bronze cross, which was later sunk here. Named the Cruz de la Bahía (Cross of the Bay), it's a tribute to everyone who has died at sea. Another option is the Barco L-55 and C-58 dive, which visits World War II boats 20 minutes off Isla Mujeres' coast.

Most dive shops offer a variety of packages with rates depending on the time of day, location, and the number of tanks.

Carey Diving

DIVING & SNORKELING | FAMILY | You can sign on for one-tank reef dives, deep dives, and two-tank cenote dives at this popular PADI dive shop. Whale-watching, fishing, and snorkeling excursions are offered as well. ⊠ *Av. Matamoros 13A, off Av. Juárez, Downtown* ☎ *998/877–0763* ⊕ *careydivecenter.com* 🅢 *Dives from $85.*

Isla Whale Sharks

DIVING & SNORKELING | Venture into the heart of whale shark territory with Isla Whale Sharks from June 1 to September 15. Owner Ramón Guerrero García is a professional diver who has dedicated more than 20 years to researching these gentle giants. Included in the boat trip are beverages, a light snack, snorkel gear, and time at the reef and beach. Tours last approximately five hours and must be prebooked online. ⊠ *Adrian's Internet Cafe, Av. Morelos, between Avs. Guerrero and Hidalgo, Downtown* ☎ *998/845–7200* ⊕ *islawhalesharks.com* 🅢 *Dives from $150.*

Sea Hawk Isla Mujeres

DIVING & SNORKELING | FAMILY | In addition to highly regarded PADI courses, Sea Hawk Divers offers one- and two-tank dives plus special excursions to the more exotic shipwrecks and underwater museum. For nondivers, snorkel trips depart daily at 8:30 and 2:30. ⊠ *Av. Arq. Carlos Lazo, near Playa Norte, Downtown* ☎ *998/877–1233, 998/137–9585* ⊕ *www.seahawkislamujeres.com* 🅢 *Dives from $70.*

Squalo Adventures

SCUBA DIVING | One of the island's more experienced dive shops, this PADI-certified outfit offers full scuba courses, as well as one- and two-tank dives to local sites including the underwater museum. ⊠ *Av. Hidalgo, Sm 1, Mz 18, Lote 27, between Matamoros and Playa Norte, Downtown* ☎ *998/274–1644* ⊕ *squaloadventures.com* 🅢 *Dives from $95.*

Side Trip to Isla Contoy

30 km (19 miles) north of Isla Mujeres.

The national wildlife park and bird sanctuary of Isla Contoy (Isle of Birds) is just 6 km (4 miles) long and less than 1 km (about ½ mile) wide. The whole island is a protected area, with visitor numbers carefully regulated to safeguard the flora and fauna. Sand dunes rise as high as 70 feet along the east coast, which is edged by black rocks and coral reefs. The west coast is fringed with sand, shrubs, and coconut palms.

More than 150 bird species—including gulls, pelicans, petrels, cormorants, cranes, ducks, flamingos, herons, doves, quail, spoonbills, and hawks—fly this way in late fall, some to nest and breed. Although the number of species is diminishing, partly as a result of human traffic, Isla Contoy remains a treat for bird-watchers.

The island is rich in sea life as well. Snorkelers will see brilliant coral and fish, while 5-foot-wide manta rays are visible in the shallow waters. All around the island are large numbers of shrimp, mackerel, barracuda, flying fish, and trumpet fish. In December, lobsters pass through in great (though diminishing) numbers on their southerly migration.

GETTING HERE AND AROUND

The trip to Isla Contoy takes 45 minutes to 1½ hours, depending on the weather and the boat, and costs $130. Everyone landing has to purchase a MX$80 authorization ticket, though this is usually included in the price of a guided tour. The standard excursion begins with a fruit breakfast on the boat and a stopover at Xlaches reef on the way to Isla Contoy for snorkeling (gear is included). As you sail, your crew trolls for the lunch it will cook on the beach: anything from barracuda to snapper (beer and soda are also included). While the catch is being barbecued, you have time to explore the island, snorkel, check out the small museum and biological station, or just laze under a palapa.

The island is officially open to a maximum of 200 visitors daily 9–5:30; overnight stays aren't allowed. Other than the birds and the dozen or so park rangers who live here, the island's only residents are iguanas, lizards, turtles, hermit crabs, and boa constrictors. Amigos de Isla Contoy (Friends of Isla Contoy ☎ 998/884–7483 in Cancún), a private foundation, jointly administers the park with the Mexican government.

TOURS

Cooperativa Isla Mujeres

BOAT TOURS | FAMILY | Daily boat trips from Isla Mujeres to Isla Contoy for 6–12 people are available through this local cooperative. ⌂ Pier 7, Av. Rueda Medina, Isla Contoy ☎ 998/240–4721 ⊕ islamujerestours.com.mx ✉ $130 per person.

Delfin Diving

BOAT TOURS | FAMILY | Besides offering scuba diving tours and courses, this company can take you to swim with the whale sharks, to see the dolphins, or to visit the nearby and protected Isla Contoy. The tour to the island includes continental breakfast, stingray encounters, and time to relax on the beaches of this natural paradise where you also get to enjoy a grilled fish lunch. ⌂ Calle 16 de Septiembre, El Pueblo ☎ 998/578–7097 ⊕ delfindiving.net ✉ $85.

Chapter 5

THE RIVIERA MAYA

Updated by
Luis F. Dominguez

⊙ Sights	🍴 Restaurants	🛏 Hotels	🛍 Shopping	🍸 Nightlife
★★★★★	★★★★★	★★★★★	★★★☆☆	★★★☆☆

WELCOME TO THE RIVIERA MAYA

TOP REASONS TO GO

★ **Tulum:** Only an hour south of Playa del Carmen, the ruins are a dramatic remnant of a sophisticated pre-Columbian people overlooking the Caribbean—one of Mexico's classic views.

★ **Casting for bonefish:** These elusive shallows dwellers, off the Chinchorro Reef near the Reserva de la Biósfera Sian Ka'an, can match wits with even the most seasoned fly-fisherman.

★ **Relaxing at a spa:** The Riviera Maya is flush with luxurious spas, some incorporating native ingredients and ancient rituals into their treatments.

★ **Snorkeling and diving outer reefs and cenotes:** The Mesoamerican Barrier Reef, Banco Chinchorro, and freshwater cenotes (cavernous sinkholes) are teeming with marine life.

★ **Soaking up local culture:** Cradled between mangrove and sea, the quaint fishing village of Puerto Morelos has maintained its authenticity despite neighboring growth.

1 Bahía Petempich (Punta Tanchacté). The Riviera Maya starts on this wide and beautiful beach.

2 Puerto Morelos. Sleepy fishing village.

3 Punta Brava. Long and secluded beach at the south end of Puerto Morelos.

4 Playa del Secreto. Considered by many as the Riviera Maya's best beach.

5 Punta Maroma. Stunning beach with restricted access.

6 Mayakoba. Glitzy resort enclave.

7 Punta Bete (Xcalacoco). One of Playa del Carmen's most popular beaches.

8 Playa del Carmen. One of Latin America's fastest-growing cities, this lively community has a plethora of shops, hotels, restaurants, and beach clubs.

9 Xcaret. Combining cultural activities and ecological theme parks, the area around Xcaret offers much more than sun and sand.

10 Puerto Aventuras. This Americanized beach community promises good snorkeling plus plenty of hotels and restaurants with all the creature comforts you'd expect back home.

11 Xpu-Há. Solitude and tranquility abound on the barren coastlines at Xpu-Há.

12 Akumal. Beautiful bay perfect for snorkeling and swimming with turtles.

13 Tankah. In this quiet town, the favorite pastime is swinging in a hammock.

14 Tulum. Eco-friendly Tulum combines breathtaking ruins with bohemian-chic beach hangouts.

15 Cobá. The less-visited (but more impressive) pyramids at Cobá are surrounded by jungle.

16 Reserva de la Biósfera Sian Ka'an. Coastal mangrove forests dotted with cenotes give way to dense inland vegetation in Mexico's second-largest wilderness reserve.

17 Felipe Carrillo Puerto. Small Maya village away from the beaches and the mass tourism.

18 Bacalar. Spectacular lagoon of seven colors.

19 Chetumal. Capital city of the state of Quintana Roo.

20 Mahahual. Gorgeous beach town already recognized as "the next Tulum."

21 Xcalak. The Riviera Maya ends on this quaint fishing village.

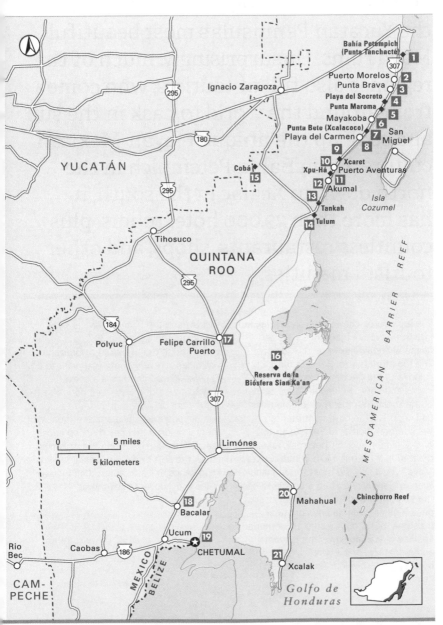

Mexico's Caribbean coast is full of treasures, from spectacular white-sand beaches and offshore reefs to some of the Yucatán Peninsula's most beautiful Maya ruins. Unsurprisingly, much of the region is also full of tourists, who come from around the world to bask in the sun and soak up the unique Mayan-Mexican culture. From Bahía Petempich in the north down to Xcalac in the south, it has more than 23,000 hotel rooms, plus countless restaurants, shops, and other tourist amenities.

The entire area can essentially be divided into three types of terrain: developed coast, national reserve, and wild coast. The top stretch from Bahía Petempich to Tulum has the greatest concentration of sights and services, and includes some of the Yucatán's most memorable ruins and cenotes. The bottom stretch, from the southern border of Sian Ka'an to Xcalak (and inland to Chetumal), is where civilization thins out. Here in the "Costa Maya" you'll find the most alluring landscapes. Sandwiched between the two is the sprawling wilderness of the Reserva de la Biósfera Sian Ka'an: a pristine preserve that is both a shelter for myriad species of wildlife (including jaguars and manatees) and a window to a time before resort development changed this coast forever.

Discovering the Riviera Maya is easy. One road, the Carretera 307, cuts all the way through to the border of Belize and will take you everywhere you want to go. The well-paved conduit is a convenient way to cover long distances between sights, but on your journey there's little to see beyond road signs and the monumental resort entrances marking access roads. Although exploring the region is about the soft sway of palms along sparkling sands, it's also about the highway miles you'll cover to get there.

Planning

When to Go

Peak season is November through April. The coastal weather is heavenly, with temperatures of 27°C (80°F) and near-constant ocean breezes. Hotel rates reflect increased demand from sun-starved northerners, especially in Playa del Carmen. During Christmas week, they often increase by 50% and hoteliers request a minimum five-night stay. If you're planning a Christmas vacation, you'd do well to book six months in advance.

June, September, and October are low season. September and October bring the worst weather, with frequent rain, mosquitoes, and the risk of hurricanes. There's also often rain in June. Breezes disappear, and humidity soars, especially inland. But if you're looking for a spa getaway and don't mind the weather outside, you'll be able to find real deals on accommodations during these months. Just keep in mind that some of the Riviera Maya's best restaurants and boutique hotels shut down during September, while larger resorts undergo renovation.

In May, July, and August, off-season prices and sunny skies make late spring and midsummer a great time to save on airfares and hotels, while having the beach to yourself.

PLANNING YOUR TIME

One week will give you enough time to enjoy the beach and explore many of the best parts of the Riviera Maya. If you use Playa del Carmen as a base, you can easily take day trips to the Xcaret theme park or Tulum's beachfront Maya ruins.

Don't miss swimming in one of the numerous cenotes along Carretera 307. The beaches at Paamul and Xpu-Há are also within driving distance, as is the Maya village of Pac Chen, the ruins at Cobá, and the Reserva de la Biósfera Sian Ka'an.

Getting Here and Around

BUS

Fifteen first-class ADO buses per day depart from Cancún between 6 am and midnight, stopping incrementally at Puerto Morelos, Playa del Carmen, Tulum, Felipe Carrillo Puerto, Limones, and Chetumal. The full trip from Cancún to Chetumal takes just over six hours and costs between MX$500 and MX$700, depending on the time of day.

CONTACTS ADO. ✉ *Quinta Av. Norte, Lote 2, Centro* ☎ *984/873–0109 in Playa del Carmen, 983/832–5110 in Chetumal* ⊕ *ado.com.mx.*

CAR

Exploring the Riviera Maya by car is easy. The entire coast from Cancún to Chetumal is connected by one highway, Carretera 307, which leads to many attractions as well as towns and cities. Indeed, sections of the highway are sometimes referred to by the towns it connects: Carretera Playa del Carmen–Tulum, Carretera Tulum–Chetumal, etc.

Between Cancún and Tulum the highway has four divided lanes, and after Tulum it's two, but it's in excellent condition the whole way. Addresses along the highway but outside towns are usually referred to by kilometer markers on small, white, upright signs at the side of the road.

Be aware that some roads off the highway are bumpy or potholed, and the road between Mahahual and Xcalak in the extreme south can be challenging after heavy rain.

DRIVING PRECAUTIONS AND SAFETY

The most dangerous place on the Caribbean coast may be the road. Before your trip, purchase travel insurance, monitor the weather, and notify your embassy and credit card company of your whereabouts. Make a copy of your passport and leave your travel itinerary with a friend or family member. To avoid unwanted situations, steer clear of remote locations, travel with a partner, and refrain from driving long distances at night.

Carretera 307 is in excellent shape, but secondary roads can be rutted with potholes. Combine that with poor lighting, unexpected speed bumps, and the occasional big crab skittering across the road, and you've got ample reason to drive slowly and carefully.

Speed bumps, called *topes,* deserve special mention: they range from well-built and-marked tarred hills to a simple but effective thick rope laid across the tarmac. When they're marked, you'll see a yellow or white sign showing bumps or reading "TOPE." Often, however, they're not, so use caution and watch the road.

Obey speed limits: police radar and sudden decreases in speed limits are easy traps for travelers. Should you get pulled over, hand over your license and expect to get it back the next day, when you pay your ticket at the police station. Most police officers are honest, but some will pull you over just to see if you'll pay them a small "tip" to avoid the hassle—don't fall for it. In many cases you'll get off with a warning when you make it clear you're prepared for the official paperwork.

⇨ *Check out our Travel Smart chapter for more information on renting cars, road rules, and safety.*

COLECTIVOS

The large white vans with the word *Colectivo* displayed prominently on their fronts or sides are how locals get from one town to another here. You'll find them running between Cancún and Playa del Carmen and Playa del Carmen and Tulum. (If you're going from Cancún to Tulum, you'll need to take the colectivo to Playa and switch to a Tulum colectivo when you get there.)

Colectivos are cheaper and faster than buses (a ride from Playa del Carmen to Tulum will run each person about MX$45 and take about 45 minutes), but most drivers won't speak English, so be prepared to speak a little Spanish. Some seats may be without seat belts or there may be standing room only; if you ever feel uncomfortable with the seats that are left, just wait for the next colectivo to pull up (they tend to run every five minutes or so).

To take a colectivo, walk out to Carretera 307 and stand on the curb as if you were hitchhiking. When you see one, wave it down, hop on, say the name of your destination, and take an empty seat. In most cases, you'll pay when you arrive. Keep in mind that colectivos are not a good option if you have a big suitcase. They often don't have trunk areas, so the bus is a better bet if you're not traveling light.

TRAIN

The Tren Maya (Maya Train) is one of the largest infrastructure projects in Mexican history, and it's expected to serve as a tourist attraction, public transit option, and boost to the regional economy. In the Riviera Maya, the train will have stations in Puerto Morelos, Playa del Carmen, Tulum, and Bacalar, with additional stops in Xcaret, Puerto Aventuras, and Akumal along the way. It will also connect with Cancún to the north and with Chetumal to the south, covering a total of 364 kilometers (226 miles) in the Riviera Maya network.

Hotels

There's lodging for every taste and budget here, from giant all-inclusive luxury resorts to small family-run cabanas on the beach. Most are in remote areas off Carretera 307. If your accommodation choice doesn't provide good shuttle service, you may want to rent a car to visit off-site attractions or restaurants. Staying at beach areas in Playa del Carmen, Akumal, or Tulum will allow you to explore on foot from your hotel.

⇨ *Hotel reviews have been shortened. For full information, visit Fodors.com. Hotel prices are the lowest cost of a standard double room in high season.*

What It Costs in U.S. Dollars			
$	$$	$$$	$$$$
HOTELS			
under $100	$101– $200	$201– $300	over $300

Restaurants

Restaurants here vary from quirky beachside affairs with outdoor tables and palapas to more elaborate and sophisticated establishments. Dress is casual at most places, so leave your tie and jacket at home. Smaller eateries may not accept credit cards, especially in remote beach villages. Bigger ones and those in hotels normally accept plastic.

Many restaurants add *propinas* (tips) to the bill; look for a charge for "servicio." If tips aren't included, a 15% gratuity is standard. It's best to order fresh local fish—grouper, dorado, red snapper, and sea bass—rather than shellfish like shrimp, lobster, and oysters, since the latter are often flown in frozen from the Gulf. Playa del Carmen has the largest selection of restaurants.

⇨ *Restaurant reviews have been shortened. For full information, visit Fodors. com. Restaurant prices are the average cost of a main course at dinner, or if dinner is not served, at lunch.*

What It Costs in Mexican Pesos			
$	$$	$$$	$$$$
RESTAURANTS			
under MP150	MP151– MP300	MP301– MP400	over MP400

Safety

With its massive resorts and tourist-oriented beach towns, the Riviera Maya is free of most big-city dangers. Though increasingly urban, Playa del Carmen is generally safe in tourist areas, and extensive police patrols keep it that way. In the past, Playa del Carmen experienced a slight rise in crime outside the major resort areas, most of it associated with criminal groups. Regardless of this, Playa del Carmen is still more secure than most North American cities and remains among the safest areas in Mexico for vacationers. Resorts all have 24-hour security guards, and most have in-room safes.

Thanks to advances in water purification, food safety has made great strides in the last decade, but Mexicans drink bottled water, and you should, too. However, there's no need to worry about ice—it's made from purified water virtually everywhere. Look for the barrel-shaped, industrial ice cubes, just to be sure.

Tours

Maya Sites Travel Services

GUIDED TOURS | This outfit uses archaeologists and other experts to lead inexpensive tours of ancient Maya sites. ⊠ *Playa del Carmen* ☎ *505/255–2279 in U.S.,*

877/620–8715 in U.S. 🌐 *www.mayasites.com* 🎫 *From $600.*

Riviera Adventours

ADVENTURE TOURS | Cycle through the ruins at Cobá, snorkel in a cenote, or get blessed by a Maya Shaman on one of Riviera Adventours's intimate four- to nine-person half- or full-day tours. Hotel pickup anywhere between Playa del Carmen and Tulum is included. ✉ *Carretera Federal 307, Tulum* ☎ *984/127–1587* 🌐 *riviera-adventours.com* 🎫 *From $120.*

Visitor Information

Online resources can help you plan your trip. Meaning "white road" in Mayan, 🌐 *Sac-Be.com* covers everything from local beaches to environmental issues. 🌐 *TravelYucatan.com* has information on transportation, hotels, and attractions, plus travel tips for both novice and veteran travelers. If you're looking for updated info on Playa del Carmen and surrounding areas, visit 🌐 *MexicanCaribbean.travel.*

Bahía Petempich (Punta Tanchacté)

23 km (14 miles) south of Cancún, 44 km (27 miles) north of Playa del Carmen.

The Riviera Maya coast starts south of Cancún at Bahía Petempich (also known as Punta Tanchacté), where the party atmosphere fades and a feeling of tranquility takes hold. Encountering this area for the first time via monotonous Carretera 307, travelers might ask, "I came all this way for this?" But just wait—beyond those towering security gates, access roads lead to an enviable collection of resorts and, ultimately, to long expanses of white sandy strands lapped by turquoise waters. Historically a fishing village, this area has recently been overtaken by Puerto Morelos's growth, and now there are new hotels and resorts here as well. Just 20 minutes south of Cancún, Bahía Petempich is quieter than neighboring towns but still close to the action.

■ TIP→ Although all beaches in Mexico are open to the public, access isn't guaranteed. When a resort snatches a prime beachfront site, it can effectively block access to nonguests.

GETTING HERE AND AROUND

Driving north on Carretera 307, turn right at Km 328. Heading south on Carretera 307, turn left at Km 27.5. The entrance is marked by a large gate reading "Bahía Petempich." This community of resorts does not offer any facilities other than those that are available within the hotels. The nearest shops, restaurants, banks, and clinics are in Cancún and Puerto Morelos.

🛏 Hotels

Azul Beach Resort Riviera Cancún

$$$$ | **ALL-INCLUSIVE** | **FAMILY** | Situated on a beautiful beach with a protected reef just offshore, this all-inclusive family-friendly resort has six pools, eight restaurants, and several categories of rooms, including swim-up rooms and family suites that accommodate two adults and three children. **Pros:** extremely family-friendly; excellent service; good food. **Cons:** noisy restaurants; not wheelchair accessible; few adult-only spaces. [$] *Rooms from: $333* ✉ *Carretera 307, Km 27.5, Bahia Petempich* ☎ *998/872-8450, 866/527-4762 in the U.S.* 🌐 *www.karismahotels.com* 🛏 *435 suites* 🍴 *All-Inclusive.*

Haven Riviera Cancun

$$$$ | **ALL-INCLUSIVE** | At this sophisticated, adults-only sanctuary—in a secluded complex just 15 minutes south of Cancún's airport—a modern Mexican design and a natural color palette with touches of turquoise blue complement

Zoëtry Paraíso de la Bonita is a unique, truly luxurious all-inclusive resort.

the outstanding ocean views. **Pros:** custom cocktails at Limes Bar; coffee bar and pastry shop; strong Wi-Fi at pool and beach. **Cons:** some restaurants are only for Serenity Club guests; oceanfront swim-out suites shady in afternoon; some hallway noise carries into first-floor rooms. $ *Rooms from: $413* ✉ *Carr. Federal 307 km. 335, Bahia Petempich* ☎ *998/889-9600* ⊕ *www.havenresorts. com* ↻ *333 suites* ¶O¶ *All-Inclusive.*

Zoëtry Paraíso de la Bonita

$$$$ | **ALL-INCLUSIVE** | A pair of stone dragons guards the entrance to this eclectic resort, where the spacious rooms—all with sweeping sea and jungle views—are elegantly styled after worldwide destinations, Italy, Mexico, and Bali among them. **Pros:** spa included; tasteful room design; every room has ocean view. **Cons:** sales pitch during the welcome; mediocre lunch; no kids' club. $ *Rooms from: $490* ✉ *Carretera 307, Km 328, Bahia Petempich* ⊕ *Turn on hwy. at signs for Paraiso de la Bonita; follow rd. about 3 km (2 miles) for gate*

to Zoëtry ☎ *888/496–3879 in the U.S., 998/872–8300* ⊕ *www.hyattinclusivecol- lection.com* ↻ *100 suites* ¶O¶ *All-Inclusive.*

🏃 Activities

★ Thalasso Center & Spa

SPAS | The 22,000-square-foot spa at the Zoëtry Paraiso de la Bonita resort is the first certified thalassotherapy spa in the Riviera Maya, meaning many of its treatments use seawater to wash your cares away. The classic hot-cold treatment cycle will take you from sauna to steam room, cold plunge pool to warm Jacuzzi, relaxing your muscles so that you can get the maximum benefit from your massage. The extensive menu features body scrubs, saltwater hydrotherapy, and proto-Maya rituals. Although most treat- ments involve getting wet, you'll also find healing dry remedies like aromatherapy, facials, massages, and acupuncture. Spa products infused with sea kelp and marine mud are said to eliminate toxins. Pilates, wellness cooking classes, and Maya healing practices are available upon

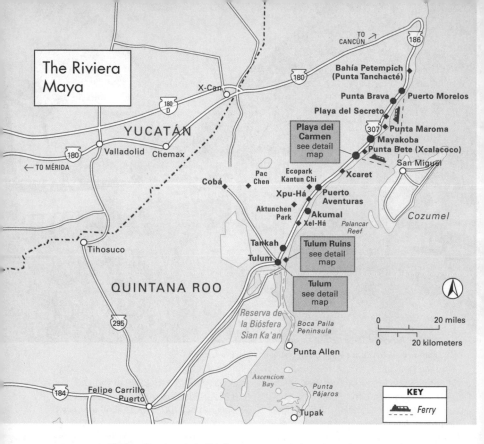

The Riviera Maya

TO CANCÚN →

Bahía Petempich (Punta Tanchacté)

Punta Brava — Puerto Morelos

Playa del Secreto

Playa del Carmen
see detail map

Punta Maroma

Mayakoba

Punta Bete (Xcalacoco)

San Miguel

YUCATÁN

X-Can

Valladolid Chemax

← TO MÉRIDA

Pac Chen

Ecopark Kantun Chi

Xcaret

Cobá

Xpu-Há

Puerto Aventuras

Aktunchen Park

Akumal

Xel-Há

Palancar Reef

Cozumel

Tihosuco

Tankah

Tulum

Tulum Ruins
see detail map

QUINTANA ROO

Tulum
see detail map

Reserva de la Biósfera Sian Ka'an

Boca Paila Peninsula

Felipe Carrillo Puerto

Punta Allen

0   20 miles

0   20 kilometers

Ascencion Bay

Punta Pájaros

Tupak

KEY

Ferry

request. ✉ *Zoëtry Paraiso de la Bonita Resort, Carretera 307, Km 328, Bahia Petempich* ☎ *998/872–8300* ⊕ *www. hyattinclusivecollection.com* ✉ *Thalasso-therapy from $69.*

Puerto Morelos

13 km (8 miles) south of Bahía Petem-pich, 32 km (20 miles) north of Playa del Carmen.

At the edge of a mangrove-tangled jungle, Puerto Morelos is one of the few coastal towns on this stretch of the Riviera Maya that's maintained a measure of authenticity. Although it's become a favorite of Canadian and American expat artists, painters, and poets, it's still essentially a salty Mexican seaside village. Environmental laws and building

restrictions have kept growth under control, nothing here has been prettied up for the gringos, and tourist traps are few and far between.

■ **TIP→ Don't miss the castle at the corner of Niños Heroes and Morelos, a carved, curvy, leaning tree-house fantasy that has to be seen to be believed.**

A wide selection of restaurants, a variety of nearby hotels, a relatively quiet beach, and a good road connecting the town with the highway make this a good base, but where Puerto Morelos really shines is out at sea. The waters here are calm and safe, and the superb Mesoamerican Barrier Reef, only 1,800 feet offshore, is an excellent place to explore with a snorkel or scuba tank.

The reef is healthy, with plenty of marine life, but it and the surrounding mangrove forests are a protected national park, so you'll also need to visit with a licensed guide and purchase a mandatory conservation bracelet (usually included in the price of the guide). Home to many species of birds, the park is also a draw for bird-watchers. (The mangroves are a haven for mosquitoes, too—bring repellent, especially after dusk.)

GETTING HERE AND AROUND

Puerto Morelos is the first major town on Carretera 307. When the center of the road rises up to an overpass, stay right, turn left underneath, and then just follow the road 2 km (1 mile) east directly to the town square and lighthouse. You can also reach Puerto Morelos by turning at the paved road at Croco Cun Zoo off Carretera 307 at Km 31. This paved road dead-ends at the entrance to Excellence Resort, where you turn right and follow the road along the mangroves to the center of town.

ADO (⊕ www.ado.com.mx) buses link Cancún, Puerto Morelos, Playa del Carmen, Tulum, Felipe Carrillo Puerto, Limones, and Chetumal. Colectivos stop along Carretera 307 just outside town.

Downtown, which can be explored by foot, is essentially the sprawling town square, bordered by Avenida Rafael Melgar at the beach, Avenida Rojo Gomez parallel, and Avenidas Tulum and Morelos to the south and north respectively. The square verges on the water, where you'll find a fisherman's shack (for boat tours) next to Pelicanos restaurant. Steps to the left take you down to the beach. The taxi stand is at the northeast corner of the square at Morelos and Rojo Gomez. Avenida Niños Heroes is the next street inland, parallel to Avenida Rojo Gomez.

TAXI CONTACTS Taxi Service. ⊠ *Sm 18, Puerto Morelos* ☎ *998/871–0090.*

Beach Safety 🏃

Deserted beaches invite thieves—never leave anything visible in your car. Remember that even the calmest-looking waters can have currents and riptides. Take note that waves are most powerful during December, and that hurricane season lasts from June into November. If visiting isolated beaches, bring sunscreen and drinking water to avoid overexposure and dehydration.

⊙ Sights

Croco Cun Zoo

ZOO | FAMILY | The biologists running the Croco Cun Zoo, an animal farm just north of Puerto Morelos, have collected specimens of many of the reptiles and some of the mammals indigenous to the area. They offer immensely informative tours—you may even get to handle a baby crocodile or feed a monkey. Be sure to wave hello to the 500-pound crocodile secure in his deep pit. ⊠ *Carretera 307, Km 31, Puerto Morelos* ☎ *998/850–3719* ⊕ *www.crococunzoo.com* ⊠ *MX$627.*

Jardín Botánico Dr. Alfredo Barrera Marín

(*Dr. Alfredo Barrera Marín Botanical Garden*)

GARDEN | This 150-acre botanical garden is the largest in Mexico. Named for a local botanist, it exhibits the peninsula's plants and flowers, which are labeled in English, Spanish, and Latin. The park features a 130-foot suspension bridge, three observation towers, and a library equipped with reading hammocks. There's also a tree nursery, a remarkable orchid and epiphyte garden, an authentic Maya house, and an archaeological site. A nature walk goes directly through the mangroves for some great birding; more than 220 species have been identified here (be sure to bring bug spray, though). Spider monkeys can usually be spotted in the afternoons, and a tree-house lookout offers a spectacular view—but the climb isn't for those afraid of heights. ✉ *Carretera 307, 1 km (½ mile) south of Puerto Morelos, Puerto Morelos* ✥ *Entrance is on northbound side of highway. From southbound side, turn around after town* ☎ *998/206–9233* 🌐 *facebook.com/JBPuertoMorelos* 🎫 *MX$150* 🕒 *Closed weekends.*

Beaches

Puerto Morelos Main Beach
BEACH | Newcomers to Puerto Morelos might be disappointed by the blankets of seaweed and boats that dock ashore—after all, this place is more about snorkeling on the reef than sunning on the sand. Your best bet is to head for the stretch of beach two blocks north of the square in front of Ojo de Agua Hotel. Park on the town square or adjacent streets. **Amenities:** food and drink; parking (no fee). **Best for:** snorkeling; walking. ✉ *North of town square, Puerto Morelos.*

Restaurants

Al Chimichurri
$$ | **SOUTH AMERICAN** | **FAMILY** | The smoky aromas of a South American *parillada* waft down the street from this Uruguayan barbecue joint. The heaping portions of short ribs, flank steak, and chorizo have developed a cult following up and down the Riviera, and locals swear by the empanadas. **Known for:** good steaks; creative empanadas; friendly staff. [$] *Average main: MP300* ✉ *Av. Javier Rojo Gomez, between Avs. Tulum and Isla Mujeres, Puerto Morelos* ☎ *998/252–4666* 🌐 *facebook.com/AlChimichurri* 🕒 *Closed Mon. No breakfast.*

Café Amancia
$ | **CAFÉ** | **FAMILY** | This colorful hangout on the corner of the main plaza is the best place in town to watch the world go by (or take advantage of free Wi-Fi) while lingering over coffee and a pastry. Most items are organic, and the fruit smoothies are delicious. **Known for:** organic fruit smoothies; vegan dishes; tasty Mexican breakfasts. [$] *Average main: MP125* ✉ *Av. Tulum at Av. Rojo Gomez, Puerto Morelos* ☎ *998/206–9242* 🌐 *cafeamancia.com* 🕒 *Closed Mon.*

★ John Gray's Kitchen
$$$ | **INTERNATIONAL** | Using only the freshest ingredients—from local fruits and vegetables to seafood right off the pier—the chefs at this jungle-side restaurant work their magic in a comfortable, contemporary setting that feels more Manhattan than Maya. Ask about the tender roasted duck breast with tequila, chipotle, and honey, or order an addictive, understated bowl of shrimp macaroni and cheese with notes of truffle. **Known for:** tuna tostadas; hamburgers and chicken wings for lunch; duck breast with honey, tequila, and chipotle sauce. [$] *Average main: MP375* ✉ *Av. Niños Heroes, 1 block north of Av. Morelos, on jungle side, Puerto Morelos* ☎ *998/871–0665* 🌐 *facebook.com/johngrayskitchen* 🕒 *Closed Sun.*

La Petita en la Playita
$$ | **SEAFOOD** | Two blocks north of the town square, the "dining room" room of this family-run eatery consists of plastic tables and chairs beneath mini palapas and tarps. What it lacks in charm it more than makes up for with food and prices—this is where locals go for seafood soup, fried fish, shrimp tacos, ceviche, and fresh guacamole. **Known for:** rice-milk horchata; toes-in-the-sand dining; closing early in the evening. [$] *Average main: MP220* ✉ *Av. Rafael Melgar, Sm 2, Puerto Morelos* ☎ *998/871–0737.*

★ La Sirena
$$$ | **INTERNATIONAL** | Overlooking the town square, La Sirena serves an eclectic mix of dishes ranging from mini sliders

and grilled grouper to hearty plates of barbecue pulled pork with shoestring fries. If you like Mediterranean food, opt for Greek specialties prepared by chef Anthony Chalas, who credits his skills to his years spent in Greece. **Known for:** Greek-style lamb chops; tequila tastings; homemade baklava. $ Average main: MP365 ⊠ Jose Maria Morelos, Sm 2, Mz 4, Lote 502, Puerto Morelos ☎ 998/293–2671 ⊕ lasirenapm.com.

Pangea Food and Music

$$ | ECLECTIC | Abutting the plaza at the beach, Pangea has it all—breakfast, lunch, and dinner served on an umbrella-shaded terrace overlooking the sea, plus live music and entertainment until late. Daily menus—all prepared with organic ingredients and without preservatives—may include grilled fresh tuna, vegetarian lasagna, or shrimp kebabs, and there's fresh ginger-lemongrass tea and pancakes for breakfast. **Known for:** fresh fish; themed menus; ginger-lemongrass tea. $ Average main: MP180 ⊠ Av. Morelos at the water, Puerto Morelos ☎ 998/159–5241 ⊕ facebook.com/pangeafoodandmusic.

★ Pelicanos Restaurant & Marina

$$ | SEAFOOD | FAMILY | Enjoy fresh seafood on the shaded patio of this family-owned restaurant in the heart of town. Try fish prepared al ajo (in a garlicky butter sauce), breaded, grilled, or tikin–xic style (marinated with adobo de achiote and sour oranges). **Known for:** fried fish by kilo; catch and cook (and eat) options; massive margaritas. $ Average main: MP275 ⊠ Av. Rafael Melgar at Av. Tulum, Puerto Morelos ☎ 998/871–0014 ⊕ www.pelicanos.com.mx.

🛏 Hotels

★ Casa Caribe & Cabañas

$ | B&B/INN | Five minutes from the town square and opposite the main beach, this charming hacienda-style bed-and-breakfast has five rooms with firm, comfortable king-size beds plus private terraces, some with partial ocean views, and six larger cabañas with kitchens. **Pros:** free beach chairs and umbrellas provided; cabañas have their own kitchen; lovely staff. **Cons:** some nighttime street noise; no pool; five-night minimum stay in high season. $ Rooms from: $95 ⊠ Av. Rojo Gómez 768, Puerto Morelos ☎ 998/251–8060 ⊕ www.casa-caribepuertomorelos.com ⟿ 11 rooms ⦿ No Meals.

Dreams Riviera Cancún

$$$$ | ALL-INCLUSIVE | FAMILY | The guest rooms at this sprawling resort—built around a lofty lobby with views across the grounds and to the sea—are lustrous, from the contemporary Mexican decor to the marble bathrooms. **Pros:** family-friendly; relatively close to the airport; plenty of activities. **Cons:** only 60% of rooms have ocean views; some visible wear and tear in guest rooms and common areas; seagrass on the beach. $ Rooms from: $427 ⊠ Carretera Federal 307, Puerto Morelos ☎ 998/872–9200, 866/237–3267 in the U.S. ⊕ www.hyattinclusivecollection.com ⟿ 486 suites ⦿ All-Inclusive.

★ Excellence Riviera Cancún

$$$$ | ALL-INCLUSIVE | Just 15 minutes from Cancún Airport, this sprawling adults-only resort is centered on an indulgent spa and six meandering pools. **Pros:** caters to honeymooners; spacious beach; rooms have private hot tubs for two. **Cons:** thin walls; adults only (18-plus); some visible wear and tear in guest rooms and common areas. $ Rooms from: $345 ⊠ Carretera Federal 307, north of Puerto Morelos, Puerto Morelos ☎ 800/953–2142, 866/211–6223 in U.S. ⊕ www.excellenceresorts.com ⟿ 440 rooms ⦿ All-Inclusive.

🛍 Shopping

Alma Libre Bookstore

BOOKS | There are more than 20,000 titles in stock at Alma Libre. You can buy outright or trade in your own books for a discount and replenish your holiday reading list. ✉ *Av. Tulum 4, Puerto Morelos* ⊕ *almalibrebookstore.com.*

Ixchel Jungle Market & Spa

MARKET | This nonprofit organization generates income for Maya women and their families. From December through April, a Sunday market features traditional dances, regional foods, and handmade crafts sold by Maya women wearing embroidered dresses. Year-round, the spa offers traditional Maya treatments such as deep-tissue massage and body wraps with aloe vera or chocolate fresh from the cacao; it's open by appointment only, with bookings at 10, noon, 2, and, when full, 4. ✉ *Villa Morelos 1, Puerto Morelos* ☎ *998/180–5424* ⊕ *www.mayaecho.com* ☉ *Closed Sun. and Mon. and May–Nov.*

Naturalmente Mexican Boutique

CRAFTS | This cute little boutique offers an interesting collection of handmade products designed by local women artists. Choose from colorful crochet bags, artisan soaps, or mystical paintings, and take an authentic piece of Puerto Morelos back with you. ✉ *Av. Tulum, under Punta Corcho restaurant, Puerto Morelos* ☎ *998/255–0261* ⊕ *www.facebook.com/naturalmentepm.*

🏃 Activities

Aquanauts Dive Adventures

SCUBA DIVING | The oldest family-run dive shop in Puerto Morelos is in the Marina El Cid resort, overlooking the ocean. It offers both scuba and snorkeling adventures at more than 40 different dive sites that range from easy reef dives to shipwreck explorations. Van service from your hotel is available for an extra fee. ✉ *Marina El Cid, Puerto Morelos* ☎ *998/126–7966* ⊕ *www.aquanauts-diveadventures.com* ☑ *2-tank dive from MX$2260.*

Selvática

ZIP-LINING | **FAMILY** | Just outside Puerto Morelos, Selvática enables you to soar over the jungle on more than 10 zip lines and a bungee swing. The highest zip is more than 12 stories above the jungle floor. The full trip—including zip lines, aerial bridges, dirt buggies, a bungee swing, a cenote swim, lunch, and transfers—takes a full day, but half-day zip line adventures are also available. Advance reservations are required. ✉ *Ruta de los Cenotes, Km 18, Puerto Morelos* ⊕ *19 km (12 miles) from turnoff on Carretera 307* ☎ *998/193–3361, 866/674-8017 in the U.S.* ⊕ *www.selvatica.com.mx* ☑ *From $69.*

Xenotes

KAYAKING | **FAMILY** | Operated by Experiencias Xcaret, Xenotes includes a trip to four cenotes where you can kayak, zip line, rappel, and snorkel. Tours begin between 8 and 10 am and take about nine hours, including transfers. Transportation, lunch, and equipment are included. Tickets for kids age 6 through 11 are half off. Only biodegradable sunscreen, makeup, and mosquito repellent are allowed during the tour. ✉ *Carretera Puerto Morelos–Leona Vicario, Km 22, Puerto Morelos* ☎ *998/883–3143, 855/326–0682 in the U.S.* ⊕ *www.xenotes.com* ☑ *$128.*

Punta Brava

5 km (3 miles) southeast of Puerto Morelos, 24 km (15 miles) north of Playa del Carmen.

Punta Brava is a long, winding sweep of sand strewn with seashells. The only direct access to this beach area is through the security gate at the Grand Velas or El Dorado Royale resorts. Past the entrance is a tropical jungle and more than 1½ km (1 mile) of coastline at

Punta Brava Beach. In an effort to calm the powerful waves, artificial sandbars have been built along the shore. Not only are these burlap sacks an eyesore, but also they have eliminated one of the few spots in the area where bodysurfing was once possible.

GETTING HERE AND AROUND

If you're heading north from Playa del Carmen, turn right into El Dorado Royale gate at Km 45. Currency exchange is available within El Dorado Royale Resort. Otherwise, the nearest banks, medical facilities, and police stations are 8 km (5 miles) north in Puerto Morelos.

Hotels

El Dorado Royale

$$$$ | ALL-INCLUSIVE | Although this beachfront property has been overshadowed by its newer neighbors, the location—amid 500 acres of lush jungle—is as alluring as ever. **Pros:** on-site health bar and ATM; sprawling property; green practices. **Cons:** slow room service; no kids under 18; rocky beach with sea grass. [$] *Rooms from: $510* ✉ *Carretera 307, Km 45, Punta Brava* ☎ *998/881–9451, 844/887–9488 in the U.S.* 🌐 *eldoradosparesorts.com* 🛏 *478 rooms* 🍴 *All-Inclusive.*

Playa del Secreto

20 km (12 miles) southwest of Punta Brava, 23 km (14½ miles) north of Playa del Carmen.

The secret is out—the ½-km (1/3-mile) stretch of white sand at Playa del Secreto is one of the most beautiful in the Riviera Maya. Surrounded by jungle and Caribbean waters, the protected shores are a favorite nesting ground for giant leatherback sea turtles weighing up to 300 pounds. From May through October, early risers can watch baby turtles struggle from their shells and skitter down to the sea.

The bordering jungle is home to foxes, deer, crocodiles, wild boars, and coatimundis. Bird-watching is excellent here, with species ranging from wild parrots and hawks to kingfishers and black-necked stilts. This coastal community is midway between Cancún and Playa del Carmen, meaning that nightclubs, shopping, and restaurants are less than 20 minutes away.

GETTING HERE AND AROUND

From Playa del Carmen, drive approximately 20 minutes north on Carretera 307 and turn right at Km 312. The entrance for Playa del Secreto is just past the Cirque du Soleil Theater. From Cancún, take Carretera 307 south. Approximately 10 km (6 miles) past Puerto Morelos, turn left at Km 312 onto the Playa del Secreto road that leads to the beach. For those staying at the Valentin resort, there's a designated entrance off Carretera 307 at Km 311. Because only private villas and a resort make up this beach community, there are no restaurants, shops, or services available. The nearest are north in Puerto Morelos.

Beaches

Playa del Secreto

BEACH | Free of rocks, seagrass, and drop-offs, Playa del Secreto is perfect for swimming, kayaking, or snorkeling. On windy days, the waves are large enough for boogie boarding or bodysurfing. At the nearby reef, divers can get down with lobster, octopus, crabs, and turtles. The powdery white sand makes it great for long walks. The stretch near Valentin Imperial Maya is especially clean, with clear warm water where fish come to eat out of your hand. Dotting the shore are vacation rentals and a private community of homeowners, meaning that there is no public access to this beach other than through the private roads off Carretera

307. Despite the fact this is a public beach, non-hotel guests will be turned away at security gates. That also means that there are no public facilities other than those offered exclusively to guests. **Amenities:** none. **Best for:** snorkeling; swimming; walking. ✉ *Carretera 307, Km 311, Playa del Secreto* ✣ *15 mins south of Cancún Airport.*

Hotels

Valentin Imperial Maya
$$$$ | **ALL-INCLUSIVE** | Nestled in thriving mangrove forests, this adults-only all-inclusive is one of the few in the region that still embraces Mexican tradition. **Pros:** enormous pools; authentic Mexican coffee; pillow menu. **Cons:** no kids under 18; slippery hallways during rainy season; evening entertainment disappointing. [$] *Rooms from: $687* ✉ *Carretera 307, Km 311.5, Playa del Secreto* ☎ *984/206–3660, 800/232–8316 in the U.S.* 🌐 *www.valentinmaya.com* 🛏 *540 rooms* 🍴 *All-Inclusive.*

Performing Arts

★ JOYÀ by Cirque du Soleil
THEATER | **FAMILY** | From the creators of Cirque du Soleil, this whimsical show follows the adventures of a rebellious teenage girl swept away to a mysterious jungle. Several ticket packages are available. ✉ *Carretera 307, Km 48, near Mayan Palace Resort, Playa del Secreto* ☎ *844/247–7837* 🌐 *www.cirquedusoleil.com* 🎟 *From MX$2,296* ⏲ *Closed Sun.*

Punta Maroma

9 km (5½ miles) southwest of Playa del Secreto, 23 km (14 miles) north of Playa del Carmen.

The waters of this protected bay stay calm even on blustery days, and the enchanting beach ranks among Mexico's finest. A string of resorts has taken advantage of its enviable position. Unfortunately, nonguests will not be able to access the beach since the only entry point is through the security gate.

GETTING HERE AND AROUND

Driving north from Playa del Carmen, turn right into the Punta Maroma gate at Km 51. Heading south from Cancún, take Carretera 307 to the east (left) turnoff at Km 306.5. Signs (and a security guard) will point you to your resort. Blue Diamond Resort is accessed by way of a private entrance at Km 298.8 off Carretera 307. Because Punta Maroma is a gated community, the only available facilities are within the resorts themselves. The closest shops, restaurants, banks, and emergency facilities are 10 minutes south in Playa del Carmen.

Beaches

Punta Maroma
BEACH | One of Mexico's most beautiful beaches has deep white sand that feels like powdered sugar and crystalline water that's free of rocks. The small waves crashing onshore make it great for bodysurfing; 10 minutes off the coast of the Blue Diamond Resort, you'll find terrific diving, too. Hotels supply lounge chairs and offer activities like volleyball, yoga, and even remote-control boat racing for guests. Unfortunately, this beach can only be accessed by way of the security gate on Carretera 307 that leads to three area resorts. Unless you plan to visit by boat or stay at one of them, you're probably out of luck. **Amenities:** food and drink; toilets (for resort guests only). **Best for:** walking. ✉ *Carretera 307, Km 306, Punta Maroma.*

Hotels

★ Belmond Maroma Resort & Spa
$$$$ | **RESORT** | Connecting jungle and beach, a labyrinth of paths threads through the grounds at this elegant, renovated-in-2023, Maya-themed hotel,

where butterflies and parrots fly, and the scent of flowers fills the air. **Pros:** exceptional beach; great place to escape the crowds; most rooms have ocean views. **Cons:** far from both Cancún and Playa del Carmen; quite expensive; difficult to find from highway. [$] *Rooms from: $2,035* ✉ *Carretera Cancún–Tulum, Km 51, Punta Maroma* ✣ *From Carretera 307, look for the peacock mural and the Burger Bar restaurant just outside the security entrance. There's no other sign* ☎ *866/454–9351 in the U.S., 984/370–0400* 🌐 *www.belmond.com* 🛏 *72 rooms* 🍴 *Free Breakfast.*

Blue Diamond Luxury Boutique Hotel
$$$$ | **ALL-INCLUSIVE** | At this resort on the south end of Maroma Beach, a 25,000-square-foot spa offers massages and body wraps made with chocolate, seaweed, and coffee, and winding paths extend over the mangroves, leading to bungalow suites that rise above the lush vegetation. **Pros:** golf carts and bikes available; huge rooms; excellent service. **Cons:** strict dress code at some restaurants; lots of mosquitoes; no children under 18. [$] *Rooms from: $367* ✉ *Carretera 307, Km 298, Punta Maroma* ☎ *984/206–4100, 833/484–0789 in the U.S.* 🌐 *www.bluediamondluxuryboutique-hotel.com* 🛏 *128 rooms* 🍴 *All-Inclusive.*

★ **Secrets Maroma Beach Riviera Cancún**
$$$$ | **ALL-INCLUSIVE** | Secrets pushes typical all-inclusive boundaries by including, well, pretty much everything—international calls, gratuities, premium drinks, greens fees at the nearby El Mayakoba Golf Course, plus a laundry list of amenities and activities like gourmet restaurants, 18 swimming pools, sailing, archery, dance classes, and tennis clinics. **Pros:** unlimited luxury; swim-up rooms; romantic property. **Cons:** dress code at all restaurants; no children under 18; huge property means walking long distances. [$] *Rooms from: $819* ✉ *Carretera 307, Km 306.5, Punta Maroma* ☎ *984/877–3641, 866/467–3273 in the U.S.* 🌐 *www.hyattinclusivecollection.com* 🛏 *412 rooms* 🍴 *All-Inclusive.*

Activities

Blue Diamond Spa
SPAS | Exclusively for guests of the Blue Diamond resort, this 25,000-square-foot spa merges ancient Maya philosophy with Asian healing rituals. Both the design and philosophy are inspired by the Maya healing elements of water, air, fire, and earth. Signature treatments include Four Hand Harmony (a four-hands massage), Temazcal Ceremony (a ritual guided by a Maya shaman), and Peace Stone Ritual (a stone massage to balance energy levels). Scrubs and wraps made with chocolate and coffee are also popular. Body treatments, ranging from one to six hours, take place in jungle palapas, Thai suites, or garden villas. ■ **TIP→ Travelers who've spent too long basking in the sun can try the sunburn remedy wrap and hydrating facial.** ✉ *Blue Diamond Riviera Maya, Carretera 307, Km 298, Punta Bete* ☎ *833/484–0789 in the U.S., 984/206–4100* 🌐 *www.bluediamondluxuryboutiquehotel.com.*

Mayakoba

13 km (8 miles) southwest of Punta Maroma, 10 km (6 miles) north of Playa del Carmen.

Mayakoba (meaning "village of water") is home to four of the world's most exclusive resorts—the Banyan Tree Mayakoba, Fairmont Mayakoba, Rosewood Mayakoba, and Andaz Mayakoba. They are connected by a network of canals that inspire the property's tagline, "the Venice of the Caribbean."

In addition to luxury lodgings, this 1,600-acre enclave supports mangrove forests, freshwater lagoons, beach dunes, and sunken cenotes. Resident wildlife includes monkeys, turtles, crocodiles, and 160 species of birds. Here, spas are perched amid jungle treetops, and thatch-roof boats drift between limestone waterways.

GETTING HERE AND AROUND

The only way to reach this resort community is by car. From Playa del Carmen, head north on Carretera 307 for approximately 15 minutes; after passing the entrance for Grand Velas, turn right at Km 298 into Mayakoba. From Cancún, take Carretera 307 south to the east turnoff at Km 298. The entrance is marked by a large metal gate with silver lettering. Security guards will direct you to the property of your choice.

Access to hotels, restaurants, spas, and the golf course are permitted by reservation only. Cars are banned, but guests can explore the jungle habitat by golf cart or bike (a paved trail connects the four properties); there's also a complimentary eco-boat that cruises through 11 km (7 miles) of waterways.

Restaurants

Agave Azul

$$$$ | ASIAN FUSION | There's more to Agave Azul than those sweeping lagoon and mangrove views. The glass-walled restaurant at the elegant Rosewood Mayakoba is hands down the best place to go for fresh sushi and premium tequila. **Known for:** more than 100 varieties of tequila; fresh fish; romantic setting. $ *Average main: MP420* ⊠ *Rosewood Mayakoba, Carretera 307, Km 298, Mayakoba* ☎ *984/875–8000* ⊕ *www.rosewoodhotels.com* ⊘ *No lunch.*

Hotels

Andaz Mayakoba Resort Riviera Maya

$$$$ | RESORT | FAMILY | At the most recent addition to Mayakoba's selection of superluxurious resorts, guest rooms are

fresh, modern—with a palette inspired by the colors of the surrounding jungle—and loaded with a wide array of deluxe amenities. **Pros:** PGA golf club next door; walk-in rain showers; all-inclusive package available. **Cons:** not all rooms are beachfront; transportation inside the resort takes its time; lagoon-front rooms get a lot of mosquitoes. $ *Rooms from: $464* ⊠ *Carretera 307, Km 298, Mayakoba* ☎ *984/149–1234* ⊕ *www.hyatt.com/andaz* ⤢ *214 rooms* ⊘ *No Meals.*

Banyan Tree Mayakoba

$$$$ | RESORT | This Thai chain has brought its own traditions to Mexico's Riviera with stunning results—in addition to vaulted ceilings, lounge areas, dining rooms, private gardens, and Talavera earthenware sinks, all rooms have outdoor bathtubs and private 376-foot swimming pools, a unique perk. **Pros:** top-notch spa; excellent food; world-class service. **Cons:** small kids' club; fee to use bicycles on property; not many activities. $ *Rooms from: $809* ⊠ *Carretera 307, Km 298, Mayakoba* ☎ *984/877–3699* ⊕ *www.banyantree.com* ⤢ *118 rooms* ⊘ *No Meals.*

Fairmont Mayakoba

$$$$ | RESORT | Set under a mangrove canopy, this sprawling luxury resort sets new standards in the Riviera Maya for sustainability and comfort—not only is it recognized for its green practices and community involvement, but it also has biodegradable bath products, a recycling program, rooftops made from recycled tires, and bicycles stationed throughout the 240-acre property. **Pros:** free shuttle to neighboring properties; bird-watching tours; access to nearby El Camaleón golf course. **Cons:** 20-minute walk from lobby to ocean; some rooms lack water views; limited free hours at kids' club. $ *Rooms from: $470* ⊠ *Carretera 307, Km 298, Mayakoba* ☎ *984/206–3000, 800/540–6088 in the U.S.* ⊕ *www.fairmont.com/mayakoba-riviera-maya* ⤢ *401 rooms* ⊘ *No Meals.*

The Rosewood Mayakoba is one of the Riviera Maya's most elegant resorts.

★ Rosewood Mayakoba

$$$$ | RESORT | FAMILY | From the moment you set foot on the palapa-roofed boat that brings you to your room's private dock, the Rosewood transports you to an exotic world—one where meandering trails lead through grounds featuring a labyrinthine network of lily-strewn lagoons. **Pros:** free kids' club; extraordinary spa; check-in takes place on the boat. **Cons:** limited food options; no meals included; narrow beach. [$] *Rooms from: $1,479* ✉ *Carretera 307, Km 298, Mayakoba* ☎ *984/875–8000, 877/737–7538 in the U.S.* 🌐 *www.rosewoodhotels.com* 🛏 *130 suites* 🍴 *No Meals.*

Activities

GOLF

El Camaleón Mayakoba

GOLF | Designed by the legendary Greg Norman, El Camaleón's 18-hole course is backdropped by jungle, mangrove, and sea. It was home to Mexico's first PGA tour event—the OHL Classic at Mayakoba, and the first LIV Golf League event—the LIV Golf Mayakoba. The layout is exceptional, from the first hole with a cenote in the middle of the fairway to the par 3s on the back with ocean views. Throughout the perfectly manicured course, each hole has a minimum of five tee blocks, so there is distance for every skill level. Holes 7 and 15 skirt the ocean; Hole 17 plays directly between a limestone canal and the Fairmont Mayakoba Resort. ✉ *Carretera 307, Km 298, Mayakoba* ☎ *984/206–4653* 🌐 *mayakoba.com/el-camaleon-golf-course* 🎟 *$259 for 18 holes* ⛳ *18 holes. 7024 yards. Par 72.*

SPAS

★ Banyan Tree Spa

SPAS | Built over freshwater lagoons, the Banyan Tree Spa draws on centuries-old Asian traditions. The therapists (most of whom are from Thailand) begin with a heavenly footbath, followed by your choice of Asian-flavored healing treatments, including scrubs with turmeric, lemongrass, or green tea. Treatments take place in private pavilions, each with its own steam room, shower, and outdoor whirlpool tub enclosed by bamboo walls. Unique to Banyan Tree are its signature Rainmist Steam Bath and the romantic couples' Rainforest Experience, which combines hydrotherapy with infrared light to release tension and revitalize the body. ⊠ *Banyan Tree Resort, Carretera 307, Km 298, Mayakoba* ☎ *984/877–3688* ⊕ *www.banyantree. com.*

Fairmont Spa at Mayakoba

SPAS | It's easy to lose yourself (literally) within this spa thoroughly renovated in 2022 at the Fairmont Mayakoba. Signature treatments include the Mexican stone massage, the Xunan Uh massage featuring a Mayan shawl technique, and the Cha Chac Rain ritual (a massage that takes place on a seven-jet Vichy table). Weary travelers will want to try the Deep Sleep treatment, a massage that purports to reverse the negative effects of flying and time zone changes. After a gym workout, ease your muscles at the rooftop vitality pool. ⊠ *Fairmont Mayakoba, Carretera 307, Km 298* ☎ *984/206– 3038, 800/540–6088 in the U.S.* ⊕ *www. fairmont.com/mayakoba-riviera-maya* 🎟 *Access to spa relaxation area $39; massages from $199.*

★ Sense, a Rosewood Spa

SPAS | Wooden walkways traverse the jungle-covered island that is the setting for Rosewood's 17,000-square-foot spa, where you'll find a swimming pool as well as a limestone cenote fed by subterranean springs. The Maya tradition of harmonizing the energy of the body is evident in treatments such as the *temazcal* ritual and the "fire and ice" therapy. The gourmet sugar body scrub and antiaging facial are both heavenly. Nonguest visitors can book a treatment, then enjoy the spa facilities, including the gym, sauna, whirlpool tub, plunge pool,

and the eucalyptus steam room for free. ⊠ *Rosewood Mayakoba, Carretera 307, Km 298, Mayakoba* ☎ *984/875–8000, 877/737–7538 in the U.S.* ⊕ *www.rosewoodhotels.com.*

Punta Bete (Xcalacoco)

13 km (8 miles) southwest of Mayakoba, 6 km (4 miles) north of Playa del Carmen.

Beyond Punta Maroma, a river spills into the sea, dividing the coastline. South of the split, Playa Xcalacoco (scala-coco) is a 7-km-long (5½-mile-long) beach dotted with bungalows; small, exclusive resort hotels; and thatched-roof restaurants, backing into dense jungle. The beach is beautiful, a more natural extension of Playa del Carmen, but the shore can be rocky. Some hotels here supply water shoes for swimming, and the Viceroy has a dock to enter deeper water.

GETTING HERE AND AROUND

Driving north from Playa del Carmen, turn right at the Coca-Cola factory and follow the road east. Heading south from Cancún on Carretera 307, turn at the huge sign for the Princess Resort at Km 296 to reach Petit Lafitte, Cocos Cabanas, the Viceroy, and the beach. (To reach Le Rêve, you'll have to take the road about 100 yards south, marked with a blue sign for Azul Fives condos.) Punta Bete has few shops, bars, or restaurants outside the hotels; however, there is a convenience store and a pizzeria on the way to Le Rêve.

🜨 Beaches

If long walks on the beach are your thing, you'll love the 6-km (4-mile) stretch from Playa Xcalacoco to Playa del Carmen. Although delightfully deserted (during weekdays), the beach itself is not the area's best; the sand is somewhat coarse and often draped in seagrass.

There's decent snorkeling, however, and the isolation is unbeatable, although on weekends it's very popular among the locals. Plus, it's a way to explore Playa from Xcalacoco without bumping over the jungle road.

Hotels

Coco's Cabañas
$ | **B&B/INN** | Tranquility and seclusion are the name of the game in these adults-only, cozy bungalows located a stone's throw from the beach. **Pros:** excellent wood-fired oven pizza; friendly staff; suites include kitchenette. **Cons:** not directly on the beach; tons of mosquitoes; tiny pool. [$] *Rooms from: $97* ✉ *Xcalacoco, Lote 2, Punta Bete* ✥ *Take the paved road at Princess Resort and follow signs. Turn left onto the dirt road. Coco's Cabanas will be on your right* ☎ *998/874–7056* 🌐 *www.cocoscabanas.com* 🛏 *6 rooms* 🍴 *Free Breakfast.*

Grand Velas Riviera Maya
$$$$ | **ALL-INCLUSIVE** | **FAMILY** | This all-inclusive resort offers Mexican luxury at its best with top-notch gastronomy, stylish rooms, a certified Blue Flag beach, an outstanding spa, and lots of activities for all ages. **Pros:** stunning spa with hydrotherapy circuit; infinity pools with volcanic stones; kids and teens clubs. **Cons:** huge property means long walks; away from downtown Playa; common areas can get too crowded at times. [$] *Rooms from: $1,300* ✉ *Carretera 307, Km 62, Punta Bete* ☎ *322/226–8689, 877/418–2963 in the U.S.* 🌐 *rivieramaya.grandvelas.com* 🛏 *506 rooms* 🍴 *All-Inclusive.*

Petit Lafitte
$$$ | **HOTEL** | **FAMILY** | Named after the famous pirate, this warm and family-friendly resort has multiunit cabanas plus freestanding bungalows on the beach's north end that are more private and charming. **Pros:** peaceful atmosphere; kids love the small animal refuge; breakfast and dinner included. **Cons:** rocky beach; plenty of mosquitoes; no TVs in bungalows. [$] *Rooms from: $224* ✉ *Carretera 307, Km 296, Punta Bete* ✥ *From Carretera 307, turn onto the paved road for the Princess Resort and follow the signs to Petit Lafitte* ☎ *984/877–4000* 🌐 *www.petitlafitte.com* 🛏 *55 rooms* 🍴 *Free Breakfast.*

★ Viceroy Riviera Maya
$$$$ | **RESORT** | Punta Bete's most luxurious jungle-beach resort is romantic and exotic, with sumptuous palapa villas that have private plunge pools, "moon bath" showers in palm-shaded gardens, and every imaginable creature comfort—from silky-soft sheets on canopy-draped king beds to soap hand-cut by your butler. **Pros:** romantic and private; luxurious villas; several meal plans available. **Cons:** bugs in jungle setting; rocky beach; no children under 14. [$] *Rooms from: $595* ✉ *Playa Xcalacoco, Carretera 307, Km 296, Fracc. 7, Punta Bete* ✥ *From Carretera 307, turn onto the paved road for Princess Resort and follow the signs to the Viceroy* ☎ *984/877–3000* 🌐 *www.viceroyhotelsandresorts.com* 🛏 *41 villas* 🍴 *Free Breakfast.*

Antojería Night 🍴

Viceroy Riviera Maya (☎ *984/877–3000* 🌐 *www.viceroyhotelsandresorts.com*) offers a wide array of traditional Mexican street food every Thursday at 6:30 pm. The resort's chef will reveal his own modern interpretation of the famous Mexican *antojitos*. Reservations are required.

🏃 Activities

Wayak Spa

SPAS | Although not as grandiose as most spas in the Riviera Maya, this small spot (whose name translates to "the dreamer") utilizes natural surroundings to create a unique pampering experience. From the shaman who greets you with a purifying waft of cobal smoke to the treatment rooms oriented toward sun, moon, and stars, the Wayak Spa makes a point of reminding you that you're in the land of the Maya. Opt for massages in jungle palapa huts surrounded by waterfalls (and mosquito curtains) or a purifying steam bath with a heavenly oculus. Client favorites include the honey-citrus scrub and mud body wrap. The Sac-Há treatment starts detoxifying the body with a coffee scrub and then applies a massage under a warm delicate rain that has a relaxing effect. ⊠ *Viceroy Riviera Maya Resort, Carretera 307, Km 296, Punta Bete ✛ From Carretera 307, turn onto the paved road at Princess Resort and follow the signs to the Viceroy.* 🕿 *984/877–3000* ⊕ *www.viceroyhotelsandresorts.com.*

Playa del Carmen

68 km (42 miles) south of Cancún.

Welcome to the party! "Playa," currently Latin America's fastest-growing community, has a population of more than 150,000 and an international flavor lent by the *estadounidenses* (United States citizens), Canadians, and Europeans who have been moving here since the early 1990s. Full of lively bars, restaurants, beach clubs, shops, and hotels, its eminently walkable downtown is one of the few places on the Riviera Maya where you can have a car-free vacation.

Sunbathe and swim at trendy beach clubs by day, then drink and dance at nightclubs until the sun comes up and start all over again. In between, there's an enjoyable array of diversions along Avenida 5, a pedestrian-only cobbled street that is the town's main drag. Its southern section, from about Calle 4 to Constituyentes, is busy, noisy, and sometimes rowdy—the place to go for nightlife, tequila shots, and souvenir shopping. Its quieter, more upscale northern end, north of Constituyentes up to about Calle 38, is the place for chic cafés and stylish boutiques.

Rapid development means a decline in Mexican culture, with chain stores and cheap souvenirs emerging on every corner (Starbucks junkies can easily get their fix). It also means businesses open and close monthly, surviving on the hope they can offer a better service than their neighbors.

Although building-height restrictions have helped to keep Playa from turning into the next Cancún, you'll have to leave town to get off the beaten path. Much of the area is developed, most recently by a slew of all-inclusive resorts opening up on the city's outskirts. If you plan on leaving the town center, be aware of your surroundings.

GETTING HERE AND AROUND

Driving from Cancún's airport, follow the signs on Carretera 307. Shortly before town, take the overpass up and descend at the Avenida Constituyentes exit. Turn left under the overpass and follow Constituyentes into town. The Playacar resort development is south of Playa del Carmen's numbered calles, starting at Avenida Juárez. To get there from Cancún, stay on the highway past the Constituyentes exit and turn left after the overpass at the Playacar sign.

The trip from Cancún takes about an hour. Note that there are several rather intimidating police checkpoints as you approach Playa del Carmen from the highway. Officers occasionally check vehicles at random, especially at night.

If you are coming from Cancún by taxi, expect to pay around MX$1,200. Shared vans from the airport generally cost MX$430 per person; if you're traveling with a group or even find some other Playa-bound travelers at the airport, a van can be a good way to go.

Buses traveling south from Cancún stop at Playa del Carmen's bus terminal at Avenida 20 and Calle 12, a short walk from downtown and the main drag, Avenida 5 (known as "la Quinta"). Buses headed to Cancún from Playa del Carmen use the main bus terminal at Avenida Juárez and Avenida 5. ADO (⊕ *ado.com. mx*) runs express, first-class, and second-class buses to major destinations. Colectivos stop on Calle 2 a few blocks (and an easy walk) from Avenida 5.

The town is set up on a grid system that's easy to navigate, if you know the rules. North–south avenidas are numbered in multiples of five, with Avenida 1 along the beach, and then moving westward through Avenidas 5, 10, 15, 20, and so on. East–west calles are even numbers only, starting with Calle 2 and progressing northward through 4, 6, 8, and so on.

■TIP→ **In Playa del Carmen, parking is prohibited at yellow curbs. If you're ticketed, your license plate will be taken to a nearby police station and returned only after the fine has been paid.**

Beaches

Playa del Carmen is famous for its pristine beaches, which have various access points staggered between the hotels on Avenida 5. Of course, it is equally famous for its thriving nightlife, and the trendy beach clubs here—all in central Playa del Carmen—offer the best of both. The combination of DJ music, cocktails, and twentysomethings makes these open-air bars a can't-miss for young singles. Outside resorts, they're also the only places you'll find beach amenities.

There are beach clubs all the way from Calle 8 to Calle 46, the hottest being at Mamita's beach between Calles 26 and 30. (In between, you can also find little ad hoc massage places for about MX$650 per hour.) Coco Beach, where Calle 46 meets the ocean, is popular with snorkelers drawn to the outer Chun-Zumbul Reef. For deserted strands, head even farther north, where the waves are small and the water is shallow.

The southern beaches of Playacar extending to the ferry dock at Avenida Benito Juárez are shored up against erosion with buried sandbags, but there's still a sharp drop-off from the beach level to the water; beaches north of the ferry dock are more level. Although all local strands are technically open to the public, those in Playacar are difficult to access since they are dominated by all-inclusive resorts. You also won't find any beach clubs in Playacar.

Playa's beaches lack protective outer reefs, but the strong wind and waves make these areas great for water sports. For an underwater adventure, organize a tour with one of the local dive companies that will take you to outer reefs and cenotes.

Mamita's Beach

BEACH | This stretch of beach north of the ferry dock, from Constituyentes to Calle 38, is known to locals as Mamita's, although it also encompasses the Coralina beach club and the Hilton and Mahekal hotels. Independent of the main beach's drop-off (and the sandbags that are sometimes visible there), it's a lovely straight stretch of flat sand and clear water, which you'll share with lots of other visitors. The trade-off is that WaveRunners, which are largely absent from the main beach, are very present here. It's a good spot for fun in the sun, not seclusion. **Amenities:** food and drink; lifeguards; toilets; water sports. **Best for:** partiers; swimming. ⊠ *Between*

Constituyentes and Calle 38, Playa del Carmen.

Playa del Carmen Main Beach

BEACH | **FAMILY** | The community's most central section of beach stretches from the ferry docks up to Calle 14 at the Wyndham Alltra Resort, a swath of deep white sand licked by turquoise water. The beach and water are clean, but there is some boat traffic that makes swimming less idyllic. Snorkelers aren't likely to see much here, but you can't beat the beach for convenience: countless bars and restaurants are a short walk away on 5th Avenue, masseurs compete (discreetly) to knead out your kinks, and it's easy to find a dive shop ready to take you out to sea. The closer you get to the docks, the more people you'll find. If you're looking for seclusion, head farther north outside Playa del Carmen. **Amenities:** food and drink; lifeguards; water sports. **Best for:** swimming; walking. ✉ *Between ferry docks and Calle 14, Playa del Carmen.*

BEACH CLUBS

Coralina Daylight Club

BEACH | A favorite of party animals and the young and beautiful, Coralina offers nonstop music all day long with an open bar, fireworks, go-go dancers, and bikini contests also included in the rates. The pool parties here are legendary, as are the champagne wars. **Amenities:** food and drink; toilets. **Best for:** partiers. ✉ *Calle 26 and The Beach, Playa del Carmen* ☎ *984/204–6009* 🌐 *coralinabeachclub.com* 🎟 *Women from MX$1,500; Men from MX$2,000* 🕒 *Closed Mon.*

Mamita's Beach Club

BEACH | Accessible by way of Calle 28, this is Playa's hottest spot to catch some rays. You can rent an umbrella and two chairs (the smallest beachfront package) for MX$600; MX$3,500 will get you a plush, shady couch in the sand (and a refund of up to MX$3,000 if you purchase that much in drinks). Expect to pay around MX$165 for a cocktail and MX$60 for a beer. Guests can relax in the VIP area while a DJ spins trance and techno beside the freshwater pool. Facilities include three restaurants, four bars, two swimming pools, and a second-floor champagne bar. **Amenities:** food and drink; toilets; water sports. **Best for:** partiers. ✉ *Calle 28 at the beachfront, Playa del Carmen* ☎ *984/239–2906* 🌐 *www.facebook.com/MamitasBeachClub* 🎟 *Starting at MX$600, with partial refunds with food or drink purchase.*

★ Zenzi

BEACH | This beach club and restaurant is one of the few open every day from morning (8:30 am) to late (1 am). Take a dip in the ocean and then catch some rays on one of the sun beds or chaise lounges. When the sun goes down, there is live music, shows, and salsa lessons on the beach. **Amenities:** food and drink; toilets. **Best for:** partiers; swimming. ✉ *Calle 10 at the beach, Playa del Carmen* ☎ *984/803–5738* 🌐 *zenzi-playa.com* 🎟 *Free with purchase of food or drink.*

🍴 Restaurants

Aldea Corazón

$$$ | **MEXICAN** | Playa's most dramatically sited restaurant sits atop a small cenote in a vast jungly garden full of strangler vines and Mayan ruins—right in the middle of Avenida 5. Designed in accordance with Maya building practices, it's a feast for the eyes, with living "green walls" covered with plants, a bar built on a stone wall, and a park in back that makes for a romantic setting at night (bring bug spray). **Known for:** exotic jungle setting; bottled water filtered from the cenote; jicama tacos. [$] *Average main: MP375* ✉ *Av. 5 between Calles 14 and 16, Playa del Carmen* ☎ *984/803–1942* 🌐 *qrco.de/aldeacorazon.*

Alux Restaurant & Lounge

$$$$ | **ECLECTIC** | Although this restaurant is a 10-minute drive from downtown, its location in an underground cavern makes it extremely popular. A candlelit rock

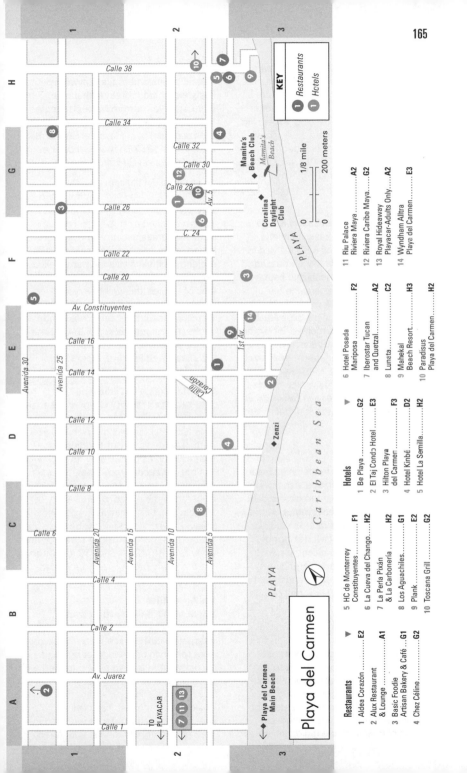

165

Playa del Carmen

Restaurants ▶

1 Aldea Corazón............**E2**
2 Alux Restaurant
   & Lounge..................**A1**
3 Basic Foodie
   Artisan Bakery & Café....**G1**
4 Chez Céline................**G2**
5 HC de Monterrey
   Constituyentes............**F1**
6 La Cueva del Chango....**H2**
7 La Perla Pixán
   & La Carbonería..........**H2**
8 Los Aguachiles............**G1**
9 Plank........................**E2**
10 Toscana Grill..............**G2**

Hotels ▶

1 Be Playa.....................**G2**
2 El Taj Condo Hotel.........**E3**
3 Hilton Playa
   del Carmen..................**F3**
4 Hotel Kinbé..................**D2**
5 Hotel La Semilla...........**H2**
6 Hotel Posada
   Mariposa....................**F2**
7 Iberostar Tucan
   and Quetzal.................**A2**
8 Lunata........................**C2**
9 Mahekal
   Beach Resort...............**H3**
10 Paradisus
   Playa del Carmen.........**H2**
11 Riu Palace
   Riviera Maya................**A2**
12 Riviera Caribe Maya......**G2**
13 Royal Hideaway
   Playacar-Adults Only....**A2**
14 Wyndham Alltra
   Playa del Carmen.........**E3**

KEY
❶ Restaurants
① Hotels

Caribbean Sea

PLAYA

Calle 1
Calle 2
Calle 4
Calle 6
Calle 8
Calle 10
Calle 12
Calle 14
Calle 16
Av. Constituyentes
Calle 20
Calle 22
C. 24
Calle 26
Calle 28
Calle 30
Calle 32
Calle 34
Calle 38

Av. Juarez
Avenida 30
Avenida 25
Avenida 20
Avenida 15
Avenida 10
Avenida 5
Av. 5
1st Av.

Calle Corazón

TO PLAYACAR

◆ Playa del Carmen Main Beach
◆ Zenzi
◆ Coralina Daylight Club
◆ Mamita's Beach Club
Mamita's Beach

0   1/8 mile
0   200 meters

stairway leads to a setting that's part Carlsbad Caverns, part *The Flintstones*. Some of the "cavernous" rooms are for lounging, some for drinking, some for eating, some for dancing. **Known for:** a unique location inside a cave; great variety of wines; shredded deer meat. [$] *Average main: MP650* ✉ *Av. Juárez between Calles 65 and 70, Playa del Carmen* ☎ *984/206–1401* 🌐 *www.aluxrestaurant.com* 🕒 *No lunch.*

★ Basic Foodie Artisan Bakery & Café
$$ | **BAKERY** | **FAMILY** | Basic Foodie is that cool bakery we all wish we had in our neighborhood, with unsurpassed baked goods and a menu that caters to organic-minded, vegan, and gluten-free customers. A modern design and laid-back atmosphere (plus reliable Wi-Fi) have made it a magnet for digital nomads. **Known for:** wide variety of handmade bread; vegetarian molletes (baguette with beans Mexican style); organic smoothies. [$] *Average main: MP160* ✉ *Av. 25, between Calles 26 and 28, Fracc. La Toscana* ☎ *984/109–1948* 🌐 *www.facebook.com/basicfoodie* 🕒 *No dinner.*

★ Chez Céline
$$ | **FRENCH** | Céline's fresh-baked breads and pastries honor France, especially exquisite desserts like the classic dark chocolate cake and bold vanilla crème brûlée. Classic bistro fare—including quiche Lorraine and flavorful croques madames—make for a light lunch *comme il faut*. **Known for:** French bistro-style croques; pastries and sweets to eat in or take away; quiche Lorraine. [$] *Average main: MP170* ✉ *Av. 5 at Calle 34, Playa del Carmen* ☎ *984/803–3480* 🌐 *chezceline.com.mx.*

HC de Monterrey Constituyentes
$ | **STEAKHOUSE** | Follow your nose to this Mexican grill house, where locals gather for some of the best-tasting steak in town. The open-air restaurant is filled with the sounds of mariachi music blaring from the radio, and a mounted bull's head hangs above the plastic tables and chairs. **Known for:** tasty arrachera (skirt steak); ample portions; lively atmosphere. [$] *Average main: MP120* ✉ *Av. Constituyentes at Gonzalo Guerrero, Playa del Carmen* ☎ *984/115–5959* 🌐 *www.facebook.com/HCdeMonterreyConstituyentes.*

★ La Cueva del Chango
$$ | **MEXICAN** | This Playa institution, in a funky jungle garden with fountains, palmettos, and a rambling koi pond, is a favorite breakfast spot. The well-prepared, authentic Mexican selections include multiple styles of *chilaquiles*, a tart mix of meat, sauce, and egg on a bed of tortillas that will have you skipping lunch. **Known for:** chilaquiles, served spicy or mild; good coffee; enchiladas with mole. [$] *Average main: MP284* ✉ *Calle 38, between Av. 5 and the beach, Playa del Carmen* ☎ *984/147–0271* 🌐 *lacuevadelchango.com* 🕒 *No dinner Sun.*

La Perla Pixán & La Carbonería
$$$$ | **MEXICAN** | **FAMILY** | If you want to try authentic Mexican and pre-Hispanic cuisine, La Perla Pixan is the place for you with its wide variety of traditional specialties such as pozole (and its vegetarian option), *barbacoa, enchiladas, tlayudas,* and more. Look for the weekend brunch buffet, and the extraordinary variety of mezcal cocktails. **Known for:** pre-Hispanic cuisine; mezcal cocktails; vegetarian pozole (traditional Mexican stew). [$] *Average main: MP420* ✉ *Calle 38, between Av. 5 and the beach, Fracc. La Toscana* ☎ *984/120-2616* 🌐 *laperlacarboneria.com.*

Los Aguachiles
$$ | **SEAFOOD** | **FAMILY** | This upscale seafood taquería is an anchor of Playa's alternative culinary scene, an in-the-know spot for lunch or dinner that reimagines tacos sautéed in olive oil and topped with cucumber or strawberry-habanero salsa. Local favorites include shrimp tacos with "black gold" (beans), fish ceviche with green salsa, and fish tacos wrapped in your choice of corn tortilla, flour tortilla,

or a giant leaf of Bibb lettuce. **Known for:** a new, modern take on tacos; unusual salsas; shrimp tacos with black gold (beans). $ *Average main: MP175* ✉ *Calle 34 at Av. 25, Playa del Carmen* ☎ *984/859–1442, 984/803–1583* ⊕ *www.facebook.com/LosAguachilesRM.*

★ Plank

$$$$ | STEAKHOUSE | The name says it all at this New York–inspired restaurant where entrées are grilled on wooden planks or Himalayan salt blocks. The smoky flavors of cedar, maple, hickory, and oak come through in signature dishes like grilled salmon or beef filet in mushroom sauce. **Known for:** entrées grilled on wooden planks; meats smoked in white cedar for over 12 hours; grilled salmon. $ *Average main: MP470* ✉ *Calle 16, between Avs. 5 and 1, Playa del Carmen* ☎ *984/452–0458* ⊕ *www.plank.mx* ⊗ *No lunch.*

Toscana Grill

$$$ | ITALIAN | FAMILY | This Italian restaurant stands out for its elegance, excellent service, extraordinary steaks, and noteworthy pizzas and cocktails. There's a great brunch on weekends and live music every night. **Known for:** delicious steaks; stylish cocktails; live music. $ *Average main: MP350* ✉ *Av. 5 at Calle 28 Norte, Playa del Carmen* ☎ *984/278–0033* ⊕ *www.facebook.com/ToscanaGrillPlaya.*

🛏 Hotels

PLAYA DEL CARMEN
Be Playa

$$ | HOTEL | This funky boutique hotel melds retro with modern, as evidenced by the red vinyl couches in the lobby and the exceedingly cool rooftop pool bar, where tables and chairs wade in the water. **Pros:** creative design; good views from rooftop bar; free use of bikes. **Cons:** four blocks from beach; rooms don't have ocean views; bland breakfast. $ *Rooms from: $140* ✉ *Calle 26, between Avs. 5 and 10, Playa del Carmen*

☎ *984/168–0911* ⊕ *beplaya.com* ⊲ *23 rooms* ❧ *Free Breakfast.*

★ El Taj Condo Hotel

$$$ | APARTMENT | A pair of curvaceous buildings contains stylish condo rentals, each complete with a fully equipped kitchen, washer-dryer, and Balinese furnishings. **Pros:** right on the beach; private kitchens; free access to neighboring fitness club, including fitness classes. **Cons:** units are mostly two- and three-bedroom; stale smell in some units; three-night minimum stay in high season (though they're flexible if not fully booked). $ *Rooms from: $280* ✉ *Calle 1 Norte at Calle 14, Playa del Carmen* ☎ *984/141–3874, 866/479–2738* ⊕ *www.eltaj.com* ⊲ *57 units* ❧ *Free Breakfast.*

Hilton Playa del Carmen

$$$$ | ALL-INCLUSIVE | If you are looking for the royal treatment, this massive, colonial-style resort has everything from laundry service and a 24-hour on-site doctor to in-room whirlpool tubs and fully stocked minibars. **Pros:** on Playa's best beach; live-entertainment evenings; hydrotherapy at the spa included. **Cons:** most rooms face the garden; adults only (18-plus); pool area can get too crowded. $ *Rooms from: $338* ✉ *Av. Constituyentes 2, Playa del Carmen* ☎ *984/877–2900, 800/445–8667 in the U.S.* ⊕ *www.hilton.com* ⊲ *524 rooms* ❧ *All-Inclusive.*

Hotel Kinbé

$ | HOTEL | An interesting fusion of Maya and contemporary decor, budget-friendly Kinbé (which means "path to the sun") is steps from the beach. **Pros:** great value; discounts at nearby beach clubs; in the heart of Playa. **Cons:** small rooms; some street noise; lots of stairs. $ *Rooms from: $95* ✉ *Calle 10 Norte, between Avs. 1 and 5, Playa del Carmen* ☎ *984/873–0441* ⊕ *www.kinbe.com* ⊲ *29 rooms* ❧ *No Meals.*

Hotel La Semilla

$$ | **B&B/INN** | From the lush jungle courtyard to the airy, stone-walled rooms to the sunny, plush rooftop deck with distant ocean views, this boutique hotel is designed to charm at every turn. **Pros:** beautiful design; laundry included; free use of bikes. **Cons:** no pool; adults only (18-plus); no phones or TVs. [$] *Rooms from: $180* ✉ *Calle 38 Norte, between Av. 5 and the beach, Playa del Carmen* ☎ *984/147–3234* 🌐 *hotellasemilla.com* 🛏 *9 rooms* 🍴 *Free Breakfast.*

Hotel Posada Mariposa

$$ | **HOTEL** | Although it has few facilities, this hotel is still a great value, with impeccable rooms set around a garden courtyard where trees grow past the third floor. **Pros:** cozy setting; beach club discounts; one hour free per day at nearby gym. **Cons:** not on the beach; few guest common areas; no pool or gym. [$] *Rooms from: $110* ✉ *Calle 24 Norte 5A, Playa del Carmen* ☎ *984/147–2278* 🌐 *posadamariposaboutiquehotel.com* 🛏 *30 rooms* 🍴 *Free Breakfast.*

Lunata

$$ | **B&B/INN** | An elegant entrance, Spanish-tile floors, and hand-crafted Guadalajara furnishings greet you at this classy inn, where guest rooms have terraces, as well as sitting areas with dark hardwood furnishings and interesting local crafts. **Pros:** prime location; warm, welcoming staff; intimate setting. **Cons:** some nighttime noise from nearby clubs; mediocre breakfast; no pool. [$] *Rooms from: $109* ✉ *Av. 5, between Calles 6 and 8, Playa del Carmen* ☎ *984/873–0884* 🌐 *lunata.com* 🛏 *10 rooms* 🍴 *Free Breakfast.*

Mahekal Beach Resort

$$$$ | **RESORT** | With three blocks of beach and grounds that include both sandy shore and cool jungle garden, this resort offers a taste of everything the Riviera landscape has to offer. **Pros:** three blocks of beachfront; excellent service; free movie nights on the beach. **Cons:** large property may feel impersonal to some; no TVs in rooms; lack of privacy in beachfront rooms. [$] *Rooms from: $377* ✉ *Calle 38 at the beach, Playa del Carmen* ☎ *984/873–0611, 877/235–4452* 🌐 *www.mahekalbeachresort.com* 🛏 *196 rooms* 🍴 *All-Inclusive.*

Paradisus Playa del Carmen

$$$$ | **RESORT** | **FAMILY** | This all-inclusive offers flash and class in a Vegas-meets-cruise-ship environment with 14 restaurants, 11 bars, and nearly 1,000 rooms housed in two buildings—the adults-only La Perla and the family-friendly La Esmeralda, where extras for the kids include PlayStations, nightly turndown with milk and cookies, and a pool area that looks like a water park. **Pros:** spa with hydrotherapy circuit; beautiful swim-up rooms; plenty of children's activities. **Cons:** rocky beach; 10-minute drive from downtown Playa; not all restaurants are open to children. [$] *Rooms from: $356* ✉ *Av. 5 Norte, Col. Luis Donaldo Colosio, Playa del Carmen* ☎ *984/877–3900, 929/207–1078 in the U.S.* 🌐 *www.melia.com* 🛏 *906 rooms* 🍴 *All-Inclusive.*

Riviera Caribe Maya

$ | **HOTEL** | It may not have the bells and whistles of other Playa hotels, but this small property, on a quiet street two blocks from the beach, is very pleasant. **Pros:** breezy rooms; outstanding pool area; huge bathrooms. **Cons:** hard mattresses; no parking lot; minimal street noise. [$] *Rooms from: $89* ✉ *Av. 10 and Calle 30, Playa del Carmen* ☎ *984/873–1193* 🌐 *www.hotelrivieramaya.com* 🛏 *25 rooms* 🍴 *No Meals.*

Wyndham Alltra Playa del Carmen

$$$$ | **ALL-INCLUSIVE** | Formerly known as the Panama Jack Resort, this property in the heart of Playa rebranded and reinvented itself as an all-inclusive, adults-only option, where the decor is modern without being flashy, and the overall atmosphere is fresh and relaxing. **Pros:** great location; rooftop swimming

pool; live entertainment. **Cons:** extra fee for pool and beach cabanas; no kids; seaweed on the beach. $ *Rooms from: $310 ✉ Av. Constuyentes 1, Playa del Carmen ☎ 984/873–4000 ⊕ alltrabyplaya. com ↝ 287 rooms* ❘◯❘ *All-Inclusive.*

PLAYACAR

South of downtown Playa del Carmen, the upscale gated community of Playacar is home to a string of all-inclusive resorts, beachfront condos, and rental properties, as well as an 18-hole golf course and the small, open-air Plaza Playacar mall. A paved bike path skirts the tree-lined streets of the development, past private neighborhoods, all the way north to downtown Playa and south to the adventure parks Xplor and Xcaret.

Iberostar Tucan and Quetzal

$$$$ | **RESORT** | **FAMILY** | Despite its size, this all-inclusive resort—consisting of the adults-only Tucan and the family friendly Quetzal sections—has managed to preserve natural surroundings that are home to flamingos, turtles, toucans, peacocks, and monkeys. **Pros:** tropical setting; bicycles for guests; great facilities for kids. **Cons:** no elevators; water at swim-up bar can be chilly; food lacks variety. $ *Rooms from: $317 ✉ Av. Xaman-Ha, Lote 2, Playacar, Playacar ☎ 984/877–2000 ⊕ www.iberostar.com ↝ 730 rooms* ❘◯❘ *All-Inclusive.*

Riu Palace Riviera Maya

$$$$ | **RESORT** | **FAMILY** | Palatial in name, scale, and decor (oversize entrance columns, crystal chandeliers, fountains), this all-inclusive is known for its breathtaking beach and exceptional service. **Pros:** sports bar open nonstop; friendly staff; lots of scheduled activities. **Cons:** no poolside service; reservations needed for certain restaurants; hallways echo at night. $ *Rooms from: $345 ✉ Av. Xaman-Ha, Mz 9 and 10, Fase II, Playacar ☎ 984/877–2280 ⊕ riu.com ↝ 460 rooms* ❘◯❘ *All-Inclusive.*

★ Royal Hideaway Playacar

$$$$ | **ALL-INCLUSIVE** | Art and antiques from around the world fill the lobby, and streams, waterfalls, and fountains fill the grounds of this 13-acre resort on a stretch of pristine beach. **Pros:** romantic setting; attentive service; taxes and gratuities included. **Cons:** adults only; pool service can be slow; restaurants require reservations. $ *Rooms from: $428 ✉ Av Xaman-Ha, Lote 6, Playacar ☎ 984/873–4500, 800/227–2356 in the U.S. ⊕ www.barcelo.com ↝ 201 rooms* ❘◯❘ *All-Inclusive.*

ⓨ Nightlife

The club scene is a major draw here, and most of the action is on Calle 12, which is lined with nightclubs and filled with lively young things ready to set the night afire. Most clubs are open-air, so this part of town gets very noisy until very late—something to keep in mind if you're planning to stay downtown and actually want to sleep. By day, Playa's lively beach clubs are packed with travelers lounging in the sun or dancing to the sounds of a live DJ.

Alux

DANCE CLUBS | Inside a cavern, Alux has a bar, disco, wine cellar, and restaurant. There's a MX$100 drink minimum. ✉ *Av. Juárez, between Avs. 65 and 70, Mz 217, Lote 2, Playa del Carmen ☎ 984/206– 1401 ⊕ www.aluxrestaurant.com.*

Bar Ranita

BARS | Attached to the Rana Cansada Hotel, Bar Ranita is a favorite among rowdy expats. The prices are unbeatable, and the margaritas pack a powerful punch. ✉ *Calle 10 Norte, between Avs. 5 and 10, Playa del Carmen ☎ 984/873–0389 ⊕ www.facebook.com/bar.ranita.*

★ Coco Bongo

DANCE CLUBS | Like its successful sister properties in Cancún, Coco Bongo has things like flying acrobats, bar-top conga lines, live bands, and DJs mixing everything from rock to hip-hop. The cover charge includes unlimited drinks. ⊠ *Calle 12 Norte at Av. 10, Playa del Carmen* ☎ *984/803–5939* ⊕ *www.cocobongo.com.*

La Bodeguita del Medio

LIVE MUSIC | Graffiti-styled La Bodeguita del Medio, a franchise of the famous Havana outpost, features live Cuban music every day. ⊠ *Av. 5 and Calle 34, Playa del Carmen* ☎ *984/803–3951* ⊕ *labodeguitadelmedio.com.mx.*

Mandala

DANCE CLUBS | The biggest, loudest, and most expensive party spot on Calle 12, trendy Mandala is divided into a street-level bar, a rooftop terrace, and a dance club. Each has its own DJ spinning anything from house and hip-hop to disco and techno. ⊠ *Av. 1 Norte at Calle 12, Playa del Carmen* ☎ *998/883–3333* ⊕ *www.mandalagroup.mx.*

🍽 Shopping

Avenida 5 between Calles 4 and 38 has the Riviera Maya's best shopping. Small galleries sell original folk art from around Mexico and clothing boutiques offer everything from chic bikinis to tacky tees. Stores dedicated to Mexican specialties sell things like silver, chocolate, and tequila. At the Calle Corazón (Calle 12) and Quinta Alegría (Calle 16) shopping malls, you'll find international brand names like Diesel and Havaianas.

BOOKS

Librería Mundo

BOOKS | This spot has an extensive selection of books on Maya culture, along with used English-language books. Profits from all English-language tomes are donated to Mexican schools to buy textbooks. ⊠ *Plaza las Américas, Calle 58 Norte, Playa del Carmen* ☎ *984/109–1566* ⊕ *www.facebook.com/americaslibreriamundo.*

CRAFTS

Candle Boutique

CRAFTS | The oversized, handmade candles that you see lighting the night so elegantly in Playa's restaurants and hotels are sold at Candle Boutique. ⊠ *Calle 2 Norte, between Calle 60 and Calle 70, Playa del Carmen* ☎ *984/114–9602* ⊕ *www.facebook.com/candleboutique.mx* ⊘ *Closed Sun.*

FOOD & DRINK

Ah Cacao

CHOCOLATE | **FAMILY** | This modish chocolate shop sells Mexico's finest, in bars, tablets, soaps, massage oils, and brownies. Locals swear by the coffee. There are other four branches around Playa del Carmen and Cancún. ⊠ *Avs. 5 and Constituyentes, Playa del Carmen* ☎ *984/803–1541* ⊕ *ahcacao.com.*

Bio-Orgánicos Playa del Carmen

GENERAL STORE | From snacks to groceries to organic soaps, lotions, and shampoos, this little shop has a little something for every health-conscious traveler. There's also an organic restaurant attached. ⊠ *Calle 12 Norte at Av. 20, Playa del Carmen* ☎ *984/803–2881.*

Hacienda Tequila

CRAFTS | More than 600 different types of tequila, plus an assortment of kitschy Mexican crafts and souvenirs, are sold at Hacienda Tequila. Free tastings are available, and the staff would love to share their deep knowledge of tequila making with you. ⊠ *Av. 5 and Calle 14, Playa del Carmen* ☎ *984/128–2195.*

MALLS

★ Paseo del Carmen

MALL | **FAMILY** | Upscale, open-air Paseo del Carmen has numerous boutiques—including Zara, Ultrafemme, and Old Navy. Seattle-coffee lovers can get their fix at the Starbucks that dominates the center of the mall. A cobblestone path makes this one of the area's most popular and pleasant shopping destinations. ⊠ *Av. 10 at Calle 1, Playa del Carmen*

☎ 984/803–3789 ⊕ paseodelcarmen.
com.

Plaza Las Américas

MALL | **FAMILY** | This family-friendly mall
features restaurants, shops, and cine-
mas. ⊠ Av Chemuyil and CTM, Playa del
Carmen ☎ 984/109–2161.

Plaza Playacar

MALL | **FAMILY** | This Mexican-colonial-style
outdoor mall in Playacar sells handcrafts,
clothes, jewelry, and specialty items like
tequila and cigars. There is also a Starbucks. ⊠ Paseo Xaman-Ha, Mz 25, Lote
19, Playacar Fase II, Playacar ☎ 984/873–
0006 ⊕ plazaplayacar.com.

★ Quinta Alegría

MALL | **FAMILY** | This three-story plaza
on Playa's main drag houses Sanborn's
department store, Harley Davidson, Forever 21, Oakley, Hurley, American Eagle
Outfitters, and much more. There's even
a Häagen-Dazs where you can cool off
with an ice cream before more shopping.
⊠ Av. 5 at Av. Constituyentes, Playa del
Carmen ☎ 984/803–2358 ⊕ www.quin-
taalegria.com.mx.

🏃 Activities

GOLF

Gran Coyote Golf

GOLF | This 18-hole championship course
was designed by Nick Price. Not as busy
(or expensive) as neighboring courses
at Mayakoba or Playacar, Gran Coyote
is challenging without being overly
intimidating. You'll face a good amount
of bunkers and water on the holes. The
greens are slow, but the course is well
maintained. If you can swing it, opt for
the all-inclusive package that covers food
and drink. Otherwise greens fees cover
only the cart, bottled water, and golf
tees. ⊠ Gran Coyote Golf, Carretera 307,
Km 294 ☎ 984/109–6025 ⊕ grancoyoteg-
olf.com ☑ $295 for 18 holes 🏌 18 holes;
7043 yards; par 71.

Hard Rock Golf Club Riviera Maya

GOLF | This 18-hole course is considered
one of the region's most challenging.
There's not a ton of water here, but
watch out for sand traps and tricky Hole
14. Signature holes are Hole 13 (342
yards, par 4) and Hole 18 (530 yards, par
5). Included in the greens fee are food
and drink, which are delivered cart-side
every few shots. Plan to lose a few balls
during your game as the greens are
tight and narrow. The fairways are well
manicured and full of wildlife. If it gets
too challenging, swing on over to the
practice area complete with a driving
range and putting green with its own
chipping, pitching, and green-side bunker
areas. ■TIP→ **Come after 1 pm for the
twilight fee.** ⊠ Paseo Xaman-Ha, near Riu
Palace, Playacar ☎ 998/881–3699 Ext.
4444, 817/567–7516 in the U.S. ⊕ www.
hardrockhotels.com/riviera-maya ☑ $250
for 18 holes 🏌 18 holes. 6775 yards. Par
72.

SCUBA DIVING AND SNORKELING

Dune Mexico Blue Dream

SCUBA DIVING | **FAMILY** | Custom snorkel
tours in Playa, Laguna Yal-Ku, Akumal,
and nearby cenotes are available through
Dune Mexico Blue Dream. Dive courses
and dive trips to Cozumel are also
arranged. ⊠ Calle 70 between Avs. 10
and 15, Playa del Carmen ☎ 984/143–
7400 ⊕ www.mexicobluedream.com ☑ 2
dives from $99.

Tank-Ha Dive Center

SCUBA DIVING | **FAMILY** | Playa's original
dive outfit has PADI-certified instructors
and runs diving and snorkeling excursions
to the reefs and caverns. Dive packages
and Cozumel trips are available, too.
⊠ Av. 1 between Calles 20 and 22, Playa
del Carmen ☎ 631/214–3347 in the U.S.,
984/873–0302 ⊕ tankha.com ☑ 2 dives
from $100.

Yucatek Divers

SCUBA DIVING | **FAMILY** | PADI-affiliated
Yucatek Divers offers cenote dives, dive
packages, and instruction. A one-tank

introductory course costs $120; the open-water diver-training course with four dives included costs $440. ⊠ *Av. 15 between Calles 2 and 4, Playa del Carmen* ☎ *984/803–1363* ⊕ *www.yucatek-divers.com.*

SKYDIVING
Skydive Playa
SKYDIVING | Adrenaline junkies can take the plunge high above Playa in a tandem skydive (where you're hooked up to an instructor the whole time). Jumps take place every hour; reserve at least one day in advance. ■**TIP**→ **For an extra MX$2,155, SkyDive Playa will shoot video of your free fall.** ⊠ *Av. 15 Sur 131, Playa del Carmen* ☎ *984/187–4868* ⊕ *www.skydive.com. mx* ⊠ *$269.*

Xcaret

6 km (4 miles) southwest of Playa del Carmen.

Xcaret (pronounced ish-*cah*-ret), formerly a sacred Maya city and port, is the site of two popular parks on a gorgeous stretch of coastline. The 250-acre ecological theme park, simply known as "Xcaret," is the Riviera Maya's most heavily advertised attraction. Billed as "nature's sacred paradise," it has its own published magazines plus a collection of stores. Just 2 km (1 mile) away is Xplor; half the size of Xcaret, this sister property is targeted at extreme-adventure seekers.

GETTING HERE AND AROUND
If you're driving, the entrance for both parks and the Occidental Grand Xcaret Resort is at Km 282 on Carretera 307. Organized day trips from Cancún will also take you to Xcaret, and a cab ride from nearby Playa del Carmen will cost about MX$220.

Navigating Xcaret ◉

You can easily spend at least a full day at Xcaret. This place is big, so it's a good idea to check the daily activities against a map of the park to organize your time. Plan to be in the general area of an activity before it's scheduled to begin—you'll beat the crowds and avoid having to sprint across the property.

◉ Sights

Museo de Arte Popular Mexicano
ART MUSEUM | FAMILY | This entrancing folk-art museum is a must for anyone interested in Mexican culture and handicrafts. It's brimming with original works by the country's finest artisans, which are arranged in fascinating tableaux. The collection represents different regions of Mexico—from nativity scenes sculpted from Oaxacan clay to the intricate *árbol de la vida* (tree of life) sculptures crafted in Metepec. Children will love the toy room, which includes an impressive display of *alebrijes* (fantastical wood carvings). Since this is one of the many attractions inside Xcaret, the only way to visit the museum is by purchasing a day pass to the theme park. ⊠ *Carretera 307, Km 282, at Xcaret, attraction No. 41, Xcaret* ☎ *998/883–3143* ⊕ *www.xcaret. com* ⊠ *Free with admission to Xcaret.*

★ Xcaret
THEME PARK | FAMILY | Take a small collection of Maya ruins and build a mammoth theme park around them, and you have Xcaret, one of the Yucatán Peninsula's most popular destinations. Among its most-visited attractions are the Paradise River raft tour that takes you on a winding, watery journey through the jungle; the Butterfly Garden, where thousands

There's plenty to do and see in Xcaret.

of butterflies float dreamily through a botanical garden while New Age music plays in the background; and an ocean-fed aquarium, where you can see local sea life drifting through coral heads and sea fans.

The park also has a wild-bird breeding aviary, nurseries for abandoned flamingo eggs and sea turtles, and a series of underwater caverns that you can explore by snorkeling or Snuba (a hybrid of snorkeling and scuba). A replica Maya village includes a colorful cemetery with catacomb-like caverns underneath; traditional music and dance ceremonies (including performances by the famed Voladores de Papantla, or Flying Birdmen of Papantla) are performed here at night. But the star performance is the evening "Xcaret Mexico Espectacular," which tells the history of Mexico through song and dance. The list of Xcaret's attractions goes on and on: you can visit a dolphinarium, a bee farm, a manatee lagoon, a bat cave, an orchid and bromeliad greenhouse, an edible-mushroom farm, and a small zoo.

You can also climb a 240-foot tower that offers a spectacular view of the park.

The entrance fee covers only access to the grounds and the exhibits; some other activities and equipment—from sea treks and dolphin tours to lockers and swim gear—are extra. The Plus Pass includes park entrance, lockers, snorkel equipment, food, and drinks. You can buy tickets from any travel agency or major hotel along the coast. ■TIP→ You can also book slightly discounted tickets through Xcaret's website. ⊠ Carretera 307, Km 282 ☎ 998/883–3143, 855/326–0682 in the U.S. ⊕ www.xcaret.com 🎟 Basic Pass $120; Plus Pass $164; Night Pass $98.   .

Xplor

THEME PARK | FAMILY | Designed for thrill seekers, this 125-acre park features underground rafting in stalactite-studded water caves and cenotes. Swim in a stalactite river, ride in an amphibious vehicle, or soar across the park on 14 of the longest zip lines in Mexico. Daytime admission (valid 8:30 am to 6 pm) includes all food, drink, and equipment. A separate evening admission from 5:30 to 11:00 pm includes "Xplor Fuego" activities, which include similar things but with a nighttime theme. Mix-and-match packages can be purchased online to include both day and evening admission and entry to Xcaret next door. ✉ *Carretera 307, Km 282* ☎ *998/883–3143, 855/326–0682 in the U.S.* 🌐 *www.xplor.travel* 🎟 *Xplor $142; Xplor Fuego $120.*

Hotels

Occidental at Xcaret Destination
$$$$ | **ALL-INCLUSIVE** | **FAMILY** | In such an enormous all-inclusive, it's surprising to find staff members who go out of their way to make your stay pleasant, beginning with a glass of tropical juice at registration and continuing with helpful concierge service throughout your stay. **Pros:** pleasant lagoon; Unlimited Xcaret Xperience provides access to Xcaret park; 11 restaurants and 11 bars. **Cons:** time-share sales reps give you the hard sell; small beach; squawking parrots in the lobby. [$] *Rooms from: $377* ✉ *Carretera 307, Km 282, Xcaret* ☎ *984/871–5400, 800/227–2356* 🌐 *www.barcelo.com* 🛏 *765 rooms* 🍴 *All-Inclusive.*

Puerto Aventuras

20 km (12 miles) southwest of Xcaret, 26 km (16 miles) southwest of Playa del Carmen.

The most Americanized of all the Riviera Maya's resorts is a 900-acre gated community and golf course more reminiscent of coastal Florida than Mexico. This has its advantages if you want to speak English exclusively and have the option to eat American food. Fatima Bay (the beach in front of the Puerto Aventuras Hotel) is glorious, but the town itself is not particularly scenic. The main marina is closed off to boat traffic and is instead home to Dolphin Discovery's dolphins and sea lions, which are fun to watch from the waterside restaurants and benches.

GETTING HERE AND AROUND

Puerto Aventuras is a 20-minute drive south of Playa del Carmen along Carretera 307. Its orientation around a small marina makes it very walkable—it's the sort of place where you can let older kids go off by themselves for the afternoon. Taxis are stationed at the small parking area near the marina outside the Puerto Aventuras hotel. You can also find them outside all major hotels. Taxis from Playa del Carmen cost about MX$330.

Sights

Ecopark Kantun Chi
THEME PARK | **FAMILY** | This Maya-owned and-operated eco-park has cenotes and a few beautiful underground caverns that are great for snorkeling and diving, as well as some small Maya ruins. It offers you a choice of three different experiences. The place is low-key—a nice break from the crowds. Bring natural mosquito repellent. ✉ *Carretera 307, Km 266, in front of Barceló Hotel, Puerto Aventuras* ☎ *984/271–0681* 🌐 *www.kantunchi.com* 🎟 *$67.*

Beaches

Fatima Bay
BEACH | **FAMILY** | Although the marina is the focus here, Puerto Aventuras's beaches are naturally stunning and seldom crowded. The main one, Fatima Bay, stretches nearly 3 km (2 miles) south between Chac Hal Al condominiums and the Grand Peninsula residence. Its shallow, calm waters are kid-friendly, especially inside the breakwater. Farther out the temperature drops, making for a refreshing swim. To the north is a smaller bay, known as Chan Yu Yum, used by guests of the Catalonia Resort;

Continued on page 180

ANCIENT ARCHITECTS:
THE MAYA

Visiting the Yucatán Peninsula and not touring any Maya sites is like going to Greece and not seeing the Acropolis or the Parthenon. One look at the monumental architecture of the Maya and you might feel transported to another world. The breathtaking structures are even more impressive when you consider that they were built 1,000 to 2,000 years ago or more without iron tools, wheels, pulleys, or beasts of burden—and in terrible heat and difficult terrain.

El Castillo, Tulum

THE ARCHITECTURAL PERIODS

Calakmul

PRECLASSIC PERIOD: Petén

Between approximately 2000 BC and AD 100, the Maya were centered around the lowlands in the south-central region of Guatemala. Their communities were family-based and governed by hereditary chiefs; their worship of agricultural gods (such as Chaac, the rain god, who they believed controlled the seasons), led them to chart the movement of heavenly bodies. Their religious beliefs also led them to build enormous temples and pyramids, such as El Mirador in the Guatemalan lowlands, where sacrifices were made and ceremonies were performed to please the gods.

The structures at El Mirador, as well as at the neighboring ruin site of Tikal, were built in what is known today as the Petén style: pyramids were steeply pitched, built on stepped terraces, and decorated with large stucco masks and ornamental (but sometimes "false" or unclimbable) stairways. Petén-style structures were also often roofed with corbeled archways. The Maya began to move northward into the Yucatán during the late part of this period, which is why Petén-style buildings can also be found at Calakmul, just north of the Guatemalan border.

EARLY-CLASSIC PERIOD: Río Usumacinta

The Classic Period, often referred to as the "golden age," spanned from about AD 100–1000. Maya civilization expanded northward and became much more complex. A distinct ruling class emerged, and hereditary kings ruled over densely populated jungle cities filled with increasingly impressive-looking palaces and temples.

During the early part of the Classic Period, Maya architecture began to take on some distinctive characteristics. Builders placed their structures on hillsides or crests, and the principal buildings were covered with bas-reliefs carved in stone. The pyramid-topped temples had vestibules and rooms with vaulted ceilings. Many chamber walls were carved with scenes recounting important events during the reign of the ruler who built the pyramid. Some of the most stunning examples of this style are at the ruins of Palenque, near Chiapas.

Palenque

Chicanná

MID-CLASSIC PERIOD: Ríos Bec and Chenes

It was during the middle part of the Classic Period (roughly between AD 60–900) that the Maya presence exploded onto the Yucatán Peninsula. Several Maya settlements were established in what is now Campeche state, including Chicanná and Xpujil, near the southwest corner of the state. The architecture at these sites was built in what is now known as the Río Bec style. As in the earlier Petén style, Río Bec pyramids had steeply pitched sides and ornately decorated foundations. Other Río Bec-style buildings, however, were long, one-story affairs incorporating two or three tall towers. These towers were typically capped by large roof combs that resembled mini-temples.

During the same part of the Classic Period, a different architectural style, known as Chenes, developed in some of the more northerly Maya cities, such as Hochob. While some Chenes-style structures share the same long, single-story construction as Río Bec buildings, others have strikingly different doorways carved in the shape of huge Chaac faces with gaping open mouths.

LATE-CLASSIC PERIOD: Puuc and Northeast Yucatán

Chichén Itzá

The fusion of two distinct Maya groups—the Chichén Maya and the Itzás—produced another striking architectural style. This style, known as Northeast Yucatán, is exemplified by the ruins at Chichén Itzá. Here, columns and grand colonnades were introduced. Palaces with row upon row of columns carved in the shape of serpents looked over grand patios, platforms were dedicated to the planet Venus, and pyramids were raised to honor Kukulcán (the plumed serpent god borrowed from the Toltecs, who called him Quetzalcoátl). Northeast Yucatán structures also incorporated carved stone Chacmool figures—reclining statues with trays carved into their midsections for sacrificial offerings.

Some of the Yucatán's most spectacular Maya architecture was built between about AD 800–1000. By this time, the Maya had spread into territory that is now Yucatán state, and established lavish cities at Labná, Kabah, Sayil, and Uxmal—all fine examples of the Puuc architectural style. Puuc buildings were beautifully proportioned, often designed in a low-slung quadrangle shape that allowed for many rooms inside. Exterior walls were kept plain to show off the friezes above, which were embellished with stone-mosaic gods, geometric designs, and serpentine motifs. Corners were edged with gargoyle-like, curved-nosed Chaac figures.

Uxmal

▼
Between 2000 BC and AD 100, the Maya are based in lowlands of south-central Guatemala and governed by hereditary chiefs.

2000 BC   1000

PETÉN

PRECLASSIC

POSTCLASSIC PERIOD: Quintana Roo Coast

Although Maya culture continued to flourish between AD 1000 and the early 1500s, signs of decline also began to take form. Wars broke out between neighboring city-states, leaving the region vulnerable when the Spaniards began invading in 1521. By 1600, the Spanish had dominated the Maya empire.

Maya architecture enjoyed its last hurrah during this period, mostly in the region along the Yucatán's Caribbean coast. Known as Quintana Roo Coast architecture, this style can be seen today at the ruins of Tulum. Although the structures here aren't as visually arresting as those at earlier, inland sites, Tulum's location is breathtaking: it's the only major Maya city overlooking the sea.

Tulum

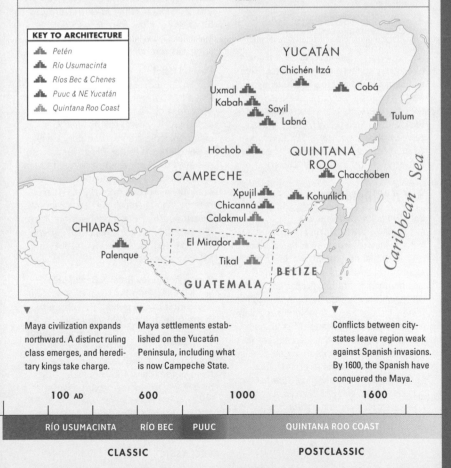

KEY TO ARCHITECTURE

- Petén
- Río Usumacinta
- Ríos Bec & Chenes
- Puuc & NE Yucatán
- Quintana Roo Coast

YUCATÁN

Chichén Itzá

Uxmal
Kabah
Sayil
Labná

Cobá

Tulum

Hochob

QUINTANA ROO

CAMPECHE

Chacchoben

Xpujil
Chicanná
Calakmul

Kohunlich

CHIAPAS

Palenque

El Mirador

Tikal

BELIZE

GUATEMALA

Caribbean Sea

▼ Maya civilization expands northward. A distinct ruling class emerges, and hereditary kings take charge.

▼ Maya settlements established on the Yucatán Peninsula, including what is now Campeche State.

▼ Conflicts between city-states leave region weak against Spanish invasions. By 1600, the Spanish have conquered the Maya.

| 100 AD | 600 | 1000 | 1600 |

RÍO USUMACINTA | RÍO BEC | PUUC | QUINTANA ROO COAST

CLASSIC | POSTCLASSIC

better beaches lie just south of Puerto Aventuras in the community of Xpu-Há. **Amenities:** food and drink. **Best for:** snorkeling; swimming. ✉ *Behind the Omni Hotel, Puerto Aventuras.*

Paamul Beach
BEACH | FAMILY | Beachcombers, campers, and snorkeling snowbirds love Paamul (pronounced pah-*mool*), a crescent-shaped lagoon 21 km (13 miles) south of Playa del Carmen with clear, placid waters sheltered by a coral reef. Shells, sand dollars, and even glass beads—some from the sunken, 18th-century Spanish galleon *Mantanceros,* which lies off nearby Akumal—wash up onto the sandy parts of the beach. (There's a sandy path into deeper water in front of the restaurant—on the rocks, watch out for sea urchins.) Sea turtles hatch here June to November. ■ **TIP→ If you'd like to stay on this piece of paradise, Hotel and Cabanas Paamul is a laid-back option.** **Amenities:** food and drink; parking (no fee); showers; toilets; water sports. **Best for:** snorkeling; swimming; walking. ✉ *Paamul Bay, Carretera 307 Cancún–Chetumal, Km 85, between Xcaret and Puerto Aventuras, Paamul* 🎟 *Free.*

🍴 Restaurants

Café Olé In Puerto Aventuras
$$ | INTERNATIONAL | FAMILY | The laid-back hub of Puerto Aventuras is this terrace café with a varied menu, including coconut shrimp and chicken with a chimichurri sauce made from red wine, garlic, onion, and fine herbs. If you and local fisherman get lucky, the nightly specials might include fresh-caught fish in garlic sauce. **Known for:** all-you-can-eat barbecue ribs; fresh-caught fish in garlic sauce; live music. [$] *Average main: MP280* ✉ *Centro Comercial Marina, Puerto Aventuras* ☎ *984/873–5125* 🌐 *www.facebook.com/cafeoleinpuertoaventuras.*

🛏 Hotels

Hard Rock Hotel Riviera Maya
$$$$ | ALL-INCLUSIVE | FAMILY | Live out your rock-star fantasies at this 85-acre all-inclusive—either in the adults-only Heaven section, a pampering resort within the resort, or the family-friendly Hacienda wing, which has a teens' club, disco, kids' pool, 100-foot climbing tower, snorkeling cove, and obstacle fitness trail. **Pros:** outstanding for-guests-only spa; great aquapark; access to neighboring golf course. **Cons:** time-share sales pitch; artificial beach; theme isn't for everyone. [$] *Rooms from: $454* ✉ *Carretera 307, Km 72, Puerto Aventuras* ✥ *3 km (2 miles) north of Puerto Aventuras* ☎ *984/875–1100, 817/567–7516 in the U.S.* 🌐 *www.hardrockhotels.com* 🛏 *1,264 rooms* 🍴 *All-Inclusive.*

Paamul Hotel
$$ | HOTEL | Located in Paamul, south of Playa del Carmen, this rustic resort sits on a perfect white-sand beach. **Pros:** some lovely views; rooms have spacious balconies; complimentary kayak or paddleboard rental. **Cons:** need car to get around; somewhat pricey restaurant with mediocre food; lots of mosquitoes at night. [$] *Rooms from: $210* ✉ *Carretera Cancún-Tulum, Km 85, 19 km (12 miles) south of Playa del Carmen, Paamul* ☎ *984/239–9484, 612/442–9577 in the U.S.* 🌐 *www.paamul.com* 🛏 *13 rooms* 🍴 *Free Breakfast.*

Puerto Aventuras Hotel & Beach Club
$$ | RESORT | Atop the main beach and in the center of the action, this property is the focal point of Puerto Aventuras, but its low-key luxury is a cut above the town's other resorts. **Pros:** pretty beach; nearby marina with dolphins; decent golf course. **Cons:** food choices could be better; no elevator; extra charge for beach amenities. [$] *Rooms from: $161* ✉ *Calle Punta Celis, Puerto Aventuras*

☎ 984/875–1950 ⊕ www.puertoaven-turashotel.com ⇆ 30 rooms ¶◯¶ Free Breakfast.

 Activities

Aquanauts Dive Shop

SCUBA DIVING | The reef here invites exploration, and this full-service operation specializes in open-water dives, including multi-tank options. Certification courses and cenote dives are also available. ✉ Calle Punta Celis, by the marina, Puerto Aventuras ☎ 984/108–7825, 877/623–2491 in the U.S. ⊕ aquanautsdiveshop.com ⌨ 2-tank dives from MX$2,500.

Dolphin Discovery

WILDLIFE-WATCHING | **FAMILY** | You can swim with dolphins in the closed-off waters of the marina or get up close and personal with manatees, stingrays, and sea lions at Dolphin Discovery. Programs are available daily from 9 to 3:30. ✉ On the marina, Calle Bahia Xcacel, Puerto Aventuras ☎ 998/193–3360, 866/393–5158 in the U.S. ⊕ www.dolphindiscovery.com ⌨ From $69.

Rock Spa

SPAS | With 75 treatment rooms, steam baths, and hydrotherapy pools, the Rock Spa is one of the largest in the Caribbean. In keeping with Hard Rock's music theme, massage therapists synchronize movements with an expertly curated playlist. From facials to wraps, each treatment connects the healing power of music with the power of touch and relaxation. There's also a yoga temple, beauty salon, and fitness center, but the hydrothermal experience is the big draw; only resort guests have access to the spa. ✉ Hard Rock Hotel Riviera Maya, Carretera 307, Km 72, Puerto Aventuras ✛ 3 km (2 miles) north of Puerto Aventuras ☎ 817/567–1100 in the U.S., 984/875–1100 ⊕ www.hardrockhotels.com.

Zero Gravity Dive Center

DIVING & SNORKELING | This dive shop rents equipment and has a staff of experienced instructors that specialize in cave diving. ✉ Carretera 307, Km 269.5, Puerto Aventuras ☎ 984/840–9030 ⊕ zerogravity.com.mx.

Xpu-Há

6 km (4 miles) southwest of Puerto Aventuras, 31 km (19 miles) southwest of Playa del Carmen.

Located 20 minutes southwest of Playa del Carmen and 20 minutes northeast of Tulum, Xpu-Há is the perfect base to relax and get away from the crowds. The beach is startling white, with soft clean sand that is raked by the few boutique hotels and villas that dot the shores. Other than the Catalonia Royal Tulum, you won't find sprawling resorts taking over the area. But this stellar stretch has recently brought in several beach clubs and restaurants, which means this hush-hush haven is now officially on the map.

GETTING HERE AND AROUND

The Xpu-Há entrance is just southwest of Puerto Aventuras at Km 265. if you're coming from the north, individual signs for Al Cielo, Esencia, and Catalonia Royal mark the three entrances on the east side of the highway. If you're coming from the south, make a U-turn at the retorno across from the Pemex gas station. Bumpy dirt roads will drop you in paradise. Since Xpu-Há is simply a beach community consisting of hotels and villas, the closest services are in Puerto Aventuras and, to the south, in Akumal.

⬆ Beaches

La Playa Xpu-Ha Beach Club

BEACH | **FAMILY** | Located at Playa Xpu-Ha, this beach club is open year-round from 10 am to 6:30 pm. Guests of nearby villas are often lured here by the plethora of amenities—including showers, lockers, hammocks, umbrellas, chaise lounges, and a rental shop that has snorkeling gear, WaveRunners, boogie boards, and kayaks. In full beach club tradition, there's a restaurant and a bar with swings instead of stools. You can burn off your lunch with a game of volleyball, or opt for hair braids and henna tattoos. **Amenities:** food and drink; showers; toilets; water sports. **Best for:** partiers; swimming; walking. ✉ *Carretera 307, Km 265, Xpu-Há* ☎ *984/133–6701* 🌐 *laplayaxpuha.com* 🎟 *MX$200 entry which is applied to food and drinks consumption.*

★ Xpu-Ha Beach

BEACH | FAMILY | Other than the occasional villa and resort, including Royal Catalonia Tulum smack-dab in the center, this stretch of white sand is fairly isolated. South of here are a few spots where you can grab a midday snack, like La Playa Beach Club. There are no hidden rocks in shallow areas, so many people come to swim or snorkel, especially when the winds are calm. The sugary sand is raked, making it a good place for an unobstructed stroll, too. Unlike many beaches, this one isn't blocked by resort security. You can access it through La Playa or by having lunch at one of the nearby restaurants and beach clubs. **Amenities:** food and drink; lifeguards; parking (fee); showers; toilets; water sports. **Best for:** partiers; snorkeling; swimming; walking. ✉ *Carretera 307, Km 265, at the entrance to La Playa Beach Club, Xpu-Há.*

Hotels

Catalonia Royal Tulum

$$$ | RESORT | This lavish, adults-only resort was designed around the surrounding jungle and has a great beach, nonstop activities, and terrific food for a resort in its price range. **Pros:** excellent beach; great diving classes; enthusiastic staff. **Cons:** no kids under 18; no elevator; nonstop action not for everyone. [$] *Rooms from: $289* ✉ *Carretera 307, Km 264.5, Xpu-Há* ☎ *984/875–1800* 🌐 *www.cataloniahotels.com* 🛏 *288 rooms* 🍴 *All-Inclusive.*

★ Hotel Esencia

$$$$ | HOTEL | Situated on 50 acres of jungle, this sprawling estate—once the home of an Italian duchess—has been converted into one of the Riviera Maya's most luxurious hotels. **Pros:** stunning beach; daily yoga; private helicopter. **Cons:** small section of the beach is rocky; not all rooms have ocean views; small gym. [$] *Rooms from: $1,305* ✉ *Carretera 307, Km 265, Predio Rústico Xpu-Há, Lotes 18 and 19, Xpu-Há* ☎ *984/873–4830* 🌐 *hotelesencia.com* 🛏 *29 rooms* 🍴 *Free Breakfast.*

Akumal

16 km (10 miles) southwest of Xpu-Há, 37 km (23 miles) southwest of Playa del Carmen.

In Mayan, Akumal (pronounced ah-koo-*maal*) means "place of the turtle," and this portion of coast is a storied nesting ground, especially at Half Moon Bay. Akumal first attracted international attention in 1926, when explorers discovered the *Mantanceros,* a Spanish galleon that sank there in 1741. In the 1960s, diver Pablo Bush Romero established the Hotel Akumal Caribe. Today Akumal is an Americanized beach community, home to divers, fishermen, and laid-back expats from the United States and Canada.

It's essentially a long string of upscale homes and condos along three bays. Akumal Bay is the best base for visits, with a good selection of hotels and restaurants plus the best all-around beach for swimming and snorkeling. Half Moon Bay, just beyond, has decent snorkeling and more condos for rent, but the beach is narrow and rocky. Laguna Yal-kú is a protected snorkeling lagoon.

■ **TIP→** Bypass the vendors at Akumal's entrance offering snorkel gear for rent. Although their rates are slightly less than you'll pay elsewhere, once you tack on conservation fees, parking, and a guide, you're better off going through an official dive shop.

GETTING HERE AND AROUND

The entrance to town is on the east side of the highway, so coming from the north you'll have to make a U-turn at the well-marked retorno; coming from the south, exit at Km 264 off Carretera 307. From either direction, follow the signs to "Akumal Playa."

Getting around is easy as there's only one road. It runs from the highway through the Arch—the town's gateway, at Hotel Akumal Caribe—and along Akumal Bay past Half Moon Bay to Laguna Yalku, a trip of about 10 minutes by car. Unlike many beach communities, this one can be entered even when a guard is stationed. Simply explain that you're heading to the beach. Akumal's tourist office is a small booth on the main road before the Arch as you enter town.

◉ Sights

★ **Aktunchen Park** (*Indiana Joe's*)
CAVE | FAMILY | The name is Mayan for "the cave with cenotes inside," and these amazing underground caverns—estimated to be about 5 million years old—are the area's largest. You walk through the underground passages, past stalactites and stalagmites, until you reach the cenote with its various shades of deep green. There's also an on-site canopy tour and one cenote where you can swim. ■ **TIP→ This top family attraction isn't as crowded or touristy as Xplor, Xel-Há, and Xcaret.** ⊠ *Carretera 307, Km 107, opposite Bahia Principe resort, between Akumal and Xel-Há, Akumal* ☎ *984/806–4962* ⊕ *www.aktun-chenpark. com* ⊠ *Cave tour $29; cenote tour $33; canopy tour $44.*

★ **Xel-Há**
WATER PARK | FAMILY | Part of the Xcaret nature-adventure park group, Xel-Há (pronounced shel-*hah*) is a natural aquarium made of coves, inlets, and lagoons cut from the limestone shoreline. The name means "where the water is born," and a natural spring here flows out to meet the salt water, creating a unique habitat for tropical marine life. There's enough to impress novice snorkelers, though there seem to be fewer fish each year, and the mixture of fresh and salt water can cloud visibility. Low wooden bridges over the lagoons allow for leisurely walks around the park, and there are spots to rest, swim, cliff-jump, zip line, or swing from ropes over the water.

Xel-Há gets overwhelmingly crowded, so come early. The grounds are well equipped with bathrooms and restaurants. At the entrance you'll receive specially prepared sunscreen that won't kill the fish; other sunscreens are prohibited. The entrance fee includes a meal, towel, locker, inner tubes, and snorkel equipment; other activities, like scuba diving, zip-lining, swimming with the dolphins, and spa treatments, are available at additional cost. ■ **TIP→ Discounts are offered when you book online.** ⊠ *Carretera 307, Km 240, Xel-Ha* ☎ *998/883–3143, 855/326–0682 in the U.S.* ⊕ *www.xelha. com* ⊠ *$114.*

Yal-Ku Akumal Lagoon & Snorkel (*Yal-kú Lagoon*)
BODY OF WATER | FAMILY | Devoted snorkelers may want to follow the unmarked dirt road to Laguna Yal-kú, about 3 km (2 miles) north of Akumal town center. A series of small mangrove-edged lagoons that gradually reach the ocean, Yal-kú is an eco-park that's home to schools of parrot fish in clear water with visibility to 160 feet in winter and spring. Snorkeling equipment can be rented in the parking lot; the site also has toilets, lockers, changing rooms, outdoor showers, and a snack bar. ■ **TIP→ Sunscreen is not**

allowed, so bring a T-shirt to keep from getting burned. ✉ *Calle de Acceso Etapa H, Lote 5, just past Half Moon Bay, Akumal* ☎ *984/875–9065* 🌐 *yalku-cenote.company.site* 🎟 *MX$280.*

Beaches

Akumal Bay

BEACH | FAMILY | Known for the sea turtles that swim in its waters, Akumal Bay is sheltered by an offshore reef—though, sadly only about 30% of it is alive. It's best to explore the waters with a certified guide available through dive shops in town. Do not wear sunscreen in the water as it can harm the reef, and, above all, do not touch the wildlife or coral. Be careful to stay clear of the red "fire reef," which stings on contact. When you drag yourself away from the snorkeling, there are plenty of palm trees for shade, as well as a variety of waterfront shops, restaurants, and cafés. If you continue on the main road, you'll reach Half Moon Bay and Laguna Yal-kú, also good snorkeling spots. **Amenities:** food and drink; lifeguards; parking (fee); showers; toilets; water sports. **Best for:** snorkeling; swimming; walking. ✉ *Enter at Hotel Akumal Caribe, Akumal.*

Half Moon Bay

BEACH | FAMILY | The crescent bay on the north end of Akumal has shallow water and almost no current, making it a safe swimming spot for children; the snorkeling is also good here (you might even see the occasional sea turtle). Beach chairs and hammocks line the narrow, rocky shore at La Buena Vida restaurant, which has a pool, restrooms, and limited street parking for patrons. The area near Casa Zama is protected by an outer reef; however, the entry point is rocky, so bring water shoes. Bring an umbrella, too—Half Moon Bay is known for its white sand and clear waters, but the lack of trees means you'll have trouble finding shade. **Amenities:** food and drink; toilets. **Best for:** snorkeling; swimming. ✉ *Beach Rd., Lote 35, North Akumal, Akumal.*

Xcacel Beach

BEACH | FAMILY | About 10 km (6 miles) south of Akumal, this beach (also written Xca-Cel), has white powdery sand and a nearby cenote that can be accessed through a jungle path to your right. Snorkeling is best on the beach's north end. To reach it from Carretera 307, turn at the dirt road that runs between Chemuyil and Xel-Há. The route is blocked by a guard who will charge you MX$97 to enter; after paying, simply continue on to the beach itself. From May through November, this area is reserved for turtle nesting. Avoid stepping on any raised mounds of sand as they could be turtle nests. Note that the beach road is open daily 10–4. **Amenities:** parking (no fee); toilets. **Best for:** snorkeling; solitude; swimming. ✉ *Carretera 307, Km 248, Akumal* 🎟 *MX$97* ⏲ *Closed Sun.*

Restaurants

La Buena Vida

$$$ | MEXICAN | FAMILY | With driftwood tables overlooking Half Moon Bay, swings at the lively bar, and salsa music keeping things moving, this might be the perfect beach restaurant. The usual Mexican fare—quesadillas, empanadas, burritos, and fish tacos with handmade tortillas—is perfectly fine, but the food isn't the point. **Known for:** incredible beachfront location; sweeping waterfront views; a two-seater tower table above the sand. [$] *Average main: MP320* ✉ *North Akumal, Beach Rd., Half Moon Bay, Lote 35, Akumal* ☎ *984/875–9061* 🌐 *labuenavidarestaurant.com* ⏲ *Closed 1st 2 wks in Sept.*

La Cueva del Pescador

$$ | SEAFOOD | FAMILY | Dig your toes in the sand floor and enjoy the catch of the day at La Cueva del Pescador. A crowd of easygoing expats hunkers down for the afternoon to feast on octopus, shrimp,

Did You Know?

At Aktunchen, you can snorkel in a cenote and see 5-million-year-old stalactites and stalagmites. Need a bit of fresh air? Try a zip line tour.

or conch ceviche prepared with lime juice and flavored with cilantro—usually with a generous helping of beer on the side. **Known for:** ceviche with octopus, shrimp, or conch; good beer; grilled garlic shrimp. $ *Average main: MP275* ✉ *Plaza Ukana, Main rd., Akumal Bay, Akumal* ☎ *984/875–9002.*

Turtle Bay Café & Bakery

$$$ | CAFÉ | FAMILY | This funky café, where expats and locals congregate, serves up smoothies, baked goods, tacos, homemade ice cream, and everything in between. The breakfast menu spans acai bowls, eggs Benedict, pancakes, and fruit plates, and for lunch and dinner you'll find blackened fish tacos, coconut shrimp, burgers, and vegetable wraps. **Known for:** sticky buns; homemade ice cream; Quintana Roo vodka. $ *Average main: MP330* ✉ *Plaza Ukana, Main rd., Akumal Bay, Akumal* ☎ *984/875–9138* ⊕ *turtlebaycafe.com.*

 ## Hotels

Bahía Príncipe Riviera Maya Resort (*Grand Bahia Principe*)

$$$$ | ALL-INCLUSIVE | FAMILY | This all-inclusive megacomplex consists of four upscale hotels (Akumal, Cobá, Tulum, and Sian Ka'an) with extensive shared facilities reachable by shuttle from 7:30 am to midnight. **Pros:** on the beach; lots of activities for children; access to golf course. **Cons:** you'll need a car to get to town; you'll need a golf cart to move around the sprawling facilities; most restaurants require advance booking. $ *Rooms from: $315* ✉ *Carretera 307, Km 250, Akumal* ✛ *Access the property through the resort gate off Carretera 307 rather than the main entrance into Akumal town* ☎ *984/875–5000, 800/607–0179* ⊕ *www.bahia-principe. com* ☚ *Akumal 758 rooms, Cobá 1,080 rooms, Tulum 976 rooms, Sian Ka'an 420 rooms* ❒ *All-Inclusive* ☞ *3-night stay minimum.*

Del Sol Beachfront

$$ | HOTEL | FAMILY | Each small room in the main building of this bright, colorful seaside hotel has an ocean view and a private terrace, and next door are more expensive condos with Spanish colonial touches. **Pros:** on beach; all rooms have ocean views; well-kept grounds. **Cons:** beach is a little rocky; beds aren't very comfortable; no meals. $ *Rooms from: $160* ✉ *Calle Caleta Yalku, Lote 41G, Akumal* ✛ *Next to La Buena Vida* ☎ *984/875–9060, 888/425–8625 in the U.S.* ⊕ *delsolbeachfront.com* ☚ *28 rooms* ❒ *No Meals.*

Hotel Akumal Caribe

$$$ | HOTEL | Back in the 1960s, Pablo Bush Romero established this resort as a place for his diving buddies to crash, and it still offers pleasant accommodations and a congenial staff. **Pros:** comfortable beds; on the beach; easy snorkeling. **Cons:** most rooms lack ocean views; no elevator; basic decor. $ *Rooms from: $239* ✉ *At Akumal Arch, Main rd., Akumal Bay, Akumal* ☎ *984/875–9012, 915/222–8634 in the U.S.* ⊕ *hotelakumal-caribe.com* ☚ *55 rooms* ❒ *No Meals.*

Shopping

Galería Lamanai

ART GALLERIES | A laid-back spot under a palapa roof, Galería Lamanai carries a mix of folk and fine art from more than 200 Mexican artists. ✉ *Hotel Akumal Caribe, Yodzonot, Akumal Bay, Akumal* ☎ *984/875–9055.*

Mexicarte

CRAFTS | FAMILY | This colorful little shop sells high-quality crafts from around the country. ✉ *Main rd., Akumal Bay, Akumal* ✛ *Next to Hotel Akumal Caribe* ☎ *984/875–9115* ⊕ *mexicarte.shop.*

Activities

Akumal Dive Center

DIVING & SNORKELING | FAMILY | The area's oldest dive operation offers reef or cenote diving as well as one-hour snorkeling tours; the latter includes gear, lockers, showers, guides, and conservation wristbands for $50 per person. Three-hour fishing trips for up to four people can also be arranged. Take a sharp right at the Akumal Arch, and you'll see the dive shop on the beach. ⊠ *Hotel Akumal Caribe, Akumal Bay, Akumal* ☎ *984/875–9025* ⊕ *www.akumaldivecenter.com* ✉ *From MX$960.*

★ Akumal Dive Shop

DIVING & SNORKELING | FAMILY | You can go snorkeling with turtles or diving at cenotes with the Akumal Dive Shop. Certification courses are also available. If boating is more your thing, it runs daytime and sunset catamaran cruises, too. ⊠ *Plaza Ukana, North Akumal Bay, Akumal* ☎ *984/875–9030, 984/875–9031* ⊕ *akumaldiveshop.com* ✉ *Snorkeling tour MX$750; diving trip MX$1,100; cruises MX$2,400.*

Akumal Guide

BIKING | FAMILY | The small booth inside Hotel Akumal Caribe rents bikes for MX$160 per day, as well as golf carts—a popular way to get around Akumal—for MX$800 per day. Tours to popular spots like Cobá or Sian Ka'an can also be arranged here. ⊠ *Hotel Akumal Caribe, Akumal Bay, Akumal* ☎ *984/114–9789* ⊕ *www.akumalguide.com.*

Budha Garden Spa

SPAS | This small day spa in Akumal offers hot stone massage, reflexology, facials, body scrubs, wraps, manicures, and pedicures. After a time in the sun, try the popular Maya clay mask, said to firm the skin and draw out impurities. Body scrub options range from essential oil to lavender-rose, while the facials incorporate ingredients like white tea and acai and goji berry to rehydrate the skin. ⊠ *Past Akumal Arch on main rd., next to Hotel Akumal Caribe, Akumal* ☎ *984/745–4942* ⊕ *www.budhagardenspa.com.*

Centro Ecológico Akumal

ECOTOURISM | FAMILY | From May through October, the ecological center in Akumal offers guided walks through sea turtle nesting sites. Learn about conservation efforts and participate in nighttime nest visits for a suggested $15 donation. Proceeds go to turtle conservation. ⊠ *Carretera Puerto Juarez Tulum, Km 104, Akumal* ☎ *984/217–3385* ⊕ *ceakumal.org* ✉ *Suggested donation $15.*

Tankah

26 km (16 miles) southwest of Akumal, 56 km (35 miles) southwest of Playa del Carmen.

In ancient times, Tankah was an important Maya trading city, and today, if you plan to visit Tulum or Cobá, it's a good place to stay if you want to avoid the crowds. Several small, reasonably priced hotels have cropped up here over the past few years, and a few expats who own villas rent them out year-round. Often overlooked by travelers, this spectacular stretch of coastline offers great snorkeling, diving, and best of all, isolation. A cenote that tunnels under the beach road and spills into the sea makes the area even more unique.

GETTING HERE AND AROUND

To reach the coastal road in Tankah, turn east off Carretera 307 at Km 237 (a sign for Nuh Hotel and a peacock mural mark the turn). At the end of the long, pitted road, turn left (north) where a string of villas and small hotels parallel the beach. The closest medical clinics, grocery stores, and emergency services are 4 km (2½ miles) south in Tulum.

Beaches

Tankah Bay

BEACH | Nestled in a protected cove, this wide stretch of beach is popular with divers and snorkelers due to the outer reef that keeps waters calm. The fine sand is perfect for a barefoot stroll, but the shallow waters have sharp rocks just below the surface. Across the road from Casa Cenote Restaurant is Manatee Cenote, an underwater cave that spills from the mangroves into the sea. This freshwater pool, coupled with the outer reef, make Tankah a snorkeler's paradise. The main draw is that the area is relatively isolated since most sun worshipers tend to bask on the shores of Playa del Carmen. **Amenities:** food and drink; toilets. **Best for:** snorkeling; solitude; walking. ✉ *Tankah Bay, Tulum.*

Restaurants

Casa Cenote Restaurant

$$$ | **MEXICAN** | **FAMILY** | The cheapest restaurant along Tankah's beachfront serves up fresh, simple, satisfying Mexican food from 8 am to 9 pm every day. Grab a table at the waterfront, and order up beef fajitas or fish tacos, topped with a healthy helping of fresh-made salsa and fresh-squeezed lime juice. **Known for:** beef and chicken fajitas; fish tacos; powerful margaritas. [$] *Average main: MP325* ✉ *Interior Fracc. Tankah, Mz 3, Lote 32, across from Cenote Manatee, Tulum* ☎ *984/115–6996, 646/634–7206 in the U.S.* 🌐 *www.casacenote.com/eat-drink.*

★ **Oscar & Lalo**

$$ | **SEAFOOD** | **FAMILY** | Enter through the massive gate and wind your way up a garden pathway through the main dining area and into the back garden where intimate four- or five-table palapas are surrounded by jungle and hung with bright white hammocks and twinkling lights. Many ingredients, as well as medicinal plants, are grown on property and the owners would be happy to cut you a piece of fresh aloe for your sunburn or brew you up some anti-food-poisoning tea. **Known for:** intimate jungle garden seating; Maya dishes; organic chicken and pork. [$] *Average main: MP270* ✉ *Carretera 307, Km 241, Tulum* ☎ *984/127–1587, 984/115–9965* 🌐 *oscarandlalo.com.*

Hotels

★ **Jashita**

$$$$ | **HOTEL** | **FAMILY** | At this sophisticated little hotel on the northern end of Soliman Bay, a large stone Buddha flanked by birds-of-paradise greets you in the lobby—which is outfitted with Indonesian carved-wood doors and Moroccan art—and two small swimming pools nestle in a garden of palms just beyond. **Pros:** kid-friendly; clear, calm bay; very private. **Cons:** not much to do in the nearby area; bay too shallow for swimming in some places; not all rooms have ocean views. [$] *Rooms from: $303* ✉ *Bahia de Soliman, Tankah Rd. IV, Tulum* ✥ *Across Carretera 307 from Oscar & Lalo* ☎ *984/179–1659* 🌐 *www.jashitahotel.com* 🛏 *30 suites* 🍴 *Free Breakfast.*

Mereva Tulum

$$$ | **HOTEL** | **FAMILY** | This boutique beach property—complete with oceanfront pool and exquisite accommodations just steps from the secluded white sand—is one of the area's best. **Pros:** sublime beachfront setting; excellent mixologist (for both juices and cocktails that will transport you to paradise); stunning rooms. **Cons:** need a car to get around; some rooms lack full ocean view; restaurant is nothing special. [$] *Rooms from: $216* ✉ *Bahía Tankah, Fracc. Tankah III, Mz 3, Lote 35, past Casa Cenote, Tulum* ☎ *984/147–6571* 🌐 *www.mereva.mx* 🛏 *25 rooms* 🍴 *No Meals.*

🏃 Activities

Due to the outer reef, calm bay, and connecting cenote, Tankah has become a popular dive spot. The closest dive shop is Maya Dive Center, but most scuba centers along Riviera Maya can organize trips to Tankah.

Cenote Manatee (*Casa Cenote*)
DIVING & SNORKELING | Directly across from Casa Cenote Hotel, this open lagoon (often referred to as Casa Cenote) is popular with experienced cave divers since a freshwater tunnel—dropping below the main road—connects directly to the ocean. Here two ecosystems collide with both fresh and salt water, offering a maximum diving depth of 26 feet. The constant currents draw in a variety of marine life including parrot fish, swimming crabs, moray eels, juvenile barracuda, and tarpon. ⚠ **Only skilled divers should enter the underwater cave since the distance between the cenote and ocean is dangerously long.** Aside from a small parking lot and a shack renting snorkeling equipment, the only facilities are those at neighboring hotels and restaurants. ✉ *Interior Fracc. Tankah, Mz 3, Lote 32, Tulum* 💰 *MX$150.*

Extreme Control Kite School
WATER SPORTS | FAMILY | All levels of kite-surfing lessons and the latest equipment are available through Extreme Control Kite School. Led by IKO (International Kiteboarding Organization) instructor Marco Cristofanelli, courses take place at Caleta Tankah Beach Club, about five minutes from Tulum. Paddleboarding, diving, and snorkeling tours, as well as lessons and equipment rentals are also offered. ✉ *Caleta Tankah Beach Club, Carretera 307, Km 230, Tulum* ☎ *984/745–4555* 🌐 *extremecontrol.net* 💰 *1-hour lessons from $90.*

Tulum

9 km (5½ miles) southwest of Tankah, 61 km (38 miles) southwest of Playa del Carmen.

It used to be that Tulum was simply known as dusty little town with a stellar archaeological site and a few palapa huts. No longer. Discovered by the international eco-set, it now has whitewashed, solar-powered bungalow hotels that line the spectacular beach 2 km (1 mile) east of town. Locals speak of a battle for Tulum's bohemian soul, and although first-time visitors may not notice the changes, it's indisputable that the free-spirited hippie days are over.

Tulum is divided into three main areas: the downtown pueblo, south from the shore along Carretera 307 (here known as Avenida Tulum); the Mayan ruins to the north on the coast; and the beach (Zona Hotelera), which extends down from the ruins.

The ancient structures were the town's original draw, and Tulum (meaning "wall" in Mayan) now lures more than 2 million people annually. Even if you couldn't care less about history, the site's waterfront location elevates it to the sublime. The pueblo, conversely, is a jumble of food stalls, souvenir shops, budget hostels, and cheap eateries—some catering to tourists, some to locals, and some to both. Although it's more appealing to stay along the shore, the town offers an authentic slice of Mexico.

Tulum's irresistible beach begins just east on the Boca Paila road. (Technically there's beach all the way from the ruins down to Sian Ka'an, but the coast by the ruins, and south to Zamas restaurant, is a series of rocky coves. The endless powdery sand you came for is south of the bridge and police checkpoint after Zamas.) Miles of magnificent white sand sparkle before the aquamarine waves,

Did You Know?

Tulum is the only ancient
Maya city overlooking
the sea, and while the
architecture may not
be as striking as inland
sites, the location is
breathtaking.

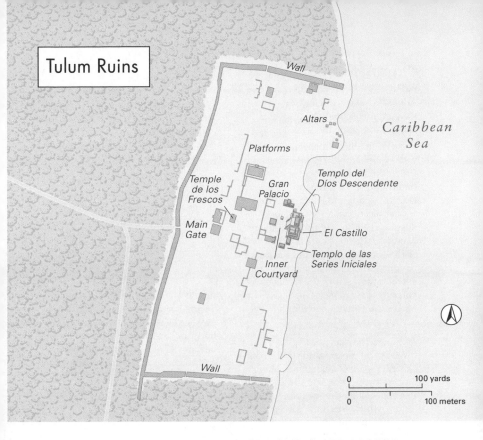

Tulum Ruins

Wall

Altars

Caribbean Sea

Platforms

Temple de los Frescos

Gran Palacio

Templo del Díos Descendente

Main Gate

El Castillo

Inner Courtyard

Templo de las Series Iniciales

Wall

| 0 | | 100 yards |
| 0 | | 100 meters |

backed by eco-hotels on one side of the narrow road, and tropical hipster restaurants, yoga centers, and the odd spa on the other.

Tulum's ongoing transformation has brought new services, including a 24-hour hospital, four gas stations, and a Chedraui supermarket. But there's still no community power supply at the beach, so eco-resorts—both rustic and chic—rely on wind turbines, solar energy, recycled water, generators, and candlelight. Rooms are usually void of TVs and phones, and they seldom have Wi-Fi or 24-hour air-conditioning (although this is slowly changing). Note, too, that some hotels draw water from cenotes, which might result in a salty shower and low water pressure.

GETTING HERE AND AROUND

Tulum is a 20-minute drive from Akumal and a 45-minute drive from Playa del Carmen. You can hire a taxi from Cancún for approximately MX$2,000. Tucan Kin (⊕ www.tucankin.com) has a direct shared shuttle service from Cancún airport for MX$1,450 per couple one way. Buses operated by ADO (⊕ www.ado.com.mx) link Cancún, Puerto Morelos, Playa del Carmen, Tulum, Felipe Carrillo Puerto, Limones, and Chetumal. Colectivos travel from Cancún to Playa and Playa to Tulum and should cost you less than MX$100.

The archaeological site entrance is 2 km (1 mile) from the pueblo and accessible on foot or by bike. You can also catch one of the shuttles that pass every few minutes.

Caribbean Coastal History

Maya culture is the enduring backdrop for Mexico's Caribbean coast. Archaeologists have divided this civilization, which lasted some 3,500 years, into three main periods: Preclassic and Late Preclassic together (2000 BC–AD 100), Classic (AD 100–1000), and Postclassic (AD 1000–1521). Considered the most advanced civilization of the ancient Americas, the Maya are credited with several major breakthroughs: a highly accurate calendar based on astronomical study; the mathematical concept of zero; hieroglyphic writing; and extraordinary ceremonial architecture.

Although the Maya's early days were centered on the lowlands in the south-central region of Guatemala, Maya culture spread north to the Yucatán Peninsula sometime around AD 987. Tulum, which was built during this period, is the only ancient Maya city constructed right on the water.

Until the 1960s, Quintana Roo (then a Mexican territory, not a state) was considered the wildest coast in Central America. The Caste War of the Yucatán, which began in 1847 and ended with a half-hearted truce in 1935, herded hardy Maya to this remote region. With the exception of *chicleros* (men who tapped *zapote* or chicle trees for the Wrigley Chewing Gum Corporation), few non-Maya lived here.

By the 1950s the Mexican government began giving tracts of land to the chicleros in hopes of colonizing Quintana Roo. At that time there were no roads. A few *cocals*, or coconut plantations, were scattered throughout the peninsula, headed by a handful of Maya families.

In 1967 the Mexican government decided to develop an international tourist destination, and was on the hunt for the location with the finest beaches, the most beautiful water, and the fewest hurricanes. A stretch of unpopulated sand at the northeast tip of the Yucatán Peninsula was the lucky winner. Soon after Cancún was born, Quintana Roo became Mexico's 31st state.

The phenomenal rise of Cancún has meant heightened exposure and economic overflow for communities farther south. Today the region extending down the coast to Tulum has developed into one of the world's most popular beach destinations.

To reach the beachfront Zona Hotelera, head south on Carretera 307 and turn left (east) at the second stoplight in Tulum. Shortly after passing the fire station, you'll come to a "T" in the road. There you'll find dozens of signs directing you to area hotels. The best beach is to the right, and the ruins are to the left. A taxi from the pueblo to the Zona Hotelera costs MX$200–MX$300. Within the Zona Hotelera, you'll have to rely on taxis, cars, or bikes to get around.

⚠ If you're driving in the area, watch out for the large beach crabs that cross the roads after dark.

TAXI CONTACTS Tucan Kin. ✉ *Carretera 307, Km 22, Carretera Cancún-Aeropuerto* ☎ *984/129–1575* ⊕ *tucankin.com.*

👁 Sights

★ Rivera's Kitchen Tulum

OTHER ATTRACTION | Join a vibrant Mexican mama from the foodie-beloved region of Oaxaca for an excellent four-hour cooking adventure in her jungle kitchen, starting at either 10:30 am or 4 pm. Classes are kept small, with a maximum of 10 people. The four-plus courses you'll make vary by season, but they often include authentic mole and ceviche. Once you're done prepping, stirring, and learning about the cuisine, you'll sit down to enjoy the meal you've prepared. Transportation is provided from Villas Tulum. ⊠ *Carretera Tulum–Cobá, Km 9.9, Tulum* ☎ *984/129–2690* ⊕ *riverakitchentulum.com* 🍴 *From $95 per person.*

★ Tulum Archaeological Site

RUINS | **FAMILY** | Tulum has long been a symbol of independence and resistance. It was a key city in the League of Mayapán (AD 987–1194), a trade center, and a safe harbor for goods from rival Maya factions who considered it neutral territory. At its height, Tulum's wealthy merchants outranked Maya priests in authority and power for the first time. It was also one of the few Maya cities known to have been inhabited when the conquistadores arrived in 1518.

Although the Spaniards never conquered Tulum, they forbade Maya traders to sail the seas. Commerce among the Maya died, and they abandoned the site about 75 years after the conquest of the rest of Mexico. The area was, however, one of the last Maya outposts during their insurrection against Mexican rule in the Caste Wars, which began in 1847. Uprisings continued intermittently until 1935, when the Maya ceded Tulum to the Mexican government.

To avoid long lines, arrive before 11 am. Although you can see the ruins thoroughly in two hours, allow extra time for a swim or a stroll on the beach. Guides are available for hire (MX$800) at the entrance, but some of their information is more entertaining than historically accurate. (Disregard that stuff about virgin sacrifices.) Also, vendors outside the entrance sell Mexican crafts, so bring some pesos for souvenirs.

To the left of the entryway is the first significant structure: the two-story **Templo de los Frescos,** whose vaulted roof and corbel arch are examples of classic Maya architecture. Faint traces of blue-green frescoes outlined in black on the inner and outer walls depict the three worlds of the Maya and their major deities, as well as decorative stellar and serpentine patterns, rosettes, and ears of maize and other offerings to the gods. One scene portrays the rain god seated on a four-legged animal—probably a reference to the Spaniards on their horses. Unfortunately, the frescoes are difficult to see from the path to which you are restricted.

The largest and most photographed structure, the **Castillo** (Castle), looms at the edge of a 40-foot limestone cliff just past the Temple of the Frescoes. Atop it, at the end of a broad stairway, is a temple with stucco ornamentation on the outside and traces of fine frescoes inside the two chambers. (The stairway has been roped off, so the top temple is inaccessible.) The front wall of the Castillo has faint carvings of the Descending God and columns depicting the plumed serpent god, Kukulcán, who was introduced to the Maya by the Toltecs.

To the left of the Castillo, facing the sea, is the **Templo del Dios Descendente**—so called for the carving over the doorway of a winged god plummeting to Earth. In addition, a few small altars sit atop a hill at the north side of the cove, where there's a good view of the Castillo and the sea. ⊠ *Carretera 307, Km 133, Tulum* ☎ *983/837–2411* ⊕ *inah.gob.mx* 🍴 *MX$90 entrance; MX$160 parking; MX$50 shuttle from parking to ruins.*

Sights ▼

Restaurants ▼

Hotels ▼

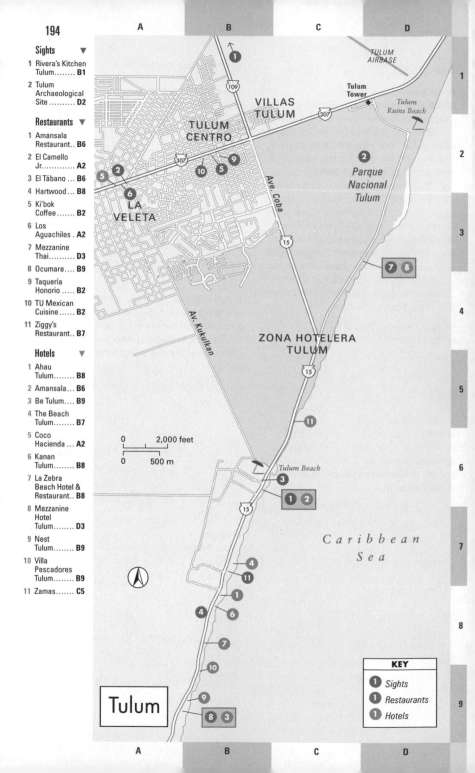

Beaches

Tulum Beach

BEACH | Extending 11 km (7 miles), Tulum's main beach is a tropical paradise comprised of glassy water and powdery sand, set off from the jungle by hip restaurants and low-slung bungalow hotels where the yoga set take their virtuous rest. It's divided by a rocky promontory into two main sections, similar to each other, although the farther south you go on the Carretera Tulum–Boca Paila beach road, the more secluded and lovelier it gets. The beach is bordered on the south by the Sian Ka'an biosphere reserve, whose coast is even more deserted. To the north, you'll find the Tulum ruins. Beach access can be tricky; even though the beach is public, the hotels and restaurants along the shore often limit access to guests only, and public access points are few and far between. If you're not staying on the beachfront, make sure to ask your hotel where the closest access point is. **Amenities:** food and drink; toilets; water sports. **Best for:** swimming; walking. ⊠ *Carretera Tulum-Boca Paila, Tulum.*

Tulum Ruins Beach

BEACH | Talk about a beach with a view! At Tulum's archaeological site, the Caribbean's signature white sand and turquoise waters are framed by a backdrop of Maya pyramids. The small cove can get crowded, especially during peak season when travelers flock to the ruins for a day of sightseeing. The south end by the rocks tends to have more breathing room. Only those who purchase a ticket to the ruins can access this beach, unless you approach the shores by boat. **Amenities:** none. **Best for:** swimming. ⊠ *Carretera 307, Km 130, Tulum* 🎫 *MX$90 for entrance via ruins.*

🍴 Restaurants

Amansala Restaurant

$$$ | **INTERNATIONAL** | For sweeping ocean views and light meals, head to this shady beachfront resort restaurant, where the smoothies are fruity but not overly sweet, the guacamole is fresh and flavorful, and the salsa selection is excellent. Don't miss the amply portioned spicy-sweet Thai curry Buddha Bowl. **Known for:** meals with a view; health-conscious cuisine; vegan and vegetarian options. $ *Average main: MP350* ⊠ *Amansala, Carretera Tulum-Boca Paila, Km 5.5, Tulum* 🕾 *559/225–2190* ⊕ *www.amansala.com.*

El Camello Jr.

$$ | **SEAFOOD** | **FAMILY** | Called "Camellito" by locals, this restaurant is famed for having Tulum's freshest seafood—and the jammed parking lot is testament to its enduring popularity. Fish or shrimp tacos are light and fresh, but the full splendor of the place is expressed by its whole grilled or fried fish, served with generous mounds of rice, beans, and *plátanos.* Come hungry. **Known for:** fresh seafood; fish or shrimp tacos; whole grilled or fried fish. $ *Average main: MP230* ⊠ *Avs. Tulum and Luna, at back end of town, Tulum* 🕾 *984/871–2036* ⊕ *www.facebook.com/RestauranteElCamelloJr* ⊘ *Closed Wed.*

El Tábano

$$$$ | **MEXICAN** | This jungle-side hangout is laid-back, casual, and comfortable, with an open kitchen and airy layout in a large, traditional palapa. Standout dishes include organic-chicken-stuffed jalapeños and organic chicken in red sauce (so tender that it practically falls off the bone). **Known for:** Mexican wines; spicy margaritas; traditional Mexican dishes. $ *Average main: MP420* ⊠ *Carretera Tulum-Boca Paila, Km 7, Tulum* 🕾 *984/182–9661* ⊕ *www.facebook.com/eltabanotulum* ⊘ *Closed Sun. Apr.–Sept.*

★ Hartwood

$$$$ | ECLECTIC | New York chefs cooking New York food for New York prices—in a jungle setting open to the night sky—that's Hartwood. Though the menu changes daily, options might include slow-roasted pork ribs marinated in agave honey or a light, fresh ceviche, and you can always finish with homemade ice cream in flavors like peanut brittle, sweet corn, and cream cheese. **Known for:** running a zero-carbon footprint operation; locally farmed rabbit; long waits in high season. $ *Average main: MP1,364* ⊠ *Carretera Tulum–Boca Paila, Km 7.6, Tulum* ⊕ *www.hartwoodtulum.com* ⊗ *Closed Mon. and Tues. and Sept. and Oct. No lunch.*

Los Aguachiles

$ | SEAFOOD | This Tulum outpost of the Playa hipster cantina has a light take on traditional tacos and seafood, which are served with lots of lime and creativity. Batter-fried shrimp on a bed of hydroponic lettuce, grouper with avocado and cucumber, and tacos de *pescado* are all good bets. **Known for:** great (but really spicy) aguachile; laid-back atmosphere; best fish tacos in town. $ *Average main: MP140* ⊠ *Av. Tulum, Mz 40, Lote 1, between San Francisco Supermarket and Chedraui, Tulum* ☎ *984/802–5482* ⊕ *losaguachiles.mx* ⊗ *Closed Mon.*

Ki'bok Coffee

$ | CAFÉ | FAMILY | Rub shoulders with cab drivers, local government officials, and expat regulars over coffee at Tulum's favorite family-owned and-run coffee shop, where espresso drinks are made with 100% Mexican-grown coffee from places like Oaxaca and Veracruz. Upstairs you'll find a small bakery, out back a quiet jungle garden, and up front a relaxed beachy bar space, all serving up coffee, baked goods, and Mexican dishes like *molletes*—spiced toast over black-bean puree with pico de gallo. ■**TIP**➔ **Add a fried egg for something special. Known for:** espresso drinks made with Mexican coffee; carrot cake muffins; homemade baked goods. $ *Average main: MP120* ⊠ *Av. Zamna, Calle 12 Sur, El Centro* ☎ *984/802–5347* ⊕ *www.facebook.com/kiboktulum.*

★ Mezzanine Thai

$$$ | THAI | People come from up and down the Riviera for the zingy flavors of this southern Thai restaurant. Popular dishes include pad Thai, drunken noodles, and money bags (crispy fried wonton wrappers filled with a Thai shrimp mix). **Known for:** pad Thai with chicken or shrimp; fresh fruit and salads; Thai whole fish with mango salad. $ *Average main: MP310* ⊠ *Carretera Tulum–Boca Paila, Km 1.5, Zona Hotelera* ☎ *984/131–1596* ⊕ *mezzaninetulum.com.*

★ Ocumare

$$$ | ECLECTIC | This jungle-chic restaurant serves up creative fine-dining fare unlike anything else you'll find in the region. Standout dishes include *al pib*–style lamb (with roasted mushrooms and birria sauce reduction), *a la talla*–style catch of the day (with adobe sauce and Mexican grasshoppers), and mole verde with curry and breaded avocado. **Known for:** decadent desserts; inventive flavor combinations; Mexican fusion gastronomy. $ *Average main: MP350* ⊠ *Be Tulum, Carretera Tulum-Boca Paila, Km 10, Tulum* ☎ *984/116–6077* ⊕ *ocumaretulum.com* ⊗ *Closed Sun. No lunch.*

Taquería Honorio

$ | MEXICAN | This collection of plastic tables under a tarp may not look like much from the outside, but it's where the locals go for some of the best (and cheapest) tacos in town. Grab a seat, and order up pork or vegetarian options and a bottle of agua fresca (water mixed with fruit and sugar). **Known for:** cheap, flavorful tacos; aguas frescas; excellent salsas. $ *Average main: MP26* ⊠ *Av. Satélite Sur, Tulum* ✢ *Between Calle Sol Oriente and Calle Andromeda Oriente* ☎ *984/745–0674* ⊕ *www.facebook.com/taqueriahonorio* ⊗ *No dinner.*

★ TU Mexican Cuisine
$$$ | **MEXICAN** | Considered by some as the best gourmet Mexican cuisine in Tulum, TU is, if nothing else, a fascinating expression of the country's rich gastronomy. Start with octopus tacos served with chipotle mayonnaise, and try the huitlacoche risotto with salmon as main dish. **Known for:** gourmet Mexican dishes; vegan options; spectacular cocktails. [$] *Average main: MP350* ✉ *Andrómeda Oriente, Mz 4, Lote 8, El Centro* ☎ *331/789–4137* 🌐 *www.tutulum.com* 🕒 *No lunch.*

Ziggy's Restaurant
$$$$ | **MEXICAN** | With tables under a palapa on the beach, this restaurant is a perfect place to sink your toes in the sand while dining. Chef Sandra offers understated appetizers like tuna nachos (tuna tartare and avocado with tortilla strips) or shrimp and chipotle *sopes* (corn flour "disks" with different toppings). **Known for:** live local music; tuna nachos; excellent beachfront location. [$] *Average main: MP560* ✉ *The Beach Tulum, Carretera Tulum-Boca Paila, Km 7.5, Zona Hotelera* ☎ *984/871–1132* 🌐 *www.ziggybeachtulum.com.*

Hotels

★ Ahau Tulum
$$$ | **HOTEL** | Named after the Maya sun god, Kin Ahau, this beachfront property has rooms ranging from simple Balinese huts to palapa suites with 20-foot vaulted ceilings, enormous decks, and two-person hammocks that make you forget the day of the week. **Pros:** good restaurant; sprawling beachfront; all furnishings built on-site by locals. **Cons:** yoga, aerial dance, and water sports cost extra; meals not included; lots of mosquitoes. [$] *Rooms from: $260* ✉ *Carretera Tulum–Boca Paila, Km 7.5, Zona Hotelera* ☎ *984/144–4415* 🌐 *ahaucollection.com* 🛏 *24 rooms* 🍴 *No Meals.*

★ Amansala
$$$ | **HOTEL** | This small, eco-friendly resort hotel caters to the yoga and meditation set, with three spacious, second-floor yoga studios—one with sweeping beachfront views. **Pros:** excellent, healthy food; intimate atmosphere; beautiful beach and ocean views. **Cons:** a/c only available in some rooms and only between 10 pm and 7 am; small pool; no door locks (though you can ask the staff to provide one). [$] *Rooms from: $245* ✉ *Carretera Tulum-Boca Paila, Km 5.5, Tulum* ☎ *559/225–2190* 🌐 *www.amansala.com* 🛏 *25 rooms* 🍴 *Free Breakfast.*

Be Tulum
$$$$ | **HOTEL** | Designed by owner-architect Sebastian Sas, this chic beachfront hotel is like a beautifully executed canvas—each room is a pure work of art, with exteriors made from the wood of reclaimed train tracks, peaceful outdoor terraces or balconies, and interior features that might include wicker couches and Brazilian wood floors draped with cowhide rugs. **Pros:** free use of bikes and Wi-Fi; every room has its own unique (though cohesive) design; two restaurants on property. **Cons:** no kids under 13; no elevators; few rooms have ocean views. [$] *Rooms from: $799* ✉ *Carretera Tulum-Boca Paila, Km 10.5, Zona Hotelera* ☎ *984/689–0577, 855/689–0577* 🌐 *www.betulum.com* 🛏 *65 suites* 🍴 *No Meals.*

★ The Beach Tulum
$$$$ | **HOTEL** | At this upscale, adults-only boutique hotel, rooms are contemporary in design, with polished concrete floors, spacious living rooms, direct beach access, and sundecks; king beds that have mosquito net canopies face double French doors that open to unobstructed views. **Pros:** excellent breakfast; all rooms are oceanfront; private rooftop decks. **Cons:** some nighttime noise in rooms closest to Ziggy's (though live music ends before 10); slow Internet; adults only (18-plus). [$] *Rooms from: $955* ✉ *Carretera Tulum–Boca Paila, Km 7.5,*

Zona Hotelera ☎ *984/871–1130, 855/246–5575 in the U.S.* 🌐 *www.thebeach-tulum.com* 🛏 *28 rooms* 🍴 *Free Breakfast.*

Coco Hacienda

$$ | **HOTEL** | **FAMILY** | Slip through the nondescript entrance, and you'll find a charming property with a lush, sprawling garden with partly tiled pathways, lights strung up from palm trees, two inviting pools, and a spacious central palapa with whirring ceiling fans. **Pros:** excellent value; great restaurant; beautiful grounds. **Cons:** location on the main road may mean traffic noise on parts of the property; 15-minute drive or cab ride from the beach; plenty of mosquitoes. [$] *Rooms from: $165* ✉ *Av. Tulum, Mz 39, Lote 1, Tulum* ☎ *984/277–2575* 🌐 *cocohaciendatulum.com* 🛏 *11 rooms* 🍴 *Free Breakfast.*

Kanan Tulum

$$$$ | **HOTEL** | A perfect spot for a romantic getaway, this lavish adults-only hotel is in the heart of Tulum's world-famous hotel zone. **Pros:** exotic sunset dinner in nest-like setting; stunning handmade wood bathtub; great beach and spa. **Cons:** no kids allowed; some rooms don't have ocean views; no meals included. [$] *Rooms from: $460* ✉ *Carretera Tulum at Boca Paila, Km 7.5, Zona Hotelera* ☎ *984/763–5837* 🌐 *ahaucollection.com* 🛏 *23 rooms* 🍴 *No Meals.*

La Zebra Beach Hotel & Restaurant

$$$$ | **HOTEL** | This jungle-chic, environmentally conscious hotel on a pristine beach is all about the details—say, colorful, traditional cotton robes made on a loom and handblown glasses from Jalisco. **Pros:** on-site beach bar with a mix-your-own-drink menu; good restaurant that uses sustainable practices; plunge pool in your private cabana. **Cons:** usually booked months in advance; high prices; no TVs in rooms. [$] *Rooms from: $784* ✉ *Carretera Tulum–Boca Paila, Km 8.2, Zona Hotelera* ☎ *303/952–0595 in the U.S., 984/115–4728* 🌐 *lazebratulum.com* 🛏 *29 suites* 🍴 *No Meals.*

Mezzanine Hotel Tulum

$$$$ | **HOTEL** | On the quieter side of Tulum's beachfront, this small, hip hotel is a 25-minute walk from the ruins along a powdery stretch of white sand. **Pros:** popular Thai restaurant on-site; fresh morning coffee basket delivered to your door; yoga mats, beach baskets, earplugs, sleeping masks, and sun hats provided. **Cons:** small pool area gets crowded; some rooms lack view; no kids under 16. [$] *Rooms from: $787* ✉ *Carretera Tulum–Boca Paila, Km 1.5, Tulum* ☎ *984/115–4728, 303/952–0595 in the U.S.* 🌐 *mezzaninetulum.com* 🛏 *9 rooms* 🍴 *No Meals.*

Nest Tulum

$$$$ | **HOTEL** | When you think of Tulum, you might have something in mind like this minimalist, beachfront, boutique hotel with luxurious, boho-chic rooms and a private villa. **Pros:** intimate atmosphere; complimentary welcome cocktail; free yoga and meditation lessons. **Cons:** no swimming pool; no kids; some rooms don't have ocean views. [$] *Rooms from: $480* ✉ *Carretera Tulum Boca Paila, Km 9.5, Zona Hotelera* ☎ *984/141–5433, 386/317–2993 in the U.S.* 🌐 *www.nesttulum.com* 🛏 *13 rooms* 🍴 *Free Breakfast.*

Villa Pescadores Tulum

$$$ | **HOTEL** | What used to be a fishermen's village is now a hip hotel consisting of thatched-roof bungalows that make great use of local woods and offer rustic-but-classy luxury and an overall feeling of authenticity. **Pros:** balconies with hammocks; non-motorized water sports available; great restaurant. **Cons:** no swimming pool; no TV; no meals included. [$] *Rooms from: $256* ✉ *Carretera Tulum at Boca Paila, Km 0.5, Zona Hotelera* ☎ *984/287–1851* 🌐 *ahaucollection.com* 🛏 *18 rooms* 🍴 *No Meals.*

Zamas

$$$ | **HOTEL** | On wild Punta Piedra (Rock Point), Zamas has small, rustic cabanas—with palapa roofs and ocean views as far as the eye can see—jungle-side rooms

overlooking a garden, palapas facing a coconut grove strung with colorful hammocks, and two spacious private houses that sleep up to 11. **Pros:** good restaurant; unspoiled views; rustic-chic budget alternative. **Cons:** four-night minimum stay in houses (no minimum for rooms); some traffic noise; parts of beach are rocky. [$] *Rooms from: $210* ✉ *Carretera Tulum–Boca Paila, Km 5, Zona Hotelera* ☎ *984/145–2602* 🌐 *www.zamas.com* 🛏 *26 cabanas* 🍴 *No Meals.*

Nightlife

Gitano Tulum

BARS | Part of the Gitano brand that also has venues in New York City and Miami Beach, this atmospheric jungle bar—with bulbs hanging from the trees and flickering candles at every table blinking like fireflies in the night—is known for its handcrafted mezcal cocktails. Cool beats come compliments of a DJ Friday nights and live bands on Wednesday and Sunday in high season. Mezcal tastings are also available. Come early (this place shuts down around 11), and bring a loaded wallet as drinks are powerful but pricey. ✉ *Boca Paila Rd., Km 7.5, jungle side, next to Hartwood, Zona Hotelera* ☎ *984/745–9068* 🌐 *www.gitano.com.*

La Zebra

COCKTAIL LOUNGES | Enjoy masterful mixology at this beachfront hot spot, where you can hear live music and enjoy creative cocktails featuring local flavors and ingredients. On Tuesday, when drinks are two for one, this is the place to be. ✉ *Carretera Tulum–Boca Paila, Km 8.2, Zona Hotelera* ☎ *303/952–0595 in the U.S., 984/115–4726* 🌐 *lazebratulum.com.*

Mezcalería Amores

COCKTAIL LOUNGES | With more than 30 varieties of mezcal from different regions of the country, this cantina is the perfect place to discover Mexico's second most popular agave-based drink (tequila is first). Come for the cocktails, but stay for the live music and friendly vibes. ✉ *Calle Andromeda, at Centauro, El Centro* ☎ *554/363–9859* 🌐 *www.facebook.com/AmoresTulum.*

★ **Papaya Playa Project**

DANCE CLUBS | Although Papaya Playa Project is a hotel, many folks simply patronize its beachfront club, where they can kick off their flip-flops and dance among the trees. Party people, in particular, appreciate the DJs spinning electronic and house music on Saturday night or the monthly full-moon events. ✉ *Carretera Tulum-Boca Paila, Km 4.5, Zona Hotelera* ☎ *984/871–1160* 🌐 *www.papayaplayaproject.com.*

Activities

Cacao Spa Tulum

SPAS | Forget the fancy facilities of the big resort spas or the expensive treatments of the hotel zone options, and head to this little downtown spa. The service is excellent, the massages are stellar (there are 11 different types), and the facials are organic. ✉ *Av. Tulum 16, between Satélite and Centauro, El Centro* ☎ *998/241–8650* 🌐 *www.cacaospatulum.com* 🎟 *Massages from MX$780; facials from MX$1,200.*

MC Kitesurf

WATER SPORTS | Located in front of the Ahau Tulum, this school gives lessons in kitesurfing and foil surfing. Its popular stand-up paddleboard tours take you to a cenote, a reef, or a gorgeous lagoon in the Sian Ka'an Biosphere. ✉ *Carretera Tulum–Boca Paila, Km 7.5, Tulum* ☎ *984/133–3896* 🌐 *www.mexicancaribbeankitesurf.com* 🎟 *Paddleboard tours from $125; kitesurf lessons from $90; foil-surfing lessons from $80.*

Morph Kiteboarding

WATER SPORTS | These certified IKO (International Kiteboarding Organization) instructors offer three-hour lessons that can be tailored for all levels. They also provide paddleboard rental services and lessons. ✉ *Hotel Coco Unlimited,*

The ruins of Cobá are best explored by bike.

Carretera Tulum–Boca Paila, Km. 7.5, Zona Hotelera ☎ *984/136–2877* ⊕ *www.morphkiteboardingtulum.com* ✉ *Private lessons from $80 per hr.*

Sanará Holistic Wellness Center & Spa
SPAS | Decorated with dreamcatchers, bamboo ladders, and whitewashed furnishings, this small, quiet spa at the Sanará boutique hotel has four treatment rooms and a rooftop relaxation area with 360-degree views over the jungle and beach. Head-to-toe relaxing massage is the specialty here, though hot-stone and crystal therapies are also available. ✉ *Sanará Hotel, Carretera Cobá–Boca Paila, Km 8.2, Tulum* ☎ *984/185–5059* ⊕ *sanarahotels.com* ✉ *1-hr massage MX$1,900.*

Cobá

42 km (26 miles) northwest of Tulum.

Near five lakes and between coastal watchtowers and inland cities, Cobá (pronounced ko-*bah*) once exercised economic control over the region through a network of at least 16 *sacbéob* (white-stone roads)—one, measuring 100 km (62 miles), is the longest in the Maya world. The city covered 70 square km (27 square miles), making it a noteworthy sister to Tikal in northern Guatemala, with which it had close cultural and commercial ties.

The site is noted for its massive temple-pyramids, including the largest and highest one in northern Yucatán (it stands 138 feet tall). Although often overlooked by visitors who opt for better-known Tulum, Cobá is less crowded, giving you a chance to immerse yourself in ancient culture.

GETTING HERE AND AROUND
Cobá is a 35-minute drive northwest of Tulum, along a road that leads straight through the jungle. Taxis from Tulum cost about MX$1,000. ADO (⊕ *www.ado.com.mx*) runs buses here from Playa del Carmen and Tulum at least three times a day: expect to pay about MX$150

between Cobá and Playa, MX$100 between Cobá and Tulum.

⊙ Sights

★ Cobá Ruins

RUINS | Mayan for "water stirred by the wind," Cobá flourished from AD 800 to 1100, with a population of as many as 55,000. Now it stands in solitude, and the jungle has overgrown many of its buildings—the silence is broken only by the occasional shriek of a spider monkey or the call of a bird. Most of the trails here are pleasantly shaded; processions of huge army ants cross the footpaths as the sun slips through openings between the tall hardwood trees, ferns, and giant palms. Cobá's ruins are spread out and best explored on a bike, which you can rent for MX$100 a day. Taxi-bike tours are available for MX$200 for an hour and 20 minutes or MX$300 for two hours. If you plan on walking instead, expect to cover 5 to 6 km (3 to 4 miles).

The main groupings of ruins are separated by several miles of dense vegetation. It's easy to get lost here, so stay on the main road, wear comfortable shoes, and bring insect repellent, sunscreen, and drinking water. Inside the site, there are no restrooms and only one small hut selling water (cash only). ■TIP➔ Don't be tempted by the narrow paths that lead into the jungle unless you have a qualified guide with you.

The first major cluster of structures, to your right as you enter the ruins, is the Cobá Group, whose pyramids are around a sunken patio. At the near end of the group, facing a large plaza, is the 79-foot-high temple, which was dedicated to the rain god, Chaac. Some Maya still place offerings and light candles here in hopes of improving their harvests. Around the rear, to the left, is a restored ball court, where a sacred game was once played to petition the gods for rain, fertility, and other blessings.

Farther along the main path to your left is the Chumuc Mul Group, little of which has been excavated. The principal pyramid here is covered with the remains of vibrantly painted stucco motifs (chumuc mul means "stucco pyramid"). A kilometer (½ mile) past this site is the Nohoch Mul Group (Large Hill Group), the highlight of which is the pyramid of the same name, the tallest at Cobá. It has 120 steps—equivalent to 12 stories—and shares a plaza with Temple 10. The Descending God (also seen at Tulum) is depicted on a facade of the temple atop Nohoch Mul.

Beyond the Nohoch Mul Group is the Castillo, with nine chambers that are reached by a stairway. To the south are the remains of a ball court, including the stone ring through which the ball was hurled. From the main route, follow the sign to Las Pinturas Group, named for the still-discernible polychrome friezes on the inner and outer walls of its large, patioed pyramid. An enormous stela here depicts a man standing with his feet on two prone captives. Take the minor path for 1 km (½ mile) to the Macanxoc Group, not far from the lake of the same name. ⊠ Cobá ✛ 42 km (26 miles) northwest of Tulum ☎ 984/206–7166 ⊕ inah.gob.mx ☜ MX$90.

Pac Chen

TOWN | This Maya jungle settlement is home to about 200 people who still live in round thatch huts and pray to the gods for good crops. ■TIP➔ You can only visit on trips organized by Alltournative, an eco-tour company based in Playa del Carmen. Alltournative pays the villagers a monthly stipend to protect the land; this money has made the village self-sustaining and has given the inhabitants an alternative to logging and hunting, which were their main means of livelihood before.

The "Cobá Maya Encounter" includes transportation, entrance to Cobá ruins, lunch, and Maya guides within Pac Chen, which accepts no more than 120 visitors on any given day. The half-day tour starts with a trek through the jungle to a cenote where you grab onto a harness and zip line to the other side. Next is the Jaguar cenote, set deeper into the forest, where you must rappel down the cavelike sides into a cool underground lagoon. You'll eat lunch under an open-air palapa overlooking another lagoon, where canoes await. The food includes such Maya dishes as grilled achiote (annatto seed) chicken, fresh tortillas, beans, and watermelon. ✉ *Cobá* ☎ *877/437–4990, 984/803–9999* 🌐 *alltournative.com* 🎫 *$139.*

🍴 Restaurants

Ki-Hanal

$$ | **MEXICAN** | You can't get any closer to the ruins than this two-story restaurant in a palapa setting with Mexican blankets draped over wooden tables. Some of the more traditional selections include fish prepared Yucatán style, chicken in banana leaves, and *cochinita pibil.* **Known for:** Yucatán-style fish; cochinita pibil; fresh salads. [$] *Average main: MP180* ✉ *Cobá* ✥ *To the right of the Cobá ruins entrance* ☎ *984/206–7159* ⏲ *No dinner.*

Reserva de la Biósfera Sian Ka'an

15 km (9 miles) south of Tulum to Punta Allen turnoff, 252 km (156 miles) north of Chetumal.

Wildlife has understandably been affected by the development of coastal resorts; however, thanks to the federal government's foresight, 1.3 million acres of coastline and jungle have been set aside for protection as the Reserva de la Biósfera Sian Ka'an. Whatever may happen elsewhere along the coast, this pristine wilderness preserve (Mexico's second largest after the Reserva de la Biósfera Calakmul) remains a haven both for thousands of species of wildlife and for travelers who seek the Yucatán of old.

GETTING HERE AND AROUND

To explore on your own, follow the beach road past Boca Paila to the secluded 35-km (22-mile) coastal strip of land that's part of the reserve. You'll be limited to swimming, snorkeling, and camping on the beaches, as there are no trails into the surrounding jungle. The narrow, rough dirt roads down the peninsula are filled with monstrous potholes, completely impassable after a rainfall. In rainy season, don't attempt it without a four-wheel-drive vehicle.

The archaeological ruins at Muyil sit on the northwestern edge of Sian Ka'an, about 16 km (10 miles) south of Tulum on Carretera 307.

TOURS

Visit Sian Ka'an

ADVENTURE TOURS | Local guide Aldo Ancona offers various tours of Sian Ka'an, including bird-watching, fly-fishing, snorkeling, and wildlife excursions. ✉ *Coastal rd. Tulum–Boca Paila–Punta Allen, Km 15.8, Sian Ka'an* ☎ *984/141–4245, 984/236–4168* 🌐 *visitsiankaan.com.*

👁 Sights

Muyil (*Chunyaxché*)

RUINS | This photogenic archaeological site at the northern end of the Sian Ka'an biosphere reserve is underrated. Once known as Chunyaxché, it's now called by its ancient name, Muyil (pronounced moo-*hill*). It dates from the late Preclassic Period, when it was connected by road to the sea and served as a port between Cobá and the Maya centers in Belize and Guatemala. A 15-foot-wide *sacbé,* built during the Postclassic Period, extended from the city to the mangrove swamp and was still in use when the Spaniards arrived.

Structures were erected at 400-foot intervals along the white limestone road, almost all of them facing west, but there are only three still standing. At the beginning of the 20th century, the ancient stones were used to build a chicle (natural gum) plantation, which was managed by one of the leaders of the Caste Wars. The most notable site at Muyil today is the remains of the 56-foot Castillo—one of the tallest on the Quintana Roo coast—at the center of a large acropolis. During excavations of the Castillo, jade figurines representing the goddess Ixchel were found. Recent excavations at Muyil have uncovered some smaller structures.

The ruins stand near the edge of a deep-blue lagoon and are surrounded by almost impenetrable jungle, so be sure to bring insect repellent. You can drive down a dirt road on the side of the ruins to swim or fish in the lagoon. The bird-watching is also exceptional here; come at dawn, before the site officially opens (there's no gate) to make the most of it. ✉ *Carretera 307* ✥ *16 km (10 miles) south of Tulum* ☎ *983/837–2411* 🌐 *inah.gob.mx* 🎟 *MX$70.*

★ Sian Ka'an

NATURE PRESERVE | **FAMILY** | One of the last undeveloped stretches of coastline in North America, Sian Ka'an was declared a wildlife preserve in 1986 and a UNESCO World Heritage site in 1987. The 1.3-million-acre reserve accounts for 10% of the land in the state of Quintana Roo and covers 100 km (62 miles) of coastline. It's amazingly diverse, encompassing freshwater and coastal lagoons, mangrove swamps, keys, savannas, tropical forests, and a barrier reef. Hundreds of species of local and migratory birds, fish, animals, and plants share the land with fewer than 1,000 Maya residents.

The area was first settled by the Maya in the 5th century AD—the name Sian Ka'an translates to "where the sky is born." There are approximately 32 ruins (none excavated) linked by a unique canal system—one of the few of its kind in Mayan Mexico. There's a MX$50 entrance charge for the reserve, but to see much of anything, you should take a guided tour.

Many species of the once-flourishing wildlife have fallen into the endangered category, but the waters here still teem with roosterfish, bonefish, mojarra, snapper, shad, permit, sea bass, and crocodiles. Fishing the flats for wily bonefish is popular, and the peninsula's few lodges also run deep-sea fishing trips. **■ TIP→ Most fishing lodges along the way close for the rainy season in August and September, and accommodations are hard to come by.**

The road ends at Punta Allen, a fishing village whose main catch is spiny lobster, which was becoming scarce until ecologists taught the local fishing cooperative how to build and lay special traps to conserve the species. There are several small, expensive guesthouses. If you haven't booked ahead, start out early in the morning so you can get back to civilization before dark. ✉ *Coastal rd. Tulum–Boca Paila–Punta Allen, Km 15.8, just beyond the Arco Maya (arch entrance), Sian Ka'an* 🎟 *MX$50.*

🛏 Hotels

Casa Blanca Lodge

$$$$ | **ALL-INCLUSIVE** | This fishing lodge is on a rocky outcrop on remote Punta Pájaros Island, reputed to be one of the best places in the world for light-tackle saltwater fly-fishing. **Pros:** remote location; comfortable rooms; Maya ruins on the island. **Cons:** 5-night minimum stay; far from anywhere else; all-inclusive pricing doesn't cover drinks. [$] *Rooms from: $6,649* ✉ *Punta Pájaros, Sian Ka'an* ☎ *877/261–8867 in the U.S.* 🌐 *casablancafishing.com* 🛏 *10 rooms* 🍴 *All-Inclusive.*

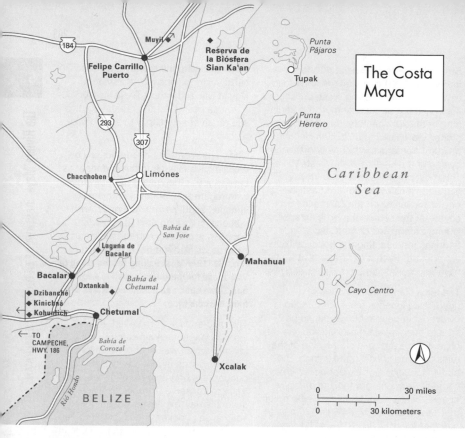

The Costa Maya

Muyil

Reserva de
la Biósfera
Sian Ka'an

Punta
Pájaros

184

Felipe Carrillo
Puerto

Tupak

Punta
Herrero

293

307

Chacchoben

Limónes

*Caribbean
Sea*

*Bahía de
San Jose*

Laguna de
Bacalar

Mahahual

Bacalar

Oxtankah

*Bahía de
Chetumal*

Cayo Centro

Dzibanché
Kinichná
Kohunlich

Chetumal

TO
CAMPECHE,
HWY. 186

*Bahía de
Corozal*

Xcalak

Río Hondo

BELIZE

0   30 miles

0   30 kilometers

Felipe Carrillo Puerto

*95 km (60 miles) southwest of Tulum,
156 km (97 miles) northeast of Chetumal.*

Named for a 1920s Yucatán governor
whose reforms helped the *campesinos*
(peasants), Felipe Carrillo Puerto sits
inland between Tulum and Chetumal
along Carretera 307. The town itself has
very little to offer visitors, though Chacchoben, a little-explored archaeological
site, isn't far.

GETTING HERE AND AROUND

Carretera 307, known locally as Avenida
Benito Juárez, runs right through the
center of town. Just drive straight and
you can't miss it. ADO (⊕ *www.ado.com.
mx*) links Cancún, Puerto Morelos, Playa
del Carmen, Tulum, Felipe Carrillo Puerto,
Limones, and Chetumal by bus.

Taxis drive up and down the street if
you arrive without your own wheels. The
tourist office is at the corner of Avenida
Juárez and Avenida Santiago Pacheco
Cruz. As you enter town, there's an HSBC
bank with an ATM and a Pemex gas
station (it's one of the few places to fuel
up between here and Chetumal).

◉ Sights

Chacchoben

RUINS | Excavated in 2005, Chaccho-
ben (pronounced *chsa*-cho-ben) is an
ancient city that was a contemporary
of Kohunlich and the most important
trading partner with Guatemala north of
the Bacalar Lagoon area. Several newly
unearthed buildings are still in good
condition. The lofty Templo Uno, the
site's main temple, was dedicated to the
Maya sun god, Itzamná, and once held a

royal tomb. (When archaeologists found it, though, it had already been looted.) Most of the site was built around AD 200, in the Petén style of the Early-Classic Period, although the city could have been inhabited as early as 200 BC. It's thought that inhabitants made their living growing cotton and extracting chewing gum and copal resin from the trees. ✥ *From Carretera 307, turn right on Carretera 293 south of Cafetal, continue 9 km (5½ miles) passing Lázaro Cardenas town* ☎ *983/837–2411* 🌐 *inah.gob.mx* 🎟 *MX$75.*

Hotels

El Faisán y El Venado
$ | HOTEL | If you absolutely need a place to stay in the area, then this simple three-story hotel is really your only remotely acceptable option. **Pros:** best place to stay in town; central location; strong a/c. **Cons:** no-frills rooms; staff speaks little English; Wi-Fi in common areas only. [$] *Rooms from: $65* ✉ *Av. Benito Juárez, Lote 781, Felipe Carrillo Puerto* ☎ *983/834–0702, 983/834–0043* 🛏 *37 rooms* 🍴 *No Meals.*

Bacalar

115 km (71 miles) southeast of Felipe Carrillo Puerto, 40 km (25 miles) northwest of Chetumal.

Founded in AD 435, Bacalar (pronounced *baa*-ka-lar) is one of Quintana Roo's oldest settlements. The town's most notable feature is a cenote-fed lake of the same name—Laguna de Bacalar. The mix of freshwater and salt water that intensifies its color has earned this long, narrow body of water the nickname "Lago de los Siete Colores" (Lake of the Seven Colors).

Marking the entrance to Bacalar is Cenote Azul, a crystalline cenote that's 300 feet deep and 600 feet across. The water is clean, and the diving is excellent here.

GETTING HERE AND AROUND

Bacalar is 30 minutes north of Chetumal, just off Carretera 307. If you're coming from Cancún, follow the well-marked signs. Upon entering the town, you'll cross over two huge speed bumps. Pass the Catholic church on your right, take a left at the first corner, and continue straight to the town square (Bacalar has no bank, but there is an ATM on this square); to your left will be the Fort of San Felipe. Northbound drivers should take Carretera 106 to 307 and enter at Km 34, marked by a sign for "Cenote Azul." Just past the cenote is a paved road that parallels Laguna de Bacalar and eventually leads to the town center.

Sights

Fuerte de San Felipe Bacalar (*San Felipe Fort*)
MILITARY SIGHT | This 17th-century stone fort was built by the Spaniards using stones from the nearby Maya pyramids. It was originally constructed as a haven against pirates and marauding bandits, then was transformed into a Maya stronghold during the Caste Wars. Today, the monolithic structure, which overlooks the enormous Laguna de Bacalar, houses government offices and a museum with exhibits on local history (ask for someone to bring a key if museum doors are locked). ✉ *Av. 3, Centro, Bacalar* ☎ *983/832–6838* 🌐 *sic.gob.mx* 🎟 *MX$55* 🕒 *Closed Mon.*

★ **Laguna de Bacalar** (*Lago de los Siete Colores*)
BODY OF WATER | Some 42 km (26 miles) long but no more than 2 km (1 mile) wide, Laguna de Bacalar is the town's focal point—renowned for both its vibrant green-and-blue waters and for the age-old limestone formations (stromatolites) that line its shores. Fed by underground cenotes, the mix of fresh

The Laguna de Bacalar is known for its giant stromatolites—limestone formations that are estimated to be 3½ billion years old.

water and salt water here creates ideal conditions for a refreshing swim. Most hotels along Laguna de Bacalar rent kayaks and paddleboats; however, there are no beaches or amenities other than those found in rental properties or hotels. English-speaking guide Victor Rosales (☎ *983/136–2827*), who organizes custom excursions throughout the Costa Maya, offers a particularly fascinating tour of the lake's 3.5-billion-year-old stromatolites. ✉ *Bacalar coastal rd., Bacalar.*

🍴 Restaurants

Jaguara Cocina Mexicana
$$$ | **MEXICAN** | This lagoon shore restaurant serves gourmet Mexican dishes and exotic cocktails to enjoy with the best view in town and live music most days. Go for the *al pastor* (shepherd-style) seared tuna as the main course, and don't leave without trying the tribute to cacao as dessert. **Known for:** organic cocktails; live music; outstanding location. [$] *Average main: MP320* ✉ *Blvd. Costero Norte 1255, Bacalar* ☎ *983/185–6929* 🌐 *www.facebook.com/jaguara.mx* 🕓 *Closed Mon.*

Restaurant Cenote Azul
$$ | **SEAFOOD** | Perched on the rim of the 300-foot-deep cenote, this palapa restaurant charges a MX$50 entrance fee to access the site. Busloads of tourists come to dine on chicken, pork, and fish dishes, as well as house specialties like the seafood platter and shrimp kebab. **Known for:** seafood platter; shrimp kebab; a lovely setting. [$] *Average main: MP250* ✉ *Carretera 307, Km 34, Bacalar* ☎ *983/834–2460.*

🛏 Hotels

Akalki Hotel & Centro Holístico (*Centro Holistico Akalki*)
$$$$ | **B&B/INN** | Considered the most upscale property on Laguna de Bacalar, Akalki offers nine luxurious cabanas built over the water, each with a private dock and direct access to the enchanting turquoise waters. **Pros:** romantic setting; immaculate rooms; overwater bungalow

experience. **Cons:** Wi-Fi in common areas only; no outlets in the rooms; tons of mosquitoes. $ *Rooms from: $484* ✉ *Carretera 307, Km 12.5, Bacalar* ☎ *983/106–1751* 🌐 *www.akalki.com* 🛏 *11 rooms* 🍴 *Free Breakfast.*

Hotal Carolina Bacalar

$$$ | **HOTEL** | **FAMILY** | This chic little hotel set right in front of the lagoon offers its guests creature comforts, an excellent restaurant, and lots of tranquility. **Pros:** private dock; balconies with hammocks; complimentary use of kayaks. **Cons:** some rooms have no lagoon views; spotty WI-FI; lots of mosquitoes. $ *Rooms from: $260* ✉ *Blvd. Costero de Bacalar Sur 625, Bacalar* ☎ *983/154–1810* 🌐 *carolinabacalar.mx* 🛏 *16 rooms* 🍴 *Free Breakfast.*

Makaabá Hotel Eco Boutique

$$$ | **HOTEL** | This eco-friendly hotel, just a block from the lagoon shore, offers a laid-back atmosphere and personalized service. **Pros:** spectacular swimming pool; great restaurant; eco-friendly practices. **Cons:** not on the lagoon shore; small rooms; lack of privacy. $ *Rooms from: $263* ✉ *Blvd. Costera de Bacalar Sur 506, Bacalar* ☎ *983/192–8024* 🌐 *hotelmakaaba.com* 🛏 *11 rooms* 🍴 *Free Breakfast.*

★ **Rancho Encantado**

$$$ | **HOTEL** | On the shores of Laguna Bacalar, Rancho Encantado's property is dotted with freestanding Maya-themed casitas, each of which is uniquely decorated with murals and hammocks and can comfortably sleep four people. **Pros:** friendly staff; huge whirlpool tub; Wi-Fi in restaurant. **Cons:** need car to get around; low water pressure; mosquitoes. $ *Rooms from: $230* ✉ *Carretera 307, Km 24, look for turnoff sign, Bacalar* ☎ *998/884–1181, 998/884–2071* 🌐 *www.encantado.com* 🛏 *16 rooms* 🍴 *Free Breakfast.*

Chetumal

328 km (283 miles) southeast of Playa del Carmen.

At times, Chetumal—the capital city of Quintana Roo—feels more Caribbean than Mexican; this isn't surprising, given its proximity to Belize. A population that includes Afro-Caribbean and Middle Eastern immigrants creates a melting pot of music (reggae, salsa, calypso) and cuisines (Yucatecan, Mexican, Lebanese).

Because this is the closest major community to Bacalar, Mahahual, and Xcalak, many residents from neighboring towns come here to do banking and stock up on supplies. Traffic can get very congested, but you will see very few tourists.

Nevertheless, this small city has a number of parks on a waterfront that's as pleasant as it is long: the Bay of Chetumal surrounds the city on three sides. Tours can take you to the fascinating nearby ruins of Kohunlich, Dzibanché, and Kinichná, a trio dubbed the "Valley of the Masks."

GETTING HERE AND AROUND

Aeropuerto Internacional Chetumal (CTM), on the city's southwestern edge, has daily Interjet flights to and from Mexico City. Chetumal's main bus terminal, at Avenida Salvador Novo 179, is served mainly by ADO (🌐 *www.ado.com.mx*). The bus trip from Cancún takes five hours and 45 minutes, with stops along the way in Puerto Morelos, Playa del Carmen, Tulum, Felipe Carrillo Puerto, and Limones; tickets costs MX$595. There's an ATM at the bus station.

On Avenida Insurgentes, there's a bank and ATM in the center of the shopping mall. If you're driving here, be sure to fill up at the Pemex station in Felipe Carrillo Puerto, one of the few stations along this stretch of Carretera 307.

VISITOR INFORMATION

CONTACTS Chetumal Tourist Information.
✉ Av. Carmen Ochoa de Merino, at Av. 5 de Mayo, Chetumal ☎ 983/129–2614 ⊕ www.visitchetumal.com.mx.

👁 Sights

Dzibanché

RUINS | FAMILY | The alliance between sister cities Dzibanché and Kinichná was thought to have made them the most powerful cities in southern Quintana Roo during the Maya Classic Period (AD 100–1000). The fertile farmlands surrounding the ruins are still used today as they were hundreds of years ago, and the winding drive deep into the fields makes you feel as if you're coming upon something undiscovered. Archaeologists have been making progress in excavating more and more ruins, albeit slowly.

At Dzibanché (which translates as "place where they write on wood" and is pronounced zee-ban-chay), several carved wooden lintels have been found. The most perfectly preserved example is in a supporting arch at the Plaza de Xibalba.

Also at the plaza is the Templo del Búho (Temple of the Owl), atop which a recessed tomb was discovered—only the second of its kind in Mexico (the first was at Palenque in Chiapas). In the tomb were magnificent clay vessels painted with white owls, messengers of the underworld gods.

More buildings and three plazas have been restored as excavation continues. Several other plazas are surrounded by temples, palaces, and pyramids, all in the Petén style. The carved stone steps at Edificio 13 and Edificio 2 (Buildings 13 and 2) still bear traces of stone masks. A copy of the famed lintel of Templo IV (Temple IV), with eight glyphs dating from AD 618, is housed in the Museo de la Cultura Maya in Chetumal. (The original was replaced in 2003 because of deterioration.) Four more tombs were discovered at Templo I (Temple I). ✉ Carretera 186 (Chetumal–Escárcega), 80 km (50 miles) west of Chetumal ✥ Following Carretera 186 (Chetumal–Escárcega), turn north at Km 58 and pass through town of Morocoy; continue 2 km (1 mile) farther, and turn right at sign for Dzibanché. The entrance is 7 km (4½ miles) away ☎ 983/837–2411 ⊕ inah.gob.mx 🎟 MX$75.

Kinichná

RUINS | FAMILY | After you've seen its sister city, Dzibanché, make your way back to the fork in the road, and head to Kinichná ("House of the Sun," pronounced kin-itch-na). At the fork, you'll see the restored Complejo Lamai (Lamai Complex), the administrative buildings of Dzibanché. Kinichná consists of a two-level pyramidal mound split into Acropolis B and Acropolis C, apparently dedicated to the sun god. Two mounds at the foot of the pyramid suggest that the temple was a ceremonial site. Here a giant Olmec-style jade figure was found. At its summit, Kinichná affords one of the finest views of any archaeological site in the area. ✉ Carretera 186 Chetumal–Escárcega, 80 km (50 miles) west of Chetumal, Chetumal ✥ Following Carretera 186 Chetumal–Escárcega, turn north at Km 58 and pass through town of Morocoy; continue 2 km (1 mile) farther, and turn right at the sign for Dzibanché. The entrance for both ruins is 7 km (4½ miles) away. Pass Dzibanché, and veer left toward the hill where Kinichná is located ☎ 983/837–2411 ⊕ inah.gob.mx 🎟 MX$75.

Kohunlich

RUINS | FAMILY | Kohunlich (pronounced Ko-hoon-lich) is renowned for the giant stucco masks on its principal pyramid, the Edificio de los Mascarones (Mask Building). It also has one of Quintana Roo's oldest ball courts and the remains of a great drainage system at the Plaza de las Estelas (Plaza of the Stelae). Masks that are about 6 feet tall are set vertically into the wide staircases at the main pyramid, called Edificio de las Estelas (Building of the Stelae). First thought to represent the Maya sun god, they're now considered to be composites of Kohunlich's rulers and important warriors. Another giant mask was discovered in 2001 in the building's upper staircase.

Kohunlich was built and occupied during the Classic Period by various Maya groups. This explains the eclectic architecture, which includes the Petén and Río Bec styles. Although there are 14 buildings to visit, it's thought that there are at least 500 mounds on the site waiting to be excavated. Digs have turned up 29 individual and multiple burial sites inside a residence building called Templo de Los Veintisiete Escalones (Temple of the Twenty-Seven Steps). This site doesn't have a great deal of tourist traffic, so it's surrounded by thriving flora and fauna. ⊠ *Off Carretera 186 (Chetumal–Escárcega), 65 km (46 miles) west of Chetumal* ✛ *Follow Carretera 186 west of Chetumal for 65 km (40 miles); continue another 9 km (5½ miles) south on side road to ruins* 🕾 *983/837–2411* ⊕ *inah.gob.mx* 🖅 *MX$90.*

★ **Museo de la Cultura Maya**
HISTORY MUSEUM | FAMILY | Dedicated to the complex world of the Maya, this interactive museum is outstanding. Exhibits in Spanish and English trace Maya architecture, social classes, politics, and customs. The most impressive display is the three-story Sacred Ceiba Tree, a symbol used by the Maya to explain the relationship between the cosmos and Earth. The first floor represents the tree's roots and the Maya underworld, called Xibalba; the middle floor is the tree trunk, known as Middle World, home to humans and all their trappings; on the top floor, leaves and branches evoke the 13 heavens of

the cosmic otherworld. ⊠ *Av. Héroes and Calle Mahatma Gandhi, Chetumal* 🕾 *983/832–2270* ⊕ *sic.gob.mx* 🖅 *MX$55* ⊗ *Closed Mon.*

Oxtankah
RUINS | FAMILY | The small ruins at Oxtankah are worth a visit if you're in the Chetumal area. Named for the Ramon trees ("ox" in Mayan) that populate the grounds, they're in a parklike setting and take about an hour to explore. The ruins include a Spanish mission, a pyramid, and several other structures. Archaeologists believe this city's prosperity peaked between AD 200 and 600. Maya groups returned to the area during the 15th and 16th centuries, using old stone to build new structures. There are toilets, free parking, and a tiny museum on-site but no food or drink available, so come prepared. ⊠ *Calderitas, 16 km (10 miles) north of Chetumal, Chetumal* ✛ *Take Carretera Chetumal-Calderitas (Av. Heroes) north of town and continue on the paved road bordering the bay; 4½ km (3 miles) to the north is the sign that marks access to the archaeological zone* 🕾 *983/837–2411* ⊕ *inah.gob.mx* 🖅 *MX$70.*

🕤 Beaches

Chetumal Bay
BEACH | FAMILY | Several grassy beach parks, including Punta Estrella and Dos Mulas, surround the bay. The latter is not recommended due to cleanliness issues. But Punta Estrella has parking, toilets, volleyball courts, and a small boat marina. The water here is calm, if cloudy, and there's plenty of shade from trees and little palapa-topped picnic tables. Popular with fishermen, the bay itself is shallow and the flats go on for miles. **Amenities:** food and drink; parking (no fee); toilets. **Best for:** walking. ⊠ *Chetumal.*

🍴 Restaurants

El Patio del 30

$$ | **INTERNATIONAL** | **FAMILY** | Come to this cozy place for the pizza, stay for the cocktails and the live music. If pizza is not your thing, though, a wide variety of salads, pastas, and steaks are also available and well-served. **Known for:** specialty pizzas; live music; original cocktail menu. [$] *Average main: MP299* ✉ *Álvaro Obregón 165, Bacalar* ☎ *983/285–3898* 🌐 *www.facebook.com/ElPatioDel30* 🕒 *No lunch.*

Sergio's Pizzas

$$$ | **PIZZA** | **FAMILY** | Locals rave about the grilled steaks and garlic shrimp at Sergio's—one of the nicest restaurants in Chetumal. The barbecued chicken (made with the owner's special sauce) and smoked-oyster or seafood pizzas are equally tasty. **Known for:** gracious staff; huge breakfast menu; free Wi-Fi. [$] *Average main: MP399* ✉ *Av. Alvaro Obregón 182, at Av. 5 de Mayo, Chetumal* ☎ *983/832–2991* 🌐 *www.sergiospizzas.com.mx.*

🛏 Hotels

★ The Explorean Kohunlich

$$$$ | **RESORT** | About 40 minutes outside Chetumal, at the edge of the Kohunlich ceremonial grounds, this luxury eco resort lets you feel adventurous without really roughing it. **Pros:** attentive staff; excellent food; tours, meals, and transportation included. **Cons:** expensive; small pool can feel too crowded; no TV or Internet. [$] *Rooms from: $361* ✉ *Carretera Chetumal–Escarega, Km 5.6, on rd. to ruins, Chetumal* ☎ *983/689–0042* 🌐 *www.explorean.com* 🔑 *40 suites* 🍴 *All-Inclusive.*

Hotel Los Cocos

$ | **HOTEL** | Large and modern by Chetumal's standards, Hotel Los Cocos has a pool framed by a pleasant garden (a boon on sweltering days) plus rooms—some with balconies or outdoor sitting areas—that are tidy, if not especially stylish. **Pros:** strong water pressure; good location; free Wi-Fi in rooms. **Cons:** loud a/c; staff speaks minimal English; uncomfortable beds. [$] *Rooms from: $78* ✉ *Av. Héroes 134, at Calle Chapultepec, Chetumal* ☎ *983/835–0430* 🌐 *hotelloscocos.com.mx* 🔑 *140 rooms* 🍴 *No Meals.*

TRYP by Wyndham Chetumal

$ | **HOTEL** | **FAMILY** | Formerly known as Hotel Villanueva and now part of the Wyndham family, this basic property is a good, functional base for exploring the region. **Pros:** centric location; nice indoor swimming pool; pet-friendly. **Cons:** uninspired design; mediocre restaurant; no gym. [$] *Rooms from: $90* ✉ *Carmen Ochoa de Merino 166, Chetumal* ☎ *983/107–9128, 800/422–1115 in the U.S.* 🌐 *www.wyndhamhotels.com/tryp* 🔑 *72 rooms* 🍴 *Free Breakfast.*

Mahahual

143 km (89 miles) northwest of Chetumal via Carreteras 186 and 307.

Tiny Mahahual (also spelled Majahual) has something of a split personality. With a population of only 600, it's a quiet beachfront outpost with clear, calm waters, good snorkeling and diving, and not a whole lot to do. That's just the way its Mexican and expat U.S. and Canadian residents like it.

When the cruise ships are in port, however, this sleepy spot gets a locally unwelcome shot in the arm. Passengers flood its waterside palapa restaurants, beach clubs, and the boardwalk fronting the town's few blocks; it's lively but can be overwhelming. That's when locals and savvy overnight visitors retreat to the handful of delightfully remote beachfront hotels and inns on Mahahual's outskirts, waiting out the crowds in a hammock, beach book in hand.

If you need a prescription for relaxation, a stay at the luxurious Almaplena Resort & Beach Club in Mahahual may be just what the doctor ordered.

GETTING HERE AND AROUND

If you're coming by car, take Carretera 307 to Carretera 10, approximately 2½ km (1½ miles) past dusty little Limones (you can't miss the road; it's marked "Mahahual"). Continue for 50 km (30 miles) until you reach the coast; then turn right at the lighthouse, and follow the road into town, where a string of hotels and restaurants line the beach.

If you're staying at the Almaplena Beach Resort (halfway between Mahahual and Xcalak), turn right at the paved road toward Xcalak and continue for 16 km (10 miles) until you see a sign for Punta Herradura; turn left on this bumpy road and follow the signs to the resort. To reach the port area of New Mahahual, turn left at Km 55, just past the mayor's office.

Be advised that the beach road south of town is rough and potholed. After it rains, driving here can be an adventure. If you're planning to drive south, check with locals for road conditions, and allow plenty of time.

There's a taxi stand at the corner of Avenida Mahahual and Calle Rubic. A full day of transportation with a private driver can be arranged for around MX$1,500. Otherwise, expect to pay around MX$15 per km (½ mile). Additional taxis are parked on the west side of the soccer field. Always ask to see a rate card before agreeing to a price.

🏖 Beaches

The three cruise ships that stop here daily have made Mahahual's beach the liveliest place in town. Seaside restaurants dish out cerveza and ceviche, and several vendors offer boat tours and rental equipment like glass-bottom kayaks.

The main beach in the center of town has fine sand and calm waters, great for swimming and snorkeling. Some hotel owners have opened beach clubs to cater to cruise passengers looking for a day (and a drink) in the sun.

BEACH CLUBS

Nacional Beach Club

BEACH | FAMILY | This colorful beach club, exclusively for overnight guests and cruise-ship passengers who purchase a VIP beach club package, is the only one on the Mahahual strip with a pool. Bungalows start at $115 a night, and VIP Beach Breaks for cruise passengers are $135 per adult. Both will get you access to the club's pool, restaurant, beach chairs, umbrellas, showers, and changing facilities.

VIP guests can also expect all-you-can-drink cocktails, all-you-can-eat food, and transportation from the port. Margaritas can be delivered to you beachside, or you can escape the heat by grabbing a bite in the enclosed patio. Free Wi-Fi is also included. There's decent snorkeling right out front, and equipment is available next door at Gypsea Divers. Even if you don't get in the water, the four shades of turquoise are breathtaking. **Amenities:** food and drink; showers; toilets. **Best for:** partiers; snorkeling; swimming. ✉ *Av. Mahahual, Mz 14, Lote 4, Mahahual* ☎ *983/834–5719* 🌐 *nacionalbeachclub.com* 🎫 *VIP Beach Break Pass from $135; bungalows from $115.*

Nohoch Kay Beach Club

BEACH | FAMILY | This beachfront restaurant on the boardwalk doubles as a beach club, offering a bar, lunch, beach chairs, umbrellas, and kayaks. There's no fee for using the beach chairs and equipment, but you'll need to consume at least $50 worth of food and drink per person. There are restrooms, showers, and an on-site massage therapist you can book for an extra fee.

The restaurant cooks up ceviche, tacos, sandwiches, and nachos, but most people opt for the fresh fish served with tortillas and homemade tartar sauce. Between tanning sessions, you can head to the outer reef on a private catamaran for a snorkeling tour. Cruise passengers flock to this simple beachfront hot spot, so reserve ahead if you want to be part of the action. **Amenities:** food and drink; showers; toilets; water sports. **Best for:** partiers; snorkeling. ✉ *Malecón, between Calles Liza and Cazón, Mahahual* ☎ *983/201–9577* 🌐 *elgrannohochkaybigfish.com* 🎫 *$50.*

Hotels

★ Almaplena Resort & Beach Club

$$ | HOTEL | One of only two fully green eco-hotels in the area, Almaplena Resort also happens to be the most luxurious, with large, rustic-chic rooms—in two-story white buildings—featuring textiles from Chiapas, rugs from Michoacan, wood from Yucatán, and iron from Jalisco, as well as stone floors, private balconies, and four-poster beds. **Pros:** spotless rooms; great snorkeling out front; stunning views from rooftop terrace. **Cons:** no TV; low water pressure; bland breakfast. [$] *Rooms from: $115* ✉ *Carretera Costera, Mahahual–Xcalak, Km 12.5, Mahahual* ☎ *983/137–5070* 🌐 *almaplenabeachresort.com* 🛏 *9 rooms* 🍴 *All-Inclusive.*

El Caballo Blanco

$ | HOTEL | Since access is only via a walk along the beach, there isn't much standing in the way of you and the ocean at this stark-white property, which, as the tallest hotel in Mahahual, also offers spectacular views from its rooftop, where you'll find a small infinity pool and a rooftop bar (open 5 to 10 pm). **Pros:** great views; rooftop bar and pool; great location. **Cons:** small bathrooms; not all rooms have ocean views; meals not included. [$] *Rooms from: $90* ✉ *Av. Mahahual, Mz 16, Lote 1, Mahahual* ☎ *983/126–0319* 🌐 *hotelelcaballoblanco.com* 🛏 *8 rooms* 🍴 *No Meals.*

★ 40 Cañones

$$ | HOTEL | Ocean breezes sweep through this pretty little hotel adorned with wicker-basket pendant lamps and mosquito-net-draped queen-size beds

Mayan Beach Garden

that swing from ropes. **Pros:** reasonably priced; comfortable beds; charming design. **Cons:** no pool; no breakfast included; mediocre restaurant. [$] *Rooms from: $104* ✉ *Malecón Mahahual, Km 1.3, at Calle Huachinango, Mahahual* ☎ *983/123–8591* 🌐 *www.40-canones.com* 🛏 *26 rooms* 🍴 *No Meals.*

Maya Luna

$$ | B&B/INN | Far from the boardwalk, this small inn on the beach is a quiet, relaxing place, where the cabanas have simple concrete rooms—with private roof decks where you watch the moon rise from the sea—and the decor is a mishmash of styles with painted murals and Mexican blankets. **Pros:** quiet, spacious beachfront location; nice restaurant open to the public; relaxed atmosphere. **Cons:** no a/c, TVs, or refrigerators in rooms; 40-minute walk to town; garbage often washes up on the beach. [$] *Rooms from: $100* ✉ *Carretera Mahahual-Xcalak, Km 5.2, Mahahual* ☎ *558/854–7945* 🌐 *hotelmayaluna.com* 🛏 *5 bungalows* 🍴 *Free Breakfast.*

★ Mayan Beach Garden

$$ | B&B/INN | There isn't another hotel for miles, so this solar-powered B&B offers blessed isolation in beachfront cabanas that have kitchenettes, king beds, Wi-Fi, and private decks. **Pros:** custom tours available; huge movie and book library; free use of bikes, kayaks, paddleboards, and snorkels. **Cons:** bumpy dirt road means 30-minute drive to town; extra fee to use the a/c; no kids under 12 during high season (Christmas to April). [$] *Rooms from: $100* ✉ *Norte Carretera Costera Majahual–Punta Herrera, 20 km (12½ miles) north of Mahahual town, Mahahual* ☎ *983/130–8568, 206/905–9665 in the U.S.* 🌐 *www.mayanbeachgarden.com* 🛏 *8 rooms* 🍴 *Free Breakfast.*

Activities

Gypsea Divers

DIVING & SNORKELING | FAMILY | Owners Catherine and Abel offer both dive trips and snorkeling tours. Group discounts are available. ✉ *Av. Mahahual, next* to Nacional Beach Club, Mahahual ☎ 983/111–2563, 983/111–2563 ⊕ gypseadivers.com ✉ 2-tank dives from $95; snorkeling tours $30.

The Native Choice

ADVENTURE TOURS | Ivan and David know all there is to know about Costa Maya sites like Chacchoben, Kohunlich, and Dzibanché. Aside from archaeology-themed outings, their company has tours that focus on adventure and contemporary Maya culture, too. ⊠ Paseo del Puerto 1301, Plaza las Fuentes Local #6, Nuevo Mahahual ☎ 983/103–5955, 998/869–4000 ⊕ thenativechoice.com ✉ From $58.

Western Caribbean Fly Fishing School

FISHING | This fly-fishing school offers trips to Sian Ka'an Biosphere Reserve, Xcalak, Chetumal Bay, or local cenotes in search of tarpon and snook. Fly-fishing instructor Nick Denbow leads beginners and experts through the fine arts of fly-tying and casting. He also customizes trips for individuals and groups. ⊠ Calle Bacalar 39, Malecón between Calles Liza and Cazón, Mahahual ☎ 983/732–3144 ✉ From $99.

Xcalak

180 km (111 miles) southwest of Chetumal.

The southernmost town in Quintana Roo, Xcalak (pronounced ish-ka-lack) is only 11 km (7 miles) from the Belize border by water, and a little of both places is evident in local life. Spanish is still the primary language, although most people speak English, and you'll sometimes hear a Caribbean patois.

Getting here is an adventure, but it's worth the effort. After all, this remote area offers excellent saltwater fly-fishing; flowers, birds, and butterflies are abundant; and the terrain is marked by savannas, marshes, streams, and island-dotted lagoons. You'll also find fabulously deserted beaches and a small town center comprised of bars, restaurants, and a few food shops.

The entire coast in this area is a designated National Marine Park, and all construction near Xcalak is bound by stringent environmental laws, which protect the natural beauty. By extension, electricity isn't very dependable, and tourist amenities are few; the community has no nightlife, and hotels (most of which close down during hurricane season) primarily cater to rugged outdoorsy types.

Since there are no standard phones here, and cell service is very limited, visitors should plan on being out of touch, or doing as the locals do and keeping connected via email or WhatsApp. The lack of phone lines means most hotels don't accept credit cards (or only do so through PayPal) either; moreover, there are no banks or ATMs in or near Xcalak—the closest ATMs are 64 km (40 miles) north in Mahahual—so bring enough cash for your entire stay.

GETTING HERE AND AROUND

The best way to get here is by car. Following Carretera 10, turn right at the intersection 2 km (1 mile) before Mahahual, and continue along the rough and tricky road until you reach Xcalak, about 61 km (37 miles) away. Pass the soccer field, and turn left onto the bumpy beach road, now heading north toward the Zona Hotelera, a 14-km (9-mile) stretch of properties lining the beach. Your hotel will probably be within this main area.

Don't rely on taxi service or local transportation to get around. Drive or stay in a property close to town or that offers bicycles. Note that this is a great launching point for day trips to Belize and for diving trips to Banco Chinchorro, a coral atoll and national park some two hours northeast by boat.

■ TIP→ On a map, the 55 km (34 miles) of bay separating Chetumal from Xcalak looks like an easy boat trip. Unfortunately, shallow sections of the bay make it impassable.

SAFETY

Make sure you have a full tank before you drive south. Although there is a Pemex gas station in Mahahual, it is sometimes closed for no apparent reason. Unlike the trafficked roads along Riviera Maya, the two-lane stretch near Belize is seldom visited by tourists. It's always best to travel with a partner and to drive during daylight hours.

⚠ **Drive with caution and be careful of wild animals and potholes.** Once you leave the paved road and enter Xcalak, the road goes from bad to worse. Be sure to rent a car that can handle pitted dirt roads.

Xcalak's growing expat community includes several nurses, who are always willing to help if health issues arise. There's a small clinic in the center of town; however, the "medic" (not always a doctor) is seldom around. Usually, a local can point you in the right direction for rudimentary first aid until you can reach the nearest staffed clinic in Bacalar. The closest small hospital (Carranza Clinic) is in Chetumal.

Beaches

Playa Xcalak

BEACH | Snorkelers and divers love this stretch of coastline, but beachgoers might be a little disappointed. The beach alongside Xcalak town is narrow—eaten away by past hurricanes—and often covered in seaweed and piles of garbage washed in on the tide. The hotels and B&Bs north of town do their best to keep their beaches clean and comfortable, making them the area's best spots for swimming or kayaking.

Sections of the beach connect to a network of protected mangroves frequented by manatees. Moreover, the offshore reef of nearby Banco Chinchorro is great for snorkeling, diving, and fishing. **Amenities:** none. **Best for:** snorkeling; swimming.

🍴 Restaurants

Coral Bar and Grill Xcalak

$$ | **INTERNATIONAL** | **FAMILY** | Just by the beach, the Coral Bar and Grill is the on-site restaurant of the Flying Cloud Hotel and part of the XTC Dive Center. The place is open all day, offering Mexican breakfasts, international food for lunch and dinner, and even some vegan dishes. **Known for:** great ocean views; outstanding margaritas; theme nights. [$] *Average main: MP235* ✉ *Camino Costero, Km 54, Xcalak* ☎ *983/836–5790* 🌐 *www.coralbarandgrillxcalak.com.*

Reel Inn Restaurant

$$ | **INTERNATIONAL** | **FAMILY** | This oceanfront, thatched-roof, palapa restaurant serves simple but tasty food. The Tex-Mex shrimp tacos accompanied with a cool beer are perfect for lunch, while dealing with the midday heat, and, for dinner, try the Poc Chuc pork or the traditional chicken with mole. **Known for:** seasonal lobster tacos; spicy chilaquiles for breakfast; specialty pizzas. [$] *Average main: MP263* ✉ *Carretera Mahahual-Xcalak, Km 52, at the Costa de Cocos Hotel, Xcalak* 🌐 *costadecocos.com/amenities/restaurant.*

Hotels

Casa Paraiso

$ | **B&B/INN** | A wonderful place to stay if you want to dive, snorkel, kayak, fly-fish, or just relax in a hammock, this hotel has spacious rooms with colorful tiles and hand-woven blankets on single or queen beds. **Pros:** on a nice beach; private fishing dock; kayaks, bikes, paddleboards, and fishing and snorkeling equipment provided. **Cons:** no restaurant; no a/c;

seaweed on the beach. $ Rooms from: $75 ✉ Carretera Majahual–Xcalak, Km 48, Xcalak ✛ Beach road "Calle Costero," 2 km (1 mile) north of Xcalak town ☎ 983/158–7008 ⊕ www.casaparaisoresort.com ⤳ 3 rooms ⦿ Free Breakfast.

Flying Cloud Hotel

$$ | B&B/INN | This small hotel is a repurposed 25-year-old house that caters mostly to divers who come to the XTC Dive Center and use it as launching point for their adventures and explorations. **Pros:** on-site restaurant; small swimming pool; accomodation and diving packages. **Cons:** no a/c; lots of mosquitoes; some rooms don't have ocean views. $ Rooms from: $125 ✉ Camino Costero at Xcalak, Km 54, Xcalak ☎ 984/179–5692 ⊕ flyingcloudhotelxcalak.com ⤳ 5 rooms ⦿ Free Breakfast.

Sin Duda Villas

$$ | B&B/INN | Set on a lovely beach, this property has accommodations—all adorned with Mexican pottery and other collectibles—that include two apartments with private kitchens; a secluded jungle studio (which the owners refer to as "a tree house for adults"); and a house divided into three suites that share a kitchen, dining room, sundeck, and library full of books and board games. **Pros:** solar powered; world-class snorkeling; sports gear included in the rate. **Cons:** getting here on the rough, potholed road isn't easy; no restaurant; lots of bugs. $ Rooms from: $135 ✉ Xcalak Peninsula, Xcalak ✛ 60 km (37 miles) south of Mahahual, 5½ km (3½ miles) north of Costa de Cocos ☎ 306/500–3240 in the U.S. ⊕ sindudavillas.com ⤳ 6 units ⦿ No Meals.

🏃 Activities

Costa de Cocos

FISHING | FAMILY | Xcalak's only full-service fishing resort offers half- and full-day fly-fishing trips plus all-inclusive, multinight packages at its 16-room wind- and solar-powered resort. Scuba diving and snorkeling are also available, and locals recommend the pizza at the on-site restaurant. ✉ Carretera Mahahual–Xcalak, Km 52, Xcalak ✛ Head north on beach rd., through Xcalak town, past the lighthouse and pier; turn left at 2-story white building (Captain's Office) and then right at next street. Cocos is less than 1 km (½ mile) north of the bridge ⊕ costadecocos. com ⛴ Fly-fishing from $175.

XTC Dive Center

SCUBA DIVING | This is the town's sole full-service dive shop and one of the few outfits licensed to take passengers to Chinchorro. In addition to recreational diving, it provides DAN and PADI instruction; fly-fishing and snorkeling can also be arranged, as well as a unique crocodile encounter experience at Banco Chinchorro Biosphere Reserve. Serious divers might be interested in renting one of the three basic rooms attached to the property. ✉ Camino Costero Mahahual–Xcalak, Km 54, Xcalak ☎ 983/836–5790 ⊕ xtcdivecenter.com ⛴ 2-tank dives from $125; snorkeling from $50.

Chapter 6

COZUMEL

Updated by
Jeffrey Van Fleet

⊙ Sights	🍴 Restaurants	🛏 Hotels	🛍 Shopping	🍸 Nightlife
★★★★☆	★★★★☆	★★★★☆	★★★★☆	★★★★☆

WELCOME TO COZUMEL

TOP REASONS TO GO

★ **Diving the Great Maya Reef:** Tropical fish, coral, and other marine creatures enliven the Mesoamerican Barrier Reef, which stretches from Cozumel to Central America over 1,000 km (621 miles).

★ **Slowing down:** Stroll along a white-sand beach, then explore the gardens above and below the waters at Chankanaab. Or just grab a table at a sidewalk café and watch the world go by.

★ **Savoring local life:** San Miguel's Plaza Central is a Sunday evening hot spot for locals who gather for music and dancing. On any major holiday, you'll see parades, processions, and food stands with seasonal treats.

★ **Visiting Maya sites:** Take a refresher course on Maya culture past and present at the Museo de la Isla de Cozumel, then explore the temples dedicated to Ixchel, the Maya goddess of childbirth, fertility, and healing, at San Gervasio.

A 490-square-km (189-square-mile) island just 19 km (12 miles) east of the Yucatán Peninsula, Cozumel is mostly flat, with an interior covered by low-scrub jungle and marshy lagoons. White beaches with calm waters line the island's leeward (western) side, which is fringed by a spectacular reef system; the windward (eastern) side, facing the Caribbean Sea, has rocky strands and powerful surf.

1 **San Miguel.** Although cruise-ship passengers throng the souvenir shops lining the seafront boulevard, Cozumel's only town retains the flavor of a Mexican village. On weekend nights, musicians, food vendors, and lively crowds gather in the main square.

2 **Zona Hotelera Norte.** Lodgings skew smaller in size and number heading north from San Miguel, giving this coastal area an exclusive feel. There's less to do here but perhaps that's exactly what you crave. Nothing is far away, and taxis are on hand.

3 **Zona Hotelera Sur.** South of San Miguel, this action-packed stretch of coast contains the largest concentration of hotels. Lots of shopping options and the presence of the island's cruise terminals give rise to what passes for an occasional traffic jam—though nothing too L.A.-like—in Cozumel.

4 **Leeward Side.** Cozumel's entire west side is *leeward*, but here the term refers to the coast heading north and south beyond the two hotel zones. Broad beaches and the island's only golf course occupy the quiet northwest tip. Farther south, mangrove lagoons and beaches shelter nesting sea turtles. Chankanaab, one of Mexico's first marine parks, is superb for snorkeling.

5 **Windward Side.** The rough Caribbean surf pounds the limestone shore here, creating pocket-size beaches that seem tailor-made for solitary sunbathing. Pay attention to tides, currents, and sudden drop-offs in the ocean floor.

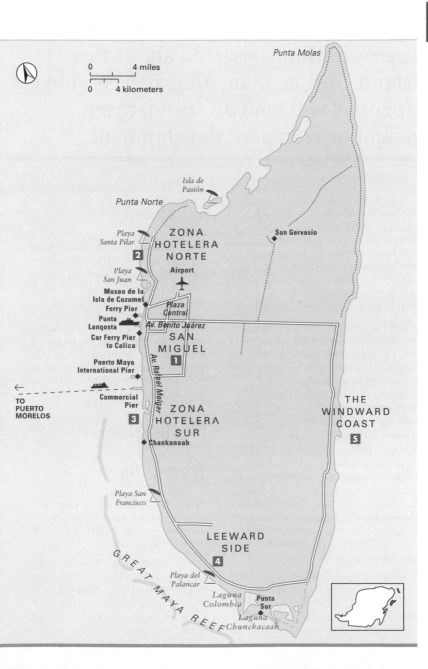

0 —— 4 miles
0 —— 4 kilometers

Punta Molas

Isla de
Pasión

Punta Norte

Playa
Santa Pilar

ZONA
HOTELERA
NORTE

San Gervasio

Airport

Playa
San Juan

Museo de la
Isla de Cozumel
Ferry Pier

Plaza
Central

Punta
Langosta

Av. Benito Juárez

Car Ferry Pier
to Calica

SAN
MIGUEL

Puerto Maya
International Pier

Av. Rafael Melgar

TO
PUERTO
MORELOS

Commercial
Pier

ZONA
HOTELERA
SUR

THE
WINDWARD
COAST

Chankanaab

Playa San
Francisco

LEEWARD
SIDE

GREAT MAYA REEF

Playa del
Palancar

Laguna
Colombia

Punta
Sur

Laguna
Chunchacaab

It's not Cancún. Should "yet" be added to that statement? Cozumel's days as a rustic divers' hangout *are* history, and there's nothing deserted about this island. Still, its many fans feel confident Cozumel will fend off its northern neighbor's rampant development.

It's rare to find such stunning natural beauty, crystal clear aquamarine seas, and vast marine life combined with top-flight visitor services and accommodations. As a result, Cozumel's devotees are legion. Divers sharing stories of lionfish and sharks sit table to table with families tanned from a day at the beach club, while Mexican couples spin and step to salsa music in the central plaza.

But the elephant in Cozumel's big and bountiful room is the throng of cruise-ship passengers who take over the countless craft and jewelry stores along the seaward boulevard downtown any day there are ships in port—which is to say, just about every day except Sunday. Take just a few steps off the beaten path, however, and you'll soon see that the country's third-largest island offers big rewards. Windswept beaches, wild and vibrant natural parks, and miles of coral reef are still yours to discover. In 2023, Cozumel was named a Pueblo Mágico ("magic town"), a government tourism designation honoring communities for their cultural or natural significance. The island won accolades for both.

Irregularly shaped, Cozumel is, at most, 48 km (30 miles) long and 15 km (9 miles) wide. Plaza Central, or just "El Centro," is the heart of San Miguel, directly across from the ferry docks that serve Playa del Carmen. Residents congregate here in the evening, especially on weekends, when free concerts begin around 8 pm.

Heading inland (east) takes you away from the tourist zone and toward residential areas of town. Most of the island's restaurants, hotels, stores, and dive shops are concentrated downtown and along the two hotel zones that fan out on the leeward (western) coast to the north and south of San Miguel. If you seek greater solitude, Cozumel's windward (eastern) side has a few beach-bar restaurants, one hotel, and miles of deserted beaches.

Planning

When to Go

When choosing vacation dates, keep in mind that the weather here is more extreme than you might expect on a tropical island.

High season extends from December until mid-April, with prices spiking around Christmas and Easter. Spring, being warm and dry, has the optimal conditions. In winter, *nortes* (north winds) occasionally blow through, churning the sea and lowering temperatures, so pack a shawl or jacket for the comparatively chilly 18°C (65°F) evenings. Note that during a norte, the windward side is calmer than the leeward one, and the interior is warmer than the coast.

June through October is the rainy season. Summer is generally hot and humid, but crowds disperse and prices drop in the low season—and, if you're a diver, warm water and the year's-best visibility might be enough to induce you to brave the heat. Mid-April through May is the sweet spot. With a lull in tourism and the fine weather that precedes the rainy season, late spring might be your all-around best bet. November is another good option, provided you avoid Thanksgiving weekend.

Getting Here and Around

AIR

The small Aeropuerto Internacional de Cozumel (CZM), 3 km (2 miles) north of San Miguel and less than 10 minutes from downtown, receives flights from a few Mexican cities and U.S. hubs. On arrival, take the shared shuttle to your hotel; fares range from MX$100 to MX$500 per person depending on where you're going. Tickets are available just outside customs, and there is no need to prepurchase.

Individual taxis are not permitted to pick up fares inside the airport—you may walk outside the airport entrance, a two-block hike from the terminal exit, to catch one. Taxis may bring you all the way into the terminal when you fly out.

Flights to Cancún are often much less expensive and much more plentiful, giving rise to a phenomenon that expats here affectionately refer to as "the Cozumel Bag Drag." This involves taking an ADO bus from Cancún airport to Playa del Carmen and then the ferry to Cozumel. If everything runs on schedule, the trip should be about three hours; the cost should be less than MX$400.

BOAT AND FERRY

Two companies, Ultramar and Winjet, provide passenger-only ferry service between Cozumel and Playa del Carmen on the mainland. Boats bound for Cozumel leave Playa del Carmen's dock about every other hour on the hour, from 6 am to 11 pm. On the return trip, they leave Cozumel's main pier approximately every other hour from 5 am to 10 pm. The 30-km (18-mile) crossing takes 45 minutes and costs about MX$250 each way. The number of trips per day varies by season, so be sure to check ferry websites for times. Purely objectively, the blue and yellow Ultramar boats are a bit nicer than the orange Winjet vessels, but old hands will tell you the best boat is the one that's the next to leave. Grab it.

Both Transcaribe and the Ultramar-owned Ultra Carga operate car-ferry service between the mainland port of Calica and Cozumel. Each company makes two or three round-trip crossings per day. The crossing takes one hour. One-way fares are approximately MX$720 for a standard passenger vehicle and MX$80 for each passenger beyond the driver. Reservations must be made at least 24 hours in advance. Check schedules carefully. Several of the runs *to* Cozumel have blackouts when no more than two adult passengers may occupy the vehicle. No such restrictions exist heading back to the mainland.

CONTACTS Transcaribe. ⊠ *Av. Melgar, Cozumel* ✛ *2⅓ km (1½ miles) south of El Centro* ☎ *998/302–9244* ⊕ *transcaribe. net.* **Ultramar.** ⊠ *Terminal Maritima San Miguel, Av. Rafael E. Melgar, Cozumel* ✛ *Directly across from El Centro* ☎ *998/881–5890* ⊕ *www.ultramarferry. com.* **Winjet.** ⊠ *Terminal Marítima Api, Av. Rafael E. Melgar and Av. Benito Juárez, Cozumel* ☎ *987/872–1508* ⊕ *winjet.mx.*

BUS

Bus service on Cozumel is basically limited to San Miguel's residential areas and mostly used by locals, so you'll need a rental car or taxi to explore.

CAR

If you want to explore Cozumel (particularly the eastern side) at your own pace, you should rent a car. Most worthwhile sites, such as the island's Maya ruins and pristine windward beaches, are readily accessible only with wheels. Fuel is available at any of the five government-owned Pemex stations around the island. Though it's tempting to drive on Cozumel's dirt roads (which lead to the least crowded beaches), most car-rental companies have a policy that voids your insurance once you leave the paved roadway.

⇨ *Check out our Travel Smart chapter for rules of the road and information on rental car agencies if you plan on driving.*

CRUISE

Cozumel is Mexico's largest cruise destination, and, depending how numbers are tallied, the world's second or fourth largest. As many as six ships a day call here during the November–April high season, tendering passengers to the downtown pier in the center of San Miguel or docking at the two international piers 6 km (4 miles) away. From the downtown pier you can walk into town or catch the ferry to Playa del Carmen; the international piers are close to many beaches, but you'll need a taxi to get into town.

A four-hour island taxi tour (four people maximum), including the ruins and other sights, costs around MX$1,500 to MX$2,000—negotiate the price before setting off. There's rarely a wait for a taxi; however, prices are high, and drivers are often aggressive, asking double or triple the reasonable fare. When in doubt, ask to see the rate card required of all taxi drivers, and always agree on the price before getting in the car. Drivers accept both U.S. dollars and pesos; tipping is not necessary but appreciated.

MOPED

We do not recommend renting a moped (*moto*) here. They are popular with visitors, but heavy traffic, potholes, and hidden stop signs make them a risky option. Accident rates are high. Mexican law requires all riders to wear helmets (it's a MX$350 fine if you don't).

If you do decide to rent a moped, drive slowly, check for oncoming traffic, and don't ride at night or when it's raining or you've been drinking. Mopeds rent for about MX$600 per day or MX$400 for a half day, including insurance.

TAXI

Cozumel's white cabs wait at all the major hotels, and you can hail them on the street, but be aware that rates can be astronomical, especially if you are headed to a far-flung beach on the windward (east) coast. The fixed rates run about MX$30–MX$60 within town; MX$75–MX$150 between town and the Zona Hotelera Norte; MX$100–MX$300 between town and the Zona Hotelera Sur; MX$200–MX$450 from most hotels to the airport; and MX$210–MX$350 from the northern hotels or town to Parque Chankanaab or Playa San Francisco. The cost from the Puerta Maya cruise-ship terminal by El Cid La Ceiba to San Miguel is about MX$130.

Ride-hailing services such as Uber or Lyft do not operate in Cozumel.

Banks and Currency Exchange

San Miguel is dotted with bank offices, and ATMs are abundant—including a few that dispense U.S. dollars. Some major hotels and resorts along the northern and southern hotel zones also have ATMs on-site, but it's best to stick with bank-affiliated machines during business hours and withdraw only pesos, since independent ones offering U.S. dollars charge exorbitant fees. The BBVA bank on the southeast side of the central plaza has several ATMs in its lobby.

■TIP→ **If you'd prefer to pay by credit card, ask first, as not all businesses accept them.**

Hotels

Small, one-of-a-kind hotels have long been the norm in Cozumel. Most of the island's accommodations are on the leeward (western) and south sides of the island, but there's one peaceful hideaway on the windward (eastern) side. The larger resorts are north and south of San Miguel, while the less expensive places are found in town. Cozumel also has a growing condo rental market; rates are competitive, and condos are easily found via any of the numerous vacation rental websites.

⇨ *Hotel reviews have been shortened. For full information, visit Fodors.com. Hotel prices are the lowest cost of a standard double room in high season.*

What It Costs in U.S. Dollars			
$	$$	$$$	$$$$
HOTELS			
under $100	$100–$200	$201–$300	over $300

Restaurants

Dining options on Cozumel reflect the island's laid-back attitude: breezy and relaxed, with casual dress and no reservations the rule at most places. Generally, restaurants emphasize fresh ingredients, simple presentation, and amiable service. As befits an island, there's lots of just-caught seafood on the menu. Regional cuisine is harder to come

by; you're more likely to find standard Mexican fare like tacos, enchiladas, and huevos rancheros.

Although some restaurants offer creative cuisine to suit the most demanding of palates, some of the best dining experiences are those in little family-owned spots—perhaps merely a tiny café with a few wobbly tables—where you might find Yucatecan dishes such as *cochinita pibil* (barbecue pork), *queso relleno* (cheese stuffed with ground meat), and *sopa de lima* (lime soup).

For authentic budget meals, head into the untouristed part of downtown, and look for the places that are filled with locals. Note that although many restaurants accept credit cards, casual cafés generally don't.

■TIP→ **Cab drivers are often paid to shill for restaurants, so take their dining suggestions with a grain (or two) of salt.**

⇨ *Restaurant reviews have been shortened. For full information, visit Fodors. com. Restaurant prices are the average cost of a main course at dinner, or if dinner is not served, at lunch.*

What It Costs in Mexican Pesos			
$	$$	$$$	$$$$
RESTAURANTS			
under MP135	MP135–MP200	MP201–MP350	over MP350

Safety

Cozumel is very safe; the most trouble you're likely to get in has two or four wheels and a motor (drive carefully). Some petty theft does exist on the island, so keep an eye on your belongings at the beach and don't leave valuables in plain sight in your car. Carry a photocopy of your passport and driver's license and keep the original tucked away at the hotel. If you plan to try water sports, make sure that your health or travel insurance has a sports rider.

Tours

Tours of the island's sights, including the San Gervasio ruins, El Cedral, Parque Chankanaab, and the Museo de la Isla de Cozumel, cost about MX$750 per person and can be arranged through travel agencies; most larger hotels have an on-site agency or tour operator. Another option is to take a private tour of the island via taxi, which costs about MX$1,200 for a half day.

Visitor Information

The tourism website has up-to-date news items and info on all things Cozumel. The website (⊕ www.cozumel4you.com) and Facebook page of Cozumel4You are edited by full-time island residents and feature insider tips on activities, sights, and places to stay and eat. You can also post questions, but use the search function first, as many of your questions may have already been asked and answered.

CONTACTS Cozumel Tourist Information Office. ⊠ Plaza del Sol, Calle 2 Norte 299B, Cozumel ☎ 987/872–7585 ⊕ www. mexicancaribbean.travel/isla-cozumel.

San Miguel

San Miguel is Cozumel's only town. The malecón, or seaside boulevard, Avenida Rafael E. Melgar, is a pleasant place to stroll. The waterfront has been taken over by large shops selling jewelry, imported rugs, leather boots, and souvenirs to cruise-ship passengers. One block inland lies the Plaza Benito Juárez, San Miguel's traditional heart. The town feels increasingly traditional as you head inland to the pedestrian streets around the

plaza, where family-owned restaurants and shops cater to residents and savvy travelers.

Even-numbered calles (streets) run perpendicular to the malecón and increase in number heading north from the plaza. Odd-numbered calles increase in number heading south from the plaza. Avenidas (avenues) run parallel to the coast and increase in number in multiples of five. Street signs are affixed to corners of buildings at most, but not all, intersections.

◉ Sights

Museo de la Isla de Cozumel (Cozumel Island Museum)
HISTORY MUSEUM | FAMILY | Filling two floors of a former hotel, Cozumel's museum has displays on natural history—the island's origins, endangered species, topography, and coral-reef ecology—as well as human history during the pre-Columbian and colonial periods. The photos of the island's transformation over the 20th and 21st centuries are especially fascinating, as are the exhibit of a typical Maya home and a room devoted to the island's carnaval traditions. Guided tours are available. ⊠ Av. Rafael E. Melgar, between Calles 4 and 6 Norte, San Miguel ☎ 987/872–0093 ⊕ cozumelparks. com/museo-de-la-isla ⊠ $9 ⊗ Closed Mon.

Parque Benito Juárez (Benito Juárez Park)
PLAZA/SQUARE | One block inland from the tourist hubbub of the waterfront sits "the plaza," the center of all things San Miguel. With its local feel, it could be the central park in any Mexican town, especially on Sunday evenings when it becomes the place to see and be seen. Join the couples and families who gather here to stroll, snack, enjoy the lighted fountains, and dance to live music around the central kiosk. You'll find plenty of benches for taking in the spectacle, too.

Cozumel's main town, San Miguel, is full of casual, local restaurants.

An orange clock tower dating from 1910 watches over the proceedings. Posing with the red-pink-yellow-grey-green-blue-orange block letters of the "Cozumel" sign here makes for the obligatory post on social media to let everyone know where you are. (Other more modern such signs dot the island, including at each of the three cruise ports.) ✉ *Calle 1 Sur, at 5 Av. Norte, San Miguel.*

🍴 Restaurants

★ Burritos Gorditos

$ | **MEXICAN** | If you've got a hankering for a hole-in-the-wall place that serves cheap, delicious meals, Burritos Gorditos fits the bill for breakfast and lunch. The made-to-order shrimp burritos are excellent and big enough to split, and a solid assortment of tacos and salads is available, but no alcohol is served. **Known for:** shrimp burritos; steak quesadillas; fast service. [$] *Average main: MP100* ✉ *Av. Norte 5A, between Calles 2 and 4, San Miguel* ☎ *987/116–7214* 🌐 *burritosgorditos.wixsite.com/burritos-gorditos* 🕓 *Closed Sun.*

Casa Denis

$$$ | **MEXICAN** | **FAMILY** | This restaurant in a little yellow house near the plaza has been satisfying cravings for Yucatecan favorites like *cochinita pibil* (spiced pork baked in banana leaves) since 1945. Locals tend to stop in between 8:30 and 1 for cheap breakfast and lunch menus that highlight tacos and empanadas, and the *tortas* (sandwiches) are also a real bargain. **Known for:** beef fajitas; Yucatán-style cooked fish; grilled seafood. [$] *Average main: MP300* ✉ *Calle 1 Sur 132, between Avs. 5 and 10, San Miguel* ☎ *987/872–0067* 🌐 *www.facebook.com/casadeniscozumel* 💳 *No credit cards* 🕓 *Closed Sun.*

Casa Mission

$ | **MEXICAN** | **FAMILY** | Part private home, part restaurant (and owned by the same family since the 1980s), this place evokes a country hacienda in mainland Mexico. Although the setting, with tables lining

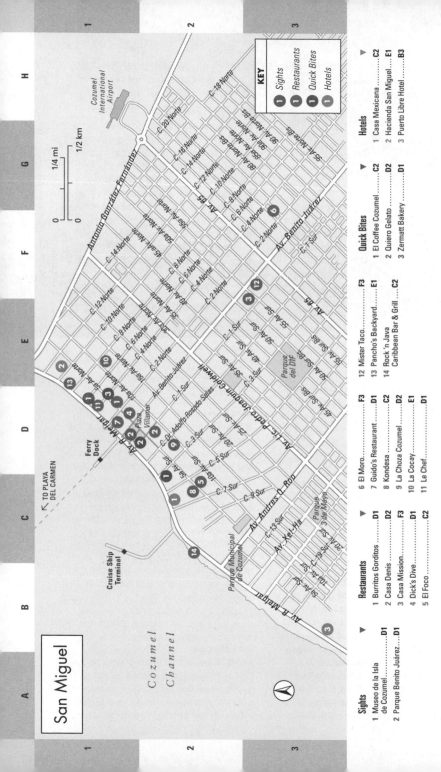

San Miguel

TO PLAYA DEL CARMEN

Cozumel Channel

Cozumel International Airport

0   1/4 mi
0   1/2 km

Sights ▶
1 Museo de la Isla de Cozumel............**D1**
2 Parque Benito Juárez.....**D1**

Restaurants ▶
1 Burritos Gorditos **D1**
2 Casa Denis **D2**
3 Casa Mission.................**F3**
4 Dick's Dive....................**D1**
5 El Foco **C2**
6 El Moro..........................**F3**
7 Guido's Restaurant **D1**
8 Kondesa **C2**
9 La Choza Cozumel.........**D2**
10 La Cocay.......................**E1**
11 Le Chef..........................**D1**
12 Mister Taco...................**F3**
13 Pancho's Backyard.......**E1**
14 Rock 'n Java
Caribbean Bar & Grill **C2**

Quick Bites ▶
1 El Coffee Cozumel **C2**
2 Quiero Gelato **D2**
3 Zermatt Bakery **D1**

Hotels ▶
1 Casa Mexicana...............**C2**
2 Hacienda San Miguel.....**E1**
3 Puerto Libre Hotel.........**B3**

KEY
1 Sights
1 Restaurants
1 Quick Bites
1 Hotels

the veranda, outshines the food, stalwart fans nevertheless rave about the huge platters of fajitas and grilled fish. **Known for:** relaxed "in-home" dining; Veracruz fish fillet; grilled lobster. [$] *Average main: MP130* ✉ *Av. 55, between Avs. Juárez and Calle 1 Sur, San Miguel* ☎ *987/105-5468* 🌐 *www.casamissionrestaurant.com.*

Dick's Dive

$$ | **AMERICAN** | Hardly a dive bar, this place's name refers to Cozumel's great diving experience. Rub elbows with friendly expats and locals alike while you dine on burritos, shrimp bruschetta, and burgers. **Known for:** Sunday barbecue; pub fare; nachos. [$] *Average main: MP200* ✉ *Av. 5, between Calles 2 and Juárez, San Miguel* ☎ *987/872-4279* 🌐 *www.facebook.com/dicksdivecozumel.*

El Foco

$$ | **MEXICAN** | Popular among locals, this *taquería* captures some of the charm of the barrios and remains open late (until 1 am daily). The soft tacos stuffed with pork, chorizo (sausage), cheese, or beef aren't the cheapest tacos on the island, but they're tasty and filling. **Known for:** good fast food; chorizo tacos; late-night atmosphere. [$] *Average main: MP180* ✉ *Av. 5 Sur, Suite 433, between Calles 5 and 7 Sur, San Miguel* ☎ *987/107-4108* 🌐 *www.facebook.com/ElFocoCozumel* 🕓 *Closed Wed.*

★ El Moro

$$$ | **MEXICAN** | **FAMILY** | You'll have to work hard to find El Moro, but your perseverance will be rewarded with one of the better meals—consisting of a wide range of seafood and beef dishes—in Cozumel. After dinner, try a taste of *xtabentun*, a traditional Yucatecan liqueur made of fermented honey and anise seeds. **Known for:** Yucatán-style food; excellent service; seafood. [$] *Average main: MP260* ✉ *75 Bis Norte 124, between Calles 2 and 4, San Miguel* ✥ *Head east on Calle 4 from Av. 65; take 4th right turn onto 75 Bis (no street signs). It's in the middle of the block on the right* ☎ *987/120-2907* 🌐 *www.facebook.com/RestauranteElMoroCozumel* 🕓 *Closed Thurs.*

★ Guido's Restaurant

$$$ | **ITALIAN** | Chef Yvonne Villiger works wonders with fresh fish—if the wahoo with capers and black olives is on the menu, don't miss it. But Guido's is best known for pizzas that are baked in a wood-fired oven and served by an incredibly attentive staff. **Known for:** fresh seafood; sangria; puffy garlic bread. [$] *Average main: MP350* ✉ *Av. Rafael E. Melgar 23, between Calles 6 and 8 Norte, San Miguel* ☎ *987/869-2589* 🌐 *guidoscozumel.com.*

Kondesa

$$$ | **MEXICAN FUSION** | **FAMILY** | Thanks to a hot-pink-and-turquoise exterior, you can't miss this restaurant, which features a palapa-covered bar that opens onto a dimly lit garden dining area. Kondesa puts a modern spin on classic dishes, and the menu emphasizes fresh fish, with favorites like the Kondesa *kake* (an interpretation of crab cakes made with lionfish) and seafood-filled enchiladas. **Known for:** fresh seafood; artisanal cocktails; lionfish "crab" cake. [$] *Average main: MP300* ✉ *Av. 5, Suite 456, between Calles 5 and 7, San Miguel* ☎ *987/869-1086* 🌐 *www.kondesacozumel.com* 🕓 *Closed Mon. No lunch.*

La Choza Cozumel

$$$ | **MEXICAN** | **FAMILY** | Locals and expats gather here for breakfasts of *migas* (scrambled eggs with bits of bacon and tortilla) and the daily lunchtime *comida corrida* (a set-priced meal with a choice of appetizers and entrées), which is a great deal. Favorite dishes include *pollo con mole poblano* (chicken in a smooth, earthy chile sauce), chile relleno *de camarón* (chile stuffed with shrimp), and pork with pumpkin-seed sauce. **Known for:** Mexican-style breakfasts; chilled avocado pie; mole poblano. [$] *Average main: MP260* ✉ *Av. 10, between Calles 3 and Adolfo Rosado Salas, San Miguel*

☎ *987/872–0958* 🌐 *www.facebook.com/lachozaczm.*

★ La Cocay

$$$$ | **MEDITERRANEAN** | This casually sophisticated dining room and garden is a local favorite. Although the menu changes frequently, you can expect to find salads with fruits, pasta dishes, steaks, and seafood entrées like seared sashimi-grade tuna or the sweet-mango-topped mahimahi. **Known for:** fresh-prepared meals; beautiful garden dining; great service. [$] *Average main: MP360* ✉ *Calle 8 Norte 208, between Avs. 10 and 15, San Miguel* ☎ *987/872–5533* 🌐 *lacocay.com/home* ⏲ *No lunch.*

★ Le Chef

$$$ | **MEDITERRANEAN** | Dining is a relaxed affair at this intimate café and restaurant with a Mediterranean-inspired menu. The lobster BLT sandwich, assorted soups, salads, or special pizzas all make a great choice, and there are daily specials as well. **Known for:** fresh salads; excellent wine selection; creative meal presentations. [$] *Average main: MP290* ✉ *Av. Rafael E. Melgar 201-4, between Calles 3 and 5, San Miguel* ☎ *987/878–4391* 🌐 *www.lechefcozumel.com/cozumel* ⏲ *Closed Mon. No lunch.*

Mister Taco

$ | **MEXICAN** | **FAMILY** | If you are looking for an authentic taco joint where the locals go, this is the place. The tacos *al pastor*, carved from a vertical spit, are big, juicy, and inexpensive. **Known for:** open till the wee hours; cheap eats; fast service. [$] *Average main: MP40* ✉ *Av. Juárez between Avs. 55 and 60, San Miguel* 🌐 *mistertaco.restaurantwebexperts.com* ⏲ *No lunch.*

★ Pancho's Backyard

$$$ | **MEXICAN** | **FAMILY** | Marimbas play beside a bubbling fountain in the charming courtyard behind one of Cozumel's best folk-art shops. The English menu is geared toward tourists and priced in pesos, but regional ingredients like smoky chipotle chile make even the standard steak stand out for a true Mexican-inspired meal. **Known for:** open-air courtyard dining; strong margaritas; vegan and vegetarian options. [$] *Average main: MP320* ✉ *Av. Rafael E. Melgar 27, between Calles 8 and 10 Norte, San Miguel* ☎ *987/872–2141* 🌐 *www.panchosbackyard.com.*

Rock 'n Java Caribbean Bar & Grill

$$ | **ECLECTIC** | **FAMILY** | A favorite of expats and locals, this restaurant has an extensive breakfast menu that includes whole-wheat French toast and cheese crepes. For lunch or dinner try the vegetarian tacos, linguine with clams, or one of the many salads. **Known for:** leisurely breakfasts; fresh ingredients; oceanfront views. [$] *Average main: MP185* ✉ *Av. Rafael E. Melgar 602-6, San Miguel* ☎ *987/869–2794* 🌐 *www.rocknjavacozumel.com.*

☕ Coffee and Quick Bites

El Coffee Cozumel

$ | **CAFÉ** | San Miguel's place to go for coffee roasts beans from Oaxaca and whips them into a variety of drinks. A selection of baked goods and salads rounds out the fare. **Known for:** good selection of coffee drinks; coffeehouse vibe; late-night hours. [$] *Average main: MP120* ✉ *Calle 4 Sur, at Av. 5, San Miguel* ☎ *987/869–0456* 🌐 *www.facebook.com/elcoffeecozumel.*

Quiero Gelato

$ | **ICE CREAM** | **FAMILY** | "I want gelato" is the translation of the name of this shop on the southwest side of central plaza. Partake of mango-, lemon-, banana-, and other tropical-flavored cones in addition to the standard chocolate and vanilla. **Known for:** fun tropical flavors; old-fashioned ice cream-parlor vibe; quick service. [$] *Average main: MP100* ✉ *Calle 1 Sur 58B, San Miguel* 🌐 *www.quierogelato.com* 💳 *No credit cards.*

San Miguel's charming streets lead to sun-soaked beaches and resorts.

Zermatt Bakery
$ | **BAKERY** | **FAMILY** | Pick out your goodies with a pair of tongs—that's the way bakeries operate in Mexico—and bring your tray to the front counter. Take your food (cakes, pastries, breads) to a table indoors or on the front porch or get it to go. **Known for:** amazing aromas; strong coffee; European-style bakery. [$] *Average main: MP100* ✉ *Av. 5 and Calle 4 Norte, San Miguel* 💳 *No credit cards* 🕑 *Closed Sun.*

🛏 Hotels

★ Casa Mexicana
$$ | **HOTEL** | Although not on the beach, this distinctive and inexpensive hotel overlooks the water, and its oceanfront rooms, with comfortable balconies from which to enjoy the views, are worth the added cost. **Pros:** near restaurants and shops; friendly staff; substantial breakfast. **Cons:** no beach; tiny pool; some street noise. [$] *Rooms from: $130* ✉ *Av. Rafael E. Melgar 457, between Calles 5 and 7 Sur, San Miguel* ☎ *987/872–9090* 🌐 *www.casamexicanacozumel.com* 🛏 *88 rooms* 🍴 *Free Breakfast.*

Hacienda San Miguel
$$ | **B&B/INN** | Five blocks south of San Miguel's main plaza, this small inn consists of two-story buildings set around a lush courtyard. **Pros:** quiet but central; plenty of great restaurants nearby; courtyard gardens make it feel like a private home. **Cons:** no parking or pool; a/c can be noisy and rooms musty; free Wi-Fi in courtyard only. [$] *Rooms from: $120* ✉ *Calle 10 Norte 1500, at Av. 5, San Miguel* ☎ *987/872–1986* 🌐 *www.hotelhaciendasanmiguel.com* 🛏 *11 rooms* 🍴 *No Meals.*

★ Puerto Libre Hotel
$$ | **HOTEL** | This newest entry into the San Miguel lodging sweepstakes is this snazzy, sleek, starkly modern hotel that offers an elegance previously unseen downtown. **Pros:** high standards of service; good value for what's offered; within walking distance of almost everything. **Cons:** balconies pick up a bit of street noise; charges for a lot of extras; small

on-site restaurant. $ *Rooms from: $174* ⊠ *Calle 8 and Av. Rafael E. Melgar, San Miguel* ☎ *987/688–3000* ⊕ *www.puertolibrehotel.com* ⊷ *26 rooms* ⊙⎮ *Free Breakfast.*

Nightlife

BARS
Fat Tuesday
BARS | On the northwest corner of the square, this watering hole draws cruise-ship crowds by day and vacationers staying on the island at night. Expect frozen daiquiris, ice-cold beers, and blaring rock at tourist prices. You'll find a second location at the Puerta Maya cruise terminal. ⊠ *Av. Juárez 2, between Av. Rafael E. Melgar and Calle 3 Sur, San Miguel* ☎ *987/872–5130* ⊕ *www.fat-tuesday.cozumel.net.*

La Internacional Cervecería Cozumel
BREWPUBS | Mexico is home to a growing number of artisanal brewers, and this is the place to try craft Mexican beers as well as additional selections from over 33 other countries. The bartenders are knowledgeable about their brews. ⊠ *Av. Rafael E. Melgar between Calles 7 and 11, San Miguel* ☎ *987/869–1289* ⊕ *www.facebook.com/lainternacionalcerveceriacozumel.*

'Ohana Café & Bar
BARS | This reggae bar serves deep-dish pizza that gets rave reviews, and the Mexican-inspired meals provide something for every palate. ⊠ *Av. 5 between Calles 6 and 8 Norte, San Miguel* ☎ *987/564–1771* ⊕ *ohanacozumel.com* ⊙ *Closed Sun.*

Señor Frog's
BARS | The *Animal House* ambience at Señor Frog's at night includes loud music and a bar-dancing, bead-throwing, balloon-hat-wearing, anything-goes drinking scene. During the day, the pub grub is better than you'd expect, the drinks are flowing, and the waiters are always entertaining. You'll find two locations here, near the Punta Langosta and the International cruise terminals. ⊠ *Punta Langosta, Av. Rafael E. Melgar between Calles 7 and 11, San Miguel* ☎ *987/869–1651* ⊕ *www.senorfrogs.com* ⊙ *Closed for breakfast.*

Viva Mexico Bar and Grill
BARS | Live bands and DJs play dance music some evenings at Viva Mexico, but it's the extensive food menu with the expected items (burgers, quesadillas, and such) that makes this second-floor bar-restaurant popular. Happy hour generally runs from 6 to 8 pm. ■**TIP**→ **The best seats overlook the waterfront and the sunset.** ⊠ *Av. Rafael E. Melgar and Calle Adolfo Rosado Salas, San Miguel* ☎ *987/872–0799* ⊕ *www.facebook.com/cozumelvivamexico.*

★ Wet Wendy's Margarita House
LIVE MUSIC | **FAMILY** | You'll find the best and largest frozen margaritas in town at Wet Wendy's. Sit at the bar, and down one of the potent concoctions, or grab a table in the outdoor garden to dine on remarkably good food and dance to the salsa, rock, and jazz bands that play here several nights a week. Service is friendly, so don't be surprised if the bartender asks you if you want "the usual" on your second visit. ⊠ *Av. 5A Norte, San Miguel* ☎ *987/872–4970* ⊕ *www.wetwendys.com.*

DANCE CLUBS
Tiki Tok Bar
DANCE CLUBS | A second-floor restaurant called Trattoria by day transforms into a salsa dance club called Tiki Tok after dark. On Friday and Saturday, local bands draw salsa aficionados of all stripes from 10 pm to about 3 am; a DJ spins Latin and reggaeton through all hours of the night. ⊠ *Av. Rafael E. Melgar 13, between Calles 2 and 4 Norte, San Miguel* ☎ *987/869–8119* ⊕ *www.facebook.com/tikitokcozumel* ⊙ *Closed Sun.*

Cozumel's History

Cozumel's name is believed to have come from the Mayan "Ah-Cuzamil-Peten" ("Land of the Swallows"). For the Maya, who lived here intermittently between about AD 600 and 1200, the island was not only a center for trade and navigation but also a sacred place. Pilgrims from all over Mesoamerica came to honor Ixchel, the goddess of fertility, childbirth, and healing. The mother of all other gods, Ixchel (also known as Lady Rainbow) was often depicted with swallows at her feet. Maya women, who were expected to visit her site at least once in their lives, made the dangerous journey from the mainland by canoe. Cozumel's main exports were salt and honey, both of which at the time were considered more valuable than gold.

In 1518 Spanish explorer Juan de Grijalva arrived on the island in search of slaves. His tales of treasure inspired Hernán Cortés, Mexico's most famous Spanish explorer, to visit the following year. There he met Gerónimo de Aguilar and Gonzalo Guerrero, Spaniards who had been shipwrecked years earlier. Initially enslaved by the Maya, the two were later accepted into the community. Aguilar joined forces with Cortés, helping set up a military base on the island and using his knowledge of the Maya to defeat them. Guerrero, in contrast, died defending his adopted people, and the Maya still consider him a hero. By 1570, most Maya islanders had been massacred by the Spanish or killed by disease, and, by 1600, the island was abandoned.

In the 17th and 18th centuries, pirates found Cozumel to be the perfect hideout. The notorious buccaneers

Jean Lafitte and Henry Morgan favored its safe harbors and hid their treasures in Mayan catacombs and tunnels. By 1843, Cozumel had again been abandoned. Five years later, 20 families fleeing Mexico's brutal Caste War of the Yucatán resettled the island, and their descendants still live here.

By the early 20th century, the island began capitalizing on its abundant supply of *zapote* (sapodilla) trees, which produce *chicle*, a chewy substance prized by the chewing-gum industry. (Now you know how Chiclets got its name.) Shipping routes began to include Cozumel, whose natural harbors made it a perfect stop for large vessels. Jungle forays in search of chicle led to the discovery of ruins, so archaeologists began visiting the island as well. Meanwhile, Cozumel's importance as a seaport diminished as air travel grew, and the demand for chicle dropped off with the invention of synthetic chewing gum.

For decades Cozumel was another backwater where locals fished, hunted alligators and iguanas, and worked on coconut plantations to produce *copra*, the dried kernels from which coconut oil is extracted. Cozumeleños subsisted largely on seafood, still a staple of the local economy. During World War II, the U.S. Army paid to have an airstrip built to hunt the German U-boats that were sinking Mexican ships. Then, in the 1960s, the underwater explorer Jacques Cousteau helped make Cozumel famous by featuring its reefs on his television show. Today, Cozumel is among the world's most popular diving destinations.

🎭 Performing Arts

Cinepolis

FILM | FAMILY | On a sweltering hot or rainy afternoon, slip into Cinepolis. The modern, multiscreen theater shows current hit films in Spanish and English at afternoon matinees and nightly shows. When buying your ticket, select your seats on the computer screen and then head over for some reasonably priced food and drinks at the snack bar. ⊠ *Av. Rafael E. Melgar 1001, between Calles 15 and 17 Sur, San Miguel* 🕾 *552/122–6060* ⊕ *cinepolis.com/cartelera/cozumel.*

🛍 Shopping

Cozumel's main souvenir-shopping area is downtown on or near the waterfront. Tourist-trap malls at the cruise-ship piers sell jewelry, perfume, sportswear, and low-end souvenirs at high-end prices.

Most downtown shops accept U.S. greenbacks, and many goods are priced in dollars. But to get better prices, pay with pesos and stick to cash—some shops tack a hefty surcharge on credit-card purchases. Shops, restaurants, and streets are always crowded between 10 am and 2 pm but slow down in the evening. Traditionally, stores are open from 9 to 9, although most do close on Sunday morning.

■ **TIP→ When you shop for souvenirs, be sure you don't buy anything made with black coral. It's an endangered species, and you'll be barred from bringing it to the United States and other countries.**

ART GALLERIES

Galería Azul

ART GALLERIES | At one of Cozumel's best galleries, Greg Dietrich creates and shows his engraved blown-glass lamps and vases along with paintings, jewelry, photography, and other works by local artists. It's open Monday through Friday from 11 to 7 (other times by appointment). The gallery is three blocks off the waterfront. ⊠ *Av. 15 Norte 449, between Calles 8 and 10, San Miguel* 🕾 *987/869–0963* ⊕ *www.cozumelglassart.com* ⊘ *Closed weekends.*

Galo Art Studio

ART GALLERIES | Local painter Galo Ramírez and a consortium of island artists display their works at this gallery. Their vibrant water colors and acrylics portray local scenes and people. ⊠ *5 Av. 691, at Calle 9 Bis, San Miguel* ⊕ *www.facebook.com/galoartstudio.*

CLOTHING

Blanc du Nil

MIXED CLOTHING | FAMILY | Be the best-dressed person at your next party wearing one of the many styles of casual, breezy, tropical white clothing for sale here. ⊠ *Av. Melgar and Calle 3, San Miguel* 🕾 *987/869–0952* ⊕ *www.blanc-dunil.com* ⊘ *Closed Sun.*

Island Outfitters

MIXED CLOTHING | FAMILY | In addition to sportswear and sarongs, the offerings here include Mexican crafts, home decor, and beach towels. ⊠ *Av. Rafael E. Melgar and Calle 4, San Miguel* 🕾 *987/872–2741* ⊘ *Closed Sun.*

CRAFTS

★ Los Cinco Soles

CRAFTS | FAMILY | This is the best one-stop shop in Cozumel for Mexican crafts and art. Numerous display rooms, covering almost a block, are filled with clothing, furnishings, home-decor items, quality tequilas, and jewelry. There are smaller branches at Puerta Maya, the international pier (SSA), the Cozumel airport, Punta Langosta, and the gift shops of some hotels. ⊠ *Av. Rafael E. Melgar and Calle 8 Norte, San Miguel* 🕾 *987/872–9004* ⊕ *www.loscincosoles.com.*

Viva Mexico

CRAFTS | FAMILY | Downstairs from the bar of the same name, Viva Mexico sells souvenirs and handicrafts from all over Mexico; it's a great place to find vanilla, T-shirts, household goods, art,

EL FARO

HAVANA CIGARS

COHIBA

and assorted trinkets. There are also branches at Puerta Maya and the international pier. ✉ *Av. Rafael E. Melgar and Calle Adolfo Rosado Salas, San Miguel* ☏ *987/872–0418* ⊕ *www.facebook.com/cozumelvivamexico.*

GROCERY STORES

Chedraui

SUPERMARKET | **FAMILY** | Open daily from 7 am to 11 pm, this big, full-service grocery store also carries clothing, kitchenware, appliances, furniture, and a terrific selection of wine. For those renting a nearby condo, this is a place to stock up on food and beverages. Brand-name sunscreens, while expensive, are available. ■**TIP**→ **The deli and bakery are excellent places to pick up picnic provisions; coolers and ice are sold here, too.** ✉ *Av. Rafael E. Melgar, between Calles 15 and 17 Sur, San Miguel* ☏ *987/872–5404* ⊕ *www.chedraui.com.mx.*

Mega Soriana

SUPERMARKET | **FAMILY** | A supermarket, pharmacy, and department store all under one big roof, Mega Soriana has a huge covered parking lot and pretty much anything you would need for a short or extended stay on Cozumel. Soriana's wine and international beer offerings are second to none. It's open daily from 8 am to 10 pm, though alcohol sales on Sunday cease at 3 as they do around the island for carryout. ✉ *Av. Rafael E. Melgar and Calle 11, San Miguel* ☏ *987/872–2116* ⊕ *www.soriana.com.*

JEWELRY

Diamonds International

JEWELRY & WATCHES | You can have pieces of jewelry that incorporate this store's selection of loose diamonds, emeralds, rubies, sapphires, or tanzanite customized to suit your taste. There is also a broad range of watches. The shop and its affiliates, Tanzanite International and Silver International, have multiple locations along the waterfront, at the cruise piers, and in the shopping malls—in fact, it's hard to avoid them. Repairs and batteries are also available. ✉ *Av. Rafael E. Melgar 599, San Miguel* ☏ *987/869–5335* ⊕ *www.diamondsinternational.com* ⊘ *Closed Sun.*

★ Pama

DUTY-FREE | Trusted, well-established Pama offers a wide array of imported jewelry, perfumes, watches, and watch repairs while you wait. Sales pitches are definitely low-pressure here, so take your time and enjoy looking around. ✉ *Av. Rafael E. Melgar Sur 9, San Miguel* ☏ *987/872–0090* ⊕ *www.facebook.com/pamacozumel* ⊘ *Closed Sun.*

Sergio's Silver

JEWELRY & WATCHES | The renowned artist's Taxco silver jewelry collections are sold at this gallery. If you have the time, they will make a custom piece for you to take home. ✉ *Av. Juárez between Avs. 5 and 10, San Miguel* ☏ *987/872–7632* ⊕ *www.sergiosilver.com* ⊘ *Closed Sun.*

MALLS

Plaza Punta Langosta

MALL | **FAMILY** | This fancy, multilevel shopping mall is across from the downtown cruise-ship dock. A covered pedestrian walkway leads over the street from the ships to the center, which houses several jewelry, sportswear, and souvenir stores, as well as ice-cream shops and chain restaurants and bars such as Hooters and Señor Frog's. ✉ *Av. Rafael E. Melgar 559, at Calle 7, San Miguel* ☏ *987/869–1127.*

MARKETS

Crafts Market

MARKET | **FAMILY** | On the northeast side of the downtown square, an unnamed artisan market sells a respectable assortment of Mexican wares. Practice your bartering skills—start low, compromise, smile—while shopping for blankets, T-shirts, hammocks, and pottery. Most sellers accept only cash. ✉ *Between Calles 1 and Benito Juárez, San Miguel.*

Mercado Municipal

MARKET | FAMILY | You'll find a few souvenirs here, but the municipal market is really a place to see where the average island resident shops for day-to-day goods like fresh produce, fish, and chiles. There are also several inexpensive places to eat serving Mexican and Asian foods. ⊠ *Calle Adolfo Rosado Salas, between Avs. 20 and 25 Sur, San Miguel.*

Zona Hotelera Norte

🛏 Hotels

Coral Princess Golf & Dive Resort

$$ | RESORT | FAMILY | Good snorkeling off the rocky shoreline and a relaxed family feel make this resort, which offers both hotel rooms and apartmentlike units, a north-coast favorite. **Pros:** decent, well-priced meals; family-friendly; snorkeling right off beach. **Cons:** can be noisy at pool; some rooms lack bathtubs; time-share pitches. $ *Rooms from: $155* ⊠ *Carretera Costera Norte, Km 2.5, Cozumel* 🕾 *987/564–5889* ⊕ *www. coralprincess.com* 🛌 *148 rooms* ✲ *Free Breakfast.*

Hotel B Cozumel

$$ | HOTEL | This sleek boutique property has quickly become the lodging of choice for a discerning young crowd. **Pros:** great snorkeling; close to town and marina; intimate atmosphere. **Cons:** small sandy beach; pool service is slow; some rooms don't have ocean views. $ *Rooms from: $174* ⊠ *Carretera Costa Norte, Km 2.5, Cozumel* 🕾 *987/872–0300* ⊕ *www. hotelbcozumel.com* 🛌 *45 rooms* ✲ *Free Breakfast.*

Hotel B Unique

$$$ | HOTEL | This hip adults-only design hotel has a wellness, holistic, and boho attitude overall. **Pros:** adults-only; chic Mexican design; quality spa. **Cons:** some rooms have no ocean views; no bathtub in rooms; rocky beach. $ *Rooms from:*

$274 ⊠ *Carretera playa San Juan, Km 2.5, Cozumel* 🕾 *987/872–0194* ⊕ *www. hotelbunique.com* 🛌 *27 rooms* ✲ *Free Breakfast.*

Meliá Cozumel

$$$ | ALL-INCLUSIVE | FAMILY | One of the first international-class hotels in Cozumel, Meliá continues to satisfy by offering guests a bit of everything, including a wide variety of restaurants and activities, including motorized and nonmotorized water sports. **Pros:** 40+ activities available every day; kids' club; great beach. **Cons:** extra charge for room service; some rooms have no ocean views; massive property. $ *Rooms from: $235* ⊠ *Carretera Costera Norte, Km 5.8, Zona Hotelera Norte, Cozumel* 🕾 *987/872–9870* ⊕ *www.melia.com* ✲ *210 rooms* ✲ *All-Inclusive.*

Playa Azul Cozumel Hotel

$$$ | HOTEL | FAMILY | Playa Azul feels like a charming, understated Mexican hacienda—there's elegance in its simplicity, and its spacious rooms overlooking the courtyard pool and ocean are tastefully decorated with Mexican furnishings. **Pros:** intimate; excellent spa; good snorkeling. **Cons:** rocky beach entry in areas; quite, so not a place to stay if you crave action; far from downtown. $ *Rooms from: $217* ⊠ *Carretera Costera Norte, Km 4, Cozumel* 🕾 *987/869–5160* ⊕ *www. playa-azul.com* ✲ *50 rooms* ✲ *Free Breakfast.*

The Westin Cozumel

$$$ | HOTEL | FAMILY | This sophisticated white tower is one of the island's most luxurious hotels, with ultramodern decor and incredible ocean views. **Pros:** modern, chic design; good snorkeling just offshore; pet-friendly up to 40 pounds. **Cons:** beach is small; rooftop pool bar is not always open; beach beverage service can be spotty. $ *Rooms from: $259* ⊠ *Carretera Costera Norte, Km 4.8, Cozumel* 🕾 *987/872–9200* ⊕ *www.marriott. com* ✲ *152 rooms* ✲ *Free Breakfast.*

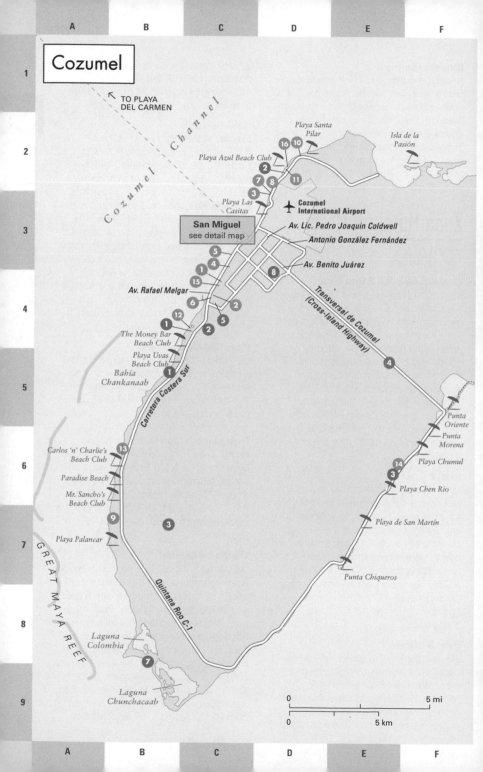

G   H   I

Laguna
Xlapak

Caribbean
Sea

Sights ▼

1 Chankanaab Beach
Adventure Park **B5**
2 Discover Mexico......... **C4**
3 El Cedral **B7**
4 Mayan Bee
Sanctuary................. **E5**
5 Planetario de Cozumel
Cha'an Ka'an **C4**
6 Punta Molas Faro......... **I1**
7 Punta Sur **B8**
8 San Gervasio............ **D3**

Restaurants ▼

1 Alfredo di Roma......... **B4**
2 Buccanos at Night...... **D2**
3 Coconuts Bar & Grill **E6**

Hotels ▼

1 Blue Angel Resort **C4**
2 Casa del Mar **C4**
3 Coral Princess Golf
& Dive Resort.......... **D2**
4 Cozumel Hotel
& Resort **C3**
5 Cozumel Palace.......... **C3**
6 El Cid la Ceiba............ **C4**
7 Hotel B Cozumel **D2**
8 Hotel B Unique.......... **D2**
9 Iberostar Cozumel...... **B7**
10 Meliá Cozumel **D2**
11 Playa Azul Cozumel
Hotel..................... **D2**
12 Presidente
InterContinental
Cozumel Resort
and Spa **B4**
13 Secrets Aura
Cozumel.................. **B6**
14 Ventanas al Mar **E6**
15 Villablanca Garden
Beach Hotel **C4**
16 The Westin Cozumel ... **D2**

KEY

1 *Sights*
1 *Restaurants*
1 *Hotels*

G   H   I

Zona Hotelera Sur

Sights

Chankanaab Beach Adventure Park
THEME PARK | FAMILY | Chankanaab, translated as "small sea," consists of a saltwater lagoon, an archaeological park, and a botanical garden, with reproductions of a Maya village and Olmec, Toltec, Aztec, and Maya stone carvings scattered throughout. You can swim at the beach, and there's plenty for snorkelers and divers to see beneath the surface, including underwater caverns, a sunken ship, crusty old cannons and anchors, a sculpture of the Virgen del Mar (Virgin of the Sea), and parrot fish and sergeant majors galore. Note, though, that to preserve the ecosystem, rules forbid touching the reef or feeding the fish. A seal show is included in the admission, and you'll find dive shops, restaurants, gift shops, a snack stand, and dressing rooms with lockers and showers right on the sand. Chankanaab also has a Dolphin Discovery facility where you can swim with the much-loved marine mammals. ✉ *Carretera Sur, Km 9, Cozumel* ☎ *987/872–0093* 🌐 *cozumelparks.com/parque-chankanaab* 🎫 *$19* 🕒 *Closed Sun.*

Discover Mexico
MUSEUM VILLAGE | FAMILY | Want to see all of Mexico while staying on the island? This theme park purports to show you the country's archaeological sites, important architectural landmarks, and cultures, without leaving Cozumel. The scale models of temples, pyramids, monasteries, and more have kitsch value, but a slickly produced film about the country and high-quality folk-art exhibits begin to touch on the real thing. A café serves tasty fruit sorbets and light meals; you can also reserve in advance for the daily tequila or chocolate tastings. **■ TIP→ The gift shop has an array of beautiful Mexican folk art for sale.** ✉ *Carretera Sur, Km 5.5, Cozumel* ☎ *987/875–2820* 🎫 *$26* 🕒 *Closed Sun.*

Planetario de Cozumel Cha'an Ka'an
(Cha'an Ka'an Cozumel Planetarium)
OBSERVATORY | FAMILY | The Maya were centuries ahead of their time in understanding the heavens. This newest addition to Cozumel's sightseeing roster mixes modern-day with pre-Columbian knowledge of astronomy, with a bit of Maya legend peppered in. A separate admission apart from the daily schedule admits you to the Velada Astronómica, hourlong stargazing programs held Thursday and Saturday nights at 8—weather permitting, of course. ✉ *Av. Claudio Canto s/n, Cozumel* ☎ *987/857–0867* 🌐 *www.planetariodecozumel.org* 🎫 *MX$90; MX$140, evening programs* 🕒 *Closed Sun. and Mon.*

Restaurants

Alfredo di Roma
$$$$ | ITALIAN | The opportunity to dine graciously amid crystal and candlelight (and blessedly cool air-conditioning) is just one reason to book a special dinner at Alfredo's. The pastas are made fresh daily, and cheeses are flown in from Italy so that the chef can prepare the house special—authentic fettuccine Alfredo—at your table. **Known for:** fresh-made pasta dishes; impressive wine selection; ocean views. [$] *Average main: MP450* ✉ *Presidente InterContinental Cozumel, Carretera Chankanaab, Km 6.5, Cozumel* ☎ *987/872–9500* 🌐 *presidenteiccozumel.com* 🕒 *No lunch.*

★ Buccanos at Night
$$$$ | MODERN MEXICAN | Sunset views and an incredible meal await you at this oceanfront restaurant, which offers fresh seafood and meats as well as seasonal salads—all presented beautifully. If you have plans for a special-occasion meal, this is the place, but be sure to make reservations in advance, as the indoor and outdoor tables fill up fast and walk-ins

are sometimes left waiting. **Known for:** seasonal fresh seafood; delicious desserts; artisanal cocktails. [$] *Average main: MP370* ✉ *Playa San Juan, Km 4.5 Norte, Cozumel* ☎ *987/114–5607* 🌐 *www.facebook.com/buccanosatnight* ⏲ *Closed Mon.*

Hotels

Blue Angel Resort

$$ | **HOTEL** | **FAMILY** | The clean and bright guest rooms at this locally owned hotel, a big favorite among hard-core divers, all have balconies or terraces with hammocks and racks for drying dive gear. **Pros:** close to town; on-site PADI outfitter; incredible sunsets. **Cons:** small pool; busy street behind the hotel; street parking only. [$] *Rooms from: $147* ✉ *Carretera Sur, Km 2.2, Cozumel* ☎ *987/872–0188* 🌐 *www.blueangelresort.com* 🔑 *22 rooms* 🍴 *Free Breakfast.*

Casa del Mar

$ | **HOTEL** | All rooms at this diver-oriented hotel are enlivened by simple Mexican artwork, but those with sea-facing balconies are lighter, airier, and don't cost that much more. **Pros:** good dive base location; optional, reasonably priced all-inclusive plan; close to other dining options. **Cons:** food choices and serving times are limited; beach is across the street; weak Wi-Fi. [$] *Rooms from: $79* ✉ *Carretera Sur, Km 4, Cozumel* ☎ *987/872–1900* 🌐 *casadelmarcozumel.com* 🔑 *89 rooms* 🍴 *All-Inclusive.*

Cozumel Hotel & Resort

$$ | **RESORT** | **FAMILY** | In high season, guests surround the enormous pool at this bright-orange Wyndham property, while activity directors enliven the crowd with games and loud music. **Pros:** near grocery stores and restaurants; 10 fully accessible rooms; breakfast-only option available. **Cons:** rocky beach area; poolside entertainment loud; outdated facilities. [$] *Rooms from: $182* ✉ *Carretera Costera Sur, Km 1.7, Cozumel* ☎ *987/872–9020* 🌐 *www.cozumelhotel.com.mx* 🔑 *181 rooms* 🍴 *All-Inclusive.*

Cozumel Palace

$$$$ | **RESORT** | **FAMILY** | Gleaming white in the afternoon sun, the Cozumel Palace seems more like a cruise ship than an upscale all-inclusive hotel, one where the music and flowing drinks in the tight confines of the pool deck area create a lively outdoor atmosphere. **Pros:** on-site spa and dive shop; extremely attentive staff; walking distance to downtown. **Cons:** time-share reps; pool and lobby get noisy at happy hour; lack of premium liquors. [$] *Rooms from: $440* ✉ *Av. Rafael E. Melgar, Km 1.5 Sur, Cozumel* ☎ *987/872–9430, 800/986–5632 in the U.S. and Canada* 🌐 *www.palaceresorts.com* 🔑 *175 rooms* 🍴 *All-Inclusive* ☞ *Day passes available for a fee.*

El Cid la Ceiba

$$ | **ALL-INCLUSIVE** | **FAMILY** | Next door to the Puerta Maya cruise pier and shopping center, this smallish resort, part of a small Mexican hotel chain, is a comfortable choice, with some condo-style rooms that have kitchenettes. **Pros:** comfy accommodations; reasonably priced all-inclusive option available; close to town and other restaurants. **Cons:** pool area is small and the scene can be boisterous; heavy boat traffic in snorkel areas; time-share reps. [$] *Rooms from: $180* ✉ *Carretera Chankanaab, Km 4.5, Cozumel* ☎ *987/872–0844, 888/733–7308 in U.S. and Canada* 🌐 *www.elcid.com* 🔑 *76 rooms* 🍴 *All-Inclusive.*

Iberostar Cozumel

$$$ | **RESORT** | **FAMILY** | Jungle greenery surrounds this all-inclusive resort at Cozumel's southernmost point, where bungalow rooms are small but pleasant. **Pros:** friendly, personal service; large pool area with plenty of lounge chairs; short trip to most dive sites. **Cons:** rocky beach entry; so-so food and reservations required; expensive cab ride to town. [$] *Rooms*

Presidente InterContinental Cozumel Resort and Spa

from: $227 ✉ Carretera Chankanaab, Km 17, past El Cedral turnoff, Cozumel ☎ 987/872–9900, 833/399–7888 in the U.S. and Canada 🌐 www.iberostar.com 🛏 306 rooms 🍴 All-Inclusive.

★ Presidente InterContinental Cozumel Resort and Spa

$$$ | RESORT | FAMILY | The luxurious InterContinental has top-notch service, expansive lawns, pristine beaches, and spacious, modern rooms. **Pros:** modern, luxurious rooms; impeccable service; four restaurants. **Cons:** pricey food; some rooms lack ocean views; marina traffic can create waves for snorkelers. [$] *Rooms from: $265 ✉ Carretera Chankanaab, Km 6.5, Cozumel ☎ 800/502–0500 in the U.S. and Canada, 987/872–9500 🌐 presidenteiccozumel.com 🛏 218 rooms 🍴 Free Breakfast.*

Secrets Aura Cozumel

$$$$ | RESORT | The elegant adults-only Aura offers the ultimate in all-inclusive service and a variety of room styles in four low-rise buildings that face a meandering pool with separate areas linked by a lazy river. **Pros:** high-tech; luxurious amenities (rare on Cozumel); intimate, sophisticated atmosphere. **Cons:** far from town; offshore snorkeling not very good; some rooms need updating. [$] *Rooms from: $323 ✉ Carretera Costera Sur, Km 12.9, Cozumel ☎ 866/467–3273 in the U.S. and Canada, 987/872–9320 🌐 www.hyattinclusivecollection.com 🛏 238 suites 🍴 All-Inclusive.*

Villablanca Garden Beach Hotel

$ | HOTEL | FAMILY | The landscaped grounds here are lovely, as are most rooms, although, as befitting the price, there's a certain budget-hotel sparseness to the place. **Pros:** lush gardens around pool; good value; dive packages offered. **Cons:** dated and minimal furnishings; spotty Wi-Fi; busy street out front. [$] *Rooms from: $88 ✉ Carretera Chankanaab, Km 3, Cozumel ☎ 987/872–0730 🌐 villablanca.net 🛏 54 rooms 🍴 No Meals.*

Nightlife

Cerveceria Punta Sur

BREWPUBS | Cozumel's first microbrewery serves a range of delicious brews from lighter ales to darker beers. The pub fare pairs well with the brews offered, and the pizzas are cooked in a wood-fired oven with excellent results. ⊠ *298A Av. 10, between AR Salas and Calle 3, Cozumel* ☎ *987/140–6744* ⊕ *www.cerveceria-puntasur.com.*

Leeward Side

⊙ Sights

El Cedral

RUINS | Spanish explorers discovered this site—once the hub of Maya life on Cozumel—in 1518, and in 1847 it became the island's first official city. Today, it's a residential community with small, well-tended houses and gardens. Conquistadores tore down much of the Maya temple, so there's little in the way of actual ruins apart from one small stone arch; if you're in the market for souvenirs, however, vendors around the main plaza display embroidered huipil blouses and hammocks. Kun Che Park, just past the village, offers an interactive tour of the Maya lifestyle. ⊠ *Off Carretera Sur, Cozumel* ⊹ *Turn at Km 17.5 off Carretera Sur or Av. Rafael E. Melgar, then drive 3 km (2 miles) inland to site* ⊠ *MX$40.*

Punta Sur

NATURE PRESERVE | **FAMILY** | This 247-acre national preserve is a habitat for numerous birds and animals, including crocodiles, flamingos, egrets, and herons. At the park's (and Cozumel's) southernmost point stands the Faro de Celarain, a lighthouse that's now a museum of navigation. Climb the 134 steps to the top for the best view of the island. Spot birds from observation towers near Laguna Colombia or Laguna Chunchacab, or visit the ancient Mayan lighthouse El Caracol, which was designed to whistle when the wind blows in a certain direction. Beaches here are wide and deserted, and there's great snorkeling offshore; snorkeling equipment is available for rent, as are kayaks. Leave your car at the Faro and take a park shuttle or rental bike to either of the two beach bars. Admission price includes a pontoon-boat ride in the crocodile-infested lagoon. If you're coming by taxi, expect to pay about MX$400 for a round-trip ride from San Miguel. ⊠ *Carretera Costera Sur, Km 30, Cozumel* ☎ *987/872–0093* ⊕ *cozumelparks.com/punta-sur* ⊠ *USD$19* ⊙ *Closed Sun.*

⊕ Beaches

Wide, sandy beaches washed with shallow waters are typical at the far north and south ends of Cozumel's west coast. The topography changes between the two, with small sandy coves interspersed with limestone outcroppings.

■**TIP→ Generally, the best snorkeling from shore is wherever piers or rocky shorelines provide a haven for sergeant majors and angelfish.**

Isla de la Pasión

BEACH | Off Punta Norte on the northwest coast, private Isla de Pasión has one of Cozumel's loveliest beaches. Most people arrive on organized excursions (from MX$1,300), but you can also get to the Isla dock independently (it's at the end of the bumpy dirt road to Punta Norte) and come over for MX$150 per person. If coming as part of an organized excursion, your visit includes the short round-trip boat ride, a buffet lunch, soft drinks, some alcoholic drinks, and use of the extensive facilities. You can easily spend a whole day here strolling the strand, floating in the shallow water, swinging in a hammock, playing volleyball, indulging in a massage (for an extra fee), or even getting married in the island's chapel. This is a favorite stop for

Cozumel's best beaches and reefs are on the leeward side.

hordes of cruise-shippers, but the beach stretches for 4 km (2½ miles), so you can still escape the crowds. **Amenities:** food and drink; showers; toilets. **Best for:** snorkeling; swimming; walking. ⊠ *Bahia Ciega Lagoon, Cozumel* ☎ *Round trip from MX$150.*

Playa Las Casitas

BEACH | FAMILY | Hugely popular with locals, Playa Las Casitas has several large palapa-style restaurant-bars, small palapas and palm trees for shade, calm waters, and a long stretch of beach. Swim out 150 yards from the north end to enjoy the fish-filled artificial reefs. Windsurfers and stand-up paddleboards are also available for rent. The beach is fairly deserted on weekdays but completely packed on Sunday, the traditional day for family outings. **Amenities:** food and drink; parking (no fee); toilets; water sports. **Best for:** snorkeling; sunsets; swimming. ⊠ *Carretera Norte and Blvd. Aeropuerto, Cozumel* ☎ *Free.*

Playa Palancar

BEACH | FAMILY | South of the resorts, down a dirt road and way off the beaten path, lies this long, serene, walkable beach with hammocks hanging under coconut palms. The on-site dive shop can outfit scuba enthusiasts for trips to the famous Palancar and Columbia reefs, just offshore; boats will take snorkelers out every two hours from 9 to 5. There's also a nice open-air restaurant-bar here if you'd rather just relax. **Amenities:** food and drink; parking (no fee); showers; toilets; water sports. **Best for:** snorkeling; swimming; walking. ⊠ *Carretera Sur, Km 19.5, Cozumel* ☎ *987/117–5863* ⊕ *face-book.com/palancarczm* ☎ *Free.*

Playa Santa Pilar

BEACH | Running along the northern hotel strip where the Meliá and El Cozumeleño hotels are located, you'll find long stretches of sand and shallow water that encourage leisurely swims. Beach hotels have all the facilities you would need, but most are all-inclusive and don't allow nonguests on the premises. If you're not staying at one, bring your own shade and slip onto the beach between properties. ■TIP➔ **Kiteboarders gather in this area when the winds are good, offering hours of entertaining acrobatics; equipment can be rented nearby from De Lille Sports. Amenities:** food and drink (for guests only); parking (no fee). **Best for:** snorkeling; swimming; walking. ⊠ *Carretera San Juan, just south of Punta Norte, Cozumel* 🖾 *Free.*

BEACH CLUBS

Carlos 'n' Charlie's Beach Club

BEACH | Easily accessible by cab from downtown or the cruise piers, this spot at Playa San Francisco is a rowdy affair with a restaurant and bar where waiters break into song and draw customers into line dances. The food is typical of the chain—burgers, barbecued ribs, tacos—and the alcohol flows generously. While there's a wide array of water sports offered, the water is shallow, not always clear, and congested with Jet Skis and water toys. **Amenities:** food and drink; parking (no fee); showers; toilets; water sports. **Best for:** partiers. ⊠ *Carretera Costera Sur, Km 14, Cozumel* 🕾 *987/564–0960 mobile* ⊕ *www.carlosandcharlies.com/cozumel* 🖾 *Entry free with food or drink purchase.*

The Money Bar Beach Club

BEACH | FAMILY | Situated on Dzul-Ha reef, the island's most upscale beach club has a small sandy beach, sunset views, and great food. Entry is free; once inside, you can pay for individual activities or choose an all-inclusive package that might cover anything from meals and massages to guided snorkel tours. (If you snorkel the fish-filled reef on your own, watch out for sea urchins on the rocks.) A water-sports center rents snorkel gear, kayaks, and small sailboats. Mingle with locals and sip frothy cocktails during the two-for-one sunset happy hour. ■TIP➔ **There's live music and dancing on weekend nights. Amenities:** food and drink; parking (no fee); showers; toilets; water sports. **Best for:** snorkeling; sunset; swimming.

⊠ *Carretera Sur, Km 6.5, Cozumel* 🕾 *987/869–5140* ⊕ *www.moneybar-beachclub.com* 🖾 *Free.*

Mr. Sancho's Beach Club

BEACH | FAMILY | There's always something going on at Mr. Sancho's. Scores of vacationers come here to swim, snorkel, drink, parasail, and ride around on Jet Skis. The restaurant, which offers a number of meal options, holds a lively, informative tequila seminar at lunchtime. Grab a swing seat under the palapa and sip a mango margarita, or opt for a massage. Lockers are available and souvenirs are for sale. This is one of the few bars on the west side that is free to enter and also offers an all-inclusive package. **Amenities:** food and drink; parking (no fee); showers; toilets; water sports. **Best for:** partiers; swimming. ⊠ *Carretera Sur, Km 15, Cozumel* 🕾 *844/856–7269 in the U.S. and Canada, 987/871–9174* ⊕ *www.mrsanchos.com* 🖾 *Free; all-inclusive from $68.*

Paradise Beach

BEACH | FAMILY | Home to one of the largest heated pools on the island, this club charges $3 for lounge chairs; a Fun Pass ($60) gives you all-day use of kayaks, stand-up paddleboards, and snorkel gear, plus numerous large floats in the water. Parasailing equipment and Jet Skis are available for rent. Food at the club's three restaurant-bars is expensive, and there's a minimum per-person consumption cost ($6) that's easily reached. **Amenities:** food and drink; parking (no fee); showers; toilets; water sports. **Best for:** swimming. ⊠ *Carretera Sur, Km 14.5, Cozumel* 🕾 *987/689–0010* ⊕ *paradisebeachcozumel.com* 🖾 *$50.*

Playa Azul Beach Club

BEACH | FAMILY | This club sits just north of the hotel of the same name. The beach is actually pockets of soft sand between limestone shelves; there's also a pool at the hotel that is open to club guests. The restaurant beneath a large palapa serves delicious ceviche and bountiful club sandwiches with a side of fries, and there's free Wi-Fi to boot. Live music on Sunday afternoon draws a crowd of fun-loving people. ■**TIP→ There's good snorkeling along the reef wall. Amenities:** food and drink; parking (no fee); showers; toilets. **Best for:** snorkeling; sunsets; swimming. ⊠ *Carretera Norte, Km 4, Cozumel* ☎ *987/869–5160* ⊕ *www. playa-azul.com/beachclub* ☞ *Free.*

Playa Uvas Beach Club

BEACH | FAMILY | Sitting on a narrow sandy beach, Uvas caters to small cruise-ship groups and independent tourists. On-site amenities include a dive shop, kayaks, massages, and more. The basic entrance fee gets you one beverage and the use of beach umbrellas, lounge chairs, and a guided snorkel tour, but additional food and drink purchases can quickly run up your tab; all-inclusive packages are also available. ■**TIP→ Phone or online reservations are required since the club limits the number of guests. Amenities:** food and drink; parking (no fee); showers; toilets; water sports. **Best for:** swimming. ⊠ *Carretera Sur, Km 8.5, Cozumel* ☎ *987/120–1420* ⊕ *cozumelexperiences. com/playa-uvas* ☞ *$15.*

Windward Side

 Sights

Mayan Bee Sanctuary

OTHER ATTRACTION | FAMILY | Experience the life and times of the Yucatán's stingless Melipona bees during an informative one-hour bilingual tour of this site near the center of the island. (The Melipona cannot sting, but it does bite when threatened.) The bees, which have been cultured since ancient Maya times, are known for producing a tangy, slightly acidic honey. ⊠ *Carretera Transversal, Km 10, Cozumel* ☎ *987/114–3299* ⊕ *www. mayanbeesanctuary.com.mx* ☞ *USD$8* ⊗ *Closed Sun.*

Punta Molas Faro (*Molas Point Lighthouse*)

LIGHTHOUSE | The lighthouse at Cozumel's northernmost point is a solitary, beautiful sight. The rutted road to Punta Molas is accessible by four-wheel-drive vehicles, dirt bikes, and ATVs only, but the scenery is awe-inspiring no matter how far you're able to go. Some tour operators travel out this way when the oceans are calm, providing a photo op from the top of the lighthouse. If making the trip, the small military garrison based there always appreciates a few snacks and soft drinks if you have some to spare. ⊠ *Cozumel* ☞ *Free.*

San Gervasio

RUINS | It's no Chichén Itzá, but rising from the jungle, these temples make an impressive sight. Cozumel's largest remaining Maya and Toltec site, San Gervasio was the island's capital and ceremonial center, dedicated to the fertility goddess Ixchel. (As with most Maya sites in Mesoamerica, the original name has been lost to history.) The Classic- and Postclassic-style buildings and temples were continuously occupied from AD 300 to 1500. Typical architectural features include limestone plazas and arches atop stepped platforms, as well as stelae and bas-reliefs. Don't miss the temple Las Manitas, with red handprints all over its altar. Water and light snacks are available to purchase, and bug spray is recommended—and be sure to wear your walking shoes for this adventure. ■**TIP→ Plaques in Mayan, Spanish, and English clearly describe each structure, but it's worth hiring a guide to fully appreciate the site.** ⊠ *Benito Juárez Transversal Rd., Km 7.5* ✛ *From San Miguel, take cross-island road east to San Gervasio access road; turn left and follow road 7 km (4½ miles)* ☎ *987/872–0093* ⊕ *cozumelparks. com/san-gervasio* ☞ *$13.*

The Quieter Side of Cozumel

Blazing-white cruise ships parade in and out of Cozumel like a regatta of floating apartment buildings. Sundays aside, there's at least one on the horizon every day of the year; some days, the island gets six or more. The day-trippers they carry pack the tourist-trap souvenir shops and bars on San Miguel's waterfront every afternoon, making the place feel more like a suburban shopping mall than a small Mexican town.

Luckily, there's plenty of Cozumel to go around. If you're fortunate enough to overnight on the island, try these tricks to avoid the crowds.

1. **Keep a low profile.** Stick close to the beach and pool when more than two ships are in port.

2. **Time your excursions.** Go into San Miguel for early breakfast and errands, then stay out of town for the rest of the day. Wander back after you hear the ships blast their departure warnings around 5 or 6 pm.

3. **Dive in.** Hide from the hordes by slipping underwater. But be sure to choose a small dive operation that travels to less popular reefs.

4. **Drive on the wild side.** Rent a car and cruise the windward coast, still free of rampant construction. You can picnic and sunbathe on private beaches hidden by limestone outcroppings, and watch the waves roll in. Use caution when swimming, though, since the surf can be rough, and there can be rip currents.

5. **Frequent the "other" downtown.** Most of Cozumel's residents live and shop far from San Miguel's waterfront. Avenidas 15, 20, and 25 are packed with taco stands, *papelerías* (stationery stores), and neighborhood markets. While driving here can be messy, park on a quieter side street and explore the shops and neighborhoods to see a whole different side of Cozumel.

⊕ Beaches

The east coast of Cozumel presents a splendid succession of deserted rocky coves and narrow powdery beaches poised dramatically against the turquoise Caribbean.

⚠ **Swimming can be treacherous here if you go out too far—in some places the strong undertow can sweep you out to sea in minutes.**

These beaches are perfect for solitary sunbathing. Several casual restaurants dot the coastline; they all close around sunset as there is no electricity on this side of the island.

Beyond Punta Oriente, the sandy road beside Mezcalitos leading to the wild northeast coast is sometimes open and sometimes gated—a shame, because the beaches there are superb. Other than ATV outings there are no tours to this part of the coast, and the road is too rutted for rental cars. Rumors abound as to this area's future—some say there will be a small-scale resort here someday, while others hope it will become an ecological reserve. A small navy bivouac at the Punta Molas lighthouse is the only settlement on the road for now, though some of the scrub jungle is divided into housing lots.

Playa Chen Rio

BEACH | FAMILY | This long and wide, white sand beach has natural rock formations that serve as protection from the waves providing calm waters that are perfect for swimming with kids. There are several palapas scattered here and there to relax under. Visit the nearby Mirador Chen Rio for some of the best views on this side of the island. **Amenities:** food and drinks; lifeguards; parking (no fee); showers; toilets; water sports. **Best for:** snorkeling; sunrise; swimming; walking. ⊠ *Carretera Costera Oriente, Cozumel* ☒ *Free.*

Playa Chumul

BEACH | About 3 km (2 miles) to the north of Playa San Martín, the island road turns hilly and offers panoramic ocean views. Coconuts, a hilltop palapa restaurant, is a prime lookout spot that also serves decent food. One hundred yards away, Ventanas al Mar (the only hotel on the windward coast) attracts travelers who value solitude. Locals picnic on the long beach directly north of the hotel. When the water is calm, there's good snorkeling around the rocks beneath Ventanas al Mar, but steer clear if it's rough. **Amenities:** food and drink; parking (no fee); toilets. **Best for:** solitude; snorkeling; surfing. ⊠ *Carretera C-1, Km 43.5, Cozumel* ☒ *Free.*

Playa de San Martín

BEACH | Not quite 3 km (2 miles) north of Punta Chiqueros, a long stretch of beach begins along the Chen Río Reef. Turtles come to lay their eggs on the section known as Playa de San Martín. Soldiers or ecologists sometimes guard the beach during full moons from May to September to prevent poaching. This is a particularly good spot for swimming when the water is calm. However, if red flags are displayed, it means there is a dangerous rip current—be cautious. When the wind is blowing from the south, though, the water is best for kiteboarders and windsurfers. When you're ready to kick back, La Palapa de St. Martin serves cold

drinks and seafood. **Amenities:** lifeguards (part-time); parking (no fee). **Best for:** solitude; surfing; swimming. ⊠ *Carretera C-1, Km 41, Cozumel* ☒ *Free.*

Punta Chiqueros

BEACH | Sheltered by an offshore reef, this secluded half-moon cove is Mexico's furthest eastern spot. Part of a longer beach that some locals call "Playa Bonita," it has fine sand, clear water, turtle nests, and moderate waves. There used to be a popular restaurant and beach club here, but it's now abandoned. The road to get here has been neglected in the last few years, so not many people frequent this beautiful beach these days. **Amenities:** parking (no fee). **Best for:** sunrise; swimming; walking. ⊠ *Carretera C-1, Km 38, Cozumel* ☒ *Free.*

Punta Morena

BEACH | FAMILY | Surfers, kiteboarders, and boogie boarders have made Punta Morena beach and the restaurant of the same name one of their official hangouts—and for good reason: it has great waves and a restaurant serving surfer-friendly burgers, fries, and Mexican fare. ■ **TIP→ If you are away from the main palapa, ask the waiter for a beverage-service flag, and settle your bill in pesos to avoid conversion costs.** **Amenities:** food and drink; lifeguards; parking (no fee); showers; toilets; water sports. **Best for:** sunrise; surfing; swimming; walking. ⊠ *Carretera C-1, Km 46, Cozumel* ☒ *Free.*

Punta Oriente

BEACH | This typical east-side beach is great for beachcombing but unsuitable for swimming due to the currents. It's nicknamed Playa Mezcalitos after the much-loved Mezcalito Café, which serves seafood and beer and has beachfront hammocks for an afternoon siesta. Señor Iguana's is the other restaurant option here. The "Naked Beach" sign here doesn't actually indicate the sector of sand where discreet nudity is tolerated. For that, walk north along the beach. **Amenities:** food and drink; parking (no fee); toilets. **Best for:** nudists (to the north); partiers; walking. ✉ *Carretera C-1, Km 49, Cozumel* 🎟 *Free.*

🍴 Restaurants

Coconuts Bar & Grill

$$ | **INTERNATIONAL** | The T-shirts and bras hanging from the palapa of this hilly, windward-side hangout at the island's highest point are good indicators of its party-time atmosphere. Classic rock and reggae tunes play in the background while crowds down cervezas, fish, fajitas, and garlic shrimp. **Known for:** adults-only party, not to everybody's taste; fantastic hilltop views; variety of cocktails. [$] *Average main: MP180* ✉ *Carretera C-1, Km 43, Cozumel* ☎ *987/107–7622* 🌐 *coconutscozumel.com* 💳 *No credit cards.*

🛏 Hotels

Ventanas al Mar

$$ | **HOTEL** | The lights of San Miguel are a distant glow on the horizon when you look west from the windward coast's only lodging, a small rustic inn that's run on generator power and has spacious, simply furnished rooms with patios or balconies. **Pros:** blissful solitude; long beach for morning walks; adults-only. **Cons:** a/c operates 8 pm–8 am only; limited food and drink options; limited Wi-Fi, no phones, no in-room TVs. [$] *Rooms from: $130* ✉ *Carretera C-1, Km 43.5, Cozumel* ☎ *984/212–9468, 987/107–1008* 🌐 *ventanasalmarcozumel.com* 🔑 *19 rooms* 🍽 *Free Breakfast.*

Activities

FISHING

The waters here teem with more than 230 species of fish, making Cozumel a premier deep-sea fishing destination. During billfish migration season from late April through June, blue marlin, white marlin, and sailfish are plentiful, and world-record catches aren't uncommon.

Larger sportfishing boats dock in the Puerto Abrigo marina just north of San Miguel. Boats also moor at the south side Marina Fonatur, near the Presidente InterContinental resort. Some sportfishing companies are affiliated with dive shops and offer a full range of water activities. Hotels can help arrange daily charters—some with boats leaving from their own docks.

Albatros Charters

FISHING | **FAMILY** | Half- and full-day outings that include boat and crew, tackle and bait, plus libations and lunch (quesadillas or your own fresh catch) are organized by Albatros Charters. Snorkeling and sightseeing trips are also available. ✉ *Calle 19 Sur near the corner of 10 Av. Sur Bis, Cozumel* ☎ *987/872–7904, 888/333–4643 in U.S. and Canada* 🌐 *www.cozumel-fishing.com* 🎟 *From $550 for a half day.*

Ocean Tours

DIVING & SNORKELING | **FAMILY** | All equipment and tackle, lunch with beer, and, of course, the boat and crew are included in Ocean Tours' full-day rates. Deep-sea fishing, scuba diving, and snorkeling tours are available. Half-day tours are also offered, and discounts are given for cash payments. ✉ *El Cozumeleño Beach Resort, Playa Santa Pilar, Zona Hotelera Norte, Km 4.5, Cozumel* ☎ *987/872–1379* 🌐 *www.cozumel-diving.net/oceantur* 🎟 *From $480 for half day.*

★ Spearfishing Today

FISHING | After a short spearfishing lesson with certified instructors, you'll launch from Puerto Abrigo on a four-hour boat trip. Expect to get shots off at grouper, snapper, or triggerfish. Snacks, water, soft drinks, and all equipment are included. The crew will also clean your catch and suggest restaurants that will cook it

Continued on page 255

COZUMEL DIVING AND SNORKELING

First comes the giant step, a leap from a dry boat into the warm Caribbean Sea. Then the slow descent to white sand framed by rippling brain coral and waving purple sea fans. If you lean back, you can look up toward the sea's surface. The water off Cozumel is so clear you can see the puffy white clouds in the sky even when you're submerged 20 feet underwater.

With more than 30 charted reefs whose depths average 50–80 feet and water temperatures around 24°C–27°C (75°F–80°F) during peak diving season (June–August, when hotel rates are coincidentally at their lowest), Cozumel is far and away the place to dive in Mexico. More than 60,000 divers come here each year.

Because of the diversity of coral formations and the dramatic underwater peaks and valleys, divers consider Cozumel's Palancar Reef (promoters now call it the Maya Reef) to be one of the top five in the world.

Sea turtles that are headed to the beach to lay their eggs swim beside divers in May and June. Fifteen-pound lobsters wave their antennae from beneath coral ledges; they've been protected in Cozumel's National Marine Park for so long they've lost all fear of humans.

Long green moray eels appear rather menacing as they bare their fangs at curious onlookers, and snaggle-toothed barracuda look ominous as they swim by.

All in all, however, diving off Cozumel is relaxing, rewarding, and addictive. You simply can't do it just once.

The reef is home to brain coral and huge sponges.

DIVE SITES

Cozumel's reefs stretch for 32 km (20 miles), beginning at the international pier and continuing to Punta Celarain at the island's southernmost tip. Here is a rundown of Cozumel's main dive destinations:

Chankanaab Reef. This inviting reef lies south of Parque Chankanaab, about 350 yards offshore. Large underground caves are filled with striped grunt, snapper, sergeant majors, and butterfly fish. At 55 feet, there's another large coral formation that's often filled with crabs, lobster, barrel sponges, and angelfish. If you drift a bit farther south, you can see the Balones de Chankanaab, balloon-shaped coral heads, at 70 feet.

Colombia Reef. Several miles off Palancar, the reef reaches 82–98 feet and is best suited for experienced divers. Its underwater structures are as varied as those of Palancar Reef, with large canyons and ravines to explore. Clustered near the overhangs are large groupers, jacks, rays, and an occasional sea turtle.

Felipe Xicotencatl (C-53 wreck). Sunk in 2000 specifically for scuba divers, this 154-foot-long minesweeper is located on a sandy bottom about 80 feet deep near Tormentos and Chankanaab. Created as an artificial reef to decrease some of the traffic on the natural reefs, the ship is open so divers can explore the interior and is gradually attracting schools of fish.

Maracaibo Reef. Considered one of the most difficult reefs, Maracaibo is a thrilling dive with strong currents and intriguing old coral formations. Although there are shallow areas, only advanced divers who can cope with the current should attempt Maracaibo.

Palancar Reef. About 2 km (1 miles) offshore, Palancar is actually a series of varying coral formations with about 40 dive locations. It's filled with winding canyons, deep ravines, narrow crevices, archways, tunnels, and caves. Black and red coral and huge elephant-ear, and barrel sponges are among the attractions. At the section called Horseshoe, a series of coral heads forms a

natural horseshoe shape. This is one of the most popular sites for dive boats and can become crowded.

Paraíso Reef. About 330 feet offshore, running parallel to the international cruise-ship pier, this reef averages 30–50 feet. It's a perfect spot to dive before you head for deeper drop-offs. There are impressive formations of star and brain coral as well as sea fans, sponges, sea eels, and yellow rays. It's wonderful for night diving.

Paseo El Cedral. Running parallel to Santa Rosa reef, this flat reef has gardenlike valleys full of fish, including angelfish, grunt, and snapper. At depths of 35–55 feet, you can also spot rays.

San Francisco Reef. Considered Cozumel's shallowest wall dive (35–50 feet), this 1-km (½-mile) reef runs parallel to Playa San Francisco and has many varieties of reef fish. You'll need to take a dive boat to get here.

Chankanaab Reef

Young yellow sponges along the Palancar Reef

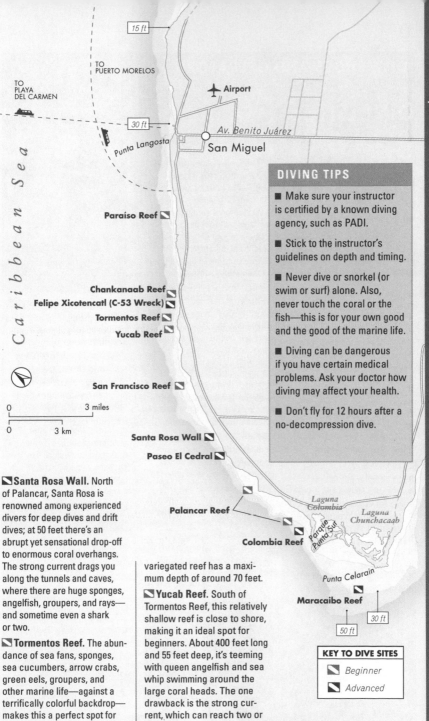

15 ft

TO PUERTO MORELOS

TO PLAYA DEL CARMEN

✈ **Airport**

30 ft

Punta Langosta

Av. Benito Juárez

○ **San Miguel**

C a r i b b e a n   S e a

Paraíso Reef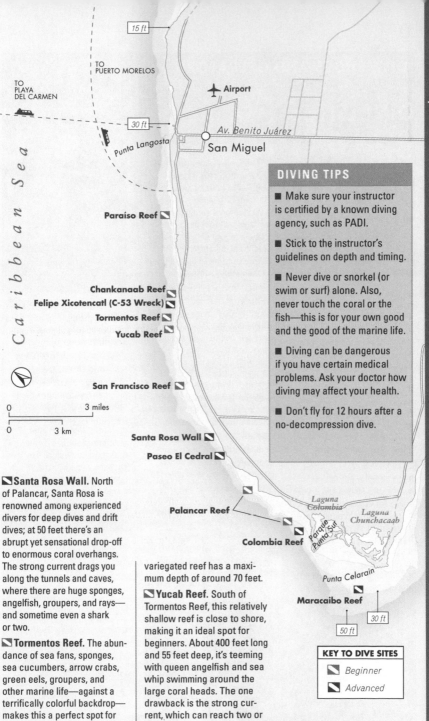

Chankanaab Reef
Felipe Xicotencatl (C-53 Wreck)
Tormentos Reef
Yucab Reef

San Francisco Reef

0 —— 3 miles
0 —— 3 km

Santa Rosa Wall
Paseo El Cedral

Palancar Reef

Colombia Reef

Parque Punta Sur

Laguna Colombia

Laguna Chunchacaab

Punta Celarain

Maracaibo Reef

30 ft

50 ft

DIVING TIPS

■ Make sure your instructor is certified by a known diving agency, such as PADI.

■ Stick to the instructor's guidelines on depth and timing.

■ Never dive or snorkel (or swim or surf) alone. Also, never touch the coral or the fish—this is for your own good and the good of the marine life.

■ Diving can be dangerous if you have certain medical problems. Ask your doctor how diving may affect your health.

■ Don't fly for 12 hours after a no-decompression dive.

Santa Rosa Wall. North of Palancar, Santa Rosa is renowned among experienced divers for deep dives and drift dives; at 50 feet there's an abrupt yet sensational drop-off to enormous coral overhangs. The strong current drags you along the tunnels and caves, where there are huge sponges, angelfish, groupers, and rays— and sometime even a shark or two.

Tormentos Reef. The abundance of sea fans, sponges, sea cucumbers, arrow crabs, green eels, groupers, and other marine life—against a terrifically colorful backdrop— makes this a perfect spot for underwater photography. This variegated reef has a maximum depth of around 70 feet.

Yucab Reef. South of Tormentos Reef, this relatively shallow reef is close to shore, making it an ideal spot for beginners. About 400 feet long and 55 feet deep, it's teeming with queen angelfish and sea whip swimming around the large coral heads. The one drawback is the strong current, which can reach two or three knots.

KEY TO DIVE SITES

Beginner
Advanced

DIVE SHOPS AND OPERATORS

It's important to choose a dive shop that suits your expectations. Beginners are best off with the more established, conservative shops that limit the depth and time spent underwater. Experienced divers may be impatient with this approach, and are better suited to shops that offer smaller group dives and more challenging dive sites. More and more shops are merging these days, so don't be surprised if the outfit you dive with one year has been absorbed by another the following year. Recommending a shop is dicey. The ones we recommend are well-established and also recommended by experienced Cozumel divers.

Because dive shops tend to be competitive, it's well worth your while to shop around. Many hotels have their own on-site operations, and there are dozens of dive shops in town. Before signing on, ask experienced divers about the place, check credentials, and look over the boats and equipment. Shops can have specialties, so if you have special needs (for example, kids) look for an outfitter comfortable with family dives.

Top: the wreck of C-53 *Felipe Xicotencatl*
Bottom: Coral, coral, and more coral

WHAT IT COSTS IN U.S. DOLLARS	
Regulator & BC	$6.30–$25
Underwater camera	$35–$45
Video camera	$75
Pro videos of your dive	$160
Two-tank boat trips	$60–$100
Specialty dives	$70–$150
One-tank afternoon dives	$45–$60
Night dives	$45–$60
Marine park fee	$5

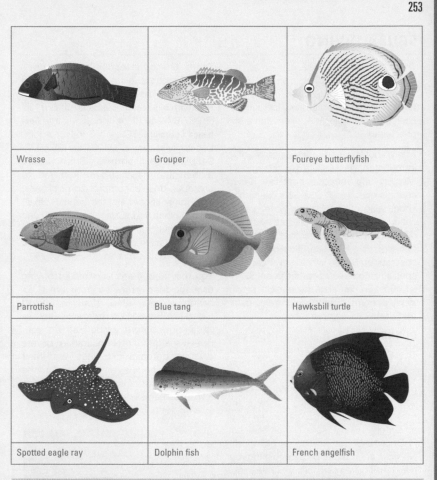

Wrasse	Grouper	Foureye butterflyfish
Parrotfish	Blue tang	Hawksbill turtle
Spotted eagle ray	Dolphin fish	French angelfish

SNORKELING TIPS

Snorkeling equipment is available at nearly all hotels and beach clubs as well as at Parque Chankanaab, Playa San Francisco, and Parque Punta Sur. Gear rents for less than $15 a day. Snorkeling tours run about $60 and take in the shallow reefs off Palancar, Chankanaab, Colombia, and Yucab.

■ Never turn your back on the ocean, especially if the waves are big.

■ Ask about rip tides before you go in.

■ Enter and exit from a sandy beach area.

■ Avoid snorkeling at dusk and never go in the water after dark.

■ Wear lots of sunscreen, especially on your back and butt cheeks.

■ Don't snorkel too close to the reef. You could get scratched if a wave pushes you.

■ Be mindful of boats.

SCUBA DIVING

There's no way anyone can do all the deep dives, drift dives, shore dives, wall dives, and night dives in one trip, never mind the theme dives focusing on ecology, archaeology, sunken ships, and photography.

Many hotels and dive shops offer introductory classes in a swimming pool. Most include a beach or boat dive. Resort courses cost about $60–$80. Many dive shops also offer full open-water certification classes, which take at least four days of intensive classroom study and pool practice. Basic certification courses cost about $390, while advanced and specialty courses cost between $270–$1,400. You can also do your classroom study at home, then do your training and test dives on Cozumel.

DIVING SAFELY There are more than 100 dive shops in Cozumel, so look for high safety standards and documented credentials. The best places offer small groups and individual attention. Next to your equipment, your dive master is the most important consideration for your adventure. Make sure he or she has PADI or NAUI certification (or FMAS, the Mexican equivalent). Be sure to bring your own certification card; all reputable shops require customers to show them before diving. If you forget, you may be able to call the agency that certified you and have the card number faxed to the shop.

Keep in mind that much of the reef off Cozumel is a protected National Marine Park. Boats aren't allowed to anchor in certain areas, and you shouldn't touch the coral or take any "souvenirs" from the reefs when you dive there. It's best to swim at least 3 feet above the reef—not just because coral can sting or cut you, but also because it's easily damaged and grows very slowly; it has taken 2,000 years to reach its present size.

There are two reputable recompression chambers in Cozumel if you need emergency medical attention: **Medicina Hiperbarica Integral** (⊠ Calle 5 Sur 37 ☎ 987/872–1430 24-hr hotline); and **Costamed Cozumel** (⊠ Calle 1 Sur 101, Adolfo López Mateos ☎ 9400 or 987/872-9400). These chambers, which aim for a 35-minute response time from reef to chamber, treat decompression sickness, commonly known as "the bends," which occurs when you surface too quickly and nitrogen bubbles form in the bloodstream. Recompression chambers are also used to treat hypothermia.

You may also want to consider buying dive-accident insurance from the U.S.-based **Divers Alert Network (DAN)** (☎ 919/684–9111 emergency hotline ⊕ dan.org) before embarking on your dive vacation. DAN insurance covers dive accidents and injuries, and their emergency hotline can help you find the best local doctors, hyperbaric chambers, and medical services. They can also arrange for airlifts.

for you. ⊠ *Puerto de Abrigo–Banco Playa, Zona Hotelera Norte, Puerto Abrigo* ☎ *987/876–0862* ⊕ *spearfishingtoday. com* ⊠ *From $300.*

Tres Hermanos

FISHING | FAMILY | This outfit specializes in deep-sea and fly-fishing trips. It also offers scuba-diving excursions and snorkel trips. Boats are available for group charters, allowing you to move at your own pace. ⊠ *Marina Puerto de Abrigo, Av. Rafael E. Melgar Norte, Puerto Abrigo* ☎ *987/107–2030* ⊕ *cozumelfishing.com* ⊠ *From $375 for a half day.*

PADDLEBOARDING AND KITEBOARDING

★ De Lille Sports

STAND-UP PADDLEBOARDING | FAMILY | Cozumel native Raul De Lille—a former world windsurf champion and national kiteboard champion—offers two- to three-hour classes in both stand-up paddleboarding (SUP) and kiteboarding. Tours depart from either the De Lille Sports shop at Hotel Barracuda or the Puerto de Abrigo Marina. The equipment is top-of-the-line. The huge, six-person paddleboard is great for a large group. Multiday courses and rental equipment are available, too. ■**TIP→ If the winds are calm, inquire about De Lille's private snorkeling tour to the northern tip of the island.** ⊠ *Av. Melgar 628, Hotel Barracuda, Cozumel* ☎ *987/103–6711* ⊕ *delillesports.com* ⊠ *SUP tour from $60* ☾ *Closed Sun.*

SNORKELING AND SCUBA DIVING

★ Aldora Divers

SCUBA DIVING | Make the most of your trip by exploring the undersea environment with Aldora Divers. Although it also works with neophytes, this outfit caters to experienced divers. Its all-day, three-tank nitrox trip gets you up close to reef sharks, eagle rays, and huge lionfish. ■**TIP→ Ask about Aldora's afternoon lionfish hunting trip to the north end of the island.** ⊠ *Calle 5 Sur, between Avs. 5 and Rafael E. Melgar, San Miguel*

☎ *987/872–3397, 210/569–1203 in U.S.* ⊕ *www.aldora.com* ⊠ *2-tank dives from $105.*

Aqua Safari

SCUBA DIVING | FAMILY | One of the island's oldest and most professional shops, Aqua Safari provides beginning and advanced PADI certification and daily introductory scuba courses. The operation uses larger, 12- to 16-passenger boats that are great in rough weather, but they are slow. ⊠ *Av. Rafael E. Melgar 429, between Calles 5 and 7 Sur, San Miguel* ☎ *987/872–9439* ⊕ *www.aquasafari.com* ⊠ *2-tank dives from $90.*

Aquatic Sports

SCUBA DIVING | FAMILY | Sergio Sandoval gets rave reviews from his clients, many of whom are repeat customers. In addition to the usual excursions, he'll take you out for wreck dives, underwater photo safaris, or lionfish hunting. He also charters his boat for full- and half-day fishing trips. ⊠ *Carretera Sur, Km 6.5, Cozumel* ☎ *987/112–5002* ⊕ *www.scubacozumel.com* ⊠ *2-tank dives from $110.*

Blue Angel Scuba and Scuba School

SCUBA DIVING | FAMILY | The combo dive-and-snorkel excursions arranged by Blue Angel allow family members to have fun together, even if not all are scuba enthusiasts. Dedicated dive trips to local reefs and PADI courses are also offered. Inquire about the snorkel trip to the crystal-blue waters called El Cielo. Dive-and-hotel packages are available at its hotel of the same name. ⊠ *Blue Angel Resort, Carretera Costera Sur, Km 2.2, Cozumel* ☎ *987/872–0819* ⊕ *www.blueangelresort.com* ⊠ *2-tank dives from $100.*

Eagle Ray Divers

SCUBA DIVING | FAMILY | Snorkeling trips and dive instruction are available through Eagle Ray Divers. (The three-reef snorkel trip lets nondivers explore beyond the shore.) As befits its name, the company keeps track of the eagle rays that appear off Cozumel from December to February and runs trips for advanced divers to walls where the rays congregate. Beginners can also see rays around some of the reefs. ⊠ *La Caleta Marina, near Presidente InterContinental, San Miguel* ☎ *987/107–2315* ⊕ *www.eagleraydivers. com* ⊠ *2-tank dives from $90.*

Fury Catamarans

SAILING | Vacationers who can't decide between snorkeling and partying can combine the two by boarding one of Fury's 65-foot catamarans. Boats visit the reef en route to a private stretch of beach south of town. Rates include equipment, lunch, soft drinks, beer, and margaritas, plus access to assorted beach toys. A sunset booze cruise is also offered, and there are numerous pickup points at different times along the west coast. ⊠ *Carretera Sur, Km 3.5, beside Casa del Mar Hotel, Cozumel* ☎ *987/872–5145, 305/433–4537 in the U.S. and Canada* ⊕ *www.furycozumel.com* ⊠ *From $79.*

Scuba Du

SCUBA DIVING | **FAMILY** | Along with the requisite Cozumel reef dives, this diver favorite organizes night dives and an advanced trip to walls off Punta Sur as well as snorkeling and fishing trips. A combination of large and smaller "six pack" boats are available. The Presidente InterContinental, Casa Mexicana, and Hotel B offer lodging-and-dive packages. A sunset pleasure ride is also offered. ⊠ *Presidente InterContinental, Carretera Sur, Km 6, Cozumel* ☎ *987/872–9505* ⊕ *www.scubadu.com* ⊠ *2-tank dives from $115.*

★ ScubaTony

DIVING & SNORKELING | Diving with ScubaTony is like diving with friends you've known for years. The personalized trips include tanks, weights, fresh fruit, and drinks. Introductory and refresher courses are available; PADI-certified instructors will also work with you to obtain additional certifications (such as nitrox). ⊠ *Puerto*

Fonatur, Carretera a Chankanaab, Km 5.75 Sur, Cozumel ☎ *987/878–2432, 469/361–6573 in the U.S.* ⊕ *www.scubatony.com* ⊠ *2-tank dives from $95.*

TOURS

★ Atlantis Submarine

BOAT TOURS | **FAMILY** | If you're curious about what's beneath Cozumel's waters but don't like getting wet, Atlantis Submarine's 1½-hour outings explore the Chankanaab Reef and surrounding area. Subs descend about 100 feet—deeper than most scuba dives go—but be warned: claustrophobes may not be able to handle the sardine-can conditions. All passengers must be at least 36 inches tall and over four years old. Three to five daily trips are offered, depending on the season and day of week. ⊠ *Carretera Sur, Km 4, across from Hotel Casa del Mar, Cozumel* ☎ *987/872–5672* ⊕ *www. atlantissubmarines.travel* ⊠ *from $115.*

Cozumel Bar Hop

FOOD AND DRINK TOURS | A popular excursion among cruise passengers (but nothing says landlubbers can't partake) is this five-hour daytime pub crawl. Cozumel offers a few such Bacchanalian tours, but this one takes in three bars on the remote windward coast of the island. (The two remaining visits are in town.) Transport, beverages, and an "I survived" T-shirt are included. ⊠ *Plaza Punta Langosta, Av. Rafael E. Melgar 559, at Calle 7, San Miguel* ☎ *987/872–2294* ⊕ *cozumelbarhop.com* ⊠ *$67* ⊙ *Closed Sun.*

Chapter 7

YUCATÁN AND CAMPECHE STATES

Updated by
John Newton

⊙ Sights	⑪ Restaurants	🛏 Hotels	🛍 Shopping	🍸 Nightlife
★★★★★	★★★★☆	★★★★☆	★★★☆☆	★★★☆☆

WELCOME TO YUCATÁN AND CAMPECHE STATES

TOP REASONS TO GO

★ **Visiting spectacular Maya sites:** Chichén Itzá, Uxmal, and Calakmul are three of the largest and most beautiful of many in these states.

★ **Living like a wealthy hacendado:** You can stay in a restored *henequen* (sisal) hacienda-turned-hotel and delight in its Old-World charm.

★ **Browsing at fantastic craft markets:** This region is known for its handmade *hamacas* (hammocks), piñatas, and other local handicrafts.

★ **Swimming in pristine cenotes:** Freshwater sink-holes, once believed to be portals to the underworld, are scattered throughout the peninsula.

★ **Tasting new flavors:** The most famous Yucatecan specialty is *cochinita pibil* (pork cooked in banana leaves with sour orange and achiote).

1 Mérida. Bustling Mérida, the capital of and largest city in Yucatán State, was a stronghold of Spanish colonialism. Tucked among the restaurants, museums, and markets are mansions built when this was one of Mexico's wealthiest cities.

2 Celestún. Nature lovers flock here to admire one of the hemisphere's largest colonies of pink flamingos.

3 Dzibilchaltún. Just off the road between Mérida and Progreso, this Maya site is best known for its Temple of the Seven Dolls.

4 Progreso. Outside this unpretentious town, empty beaches, fishing villages, estuaries, and salt flats stretch for miles in either direction.

5 Xcambo. Archaeological evidence suggests that salt, a coveted commodity in the ancient world, made the residents of this Maya site prosperous.

6 Reserva de la Biósfera Ría Lagartos. This coastal reserve is popular with birders who come to see flamingos.

7 El Cuyo. A quiet but windy coastal town that attracts kitesurfers.

8 Isla Holbox. This island has a more casual, barefoot feel than the beach towns of the Riviera Maya.

Gulf of Mexico

9 Aké. You can readily explore this lesser-known Maya site while based at one of the area's charming hacienda hotels.

10 Izamal. This town is dominated by the 16th-century Convent of San Antonio, and most of its buildings are painted in the same mustard-yellow hue, creating a vivid backdrop.

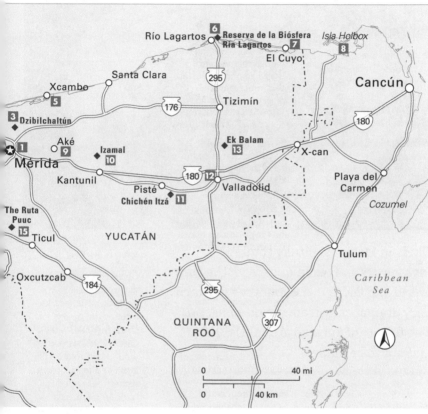

11 Chichén Itzá. More than a million visitors a year come to this magnificent and mysterious Maya site.

12 Valladolid. One of the state's most important colonial towns is a convenient base for day trips.

13 Ek Balam. This Maya site near Valladolid is known for the restored façades on its enormous El Torre pyramid.

14 Uxmal. South of Mérida, beautiful Uxmal is less well known (and less crowded) than Chichén Itzá.

15 The Ruta Puuc. Small Maya sites—some hardly visited—lie along the Ruta Puuc, an informal designation for the hilly area southeast of Uxmal.

16 Campeche State. The most happening spot in this state south of Yucatán is its capital, Campeche City, a walled colonial enclave on the edge of the Gulf of Mexico. The state's Maya sites include spectacular Edzná and remote Calakmul.

YUCATÁN CUISINE

Cochinita pibil can vary from restaurant to restaurant.

Chefs in Mexico skillfully combine ingredients and techniques from the New World and Old, but the country's cuisines vary dramatically from region to region. The flavors of Yucatán are subtle, unique, and not to be missed.

In terms of culinary traditions, the country can be divided into four broad regions. Foods from the north tend to be unpretentious; you'll find dishes like barbecued meats that were originally served on ranches and haciendas. Seafood dominates along both coasts. The central region includes the area in and around Mexico City, where many of the country's most characteristic plates were invented in convent kitchens during colonial times. Foods from the south, including the Yucatán, are singular within Mexico. The culinary traditions that developed on the once-isolated peninsula are particularly unique. At the same time, centuries of commercial and cultural trade with Cuba, Europe (especially France), and New Orleans have left their mark on Yucatecan cuisine, along with more recent Middle Eastern influences.

AGUA FRESCA

Given the Yucatán's warm climate, nothing satisfies like a cool *agua fresca* (fruit-infused water). One drink that you won't want to miss is *agua de chaya*. Chaya, sometimes called "tree spinach," is a nutritious leafy green that's used in a wide variety of recipes, including soups, omelets, tamales, and a sweet agua fresca.

REGIONAL CUISINES

Visitors to the Yucatán often discover a wide variety of dishes they've never seen before. This is because Yucatán cuisine is not often served in Mexican restaurants north of the border or even in other areas of the country. Here are some of the most typical dishes—all of them well worth a try.

Huevos motuleños. This is a popular breakfast dish that originated in Motul, a small town east of Mérida, where the ancient Maya city of Zacmotul once stood. Eggs, sunny-side up, are covered with black beans and cheese and served on a crispy tortilla. Other ingredients like red salsa, ham, and green peas are usually heaped on top. Fried plantains are often served on the side.

Sopa de lima. This soup is traditionally prepared with turkey, indigenous to the Yucatán, and includes tomatoes, sweet chile or green pepper, and lime juice. It's garnished with strips of lightly fried tortilla.

Queso relleno. Legend has it that, in the 19th century, a boat from Holland was forced to land on the peninsula because of bad weather, and the locals were delighted with the cargo of Dutch cheese. From this trip, a typical Yucate-can dish made with Gouda or Edam

Huevos motuleños

cheese was born. A salty cow's-milk cheese is stuffed with spiced ground meat and served with two sauces: a tomato-caper sauce and a milder creamy sauce.

Cochinita pibil. This is perhaps the most representative dish in the Yucatecan repertoire. The word *pibil* means "roast-ed in the hole," which describes just how this dish is classically prepared. The Maya used to roast venison in this way, but the Spanish-introduced pork is now the standard. The meat is first marinated in a mixture of bitter orange juice (from the Seville oranges that grow in this region), achiote (a peppery paste that some describe as having a nutmeg-like flavor, made from annatto seeds), oregano, salt, and pepper. Next, it's wrapped in banana leaves and placed in a hole lined with stones that have been heated with fire. The meat cooks slowly.

Panuchos and salbutes. These culinary cousins are the Yucatecan version of tostadas—a fried tortilla topped with protein (typically turkey or cochinita pibil), lettuce, tomatoes, and pickled onions. The difference between the two is that the tortillas used with panuchos are stuffed with black beans.

Sopa de lima

In sharp contrast to the Riviera Maya, the states of Yucatán and Campeche cater to a more tranquil traveler who wants to avoid the spring-break atmosphere. Here you'll find innumerable historic and natural wonders, including spectacular Maya sites, quaint colonial villages, mangrove forests, unspoiled beaches, and myriad bird species.

Unlike Quintana Roo, Yucatán has fewer international residents (though the state capital of Mérida has a growing expat community), and there's much less emphasis on beach activities. With large indigenous populations, both Yucatán and Campeche states are defined by Maya culture and traditions. The history and food also set them apart from the rest of Mexico.

One of Yucatán's biggest draws is its capital, Mérida. It is the handsome regional hub of art and culture, and locals and travelers alike gather in the main square for weekend music and dance performances. The eponymous capital of Campeche State has its appeals, too, with a charming walled historic center overlooking the Gulf of Mexico.

Along the Yucatán coast, the beach town of Celestún west of Mérida is a gateway to a reserve known for its pink flamingos. North of Mérida, Progreso, a port of call for cruise ships, and its nearby beach towns are other coastal favorites. To combine wildlife with adventure, head to Río Lagartos where you can kayak through mangroves. Off the coast of Isla Holbox, a small island devoid of cars, you can dive

with whale sharks from June through August. Neighboring El Cuyo is popular with kitesurfers and less developed than Holbox—for now, anyway.

East of Mérida, Izamal, the oldest town in the Yucatán, will take you back in time with its cobblestone streets, yellow-painted buildings, and horse-drawn carriages. Near Yucatán's eastern border, the budding cosmopolitan town of Valladolid offers a bit of history as well as mysterious freshwater cenotes to explore.

More than 2,000 Maya sites lie within Yucatán and Campeche, though only a fraction of them are open to tourists. Nestled amid rampant jungles are the magnificent archaeological sites of Uxmal, Kabah, Labná, Sayil, Dzibilchaltún, and the world-famous Chichén Itzá—a UNESCO World Heritage site. Campeche is home to the less-touristed Edzná, a once-flourishing commercial and ceremonial city that features an array of Maya architectural styles. At Calakmul, you'll enjoy relative solitude as you wander amid almost 7,000 structures set in Mexico's largest forest reserve.

Planning

When to Go

High season begins in late November and continues until early April. The weeks around Christmas and Easter are peak times for visiting; making reservations up to a year in advance is common. Fortunately, Yucatán doesn't get the spring-break crowds like Cancún, but you may see a slight increase in travelers (and prices) during August, when many Europeans take their vacations.

May is usually the hottest month of the year, and the rainfall is heaviest between June and October, bringing with it an uncomfortable humidity. Provided you can avoid Thanksgiving weekend, November is one of your best bets: the rainy season is over, the humidity has faded, and temperatures are pleasantly cooler—plus you won't have to deal with holiday hordes, which means you're more likely to find airfare and hotel deals.

FESTIVALS

El Festival de Mérida, which commemorates the founding of the city, runs through most of January and includes nearly 200 free concerts, dance performances, art exhibits, and other events.

In February or March, Campeche City lays claim to Mexico's oldest Carnaval celebration, and Mérida holds the country's second largest.

Thousands swarm Chichén Itzá for the spring and fall equinoxes (March 21 and September 21), when the sun creates a snakelike shadow—meant to evoke the ancient serpent god, Kukulcán—that moves slowly down the side of the main pyramid.

If you like music and dance, Mérida hosts its Otoño Cultural during the last week of October and first week of November; events take place almost nightly at theaters and open-air venues around the city.

El Día de los Muertos (October 31 to November 2) brings street processions to Mérida and many other towns—some somber, some merry—with participants painting their faces white to look like skeletons. Yucatán's smaller towns have their own local festivals and celebrations of patron saints. In Espita, for example, the town square bustles with music and displays of horsemanship during the week that includes Christmas. The Virgin of Izamal is celebrated in the weeks leading up to her feast day, December 8, with concerts and other events, some solemn and others festive.

PLANNING YOUR TIME

Plan to spend at least five days in Yucatán and Campeche states, starting with a day or two in Mérida. Of course, visiting Yucatán State's capital without taking day trips to Maya sites like Chichén Itzá and/or Uxmal is like driving to the beach and not getting out of the car. There are also many other Maya sites, as well as atmospheric colonial towns like Valladolid and Izamal, to explore. Spending a night in a restored hacienda is a highlight for many travelers.

Campeche City, the state's small though charming capital, can be an overnight trip from Mérida. Calakmul, the enormous biosphere and Maya site in the south, requires at least two full days given its size and the travel time to reach it, regardless of your starting point.

Getting Here and Around

AIR

Aeroméxico, Interjet, and Volaris all fly from Mexico City to Mérida's Aeropuerto Manuel Crescencio Rejón (MID). International flights land in Mérida as well: United flies nonstop daily from Houston;

American from Miami; and Delta and Aeroméxico from Atlanta. WestJet operates seasonal (winter) nonstop flights from Toronto. Aeroméxico and Interjet also fly several times daily from Mexico City to Aeropuerto Internacional Alberto Acuña Ongay in Campeche City.

BUS
ADO (⊕ www.ado.com.mx) runs direct buses to many coastal cities and colonial towns from Mérida. They depart from the ADO Mérida Centro Histórico station on Calle 69 between Calle 68 and Calle 70. Regional bus lines to intermediate or more out-of-the-way destinations also leave from here. ADO buses also connect Campeche City to points all over the Yucatán Peninsula.

CAR
From Mérida, highways radiate in every direction. To the east, Carreteras 180D cuota and 180 libre are, respectively, the toll and free roads to Cancún; driving the full length of the former costs about MX$600. The toll road has exits for Chichén Itzá and the low-key colonial city of Valladolid; the free road passes through these and many smaller towns. Although it's a dull drive, the toll road is faster, better maintained, and void of detours.

Heading south from Mérida on Carretera 261 (Carretera 180 until the town of Umán), you come to Uxmal and the Ruta Puuc, a series of small Maya sites of a relatively uniform style (most have at least one outstanding building). Carretera 261 north from Mérida takes you to the port and beach resort of Progreso. To the west, the laid-back fishing village of Celestún—which borders protected wetland—can be accessed by a separate highway from Mérida.

Campeche City is about 180 km (112 miles) southwest of Mérida along Carretera 180. If you have more time

and want to pass some Maya ruins while traveling between the two cities, consider taking the the 250-km (155-mile) Carretera 261.

⇨ *Check out the Travel Smart chapter for rules of the road and information on rental car agencies if you plan on driving.*

TRAIN
The new-in-2024 Tren Maya (Maya Train) features high-speed trains traversing a 1,525-km (950-mile) network through the states of Quintana Roo, Yucatán, and Campeche. One route from Cancún heads south to Playa del Carmen, Tulum, and Chetumal. Another heads west from Cancún, connecting Valladolid, Chichén Itzá, Izamal, Mérida, and Campeche. Both portions meet in southern Campeche State and continue farther south through Tabasco and Chiapas states before terminating near the famous Maya ruins of Palenque.

Hotels

Although Yucatán and Campeche states have fewer offerings than neighboring Quintana Roo, the number of options is growing. Urban hotels range from boutique properties to international brands. For a taste of the slow-paced countryside, consider staying at a hacienda or at a lodging in an inland town such as Valladolid and Izamal.

There are several charming hotels near the major archaeological sites Chichén Itzá and Uxmal as well as in seaside towns such as Progreso, Sisal, Celestún, and El Cuyo. In addition, as more and more historic homes are being renovated and offered as rentals, an increasing number of travelers are opting to live like well-heeled locals by taking advantage offerings on Airbnb, VRBO, and similar sites.

⇨ *Hotel reviews have been shortened. For full information, visit Fodors.com. Hotel prices are the lowest cost of a standard double room in high season.*

What It Costs in U.S. Dollars

$	$$	$$$	$$$$
HOTELS			
under $100	$100–$200	$201–$300	over $300

Restaurants

Expect a superb variety of cuisines—Yucatecan, of course, but also Italian, French, Japanese, Italian, vegetarian, Mexican, and more—at reasonable prices. In beach towns, such as Progreso, Sisal, and Celestún, waterfront restaurants serve fresh, simply prepared seafood. Specialties include fish and shellfish stews, cream soups, shrimp cocktail, squid and octopus, and *panuchos* (chubby rounds of fried cornmeal covered with refried beans and topped with onion and shredded turkey or chicken).

Mexicans generally eat lunch in the afternoon—certainly not before 2. If you want to eat at noon, call ahead to verify hours. In Mérida locals make a real event of late dinners, especially in summer. Reservations are recommended for pricier restaurants on weekends and in high season.

Casual (but neat) dress is acceptable at all restaurants. Avoid wearing shorts or casual sandals in the more expensive places, and anywhere at all—especially in the evening—if you don't want to look like a tourist.

Although food servers at most restaurants are kind and hospitable, the language barrier may cause them to come across as more reserved than their compatriots in the United States.

■ **TIP**➔ **Some restaurants include a gratuity in the bill, so double-check before adding a tip.**

⇨ *Restaurant reviews have been shortened. For full information, visit Fodors. com. Restaurant prices are the average cost of a main course at dinner, or if dinner is not served, at lunch.*

What It Costs in Mexican Pesos

$	$$	$$$	$$$$
RESTAURANTS			
under MP200	MP200–MP300	MP301–MP500	over MP500

Visitor Information

CONTACTS Turismo de Campeche. ✉ *Plaza Moch Couoh, Av. Ruíz Cortínez s/n, Centro* 🕾 *981/127–3300* ⊕ *www.campeche. travel.* **Oficina de Turismo de Yucatán.** ✉ *Centro Cultural de Mérida Olimpo, Calle 62, between Calles 61 and 63, Centro* 🕾 *999/942–0000 main office* ⊕ *www. yucatan.gob.mx.*

Mérida

307 km (184 miles) west of Cancún.

Bustling streets, lively parks, a tropical version of the Champs-Elysées, endless cultural activities, and a varied nightlife: Mérida is the beating urban heart of the state of Yucatán. The hubbub of the city can seem frustrating—especially if you've just spent a peaceful few days on the coast or visiting Maya sites—but as the cultural and intellectual hub of the peninsula, Mérida is rich in art, history, and tradition. A sizable expatriate population serves as testament to its desirability as a place to live, and Mérida consistently appears on lists of best places to retire overseas.

On Saturday nights and Sundays, locals gather in or around Plaza Grande (the *zócalo,* or main square) in the Centro Histórico to socialize and watch live entertainment. Calle 60 between Parque Santa Lucía and Plaza Grande gets especially lively. Restaurants set out tables in the streets, which quickly fill with patrons enjoying the free tango, salsa, or jazz performances. On Sunday mornings, downtown streets are closed to all but pedestrians and cyclists from Parque de la Ermita through Plaza Grande to Paseo de Montejo.

GETTING HERE AND AROUND

Most streets in Mérida are numbered, not named, and most run one way. North–south streets have even numbers, which ascend from east to west; east–west streets have odd numbers, which ascend from north to south.

Street addresses, however, can be confusing because they don't progress in even increments by blocks. The 600s, say, might occupy two or more blocks, so a location is usually identified by indicating the street number and the nearest cross street, as in "Calle 64 and Calle 61," or "Calle 64 between Calles 61 and 63," which is written "Calle 64 x 61 y 63." Take heart: the system does make sense once you're on the ground and wandering around.

As many streets are one-way, you're better off parking your car downtown and walking to key attractions. Most are around Plaza Grande, bordered by Calles 61 and 63 (on its north and south sides) and Calles 60 and 62 (on its east and west sides). Using the zócalo as your starting point is a great way to get to know the layout of the city. If you need extra help getting oriented, stop by the tourism offices on the square; the friendly, helpful staff have loads of information.

Mérida's airport, Aeropuerto Manuel Crescencio Rejón, is 7 km (4½ miles) west of the city on Avenida Itzáes.

Getting from it to the downtown area usually takes 20 to 30 minutes by taxi, and the fare will be about MX$220. Note that while Uber is a popular service in Mérida, Uber drivers are not allowed to pick up passengers at the airport.

Municipal buses charge MX$12 for trips around Mérida; having the correct change is helpful but not required. Riding the red, double-decker Turibus is a fun and informative alternative. You can buy your ticket (MX$120) onboard the open-roof vehicle and get on and off as you please at seven key stops, enjoying recorded commentary along the way. The full route takes an hour and 45 minutes to complete, and buses operate from 9 am until 8:30 pm, daily except Sunday.

A smaller bus operator, Carnavalito, visits many of the same sites. The upside to this tour is that it's given by real people (in both Spanish and English), so you can ask questions; the downside is that you can't hop on and off at will. Tours cost MX$120 and last around two hours, with a 20-minute break at a small shopping center where you can stretch your legs or buy a drink. The colorful Carnavalito bus takes off from Parque Santa Lucía Monday to Saturday at 1, 4, and 6 pm; Sunday departures are at 1 and 3 pm.

CONTACTS Carnavalito. ⊠ *Mérida* ☎ *999/924–1199* ⊕ *www.carnavalitocitytour.com.mx.* **Turibus.** ⊠ *Mérida* ☎ *55/5133–2444* ⊕ *www.turibus.com.mx.*

One popular way to get a feel for the city is to hire a *calesa,* or horse-drawn carriage. You can hail one of these at Plaza Grande or, during the day, at Palacio Cantón, site of the archaeology museum on Paseo de Montejo. Choose your horse and driver carefully, as some of the animals look dispirited, but others are fairly well cared for.

It costs about MX$400 for an hour-long circuit around downtown and up Paseo de Montejo; an extended tour costs about MX$600. Along the route, drivers point out notable buildings and provide a little historic background, though their English-language skills range from capable to halting.

Some taxis in Mérida charge beach-resort prices, and most don't use meters. Those that do have a sign that reads *taxímetro* on the roof; these are recommended because they offer fair rates. Expect to pay MX$30 to MX$50 for a trip around Centro and between MX$70 to MX$100 for longer trips within the city.

The ride-sharing apps Uber and its local competitor, DiDi, have added some healthy competition, and they make it easier to get a lift—taxis can be difficult to find outside of the busiest areas of Centro.

TOURS

Mérida has more than 50 tour operators, and they generally take you to the same places. Because there are so many reputable, reasonably priced companies, there's no reason to opt for the less predictable *piratas* ("pirates") who sometimes lurk outside tour offices offering to sell you a cheaper trip and don't necessarily have much experience or your best interests at heart.

■TIP→ **The city's tourist office (Oficina de Turismo de Mérida) conducts free 90-minute walking tours in both English and Spanish.** They depart from the Centro Cultural de Mérida Olimpo, on the main plaza, at 9:30 am and are offered Monday through Saturday year-round.

Amigo Yucatán

GUIDED TOURS | FAMILY | This operator offers private and group visits to major archaeological sites and also to Celestún, a town known for its massive flamingo colonies. ⊠ *Av. Colón 508C, Col. García Ginerés* ☎ *999/920–0105* ⊕ *www.amigoyucatan.com.*

Casa Misterio Mérida

FOOD AND DRINK TOURS | FAMILY | Erin Gomez, who worked as a chef in San Francisco before moving to Mérida, now leads market tours followed by cooking classes. Her excursions are tailored around clients' interests and she'll select dishes for vegans, vegetarians, or carnivores as requested. You'll enjoy an introduction to some of the tropical ingredients typical of the Yucatán, and then learn how to prepare them. ⊠ *Mérida* ☎ *999/197–6696* ⊕ *www.casamisteriomerida.com.*

EcoTurismo Yucatán

ECOTOURISM | FAMILY | A good mix of day trips, overnight tours, and customized excursions throughout the region is available through this tour operator, based in Mérida. A one-day biking adventure includes cycling plus brief visits to two archaeological sites, a cave, an hacienda, and two cenotes. ⊠ *Calle 3 235, between Calles 32A and 34, Col. Pensiones* ☎ *999/920–2772* ⊕ *www.ecoyuc.com* ⊠ *From MX$875.*

Mérida English Library

WALKING TOURS | FAMILY | If you enjoy walking and are curious about what's behind the doors of those old homes, the Mérida English Library conducts two-hour house and garden tours every Wednesday morning from November through the end of March. Meet at the library at 9 am for registration. ⊠ *Calle 53 524, between Calles 66 and 68, Centro* ☎ *999/924–8401* ⊕ *www.meridaenglishlibrary.com* ⊠ *MX$500.*

VISITOR INFORMATION

CONTACTS Oficina de Turismo de Mérida. ⊠ *Centro Cultural de Mérida Olimpo, Calle 62, between Calles 61 and 63, Centro* ☎ *999/942–0000* ⊕ *www.merida.gob.mx.*

KEY

1 Sights

1 Restaurants

1 Quick Bites

1 Hotels

i Tourist Information

Sights ▼

1 Catedral de Mérida...... **F5**
2 Centro Cultural de Mérida Olimpo **E5**
3 Ermita de Santa Isabel............. **D9**
4 Gran Museo del Mundo Maya......... **E1**
5 Iglesia de la Tercera Orden de Jesús.......... **F5**
6 Museo Casa de Montejo **G1**
7 Museo de Arte Popular de Yucatán **H5**
8 Museo Fernando García Ponce—MACAY......... **F6**
9 Palacio Cantón.......... **G2**
10 Palacio de la Música.... **F5**
11 Palacio del Gobierno.... **F5**
12 Parque Hidalgo **F5**
13 Parque Santa Lucía **F4**
14 Parque Zoológico El Centenario............ **A4**
15 Paseo de Montejo **H1**
16 Plaza Grande............. **F5**

Restaurants ▼

1 Apoala **F4**
2 Café Crème.............. **G1**
3 Casa Chica **G3**
4 Cuna...................... **E1**
5 Hacienda Teya **I7**
6 K'u'uk..................... **H1**
7 La Negrita Cantina....... **F3**
8 La Poderosa............. **D4**
9 La Tratto Santa Lucía ... **F4**
10 Los Almendros **H5**
11 Micaela Mar y Leña.... **H3**
12 Museo de la Gastronomía Yucateca **F4**
13 Oliva Enoteca **H3**
14 Pancho Maiz **I5**
15 Restaurante Amaro...... **F5**
16 Rosas & Xocolate Restaurant.............. **G2**
17 Salón Gallos............. **H6**
18 Trotter's Grill House...... **F1**
19 Wayan'e **F1**

Quick Bites ▼

1 El Colón Sorbetes y Dulces Finos............. **F5**
2 Latte Quattro Sette **G3**
3 Pan & Koffee............ **G2**
4 Pola........................ **E4**

Hotels ▼

1 Casa Azul **F1**
2 Casa del Balam **F5**
3 Casa Lecanda........... **G3**
4 Casa Puuc **B1**
5 Casa San Ángel.......... **G3**
6 Cigno Hotel **D8**
7 Courtyard by Marriott.... **F1**
8 Decu Downtown.........**G4**
9 Fiesta Americana Mérida **F1**
10 Gran Hotel **F5**
11 Hacienda Xcanatún by Angsana.............. **E1**
12 Hotel Hacienda Mérida **F4**
13 Hotel Julamis............ **G4**
14 Hotel Marionetas **E3**
15 Hyatt Regency Mérida **F1**
16 La Misión de Fray Diego **E5**
17 Piedra de Agua **A9**
18 Rosas & Xocolate....... **G2**
19 Villa Mercedes........... **F1**
20 Wayam Mundo Imperial **E1**

◉ Sights

★ Catedral de Mérida

CHURCH | FAMILY | Begun in 1561, Mérida's cathedral is one of the oldest on the North American mainland (an older one can be found in the Dominican Republic). It took several hundred Maya laborers, working with stones from the pyramids of the ravaged Maya city, 37 years to complete it. Designed in the somber Renaissance style by an architect who had worked on El Escorial in Madrid, its facade is stark and unadorned, with gunnery slits instead of windows and faintly Moorish spires.

Inside, the black Cristo de las Ampollas (Christ of the Blisters) occupies a side chapel to the left of the main altar. At 23 feet tall, it's the tallest Christ figure inside a Mexican church. The statue is a replica of the original, which was destroyed during the revolution in 1910 (also when the gold that once adorned the cathedral was carried off). According to one of many legends, the Christ figure burned all night and appeared the next morning unscathed—except for its namesake blisters. You can hear the pipe organ play at the 11 am Sunday Mass. ⊠ *Calles 60 and 61, Mérida* ☎ *999/924-7777* ⊕ *catedraldemerida.org.mx* ⊠ *Free.*

Centro Cultural de Mérida Olimpo

ARTS CENTER | FAMILY | Referred to as simply the "Olimpo," this beautiful porticoed cultural center was built adjacent to city hall in late 1999. Its marble interior hosts international art exhibits, classical-music concerts, conferences, and theater and dance performances. The adjoining 1950s-style movie house shows both classic art films and animated features targeting younger viewers. The center also houses a planetarium with 60-minute shows explaining the solar system (narration is in Spanish); they run Tuesday through Sunday at 6 pm and Sunday at 10, 11, noon, 6, and 7—be sure to arrive 15 minutes early as nobody is allowed to sneak in once the show has begun. ⊠ *Calle 62, between Calles 61 and 63, Mérida* ☎ *999/942-0000* ⊕ *www.facebook.com/centroculturalolimpo* ⊠ *Free; MX$56 for planetarium.*

Ermita de Santa Isabel

CHURCH | Several blocks south of the city center, the restored Hermitage of St. Isabel, also known as the Hermitage of the Good Trip stands on a square that is the heart of the neighborhood named after the church—La Ermita. Completed in 1748, the beautiful edifice served as a resting place for colonial-era travelers headed to Campeche. It's one of the most peaceful places in the city and a good destination for a ride in a horse-drawn carriage, though it's typically open only during mass. Behind the hermitage are huge tropical gardens, which have a waterfall and footpaths and which are usually unlocked during daylight hours. ⊠ *Calles 66 and 77, Mérida* ⊠ *Free.*

Gran Museo del Mundo Maya

HISTORY MUSEUM | FAMILY | Whether or not the Grand Museum of the Mayan World lives up to its lofty name depends on your tastes and expectations, but the institution certainly makes a big architectural splash. The starkly modern building was designed to resemble a giant ceiba tree, sacred to the Maya, and it looms over the northern outskirts of town on the highway to Progreso. (Plan on a MX$150 Uber or DiDi ride from downtown.)

The museum's amazing collection of Maya artifacts are exhibited in four themed halls: The Mayab, Nature, and Culture; Ancestral Maya; Yesterday's Maya; and Today's Maya. Much of the space is given over to multimedia presentations, including interactive screens that are enormously popular, especially with younger visitors. One all-the-rage panel of screens, for instance, lets you tap in your birth date, convert it to the corresponding date on the Maya calendar, and email yourself your Maya

horoscope. Everything here—artifact labeling and multimedia narration—is trilingual (Spanish, English, and Mayan). The adjoining Mayamax theater screens films, and there is an on-site concert hall, too. ⊠ *Calle 60 Norte, Mérida* ☎ *999/341–0435* ⊕ *www.granmuseodelmundomaya.com.mx* ⌑ *MX$150* ☉ *Closed Tues.*

Iglesia de la Tercera Orden de Jesús

CHURCH | Just north of Parque Hidalgo is one of Mérida's oldest buildings and the first Jesuit church in the Yucatán. It was built in 1618 from the limestone blocks of a dismantled Maya temple, and faint outlines of ancient carvings are still visible on the west wall. Although the church is a favorite place for society weddings, its interior is not ornate. In former convent rooms at the rear of the building, however, you'll find the Pinoteca Juan Gamboa Guzmán, a small but interesting art collection. The most engaging pieces are the striking bronze sculptures of indigenous Maya crafted by celebrated 20th-century sculptor Enrique Gottdiener Soto. On the second floor are about 20 forgettable oil paintings—mostly of past civic officials. ⊠ *Calle 60, between Calles 57 and 59, Mérida* ☎ *999/924–9712* ⊕ *www.inah.gob.mx/red-de-museos* ⌑ *Free.*

Museo Casa de Montejo

NOTABLE BUILDING | Three Franciscos de Montejo—father, son, and nephew—invaded the peninsula and founded the city of Mérida in January 1542, on the site of T'Hó, a Maya city. They completed construction of this stately home on the south side of the central plaza in 1549. All that remains of the original structure is the facade, which is the city's oldest and finest example of colonial plateresque architecture, a Spanish architectural style popular in the 16th century and typified by elaborate ornamentation. A bas-relief on the doorway depicts Francisco de Montejo the younger, his wife, and daughter, as well as Spanish soldiers, standing on the heads of the vanquished

Maya. An on-site museum showcases several rooms that have been restored and are furnished as they would have been at the end of the 19th century. ⊠ *Calle 63 506, Mérida* ☎ *999/253–6732* ⊕ *fomentoculturalbanamex.org/casaMontejo.html* ⌑ *Free* ☉ *Closed Mon.*

Museo de Arte Popular de Yucatán

ART MUSEUM | FAMILY | This excellent museum at the northwest corner of Parque Mejorada offers an introduction to Mexican arts and crafts including ceramics, textiles, stonework, woodwork, and glass. The first floor gallery is typically used for temporary exhibitions, with the permanent collection displayed in six second-floor rooms. Allow time to peruse the on-site gift shop, which sells shawls, baskets, dolls, and masks. ⊠ *Calle 50 487, between Calles 57 and 59, Mérida* ☎ *999/928–5263* ⊕ *www.facebook.com/artepopularyucatan* ⌑ *Free* ☉ *Closed Mon. and Tues.*

Museo Fernando García Ponce—MACAY

ART MUSEUM | Located next to the cathedral, the building that houses this museum has served in the past as a seminary, an art school, and even a military barracks. It now showcases the works of contemporary Yucatecan artists and hosts a variety of temporary exhibits featuring leading Mexican and international contemporary artists. It's free to visit; just sign the guestbook. ⊠ *Plaza Grande, Pasaje de la Revolución 1907, between Calles 58 and 60, Mérida* ☎ *999/928–0006* ⊕ *www.macay.org* ⌑ *Free* ☉ *Closed Wed. and Sun.*

Palacio Cantón

HISTORY MUSEUM | FAMILY | The most compelling of the mansions on Paseo de Montejo, this stately residence was built for General Francisco Cantón between 1909 and 1911. Designed by Enrique Deserti, who also drew up the plans for the Teatro Peón Contreras, the building has a grandiose air that seems more characteristic of a mausoleum than a home: there's marble everywhere, as well as Doric and Ionic columns and other Italianate Beaux-Arts flourishes. It now houses the Museo Regional de Antropología de Yucatán which focuses mostly on Maya history, art, and culture and sometimes other aspects of Yucatecan life. The exhibitions are generally excellent although signage is often only in Spanish, or Spanish and Mayan. ⊠ *Paseo de Montejo 485, at Calle 43, Mérida* ☎ *999/923–0557* ⊕ *www.inah.gob.mx/red-de-museos* ▤ *MX$60* ☾ *Closed Mon.*

Palacio de la Música

OTHER MUSEUM | FAMILY | This dramatic museum in the heart of the historic center, designed in a collaboration between four leading architecture firms, opened in 2019 and is devoted to the history of Mexican music. Dozens of listening stations enable you to hear everything from classical compositions and traditional *rancheras* to current pop and rock songs. The museum also hosts concerts, featuring music from a variety of genres. ⊠ *Calle 59 497, Mérida* ☎ *999/923–0641* ⊕ *palaciodelamusica.yucatan.gob.mx* ▤ *MX$150* ☾ *Closed Mon.*

Palacio del Gobierno

GOVERNMENT BUILDING | Visit the seat of state government on the north side of Plaza Grande. You can see Fernando Castro Pacheco's murals of the bloody history of the conquest of the peninsula, painted in bold colors and influenced by the Mexican muralists José Clemente Orozco and David Alfaro Siqueiros. On the main balcony (visible from outside on the plaza) stands a reproduction of the Bell of Dolores Hidalgo, on which Mexican independence rang out on the night of September 15, 1810, in the Guanajuato town of Dolores Hidalgo. On the anniversary of the event, the governor rings the bell and leads the crowds below in the Grito (battle cry), a ritual performed in town squares across the country. ⊠ *Calle 61, between Calles 60 and 62, Mérida* ☎ *999/930–3101* ⊕ *www.yucatan.gob.mx* ▤ *Free.*

Parque Hidalgo (*Plaza Cepeda Peraza*)

CITY PARK | FAMILY | A half block north of the main plaza is this small, cozy park, officially known as Plaza Cepeda Peraza. Historic mansions, now reincarnated as hotels and sidewalk cafés (including a Starbucks), line its southern and eastern sides, and at night the area comes alive with marimba bands and street vendors. On Sunday, the streets are closed to vehicular traffic, and there's free live music performed throughout the day. ⊠ *Calle 60, between Calles 59 and 61, Mérida.*

Parque Santa Lucía

CITY PARK | FAMILY | This park at Calles 60 and 55 is lined with popular, if a bit touristy, restaurants and draws crowds with its Thursday-night music and dance performances (shows start at 9, but come early if you want to sit close to the performers). On Sunday, couples also come to dance to a live band and dine on food from carts set up in the plaza. The Iglesia de Santa Lucía opposite the park dates from 1575 and was built as a place of worship for the Maya, who weren't allowed to worship at just any Mérida church. ⊠ *Calles 60 and 55, Mérida.*

Parque Zoológico El Centenario

ZOO | FAMILY | Mérida's top children's attraction features pleasant wooded paths, playgrounds, inexpensive amusement-park rides, an inline skating rink, a small lake you can row on, and a little train that circles the property. It also includes cages that house more than 300 native animals, including exotic ones like lions and tigers (a modern zoo this is not, and you might not approve of those cages). At the exit, you'll find snack bars and vendors; there are on-site picnic areas, too. The French Renaissance–style arch commemorates the 100th anniversary (in 1910) of Mexican independence. ⊠ *Av. Itzáes, between Calles 59 and 65 (entrances on Calles 59 and 65), Mérida* ☎ *999/928–5815* ⊕ *www.merida.gob.mx/*

centenario/centenario/centenario.phpx 🎟 *Entry free, activities extra* 🕒 *Closed Mon.*

Paseo de Montejo

PROMENADE | FAMILY | North of downtown, this 10-block-long street was *the* place to reside in the late-19th and early-20th centuries, when wealthy hacienda owners sought to outdo each other with the opulence of their city mansions. They typically opted for the decorative styles popular in New Orleans, Cuba, and Paris (imported Carrara marble, European antiques). Many mansions are now used as office buildings, but four are open to the public: the Palacio Cantón, which houses a museum focused on Maya culture; Casas Gemelas and Quinta Montes Molina, both of which are house museums; and El Minaret, home to the Yerba Santa restaurant. Although the broad boulevard has lost some of its panache, lined as it is with breadfruit, tamarind, and laurel trees, it's still a lovely place to explore—on foot or in a horse-drawn carriage—and enjoy a drink or meal at a restaurant with outdoor seating. ✉ *Mérida.*

Plaza Grande

PLAZA/SQUARE | FAMILY | Locals generally refer to the city's main square as Plaza Grande or Plaza de la Independencia; others (mostly foreigners) call it the *zócalo.* Laid out in 1542 on the ruins of T'Hó, the Maya city demolished to make way for Mérida, it's still a focal point—one that's surrounded by important public buildings and makes a good place to start a city tour. It's also a Wi-Fi hot spot; just don't be so glued to your smartphone that you fail to take in the parade of activity, enjoy dance or music performances, and buy souvenirs from low-key vendors. Laurel trees provide shade, *confidenciales* (*S*-shaped benches) invite tête-à-têtes, and lampposts keep things beautifully illuminated at night. ✉ *Bordered by Calles 60 and 62, 61 and 63, Mérida.*

🍴 Restaurants

With myriad restaurants, as well as street-food stands and markets, Mérida has plenty of dining options. Regional cuisine is the norm, but you can also find places that serve burgers if you're craving something familiar.

Apoala

$$ | MEXICAN | Apoala is one of the best choices for Mexican food on the lively restaurant-lined Parque Santa Lucia. The menu includes both Oaxacan and Yucatecan dishes—moles and beef dishes from the former, ceviches and cochinita pibil from the latter. **Known for:** Oaxacan and Yucatecan dishes; outdoor seating; elevated approach to Mexican cuisine. [$] *Average main: MP270* ✉ *Calle 60 471, Mérida* ✣ *On Parque Santa Lucia* ☎ *999/923–1979* 🌐 *www.apoala.mx.*

Café Crème

$ | FRENCH | FAMILY | This casual spot north of Parque Santa Ana has a French flair, with vintage posters and antique signs, and its French owner, Eric Sureau, is on the premises most days, assuring that the quiches, crêpes, and salads all leave the kitchen *comme il faut.* There are tables in the lovely and shady yard in the back. In addition Sureau has a small but excellently curated selection of wines and some of the best cheeses in the city if you want to buy the essentials for a little gathering around the pool at your rental or hotel. **Known for:** well-curated wine selection; excellent cheeses; French favorites. [$] *Average main: MP120* ✉ *Calle 41 386B, Mérida* ☎ *999/192–9565* 🌐 *www.facebook.com/cafecrememerida.*

Casa Chica

$ | MEXICAN | Though it serves good basic pastas, salads, and burgers, as well as some Mexican bar-food favorites, this restaurant's popularity is primarily due to its delicious cocktails, aguas frescas, and lively atmosphere. You can dine outside, enjoying the activity on Paseo Montejo, or inside, where the people-watching is just as interesting. **Known for:** lively atmosphere; outdoor seating on Paseo de Montejo; good value. [$] *Average main: MP120* ✉ *Paseo Montejo 498B, Mérida* 🌐 *www.facebook.com/casachicabar.*

★ Cuna

$$ | **MEXICAN FUSION** | This contemporary restaurant at the Wayam Mundo Imperial hotel in the García Ginerés neighborhood has floor-to-ceiling windows overlooking a plant-filled terrace. Chef Maycoll Calderón allows fresh ingredients to take center stage, avoiding anything too fussy in such flavorful Italian and Latin American dishes as ceviche, arroz con pollo, pizza, and pasta. **Known for:** stylish decor; innovative dishes; large terrace. [$] *Average main: MP200* ✉ *Av. Colón 508, near Av. Reforma, Mérida* 🌐 *www.cuna.mx.*

★ Hacienda Teya

$$ | **MEXICAN** | A henequen plantation in the 17th century, this beautiful hacienda just outside Mérida serves some of the best regional food around, primarily attracting well-to-do Meridanos for a leisurely lunch (let that be your guide on what to wear). Start with sopa de lima, then move on to standout mains like *poc chuc* (slices of pork in a sour-orange sauce) or cochinita pibil—both served with homemade tortillas—perhaps followed by dessert, which comes with a complimentary digestif. **Known for:** largest wine selection in town; country setting with lovely gardens; elegant atmosphere. [$] *Average main: MP270* ✉ *Carretera 180, Mérida* ✣ *12½ km (8 miles) east of Mérida* ☎ *999/988–0800* 🌐 *haciendateya.com* 🕓 *No dinner.*

K'u'uk

$$$$ | **MEXICAN** | K'u'uk, which means "sprout" in Mayan, is chic in every sense of the word, from the suave waiters to the molecular gastronomy dining experience in a historic mansion facing the Monumento a la Patria on Paseo de Montejo. The presentation is artistic—picture dollops of baby pumpkin dusted with goat cheese the texture of powdered snow, potatoes slices as thin as tissue paper, and desserts sprinkled with dehydrated berries or honey-soaked seeds. **Known for:** pibil-style (Maya oven) cooking; leisurely—some say "slow"—dining experience; eight-course tasting menu. [$] *Average main: MP600* ✉ *Av. Rómulo Rozo 488, Mérida* ☎ *999/944–3377* 🌐 *www.kuukrestaurant.com* 🕓 *Closed Mon. No dinner Sun.*

La Negrita Cantina

$ | **MEXICAN** | This cantina at the corner of Calles 62 and 49 is popular with locals, expats, and visitors thanks to its large courtyard and likewise large cocktails. You'll be offered free bar snacks as long as you keep ordering drinks, though it's worth trying some of the delicious (if basic) ceviches, enchiladas, and tacos, too. **Known for:** live music; Mexican bar snacks; oversized cocktails. [$] *Average main: MP120* ✉ *Calle 62 415, at Calle 49, Mérida* ☎ *999/121–0411* 🌐 *www.facebook.com/LaNegritaMerida.*

La Poderosa

$ | **MEXICAN** | Residents of Mérida have strong opinions on who makes the best *salbutes* and *panuchos,* two signature Yucatecan dishes, and La Poderosa is at the top of many lists. All the seats at this restaurant in the southern part of Centro—near San Sebastian's square and market—are outdoors, and it's an especially lovely spot on warm evenings. **Known for:** outdoor seating; excellent panuchos and salbutes; cheap eats. [$] *Average main: MP100* ✉ *Calle 70 568D, Mérida* 💳 *No credit cards.*

La Tratto Santa Lucía

$$$ | **ITALIAN** | **FAMILY** | This lively family-owned eatery on Parque Santa Lucía has outdoor seating that's the perfect place to eat on cool evenings, as well as plenty of tables in an air-conditioned dining room for days when the heat doesn't break. The menu is made up of filling salads, thin-crust pizzas, and pasta

dishes. **Known for:** good pizza selection; huge salads; great wine list. $ *Average main: MP350* ✉ *Calle 60 471, Mérida* ☎ *999/927–0434* ⊕ *latratto.mx.*

Los Almendros

$$ | **MEXICAN** | This vintage Yucatecan restaurant with high colonial ceilings and an elegant atmosphere is a longtime local favorite. The *combinado yucateco* (Yucatecan combination plate) is a great way to try different dishes like cochinita pibil, *longaniza asada* (grilled pork sausages), *escabeche de Valladolid* (turkey with chiles, onions, and seasonings in an acidic sauce), and poc chuc (slices of pork in a sour-orange sauce). **Known for:** spectacular cheese soup; classic Yucatecan dishes; reasonable prices. $ *Average main: MP245* ✉ *Calle 50A 493, between Calles 57 and 59, facing Parque La Mejorada, Mérida* ☎ *999/928–5459* ⊕ *www. restaurantelosalmendros.com.mx.*

★ Micaela Mar y Leña

$$$ | **MODERN MEXICAN** | **FAMILY** | Located on Calle 47, which was pedestrianized in 2023 as its status as Mérida's restaurant row became more official, this colorful restaurant specializes in grilled fish and meat dishes, though the cocktail menu of mezcal and tequila favorites is a draw as well. The scene is lively but not excessively so, making this a perfect option for a special-occasion celebration. **Known for:** grilled entrées; generous cocktails; festive atmosphere. $ *Average main: MP350* ✉ *Calle 47 458, Mérida* ☎ *999/518–1702* ⊕ *www.restaurantemicaela.com.*

Museo de la Gastronomía Yucateca

$$ | **MEXICAN** | **FAMILY** | The menu here is as an encyclopedic take on Yucatecan cuisine, with everything from salbutes to start to *manjar blanco* (a milk-based delicacy) for dessert. Before sitting down to eat in the courtyard or one of the rooms that open onto it, explore the modest displays on regional food in the colonial-style building and Maya-style houses in the garden. **Known for:** traditional Yucatecan

Market Snacks 🍴

Parque Santa Ana. The simple market in Parque Santa Ana, just to the west of Paseo Montejo and north of Calle 47, is a popular breakfast spot, where locals happily start their days with regional dishes and fresh juices at plastic tables. The tamales are good, and the *tortas de cochinita* (pork sandwiches flavored with a few drops of sour-orange chile sauce) are heavenly. Most vendors close at 1:30 pm, but some reopen to sell snacks from 7 pm until late in the evening. ✉ *Calle 60, between Calles 45 and 47, Mérida.*

dishes; an elegant setting in a colonial-style building; cooking demonstrations. $ *Average main: MP220* ✉ *Calle 62 466, Mérida* ☎ *999/518–1645* ⊕ *mugy.com. mx.*

★ Oliva Enoteca

$$ | **ITALIAN** | At this eatery on Mérida's restaurant row, the salads, pizzas, and pasta dishes could hold their own against any served by establishments in Italy itself. The restaurant group also has other locations, including Oliva Patio and Olivia Pizzeria in the north of the city. **Known for:** fresh pastas; elegant-yet-casual atmosphere; excellent wine list. $ *Average main: MP200* ✉ *Calles 47 and 54, Mérida* ☎ *999/923–3081* ⊕ *www.olivamerida. com.*

Pancho Maiz

$ | **MEXICAN** | Don't let the bare walls and basic furniture fool you—this restaurant, a few blocks east of Parque Mejorada, offers one of Mérida's best dining experiences. Chefs Xóchitl Valdés and Selena Cárdenas have impressed gourmets with their celebration of corn, the basis of many of the dishes served here. **Known for:** Oaxacan favorites; freshest and best ingredients; excellent value. $ *Average* main: MP100 ✉ Calle 59 437A, Mérida ☎ 999/750–3589 ⏰ Closed Sun. No dinner.

★ Restaurante Amaro

$$ | **MEXICAN** | The patio of this historic home glows with candlelight in the evening, but during the day, things feel a lot more casual. Although the menu has a few fish or meat dishes (cochinita pibil, say, or butterfly chicken breast in a cream sauce), the emphasis is on vegetarian dishes such as chaya soup (made from a green plant similar to spinach), stuffed mushrooms, spinach lasagna, and avocado pizza. **Known for:** upscale Yucatecan cuisine; healthful juices; romantic atmosphere. [$] *Average main: MP280* ✉ *Calle 59 507, between Calles 60 and 62, Mérida* ☎ *999/928–2451* 🌐 *www.facebook.com/restauranteamaromerida.*

Rosas & Xocolate Restaurant

$$$ | **ECLECTIC** | This elegant restaurant at the inn of the same name is beautifully designed in hues of pink and brown, with long-stem roses on every table. Chef David Segovia's menu is an haute interpretation of Mexican and Yucatecan cuisines, with sauces incorporating local chiles, tamarind, and hibiscus (or jamaica) flowers. **Known for:** six-course tasting menu; rib eye with cardamom-seasoned eggplant; stylish hotel setting. [$] *Average main: MP500* ✉ *Paseo de Montejo 480, at Calle 41, Mérida* ☎ *999/924–2992* 🌐 *www.rosasandxocolate.com/restaurant.*

★ Salón Gallos

$$ | **MODERN MEXICAN** | An oat-processing facility, in an area that's busy by day but quiet at night, has been converted into an innovative cultural complex. In addition to this restaurant offering creatively updated Yucatecan dishes, you'll also find several bars, a gallery, an arthouse cinema, and a pop-up space that typically features the work of a local artisan or collective. **Known for:** art gallery; innovative Yucatecan and Middle Eastern dishes; movie theater. [$] *Average main: MP300* ✉ *Calle 63 459B, Mérida* ☎ *999/189–6564* 🌐 *salongallos.mx.*

Trotter's Grill House

$$$ | **STEAKHOUSE** | **FAMILY** | Menu highlights at this beautifully designed, upscale restaurant include tuna steak in a black-pepper crust and Angus beef served with rosemary potatoes. A glass wall separates the formal indoor dining room from the less-formal patio seating area, which is surrounded by lush vegetation that helps you forget that you are on a bustling avenue. **Known for:** contemporary decor; steaks; excellent starters. [$] *Average main: MP400* ✉ *Circuito Colonias, between Calles 34 and 36, Mérida* ☎ *999/927–2320* 🌐 *trottersrestaurants.com* ⏰ *No dinner Sun.*

Wayan'e

$ | **MEXICAN** | This oasis of carnivorous delights serves tortas—Mexico's answer to the sandwich—and tacos at four locations in Mérida. In addition to ham and cheese tortas, you can get pork loin in smoky chipotle-chile sauce, chorizo sausage, turkey strips sautéed with onions and peppers, and several other delicious combos guaranteed to go straight to your arteries. **Known for:** fun, informal vibe; astounding taco selection; torta-style sandwiches. [$] *Average main: MP180* ✉ *Calle 59 408, at Calle 4, Mérida* ☎ *999/938–0676* ⏰ *No dinner. Closed Sun.*

Coffee and Quick Bites

El Colón Sorbetes y Dulces Finos

$ | **ICE CREAM** | **FAMILY** | The homemade ice cream and sorbet at El Colón have been keeping locals cool since 1907. Served in a pyramid-shape scoop, the tropical fruit flavors (like *chico zapote*, a brown fruit native to Mexico that tastes a little like cinnamon and comes from a tree used in chewing-gum production) are particularly refreshing. **Known for:** tropical fruit flavors; sidewalk seating; local institution. [$] *Average main: MP80* ✉ *Calle 56 474A,* *on Paseo de Montejo, Mérida* 🌐 *www.facebook.com/SorbeteriaColon.*

Latte Quattro Sette

$ | **CAFÉ** | **FAMILY** | This bright, sunny café on Mérida's restaurant row is an appealing spot for a cappuccino, latte, or tea, paired with an avocado toast, yogurt and fruit, or a pastry. **Known for:** cheerful atmosphere; delicious pastries; variety of coffees and teas. [$] *Average main: MP120* ✉ *Calle 47 465, between Calles 54 and 56, Mérida* ☎ *999/924–8895* ⏲ *Closed Sun. No dinner.*

Pan & Koffee

$ | **BAKERY** | **FAMILY** | This bakery just a few blocks north of Parque Santa Ana is a great place to start your day with a light breakfast of a pastry and a coffee. It has a small garden and plenty of seating if you want to linger for awhile at your laptop. **Known for:** coffee drinks; garden; delicious pastries, savory and sweet. [$] *Average main: MP60* ✉ *Calle 43 485, Mérida* 🌐 *www.facebook.com/panandkoffee* ⏲ *No dinner.*

Pola

$ | **DESSERTS** | **FAMILY** | On any given day, the flavors at this little historic-center gelato shop vary, but you can typically expect between five and ten sorbets and the same number of gelatos. In addition to classics like chocolate and chocolate chip, you'll find options inspired by regional cuisine and produce—perhaps, chocolate with chiles, flan, pineapple with chaya, or lemon with rosemary. **Known for:** locally inspired flavors; excellent gelato and sorbets; cheerful store. [$] *Average main: MP60* ✉ *Calle 55 467D, Mérida* ☎ *999/923–1107* 🌐 *www.polagelato.com* 💳 *No credit cards.*

Hotels

Generally, you'll find smaller options in the downtown area, within walking distance of most sights; nights are inevitably a little louder here, especially if your room faces the street. Note that small lodgings often have small, easy-to-miss signs, so you might need to spin around the block a time or two to find your hotel.

A few larger chain hotels around the Paseo de Montejo, a short ride from downtown, offer quieter accommodations. If you want true peace, however, consider booking into one of the restored hacienda hotels just outside the city.

★ Casa Azul

$$$ | **B&B/INN** | Declared a historical monument and a Yucatán Heritage site, the French-style "Blue House" is notable for its extraordinary antiques, luxurious fabrics, rose-filled bouquets, and superior service. **Pros:** flawless service; modern comforts in colonial home; filtered tap water. **Cons:** small pool; some street noise; no children under 12. [$] *Rooms from: $300* ✉ *Calle 60 343, between Calles 35 and 37, Mérida* ☎ *999/925–5016* 🌐 *www.casaazulhotel.com* 🛏 *8 rooms* 🍴 *Free Breakfast.*

Casa del Balam

$ | **HOTEL** | This property just two blocks from Plaza Grande feels more like a home than a hotel thanks to colonial-style details like red-and-white tile floors, wrought-iron headboards, and carved cedar doors, as well as such thoughtful touches as minibars, double-paned windows, and rocking chairs on wide verandas. **Pros:** easy walk to many sights; spacious rooms; great restaurant service. **Cons:** slow elevator; street noise can be a problem; rooms are due for a refresh. [$] *Rooms from: $70* ✉ *Calle 60 488, at Calle 57, Mérida* ☎ *999/924–8844, 800/624–8451* 🌐 *www.casadelbalam.com* 🛏 *43 rooms* 🍴 *Free Breakfast.*

★ Casa Lecanda

$$$$ | **B&B/INN** | Housed in a fully restored former residence on Mérida's newly pedestrianized restaurant corridor, this stately boutique hotel has wrought-iron chandeliers and antique furniture that nod to a bygone era, as well as photographs of the modern-day city that

Hacienda Xcanatún by Angsana opens up to 3 acres of manicured gardens.

anchor you in the present. **Pros:** local flavor; elegant atmosphere; excellent service. **Cons:** street can be busy at night; no children under 12; pool is more of a showpiece than a place to swim. $ *Rooms from: $320* ✉ *Calle 47 471, between Calles 54 and 56, Mérida* ☎ *999/928–0112* ⊕ *www.casalecanda. com* 🛏 *7 rooms* ○ *Free Breakfast.*

★ Casa Puuc

$$ | HOTEL | Well-known Mexican artist and boutique owner Claudia Fernández helped convert this 1914 house in García Ginerés into a six-room, flawlessly styled inn, where every room has unique design elements, both vintage and new, and the understated beauty of the original architecture—featuring things like pasta tile floors and soaring ceilings—shines, too. **Pros:** exquisite design; intimate atmosphere; a quiet retreat. **Cons:** outside the historic center; lacks the facilities and services of a larger property; small pool. $ *Rooms from: $190* ✉ *Calle 22 199B, Mérida* ☎ *55/9195–5646* ⊕ *casapuuc.com* 🛏 *6 rooms* ○ *Free Breakfast.*

Casa San Ángel

$$ | HOTEL | Set at the southern end of Paseo de Montejo, this small hotel has an open-air central courtyard and uniquely decorated rooms, each with a hammock, foot massager, and flat-screen TV. **Pros:** unique setting; colorful rooms with spacious bathrooms; fantastic service. **Cons:** small pool; no children under 15; those with allergies might have issues with two resident cats. $ *Rooms from: $170* ✉ *Paseo de Montejo 1, at Calle 49, Mérida* ☎ *999/928–0800* ⊕ *www. hotelcasasanangel.com* 🛏 *12 rooms* ○ *No Meals.*

Cigno Hotel

$$ | HOTEL | The setting for this small, chic, adults-only property is a restored colonial-style house located south of Plaza Grande in Ermita, a neighborhood with a lovely square and cobblestone streets that was recognized as one of Mexico's Barrios Mágicos in 2023. **Pros:** intimate; excellent restaurant; good value. **Cons:** far from other sights; lacks the services of larger hotels; no kids allowed. $ *Rooms* *from: $170 ✉ Calle 66 593, Mérida ☎ 55/1328–4105, 956/552–9774 in the U.S. 🌐 www.cignohotel.com 🛏 10 rooms 🍴 Free Breakfast.*

Courtyard by Marriott

$$ | **HOTEL** | **FAMILY** | With its contemporary design in concrete, the Courtyard by Marriott is a commanding presence amid the other major-brand hotels along Avenida Colón near Paseo de Montejo. **Pros:** rooms with all the latest amenities; city views from the rooftop bar; rooftop pool. **Cons:** historic center is a short taxi ride or long walk away; generic big-brand experience; some don't love the contemporary design. [$] *Rooms from: $120 ✉ Av. Colón 504, Mérida ☎ 999/454–3000 🌐 www.marriott.com 🛏 208 rooms 🍴 No Meals.*

Decu Downtown

$$$$ | **HOTEL** | The small group of Decu hotels—there are also four in Mexico City and one in Tulum—entered Mérida with this understated, discreet property situated east of Plaza Grande, in a colonial-style house whose rooms have either colonial or Maya design elements, such as traditional pasta tile floors or walls of chukum (a form of plaster that has been used by the Maya for millennia). **Pros:** elegant design; intimate atmosphere; spacious rooms. **Cons:** slightly removed from most of the sights and restaurants; on the expensive side; small pool area. [$] *Rooms from: $350 ✉ Calle 56 468, Mérida ☎ 999/191–4575 🌐 decuhotels.com 🛏 8 rooms 🍴 No Meals.*

Fiesta Americana Mérida

$$ | **HOTEL** | **FAMILY** | This popular choice, a branch of a dependable Mexican chain, attempts to evoke the grandeur of the mansions on Paseo de Montejo with colonial accents, plush armchairs, gleaming marble, and a stained-glass ceiling in the lobby. **Pros:** tasty breakfast buffet; shopping downstairs; comfortable beds. **Cons:** a taxi ride from downtown; some amenities cost extra; lacks intimacy of other properties. [$] *Rooms from: $160 ✉ Paseo de Montejo 451, at Av. Colón, Mérida ☎ 999/942–1111, 877/927–7666 🌐 www.fiestamericana.com 🛏 350 rooms 🍴 Free Breakfast.*

Gran Hotel

$ | **HOTEL** | Located on leafy Parque Hidalgo, this legendary 1901 hotel has high ceilings, wrought-iron balcony and stair rails, and ornately patterned tile floors. **Pros:** beautiful antique decorations; great rates; in the middle of downtown shops and services. **Cons:** downtown noise; no elevator makes upstairs rooms a hike; parking is sometimes unavailable (check ahead if you are driving). [$] *Rooms from: $60 ✉ Calle 60 496, at Parque Hidalgo, Mérida ☎ 999/924–7622 🌐 www.granhoteldemerida.com 🛏 28 rooms 🍴 No Meals.*

★ Hacienda Xcanatún by Angsana

$$$ | **HOTEL** | This restored 18th-century henequen hacienda 13 km (8 miles) from Mérida has a mix of historic and new suites—all of them spacious and understatedly elegant, with beige and taupe color schemes and a design that marries Asian minimalism with Mexican details. **Pros:** stellar service; expansive gardens and Olympic-size pool; outstanding restaurant and innovative spa. **Cons:** a drive from the city; pricey; not suitable for children. [$] *Rooms from: $285 ✉ Carretera 261, Km 12, Mérida ✣ 13 km (8 miles) north of Mérida ☎ 999/930–2140, 888/883–3633 in the U.S. 🌐 www.angsana.com 🛏 54 rooms 🍴 No Meals.*

Hotel Hacienda Mérida

$$ | **HOTEL** | A dramatic pool—surrounded by pillared archways draped with white curtains—serves as a focal point at this urban oasis, where small but chic guest rooms have satellite TVs, air-conditioning, hardwood floors, and four-poster beds with silk pillows and 600-thread-count Egyptian cotton sheets. **Pros:** walking distance to city center; great service; very child-friendly. **Cons:** sometimes slow Internet; no restaurant; building showing a bit of wear. [$] *Rooms from: $129 ✉ Calle 62 439, between Calles 51 and*

Hotel Julamis features hand-painted murals that complement the original tile floors.

53, Mérida ☎ *999/924–4363* 🌐 *hotelhaciendamerida.com* 🛏 *14 rooms* 🍴 *No Meals.*

★ Hotel Julamis

$ | **B&B/INN** | Service and value are hallmarks of this artist-owned hotel in a 200-year-old building, where tastefully decorated guest rooms have murals—painted by the owner to match the original tile floors—air-conditioning, organic toiletries, and complimentary minibar drinks. **Pros:** remarkable rates; roughly halfway between Paseo de Montejo and Plaza Grande; great views from rooftop bar. **Cons:** no children under 12; note the fine print about the cancellation policy before you book; Wi-Fi can be spotty in some rooms. [$] *Rooms from: $72* ✉ *Calle 53 475B, at Calle 54, Mérida* ☎ *999/924–1818* 🌐 *www.hoteljulamis.com* 🛏 *9 rooms* 🍴 *Free Breakfast.*

Hotel Marionetas

$ | **B&B/INN** | Attentive proprietors Daniel and Sofija Bosco have ensured that this lovely bed-and-breakfast, set on a quiet street seven blocks from the main plaza, has lots of thoughtful touches, from carefully chosen folk-art decor and fine cotton linens to remote-controlled air-conditioning and pressurized shower heads. **Pros:** intimate feel; personal attention from proprietors and staff; calming courtyard and pool area. **Cons:** restaurant only serves breakfast; no children under 12; off-site parking. [$] *Rooms from: $94* ✉ *Calle 49 516, between Calles 62 and 64, Mérida* ☎ *999/928–3377* 🌐 *www.hotelmarionetas.mx* 🛏 *8 rooms* 🍴 *Free Breakfast.*

Hyatt Regency Mérida

$$ | **HOTEL** | The city's first deluxe hotel is still one of its most elegant, with a beautiful marble lobby and contemporary rooms that are tastefully done in taupe color schemes set off by dark-wood furniture. **Pros:** reasonable prices; popular bistro; nice fitness center. **Cons:** far from downtown; extra charge for Internet and in-room coffee; breakfast menu could include more light and healthy options. [$] *Rooms from: $110* ✉ *Av. Colón s/n, at Calle 60, Mérida* ☎ *999/942–1234,*

800/633–7313 in the U.S. 🌐 *www.hyatt.com* 🛏 *285 rooms* 🍴 *No Meals.*

La Misión de Fray Diego

$$ | **HOTEL** | With high ceilings, arched doorways, and checkered-tile floors, the elegant accommodations in this former convent retain their colonial charm, and tasteful ecclesiastical art and other items ensure they look divine. **Pros:** great restaurant; charming property; courteous staff. **Cons:** a bit of a climb to third-floor rooms; no children under 12; stairwell not well lit at night. [$] *Rooms from: $128* ✉ *Calle 61 524, between Calles 64 and 66, Mérida* ☎ *999/924–1111, 866/639–2933* 🌐 *www.lamisiondefraydiego.com* 🛏 *26 rooms* 🍴 *Free Breakfast.*

Piedra de Agua

$$ | **HOTEL** | Renovated for maximum comfort without compromising historical charm, this hotel in an 1840s mansion features a striking antique-meets-contemporary decor, including in guest rooms, which have tile floors, high ceilings, period details, and sleek modern furnishings and amenities. **Pros:** centrally located; decent rates; wonderful decor. **Cons:** small bathrooms; some street noise; off-site parking. [$] *Rooms from: $106* ✉ *Calle 60 498, between Calles 59 and 61, Mérida* ☎ *999/924–2300* 🌐 *www.piedradeagua.com* 🛏 *20 rooms* 🍴 *No Meals.*

Rosas & Xocolate

$$$ | **B&B/INN** | Designed with romance in mind, this boutique hotel has a roses-and-chocolate theme that carries from the pink exterior through to the Belgian truffles sold in the gift shop and the chocolate soaps provided in the bathrooms. **Pros:** great breakfasts; excellent showers and mattresses; beautiful architecture. **Cons:** small pool in a very public area; no elevator; not suitable for children. [$] *Rooms from: $245* ✉ *Paseo Montejo 480, at Calle 41, Mérida* ☎ *999/924–2992* 🌐 *www.rosasandxocolate.com* 🛏 *17 rooms* 🍴 *Free Breakfast.*

Villa Mercedes

$$ | **HOTEL** | In contrast to the traditional-looking, blue-and-white exterior of this hotel, which is part of Hilton's Curio Collection, its lobby is austerely modern, and its guest rooms are contemporary, though with little to remind you that you're in Mexico. **Pros:** excellent Japanese restaurant; perfect for business travelers; recently refurbished. **Cons:** pool is in the shadow of the hotel; generic room decor; other options are more convenient to the historic center. [$] *Rooms from: $110* ✉ *Av. Colón 500, Mérida* ☎ *999/942–9000, 844/442–8746 in the U.S.* 🌐 *www.hilton.com* 🛏 *127 rooms* 🍴 *No Meals.*

Wayam Mundo Imperial

$$ | **HOTEL** | This all-suites hotel in García Ginerés blurs the line between indoors and outdoors—after checking into a mid-20th-century house, you'll pass through lush gardens with seating areas, fountains, and contemporary sculptures on the way to your accommodations. **Pros:** stylish design; quiet neighborhood; excellent restaurant. **Cons:** outside the historic center; on the pricier side; rooftop pool area is small. [$] *Rooms from: $200* ✉ *Av. Colon 508, Mérida* ☎ *800/969–2926* 🌐 *www.mundoimperial.com/wayam* 🛏 *52 suites* 🍴 *No Meals.*

🍸 Nightlife

Mérida has always been a great city to walk in by day and dance in by night. Meridanos love music, and they love to dance, but since they also have to work, many clubs are open only on weekend nights, or Thursday through Sunday. **■ TIP→ Discos and restaurants with live music and comedy acts (geared toward young people) often invite patrons onstage for some interesting audience participation acts. Locals don't seem to mind.**

The city center and Paseo de Montejo area are largely safe at night with throngs of people out enjoying themselves.

(Standard precautions about watching your things apply, of course.) Restaurants and nightspots are happy to call you a taxi or you can opt for a ride-share service if you would rather not walk back to your hotel.

Bird

BREWPUBS | The owner of Dzalbay Cantina has this low-key alternative on the opposite side of Centro. Instead of live music, most nights, the soundtrack is provided by the extensive and curated vinyl collection. The bar serves pizza and beer—there are 12 different artisanal brews on tap every night. ⊠ *Calle 56 465, Mérida* ⊕ *thebird.mx.*

Café Peón Contreras

LIVE MUSIC | The café-bar at Mérida's landmark 1908 theater is one of the most happening nightspots in town. Tables spill onto the street, where locals gather to hear balladeers singing romantic and politically inspired songs. The drinks are expensive, and the food is nothing special, so only go if you want culture, live music, and an opportunity to splurge. ⊠ *Teatro Peón Contreras, Calle 60, between Calles 57 and 59, facing Parque de la Madre, Mérida* ☎ *999/924–7003* ⊗ *Closed Tues.*

DIX Bar

CABARET | This small bar in Centro has lively drag performances each night from Wednesday to Sunday. While it is predominantly a gay bar, everyone is welcome. ⊠ *Calle 53 495, Mérida* ☎ *999/100–6953* ⊗ *Closed Mon. and Tues.*

Dzalbay Cantina

LIVE MUSIC | One of Mérida's historic traditional cantinas, Dzalbay is experiencing a second life in the hands of a group of expat musician-owners. The bar has a crowded calendar of performances by blues and jazz acts, both local musicians and ones passing through Mérida. A large outdoor terrace and menus of signature cocktails, microbrews, and bar snacks also help make Dzalbay a local favorite. If a low-key, welcoming cantina is what you are searching for, it may become your favorite, too. ⊠ *Calle 64 443, Mérida* ⊕ *dzalbaycantina.com.*

La Parrilla Colonial

LIVE MUSIC | Just a block from Plaza Grande, in the heart of the historic center, this loud, colorful bar is one of the best spots to grab a beer, listen to live music, and watch Mérida in action. ■TIP→ **Check the website for weekly promotions.** ⊠ *Calle 60 502, between Calles 59 and 61, Mérida* ☎ *999/445–8296* ⊕ *www.facebook.com/laparrillacolonialmerida.*

Mayan Pub

LIVE MUSIC | A pleasant atmosphere, flowing beer, and live music are what make this bar one of Mérida's best-kept secrets (you might want to pass on the food). Grab a spot in the beer garden where you can listen to live reggae, rock, or jazz. A rather worn billiard table and occasional entertainment—such as belly dancers and fire spinners—draw a decent crowd. ⊠ *Calle 62 473, between Calles 55 and 57, Mérida* ☎ *999/923–1271* ⊗ *Closed Mon. and Tues.*

Parque de Santiago

GATHERING PLACES | FAMILY | If dancing to the likes of romantic trios of the 1940s is your style, don't miss the Tuesday-night ritual at Parque de Santiago, where older folks and the occasional young lovers gather for dancing under the stars at 8:30 pm. ⊠ *Calles 59 and 72, Mérida.*

⊕ Performing Arts

Mérida's vibrant and diverse cultural life includes free government-sponsored music and dance performances many evenings, as well as sidewalk art shows in local parks. On Thursday at 9 pm, Meridanos enjoy outdoor entertainment at the Serenata Yucateca, held in Parque Santa Lucía (Calles 60 and 55). You'll see trios, the local orchestra, and soloists performing compositions by Yucatecan composers. On Saturday evenings after 7 pm, the Noche Mexicana (at the southern end of Paseo de Montejo, where it meets Calle 47) hosts different musical and cultural events.

More free music, dance, comedy, and regional handicrafts can be found at the Corazón de Mérida, on Calle 60 between the main plaza and Calle 55. On Friday and Saturday evenings, multiple bands entertain locals and visitors while the area is closed to through traffic.

Throughout the year, but especially in the fall and winter, various concerts and performances take place on Plaza Grande, Plaza Santa Lucía, Plaza Santa Ana, and Parque Hidalgo. For a schedule of current performances, consult the tourist office, the local newspapers, or the posters at the Teatro Peón Contreras and Centro Cultural de Mérida Olimpo.

Teatro Mérida

THEATER | The Teatro Mérida, also known as the Teatro Armando Manzanero, opened as a movie theater in 1949. Today it hosts mostly live performances which range from classical and even some experimental acts to more family-friendly dance spectacles. ⊠ *Calle 62 495, between Calles 59 and 61, Mérida* ☎ *999/924–0040* ⊕ *www.facebook.com/ TeatroArmandoManzaneroOficial.*

Universidad Autónoma de Yucatán

THEATER | FAMILY | Pop into the university's main building to check the bulletin boards just inside the entrance for upcoming cultural events. The Ballet Folklórico de la Universidad Autónoma de Yucatán presents a combination of music, dance, and theater performances (think Mexico City's famous Ballet Folklórico de México, but on a smaller scale). The shows are typically free, though the schedule is inconsistent. ⊠ *Calle 60, between Calles 57 and 59, Mérida* ☎ *999/924–6729* ⊕ *www.uady.mx.*

🛍 Shopping

You'll find reasonably priced crafts for sale not only in markets but also parks and plazas. Although most vendors are honest, it's still a good idea to shop around, acquainting yourself with the kinds of crafts, the levels of quality, and the pricing. In addition, the city's art scene is burgeoning, with many galleries selling pieces by local artists.

If you're looking for a more standard shopping experience, or need to grab some new tennis shoes or a pair of jeans, the northern part of the city has a few malls. As is true in much of Mexico, stores tend to remain open only until 1 or 2 pm on Saturdays and to be closed entirely on Sundays and holidays.

BOOKS
Between the Lines

BOOKS | Mérida's biggest English-language bookstore is relatively small, but it still offers a nicely curated selection of recent popular titles as well as a number that are focused on Mexican culture, cuisine, and history. The store also has bookish gifts including journals, bookmarks, and more. Several stores in the Carmesí complex, where the bookstore is located, are worth a stop, too; they mostly sell local, high-quality handicrafts. There's also Volta Café for a snack and drink. ⊠ *Calle 62 450, Mérida* ☎ *999/242– 3528* ⊕ *www.between-the-lines.com.mx* ⊙ *Closed Mon. and Tues.*

Librería Dante

BOOKS | FAMILY | The Mérida-based bookstore chain Dante, with a location on Plaza Grande as well as eight others around the city, has the best selection of Spanish-language books about the peninsula's history, culture, cuisine, and more. It is especially strong on books for kids and works dealing with Yucatecan flora and fauna. This branch is the largest of its locations, a little north of central Mérida on the Prolongación Paseo de Montejo. ⊠ *Calle 17 138B, at Prolongación Paseo*

Hamacas: A Primer ⬤

Yucatecan artisans are known for creating some of the finest *hamacas*, or hammocks, in the country. For the most part, the shops of Mérida are the best places in Yucatán to buy these beautiful, practical items, and you'll find lots of them near the municipal market on Calle 58, between Calles 69 and 73. That said, if you travel to some of the outlying small towns, like Tixkokob, Izamal, and Espita, you may find cheaper prices.

One of the first decisions you'll have to make is whether to buy a hamaca made from cotton or nylon. Nylon dries more quickly and is therefore well suited to humid climates, but cotton is softer and more comfortable (though its colors tend to fade faster). You'll also see both single-thread and sturdier, more densely woven double-thread versions.

Hamacas come in a variety of sizes, too. A *sencillo* (sen-*see*-yoh) is meant for just one person (although most people find it's a rather tight fit). A *doble* (doh-blay), on the other hand, is very comfortable for one but crowded for two. *Matrimonial* or king-size hammocks accommodate two, and *familiares* or *matrimoniales especiales* can theoretically sleep an entire family. (Yucatecans tend to be smaller than many Americans, and they also lie diagonally in hammocks rather than end-to-end.)

For a good-quality, king-size, nylon or cotton hamaca, prices start at MX$500; sencillos begin at MX$400. Unless you're an expert, it's best to shop at a specialty store, where you can climb into them and try them out. The proprietors will also give you tips on washing, storing, and hanging your hammock.

---

de Montejo, Mérida ☎ 999/927–7676 ⊕ www.libreriadante.com.mx.

CLOTHING

Amerindio Hombre

MEN'S CLOTHING | Once you return home, traditional huaraches, guayaberas, and straw hats might not look as appropriate as they did when you were on vacation. The items from Mexican designers at men's store Amerindio, however, have a cool factor that will be stylish even back at home. ⊠ Calle 62 469, Mérida ☎ 999/923–0945 ⊕ www.facebook.com/Amerindiomx ⊙ Closed Sun.

Happening Mérida

MIXED CLOTHING | If you are looking for a guayabera, there's no shortage of shops in Mérida's historic center that will provide you with a lovely version of this tropical garment. If, on the other hand,

you want edgier T-shirts, sweatshirts, and other attire—sold alongside beautiful Michoacan water pitchers in dazzling pastels, Mexican-themed notebooks and journals, and organic beauty products—then you'll want to drop by this shop on Paseo de Montejo. ⊠ Paseo de Montejo 468, Mérida ☎ 999/931–0929 ⊕ www.facebook.com/HappeningMerida.

CRAFTS

Expendio Doméstico

CRAFTS | Some visitors have a moment of disappointment when they learn that the Yucatán is not especially known for regional handicrafts unlike, say, Chiapas, Michoacan, or Oaxaca. Fortunately, Expendio Doméstico has opened its third location (after two in Mexico City) just to the east of Parque Mejorada. The wonderfully curated collection of typically Mexican objects includes black barro pottery, blown-glass pitchers, and embroidered tablecloths. ⊠ *Calle 57 441, Mérida* ⊕ *expendiodomestico.mx.*

Hamacas El Aguacate

CRAFTS | FAMILY | This family-run outfit specializes in hammocks and has many sizes and designs. ⊠ *Calle 58 604, at Calle 73, Mérida* ☎ *999/947–4641* ⊕ *www.facebook.com/hamacas.elaguacate* ⊗ *Closed Sun.*

La Casa de las Artesanías

CRAFTS | FAMILY | This government-run craft store offers all kinds of items, both from the state of Yucatán and other parts of Mexico, at fair prices. There's a smaller location in front of the Palacio Cantón on the Paseo de Montejo, but this main branch offers the best selection. ⊠ *Calle 63, 513, between Calles 64 and 66, Mérida* ☎ *999/928–6676* ⊗ *Closed weekends.*

Miniaturas Felguérez

CRAFTS | Although this store specializes in miniatures made of ceramics, tin, and other materials, it also has an assortment of other craft items. ⊠ *Calle 59 507A, between Calles 60 and 62, Mérida* ☎ *999/928–6503* ⊗ *Closed Sun.*

DEPARTMENT STORE

★ Casa T´Hō Concept House

DEPARTMENT STORE | Located in one of the grand mansions from the early 20th century on Paseo de Montejo, this establishment caters to well-heeled visitors and locals. The 10 boutiques housed here include an outpost from top Mexican designer Carla Fernández, Xinú (a Mexican fragrance line), and Casa Lima, which has an excellent selection of charming gifts that will fit easily into your luggage. There's also a café serving pastries and small bites with tables overlooking Paseo Montejo. ⊠ *Paseo de Montejo 498, Mérida* ☎ *999/923–2350* ⊕ *www.casatho.com.*

JEWELRY

Joyería Colonial

JEWELRY & WATCHES | Shop for malachite, turquoise, and other semiprecious stones set in silver at Joyería Colonial. ⊠ *Calle 60 502B, between Calles 61 and 63, Mérida* ☎ *999/923–5838* ⊗ *Closed Sun.*

MALLS

The Harbor Mérida

MALL | FAMILY | One of the nicest malls in Mérida wraps around an artificial lake—you can even zip-line over it. Its main anchor is Gran Chapur, a department store, sitting amid a number of smaller boutiques. The Harbor also has a movie theater as well as a number of restaurants: Maya de Asia has delicious Maya-Asian fusion dishes; Porfirio's is a lively Mexican bar and restaurant; and there are smaller venues including a Starbucks, Mr. Sushi, and Hamburgesia for, yes, burgers. ⊠ *Prolongación Paseo Montejo, Mérida* ☎ *999/921–1252* ⊕ *theharbormerida.com.*

La Isla

MALL | FAMILY | La Isla inches ahead of The Harbor when it comes to store selection, though both have pulled ahead of their competitors for the title of most-luxe mall in town. The department store Liverpool is the anchor at La Isla, but Zara and H&M are also big draws. The back of the mall has a row of restaurants overlooking a man-made lake. As with any of Mérida's malls, it may not be on your sightseeing shortlist, but if you have a longer stay in the city, air-conditioned window shopping may be appealing on warm days. ⊠ *Calle 24 608, Mérida* ☎ *999/518–3522* ⊕ *www.laislamerida.mx.*

MARKETS

Bazar de Artes Populares

MARKET | FAMILY | As its name implies, "popular art," or handicrafts, are sold at the Parque Santa Lucía on Sundays beginning at 9 am. ⊠ *Parque Santa Lucía, at Calles 60 and 55, Mérida.*

Mercado de Artesanías García Rejón

MARKET | FAMILY | Although many deal in the same wares, the shops and stalls of the García Rejón Crafts Market sell some quality items, and the shopping

The estuaries of Reserva de la Biósfera Ría Celestún are filled with pink flamingos.

experience here can be less of a hassle than at the nearby municipal market. You'll find reasonable prices on palm-fiber hats, hammocks, leather sandals, jewelry, handmade guitars, and locally made liqueurs. Persistent but polite bargaining might get you even better deals. ⊠ *Calles 65 and 60, Mérida.*

Mercado Lucas de Gálvez

MARKET | FAMILY | Sellers of chilis, herbs, seafood, and produce fill this pungent and labyrinthine municipal market. Early in the morning, the first floor is jammed with housewives and restaurateurs shopping for the freshest fish and produce. The stairs at Calles 56 and 57 lead to the second-floor Bazar de Artesanías Municipales, where you'll find local pottery, embroidered clothes, guayabera shirts, hammocks, straw bags, sturdy leather huaraches, and piñatas. Note that most initial prices are inflated as vendors expect you'll bargain—one way to begin is to politely request a discount. ⊠ *Calles 56 and 67.*

Celestún

90 km (56 miles) west of Mérida.

Think pink when someone says "Celestún." The estuaries of the Reserva de la Biósfera Ría Celestún are home to an amazing flock of flamingos. The gateway to this biosphere reserve, a tranquil fishing village of the same name, sits at the end of a spit of land separating the estuaries from the Gulf of Mexico.

GETTING HERE AND AROUND

Every Mérida tour operator offers Celestún excursions several times per week. If you'd rather come independently, you can drive—a spiffy highway gets you there in under an hour. Alternatively, take a second-class bus from Mérida's Noroeste Terminal (Calle 67 at Calle 50); there are multiple departures each day, and the round-trip fare is about MX$80.

Within Celestún, moto-taxis are your best bet. They charge about MX$20 around town and MX$40 to go out to the boats from the central plaza. Make sure you establish the fare before you get on, as some drivers try to charge foreigners significantly higher rates.

◎ Sights

Reserva de la Biósfera Ría Celestún

NATURE PRESERVE | FAMILY | Celestún is the point of entry to this 146,000-acre wildlife reserve with extensive mangrove forests and one of North America's largest flamingo colonies. Clouds of the pink birds soar above the estuary all year, but the best months for seeing them in abundance are November through March. This is also the fourth-largest wintering ground for ducks of the Gulf coastal region, and more than 365 other bird species make their home here, as do sea turtles. Mexican and American conservation programs protect the birds, as well as the endangered hawksbill and loggerhead marine tortoises, and species such as the blue crab and crocodile. Other endangered species that inhabit the area are the ocelot, the jaguar, and the spider monkey.

The park, which is set among rocks, islets, and white-sand beaches has several cenotes that are wonderful for swimming. The fishing is good here, too. Popular with Mexican vacationers, the park's sandy beach is pleasant during the morning but tends to get windy in the afternoon. And, unfortunately, mosquitoes gather in great numbers on the beach at dawn and dusk, particularly during winter months, making a walk on the beach uncomfortable. Area hotels generally drape their beds with mosquito netting, but bring along a good cream or spray to keep the bugs away.

Most Mérida tour operators run boat excursions of the *ría* (estuary) in the early morning or late afternoon, and it's not usually necessary to make a reservation in advance. Alternatively, you can hire a fishing boat at the entrance to town (they hang out under the bridge leading

into Celestún). A 75-minute tour for up to six people costs about MX$1,200; a two-hour tour costs around MX$2,500. Although more expensive (MX$990 per person), local expert Alex specializes in ecotours and donates a portion of the proceeds to the Celestún Conservation Program (call Hotel Eco Paraíso to book). ✉ *90 km (56 miles) west of Mérida, Celestún* ☎ *998/916–2100 tours booked through Hotel Eco Paraíso.*

⛱ Beaches

Playa Celestún

BEACH | FAMILY | This village may not have the classic beaches of the Caribbean, but it does have several kilometers of lovely coastline, perfect for long walks and seashell collecting. There are no crowds, even at the main beach in town, and the water is a pretty emerald-green color. The nicest stretch is near Hotel Eco Paraíso, home to 5 km (3 miles) of white sandy beaches, where turtles nest from April through July and bottlenose dolphins can be seen swimming. The waters are usually tranquil until late afternoon; when winds pick up, this isn't the best place for a dip—but it's perfect for relaxing or kayaking (rentals are available at the hotel). There are no lifeguards on duty, so ask hotel staff about rip currents and incoming swells. **Amenities:** food and drink; water sports (through the hotel). **Best for:** walking. ✉ *Celestún.*

🛏 Hotels

Casa de Celeste Vida

$$ | B&B/INN | Owned by Canadian expats, this small guesthouse directly on the beach has accommodations with fully equipped kitchens, purified water, Wi-Fi, and ocean views. **Pros:** isolated beach; less than a mile from town; gated property with secure parking. **Cons:** mosquitoes can be a problem; no air-conditioning; two-night minimum stay. $ *Rooms from: $105* ✉ *49E Calle 12, Celestún*

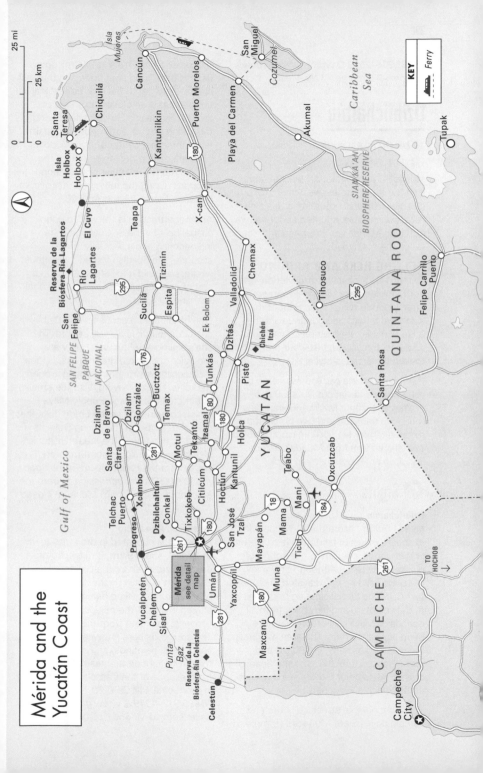

☎ 988/916–2536 ⊕ www.hotelcelestevida.com ⌕ 3 rooms ⏀ No Meals.

Dzibilchaltún

16 km (10 miles) north of Mérida.

Meaning "the place with writing on flat stones," Dzibilchaltún (dzi-bil-chal-*toon*) isn't the most impressive Maya site, but it is, nevertheless, interesting. It's also readily accessible, situated about halfway between Mérida and Progreso and not far off the main road.

GETTING HERE AND AROUND
To reach Dzibilchaltún from Mérida, drive north on Carretera Mérida–Progreso; after 10 km (6 miles), turn right at the sign for the ruins and continue another 3 km (2 miles) until you reach a village. Just past the village, take your first right toward the archaeological site.

If you don't have a car, you can come by cab from Mérida (about MX$350 one way) or Progreso (about MX$1,130, including round-trip transport and two hours at the ruins). Alternatively, you can catch a *colectivo* (shared van) from Mérida's Parque San Juan or Progreso's main dock.

◉ Sights

Dzibilchaltún
RUINS | FAMILY | More than 16 square km (6 square miles) of land here is cluttered with mounds, platforms, piles of rubble, plazas, and stelae. Although only a few buildings have been excavated, historians find Dzibilchaltún fascinating because of the sculpture and ceramics from all periods of Maya civilization that have been unearthed here. The area may have been settled as early as 500 BC and was inhabited until the time the Spanish arrived. At its height, there were around 40,000 people living here.

The most notable structure is the tiny Templo de las Siete Muñecas (Temple of the Seven Dolls). It's a long stroll down a flat dirt track lined with flowering bushes and trees to get to the low, trapezoidal temple that is an elegant example of the late Preclassic Period style. During the spring and fall equinoxes, sunbeams fall at the exact center of two windows opposite each other inside one of the temple rooms. A similar phenomenon happens during the full moon that occurs between March 20 and April 20.

Another attraction is the ruined open chapel built by the Spaniards for the indigenous people. Actually, to be accurate, the Spanish forced indigenous laborers to build it for themselves, in a sort of pre-Hispanic "separate but equal" scenario.

One of the best reasons to visit Dzibilchaltún, though, is Xlacah Cenote. The site's sinkhole, with crystalline water the color of smoked green glass, is ideal for a cooling swim after walking around the ruins. Before leaving, visit the small but impressive Museo Pueblo Maya, which contains the seven crude dolls that gave the Temple of the Seven Dolls its name. It also traces the area's Hispanic history, and highlights contemporary crafts from the region. ⊕ *www.inah.gob.mx* ⊡ *MX$200 for admission to both the site and the museum* ⊘ *Museum closed Mon.*

Galería de Arte Sacro
ART MUSEUM | Located in the small town of Conkal, about 9 km (6 miles) southeast of Dzibilchaltún, the Gallery of Sacred Art is is run by the Archdiocese of Yucatán. It's tucked behind a colonial church in one of the peninsula's 20 or so convents that date from the 16th century. The six rooms here showcase sculptures, vestments, paintings, and other objects that shine light on the nearly 500-year-old presence of the Catholic Church in the Yucatán. ⊠ *Calle 20 14, Mérida* ☎ *999/912–4049* ⊕ *www.galeriadeartesacro.com* ⊡ *MX$50* ⊘ *Closed Mon.*

Progreso

16 km (10 miles) north of Dzibilchaltún, 32 km (20 miles) north of Mérida.

The waterfront town closest to Mérida is not particularly historic or picturesque, but it provokes a certain sentimental fondness for those who know it well. On weekdays during most of the year the beaches are deserted, but over Easter and in summer they're packed with families from Mérida. Progreso has also started attracting cruise ships, and twice-weekly arrivals bring in tourist traffic.

The town's charm—or lack thereof—seems to hinge on the weather. When the sun is shining, the water appears a translucent green and feels bathtub-warm, and the fine sand makes for lovely long walks. When the wind blows during one of Yucatán's winter *nortes,* gray water churns with whitecaps and sand blows in your face. Whether the weather is good or bad, however, everyone ends up eventually at one of the restaurants lining the main street, Calle 19, across from the oceanfront *malecón* (boardwalk). These all serve cold beer, seafood cocktails, and freshly grilled fish. There's also a small downtown area, between Calle 80 and Calle 31, with shops, banks, supermarkets, and eateries, which dish out simpler fare (like tortas and tacos).

Although Progreso is close enough to Mérida to make it an easy day trip, several smaller hotels that have cropped up over the past few years make it a decent alternative base for those wanting to explore more of the untouristy coast. Just west of Progreso, the fishing villages of Chelem and Chuburna are beginning to offer walking, kayaking, and cycling tours ending with a boat trip through the mangroves for about MX$400. This is ecotourism in its infancy,

and excursions are best set up ahead of time through the Progreso tourism office.

Experienced divers can explore sunken ships at the Alacranes Reef, about 120 km (74 miles) offshore, although infrastructure is limited. Pérez Island, part of the reef, supports a large population of sea turtles and seabirds. Arrangements for the boat trip can be made through individuals at the private marina at neighboring Yucaltepén, which is 6 km (4 miles) from Progreso.

GETTING HERE AND AROUND

To drive from Mérida, head out of town via Paseo de Montejo and keep going north. It's a straight shot to the beach. Buses bound for Progreso leave Mérida from Calle 62 524, between Calles 65 and 67.

A taxi ride from Mérida to Progreso runs about MX$450, and most drivers charge around MX$200 per hour to show you around. If you plan on renting the cab for a good part of the day, talk about the number of hours and the cost with the driver before you take off. The bright blue, open-air, double-decker vehicles that tool through town cost only MX$25.

CRUISE SHIP

Carnival, Norwegian, and Royal Caribbean cruise ships call at Progreso on select western Caribbean itineraries. The pier here is long, and vessels dock at its end, so passengers are shuttled to the terminal at foot of the pier. It houses small restaurants and shops that sell locally produced crafts and are some of the town's best retail options. The beach lies just east of the pier and can easily be reached on foot. If you want to enjoy the sun and a peaceful afternoon, a drink at one of the small palapa-roof restaurants that line the beach is a good bet.

Plenty of taxis congregate around the pier. A trip through town shouldn't cost more than MX$80, but ask the taxi driver for a quote. If you want to see more of Progreso, a cab can also take you to the

Casa de Cultura, where the bright-blue, open-air, double-decker sightseeing buses depart about every 10 minutes and cost MX$25.

Most cruise visitors who want to visit Mérida band together and share a taxi (MX$450) as it's hard to rent a car here. Drivers generally charge around MX$200 per hour to show you around. Just be sure to agree on rates before you head out.

VISITOR INFORMATION

CONTACTS Oficina de Turismo. ✉ *Casa de la Cultura, Calle 80, between Calles 31 and 33, Centro* ☎ *969/103–0169* 🌐 *www.ayuntamientodeprogreso.gob.mx.*

Beaches

Progreso Beach

BEACH | FAMILY | If you want a pristine Caribbean-style strand, you'd better look elsewhere. The primary draw of Progreso's main beach is the distinctive little beach town and its proximity to Mérida, which often leaves the sand packed with tourists and locals alike during summer weekends and holidays. Water shoes are recommended since sharp, slippery rocks lurk below the surface, making this a poor spot for diving or snorkeling. The beach is void of shade, so your best bet is to find refuge in one of the eateries on the malecón that lines the shore. Several restaurant owners rent beach chairs by the hour, but beware: Progreso's peddlers are relentless and leave only once they receive a small tip. Despite its drawbacks, the water here offers a refreshing escape from the bustling city. **Amenities:** food and drink; toilets (restaurant patrons only). **Best for:** partiers; walking. ✉ *Av. Malecón and Calle 28, Progreso.*

Restaurants

Crabster Seafood & Grill

$$ | SEAFOOD | A notch above its malecón neighbors, this restaurant has contemporary Yucatecan-inspired decor (think: pasta tiles, tzalam wood details, and florescent pink chairs). The menu is extensive but almost everything is from the sea, including shrimp cocktails, Baja-style fish tacos, and platters of crab. **Known for:** ocean views; stylish decor; extensive seafood menu. [$] *Average main: MP200* ✉ *Av. Malecón, Progreso* ☎ *969/103–6522* 🌐 *www.facebook.com/CrabsterMX.*

Eladio's

$ | MEXICAN | FAMILY | An outpost of Eladio's in Mérida, this lively bar and restaurant on the malecón is popular with beachcombers and cruise-ship passengers. You can sample typical Yucatecan dishes like *longaniza asada* (baked sausage) and *pollo pibil* (citrus-pickled chicken) while seated beneath a tall palapa on the beach. **Known for:** yummy free appetizers; ocean breezes; fresh seafood. [$] *Average main: MP175* ✉ *Av. Malecón and Calle 80, Progreso* ☎ *969/935–5670* 🌐 *www.eladios.com.mx.*

Hotels

Although there are many Airbnb and other rental options in Progreso and its neighboring beach towns, many travelers prefer to return after a day at the beach to Mérida, where the options are generally better.

Playa Linda Hotel

$ | HOTEL | FAMILY | Located directly across from the beach, the Playa Linda not only has great views but also rooms that look like something straight out of an Ikea catalog, with recessed lighting, modern furnishings, and sleek kitchens. **Pros:** great views; suites have an added dining area and balcony; discounts available for longer-term stays. **Cons:** no restaurant; staff speaks little English; no amenities. [$] *Rooms from: $60* ✉ *Calle 76, between Calles 19 and 21, Progreso* ☎ *985/858–0519, 999/220–8318* 🌐 *hotelplayalinda.com* 🛏 *7 rooms* 🍴 *No Meals.*

Xcambo

37 km (23 miles) east of Progreso

Surrounded by a plantation where disease-resistant coconut trees are being developed, the Xcambo (*ish*-cam-bo) Maya site is a couple of miles inland following the turnoff for Xtampu.

Sights

Xcambo
RUINS | FAMILY | At this Maya site, two plazas, surrounded by rather plain structures, have been restored so far. The tallest temple is the Xcambo, also known as the Pyramid of the Cross. Salt, a much-sought-after commodity in the ancient world, was produced in this area and made it prosperous. Indeed, the bones of 600 former residents discovered in burial plots showed they had been healthier than the average Maya. In addition, unearthed ceramics indicate that the city traded with other Maya groups as far afield as Guatemala and Belize. The Catholic church here was built by dismantling some of the ancient structures, and, until recently, locals hauled off the cut stones to build fences and foundations. ⊠ *37 km (23 miles) west of Progreso* ✛ *Located between Progreso and Telchac Puerto, 3 km (2 miles) south of the coastal road; turn off Carretera Progreso–Dzilam de Bravo at Xtampu* ⌑ *MX$90.*

Reserva de la Biósfera Ría Lagartos

240 km (149 miles) east of Progreso, 216 km (134 miles) northeast of Mérida.

The mangroves of this biosphere reserve make up one of southern Mexico's most important wildlife sanctuaries. Birds are the big draw here, and with 300-plus resident and migratory species, there's plenty for avian enthusiasts to see. ■ **TIP→ Although the reserve is called Ría Lagartos, the town that is its hub is called Río Lagartos—***río* **means "river" in Spanish;** *ría* **means "estuary."**

GETTING HERE AND AROUND
The drive from Progreso takes the better part of 3 hours; that from Mérida is 2½. Buses from Mérida depart regularly from the second-class terminals bound for either Río Lagartos or San Felipe, which is 10 km (6 miles) west of the park.

TOURS
★ Río Lagartos Adventures
ECOTOURISM | FAMILY | Booking an excursion is the easiest way to visit the 149,000-acre park, and Río Lagartos Adventures is an excellent and experienced operation. Boat trips will take you through mangrove forests to flamingo feeding grounds. Tours are priced per boat, not person, and include one-hour tours for MX$1,000 to longer tours of up to four hours for around MX$4,500. Whether you are interested in a nocturnal crocodile adventure, a fishing expedition, or an expedition with plenty of time to stop on beaches accessible only to private boats, the outfitter can arrange one that is the right fit for your group. ⊠ *Calle 19 134, Río Lagartos* ☎ *986/100–8390* ⊕ *riolagartosaventuras.com.*

◉ Sights

Reserva de la Biósfera Ría Lagartos
NATURE PRESERVE | FAMILY | This reserve which encompasses a long estuary, was developed with ecotourism in mind—although few of the crocodiles for which it and the village were named remain. The real spectacle is provided by birds. April through September, thousands of the bright pink, black-tipped flamingos—90% of the Western Hemisphere's entire flamingo population—come to here from their "summer homes" in Celestún, on the Yucatán's west coast, as well as from northern latitudes to mate,

nest, and raise their chicks. The largest flock of bird-watching enthusiasts also descends on the reserve during this time.

Although the long-legged pink creatures are the most famous winged beasts found in Ría Lagartos, its red, white, black, and buttonwood mangrove swamps are also home to hundreds of other birds, including including snowy and red egrets, white ibis, great white herons, cormorants, pelicans, and peregrine falcons. Of the reserve's estimated 380 different species, one-third are winter-only residents. Twelve of the region's resident species are found nowhere else on Earth.

In addition, protected leatherback, hawksbill, and green turtles lay their eggs on the beaches at night. The fishing is good here, too. **■ TIP→ Mosquitoes can gather at dusk in unpleasantly large swarms in May, June, and July. Bring repellent to fend them off.** ✉ *Río Lagartos* 🌐 *www.gob.mx* 🎟 *MX$40.*

🍴 Restaurants

Restaurante Ría Maya

$ | **SEAFOOD** | **FAMILY** | Grab a seat in this palapa restaurant directly across from the water and watch the day's catch come straight from the docks. The menu features local specialties like ceviche, seafood soup, fish fillet stuffed with shrimp, and breaded seafood rolled into a ball and deep-fried. **Known for:** quality seafood; beachy vibe; lobster and octopus in season. [$] *Average main: MP180* ✉ *Calle 19 134, on the waterfront, 50 meters from the lighthouse, Río Lagartos* ☎ *986/100–8390* 🌐 *riamaya.com.*

🛏 Hotels

Hotel Tabasco Río

$ | **HOTEL** | **FAMILY** | Right on the plaza, this hotel has a bright center courtyard covered with skylights that allow light to shine on the tables where breakfast is served. **Pros:** well-appointed rooms; hotel package can include meals and tours; budget-friendly. **Cons:** hot water can be inconsistent; Wi-Fi in common areas only; some rooms are spartan. [$] *Rooms from: $40* ✉ *Calle 12 115, Río Lagartos* ☎ *986/862–0016* 🌐 *hoteltabascorio.com* 🔑 *19 rooms* 🍽 *No Meals.*

Hotel Villa de Pescadores

$ | **HOTEL** | Rooms at the nicest hotel in Río Lagartos have private balconies, water views, colorful decor and stone walls and tile floors that keep them rather cool, though there are fans and air-conditioning as well. **Pros:** clean rooms; best location in town; great views. **Cons:** restaurant closed for dinner in low season; four floors but no elevator; weak water pressure. [$] *Rooms from: $65* ✉ *Calle 14 and Av. Malecón, Río Lagartos* ☎ *986/862–0020* 🌐 *www.hotelvilladepescadores.com* 🔑 *12 rooms* 🍽 *No Meals.*

El Cuyo

262 km (163 miles) east of Mérida, 163 km (101 miles) west of Cancún.

The little town of El Cuyo's remote location on a barrier island near the border with Quintana Roo has left it relatively undiscovered by most visitors to the Yucatán coast. It is, however, popular with kitesurfers, who appreciate its frequently windy conditions. Although other places on the peninsula have calmer waters and more amenities, El Cuyo offers the chance to experience what is becoming increasingly rare in Mexico—a quiet beach town where you can relax with good company and a good book.

GETTING HERE AND AROUND

El Cuyo is a 3½-hour drive from Mérida and a 2½-hour drive from Cancún. It is possible to get to El Cuyo relying only on public transportation, but you'll most likely have to take several buses.

From Mérida, you can take an ADO bus (⊕ *www.ado.com.mx*) to Valladolid, then a second bus to Tizimín, and a third to El Cuyo. It's a little easier from Cancún, but you will still need to change buses in Colonía Yucatán.

That said, a car is helpful even once you've arrived. Although the town is small, it sprawls along the coast. If you are staying, say, at the LunArena hotel, at one end of town, and having dinner at La Casa Palma, near the opposite end, it is about a 25-minute walk.

🍴 Restaurants

★ El Chile Gordo

$$$$ | **MEXICAN** | On the inland side of the barrier island, a charming little house painted sky-blue and cherry-red contains El Cuyo's best restaurant. Here, Oscar Flores, who presides in the kitchen, and his English wife, Cathy Sissens, lead guests—never more than 20 on any night—on a nine-course journey through Mexico's culinary regions, with Cathy sharing some background on each mole, ceviche, or taco that's served. **Known for:** beautiful, intimate setting; excellent Mexican dishes; warm and welcoming hosts. $ *Average main: MP1,750* ⊠ *Calle Laguna 220* ☎ *999/169–9714* ⊕ *elchilegordo.com* ⊗ *Closed Sun.–Tues.*

La Casa Palma

$ | **PIZZA** | **FAMILY** | You'll know that a fun evening lies ahead even before you are seated at your table at this outdoor restaurant, where the pizzas and empanadas are cooked in a wood oven and several different pasta dishes are offered each day. A food truck serves as the main kitchen, kids (and adults) can make their own s'mores around a fire, and strings of taverna lights glow overhead. **Known for:** pizzas from a wood oven; fun atmosphere; make your own s'mores. $ *Average main: MP160* ⊠ *Calles 46 and 49* ⊗ *Closed Mon. and Tues.*

🛏 Hotels

Casa Mate

$ | **HOTEL** | **FAMILY** | At this hotel on the beach, which opened in 2021, the restaurant and reception area have a boho vibe, the rooms are very basic, and the service is more friendly than polished—a description that fits much of El Cuyo. **Pros:** bargain rates; friendly staff; beachfront locaton. **Cons:** spartan rooms; small pools; linens and towels need an upgrade. $ *Rooms from: $70* ⊠ *Av. Veraniega 94* ☎ *999/221–7853* ⊕ *www.facebook.com/CasaMateCuyo* ⋑ *10 rooms* ⏩ *Free Breakfast.*

LunArena

$$ | **HOTEL** | Situated as it is at the eastern end of El Cuyo, LunArena offers a trade-off—on the one hand, the beach here is quiet, but, on the other hand, the location means that you'll have to walk a ways to reach other area amenities. **Pros:** comfortable, beach-chic rooms; hammocks with ocean views; kitchenettes. **Cons:** a bit removed; restaurant is on the expensive side; small pool. $ *Rooms from: $120* ⊠ *Av. Veraniega, El Cuyo* ☎ *984/133–0810* ⊕ *lunarena.com.mx* ⋑ *10 rooms* ⏩ *Free Breakfast.*

Isla Holbox

141 km (87 miles) northeast of Valladolid.

Only 25 km (16 miles) long, tiny Isla Holbox sits at the eastern end of the Ría Lagartos estuary and is just across the state line in neighboring Quintana Roo. Fishing fans come for the ample supply of pampano, bass, and barracuda, while birders appreciate the many avian species that fill the mangrove estuaries on the island's leeward side. Beach bums love the sandy strands strewn with seashells. Although the water is often murky—the Gulf of Mexico and the Caribbean come together here—it's shallow and warm, and there are some nice places to swim.

Sandy streets lead to simple seafood restaurants where conch, octopus, and other delicacies are always fresh. Lodgings here range from bare-bones to beach-luxe, and hotel owners can help set up fishing and bird-watching excursions, as well as expeditions to see the whale sharks that cruise offshore June through August.

Holbox's population numbers some 2,000 lucky souls, and in summer it seems there are as many biting bugs per person. Bring plenty of mosquito repellent. Many locals use baby oil as a natural protection against no-see-ums, also known as biting midges.

■TIP→ Isla Holbox lies in the state of Quintana Roo and falls in a different time zone than other destinations in this chapter. Like Cancún, Holbox is an hour later than Yucatán State during the winter and the same time the rest of the year.

GETTING HERE AND AROUND

From Río Lagartos, take Carretera 176 to Kantunilkin, and then head north on the unnumbered road for 44 km (27 miles) to the port town of Chiquilá (road signs direct you simply to "Holbox"). From Cancún, take the 180 free road toward Mérida and pass through the small town of Leona Vicario; follow the signs to Kantunilkin and continue 40 km (25 miles) until you reach Chiquilá.

The drive from Cancún to Chiquilá takes about three hours depending on road conditions. The road is long and pitted with potholes, so avoid driving at night. You can park at 5 Hermanos, which has covered stalls across from the port for MX$56 a day, and continue by boat to the island.

Ferry schedules vary, but there are normally crossings on the hour from around 6 am to 7 pm. The fare is MX$220, and the trip takes about 35 minutes.

Speedboats will take you over for double the price in half the time. A car ferry makes the trip at 6 am daily, returning at 1 pm, but it's recommended to leave your car in Chiquilá.

If you're feeling flush, Isla Holbox has a rustic airport with a shell-bordered runway that receives small airplanes. You can fly to the island aboard a five-passenger Cesna through AeroSaab. For one person, round-trip airfare from Playa del Carmen, Cozumel, or Cancún costs (in U.S. dollars) $1,234, $1,551, or $1,661 respectively. The total prices go up for more people, but only by small increments, which might make this a better deal if you have a large group and can split the cost.

Little golf-cart taxis ply the island for about MX$300 an hour; you can rent your own for MX$200 an hour—12-hour or full-day rentals normally come out to less per hour. Some hotels also offer their guests complimentary bikes.

AIRLINE CONTACTS AeroSaab.
☎ 998/865–4225 in Playa del Carmen ⊕ aerosaab.com.

TOURS
Holbox Tours
SPECIAL-INTEREST TOURS | FAMILY | Hotel Puerto Holbox offers a variety of tours, from swimming with whale sharks (offered only from June to September) and a bioluminescent bay tour (offered only on moonless nights) to sunset cruises and fishing expeditions. Most are priced per person. ✉ Hotel Puerto Holbox, Av. Pedro Joaquín Coldwell s/n, Isla Holbox ☎ 984/875–2157 ⊕ www. hotelpuertoholbox.com ✉ MX$350 for bioluminescent bay tour.

🍴 Restaurants

Casa Nostra Roof Restaurant
$$ | ITALIAN | The creative menu developed by the Sicilian chef, Giuseppe Genovese (commonly known as

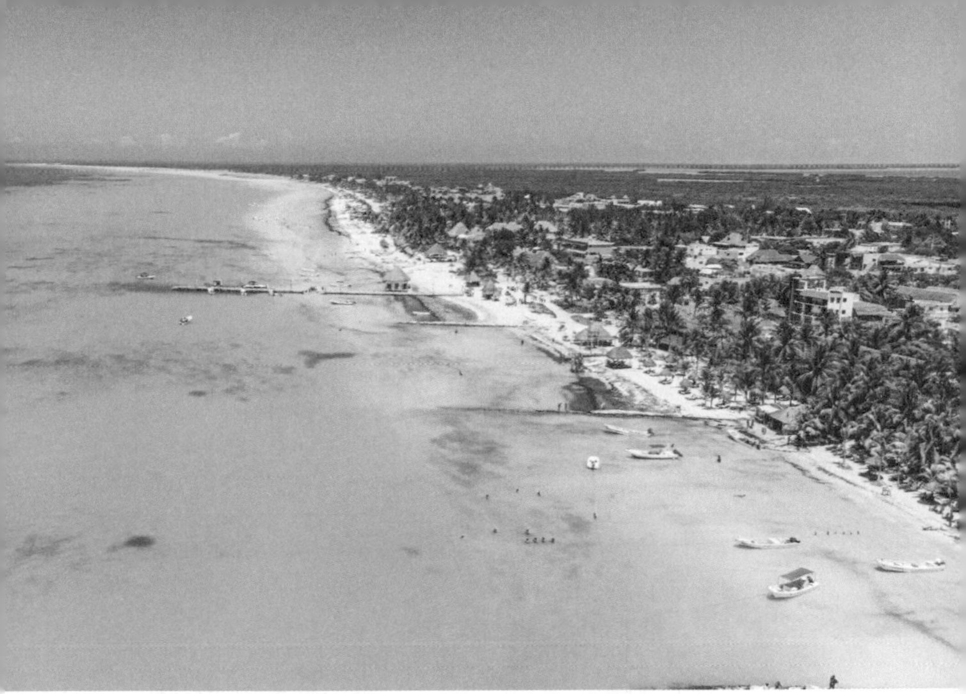

Most visitors access Isla Holbox by ferry.

"Beppe"), offers a mix of Italian, Mediterranean, and Caribbean cuisine. Locals gather for seafood pasta, grilled lobster, octopus salad, and fresh ceviche, all bathed in garlic and olive oil, and breads, sausages, and pizzas are made from scratch in the small kitchen where Beppe works his magic. **Known for:** smoked-ham pizza; authentic tiramisu; gourmet coffee. [$] *Average main: MP220* ✉ *Av. Morelos 231, at Hotel La Palapa* ☎ *984/875–2214.*

El Sushi de Holbox

$$ | **JAPANESE** | This tiny restaurant fills a void in island cuisine with the day's catch transformed into the sushi roll of your choice. Local favorites include the Holbox Rainbow made with shrimp, salmon, tuna, and sea bass. **Known for:** ginger margaritas; terrific sake; creative (if inauthentic) sushi. [$] *Average main: MP250* ✉ *Plaza El Pueblito, Av. Tiburón Ballena, top fl., Isla Holbox* ☎ *1984/132–9507* 🌐 *www.facebook.com/elsushideholbox* 🕒 *Closed Mon. No lunch.*

Mandarina Beach Club & Seaside Restaurant

$$$ | **ECLECTIC** | Chef Jorge Melul, a master baker, has become known on the island for his breads, cakes, and pastas, made from organic, local grown ingredients. For a memorable meal, start with shrimp tempura dipped in chipotle cream or homemade pesto and then order the fish cooked in white wine and topped with spinach and pears. **Known for:** fresh seafood; rooftop bar; beachside setting. [$] *Average main: MP400* ✉ *Casa Las Tortugas, Calle Igualdad s/n, Isla Holbox* ☎ *984/875–2129* 🌐 *www.holboxcasalastortugas.com.*

🛏 Hotels

Hotel Mawimbi

$$ | **HOTEL** | Made up of brightly painted beachside bungalows, this small hotel has rooms that are cozy, simple, and tastefully decorated, featuring pops of color that contrast with the white linens and the exposed wooden beams of the palapa-style roofs. **Pros:** decent rates;

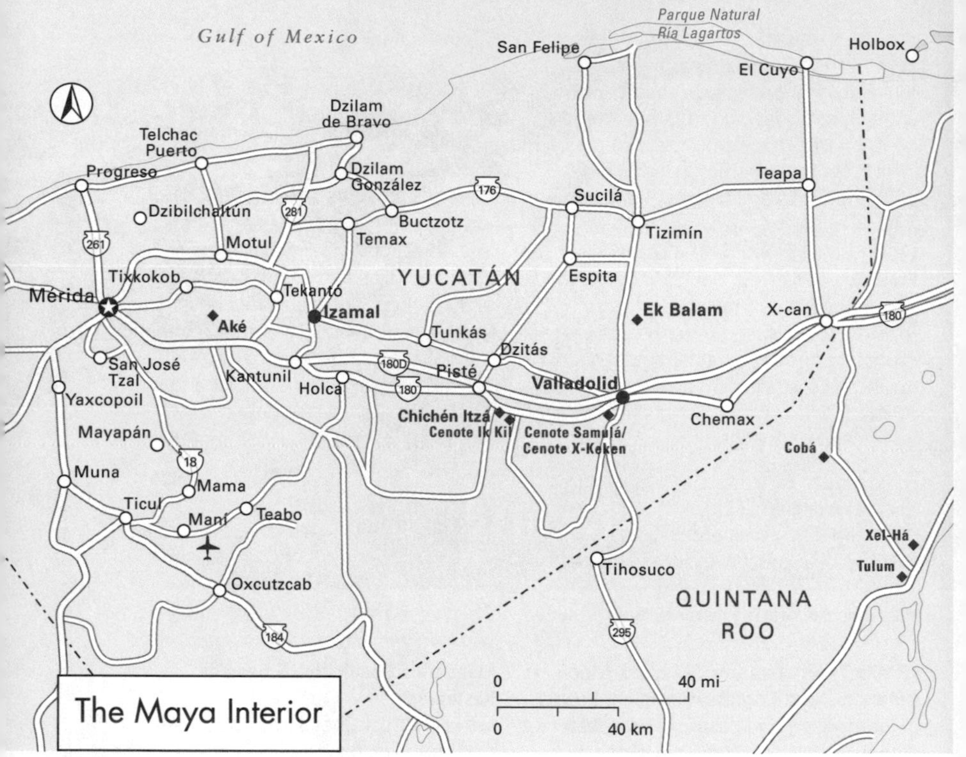

Gulf of Mexico
Parque Natural Ría Lagartos
San Felipe
Holbox
El Cuyo
Dzilam de Bravo
Telchac Puerto
Progreso
Dzilam González
Teapa
176
Sucilá
Dzibilchaltún
281
Buctzotz
Tizimín
261
Motul
Temax
Tixkokob
YUCATÁN
Espita
Mérida
Tekantó
Izamal
Ek Balam
X-can
180
Aké
Tunkás
San José Tzal
Kantunil
180D
Dzitás
Pisté
Holca
180
Valladolid
Yaxcopoil
Chichén Itzá
Cenote Ik Kil
Cenote Samulá/ Cenote X-Keken
Chemax
Mayapán
Cobá
18
Muna
Mama
Ticul
Teabo
Maní
Xel-Há
Tihosuco
Tulum
Oxcutzcab
QUINTANA ROO
184
295
0
40 mi
0
40 km
The Maya Interior

suspended beach beds are great for relaxing; restaurant food couldn't be fresher. **Cons:** cement floors aren't optimal; entryway rooms lack privacy; not all rooms have ocean views. [$] *Rooms from: $160* ✉ *Calle Igualdad s/n, Isla Holbox* ☎ *984/875–2003* 🌐 *www.mawimbi.com* 🛏 *11 rooms* 🍴 *Free Breakfast.*

★ Las Nubes de Holbox

$$$ | **HOTEL** | On the island's remote northeast side, this luxurious waterfront retreat has rooms in four white buildings, complete with tile floors, beamed ceilings, thatched roofs, and contemporary decor. **Pros:** Wi-Fi in every room, plus turndown and room service (all rarities on Holbox); peaceful location; on-site spa and free bikes for exploring. **Cons:** expensive; small beach; far from town. [$] *Rooms from: $250* ✉ *Paseo Kuka s/n, Esq. Calle Camarón* ☎ *984/875–2300* 🌐 *www.lasnubesdeholbox.com* 🛏 *28 rooms* 🍴 *Free Breakfast.*

Punta Caliza

$$ | **HOTEL** | If you follow design blogs or Instagram accounts, photos of Punta Caliza may have already caught your eye—its central pool is surrounded by three white-washed, thatched-roof buildings containing rooms that are elegantly minimalist, with cedar-planked walls and ceilings, concrete floors, crisp white linens, and private plunge pool areas that connect to the main one. **Pros:** innovative layout featuring traditional architectural details; excellent restaurant; spacious, understated rooms. **Cons:** not on the beach; service can be inconsistent; fewer facilities than larger resorts. [$] *Rooms from: $190* ✉ *Paseo Kuka s/n, Isla Holbox* ☎ *998/316–8140* 🌐 *puntacaliza.com* 🛏 *12 rooms* 🍴 *No Meals.*

★ Ser Casasandra

$$$$ | HOTEL | Rustic meets five-star at this elegantly landscaped resort, where winding paths leading to thatched-roof, bougainvillea-draped, white-stucco casitas where accommodations have soothing white-and-beige color schemes, artwork done by the owner, wooden beam ceilings, and hand-painted lamps. **Pros:** Ayurveda treatments; 500-thread-count Egyptian cotton sheets; good restaurant. **Cons:** some rooms get kitchen noise; expensive restaurant; not all rooms have ocean views. $ *Rooms from: $344* ✉ *Calle de la Igualdad s/n, Isla Holbox* ☎ *998/120–7061* ⊕ *www.casasandra.com* ⟿ *19 units* ⦿ *Free Breakfast.*

Villas Flamingos

$$$$ | HOTEL | Rooms at this tranquil, eco-friendly hotel have ocean or garden views, extra large windows, and hammocks, making them perfect for those who want to feel the sea breeze or fall asleep to the sound of crashing waves. **Pros:** eco-friendly property; nice pool; only beach house on the island. **Cons:** 20-minute walk to town; rustic design isn't for everyone; rooms could use some upgrades. $ *Rooms from: $320* ✉ *Calle Paseo Kuka s/n, Isla Holbox* ☎ *984/875–2167* ⊕ *www.villasflamingos.com* ⟿ *30 rooms* ⦿ *Free Breakfast.*

Villas HM Paraíso del Mar

$$ | RESORT | Not only is the island's largest property right on the beach, but it has everything you need to be comfortable—an open-air palapa lobby, a *temazcal* (Maya sweat lodge), a large pool, a buffet-style restaurant, manicured gardens laced with sandy paths leading to freestanding, bungalow-style accommodations. **Pros:** island's only all-inclusive property; nice breakfast buffet; massage services available. **Cons:** some rooms lack ocean views; beach could use more cleaning; Wi-Fi in common areas only. $ *Rooms from: $150* ✉ *Av. Plutarco Elias s/n, Isla Holbox* ☎ *984/875–2062* ⊕ *www.villashmparaisodelmar.com* ⟿ *58 rooms* ⦿ *All-Inclusive.*

🛍 Shopping

Lolita Holbox

WOMEN'S CLOTHING | This boutique right in the center of town has an excellent selection of beach-chic essentials including wraps, swimsuits, beach bags, and flip-flops. Lolita also has jewelry and some home goods. Their men's offerings are not as extensive as their women's, but they do carry some trunks and shirts. ✉ *Av. Damero, Isla Holbox* ☎ *984/875–2478* ⊕ *www.facebook.com/holboxlolita.*

Aké

36 km (22 miles) east of Mérida

This compact archaeological site features architecture that spans two millennia.

👁 Sights

Aké

RUINS | FAMILY | Experts estimate that Aké was populated between AD 250 and 900; today many people in the area have Aké as a surname. The city seems to have been related to the very important and powerful one at present-day Izamal. In fact, the two cities were once connected by a *sacbé* (white road) 13 meters (43 feet) wide and 33 km (20 miles) long. All that has been excavated so far are two pyramids, one with rows of columns (35 total) at the top, reminiscent of the Toltec columns at Tula, north of Mexico City.

Nearby, workers process sisal in a rusty-looking factory, which was built in the early 20th century. To the right of this dilapidated building are the ruins of the Hacienda and Iglesia de San Lorenzo Aké, both constructed of stones taken from Maya buildings. ✉ *Near Tixkokob, 32 km (19 miles) east of Mérida, Mérida* ⊕ *www.inah.gob.mx* 🎟 *MX$70.*

Hotels

Hacienda San José
$$$ | **HOTEL** | The perfect base for exploring the Aké ruins and Izamal to the east, as well as Mérida, a short drive west, this restored cattle ranch transports you back in time with its hammock-adorned sitting areas, 18-foot ceilings, exposed beams, wooden double doors, canopy beds, and tile floors. **Pros:** authentic hacienda experience; suites and villas have private plunge pools; a world-class spa. **Cons:** too remote for some; difficult to find; just one on-site restaurant (though it serves all meals). [$] *Rooms from: $250* ✉ *Carretera Tixkobob-Tekanto, Km 30, Mérida* ☎ *999/924–1333* 🌐 *www.ihg.com/spnd/hotels/us/en/tixkokob/midsj/hoteldetail* 🛏 *15 rooms* 🍴 *No Meals.*

Izamal

68 km (42 miles) east of Mérida.

One of the best examples of a Spanish colonial community in the Yucatán, Izamal is nicknamed "la Ciudad Amarilla" (the Yellow City), because so many buildings in its historic center are painted a golden ocher, which contrasts strikingly with the blue sky. It's also sometimes called "the City of Three Cultures" because of its combination of pre-Hispanic, colonial, and contemporary influences. Izamal makes a charming and lower-key alternative to the sometimes frenetic Mérida. Hotels are humble, and the few restaurants here offer basic fare. If you enjoy a quieter and slower-paced vacation, it's worth considering it as a base.

GETTING HERE AND AROUND

The drive east from Mérida takes less than an hour on Carretera 180. Calesas (horse-drawn carriages) are stationed at the town's large main square, fronting the lovely cathedral, day and night. Drivers—whose English capabilities vary widely—charge about MX$100 an hour for sightseeing, and many will also take you on a shopping tour to purchase items like hammocks or jewelry. Pick up a brochure at the visitor center for details.

VISITOR INFORMATION

CONTACT Oficina de Turismo. ✉ *Calle 30 323, between Calles 31 and 31A, Centro* ☎ *988/954–1096.*

Sights

Centro Cultural y Artesanal Izamal
ART MUSEUM | Banamex has set up this small, well-organized art museum right on the main plaza. The beautiful crafts on display include textiles, ceramics, papier-mâché, and woodwork. The center also has a little on-site café and gift shop. ✉ *Calle 31 s/n 201, Izamal* ☎ *988/954–1012* 🎟 *MX$30* 🕒 *Closed Mon.*

Ex-Convento e Iglesia de San Antonio de Padua
CHURCH | **FAMILY** | Facing the main plaza, the enormous 16th-century former monastery and church of St. Anthony of Padua is perched on—and built from—the remains of a Maya pyramid devoted to Itzamná, god of the heavens. The monastery's ocher-painted church, where Pope John Paul II led prayers in 1993, has a gigantic atrium (supposedly second in size only to the Vatican's) facing a colonnaded facade and rows of 75 white-trimmed arches. The Virgin of the Immaculate Conception, to whom the church is dedicated, is the patron saint of the Yucatán. A statue of Nuestra Señora de Izamal, or Our Lady of Izamal, was brought here from Guatemala in 1562 by Bishop Diego de Landa. Miracles are ascribed to her, and a yearly pilgrimage takes place in her honor. Frescoes of saints at the front of the church, once plastered over, were rediscovered and refurbished in 1996.

The monastery and church are now illuminated in a light-and-sound show of the type common at some archaeological sites. You can catch a Spanish-only

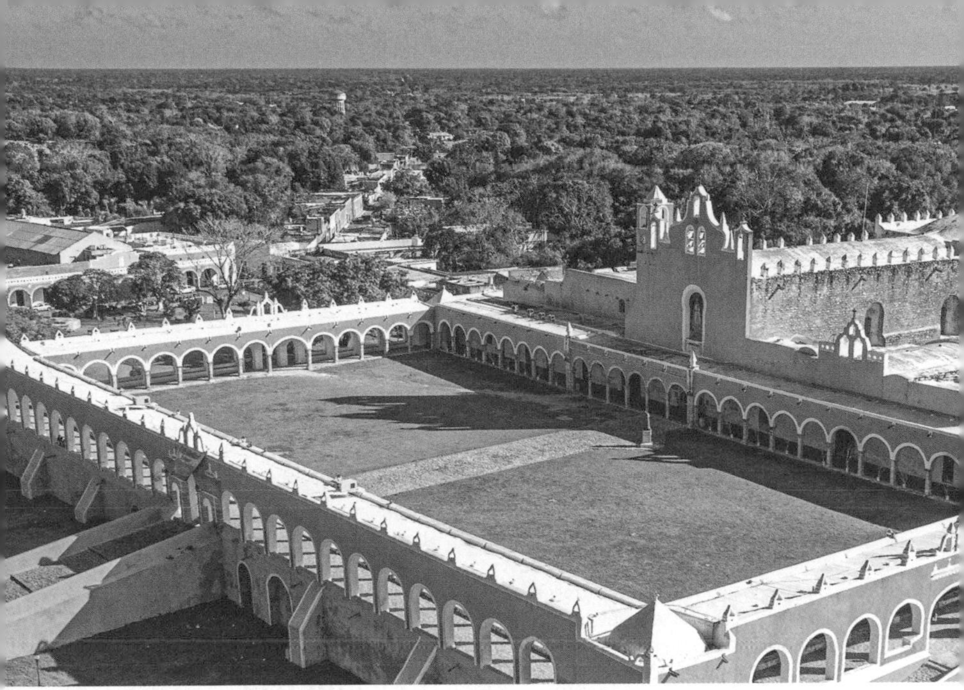

Izamal's San Antonio de Padua was built atop a Maya pyramid.

narration and the play of lights on the nearly 500-year-old structure at 8:30 every night but Sunday. ■ **TIP→ Diagonally across from the cathedral, the small municipal market is worth a wander. It's the kind of place where if you stop to watch how the merchants prepare food, they may let you in on their cooking secrets.** ✉ *Bounded by Calles 31, 28, 33, and 30, Izamal.*

Kinich Kakmó

RUINS | **FAMILY** | The Kinich Kakmó pyramid was the largest pre-Hispanic construction in the Yucatán and is the third-largest pyramid in Mexico, after the Pyramid of the Sun at Teotihuacan and the Cholula Pyramid near Puebla. It's all that remains of the royal Maya city that flourished here between AD 250 and 600. Dedicated to a Maya sun god, the massive structure is more remarkable for its size than for any remaining decoration. ✉ *Calles 39 and 40, Izamal* 🎫 *Free.*

🍴 Restaurants

Restaurante Kinich

$ | **MEXICAN** | **FAMILY** | At the town's most comfortable eatery, tables draped in white linen sit under a wide palapa that's surrounded by plants and with a burbling fountain. In a small hut in the back, the cooks make tortillas by hand, and menu highlights include locally made *longaniza* (a tasty grilled pork sausage) and excellent sopa de lima. **Known for:** longaniza (a local sausage); folk art; traditional atmosphere. [$] *Average main: MP190* ✉ *Calle 27 299, between Calles 28 and 30, Izamal* ☎ *999/900–2316* 🌐 *restaurantekinich.com.*

Restaurante Muul

$ | **MEXICAN** | **FAMILY** | Residents of Izamal have strong opinions on which restaurants make the best panuchos, salbutes, papadzules, and other local specialities, but Restaurante Muul is on many short lists. The atmosphere is no-frills, though the location is convenient, right on the main plaza just steps from the ex-convent. **Known for:** location on the main plaza; local specialties; good value. [$] *Average main: MP100* ✉ *Calle 28 300, near Calle 31, Izamal* ☎ *988/967–8006* 🌐 *www.facebook.com/muul.restaurante.*

Hotels

Hacienda Sacnicte

$$ | B&B/INN | Three miles north of town, this 1811 hacienda strikes a perfect balance between the old and the new in dramatic rooms and suites with contemporary paintings, antique mirrors, polished cement floors, handcrafted Mexican furnishings, and spacious bathrooms that feature vanity areas and walk-in showers built with local stones. **Pros:** delicious breakfast; beautiful landscaping; wonderful staff. **Cons:** owners rarely on-site; pricey; not centrally located. [$] *Rooms from: $120* ✉ *Carretera a Tekal de Venegas, Km. 5, Izamal* ☎ *988/967–4668 cell phone* 🌐 *www.haciendasacnicte.mx* 🛏 *10 rooms* 🍴 *Free Breakfast.*

★ Hacienda Santo Domingo

$ | B&B/INN | Amid gardens full of exotic plants and fruit trees, as well as sheep and two friendly dogs, this 20-acre property has spacious, freestanding rooms that are sparingly decorated with folk art (some even have carved Maya stones incorporated into their walls). **Pros:** exceptional restaurant; close to town center; cooking lessons available. **Cons:** Wi-Fi in common areas only; not everyone loves animals; the lush gardens also come with mosquitoes at times. [$] *Rooms from: $70* ✉ *Calle 18, between Calles 33 and 35, Izamal* ☎ *988/967–6136* 🌐 *www.izamalhotel.com* 🛏 *10 rooms* 🍴 *Free Breakfast.*

Macan Ché Garden Hotel

$ | B&B/INN | Each artsy bungalow here has its own themed decor—the Asian room has a Chinese checkers board and origami decorations, while the Safari room has artifacts from Mexico and Africa. **Pros:** great price; private yoga classes available; feels like a hidden village. **Cons:** several blocks from central plaza; some rooms lack a/c; mosquitoes can be an issue. [$] *Rooms from: $60* ✉ *Calle 22 305, between Calles 33 and 35, Izamal* ☎ *988/954–0287* 🌐 *www.macanche.com* 🛏 *15 rooms* 🍴 *Free Breakfast.*

Shopping

Hecho a Mano

CRAFTS | FAMILY | The only place in town to buy folk art from all over Mexico is just off the main square at the San Miguel Hotel. You'll find something to suit any budget, including a collection of textiles. ✉ *Calle 31A 308, Izamal* ☎ *988/954–0344* 🌐 *www.sanmiguelhotel.com.mx/hotel/handicrafts.*

Chichén Itzá

120 km (74 miles) east of Mérida, 76 km (47 miles) east of Izamal, 48 km (30 miles) west of Valladolid.

In 2007, this sublime Maya city was named one of the "New Seven Wonders of the World"—a distinction that puts Chichén Itzá on par with Peru's Machu Picchu and the Great Wall of China. Now, more than a million people per year come from all over the world to admire it.

If you want to devote more than a day to the magnificent and mysterious ruins, consider staying 2 km (1½ miles) west in Pisté, a tiny town that feels more like a base camp. Hotels, restaurants, and shops there tend to be less expensive than those just outside the ruins in the Zona Hotelera (Hotel Zone).

GETTING HERE AND AROUND

From Mérida, you can reach Chichén Itzá along the Carretera 180D or Carretera 180 in two or three hours respectively. For a more scenic and interesting alternative, head east on Carretera 281 to Tixkokob (a Maya community famous for its hammock weavers) and continue on through Citilcúm and Izamal. From there, drive through the small, untouristy towns of Dzudzal and Xanaba en route to Kantunil, where you can hop on the toll road or continue on the free road that parallels it through Holca and Libre Unión (both of which have very swimmable cenotes). The trip will take four to five hours.

■ TIP→ **If coming from Cancún or the Riviera Maya on a day trip, don't forget that Chichén Itzá is an hour earlier—Yucatán is on Central Standard Time while Quintana Roo is on Eastern Standard Time. Neither state follows daylight savings time.**

◉ Sights

Cenote Ik Kil
BODY OF WATER | FAMILY | When you've exhausted your interest in archaeology—or are just plain exhausted—Cenote Ik Kil (meaning "place of the winds") offers a refreshing change of pace. Located across from the Doralba Inn in Pisté, this is an especially photogenic cenote to swim in. Lockers, changing facilities, showers, and life jackets are available. ✉ *Carretera 180, Km 122, Chichén-Itzá* ☎ *999/437–0148* ⊕ *cenoteikkil.com* 🎫 *MX$180.*

★ Chichén Itzá
RUINS | FAMILY | Little is known about those who founded this dramatic, 6-square-km (2¼-square-mile) metropolis. Some structures, likely built in the 5th century, predate the arrival of the Itzá, the people who occupied the city starting around the late 8th and early 9th centuries. Why they abandoned it in the early 1200s is also unknown, as is its subsequent role. What is known is that the city's name means "the mouth of the well of the Itzá," likely referring to the site's several cenotes—valuable sources of water.

Dominating Mexico's most stunning and well-preserved Maya site is El Castillo (The Castle), also known by its Mayan name, Kukulkán. The much-photographed pyramid is remarkable not only for its size, but also for its perfectly proportioned symmetry. Adorning the corners of its four stairways (no, climbing is *not* allowed) are open-jawed serpent statues that honor the priest-king Kukulcán (aka Quetzalcóatl), an incarnation of the feathered serpent god. More serpents appear in sculpted columns atop the building.

At the spring and fall equinoxes, the afternoon light strikes the pyramid so that the snake god's shadow appears to undulate down the side of it to bless the fertile earth. Thousands of people, from sightseers to shamans, travel here to witness this phenomenon. Make lodging reservations far in advance if you hope to join them.

Archaeologists are still abuzz about the 2015 discovery of a subterranean river flowing underneath the pyramid, detected via "electrical resistance survey." Although the Maya would likely have intentionally constructed El Castillo over such a river cavern, there is concern that this will lead to the formation of a gigantic sinkhole that would threaten the structure's foundation. Although experts say this would probably not happen for several generations, time will tell.

Just west of El Castillo is another highlight: the Anexo del Templo de los Jaguares (Annex to the Temple of the Jaguars), where bas-relief carvings represent still other important deities. To its west is the Juego de Pelota, the city's main ball court. Remarkably, if you stand at one end of it and whisper something, it will be heard all the way at the other end. The game played on this ball court was apparently something like soccer (no hands were used), but it likely had some sort of ritualistic significance. (Note that the Mérida tourist offices stages a popular demonstration of the ball game each Friday evening in front of the cathedral.)

Continued on page 312

7

Yucatán and Campeche States CHICHÉN ITZÁ

The towering El Castillo pyramid, nearly 80 feet high, is the most striking structure at Chichén Itzá. Each side of the pyramid has 91 steps, which, with the addition of the topmost platform, equal 365, one for each day of the calendar year. At the vernal and autumnal equinoxes, thousands of people gather to watch as the shadow of the serpent god Kukulcán seems to slither down the side of the pyramid.

CHICHÉN ITZÁ

One of the most beautiful of the ancient Maya cities, Chichén Itzá draws some 3,000 visitors a day from all over the world. Since the remains of this once-thriving kingdom were explored by Europeans and Americans in the mid 1800s, many of the travelers who make the pilgrimage here have been archaeologists and scholars who study the structures and glyphs and try to piece together the mysteries surrounding them. While the artifacts here give fascinating insight into the Maya civilization, they also raise many, many unanswered questions.

The name of this ancient city, which means "the mouth of the well of the Itzás," is a mystery in and of itself. Although it likely refers to the valuable water sources at the site (there are several sinkholes here), experts have little information about who might have actually founded the city—some structures, likely built in the 5th century, pre-date the arrival of the Itzás who occupied the city starting around the late-8th and early-9th centuries. The reason why the Itzás abandoned the city, around 1224, is also unknown.

Scholars and archaeologists aside, most of the visitors who converge on Chichén Itzá come to marvel at its beauty, not ponder its significance. This ancient metropolis, which encompasses 6 square km (2½ square miles), is known around the world as one of the most stunning and well-preserved Maya sites in existence.

Opposite: The main pyramid, El Castillo, is also called the Temple of Kukulcán.
Top: Carvings of ball players adorn the walls of the Juego de Pelota.
Bottom: Maya statue

MAJOR SITES AND ATTRACTIONS

Rows of freestanding columns where the roof has long since disintegrated

The sight of the immense ❶ **El Castillo** pyramid, rising imposingly yet gracefully from the surrounding plain, has been known to produce goose pimples on sight. El Castillo (The Castle) dominates the site both in size and in the symmetry of its perfect proportions. Open-jawed serpent statues adorn the corners of each of the pyramid's four stairways, honoring the legendary priest-king Kukulcán (also known as Quetzalcóatl), an incarnation of the feathered serpent god. More serpents appear at the top of the building as sculpted columns. At the spring and fall equinoxes, the afternoon light strikes the trapezoidal structure so that the shadow of the snake-god appears to undulate down the side of the pyramid to bless the fertile earth. Thousands of people travel to the site each year to see this phenomenon.

At the base of the temple's north side, an interior staircase leads to two marvelous statues deep within:

a stone jaguar and the god Chacmool, who is, as usual, in a reclining position, with a flat spot on his belly for receiving sacrifices. (Although El Castillo's interior isn't generally open to visitors, the site has four other Chacmool figures, including a prominent one at the Templo de los Guerreros.)

On the ❷ **Anexo del Templo de los Jaguares** (Annex to the Temple of the Jaguars), just west of El Castillo, bas-relief carvings represent other deities. On the bottom of the columns, for instance, you can see the Toltec rain god, Tlaloc. It's no surprise that his tears represent rain, but why is he honored here, instead of his Maya counterpart, Chaac? That's one of many questions that archaeologists and epigraphers have been trying to answer ever since explorers John Lloyd Stephens and Frederick Catherwood first encountered the site in 1840.

Scholars once thought that the depictions of foreign gods and differing architectural styles and features—including a Toltec-style tzompantli, a stone platform decorated with row upon row of sculpted human skulls—proved that the Toltecs of central Mexico conquered Chichén Itzá. Most experts now agree, however, that Chichén Itzá was merely influenced by Toltec trading partners.

The flat part of a reclining Chacmool statue is where sacrificial offerings were laid.

Below: Court where players passed a ball through high stone loops.
Right: Site carvings indicate that games may have ended with beheadings.

Just west of the Anexo del Templo de los Jaguares is another puzzle: the auditory marvel of Chichén Itzá's main ball court. At 149 meters, this ❸ **Juego de Pelota** is the largest in Mesoamerica. Yet if you stand at one end of the playing field and whisper something to a friend at the other end, incredibly, you will be heard. The game played on this ball court was apparently something like soccer (no hands were used), but it likely had some sort of ritualistic significance. Carvings on the low walls surrounding the field show a decapitation, blood spurting from the victim's neck to fertilize the earth. Whether this is a historical depiction (perhaps the losers or winners of the game were sacrificed?) or a symbolic scene, we can only guess.

North of El Castillo, a ruined *sacbé* (white road) leads from a small temple dedicated to the planet Venus to the deep, straight-sided ❹ **Cenote Sagrado** (Holy Sinkhole), where Jacques Cousteau recovered about 80 skeletons and thousands of pieces of jewelry and figures of jade, obsidian, wood, bone, and turquoise. South of El Castillo and directly aligned with this cloudy green sinkhole, which was probably used for rituals, is the pristine ❺ **Cenote Xtaloc**, which was likely used for bathing and drinking.

Adjacent to this water source is a steam bath, its interior lined with benches along the wall like those you'd see in any steam room today. Outside, a tiny pool was used for cooling down during the ritual.

VISITING INFO

■ The question on everybody's lips is: "May I climb the pyramid?" The answer is a resounding "No." Wear on the staircases and visitor injuries have necessitated an end to the climbing.

■ The site is open daily 8–5; admission is MX$90. For greater insight, hire a multilingual guide at the ticket booth. Tours last about two hours and cost about MX$750 for up to seven people.

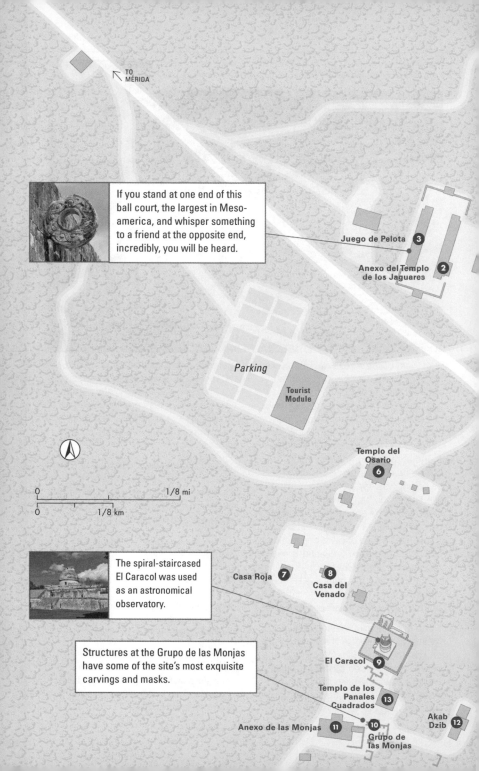

TO MÉRIDA

If you stand at one end of this ball court, the largest in Meso-america, and whisper something to a friend at the opposite end, incredibly, you will be heard.

Juego de Pelota **3**

Anexo del Templo de los Jaguares **2**

Parking

Tourist Module

Templo del Osario **6**

0 ——————— 1/8 mi
0 ——————— 1/8 km

The spiral-staircased El Caracol was used as an astronomical observatory.

Casa Roja **7**

Casa del Venado **8**

El Caracol **9**

Structures at the Grupo de las Monjas have some of the site's most exquisite carvings and masks.

Templo de los Panales Cuadrados **13**

Akab Dzib **12**

Anexo de las Monjas **11**

10

Grupo de las Monjas

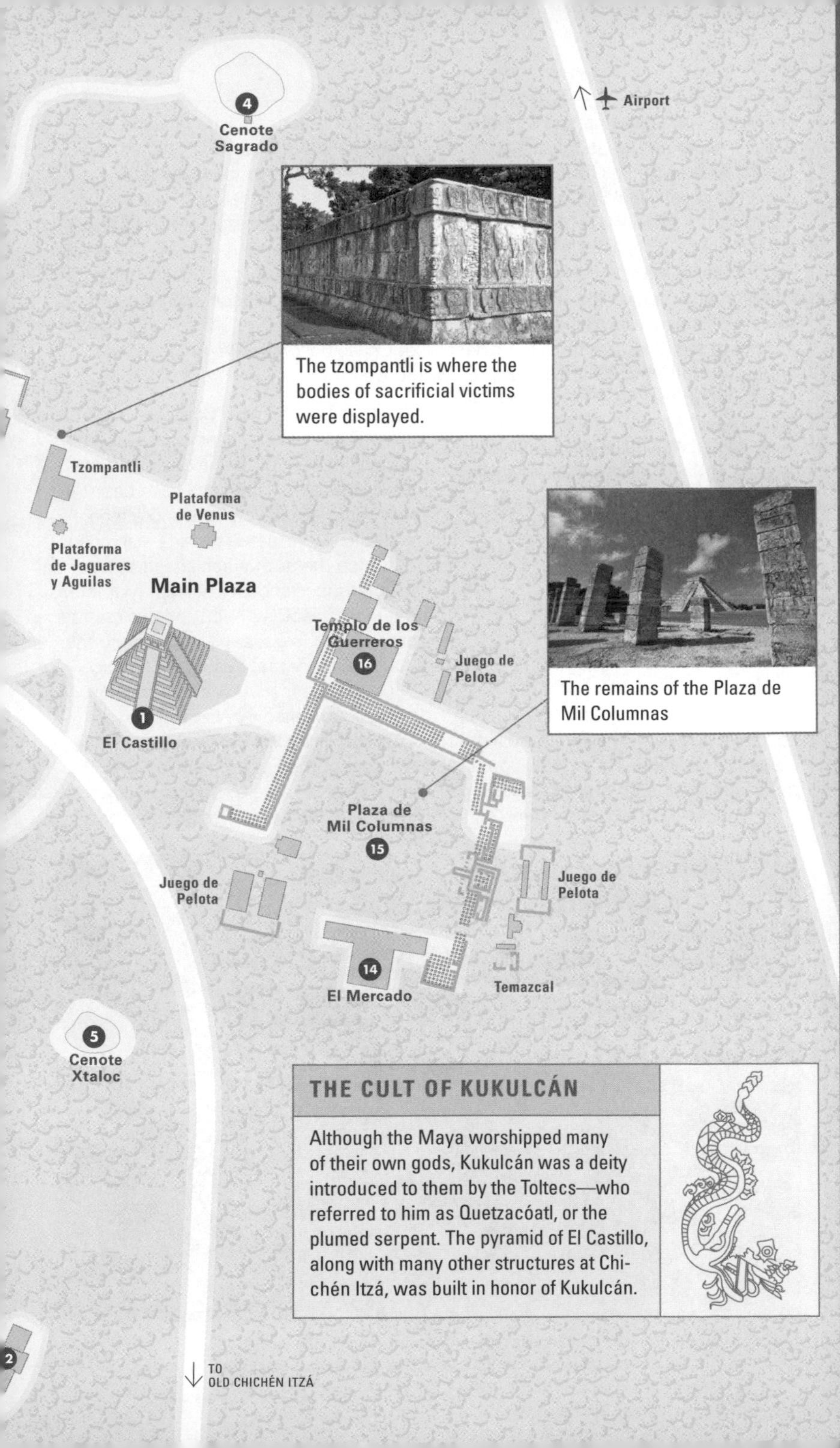
Airport
4
Cenote Sagrado
Tzompantli
Plataforma de Venus
Plataforma de Jaguares y Aguilas
Main Plaza
Templo de los Guerreros
16
Juego de Pelota
1
El Castillo
Plaza de Mil Columnas
15
Juego de Pelota
Juego de Pelota
14
El Mercado
Temazcal
5
Cenote Xtaloc
2
TO OLD CHICHÉN ITZÁ

The tzompantli is where the bodies of sacrificial victims were displayed.

The remains of the Plaza de Mil Columnas

THE CULT OF KUKULCÁN

Although the Maya worshipped many of their own gods, Kukulcán was a deity introduced to them by the Toltecs—who referred to him as Quetzacóatl, or the plumed serpent. The pyramid of El Castillo, along with many other structures at Chichén Itzá, was built in honor of Kukulcán.

The older Maya structures at Chichén Itzá are south and west of Cenote Xtaloc. Archaeologists have been restoring several buildings in this area, including the ❻ **Templo del Osario** (Ossuary Temple), which, as its name implies, concealed several tombs with skeletons and offerings. Behind the smaller ❼ **Casa Roja** (Red House) and ❽ **Casa del Venado** (House of the Deer) are the site's oldest structures, including ❾ **El Caracol** (The Snail), one of the few round buildings built by the Maya, with a spiral staircase within. Clearly built as a celestial observatory, it has eight tiny windows precisely aligned with the points of the compass rose. Scholars now know that Maya priests studied the planets and the stars; in fact, they were able to accurately predict the orbits of Venus and the moon, and the appearance of comets and eclipses. To modern astronomers, this is nothing short of amazing.

The Maya of Chichén Itzá were not just scholars, however. They were skilled artisans and architects as well. South of El Caracol, the ❿ **Grupo de las Monjas** (The Nunnery complex) has some of the site's most exquisite facades. A combination of Puuc and Chenes styles dominates here, with playful latticework, masks, and gargoyle-like serpents. On the east side of the ⓫ **Anexo de las Monjas** (Nunnery Annex), the facade celebrates the rain god Chaac. In typical Chenes style, the doorway represents an entrance into the underworld; figures of Chaac decorate the ornate facade above.

South of the Nunnery Complex is an area where field archaeologists are still excavating (fewer than a quarter of the structures at Chichén Itzá have been fully restored). If you have more than a superficial interest in the site—and can convince the authorities ahead of time of your importance, or at least your interest in archaeology—you can explore this area, which is generally not open to the public. Otherwise, head back toward El Castillo past the ruins of a housing compound called ⓬ **Akab Dzib** and the ⓭ **Templo de los Panales Cuadrados** (Temple of the Square Panels). The latter shows more evidence of Toltec influence: instead of weight-bearing

The doorway of the Anexo de las Monjas represents an entrance to the underworld.

The Templo de los Guerreros shows the influence of Toltec architecture.

Maya arches—or "false arches"—that traditionally supported stone roofs, this structure has stone columns but no roof. This means that the building was once roofed, Toltec-style, with perishable materials (most likely palm thatch or wood) that have long since disintegrated.

Beyond El Caracol, Casa Roja, and El Osario, the right-hand path follows an ancient sacbé (an ancient stone road network) now collapsed. A mud-and-straw hut, which the Maya called a na, has been reproduced here to show the simple implements used before and after the Spanish conquest. On one side of the room are a typical pre-Hispanic table, seat, fire pit, and reed baskets; on the other, the Christian cross and colonial-style table of the post-conquest Maya.

Behind the tiny oval house, several unexcavated mounds still guard their secrets. The path meanders through a small grove of oak and slender bean trees to the building known today as **14 El Mercado.** This market was likely

one end of a huge outdoor market whose counterpart structure, on the other side of the grove, is the **15 Plaza de Mil Columnas** (Plaza of the Thousand Columns). In typical Toltec-Maya style, the roof once covering the parallel rows of round stone columns in this long arcade has disappeared, giving the place a strangely Greek—and distinctly non-Maya—look. But the curvy-nosed Chaacs on the corners of the adjacent **16 Templo de los Guerreros** are pure Maya. Why their noses are pointing down, like an upside-down "U," instead of up, as usual, is another mystery to be solved.

Columns at Templo de los Guerreros.

On the other side of El Castillo, just before a small temple dedicated to the planet Venus, a ruined *sacbé,* or raised white road, leads to the Cenote Sagrado (Holy Well), which was probably for ritualistic purposes. The nearby Cenote Xtaloc was kept pristine, undoubtedly for bathing and drinking. Adjacent to it is a steam bath, outside of which is a tiny pool that was used for cooling down.

Older Maya structures lie south and west of Cenote Xtaloc. Archaeologists have been restoring several buildings in this area, including the Templo del Osario (Ossuary Temple), which concealed several tombs with skeletons and offerings. Behind the smaller Casa Roja (Red House) and Casa del Venado (House of the Deer) are the site's oldest structures, including El Caracol (The Snail), a round building—rare in Maya architecture—with an interior spiral staircase. With eight tiny windows precisely aligned with the points of the compass rose, it was seemingly built as a celestial observatory.

■ **TIP→ If the Maya gods are smiling, the evening sound-and-light show—which features images projected on El Castillo—won't be plagued by technical issues during your visit.** Though some say the show is cheesy, others say it's stunning. Regardless, it offers a different perspective on this remarkable site. It takes place at 8 pm from April through October and at 7 pm the rest of the year. Reservations are required, and you can make them online (🌐 *nochesdekukulkan.com.mx*) or through a tour operator. Tickets are pricey but include a 30-minute pre-show guided walk and use of a translation device (original narration is in Spanish only). ✥ *Off Carretera 180, 2 km (1½ miles) east of Pisté* ☎ *985/851–0137* 🌐 *www.inah.gob.mx* 🎫 *Site: MX$90. Sound-and-light show: MX$630.*

Hotels

Doloralba Inn

$ | HOTEL | FAMILY | A longtime favorite of international travelers, this family-run spot with a small motel feel is the best budget choice near the ruins. **Pros:** convivial vibe and cheap prices; close to ruins; transport to ruins is included (return transport is not). **Cons:** small rooms; some rooms lack a/c; weak Wi-Fi signal. [$] *Rooms from: $50* ✉ *Carretera 180, Km 122, 3 km (2 miles) east of Chichén Itzá, Chichén-Itzá* ☎ *985/851–0117* 🌐 *www.doloresalba.com* 🛏 *30 rooms* 🍴 *Free Breakfast.*

★ Hacienda Chichén & Yaxkin Spa

$$ | HOTEL | At this refurbished butter-yellow hacienda, cottages are all uniquely decorated with the owner's artwork and vintage furniture and are connected by pathways that wind through beautiful grounds complete with pool surrounded by palms. **Pros:** short walk from ruins; amazing spa and gardens; on-site organic farm. **Cons:** pricey; no in-room TV or Internet; restaurant is just OK. [$] *Rooms from: $179* ✉ *Carretera 180, Km 120, Chichén-Itzá* ☎ *999/924–4222, 877/631–4005* 🌐 *www.haciendachichen.com* 🛏 *28 rooms* 🍴 *No Meals.*

Hotel Chichén Itzá

$ | HOTEL | FAMILY | Just over 1½ km (1 mile) from Chichén Itzá in the town of Pisté, this two-story hotel surrounding a pool feels like a motel in a very unlikely setting—a large grassy area edged with banana plants and other tropical trees and flowers. **Pros:** minutes from ruins; big pool; kind staff. **Cons:** no room service; mediocre food; room amenities vary (check out a few if possible). [$] *Rooms from: $69* ✉ *Calle 15 45, Chichén-Itzá* ☎ *985/851–0022, 877/240–5864 in the U.S.* 🌐 *www.mayaland.com* 🛏 *44 rooms* 🍴 *No Meals.*

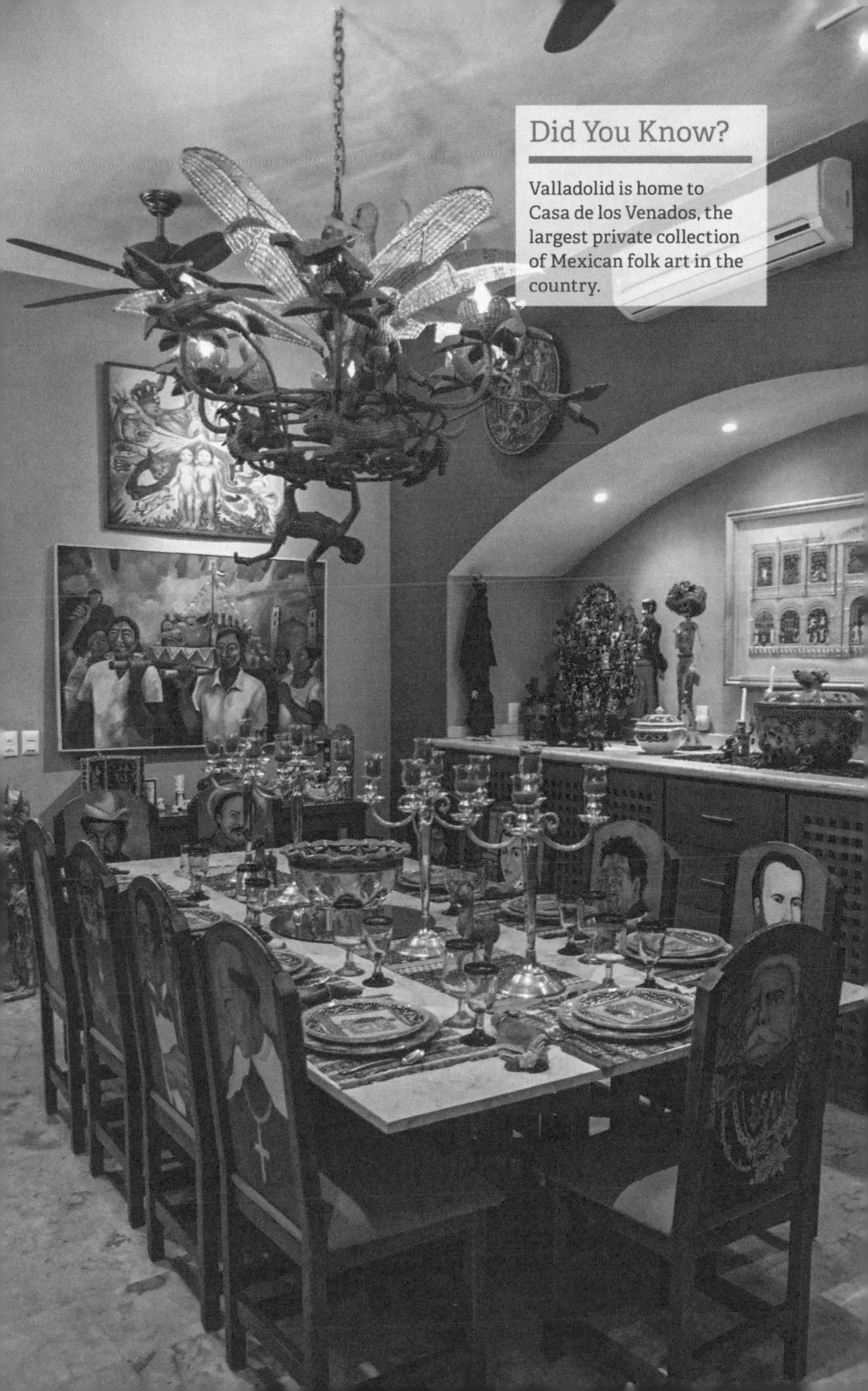

Did You Know?

Valladolid is home to Casa de los Venados, the largest private collection of Mexican folk art in the country.

You can swim in Cenote X-Keken (for a price).

Valladolid

161 km (97 miles) east of Mérida, 44 km (27 miles) east of Chichén Itzá, 146 km (88 miles) west of Cancún.

The second-largest city in Yucatán State, picturesque Valladolid (pronounced vye-ah-do-*leed*) has seen a big boom in popularity among travelers en route to or from Chichén Itzá. (It's a far closer base for exploring the ruins than either Mérida or Cancún.)

Francisco de Montejo founded Valladolid in 1543 on the site of the Maya town of Sisal. The city suffered during the Caste War of the Yucatán—when the Maya in revolt killed nearly all Spanish residents—and again during the Mexican Revolution.

Despite its turbulent history, Valladolid's downtown contains many colonial and 19th-century structures. For a taste of local life, check out the Sunday-morning demonstrations of Yucatecan folk dancing in the main square; you can return at 8 pm, when the city's orchestra plays elegant, stylized *danzón*—waltzlike music to which expressionless couples swirl (think tango: no smiling allowed).

If you need help getting oriented, Valladolid's phenomenal municipal tourist office is open daily on the southeast corner of the square. You can also look for the bilingual tourist police dressed in spiffy white polo shirts and navy-blue baseball caps and trousers.

GETTING HERE AND AROUND

The drive from Mérida to Valladolid via the toll road takes about 2 hours; budget about 2½ hours if driving from Cancún. The tolls will be about MX$223 and MX$385 respectively. The free road cuts through several small towns where speed bumps, street repairs, and traffic increases travel time significantly. ADO (⊕ *www.ado.com.mx*) has direct buses from Mérida and Cancún to Valladolid, and other Mexican cities.

Sacred Cenotes

Like their ancient forebears, tradition-bound modern-day Maya consider holes in the ground—be they sinkholes, cenotes, or caves—conduits to the world of the spirits. As sources of water in a land of no surface rivers, sinkholes are of special importance. Cenotes were used as prayer sites and shrines. Indeed, sacred objects and sacrificial victims were thrown in the sacred cenote at Chichén Itzá, and in others near large ceremonial centers in ancient times.

There are at least 2,800 known cenotes in the Yucatán. Rainwater sinks through the peninsula's thin soil and porous limestone to create underground rivers, while leaving the dry surface river-free.

Some pondlike sinkholes are found near ground level; most require a bit more effort to access, however. Near downtown Valladolid, Cenote Zací is named for the Maya town conquered by the Spanish. It's a relatively simple saunter down a series of cement steps to reach the cool green water.

Lesser-known sinkholes are yours to discover, especially in the so-called "zona de cenotes." To explore this area southeast of Mérida, you can hire a guide through the Yucatán State tourism office or, if you're in Valladolid, through its city tourism office. Another option is to head directly for the ex-hacienda of Chunkanan, 3 km (2 miles) from the town of Cuzama, about 30 minutes southeast of Mérida. Here former henequen workers will hitch their horses to tiny open railway carts and take you along the unused train tracks. The reward for this bumpy, sometimes dusty ride is a swim in several incredible cenotes.

Almost every local has a "secret" cenote; ask around, and perhaps you'll find a favorite of your own.

VISITOR INFORMATION

CONTACT Oficina de Turismo. ⊠ *Palacio Municipal, Calles 40 and 41, Valladolid* ☎ *985/856–2551* ⊕ *valladolidmx.travel.*

◉ Sights

★ Casa de los Venados

ART MUSEUM | FAMILY | A historic mansion just south of Valladolid's central square contains Mexico's largest private collection of folk art. Rooms around the gracious courtyard contain some 3,000 pieces, with Día de los Muertos (Day of the Dead) figures being a specialty. The selection is impressive, but even without it, the house would be worth touring. This hacienda-style building dates from the early 17th century, and the restoration was led by the same architect who designed Mérida's ultramodern Gran Museo del Mundo Maya (don't worry—the results here preserved its colonial elegance). Casa de los Venados opens to the public each morning for a 90-minute bilingual tour. Just show up; no reservations are needed. The suggested donation of MX$100 is a bargain, and all proceeds help fund local health-care projects. ⊠ *Calle 40 204, Valladolid* ☎ *985/856–2289* ⊕ *www.casadelosvenados.com* ⊠ *MX$100 suggested donation.*

Cenote Samulá

NATURE SIGHT | FAMILY | Perhaps the most photographed cenote in the Yucatán, this sinkhole is across the road from another one, Cenote X-Keken, about 5 km (3 miles) west of the main square. A narrow stairway leads to crystal clear water where tree vines dangle overhead and hundreds of birds nest between the stalactites. Don't be alarmed by the tiny *Garra rufa* fish that nibble at your feet—they are actually eating away the dead skin cells. Guides offer tours for tips. ✉ *On old hwy. to Chichén Itzá, Valladolid* 🎫 *MX$125 combo ticket with Cenote X-Keken.*

Cenote X-Keken

NATURE SIGHT | FAMILY | Five kilometers (3 miles) west of the main square, you can swim with the catfish in a lovely, mysterious cave illuminated by a small natural skylight. There are toilets and changing facilities but no lockers. Directly across the street is the equally stunning Cenote Samulá. Guides offer tours for tips. ✉ *On old hwy. to Chichén Itzá, Valladolid* 🎫 *MX$125 combo ticket with Cenote Samulá.*

Cenote Zací

NATURE SIGHT | FAMILY | A large, round, and beautiful sinkhole right in town, Cenote Zací—*zací* means "white hawk" in the Mayan language—is sometimes crowded with tourists and local boys clowning it up; at other times, it's deserted. Leaves from the tall old trees surrounding the sinkhole float on the surface, but the water itself is quite clean. If you're not up for a dip, visit the adjacent handicraft shop or have a bite at the popular, thatched-roof restaurant overlooking the water. ⚠ **We recommend paying the extra MX$30 to rent a life vest here.** ✉ *Calles 36 and 37, Valladolid* ☎ *985/856–0721* 🎫 *MX$60.*

Ex-Convento e Iglesia San Bernardino

CHURCH | FAMILY | Five long blocks away from the main plaza is the 16th-century, terra-cotta Ex-Convento e Iglesia San Bernardino, a Franciscan church and former monastery. The church was actually built over Cenote Sis-Há, which provided the monks with a clean water source. You can view the cenote through a grate in the well house, where much of the original stone still remains. ■ **TIP→ If a priest is around, ask him to show you the 16th-century frescoes, protected behind curtains near the altarpiece.** The lack of proportion in the human figures shows the initial clumsiness of indigenous artisans in reproducing the Christian saints. ✉ *Calle 41A, Valladolid* ☎ *985/856–2160* 🎫 *MX$40* 🕓 *Closed weekends.*

Did You Know? 🍴

Valladolid is renowned for its *longaniza en escabeche*—a sausage dish made with pork, beef, or venison, served in many of the restaurants facing the square. While you're here, also be sure to sample *xtabentún* (pronounced eesh-tah-ben- *toon*), a liqueur that combines anise, honey, and rum.

Iglesia de San Servacio

CHURCH | FAMILY | On the south side of the town's main plaza stands the large Iglesia de San Servacio, sometimes spelled "San Gervasio." Although many refer to it as a *catedral*, it is not the seat of the diocese—that's in Mérida. Its limestone exterior is impressive, but the interior is rather plain. The church makes a stunning anchor for the plaza when illuminated at night. ✉ *Calle 41, between Calles 40 and 42, Valladolid* 🎫 *Free.*

🍴 Restaurants

Casa Italia

$$ | ITALIAN | FAMILY | This restored colonial gem a couple of blocks north of the main square deserves a place on any list of Mexico's best pizza restaurants. Lots of reds and yellows brighten the interior, and the outdoor patio overlooking Parque de la Candelaria becomes prime real estate on beautiful evenings. **Known for:** impressive variety of quality pizza; good wine selection; fun vibe on outdoor patio. [$] *Average main: MP220* ✉ *Calle 35 202J, between Calles 42 and 44, Valladolid* ☎ *985/856–5539* 🌐 *www.casaitalia.uzimenu.com* 🕓 *Closed Sun. and Mon. No lunch.*

Did You Know?

Valladolid's Iglesia de San Servacio dates back to 1545, but much of the structure you see today was constructed in the 1700s.

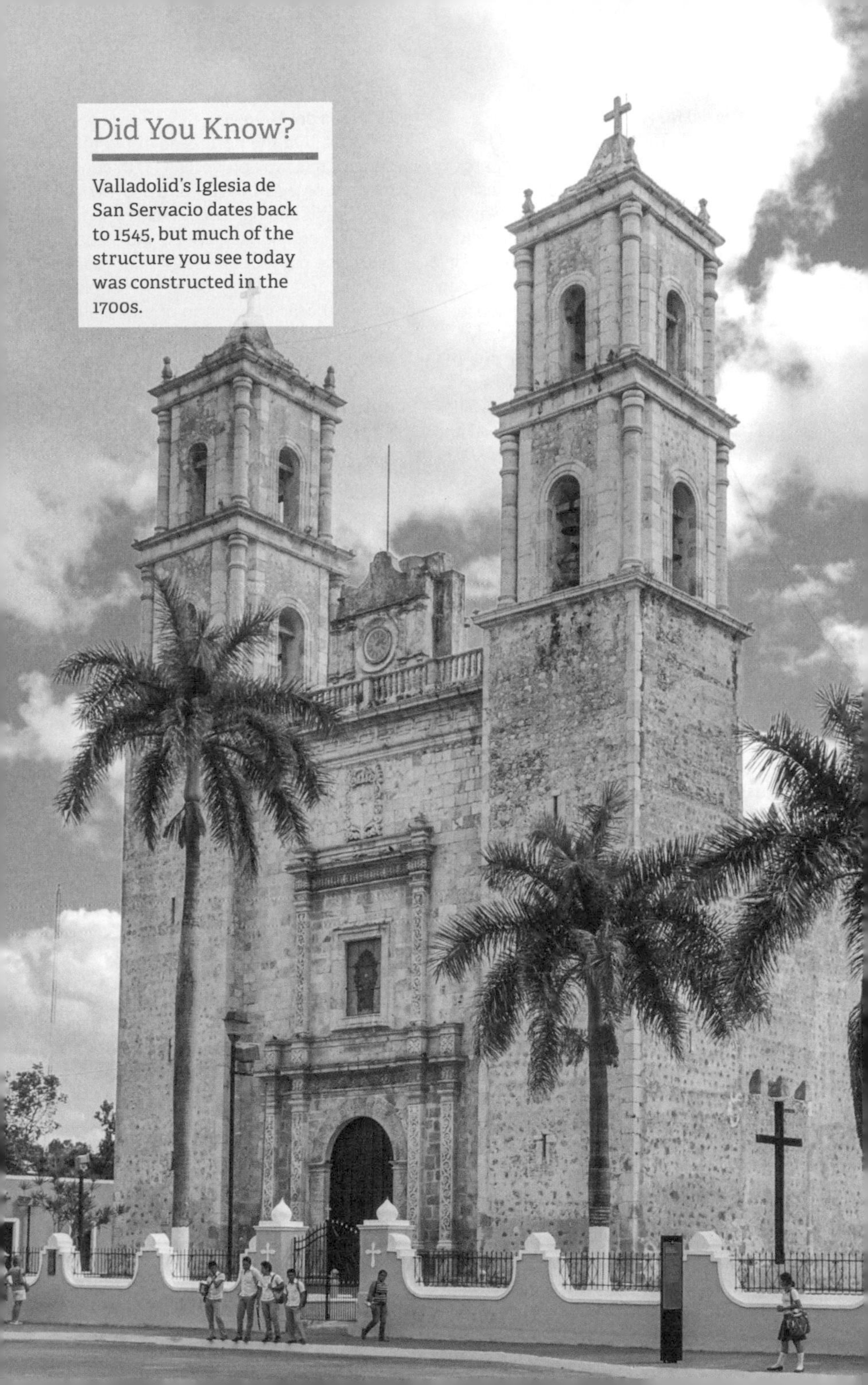

El Atrio del Mayab
$ | **MEXICAN** | This elegant colonial house on the south side of the main square specializes in hearty Yucatecan cuisine, with such menu highlights as *pollo X'cat-ik* (chicken baked in butter cream) and *lomitos* de Valladolid (cubed pork loin in a tomato-chile sauce). If you're not feeling quite so adventurous, you can choose from *mar y tierra* (meaning, basically, surf and turf) options. **Known for:** stylish setting and lush courtyard; local flavors; stays open late. [$] *Average main: MP190* ✉ *Calle 41 204A, between Calles 40 and 42, Valladolid* ☎ *985/856–2394* 🌐 *www.elatriodelmayab.com.*

Hotels

★ Casa Tía Micha
$$ | **B&B/INN** | More than a century old, this colonial-style home has been beautifully transformed into family-run hotel, where attractive rooms have beamed ceilings and antique furnishings, as well as subtle modern touches like flat-screen TVs hidden inside rustic armoires, quiet air-conditioning units, and rain shower heads inside marble bathrooms. **Pros:** friendly staff; homemade breakfast; secure parking. **Cons:** lacks the amenities of a larger property; some street noise; some rooms are dark. [$] *Rooms from: $120* ✉ *Calle 39 197, between Calles 38 and 40, Valladolid* ☎ *985/110–5404* 🌐 *www.casatiamicha.com* 🛏 *5 rooms* 🍴 *Free Breakfast.*

Ecotel Quinta Regia
$ | **HOTEL** | **FAMILY** | Mixing the colonial with modern Mexican, this hotel's whitewashed rooms have wrought-iron fixtures and hand-carved furniture. **Pros:** lively palapa bar; Wi-Fi throughout; frequent web-only discounts. **Cons:** some rooms overlook the parking area; 15-minute walk to central plaza; bland restaurant. [$] *Rooms from: $55* ✉ *Calle 40 160A, at Calle 27, Valladolid* ☎ *985/856–3472* 🌐 *www.ecotelquintaregia.com.mx* 🛏 *110 rooms* 🍴 *No Meals.*

El Mesón del Marqués
$ | **HOTEL** | On the north side of the main square, this well-preserved, 17th-century house was built around a lovely, open patio and has comfortable rooms with air-conditioning, Wi-Fi, and safes. **Pros:** nice outdoor areas; 24-hour room service; free parking. **Cons:** food could be better; rooms lack charm of public areas; mostly shaded pool. [$] *Rooms from: $90* ✉ *Calle 39 203, between Calles 40 and 42, Valladolid* ☎ *985/856–3042* 🌐 *www.mesondelmarques.com* 🛏 *85 rooms* 🍴 *Free Breakfast.*

★ Mesón de Malleville
$$$ | **B&B/INN** | The Coqui Coqui hotel group brings a contemporary feel to this luxurious property filled with vintage and handcrafted decor. **Pros:** intimate; exquisitely decorated; private and discreet atmosphere. **Cons:** few rooms, so tends to book up; lacks amenities of larger properties; expensive. [$] *Rooms from: $257* ✉ *Calle 41A 225, Valladolid* ☎ *985/856–5806* 🌐 *www.coquicoqui.com/valladolid-meson-de-malleville* 🛏 *4 suites* 🍴 *No Meals.*

Shopping

Kaxtik Arte Mexicano
CRAFTS | **FAMILY** | Located on the main square—right next to the restaurant Atrio de Mayab—this small shop sells a well-curated and diverse selection of clothing, crafts, jewelry, pottery, and masks from throughout Mexico. ✉ *Calle 41 204, between Calles 40 and 42, Valladolid* ☎ *985/856–1969* 🌐 *yalat.negocio.site.*

Ek Balam

30 km (18 miles) north of Valladolid.

The large Ek Balam ("black jaguar") site was known to 19th-century archaeologists; however, excavation and mapping didn't really get underway until the

1990s, making this one of the "newest" rediscovered Maya complexes.

GETTING HERE AND AROUND

If you don't have your own vehicle, colectivos (shared taxis) to Ek Balam leave from Calle 44 between Calles 35 and 37 in Valladolid throughout the day; the fare is MX$50 per person. You'll pay a private taxi driver MX$300 to MX$350 for the round-trip and an hour's wait.

Sights

Ek Balam

RUINS | FAMILY | The Maya site of Ek Balam is best known for the amazingly well-preserved stucco panels on the Templo de los Frisos. A giant mask crowns its summit, and its friezes contain wonderful carvings of figures often referred to as "angels" (because they have wings)—but which more likely represented nobles in ceremonial dress.

As is common with ancient Maya structures, this temple, styled like those in the lowland region of Chenes, is superimposed upon earlier ones. The temple was a mausoleum for ruler Ukin Kan Lek Tok, who was buried with priceless funerary objects, including perforated seashells, jade, mother-of-pearl pendants, and small bone masks with movable jaws. At the bases at either end of the temple, the leader's name is inscribed on the forked tongue of a carved serpent. (Maya culture ascribed no negative connotation to the snake.) A contemporary of Uxmal and Cobá, the city may have been a satellite city to Chichén Itzá, which rose to power as Ek Balam waned.

This site is also notable for its two concentric walls—a rare configuration in the Maya world—that surround the 45 structures in the main sector. They may have provided defense or, perhaps, symbolized the ruling elite that lived within. In addition, Ek Balam has a ball court and many freestanding stelae (stone pillars carved with commemorative glyphs or images). New Age groups occasionally converge here for prayers and seminars, but the site usually has few visitors, which adds to its allure. ✉ *30 km (18 miles) north of Valladolid, off Carretera 295* 🌐 *www.inah.gob.mx* 🎟 *MX$90.*

Hotels

★ Casona Los Cedros

$$$ | B&B/INN | Located a half-hour from Ek Balam, in the low-key town of Espita, this contemporary cool hotel opened in 2021 and consists of a restored historic building (with the reception area, a shop, and a coffee bar) and 10 rooms on landscaped grounds. **Pros:** stylish design; intimate setting; excellent restaurant. **Cons:** limited things to do in Espita; location may be too quiet for some; 30 minutes from Ek Balam. [$] *Rooms from: $230* ✉ *Calle 26 199, Espita, Espita* ☎ *999/114–3320* 🌐 *www.casonaloscedros.com* 🛏 *10 rooms* 🍴 *No Meals.*

Genesis Eco-Oasis

$ | HOTEL | FAMILY | Close to the Ek Balam ruins, this simple retreat is modeled on local dwellings—cabins of stucco, wood, and thatch surround a casually maintained open area with a ritual sweat lodge, meditation room, and bio-filtered swimming pool. **Pros:** intimate and eco-friendly; cultural programs; close to Ek Balam. **Cons:** early-morning crowing roosters; sometimes difficult to make phone reservations; pitted road to hotel. [$] *Rooms from: $65* ✉ *2 km (1 mile) northwest of Ek Balam* ✥ *Turn left on last rd. before entrance to Ek Balam ruins. Continue 2 km (1 mile) northwest toward Ek Balam village and follow signs to Genesis* ☎ *985/101–0277 cell phone* 🌐 *genesisecooasis.com* 🛏 *9 cabins* 🍴 *No Meals.*

Uxmal is an example of the Puuc architectural style.

Uxmal

78 km (48 miles) south of Mérida on Carretera 261; 159 km (99 miles) northeast of Campeche City on Carretera 180.

If Chichén Itzá is the most expansive Maya ruin in Yucatán, Uxmal is arguably the most elegant. Its architecture reflects the late classical renaissance of the 7th to 9th century and is contemporary with that of Palenque and Tikal, among other great Maya cities of the southern highlands. Uxmal is considered the finest and most extensively excavated example of Puuc architecture, which embraces such details as ornate stone mosaics and friezes on the upper walls, intricate cornices, rows of columns, and soaring vaulted arches.

You need the better part of a day to fully explore the ruins. Two days would allow for a more leisurely pace, and three would enable you to also visit a couple of interesting sights to the north of Uxmal. Just keep in mind that the only other entertainment in the area is that provided by hotels and the odd restaurant. The upside is that, unlike some other remote ruins, you can buy food, drinks, and souvenirs at the entrance to Uxmal.

GETTING HERE AND AROUND

If you plan to drive, take Carretera 180 south out of Mérida, and then exit on Carretera 261 in Umán. This will take you south all the way to Uxmal.

◉ Sights

Choco-Story México

OTHER MUSEUM | FAMILY | Located on a cacao plantation near the Uxmal ruins, this museum highlights the history of cacao and cocoa (the product derived from cacao) and their relationship with Maya culture. Tours take place in traditional homes where you can learn about the cultivation of cacao and the process of making chocolate. At the end, you'll be treated to a traditional Maya drink, prepared with organic cocoa and local spices. ⊠ *Carretera 261, Km 78, near*

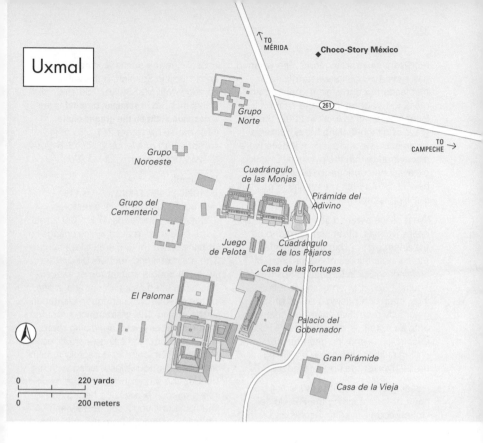

Uxmal

TO MÉRIDA

◆ Choco-Story México

261

TO CAMPECHE →

Grupo Norte

Grupo Noroeste

Cuadrángulo de las Monjas

Pirámide del Adivino

Grupo del Cementerio

Juego de Pelota

Cuadrángulo de los Pájaros

Casa de las Tortugas

El Palomar

Palacio del Gobernador

Gran Pirámide

Casa de la Vieja

| 0 | | 220 yards |
| 0 | | 200 meters |

Hacienda Uxmal, Uxmal ☎ 999/289–9914 ⊕ choco-storymexico.com ⌦ MX$180.

Oxkintok

RUINS | FAMILY | The archaeological site of Oxkintok (osh-kin-*tok*)—44 km (27 miles) northeast of Uxmal near the town of Maxcanú—was an important Maya capital that dominated the region from about AD 300 to 1100. Little was known about it until excavations began here in 1987. Structures that have been excavated so far include two tall pyramids and a palace with stone statues of several ancient rulers. Archaeologists debate the meaning of the name: Some say the site's name means "three days of flame"; others interpret it as "three days of hardship." To get here from Uxmal, follow Carretera 261 north to Muna and then take Carretera 184 northeast. ⊠ 1½ km (1

mile) east of Carretera 180 ⊕ www.inah. gob.mx ⌦ MX$70.

★ Uxmal

RUINS | FAMILY | Uxmal rivals Chichén Itzá, Coba, and other Maya sites in terms of its beauty and drama, but its distance from Cancún and the Riviera Maya helps assure that it is relatively less crowded. Although much of Uxmal has yet to be excavated, what is visible reflects the especially decorative style of Puuc Maya sites.

At 125 feet high, the Pirámide del Adivino is the site's most prominent structure. Unlike most Maya pyramids, which are stepped and angular, the so-called Pyramid of the Magician has a softer, more refined, round-corner design. This structure was rebuilt five times over hundreds of years, each time on the same foundation, so artifacts found here represent several kingdoms. The pyramid has a stairway on its western side that leads through a giant open-mouth mask to two temples at the summit. During restoration work in 2002, the grave of a high-ranking Maya official, a ceramic mask, and a jade necklace were discovered within the pyramid. Ongoing excavations continue to reveal exciting new finds. As with most ruins in Yucatán, climbing is prohibited.

West of the pyramid lies the Cuadrángulo de las Monjas, often considered to be the finest part of Uxmal. It reminded the conquistadores of typical convent buildings in Spain (*monjas* is Spanish for "nuns"). You may enter the four buildings, each comprising a series of low, gracefully repetitive chambers that look onto a central patio. Elaborate symbolic decorations—masks, geometric patterns, coiling snakes, and some phallic figures—blanket the upper facades.

Heading south, you'll pass a small ball court before reaching the Palacio del Gobernador. Covering 5 acres and rising over an immense acropolis, the palace lies at the heart of what may have been the city's administrative center. It faces east while the rest of Uxmal faces west, and archaeologists suggest this allowed the structure to serve as an observatory for the planet Venus.

The Cuadrángalo de los Pájaros (Quadrangle of the Birds) takes its name from the repeating pattern of doves that decorates the upper part of the building's frieze. In one of the building small chambers archaeologists discovered a statue of the ruler Chac (not to be confused with Chaac, the rain god), who was thought to have dwelled there.

A nightly sound and light show (8 pm April–October, 7 pm November–March) recounts Maya legends, though the spectacle is not cheap at MX$640. Still, the colored light brings out details of carvings and mosaics that are easy to miss when the sun is shining. The show is narrated in Spanish, but earphones (for an additional MX$39) provide an English translation. ⚠ **In summer, tarantulas are a common sight on the grounds here.** ✉ *Uxmal* ✛ *Carretera 261, 78 km (48 miles) south of Mérida* ☎ *997/976–2064* ⊕ *www.inah.gob.mx* ✒ *MX$90.*

Yaxcopoil

HISTORIC HOME | FAMILY | A visit to Yaxcopoil (yash-co-po-il), a restored 17th-century hacienda 47 km (29 miles) north of Uxmal, makes a nice change of pace while touring area Maya sites. The main building, with its distinctive Moorish double arch at the entrance, has been used as a film set and is one of the best-known henequen plantation in the region. The great house's rooms—including library, kitchen, dining room, drawing room, and salons—are fitted with late-19th-century European furnishings. You can tour these, along with the chapel, the storerooms, and the machine room used in processing henequen. In the museum, you'll see pottery and other artifacts recovered from the still-unexplored Classic Period Maya site for which the hacienda is named. ■**TIP**→ **Yaxcopoil has restored a one-room guesthouse (reserve online) for overnighters and will serve a continental breakfast and simple dinner of traditional tamales and horchata (rice-flavored drink) by prior arrangement.** ✉ *Carretera 261, Km 186* ☎ *999/900–1193* ⊕ *www.yaxcopoil.com* ✒ *MX$150* ⊘ *Closed Sun.*

🛏 Hotels

★ Chablé Yucatán

$$$$ | RESORT | Set on 740 acres, this meticulously restored hacienda is the state's most expensive resort, but it's a splurge-worthy choice—not only does it have spacious, luxuriously appointed, freestanding villas but it also makes an elegant base for exploring Mérida, a 40-minute drive north, as well as area Maya sites, including Oxkintok, Yaxcopoil, and Uxmal. The decor is contemporary with Mexican accents, the spa is world class, and there are delightful details at every turn—from honey made on-site to the world's largest collection of tequilas. **Pros:** contemporary design with Mexican accents; world-class spa and dining; all villas have private pools. **Cons:** very expensive; remote location; might be too quiet for some. Ⓢ *Rooms from: $800* ✉ *Tablaje 642, Chocolá* ☎ *55/4161–4262* ⊕ *yucatan.chablehotels.com* ⇆ *40 suites* ⦿ *Free Breakfast.*

The Lodge at Uxmal

$$$ | **HOTEL** | **FAMILY** | The outwardly rustic, thatched-roof buildings here have red-tile floors, hand-carved doors and rocking chairs, stained-glass windows, and local weavings—the effect is comfortable yet luxuriant, making the property feel like a peaceful ranch. **Pros:** big pools; gracious staff; directly across from Uxmal entrance. **Cons:** can book up given its proximity to Uxmal; breakfast not included; expensive for rustic rooms. Ⓢ *Rooms from: $219* ✉ *Carretera Uxmal, Km 78, Uxmal* ☎ *998/887–2495, 877/240–5864* ⊕ *www.mayaland.com* ⇆ *40 rooms* ⦿ *No Meals.*

The Pickled Onion B&B

$ | **B&B/INN** | Owner Valerie Pickles has carved out a lovely little paradise with six bungalows, beautifully maintained gardens, and a wonderful restaurant on the outskirts of Santa Elena. **Pros:** wonderful Yucatecan restaurant; amazing rates; wonderful owner. **Cons:** rustic setting is not for everyone; no in-room a/c; small pool. Ⓢ *Rooms from: $95* ✉ *Carretera 261, between Uxmal and Kabah, just after Santa Elena Centro, Uxmal* ☎ *997/111–7922* ⊕ *www.thepickledonionyucatan.com* ⇆ *8 rooms* ⦿ *Free Breakfast.*

The Ruta Puuc

Although Uxmal, meaning thrice-built city, is the largest site along the Ruta Puuc—an informal designation for the slightly hillier area southeast of Uxmal—smaller satellite sites such as Kabah, Sayil, and Labná are all well worth a visit. The series of secondary roads that wind through one of the state's least populated areas not only lead you from one fantastic Maya site to the next but also to numerous villages where you can stop for a bite to eat and feel the unique rhythm of the Yucatecan countryside.

The area also has a number of cave systems, some of which served as shelters or important religious sites for the ancient Maya. Calcehtok and Xpukil are open to visitors though two others that have long been popular with spelunkers, Lolutún and Balamcanché, remain indefinitely closed due to storm damage and flooding.

PLANNING YOUR TIME

You can visit the Ruta Puuc sites in one long day or over the course of two days. Most Mérida-based tour operators offer the former, but the latter is recommended if you have the time and your own transportation. Roads are well-marked, and the area is easy to navigate since the archaeological attractions line up one right after another. Most sites are open from 8 to 5 only, so to devote any less time means either skipping deserving locales or rushing through them.

∎ **TIP→ Fill up on fuel and cash before entering the area, because both gas stations and ATMs are hard to come by.**

Ticul

28 km (17 miles) east of Uxmal, 100 km (62 miles) south of Mérida.

One of the larger communities in the Yucatán, Ticul (with a population of

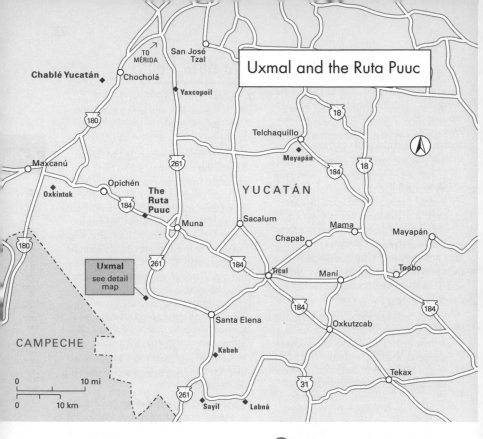

Uxmal and the Ruta Puuc

around 21,000) is a good base for exploring the Puuc region—provided you don't mind that most of the hotels are rudimentary and most of the limited selection of restaurants are simple. Many descendants of the Xiu Dynasty, which ruled Uxmal until the conquest, still live here.

Industries include the fabrication of shoes and *huipiles* (the traditional white embroidered dresses worn by indigenous women) as well as much of the pottery you see around the Yucatán. Ticul also has a handsome 17th-century church.

GETTING HERE AND AROUND
Ticul is an easy drive south of Mérida. Follow Carretera 180 to Umán, where you'll get on the Carretera 261 to Muná; from Muná, simply follow the signs to Ticul by way of Carretera 184.

◉ Sights

Iglesia de San Antonio de Padua
CHURCH | FAMILY | This evocatively faded red church is typical of Yucatán's colonial sanctuaries. It has been ransacked on more than one occasion, but the Cristo Negro (Black Christ) altarpiece is original. The best view might be from the outside, where you can take in the facade and savor the slow pace of the town as families ride by in carts attached to bicycles and locals mill around in traditional Maya dress. ⊠ *Town Sq., Centro.*

Mayapán
RUINS | FAMILY | Mayapán, which has an architectural style reminiscent of Uxmal, flourished during the Post-Classic Period, making it one of the peninsula's last major Maya city-states. Though it was destroyed in 1450, presumably by war,

Yucatán's History

The conquest of the Yucatán Peninsula by the three Franciscos de Montejo—father, son, and nephew—took three gruesome wars over a total of 24 years. The resolute Maya, their ancestors long incorrectly portrayed by archaeologists as docile and peace-loving, provided the Spaniards and their indigenous allies with one of their greatest challenges in the New World. Rebellious pockets of Maya communities held out against the dzulo'obs (dzoo-loh-obs)—the upper class, or outsiders—as late as the 1920s and '30s.

Yucatecans are proud of their heritage and culture, and with good reason. Although in a state of decline when the conquistadores clanked into their world with iron swords and fire-belching cannons, the Maya were one of the world's greatest ancient cultures. As mathematicians and astronomers they were perhaps without equal among their contemporaries, and their architecture in places like Uxmal was as graceful as that of the ancient Greeks.

To "facilitate" Catholic conversion among the conquered, the Spaniards superimposed Christian rituals on existing beliefs whenever possible, creating the syncretic Catholicism that's alive and well today. (Those defiant Maya who resisted the new ideology were burned at the stake, drowned, and hanged.) Having enslaved a huge workforce of indigenous labor, Spanish agricultural estates prospered. Mérida soon became a thriving administrative and military center and the gateway for agricultural products headed to Cuba and Spain. By the 18th century, enormous maize and cattle plantations were making the hacendados incredibly rich.

Insurrection came during the Caste War in the mid-1800s, when the enslaved indigenous people rose up with long-repressed furor and massacred thousands of settlers. The United States, Cuba, and Mexico City finally came to the aid of the ruling elite, and between 1847 and 1850, the indigenous population of Yucatán was effectively halved. Those Maya who didn't escape into the remote jungles of neighboring Quintana Roo or Chiapas, or get sold into slavery in Cuba, found themselves even worse off under the dictatorship of Porfirio Díaz (who was president for 31 years at the end of the 19th and beginning of the 20th centuries).

Their hopeless status changed little as the economic base segued from one industry to the next. After the thin limestone soil failed to produce fat cattle or impressive corn, entrepreneurs turned to dyewood and then to henequen, a natural fiber used to make rope. (Henequen is better known in English as sisal, after the Yucatán port of the same name through which much of the fiber was exported.)

After the widespread acceptance of synthetic fibers, the peninsula's land barons used local laborers to convert the resin of zapote trees into a latex that is the basis of chewing gum, as well as adhesives. The imposing French-style mansions that stretch along Mérida's Paseo de Montejo exemplify the wealth generated by this industry.

the city is thought to have once been as big as Chichén Itzá, with a population of 12,000 or more at its peak. Of the site's more than 4,000 mounds, only a half-dozen have been excavated, including the palaces of Maya royalty and the temple of the benign god Kukulcán, where stucco sculptures and murals in vivid reds and oranges have been uncovered.

The site is 42 km (26 miles) northeast of Ticul and 43 km (27 miles) south of Mérida. ■ **TIP→ Be sure you head toward the Mayapán ruins (just south of Telchaquillo) and not the town of Mayapán, since they are far apart.** ✉ *Off rd. to left before Telchaquillo (follow signs)* 🌐 *www.inah.gob.mx* 🎟 *MX$70.*

🍴 Restaurants

★ El Príncipe Tutul-Xiu

$ | **MEXICAN** | **FAMILY** | Shaded by a giant palapa roof, this open-air restaurant is an inviting spot for lunch or an early dinner (it closes at 7 pm). Though you'll find the same Yucatecan dishes (pollo pibil, sopa de lima) here as elsewhere, the preparation is excellent. **Known for:** tasty poc chuc; huge portions at reasonable prices; authentic, local atmosphere. [$] *Average main: MP140* ✉ *Calle 29 191, between Calles 20 and 22, Ticul* ☎ *997/978–4257* 🌐 *elprincipetutulxiu.wixsite.com/website.*

Pizzería La Góndola

$ | **PIZZA** | **FAMILY** | Wonderful smells waft from this small corner establishment, where scenes of old Italy and the Yucatán adorn bright yellow walls, and patrons pull padded folding chairs up to yellow-tile tables or take their orders to go. Pizza is the name of the game here, but tortas and pastas are also served. **Known for:** impressive variety of pizza; fun, informal vibe; the only nighttime dining option in town. [$] *Average main: MP170* ✉ *Calle 23 208, at Calle 26A, Ticul* ☎ *997/972–0112* 🕒 *No lunch.*

Kabah

23 km (14 miles) southeast of Uxmal.

The most important buildings at Kabah (meaning "lord of the powerful hand" in Mayan) were built between AD 600 and 900, during the later part of the Classic Period. ■ **TIP→ Although the site officially opens at 8 am, the staff often doesn't show up until 9.**

👁 Sights

Kabah

RUINS | **FAMILY** | A ceremonial center of almost Grecian beauty, Kabah was once linked to Uxmal by a *sacbé,* or raised paved road, at the end of which looms a great independent arch—now across the highway from the main ruins. The 151-foot-long Palacio de los Mascarones (Palace of the Masks) boasts a three-dimensional mosaic of 250 masks. On the central plaza, you can see ground-level wells called *chultunes,* which were used to store precious rainwater. ✉ *23 km (14 miles) south of Uxmal on Carretera 261* 🌐 *www.inah.gob.mx* 🎟 *MX$75.*

Sayil

9.5 km (6 miles) south of Kabah. Follow Highway 261 for 5 km and then take a left to Sayil.

Experts believe that Sayil, or "place of the red ants," flourished between AD 800 and 1000.

👁 Sights

Sayil

RUINS | **FAMILY** | Sayil is best known for its setting in a narrow valley surrounded by rolling hills and its majestic Gran Palacio. Built on one of those hills, the three-story structure is adorned with decorations of animals and other figures, and contains more than 80 rooms. The structure recalls Palenque in its use of multiple planes, columned porticoes, and sober cornices. Also on the grounds is a stela in the shape of a phallus—an obvious symbol of fertility. ✉ *9 km (5½ miles) south of Kabah on Carretera 31E* ⊕ *www. inah.gob.mx* ✍ *MX$70.*

Labná

8 km (5 miles) east of Sayil on a narrow (though well-maintained) road through the Puuc Biocultural Reserve.

Like many of its Puuc region neighbors, the small but important settlement of Labná, whose name means "old house" or "abandoned house," flourished roughly between AD 600 and 900.

◉ Sights

Labná

RUINS | FAMILY | Although it has a palace and a small pyramid, the most photographed building at Labná is a striking monumental corbeled arch. With its elaborate latticework and a small chamber on each side, it provided a grand entrance into a sacred precinct for anyone arriving on the road to and from Uxmal. It is believed that Labná was used mainly by royalty and the military elite. ✉ *9 km (5½ miles) south of Sayil on Carretera 31E* ⊕ *www.inah.gob.mx* ✍ *MX$70.*

Campeche State

" ¡Quiero estar ahí!" proclaim the colorful license plates in the state of Campeche. "I want to be there!" After one visit, you might say the same. Campeche City, the state capital, is one of the best-kept secrets in the Yucatán. Its beautifully preserved colonial district is brimming with historic sites, museums, cafés, and restaurants—all within easy walking distance of each other. Yet the city is

far smaller and more easygoing than its Yucatecan cousin, Mérida.

Its unique history (it was once a favorite target of seafaring pirates) has left a mark. Many of the protective walls that were built to safeguard inhabitants are still standing, and the colorful colonial buildings were constructed with safety in mind; they're markedly less ornate than their counterparts elsewhere on the peninsula, with well-barred windows and impressively heavy-looking doors. The 18th-century fort at the south end of town lets you imagine Campeche's dangerous past, and is home to a fascinating collection of Mayan artifacts taken from area archaeological sites.

Although the city is the state's most accessible spot and a good hub for exploring, there's much more to Campeche than its capital. Beyond the city lie the famous ruins of Edzná, a short detour south of Carreteras 180 and 188. The southern reaches of the state turn a bit wilder with the remnants of 10 Mayan cities strung out through the rain forest on or near Carretera 186. Just be advised that dining and accommodation options get more basic when you venture this far from the city. You'll encounter fewer English speakers off the beaten path, too, so pack a Spanish-English dictionary if you don't have at least rudimentary Spanish.

■ **TIP→ Anglophones use "Campeche City" to distinguish the capital from the rest of the state. Spanish speakers call both simply "Campeche," so let context be your guide.**

Campeche City

174 km (108 miles) southwest of Mérida.

In picturesque Campeche (aka San Francisco de Campeche), block upon block of restored buildings with lovely facades, all painted in bright colors, meet the sea. Tiny balconies overlook clean, geometrically paved streets, and charming old street lamps illuminate the scene at

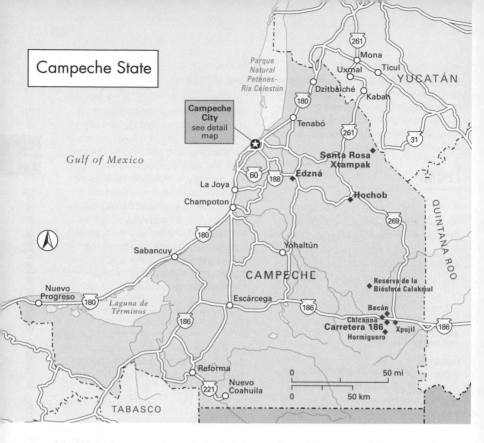

night. While the heart of the city, a UNESCO World Heritage site, looks as if it has been constructed purely for touristic purposes, you'll find just as many workaday businesses here as you will trendy restaurants and boutique hotels.

In colonial days, the city center was completely enclosed within a 10-foot-thick wall. Two stone archways (originally there were four)—one facing the sea, the other the land—long provided the only access. The defensive walls also served as a de facto class demarcation. Within them lived the ruling elite. Outside were the barrios, home to slaves from Cuba and everyone else.

On strategic corners, seven *baluartes,* or bastions, gave militiamen a platform from which to fight off the pirates and the other ruffians who continually plagued this beautiful city on the bay. It wasn't

until 1771, when the hilltop Fuerte de San Miguel was built outside town, that pirates finally stopped attacking the city.

■TIP➔ **Campeche's historic center is easily navigable—walking is always your best bet.** Narrow streets and lack of parking spaces make driving frustrating, although motorists here are polite and mellow. Streets running roughly north–south are even numbered, and those running east–west are odd numbered. The historic center has a perimeter stretching 2½ km (1½ miles).

GETTING HERE AND AROUND

Aeropuerto Internacional Alberto Acuña Ongay is just north of downtown. Taxis—the only means of transportation to and from the facility—charge about MX$200 for the 16-km (10-mile) trip.

Buses operated by ADO (⊕ *www.ado.com.mx*) connect Campeche City to destinations throughout the Yucatán Peninsula. If you're driving, Campeche City is about 2 to 2½ hours from Mérida on the 180-km (112-mile) Carretera 180, also known as the *via corta* (short way). The alternative 250-km (155-mile) Carretera 261, or *via ruinas* (ruins route), takes three to four hours, but passes some major Mayan sites.

Within Campeche City, the route of interest to most visitors is along Avenida Ruíz Cortínez. A ride on a bus costs the equivalent of about 30¢. In addition, tourist trams/trolleys (MX$100) let you take in city highlights with commentary in Spanish and, possibly, English. You can hail taxis on the street, and there are stands by the bus stations, the municipal market, and Parque Principal. The minimum fare is MX$25; after 11 pm, prices may be slightly higher. There's a small fee (MX$10) to call for a cab through Radio Taxi.

TRAM CONTACTS El Guapo and Super Guapo trams. ⊠ *Parque Principal, Centro.*

TAXI CONTACTS Radio Taxi. ⊠ *Campeche City* ☎ *981/815–8888.*

VISITOR INFORMATION

You'll see numerous Información Turística signs around town, but most are storefront tour outfits hoping to sell you excursions rather than unbiased sources of information. The city and state of Campeche each operates official tourist-information offices staffed by phenomenal people who can answer your questions.

CONTACTS Oficina de Turismo de Campeche. (*Municipal Tourist Office*) ⊠ *Parque Principal, Calle 55, between Calles 8 and 10, Centro* ☎ *981/811–3989* ⊕ *www.campeche.travel.* **Turismo de Campeche.** ⊠ *Plaza Moch Couoh, Av. Ruíz Cortínez s/n, Centro* ☎ *981/127–3300* ⊕ *www.campeche.travel.*

Trolley Tours ◉

Guided tram/trolley tours of historic Campeche City leave from Calle 10 on Parque Principal on the hour from 9 to 9. Note, though, that departures only actually happen once at least eight tickets have been sold. Buy yours ahead of time at the adjacent kiosk or wait until you're onboard. The one-hour tour costs MX$100, and, if asked, guides will do their best to speak English. The Guapo (which translates to "handsome") trolley covers the historic center and malecón; the Superguapo takes in the city center, Reducto de San José, and Fuerte San Miguel.

◉ Sights

Baluarte de la Soledad/Museo de Arquitectura Maya

HISTORY MUSEUM | FAMILY | The largest of the city's bastions contains the Museo de Arquitectura Maya with artifacts from several Campeche State Mayan sites. The bastion was originally built to protect the Puerta de Mar, a sea gate that served as one of four original entrances to the city. Because it uses no supporting walls, it resembles a Roman triumphal arch. Its relatively complete parapets and embrasures afford views of the cathedral, municipal buildings, and old houses along Calle 8. ⊠ *Calle 8, between Calles 55 and 57, Campeche City* ☎ *981/816–9136* ⊕ *www.inah.gob.mx/red-de-museos* ⊠ *MX$70.*

Baluarte de San Carlos/Museo de la Ciudad

HISTORY MUSEUM | FAMILY | This bastion, where Calle 8 curves around and becomes Circuito Baluartes, houses the Museo de la Ciudad with a small collection of artifacts, including several Spanish suits of armor and a beautifully

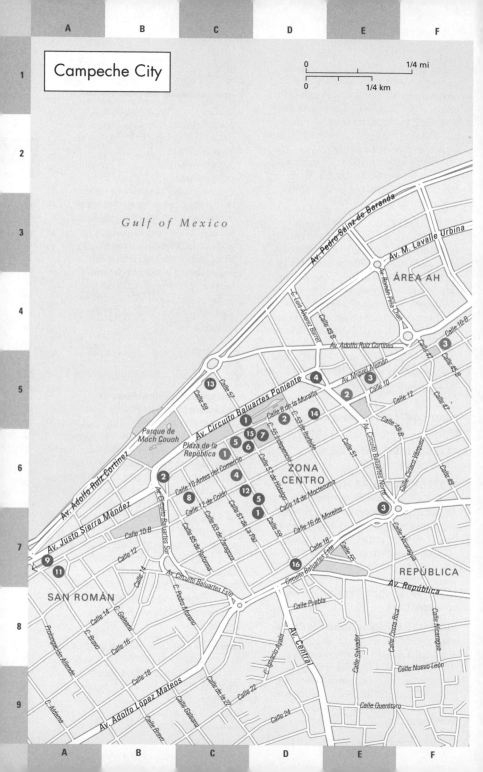

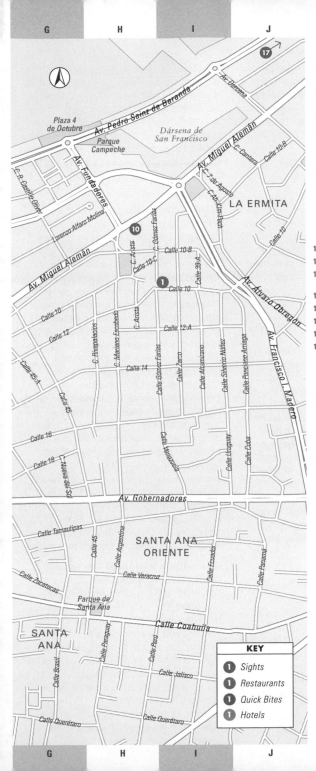

Sights ▼

1 Baluarte de la Soledad/
Museo de Arquitectura Maya.....**C5**

2 Baluarte de San Carlos/
Museo de la Ciudad **B6**

3 Baluarte de San Pedro.............**E6**

4 Baluarte de Santiago/
Xmuch-Haltún
Botanical Gardens................. **D5**

5 Calle 59............................... **D6**

6 Casa Seis **C6**

7 Catedral de la
Inmaculada Concepción.......... **D6**

8 Ex-Templo de San José............**C6**

9 Fuerte de San Miguel/
Museo de la
Arqueología Maya................. **A7**

10 Iglesia de San Francisco **H3**

11 Iglesia de San Román............. **A7**

12 Iglesia y Ex-Convento
de San Roque **C6**

13 Malecón **C5**

14 Mansión Carvajal.................. **D5**

15 Parque Principal....................**C6**

16 Puerta de Tierra.................... **D7**

17 Reducto de San José el Alto/
Museo de Armas y Barcos........**J1**

Restaurants ▼

1 Cenaduría Portales de
San Francisco....................... **I4**

2 La María Cocina Peninsular...... **D5**

3 La Pigua.............................. **E5**

4 Luz de Luna......................... **C6**

5 Marganzo............................**C6**

Quick Bites ▼

1 Chocol Ha......................... **D7**

Hotels ▼

1 Casa Don Gustavo................. **C6**

2 Hotel Plaza Campeche............. **E5**

3 Las Lupitas **F4**

KEY

① Sights

① Restaurants

① Quick Bites

① Hotels

inscribed silver scepter. Captured pirates were once jailed in the stifling basement dungeon. ■TIP→ **The unshaded rooftop provides an ocean view that's lovely at sunset.** ✉ *Calle 8, between Calles 65 and 63, Circuito Baluartes, Campeche City* ⊕ *sic. cultura.gob.mx.*

Baluarte de San Pedro

STORE/MALL | **FAMILY** | Built in 1686 to protect the city from pirate attacks, this bastion flanked by watchtowers now houses one of the city's few worthwhile handicraft shops. The collection is small but of high quality, and prices are reasonable. On the roof are well-preserved corner watchtowers. You can also check out (but not use) the original 17th-century toilet. ✉ *Calles 18 and 51, Circuito Baluartes, Campeche City* ⊕ *turismocampeche. com/folio/baluarte-de-san-pedro* 🎫 *Free.*

Baluarte de Santiago/Xmuch-Haltún Botanical Gardens

GARDEN | **FAMILY** | The last of the bastions to be built has been transformed into the Xmuch-Haltún Botanical Gardens with more than 200 plant species, including the enormous ceiba tree, which had spiritual importance to the Maya, symbolizing a link between heaven, Earth, and the underworld. The original bastion, erected in 1704, was demolished at the turn of the 20th century, then rebuilt in the 1950s. ✉ *Calles 8 and 49, Circuito Baluartes, Campeche City* ⊕ *turismocampeche.com/folio/baluarte-de-santiago* 🎫 *MX$15.*

Calle 59

STREET | Some of Campeche's finest homes were built on this street between Calles 8 and 18. Most of the two-story structures were originally dual-purpose, with warehouses on the ground floor and living quarters above. These days, behind the delicate grillwork and lace curtains, you can glimpse genteel scenes of local life. The best-preserved houses are between Calles 14 and 18 (many of those closer to the sea have been remodeled or destroyed by fire). Campeche's INAH

(Instituto Nacional de Antropología e Historia) office, between Calles 14 and 16, is a prime example; each month it displays a different artifact in its courtyard. At the end of Calle 59 is Puerta de Mar, a main entrance to the historic city. ■TIP→ **Look for the names of the apostles carved into the lintels of houses between Calles 16 and 18.** ✉ *Campeche City.*

Casa Seis

HISTORIC HOME | **FAMILY** | One of the city's earliest colonial homes now serves as a cultural center. Its fully restored rooms are furnished with period antiques and a few well-chosen reproductions; original frescoes at the tops of the walls remain, and you can see patches of the painted "wallpaper" that once covered the walls, serving to simulate European trends in an environment where real wallpaper wouldn't adhere due to the humidity. There is a small coffee shop on-site, plus a gift shop selling products from Campeche. The Moorish courtyard is occasionally used as a space for exhibits and lectures. Activities occur several evenings a week. *Vivo Recuerdo*, a musical/theater interpretation of Campeche's history, is presented Thursday through Sunday; Con Sabor a Chocolate, a chocolate-making demonstration, takes place on Friday and Saturday. ✉ *Parque Principal, Calle 57, between Calles 10 and 8, Campeche City* ☎ *981/816–1782* 🎫 *House MX$30; Vivo Recurrdo MX$120; Con Sabor a Chocolate MX$90.*

Catedral de la Inmaculada Concepción

CHURCH | **FAMILY** | It took two centuries (from 1650 to 1850) to finish this cathedral and, as a result, it incorporates both neoclassical and Renaissance elements. On the simple limestone exterior, sculptures of saints in niches are covered in black netting to discourage pigeons from unintentional desecration. The church's neoclassical interior is also somewhat plain and sparse. The high point of its collection, now housed in the side chapel museum, is a magnificent

Campeche's History

Campeche City's gulf location played a pivotal role in its history. Ah-Kim-Pech (Mayan for "lord of the serpent tick," from which the name Campeche is derived) was a capital long before the Spaniards arrived in 1517. In 1540 the conquerors—led by Francisco de Montejo and later by his son and nephew—established a foothold at Campeche (originally—and still officially—San Francisco de Campeche), using it as a base for the conquest of the peninsula.

At the time, Campeche City was the region's only port, so Spanish ships, loaded with treasure plundered from Maya, Aztec, and other indigenous civilizations, dropped anchor here en route from Veracruz to Cuba, New Orleans, and Spain. As news of the riches spread, Campeche's shores were soon overrun with pirates. From the mid-1500s to the early 1700s, such notorious corsairs as Diego the Mulatto, Lorenzillo, Peg Leg, Henry Morgan, and Barbillas swooped in repeatedly from Tris—or Isla de Términos, as Isla del Carmen was then known—pillaging and burning the city and massacring its people.

Finally, after years of appeals to the Spanish crown, Campeche received funds to build a protective wall, with four gates and eight bastions, around the town center. For a while afterward, the city thrived on its exports,

especially *palo de tinte*—a valuable dyewood more precious than gold due to the nascent European textile industry's demand for it—but also hardwoods, chicle, salt, and henequen. However, when the port of Sisal opened on the northern Yucatán coast in 1811, Campeche's monopoly on gulf traffic ended, and its economy quickly declined.

During the 19th and 20th centuries, Campeche, like most of the Yucatán Peninsula, had little to do with the rest of Mexico. Left to their own devices, *campechanos* lived in relative isolation until the petroleum boom of the 1970s brought businessmen from Mexico City, Europe, and the United States to its provincial doorstep.

Campeche retains an air of antiquity, though. Remnants of its gates and bastions split the city into two main districts: the historic center and the newer residential areas. Because the city was long preoccupied with defense, the colonial architecture is less flamboyant here than elsewhere in Mexico. The narrow flagstone streets reflect the confines of the city's walls, and homes here emphasize the practical over the decorative. Still, government decrees, bolstered by the historic center's status as a UNESCO World Heritage site, have resulted in the preservation of colonial structures.

Holy Sepulchre carved from ebony and decorated with stamped silver angels, flowers, and decorative curlicues. Each angel holds a symbol of the Stations of the Cross. ⊠ *Parque Principal, Calle 55, between Calles 8 and 10, Campeche City* ☎ *981/816–2524* ⊕ *www.facebook.com/ CatedralCampeche* ⊠ *Free.*

Ex-Templo de San José

CHURCH | FAMILY | The Jesuits built this fine baroque church in honor of St. Joseph just before they were booted out of the New World in 1767. Its block-long facade and portal are covered with blue-and-yellow Talavera tiles and crowned with seven narrow stone finials—resembling both the roof combs on many Mayan temples and the combs Spanish women once wore in their elaborate hairdos. You can ask the guard (who should be somewhere on the grounds) to let you in. From the outside you can admire Campeche's first lighthouse, built in 1864 and perched atop the right-hand tower. ⊠ *Calles 10 and 63, Campeche City* ☎ *981/816–2292* ⊕ *turismocampeche.com/folio/ex-templo-de-san-jose.*

Fuerte de San Miguel/Museo de la Arqueología Maya

HISTORY MUSEUM | FAMILY | Near the city's southwest end, Avenida Ruíz Cortínez winds to this hilltop fort with a breathtaking view of the Bay of Campeche. Built between 1779 and 1801 and dedicated to the archangel Michael, the fort was positioned to blast enemy ships with its long-range cannons. As soon as it was completed, pirates stopped attacking the city. In fact, the cannons were fired only once, in 1842, when General Santa Anna used Fuerte de San Miguel to put down a revolt by Yucatecan separatists.

The fort houses the 10-room Museo de la Arqueología Maya. Exhibits include the skeletons of long-ago Maya royals, complete with jewelry and pottery, which are arranged just as they were found in Calakmul tombs. Other archaeological treasures are funeral vessels, wonderfully expressive figurines and whistles from Isla de Jaina, stelae and stucco masks, and an excellent pottery collection. Most information is in Spanish only, but many of the pieces speak for themselves.

■TIP→ **The gift shop sells replicas of artifacts.** ⊠ *Av. Francisco Morazán s/n, Campeche City* ☎ *981/816–9111* ⊕ *www.inah.gob.mx/red-de-museos* ⊠ *MX$70* ⊘ *Closed Mon.*

Iglesia de San Francisco

CHURCH | With its flat, boldly painted facade and bells ensconced under small arches instead of in bell towers, the Church of St. Francis looks more like a Mexican city hall than a Catholic church.

Outside the city center in a residential neighborhood, the beautifully restored temple is Campeche's oldest. It marks the spot where some say the first Mass on the North American continent was held in 1517—though the same claim has been made for Veracruz and Cozumel. One of conquistador Hernán Cortés's grandsons was baptized here, and the baptismal font still stands. ⊠ *Avs. Miguel Alemán and Mariano Escobedo, Campeche City* ☎ *981/816–2925* ⊠ *Free* ⛪ *turismocampeche.com/folio/iglesia-de-san-francisco.*

Iglesia de San Román

CHURCH | FAMILY | Like most Franciscan churches, this one is sober and plain, and its single bell tower is the only ornamentation. The equally sparse interior is brightened a bit by some colorful stained-glass windows, and the carved and inlaid altarpiece serves as a beautiful backdrop for an ebony image of Jesus, the "Black Christ," brought from Italy in about 1575. Although understandably skeptical of Christianity, the indigenous people, who the Spaniards forced into perpetual servitude, eventually came to associate this Black Christ figure with miracles. As legend has it, a ship that refused to carry the holy statue was lost at sea, while the ship that accepted it reached Campeche in record time. To this day, the Feast of San Román—when worshippers carry a black-wood Christ and silver filigree cross through the streets—remains a solemn but colorful affair. ⊠ *Calles 10 and Bravo, Campeche City* ☎ *981/816–3303* ⊕ *turismocampeche.com/folio/iglesia-de-san-roman* ⊠ *Free.*

Iglesia y Ex-Convento de San Roque

CHURCH | FAMILY | The elaborately carved main altarpiece and matching side altars here were restored inch by inch, and this long, narrow house of worship now adds more than ever to historic Calle 59's old-fashioned beauty. Built in 1565, it was originally called Iglesia de San Francisco for St. Francis. In addition to a statue of Francis, humbler-looking saints peer out from smaller niches. ✉ *Calles 12 and 59, Campeche City* 🕾 *981/816–3144* ⊕ *turismocampeche.com/folio/iglesia-de-san-roque-san-francisquito* 🎟 *Free.*

Malecón

PROMENADE | FAMILY | A broad sidewalk, more than 4 km (2½ miles) long, runs the length of Campeche's waterfront boulevard, from northeast of the Debliz hotel to the Justo Sierra Méndez monument at downtown's southwestern edge. With its landscaping, sculptures, rest areas, and fountains lighted up at night in neon colors, the promenade attracts walkers, joggers, and cyclists. (Note the separate paths for each.) On weekend nights, students turn the malecón into a party zone, and families with young children fill the parks on both sides of the promenade after 7 or 8 pm, staying out surprisingly late to enjoy the cooler evening temperatures. ✉ *Av. Rodolfo Ruiz Cortínez, Campeche City.*

Mansión Carvajal

HISTORIC HOME | Built in the early 20th century by one of the Yucatán's wealthiest plantation owners, Fernando Carvajal Estrada, this eclectic mansion is a reminder of the city's heyday, when Campeche was the peninsula's only port. Local legend insists that the art nouveau staircase with Carrara marble steps and iron balustrade, built and delivered in one piece from Italy, was too big and had to be shipped back and redone. These days the mansion is filled with government offices—you'll have to stretch your imagination a bit to picture how it once was. ✉ *Calle 10 584, between Calles 51 and 53, Campeche City* 🕾 *981/816–7419* ⊕ *turismocampeche.com/folio/mansion-carvajal* 🎟 *Free* ⊗ *Closed weekends.*

Parque Principal (*Plaza de la Independencia*)

CITY PARK | FAMILY | Though small by Mexican standards, this central park is picturesque with a beautiful view of Catedral de la Inmaculada Concepción. Half of the old-fashioned kiosk in the park's center contains a branch of the municipal tourist office. The other half houses a pleasant café-bar, where you can sit and watch residents out for a stroll and listen to the itinerant musicians who often show up to play traditional ballads in the evenings. ✉ *Bounded by Calles 8, 10, 55, and 57, Campeche City.*

Puerta de Tierra

MILITARY SIGHT | FAMILY | The Land Gate, where Old Campeche ends, is the only one of Campeche's four gates with its basic structure intact. The stone arch interrupts a stretch of the partially crenellated wall, 26 feet high and 10 feet thick, that once encircled the city. Walk the wall's full length to the Baluarte San Juan for excellent views of both the old and new cities. The staircase leads down to an old well, underground storage area, and dungeon. Thursday through Sunday at 8 pm, the gate is the site of a one-hour light show accompanied by music and dance. ✉ *Calles 18 and 59, Campeche City* ⊕ *turismocampeche.com/folio/puerta-de-tierra* 🎟 *Sound-and-light show MX$60.*

Reducto de San José el Alto/Museo de Armas y Barcos

HISTORY MUSEUM | FAMILY | This lofty redoubt, or stronghold, at the northwest end of town, is home to the Museo de Armas y Barcos. Displays in former soldiers' and watchmen's rooms focus on 18th-century weapons of siege and defense. You'll also see manuscripts, religious art, and ships in bottles. The view is terrific from the top of the ramparts, which were once used to spot invading ships. ✉ *Av. Escénica s/n, Campeche City* 🕾 *981/816–2460* ⊕ *www.inah.gob.mx/red-de-museos* 🎟 *MX$70* ⊗ *Closed Mon.*

🍴 Restaurants

Cenaduría Portales de San Francisco

$ | MEXICAN | Campechano families come here to enjoy a light supper, perhaps a delicious sandwich *claveteado* of honey-and-clove-spiked ham, along with a typical drink like agua de chaya, a mixture of pineapple water and chaya (a leafy vegetable similar to spinach). The dining area is a wide colonial veranda with marble flooring and tables decked out in plastic tablecloths. **Known for:** alfresco dining on the picturesque plaza de San Francisco; stylish veranda; tamales wrapped in banana leaves. [$] *Average main: MP160* ✉ *Calle 10 86, at Portales San Francisco, 8 blocks northeast of Parque Principal, Campeche City* ☎ *981/811–1491* 🌐 *www.facebook.com/CenaduriaPortales* 🕒 *No lunch.*

La María Cocina Peninsular

$$ | **MEXICAN** | Calle 8, which runs along the north side of the historic center and roughly follows the route of the old sea wall, is now a bit of a restaurant row, home to this and other eateries. Seafood is the specialty here, though it also has a number of signature cocktails, like the Pregonero, made with a chile liquor, tamarind, and pineapple. **Known for:** ceviche and grilled fish; signature cocktails; historic center location. [$] *Average main: MP210* ✉ *Calle 8 173, Campeche City* ☎ *999/445–7635* 🌐 *la-maria-cocina-peninsular-restaurant.negocio.site.*

★ **La Pigua**

$$ | **SEAFOOD** | At the town's favorite lunch spot, glass walls replicate an oblong Maya house, which is surrounded by a profusion of plants. Seafood, with a *campechano* twist, reigns supreme here, and a truly ambitious meal might start with calamari, stone-crab claws, or *camarones al coco* (coconut-encrusted shrimp), perhaps followed by *pan de cazón* (a shark-meat casserole that's one of Campeche's most distinctive dishes) or robalo fish topped with puréed cilantro, parsley, orange, and olive oil. **Known for:** pan de cazón (shark-meat) casserole; unusual terrarium setting; coconut cake. [$] *Average main: MP220* ✉ *Av. Miguel Alemán 179A, between Calles 49A and 49B, Campeche City* ☎ *981/811–3365* 🌐 *www.facebook.com/lapiguacam.*

Luz de Luna

$ | **MEXICAN** | Inside a colonial-era building, this small (just five tables) family-run restaurant is decorated with Mexican crafts and has an enormous menu of familiar favorites like burritos and fajitas. Grilled fish and steak are served with rice and shredded lettuce, as are the rolled tacos and enchiladas topped with red or green chile sauce. **Known for:** traditional Mexican favorites; hearty breakfasts; good selection of coffees (but no alcohol). [$] *Average main: MP120* ✉ *Calle 59 6, between Calles 10 and 12, Campeche City* ☎ *981/100–8556* 🌐 *www.facebook.com/restaurantluzdeluna* 🕒 *Closed Sun.*

Marganzo

$$ | **MEXICAN** | Traditional Yucatecan dishes—like *panuchos* (fried masa cakes stuffed with beans and piled high with shredded meat, lettuce, sour onions, and other toppings) or *chile mestizo* (poblano pepper stuffed with shredded meat)—are the specialties here. Although waitresses dressed in colorful regional-style skirts will explain the dishes, if you're unsure what to order ask to see the album containing photos of top dishes with multilingual captions. **Known for:** colorful local flavor; attentive service; stylish colonial decor. [$] *Average main: MP290* ✉ *Calle 8 267, between Calles 57 and 59, Campeche City* ☎ *981/811–3898* 🌐 *www.facebook.com/marganzo.*

☕ Coffee and Quick Bites

Chocol Ha

$ | **BAKERY** | **FAMILY** | Follow your nose to this dessert café, where the aromas of French pastries and rich cocoa waft into Campeche's narrow streets. Tucked inside a stone-walled colonial building are small wooden tables and a collection of antiques, like a vintage cash register still used for ringing up transactions. **Known for:** pretty courtyard; relaxed atmosphere; cocoa-infused everything. $ Average main: MP100 ⊠ Calle 59 30, between Calles 12 and 14, Campeche City ☎ 981/811–7893 ⊕ chocolha.mx ⊙ Closed Sun.

🛏 Hotels

★ Casa Don Gustavo

$$$ | **HOTEL** | At this antiques-filled 18th-century mansion, which is one of Campeche's historic masterpieces, guest rooms are wrapped around a central courtyard and feature elaborate chandeliers, French balconies, and hand-painted floors, yet have modern comforts like plasma TVs, iPod docs, and air-conditioning. **Pros:** colonial touches; surprisingly quiet despite central location; lovely restaurant. **Cons:** some stairs to access parts of the property; no children under eight; small pool. $ Rooms from: $270 ⊠ Calle 59 4, between Calles 10 and 8, Campeche City ☎ 981/816–8090 ⊕ www. casadongustavo.com ☞ 10 suites ‖◎‖ Free Breakfast.

Hotel Plaza Campeche

$$ | **HOTEL** | Across from Plaza St. Martín, this ocher hotel is one of the largest and grandest in Campeche, and although the rooms lack some of the character found in more historic lodgings, they are clean, comfortable, and equipped with TVs, air-conditioning, phones, safes, and free Wi-Fi. **Pros:** designated parking area; spacious rooms; good location. **Cons:** no children under 13; street noise and must cross a very busy street if walking; small pool. $ Rooms from: $113 ⊠ Calle 10 126, between Calles 49B and 49C, Campeche City ☎ 981/811–9900 ⊕ hotelplazacampeche.com ☞ 83 rooms ‖◎‖ No Meals.

★ Las Lupitas

$$ | **HOTEL** | Set in Barrio de Guadalupe, which has all the charm of the historic center while being quieter, one of the newest additions to the hotel scene has spacious suites with separate living areas, full kitchens, and lovely plaza views. **Pros:** excellent location; full kitchens; contemporary-chic design. **Cons:** small pool; no lobby; limited services. $ Rooms from: $160 ⊠ Parque de Guadalupe C 10B, Campeche City ⊕ www. laslupitas.com ☞ 6 suites ‖◎‖ Free Breakfast.

▼ Nightlife

The monthly minimagazine *Cartelera Cultural* lists events on Campeche City's active cultural calendar. Pick it up at any hotel. (It can also be found online at ⊕ *culturacampeche.mx*) Listings are in Spanish, but they're easily deciphered.

In December, concerts and other events take place as part of the Festival del Centro Histórico. Year-round, a few restaurant bars are open along the malecón. Locals like to show up around 10 pm to enjoy the cool evening air.

🛍 Shopping

Bazar Artesanal

CRAFTS | **FAMILY** | This government-run bazaar offers a wide range of local crafts, including some that are hard to come by—like bull horns carved into necklaces and earrings using an old technique that only a small number of families in Campeche State still know about. All prices are fixed, so there's no need to bargain. ⊠ Plaza Ah Kim Pech, Campeche City ⊕ www.facebook.com/ bazarartesanalcampeche.

Mercado Principal

MARKET | **FAMILY** | The city's commercial heart is its main market, where locals shop for seafood, produce, and housewares in a newly refurbished setting. You'll find little of tourist interest here, but the clothing section has some nice, inexpensive embroidered and beaded pieces among the jeans and T-shirts. Adventurous eaters can also find a bargain meal of local dishes like *salbutes* (a deep-fried tortilla dish). Next to the market is a small yellow bridge aptly named Puente de los Perros—four white plaster dogs guard the area. ⊠ *Av. Baluartes Este and Calle 53, Campeche City.*

Activities

Campeche Tarpon
FISHING | FAMILY | Alejandro, and other local fishermen from Campeche Tarpon, can arrange fly-fishing excursions to nearby mangroves, flats, creeks, and lagoons. The same operator will also arrange city tours and excursions to Edzná. ⊠ *Ix-Lol-Be, Puerto de Arribó, Área Ah, Campeche City* ☎ *981/120–4708 cell phone* ⊕ *campechetarpon.com.*

Tarpon Town
FISHING | This company offers the city's only fully licensed fishing tours, and they're experts in tailoring fishing trips to individual needs. ⊠ *Marina Bahía Azul s/n* ☎ *981/133–2135 cell phone* ⊕ *www.tarpontown.com.*

Edzná

61 km (37 miles) southeast of Campeche City.

With its smorgasbord of Maya architectural styles, Edzná is considered by archaeologists to be one of the peninsula's most important ruin complexes. It's less than an hour's drive southeast of Campeche City, but it sees fewer tour groups, and the scarcity of camera-carrying visitors intensifies the feeling of communion with nature and with the history of this once-flourishing commercial and ceremonial city.

GETTING HERE AND AROUND
From Campeche, take Carretera 261 heading east toward Holpechén. The turnoff for Edzná is clearly marked about 55 km (34 miles) southeast of Campeche City.

◉ Sights

★ Edzná
RUINS | FAMILY | A major metropolis in its day, Edzná was situated at a crossroads between cities in modern-day Guatemala and the states of Chiapas and Yucatán, hence it features a mélange of Maya architectural elements. Roof combs and corbeled arches evoke those at Yaxchilán and Palenque, in Chiapas, and giant stone masks resemble the Petén-style architecture of southern Campeche and northern Guatemala.

Edzná began as a humble agricultural settlement around 300 BC, reaching its pinnacle in the Late-Classic Period, between AD 600 and 900, then gradually waning in importance until being all but abandoned in the early 15th century. Today, soft breezes blow through groves of slender trees where brilliant orange and black birds spring from branch to branch. Clouds scuttle across a blue backdrop, perfectly framing the mossy remains of once-great structures.

One highlight is the five-story Pirámide de los Cinco Pisos, which was built on the raised platform of the Gran Acrópolis (Great Acropolis). Hieroglyphs carved into the vertical faces of the 15 steps between each level (some re-cemented in place by archaeologists, although not necessarily in the correct order), as well as into stelae throughout the site, depict the opulent attire once worn by the Maya ruling class—quetzal feathers, jade pectorals, and jaguar-skin skirts. On the pyramid's top level sit the ruins of three temples and a ritual steam bath.

The Pirámide de los Cinco Pisos was constructed so that on certain dates the setting sun would illuminate the mask of the creator-god, Itzamná, inside one of the pyramid's rooms. This still happens on May 1, 2, and 3, the beginning of the Maya planting season, and on August 7, 8, and 9, the days of harvesting and giving thanks.

West of the Great Acropolis, the Puuc-style Plataforma de los Cuchillos (Platform of the Knives) was so named by the archaeological team that found a number of flint knives inside. To the south, four buildings surround a smaller structure called the Pequeña Acrópolis (Small Acropolis). Twin sun-god masks with huge protruding eyes, sharp teeth, and oversize tongues flank the Templo de los Mascarones (Temple of the Masks, or Building 414), adjacent to the acropolis. The mask at the bottom left (east) represents the rising sun; the mask to the right represents the setting sun.

If you're not driving, consider taking one of the inexpensive day trips offered by tour operators in Campeche. Convenience aside, a guide can point out features often missed by the untrained eye, such as the remains of arrow-straight sacbéob. These raised roads in their day connected one important ceremonial building within the city to the next, and also linked Edzná to trading partners throughout the peninsula. ⊠ Carretera 188, 61 km (37 miles) southeast of Campeche City ☏ 981/816–9111 in Campeche City ⊕ www.inah.gob.mx ⊠ MX$90.

Santa Rosa Xtampak

131 km (81 miles) east of Campeche City.

The importance of this Maya city during the Classic Period is evidenced by the large number of public buildings and ceremonial plazas.

◉ Sights

Santa Rosa Xtampak
RUINS | FAMILY | Archaeologists believe there are around 100 structures at this site, although only 12 have been cleared. The most exciting find was the colossal Palacio in the western plaza. Inside, two inner staircases run the length of the

structure, leading to different levels and ending in subterranean chambers. Such a combination was extremely rare in Maya temples. Also noteworthy is the Casa de la Boca del Serpiente (House of the Serpent's Mouth), with its perfectly preserved and integrated entrance: the mouth of the creator-god Itzamná stretches wide to reveal a perfectly proportioned inner chamber. Such zoomorphic features are typical of the Chenes architectural style (circa AD 100 to 1000). ⊠ Off Carretera 261, Km 79, 30 km (18 miles) down signed side road ⊕ www. inah.gob.mx ⊠ MX$70.

Hochob

140 km (87 miles) southeast of Campeche City.

This small Maya site is an excellent example of the Chenes architectural style, which flowered from about AD 100 to 1000—though Hochob was occupied roughly beginning around AD 300. Most ruins in this area were built on the highest possible elevation to prevent flooding during the rainy season, and Hochob is no exception. It rests high on a hill overlooking the surrounding valleys.

GETTING HERE AND AROUND
If you're driving from Campeche, take Carretera 180 toward Holpechén and continue until you reach Carretera 261. Follow the road approximately 40 km (25 miles) toward Dzibalchén, then take the dirt road toward the town of Chencoh until you reach Hochob, 15 km (9 miles) ahead.

◉ Sights

Hochob
RUINS | FAMILY | Since work began at Hochob in the early 1980s, four temples and palaces have been excavated, including two that have been fully restored. Intricate and perfectly preserved

geometric designs, typical of the Chenes style, cover the temple known as Estructura II.

The temple doorway represents the open mouth of Itzamná, the creator god, and above it the eyes bulge and fangs are bared on either side of the base. It takes a bit of imagination to see the structure as a mask, as, at one time, color no doubt originally enhanced the effect. Squinting helps a bit: the figure's "eyes" are said to be squinting as well. But anyone can appreciate the intense geometric relief carvings decorating the facades, including long cascades of Chaac masks along the sides. Evidence of roof combs can be seen atop the building.

Ask the guard to show you the natural and man-made *chultunes* (cisterns) that extend into the forest. They also indicate that these are Chenes ruins. ⊠ *Dzibalchén–Chencho Rd., 15 km (9 miles) west of Dzibilnocac* ☎ *981/816–9111 in Campeche City* ⊕ *www.inah.gob.mx* ⊠ *MX$70.*

Carretera 186

Xpujil, Chicanná, Calakmul … exotic, far-flung-sounding names dot the map along this stretch of jungle territory. These are places where the creatures of the forest outnumber the tourists. In the Reserva de la Biósfera Calakmul, four- and five-story ceiba trees sway as families of spider monkeys swing through the canopy; in Xpujil, brilliant blue motmots fly from tree to tree in long, swoopy arcs.

The vestiges of at least 10 little-known Maya cities lie hidden off Carretera 186 between the town of Escárcega, 149 km (93 miles) south of Campeche City, and Chetumal, the capital of neighboring Quintana Roo State. You can see Chicanná, Becán, Hormiguero, and Xpujil in one rather rushed day by starting out early from Campeche City or Chetumal and overnighting in Xpujil.

If you plan to visit the Reserva de la Biósfera Calakmul, spend the first night at a nearby hotel or one in in Xpujil, and arrive at the reserve as soon as it opens the next day. This provides the best chance to see armadillos, wild turkeys, families of howler and spider monkeys, and other wildlife.

TOURS
Río Bec Dreams
CULTURAL TOURS | FAMILY | Rick Bertram and Diane Lalonde (owners of the Río Bec Dreams hotel in Xpujil) join forces with knowledgeable archaeologist Dan Griffin to lead comprehensive tours around ancient local sites. All three are native English speakers and enthusiastic guides. Expect to pay between MX$550 and MX$2,150, depending on the site. Be sure to book ahead. ⊠ *Carretera 186, Km 142, Xpujil* ☎ *981/124–0501 cell phone* ⊕ *riobecdreams.com* ⊠ *From MX$550.*

CHICANNÁ
264 km (164 miles) southeast of Campeche City, 130 km (81 miles) west of Chetumal.

Thought to have been a satellite community of the larger, more commercial city of Becán, a couple of miles farther west, Chicanná (House of the Serpent's Mouth) was also in its prime during the Late-Classic Period.

Chicanná
RUINS | FAMILY | Of the four buildings surrounding the main plaza at Chicanná, Estructura II, on the east side, is the most impressive. On its intricate facade are well-preserved sculpted reliefs and faces with long twisted noses—symbols of Chaac. In typical Chenes style, the doorway is zoomorphic, representing the mouth of the creator-god Itzamná. Surrounding the opening are large crossed eyes, fierce fangs, and earrings to complete the stone mask, which still bears traces of blue and red pigments. ⊠ *Off Carretera 186, Km 141, 10 km (6½ miles) west of Xpujil* ☎ *981/816–9111*

in Campeche City ⊕ www.inah.gob.mx ✉ MX$70.

BECÁN
3 km (½ mile) east of Chicanná.

Becán (usually translated as "canyon of water," referring to the moat) is thought to have been an important city within the Río Bec group, which also encompassed Chicanná, Xpujil, and Río Bec.

Becán
RUINS | FAMILY | An interesting feature here is the defensive moat—unusual in ancient Maya cities—though barely evident today. Seven gateways, once the only entrances to the guarded city, may have clued archaeologists to its presence. Most of the site's many buildings date from between about AD 600 and 1000, but since there are no traditionally inscribed stelae listing details of royal births, deaths, battles, and ascendancies to the throne, archaeologists have had to do a lot of guessing about what transpired here.

Duck into Estructura VIII, where underground passages lead to small rooms and a concealed staircase that reaches the top of the temple. One of several buildings surrounding a central plaza, this structure has lateral towers and a giant zoomorphic mask on its central facade. It was used for religious rituals, including bloodletting rites during which the elite pierced earlobes and genitals, among other sensitive body parts, in order to present their blood to the gods. ⊠ *Off Carretera 186, Km 145, 8 km (5 miles) west of Xpujil, Becán* ⊕ *www.inah.gob. mx* ✉ *MX$75.*

HORMIGUERO
9 km (6 miles) west of Becán.

Bumping down the badly potholed, 8-km (5-mile) road off Carretera 186 leading to this site might give you an appreciation for the explorers who first found and excavated it in 1933. Hidden throughout the forest are at least five magnificent temples, two of which have been excavated to reveal ornate facades covered with zoomorphic figures whose mouths are the doorways.

Hormiguero
RUINS | FAMILY | *Hormiguero* is Spanish for "anthill," referring both to the looters' tunnels that honeycombed these ruins when archaeologists discovered them and the number of enormous anthills in the area. The buildings here were constructed roughly between 400 BC and AD 1100 in the Río Bec style, with rounded lateral towers and ornamental stairways, the latter built to give an illusion of height, which they do wonderfully.

Note the intricately carved and well-preserved facade of the site's largest structure, Estructura II. Estructura V is also noteworthy owing to the Chaac masks arranged in a cascade atop a pyramid. Nearby is a perfectly round *chultun* (water-storage tank), and, seemingly emerging from the earth, the eerily etched designs of a still unexcavated structure. ⊠ *30 km (18 miles) southwest of Xpujil* ⊕ *www.inah.gob.mx* ✉ *MX$75.*

XPUJIL
8 km (5 miles) east of Becán, 300 km (186 miles) southeast of Campeche City, 125 km (78 miles) west of Chetumal.

Carretera 186 briefly widens to four lanes around the town of Xpujil, which is the place to stock up on food and sundries as it's the hub for exploring the region's string of Maya ruins, including one site that shares the town's name.

Avoid driving to Xpujil late in the day. Although Carretera 186 is in good condition, it's not well lighted. In addition, area hotels tend to close at around 11 pm, and, even if you have a reservation, you may find yourself locked out of all but the seediest lodgings—all the more reason to avoid driving at night. The ruins are just west of town.

Xpujil

RUINS | FAMILY | Xpujil (sometimes spelled "Xpuhil," meaning "cat's tail," and pronounced ish-poo-*hil*) takes its name from the reedy plant that grows in the area. Elaborately carved facades and doorways in the shape of monsters' mouths reflect the Chenes style, while adjacent pyramid towers connected by a long platform show the influence of Río Bec architects.

Some buildings have lost a lot of their stones, making them resemble "day after" sand castles. In Edificio I, three towers—believed to have been used by priests and royalty—were once crowned by false temples, and at the front of each are the remains of four vaulted rooms, each oriented toward one of the compass points. On the back side of the central tower is a huge mask of the rain god Chaac. Quite a few other building groups amid the forests of gum trees and *palo mulato* (so called for its bark with both dark and light patches) have yet to be excavated. ⊠ *Off Carretera 186, Km 150, west of the town of Xpujil, Xpujil* ⊕ *www.inah.gob.mx* ⊠ *MX$70.*

🛏 Hotels

Chicanná Ecovillage Resort

$ | HOTEL | FAMILY | Surrounded by lush gardens, this property has two-story, thatched-roof, stucco duplexes that house rooms with tile floors, an overhead fan, screened windows, a wide porch or balcony, and one king or two double beds. **Pros:** close to several area ruins and the biosphere reserve; spacious rooms; eco-friendly design. **Cons:** restaurant is just okay; Wi-Fi in reception area only; no a/c. $ *Rooms from: $75* ⊠ *Carretera 186, Km 144, 9 km (5½ miles) west of Xpujil, Xpujil* ☎ *981/871–6075* ⊕ *www.chicannaecovillageresort.com* ⇥ *46 rooms* ⦿ *No Meals.*

Río Bec Dreams

$$ | B&B/INN | The moment you arrive at this jungle hotel, you'll be invited to pull up a chair at the bar, flip through literature about the area, and swap stories with the owners and other guests before retiring to your freestanding "jungalow" or palapa cabana. **Pros:** laundry service; wonderful restaurant; owners are attentive and excellent guides. **Cons:** some rooms lack private bathrooms; no a/c; might seem too rustic for some. $ *Rooms from: $101* ⊠ *Carretera 186, Km 142, Xpujil* ☎ *983/126–3526* ⊕ *www.riobecdreams.com* ⇥ *7 units* ⦿ *No Meals.*

RESERVA DE LA BIÓSFERA CALAKMUL

365 km (227 miles) southeast of Campeche City, 107 km (66 miles) southwest of Xpujil.

Vast, lovely, green, and mysterious Calakmul may not stay a secret for much longer. You won't see any tour buses in the parking lot, and, on an average day, site employees and laborers still outnumber the visitors traipsing along the moss-tinged dirt paths that snake through the jungle. But things are changing. The arrival of the Tren Maya might make this fascinating reserve not only more accessible but also more appealing. Come sooner rather than later to beat the crowds.

If you don't have your own vehicle, private drivers in Xpujil charge about MX$1,500 for round-trip transportation to the reserve. But the easiest option is to arrange a guided excursion with Río Bec Dreams or Servidores Turísticos Calakmul.

★ Reserva de la Biósfera Calakmul

NATURE PRESERVE | FAMILY | Encompassing some 1.8 million acres along the Guatemalan border, Calakmul was declared a protected biosphere reserve in 1989 and is the largest of its kind in Mexico (Sian Ka'an in Quintana Roo is second with 1.3 million acres). All kinds of flora and fauna thrive here, including wildcats, spider and howler monkeys, hundreds of exotic birds, orchid varieties, butterflies, and reptiles. There's no shortage of insects, either, so don't forget the bug repellent.

The reserve's centerpiece, however, is the Maya city that shares the name Calakmul (which translates as "two adjacent towers"). Although Carretera 186 runs right through the reserve, you'll need to drive about 1½ hours from the highway along a 60-km (37-mile) authorized entry road to get to the site. Structures here are still being excavated, but fortunately the dense surrounding jungle is being left in its natural state: as you walk among the ruined palaces and tumbled stelae, you'll hear the guttural calls of howler monkeys and see massive strangler figs enveloping equally massive trees.

Anthropologists estimate that in its heyday (between AD 542 and 695) the region was inhabited by more than 50,000 Maya. Archaeologists have mapped more than 6,800 structures and found 180 stelae. Perhaps the most monumental discovery thus far has been the remains of royal ruler Gran Garra de Jaguar (Great Jaguar Claw). His body was wrapped (but not embalmed) in a shroud of palm leaf, lime, and fine cloth, and locked away in a royal tomb in about AD 700. In an adjacent crypt, a young woman wearing fine jewelry and an elaborately painted wood-and-stucco headdress was entombed together with a child. Their identity remains a mystery. The artifacts and skeletal remains have been moved to the Museo de la Arqueología Maya in Campeche City.

You can explore the site along a short, medium, or long path, but all three eventually lead to magnificent Templo II and Templo VII —twin pyramids separated by an immense plaza. Templo II, at 175 feet, is the peninsula's tallest Maya building. Scientists are studying a huge, intact stucco frieze deep within this structure, so it's not currently open to visitors.

Arrangements for an English-speaking tour guide should be made beforehand with Servidores Turísticos Calakmul, Río Bec Dreams, or through Chicanná Ecovillage near Xpujil. Camping is permitted at Km 6 with the Servidores Turistícos Calakmul after paying caretakers at the entrance gate. You can set up camp near the second checkpoint. Even if day-tripping, though, you'll need to bring your own food and water, as the only place to buy a snack is near the second entrance inside the museum. **■ TIP→ In addition to separate fees to enter the reserve and the archaeological site, you'll also pay MX$42 per person and MX$70 per vehicle to access the first 20 km (12½ miles) of road into the reserve, which runs through private land.** ✉ *Off Carretera 186, Km 65, 107 km (66 miles) southwest of Xpujil* ✣ *Drive 98 km (60 miles) east of Escárcega to turnoff at Cohuás, then 60 km (37 miles) south to Calakmul* 🌐 *www.inah.gob.mx/zonas/zona-arqueologica-de-calakmul* 🎟 *Reserve MX$70; archaeological site MX$90; vehicle-access fees vary based on the number of passengers.*

Hotel Puerta Calakmul

$$ | **HOTEL** | **FAMILY** | Just outside the entrance to Reserva de la Biósfera Calakmul, this ecological retreat has gravel pathways that wind through the jungle to 15 private cabanas, each rustic in design with palapa roofs, tree stump nightstands, and parchment paper lampshades inlaid with leaves and bits of bark. **Pros:** closest lodgings to biosphere reserve; peaceful setting; guided tours available. **Cons:** Wi-Fi in restaurant only; pricey for what you get; back cabanas experience some highway noise. [$] *Rooms from: $155* ✉ *Carretera 186, Km 98, Calakmul* ☎ *998/166–5052* 🌐 *www.puertacalakmul.com* 🛏 *15 cabanas* 🍴 *No Meals.*

Index

Photo Credits

Front cover: Marako85/Getty Images [Descr.: Caribbean coast of Mexico - Quintana Roo - Cancun - Riviera Maya]. **Back cover, from left to right:** Elijah-Lovkoff/iStockphoto. Delbars/iStockphoto. Seckin Ozturk/iStockphoto. **Spine:** Carmengabriela/iStockphoto. **Interior, from left to right:** Simon Dannhauer/Shutterstock (1). Alexander Sviridov/Shutterstock (2-3). Cancuncd (5). **Chapter 1: Experience Cancún and the Riviera Maya:** Javarman3/iStockphoto (6-7). Aleksandar Todorovic/Dreamstime (8-9). Xcaret by Mexico (9). Flocutus/Dreamstime (9). Lrafael/Dreamstime (10). Grand Fiesta Americana Coral Beach Cancun (10). Nialldunne2/Dreamstime (10). Xan/Shutterstock (10). Ahaswerus/Dreamstime (11). Yucatán Tourism Board (11). SCStock/Shutterstock (12). Giuseppemasci/Dreamstime (12). Nialldunne24/Dreamstime (12). Chad Zube/Shutterstock (12). Elvistudio/Dreamstime (13). Kravka/Shutterstock (13). BlueOrange Studio/Shutterstock (13). Gitano Bar Tulum (13). Javarman/Shutterstock (14). Alfredo Azar Photography (14). Son of Groucho/Flickr (15). Guajillo Studio/Shutterstock (20). S.Pereira/Shutterstock (21). Georgia Evans/Shutterstock (22). John Mitchell/Alamy Stock Photo (23). Alex W/Shutterstock (24). Lunamarina/Shutterstock (24). Elijah-Lovkoff/iStockphoto (24). Wangkun Jia/Shutterstock (24). SL_Photography/iStockphoto (25). Joana Villar/Shutterstock (26). Under the Sea/Shutterstock (26). Lorena Difulvio/Shutterstock (26). Rob Atherton/Shutterstock (27). Aquapix/Shutterstock (27). Ivan Soto Cobos/Shutterstock (28). Byelikova/Dreamstime (28). Mexican Caribbean (28). Smokelmt/Dreamstime (28). Mexican Caribbean (28). Rchphoto/Dreamstime (29). Mexican Caribbean (29). Bophil/Dreamstime (29). Izanbar/Dreamstime (29). Atomazul/Dreamstime (29). **Chapter 3: Cancún:** Frederick Millett/Shutterstock (71). Cancun CVB (74). Thelmadatter/Wikipedia (75). Guajillo studio/Shutterstock (75). Arkadij Schell/Shutterstock (94). Marriott International (101). Courtesy of NIZUC Resort & Spa (103). Cancun CVB (110). **Chapter 4: Isla Mujeres:** Cancun CVB (113). Eddy Galeotti/Shutterstock (129). Robatherton/Dreamstime (132). **Chapter 5: The Riviera Maya:** YuziS/Shutterstock (139). AmResorts (147). Rosewood Hotels & Resorts (157). Lunamarina/Shutterstock (162-163). Kmiragaya/Dreamstime (173). GmbH & Co. KG/Alamy Stock Photo (175). Agefotostock/Alamy Stock Photo (176). Ales Liska/Shutterstock (177). Marketanovakova/Dreamstime (177). Findlay/Alamy Stock Photo (178). Qing Ding/Shutterstock (178). Philip Coblentz/Brand X Pictures (179). Cancun CVB (185). Andrmoel/Shutterstock (190). Nataliya Hora/iStockphoto (200). Urosr/Shutterstock (206). Almaplena Eco Resort & Beach Club (211). LindaVermeulen_MermaidsKissGallery (213). **Chapter 6: Cozumel:** Agefotostock /Alamy Stock Photo (217). Elovkoff/Dreamstime (225). Ramunas Bruzas/Shutterstock (229). Marso/Shutterstock (233). Agefotostock /Alamy Stock Photo (239). The Leading Hotels of the World (241). Phortun/Shutterstock (243). Cancuncd (249). Tslane888/Flickr (250). Tslane888/Flickr (250). Pato_Garza/Flickr (250). Mike Bauer/Shutterstock (250). Sethbienek/Flickr (252). Tubuceo/Shutterstock (252). Tzara/iStockphoto (253). Jerry McElroy (254). **Chapter 7: Yucatán and Campeche States:** Emicristea/Dreamstime (257). Robert Briggs/Shutterstock (260). Anderson Czarnesky/Shutterstock (261). Mathes/Dreamstime (261). Hemis/Alamy Stock Photo (271). Hacienda Xcanatun (279). Manuel Manso/Hotel Julamis (281). Witr/Dreamstime (287). Zstock/Shutterstock (297). Schaub/Shutterstock (301). DnDavis/Shutterstock (304). Corbis (305). Fedor Selivanov/Shutterstock (305). Bernard Gagnon/Wikimedia Commons (306). Mysticenergy/iStockphoto (306). José A. Granados/Cancun CVB (307). SL_Photography/iStockphoto (307). Colin13362/iStockphoto (308). Fcb981/Wikimedia Commons (308). Philip Baird/Anthroarcheart (309). Mexico Tourism Board (309). Jo Ann Snover/Dreamstime (310). MarkusSevcik/iStockphoto (311). Uros Ravbar/Dreamstime (311). Robert Rosenblum/Alamy Stock Photo (313). Alex James Bramwell/Shutterstock (314). Brandon Bourdages/Shutterstock (317). Dmitry Rukhlenko/iStockphoto (320). **About Our Writers:** All photos are courtesy of the writers.

*Every effort has been made to trace the copyright holders, and we apologize in advance for any accidental errors. We would be happy to apply the corrections in the following edition of this publication.